Creating a
Website

Fourth Edition

the missing manual®

The book that should have been in the box®

Matthew MacDonald

O'REILLY®

Beijing | Boston | Farnham | Sebastopol | Tokyo

Creating a Website: The Missing Manual, Fourth Edition

by Matthew MacDonald

Published by O'Reilly Media, Inc.,
1005 Gravenstein Highway North, Sebastopol, CA 95472.

O'Reilly books may be purchased for educational, business, or sales promotional use. Online editions are also available for most titles (*https://www.safaribooksonline.com*). For more information, contact our corporate/institutional sales department: (800) 998-9938 or *corporate@oreilly.com*.

June 2015:   First Edition.

Revision History for the First Edition:

2015-06-08	First release
2015-07-24	Second release

See *http://www.oreilly.com/catalog/errata.csp?isbn=0636920036364* for release details.

ISBN-13: 978-1-4919-1807-4

[LSI]

Contents

Part One: **Building Basic Web Pages**

Part Two: **From Web Page to Website**

Part Three: Connecting with Your Audience

Part Four: Interactivity and Multimedia

The Missing Credits

ABOUT THE AUTHOR

 Matthew MacDonald is a science and technology writer with well over a dozen books to his name. He's taken countless readers onto the Web with books like *WordPress: The Missing Manual* and *HTML5: The Missing Manual*. He's also shown people just how strange they really are with the mind-bending weird science of *Your Brain: The Missing Manual* and *Your Body: The Missing Manual*.

ABOUT THE CREATIVE TEAM

Peter McKie (editor) had the pleasure of working on previous editions of this book. He lives in New York, where he researches the history of abandoned buildings and, every once in a while, sneaks into them. Email: *pmckie@oreilly.com*.

Kara Ebrahim (production editor) lives, works, and plays in Cambridge, MA. She loves graphic design and all things outdoors. Email: *kebrahim@oreilly.com*.

Shelley Powers (technical reviewer) is a web developer and tech writer currently living in St. Louis, Missouri. Her areas of interest are HTML5, JavaScript, and other web technologies.

Julie Van Keuren (proofreader) quit her newspaper job in 2006 to move to Montana and live the freelancing dream. She and her husband, M.H. (who is living the novel-writing dream), have two sons, Dexter and Michael. Email: *little_media@yahoo.com*.

Ron Strauss (indexer) specializes in the indexing of information technology publications of all kinds. Ron is also an accomplished classical violist and lives in Northern California with his wife and fellow indexer, Annie, and his miniature pinscher, Kanga. Email: *rstrauss@mchsi.com*.

ACKNOWLEDGEMENTS

No author could complete a book without a small army of helpful individuals. I'm deeply indebted to the whole Missing Manual team, especially my editor, Peter McKie, who kept me on track with relatively gentle prodding, and HTML-whiz tech reviewer Shelley Powers, who lent her keen insight about all things Web-related. I also owe a hearty thanks to those who left their mark on the previous editions of this book, including Sarah Milstein, Peter Meyers, and tech reviewers Jim Goodenough, Rhea Howard, Mark Levitt, Tony Ruscoe, and Megan Sorensen. As always, I'm also deeply indebted to numerous others who toiled behind the scenes indexing pages, drawing figures, and proofreading the final copy.

Finally, I'd never write *any* book without the support of my parents, Nora and Paul, my extended parents, Razia and Hamid, and my wife, Faria. (I'd probably write many more without the challenges of my three lovable daughters, Maya, Brenna, and Aisha.) Thanks, everyone!

THE MISSING MANUAL SERIES

Missing Manuals are witty, superbly written guides to computer products that don't come with printed manuals (which is just about all of them). Each book features a handcrafted index and cross-references to specific pages (not just chapters). Recent and upcoming titles include:

Access 2013: The Missing Manual by Matthew MacDonald

Adobe Edge Animate: The Missing Manual by Chris Grover

Buying a Home: The Missing Manual by Nancy Conner

Creating a Website: The Missing Manual, Third Edition by Matthew MacDonald

CSS3: The Missing Manual, Third Edition by David Sawyer McFarland

Dreamweaver CS6: The Missing Manual by David Sawyer McFarland

Dreamweaver CC: The Missing Manual by David Sawyer McFarland and Chris Grover

Excel 2013: The Missing Manual by Matthew MacDonald

FileMaker Pro 13: The Missing Manual by Susan Prosser and Stuart Gripman

Flash CS6: The Missing Manual by Chris Grover

Galaxy Tab: The Missing Manual by Preston Gralla

Galaxy S5: The Missing Manual by Preston Gralla

Google+: The Missing Manual by Kevin Purdy

HTML5: The Missing Manual, Second Edition by Matthew MacDonald

iMovie: The Missing Manual by David Pogue and Aaron Miller

iPad: The Missing Manual, Sixth Edition by J.D. Biersdorfer

iPhone: The Missing Manual, Seventh Edition by David Pogue

iPhone App Development: The Missing Manual by Craig Hockenberry

iPhoto: The Missing Manual by David Pogue and Lesa Snider

iPod: The Missing Manual, Eleventh Edition by J.D. Biersdorfer and David Pogue

iWork: The Missing Manual by Jessica Thornsby and Josh Clark

JavaScript & jQuery: The Missing Manual, Second Edition by David Sawyer McFarland

Kindle Fire HD: The Missing Manual by Peter Meyers

Microsoft Project 2013: The Missing Manual by Bonnie Biafore

Motorola Xoom: The Missing Manual by Preston Gralla

NOOK HD: The Missing Manual by Preston Gralla

Office 2011 for Macintosh: The Missing Manual by Chris Grover

Office 2013: The Missing Manual by Nancy Conner and Matthew MacDonald

OS X Mavericks: The Missing Manual by David Pogue

Personal Investing: The Missing Manual by Bonnie Biafore

Photoshop CS6: The Missing Manual by Lesa Snider

Photoshop CC: The Missing Manual, Second Edition by Lesa Snider

Photoshop Elements 13: The Missing Manual by Barbara Brundage

PHP & MySQL: The Missing Manual, Second Edition by Brett McLaughlin

Switching to the Mac: The Missing Manual, Mavericks Edition by David Pogue

Windows 7: The Missing Manual by David Pogue

Windows 8: The Missing Manual by David Pogue

WordPress: The Missing Manual, Second Edition by Matthew MacDonald

Your Body: The Missing Manual by Matthew MacDonald

Your Brain: The Missing Manual by Matthew MacDonald

Your Money: The Missing Manual by J.D. Roth

For a full list of all Missing Manuals in print, go to *www.missingmanuals.com/library. html*.

Introduction

Congratulations! You're living in the golden age of website-building. The world has never had better, more powerful, or easier-to-use tools for making top-notch websites.

However, there's a catch—all these great tools make for some seriously confusing choices. If you're new to web design, you'll need to sort through a dizzying assortment of technologies before you can actually start building web pages. Depending on your ambitions and skills, some of these tools will be downright essential to your site, while others will be nearly irrelevant.

That's where this book, the fourth edition of *Creating a Website: The Missing Manual*, comes into the picture. Think of it as your personal trainer for site-building. You'll start by learning how to create basic web pages, using the standards that underpin every page on the Web (that's HTML and CSS). You'll then branch out to explore the services provided by companies like Google that can help you popularize your site, count your visitors, and even make you some money. You'll even take a condensed tour of JavaScript, the programming language that powers almost every interactive page you meet online.

In short, this book is the perfect guide for people who want to build a site on their own, starting from scratch, but with all the goodies the modern-day Web has to offer. It's also a gentle starting point for anyone who wants to get deeper into the field of website design (and Appendix A has plenty of suggestions for ambitious readers who want to learn more). If either of these descriptions describes you, welcome aboard!

Who Shouldn't Read This Book

It's worth pointing out that this book isn't for everyone. If you're familiar with web technologies like HTML and CSS, and you just want to learn what's new in their most recent incarnations (HTML5 and CSS3), you'll probably prefer the fast route offered in *HTML5: The Missing Manual* (O'Reilly).

If you're planning to build your website with the fantastically popular WordPress blogging-and-so-much-more framework, you should detour to *WordPress: The Missing Manual* (O'Reilly). (That said, if you want to build a traditional website and then *supplement* it with a blog, this book has you covered.)

If you're a programmer who's planning to create a highly interactive website or web application, you're cooking a different kettle of fish. First, you need to learn how to write code that works on a web server, the high-powered but mostly unseen computers that run the Internet. Starting down this path can be tricky, because there are more web programming languages in the world than there are contestants on *The Bachelor*. However, you'll find a good, gentle introduction in the book *Learning PHP, MySQL, JavaScript, CSS & HTML5* (O'Reilly). (Fair warning: If you really want to program everything yourself without shooting yourself in the foot or opening gaping security holes, you may actually need a whole *team* of web developers working with you.)

■ The Glory of Building a Website from Scratch

There are many ways to establish your web presence. You can chat with friends through a Facebook page, share your snaps on Instagram or Flickr, put your home videos on YouTube, or write short diary-style blurbs on a blog hosted by a service like Blogger. But if you're ambitious enough to have picked up this book, you're after the gold standard of the Web: a completely personalized, built-from-scratch site to call your own.

So what can you accomplish with a website that you can't do with email, social networking, and other web-based services? In a word: *anything*.

Depending on your goals, your website can be anything from a handy place to stash your resumé to the hub of an ecommerce warehouse that sells personalized underpants (hey, it's made more than one Internet millionaire). The point is that creating your own website gives you the power to decide exactly what that site is—and the control to change everything on a whim. And if you already use other web-based services, like YouTube and Facebook, you can make them a part of your website, too, as you'll learn in this book. For example, you can put the YouTube videos of your cat playing pool right next to your personalized cat merchandise.

Of course, with great power comes great responsibility—meaning that if you decide to build your own site, it's up to you to make sure it doesn't look as hokey as a 1960s yearbook portrait, or run as clunkily as a 1970s Chevy. To help you dodge these dangers, this book starts out by giving you a solid grounding in the nerdy-seeming HTML and CSS languages. Don't panic—these standards are surprisingly easy to learn for both computer whizzes *and* normal people. You'll even get some exercises to help you practice.

That's not to say that you have to do everything the hard way. This book spends plenty of time covering free website services that can do the difficult jobs you definitely don't want to tackle on your own, like tracking visitors or building a shopping cart. And the do-it-yourself web smarts you pick up will serve you well, even if you step up to handy website-building tools like Adobe's popular Dreamweaver software. (In fact, you'll learn how to choose from a few completely *free* web design tools in Chapter 5, including a professional site-designing tool from Microsoft that once cost hundreds of dollars, and a new upstart from Adobe.)

Types of Sites

You don't have much chance of creating a successful site if you haven't decided what it's for. Some people have a very specific goal in mind (like getting hired for a job or promoting a concert), while others are just planning to unleash their self-expression. Either way, take a look at the following list to get a handle on the different types of sites you might want to create:

- **Personal** sites are all about you. Whether you want to share pictures of Junior with the relatives, chronicle a trip to Kuala Lumpur, or just post your latest thoughts and obsessions, a personal website is the place to do it. These days, you can use social networking sites like Facebook and Instagram to share your life with friends, but a personal site is a good choice if you're more ambitious (say you want to chart five generations of family history) or you want complete design control (forget Facebook blue).

- **Resumé** sites are a specialized type of personal site and a powerful career-building tool. Rather than photocopy a suitcase full of paper resumés, why not send emails and distribute business cards that point to your online resumé? Best of all, with a little planning, your online vita can include more details than its tree-based counterpart, like links to former companies, an online portfolio, and even background music playing "YMCA" (which is definitely not recommended).

- **Topical** sites focus on a particular subject that interests you. If you're more interested in talking about your favorite music, art, books, food, or political movement than you are in talking about your own life, a topical website is for you.

TIP Before you set out to create a site, consider whether other people with a similar interest will want to visit it, and take a look at existing sites on the topic. The best topical websites attract people who share the same interest. The worst sites present the same dozen links you can find anywhere else. Remember, the Web is drowning in information. The last thing it needs is another *Justin Bieber Fan Emporium*.

- **Event** sites aren't designed to weather the years—instead, they revolve around a specific event. A common example is a wedding website. The event hosts create it to provide directions, background information, links to gift registries, and a few romantic photos. When the wedding is over, the site disappears—or morphs into something different (like a personal site chronicling the honeymoon). Other events you might treat in a similar way include family reunions, costume parties, or do-it-yourself protest marches.

- **Promotion** sites are ideal when you want to show off your personally produced CD or hot-off-the-presses book. They're geared to get the word out about a specific item, whether it's handmade pottery or your own software. Sometimes, these websites evolve into small-business sites, where you actually sell your wares (see the "Small business" bullet point below).

- **Small business (or ecommerce)** sites show off the most successful use of the Web—selling everything from portable music players to prescription drugs. Ecommerce sites are so widespread now that it's hard to believe that making a buck was far from anyone's mind when the Web first debuted.

NOTE Creating a full-blown ecommerce site like Amazon.com or eBay is far beyond the abilities of a single person. These sites need a team of programmers working with complex programming languages and sophisticated programming techniques. But if you've come to the Web to make money, don't give up hope! Innovative companies like PayPal and Yahoo provide services that can help you build shopping cart–style sites and accept credit card payments. You can also host Google ads or hawk products from Amazon's website to rake in some cash. You'll learn more in Chapter 13.

Once you pinpoint your website's *raison d'être*, you should have a better idea about who your visitors will be. Knowing and understanding your audience is crucial to creating an effective site. (And don't even try to suggest that you're creating a site just for yourself—if you are, there's no reason to put it on the Internet at all!)

■ About This Book

No one owns the Web. As a result, no one is responsible for teaching you how to use it or how to build an online home for yourself. That's where *Creating a Website: The Missing Manual* comes in. If the Web *did* have an instruction manual—one that detailed the basic ingredients and time-saving tricks every site needs—this book would be it.

What You Need to Get Started

This book assumes that you don't have anything more than a reasonably up-to-date computer and raw ambition. Although there are dozens of high-powered web page editing programs that can help you build a site, you *don't* need one to use this book. In fact, if you use a web editor before you understand how websites work, you're liable to create more problems than you solve. That's because, as helpful as those programs are, they shield you from learning the principles of good site design—principles that can mean the difference between an attractive, easy-to-maintain web creation and a disorganized design nightmare.

Once you master the basics, you're welcome to use a fancy web page editor like Adobe Dreamweaver. In this book, you'll get an overview of how Dreamweaver works, and you'll discover a few great free alternatives (in Chapter 5).

> **NOTE** Under no circumstances do you need to know anything about complex web programming technologies like Java or ASP.NET. You also don't need to know anything about databases or XML. These topics are fascinating but insanely difficult to implement without some solid programming experience. In this book, you'll learn how to create the best possible website without becoming a programmer. (You *will*, however, learn just enough about JavaScript to use many of the free script libraries you can find online.)

About the Outline

This book is divided into five parts, each with several chapters:

- **Part One: Building Basic Web Pages.** In this part, you'll learn the basics behind HTML, the language of the Web (Chapters 1 and 2). Next, you'll learn your way around the CSS standard, which lets you apply fancy colors, fonts, and borders to your pages (Chapter 3) and you'll add pictures, too (Chapter 4). Finally, you'll look at how you can simplify your life using web page editing programs (Chapter 5).

- **Part Two: From Web Page to Website.** This section shows you how to scale up to a complete website made up of multiple pages. You'll learn how to link your pages together (Chapter 6), style your entire site in one blow (Chapter 7), and master some slick layouts (Chapter 8). Finally, you'll put your pages online with a reputable hosting company (Chapter 9).

- **Part Three: Connecting with Your Audience.** The third part of the book explains how to get your site noticed by search engines like Google (Chapter 10), and how to reel in web traffic (Chapter 11). You'll also take a look at *blogs* (short for *web logs*) and the free programs that help you create them (Chapter 12). Finally, you'll learn how to get on the path to web riches by displaying ads or selling your own products (Chapter 13).

- **Part Four: Interactivity and Multimedia.** Now that you can create a professional, working website, why not deck it out with fancy features like glowing buttons and pop-out menus? You won't learn the brain-bending details of how to become a hardcore JavaScript programmer, but you'll learn enough to use free JavaScript mini-programs in your own pages to perform basic tasks (Chapters 14 and 15). You'll also dabble with movie clips and add an MP3 music player right inside an ordinary web page (Chapter 16).

- **Part Five: Appendixes.** At the end of this book, you'll find two appendixes. The first appendix points to additional site-building resources for ambitious web designers who want to keep improving their skills. The second one gives you a quick reference for HTML. It lists and defines the essential HTML elements and points you to the appropriate chapter of this book for more detailed discussions.

Of Windows and Macintosh PCs

One of the best things about the World Wide Web is that it truly is worldwide: Wherever you live, from Aruba to Zambia, the Web eagerly awaits your company. The same goes for the computer you use to develop your site. From an early-model Windows PC to the latest and greatest MacBook Pro, you can implement the tactics, tools, and tricks described in this book with pretty much whatever kind of computer you have. (Of course, a few programs favor one operating system over another, but you'll hear about those differences whenever they come up.) The good news is that this book is usable and suitable for owners of computers of all stripes.

About→These→Arrows

Throughout this book, you'll find sentences like this one: "To save your document in Notepad, choose File→Save." That's shorthand for a somewhat longer set of instructions that goes like this: "Open the File menu by clicking File in the menu bar. Then, in the File menu, click Save." Figure I-1 gives you a closer look.

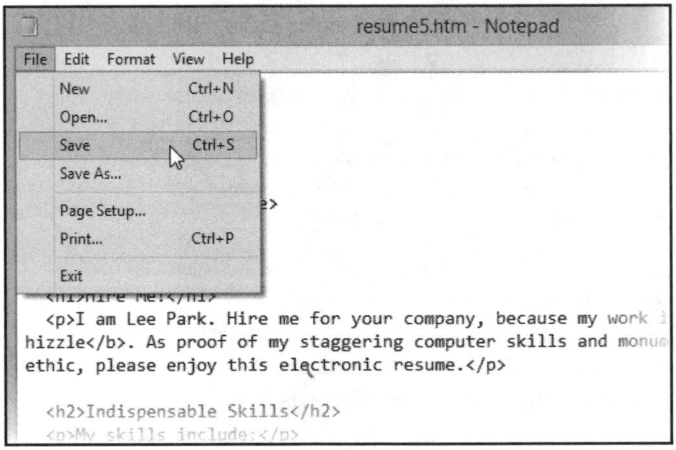

FIGURE I-1

In this book, arrow notations simplify folder and menu instructions. For example, "Choose File→Save" is a more compact way of saying, "From the File menu, choose Save," as shown here.

■ About the Online Resources

As the owner of a Missing Manual, you've got more than just a book to read. Online, you'll find example files that will give you hands-on experience, as well as links to all the websites mentioned in this book. Head over to *www.missingmanuals.com*, or go directly to one of the following sections.

The Missing CD

This book doesn't have a CD pasted inside the back cover, but you're not missing out on anything. You can download all the companion content for this book from its

Missing CD page at *www.missingmanuals.com/cds/caw4* or the book's companion site at *http://prosetech.com/web*.

The companion site includes three useful things:

- **Sample web pages.** You can never have too many examples. The Missing CD has you covered, with a collection that includes all the sample web pages featured in this book. You download them as a single ZIP file, and then unzip them on your computer. The sample files are organized in folders by chapter (so the files from Chapter 1 are in a folder named *Chapter 1*), making it easy to find the examples that interest you.

> **TIP** If you want to work on a specific example file, here's a quick way to find it: Look at the corresponding figure in this book. The filename is usually visible at the end of the web browser's address box. For example, if you see the URL *c:\Creating a Website\Chapter 1\popsicles.htm* (Figure 1-6, page 11), you'll know that the corresponding example file is *popsicles.htm*.

- **Tutorials.** The Missing CD download also includes super-useful tutorial files, which you use with the practice exercises in this book. Here's how it works: When you start one of the book's tutorials, we'll refer you to a numbered tutorial folder. For example, if you're working on the first exercise in Chapter 2, you'll be sent to a folder named *Tutorial-2-1*. In that folder, you'll find any starter files you need to get going and the tutorial's solution files—the final, finished product. So if you try a tutorial and it doesn't quite work out, you can check your work and track down the problem.

> **NOTE** This book features two types of tutorials. The most important, thorough exercises appear in their own sections of the book, with titles that begin with the word "Tutorial," as in "Tutorial: Creating an HTML File." These lessons teach key skills, so you should definitely give them a try. You'll also come across shorter, optional tutorials for extra practice. These tutorials appear in the "Sharpen Up" sidebars.

- **Links.** This book mentions plenty of useful websites and online services. Fortunately, you don't need to wear down your fingers typing long web addresses into your browser. Instead, the companion site offers a list of clickable links for all the websites mentioned, organized by chapter, and listed in the order that they appear in the book.

Registration

If you register this book at *www.oreilly.com*, you'll be eligible for special offers—like discounts on future editions of *Creating a Website: The Missing Manual*. Registering is free and takes only a few clicks. Type *http://tinyurl.com/registerbook* into your browser to hop directly to the registration page.

Contact Us

Got questions? Need more information? Drop us a line at *bookquestions@oreilly.com*.

Errata

To keep this book as up to date and accurate as possible, each time we print more copies, we'll make any confirmed corrections you suggest. We also note such changes on the book's errata page, so you can mark important corrections in your own copy of the book, if you like. Go to *http://tinyurl.com/cws-errata* to report an error and view existing corrections.

◼ Safari® Books Online

Safari Books Online is an on-demand digital library that delivers expert content in both book and video form from the world's leading authors in technology and business.

Technology professionals, software developers, web designers, and business and creative professionals use Safari Books Online as their primary resource for research, problem solving, learning, and certification training.

Safari Books Online offers a range of plans and pricing for enterprise, government, education, and individuals.

Members have access to thousands of books, training videos, and prepublication manuscripts in one fully searchable database from publishers like O'Reilly Media, Prentice Hall Professional, Addison-Wesley Professional, Microsoft Press, Sams, Que, Peachpit Press, Focal Press, Cisco Press, John Wiley & Sons, Syngress, Morgan Kaufmann, IBM Redbooks, Packt, Adobe Press, FT Press, Apress, Manning, New Riders, McGraw-Hill, Jones & Bartlett, Course Technology, and hundreds more. For more information about Safari Books Online, please visit us at *www.safaribooksonlilne.com*.

Building Basic Web Pages

Creating Your First Page

Every website is a collection of web pages, so it should come as no surprise that your journey to build a complete site starts *here*, with the writing of a single web page.

Technically, a web page is a special type of document written in a computer language called *HTML* (that's short for HyperText Markup Language). Web pages are written for web *browsers*—programs like Internet Explorer, Google Chrome, and Safari. These browsers have a simple but crucially important job: they read the HTML in a web page document and display the perfectly formatted result for you to read.

This chapter will introduce you to HTML. You'll see how a basic web page works and learn how to create one of your own. For now, you'll be working with web pages you store on your computer, visible only to you. Later on, in Chapter 9, you'll learn to put web pages online so anyone with a web connection can see them.

■ HTML: The Language of the Web

HTML is the single most important standard in web design—and the only one that's absolutely *required* if you plan to create a web page. Every web page is written in HTML. It doesn't matter whether your page contains a series of blog entries, a dozen pictures of your pet lemur, or a heavily formatted screenplay—odds are that, if you're looking at it in a browser, it's an HTML page.

HTML plays a key role in web pages: It tells browsers how to display the contents of a page, using special instructions called *tags* that tell a browser when to start a paragraph, italicize a word, or display a picture. To create your own web pages, you need to learn to use this family of tags.

HTML is such an important standard that you'll spend a good portion of this book digging through its features, frills, and occasional shortcomings. Every web page you build along the way will be a bona fide HTML document.

> **NOTE** The HTML standard doesn't have anything to do with the way a web browser *retrieves* a page on the Web. That task is left to another standard, called HTTP (HyperText Transport Protocol), which is a communication technology that lets two computers exchange data over the Internet. To use the analogy of a phone conversation, the telephone wires represent HTTP, and the juicy tidbits of gossip you exchange with Aunt Martha are the HTML documents.

FREQUENTLY ASKED QUESTION

The Web vs. the Internet

Is there a difference between the Web and the Internet?

Newscasters, politicians, and regular people often use these terms interchangeably. Technically, however, the concepts are different—and confusing them is likely to put computer techies and other self-respecting nerds on edge.

The *Internet* is a network of connected computers that spans the globe. These computers are connected together to share information, but there are a number of ways to do that, includ-

ing by email, instant messaging, file sharing, transferring files through *FTP* (short for File Transfer Protocol), and through HTTP (with the help of a web browser).

The *World Wide Web* is a term that describes the billions of public web pages that you can visit on the Internet. In other words, the Web is just one way to use the Internet, although it's undeniably the most popular—and the one that interests us in this book.

Cracking Open an HTML File

On the inside, an HTML page is actually nothing more than a plain-vanilla text file. That means that the raw code behind every web page you create will consist entirely of letters, numbers, and a few special characters (like spaces, punctuation marks, and everything else you can spot on your keyboard). Figure 1-1 dissects an ordinary (and very simple) HTML document.

Here's one of the secrets of web page writing: You don't need a live website to start creating your own web pages. That's because you can easily build and test pages using only your own computer. In fact, you don't even need an Internet connection. The only tools you need are a basic text editor and a standard web browser.

Your Text Editor

A text editor lets you create or edit an HTML file (in a window like the one you can see in Figure 1-1, bottom). Even many professional web designers stick with simple text-editing tools. There are plenty of fancier editing tools that are designed specifically for editing websites, but you don't actually *need* any of them. And if you start using them too soon, you're likely to end up drowning in a sea of extra frills and features before you really understand how HTML works.

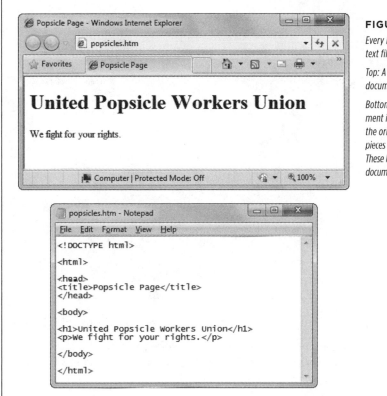

FIGURE 1-1

Every HTML document is actually an ordinary text file.

Top: A web browser displays a simple HTML document, showing all its glorious formatting.

Bottom: But when you open the same document in a text editor, you see all the text from the original document, along with a few extra pieces of information inside angle brackets < >. These HTML tags convey information about the document's structure and formatting.

The type of text editor you use depends on your computer's operating system:

- If you have a Windows computer, you use the bare-bones Notepad editor. Sail on to the next section.

- If you have a Mac computer, you use the built-in TextEdit editor. But first, you need to make the adjustments described below.

Mac fans need to tweak the way TextEdit works because the program has an "HTML view" that hides the tags in an HTML file and shows you the formatted page instead. This behavior is aimed at making life simpler for newbies, but it presents a serious danger for anyone who wants to write a real web page. To avoid confusion and to make sure you write real, raw HTML, you need to turn HTML view off. Here's how:

1. **Choose TextEdit→Preferences.**

   This opens a tabbed window of TextEdit options (Figure 1-2).

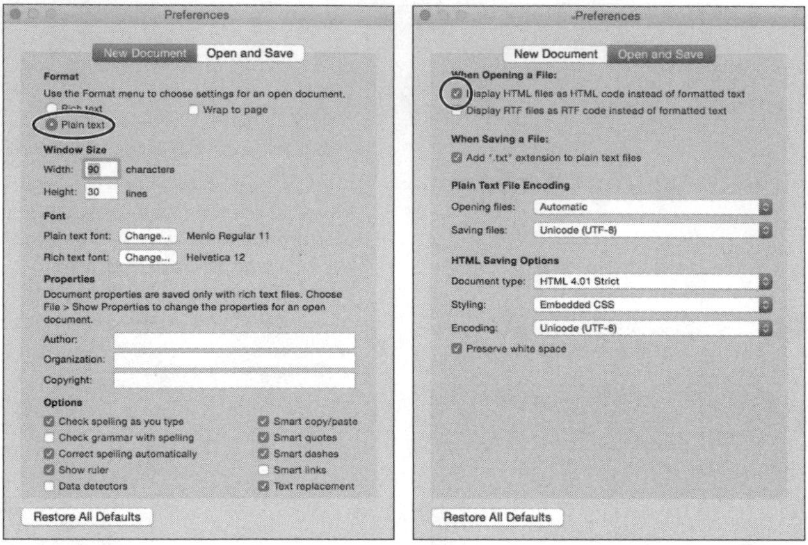

FIGURE 1-2

TextEdit's Preferences window has two tabs of settings: "New Document" (left) and "Open and Save" (right).

2. **Click "New Document" and then, in the Format section, choose "Plain text."**

   This tells TextEdit to start you out with ordinary, unformatted text and to dispense with the formatting toolbar and ruler that would otherwise appear onscreen, which aren't relevant to creating HTML files.

3. **Click "Open and Save" and switch on the first option, "Display HTML files as HTML code instead of formatted text."**

   This tells TextEdit to let you see (and edit) the real HTML markup, tags and all, not the formatted version of the page as it would appear in a web browser.

4. **Close the Preferences window, and then close TextEdit.**

   Now, the next time you start TextEdit, you'll begin in the plain-text mode that every self-respecting web developer uses.

Your Web Browser

As you no doubt know, a web browser is a program that lets you navigate to and display web pages. Without browsers, the Web would still exist, but you wouldn't be able to look at it.

A browser's job is surprisingly simple—in fact, the bulk of its work consists of two tasks. First, it requests web pages, which happens when you type in a website address (like *www.google.com*) or click a link in a web page. The browser sends that request to a far-off computer called a *web server*. A server is typically much more powerful than a home computer because it needs to handle multiple browser requests at once. The server heeds these requests and sends back the content of the desired web pages.

When the browser gets that content, it puts its second skill into action and *renders*, or draws, the web page. Technically, this means the browser converts the plain text it receives from the server into a display document based on formatting instructions embedded in the page. The end result is a graphically rich page with different typefaces, colors, and links. Figure 1-3 illustrates the process.

FIGURE 1-3

A web browser is designed to do two things really well: contact remote computers to ask for web pages, and then display those pages on your computer.

Although you usually ask your browser to retrieve pages from the Web, you can also use it to view a web page that's stored on your computer, which is particularly handy when you're practicing your HTML skills. In fact, your computer already knows that files that end in *.htm* or *.html* have web page content. So if you double-click one of these files, your computer launches your web browser automatically. (You can get the same result by dragging a web page file and dropping it on an already-open browser window.)

Although ordinary people need only a single web browser, it's a good idea for web developers-in-training (like yourself) to become familiar with the most common browsers out there (see Figure 1-4). That's because, when you design your website, you need to prepare for a wide audience of people with different browsers. To make sure your nifty pages don't turn funky when other people look at them, you should test your site using a variety of browsers, screen sizes, and operating systems.

The following list describes the most popular browsers of today:

- **Google Chrome** is the current king of web browsers, despite the fact that it's the newest kid on the block. Tech-savvy web fans love its features, like bookmarks you can synchronize across different computers, and its blistering speed.

  Get with Google Chrome at *www.google.com/chrome*.

- **Internet Explorer** is the longest-lived browser and the official standard in many corporate and government environments. It's also the browser that comes pre-installed on Windows, so it's the one non-techie people use if they don't want (or don't know how) to install something new. Even hotshot web designers need to check that Internet Explorer understands their pages, because even old versions of IE, like IE 8, remain popular.

To download the most recent version of Internet Explorer, visit *www.microsoft. com/ie.*

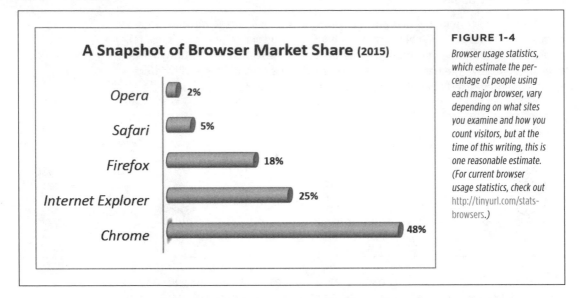

A Snapshot of Browser Market Share (2015)

- Opera — 2%
- Safari — 5%
- Firefox — 18%
- Internet Explorer — 25%
- Chrome — 48%

FIGURE 1-4

Browser usage statistics, which estimate the percentage of people using each major browser, vary depending on what sites you examine and how you count visitors, but at the time of this writing, this is one reasonable estimate. (For current browser usage statistics, check out http://tinyurl.com/stats-browsers.)

- **Firefox** started life as the modern response to Internet Explorer. It's still ahead of the game with its incredibly flexible *add-ons*, tiny programs that other people develop to enhance Firefox with extra features, like a web mail notifier and thumbnails of the sites that show up in a page of search results. Best of all, an army of volunteer programmers keep Firefox rigorously up to date.

   Give Firefox a go at *www.mozilla.org/firefox.*

- **Safari** is an Apple-designed browser that comes with current versions of the Mac OS operating system. Apple products like the iPhone, the iPad, and the iPod Touch also use the Safari browser (albeit a mobile version that behaves a bit differently). The fine folks at Apple created an incarnation of Safari for Windows computers but have since abandoned it, making Safari an Apple-only option.

   Go on Safari at *www.apple.com/safari.*

- **Opera** is a slimmed-down, easy-to-install browser that's been around for well over a decade, serving as an antidote to the bloated size and pointless frills of Internet Explorer. For years, Opera was held back by an unfortunate detail—if you wanted an ad-free version, you needed to pay. Today, Opera is free and ad-free, too, just like the other browsers on this list. It has a small but loyal following but runs a distant fifth in web browser standings.

   Check out Opera at *www.opera.com.*

Reaching as Many People as Possible

As you create your website, you need to consider not just what your audience wants to see, but what it *can* see as well. Good web designers avoid using frills on their pages unless *everyone* can experience them. Nothing is more disappointing than visiting a site that's supposed to have a nice animation and seeing a blank box, simply because your computer doesn't have the right browser plug-in (an add-on program that gives your browser more capabilities). Nor is it any fun finding a website that's all decked out for wide-screen monitors, but unbearably cramped (or, even worse, partly amputated) on the smaller screen of an iPad.

The creators of the most popular websites carefully consider these sorts of issues. For example, think about the number of people whose computers won't let them buy a book on Amazon.com, make a bid on eBay, or conduct a search on Google. (Are you thinking of a number that's close to zero?) To make your website as accessible as these top sites, you need to stick to widely accepted web standards, follow the advice in this book, and try your site on different computers.

It's been widely remarked that the average web designer goes through three stages of maturity: 1) "I'm just learning, so I'll keep it simple"; 2) "I'm a web guru, and I'll prove it by piling on the features"; and 3) "I've been burned by browser compatibility problems, so I'll keep it simple and classy."

Tutorial: Creating an HTML File

Now that you've prepped your web kitchen, you're ready to create your very own web page. In this tutorial, you'll build the basic page that you saw in Figure 1-1.

> **TIP** Like all the tutorials in this book, you'll find the solution for this exercise on the companion site at *http://prosetech.com/web*. Just look in the folder named *Tutorial-1-1* (which stands for "Chapter 1, first tutorial," if you're curious).

Ready to begin? Here's what to do:

1. **Fire up your text editor.**

   On a Windows computer, that's Notepad. To open Notepad, click the Start button, type "notepad," and then click the Notepad icon that appears.

   On a Mac, that's TextEdit. To launch it, go to the Applications folder and then double-click TextEdit.

   When you load up your text editor, it starts you out with a new, blank document, which is exactly what you want.

2. **Start writing your HTML code.**

   This task is a little tricky because you haven't explored the HTML standard yet. Hang on—help is on the way in the rest of this chapter. For now, you can use the following very simple HTML snippet. Just type it in exactly as it appears, text, slashes, pointy brackets, and all:

```
<h1>United Popsicle Workers Union</h1>
<p>We fight for your rights.</p>
```

Technically, this two-line document is missing a few structural details that self-respecting web pages should have. However, every browser can read this HTML fragment and correctly interpret what you want: the two lines of formatted text shown in Figure 1-1, top.

3. **When you finish your web page, choose File→Save.**

That brings up the Save or Save As window, where you fill in the details for your new file (Figure 1-5).

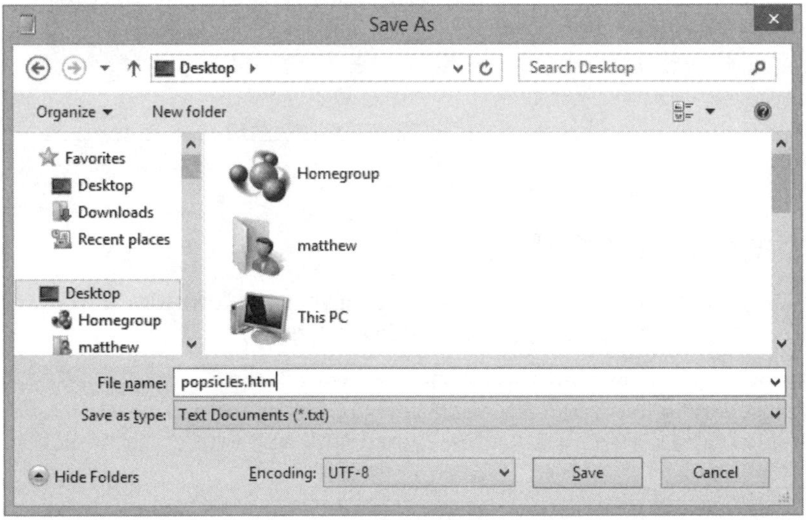

FIGURE 1-5

Whether you use Notepad (shown here) or TextEdit, there's nothing tricky about saving your file. Just make sure to include ".htm" or ".html" at the end of the filename to identify it as an HTML document.

4. **Pick a save location for your file, and give it the name** *popsicles.htm***.**

If you're not sure where to stash your file, you can save it right on your desktop for now.

When you name your file, make sure you include the extension .htm or .html at the end of the filename. For example, by using the name *popsicles.htm* or *popsicles.html*, you ensure that your computer will recognize your document as an HTML file.

Note for the paranoid: There's no difference between .htm and .html files. Both are 100% the same—text files that contain HTML content.

NOTE Technically speaking, you can use any file extension you want. However, using .htm or .html saves confusion (you immediately know the file is a web page) and helps avoid common problems. For example, using an .htm or .html file extension ensures that when you double-click the filename, your computer will know to open it in a web browser and not some other program. It's also important to use the .htm or .html extension if you plan to upload your files to a web server; prickly servers may refuse to hand out pages that have nonstandard file extensions.

5. **If necessary, change the way your text editor encodes your file to UTF-8.**

   This is the TextEdit standard, so Mac users can skip this step. But in Notepad, you need to choose UTF-8 in the Encoding list at the bottom of the Save As window.

   Your web page will work even if you don't take this step, but doing so ensures that you won't run into problems if you use special characters or a different language in your page.

6. **Click Save to make it official.**

   If you use TextEdit, the program may ask if you really want to use the *.htm* or *.html* extension instead of *.txt*, the text file standard; click "Use .htm." No such step is required in Notepad. However, you won't actually see your HTML files in the list unless you choose "All Files (*.*)" in the "Save as type" box (which initially has "Text Documents (*.txt)" selected).

7. **To view your work, open the file in a browser (Figure 1-6).**

   If you use the extension .htm or .html, opening a page is usually as easy as double-clicking the filename. Or you can drag your web page file and drop it onto an open browser window.

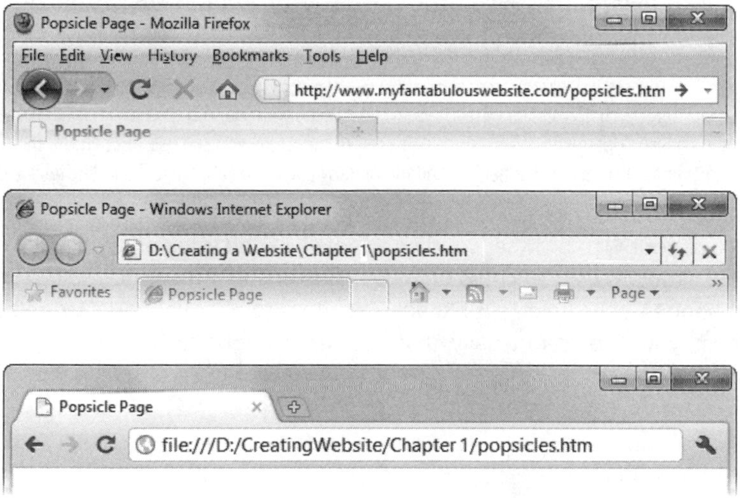

FIGURE 1-6

A browser's address bar reveals where the current web page is really located. If you see "http://" in the address, it comes from a web server on the Internet (top). If you look at a web page that resides on your own computer, you see just an ordinary local file address (middle, showing a Windows file location in Internet Explorer), or you see a URL that starts with the prefix "file:///" (bottom, showing a file location in Chrome).

If Your First Web Page Doesn't Look Right...

... the trouble is probably in the3 way you saved the file.

For example, one common problem is having your document appear in the web browser without formatting and with all the HTML tags showing. In other words, your document looks the same in your browser as it does in your text editor. Any one of several oversights can cause this problem:

- **You used the wrong file extension.** When you open files directly from your computer (rather than from a remote website), your browser may attempt to identify the file type by its extension. If you give your web page the extension .txt, the browser may assume that it's a text file and simply show the file's raw text content. To avoid this headache, use the .htm or .html extension.

- **You saved the document in a word processor.** Word processors automatically convert special HTML characters, like angle brackets, into HTML codes called *character*

entities (see page 63). For example, a word processor converts a tag like <h1> into the HTML text &lth1> by replacing the angle brackets with their character entities. The result is that the browser no longer recognizes your tag as a formatting instruction. Instead, it shows the text "<h1>" right on your web page. To avoid this tag tampering, write your HTML in a text editor.

- **You didn't save the document as a text file.** Some text editors let you save your documents in different formats. Notepad doesn't, but TextEdit does, and if you inadvertently save your web page as a rich text file, a browser won't treat it as a web page. To avoid this problem in TextEdit, make sure you configure it as described on page 5 (or just choose Format→Make Plain Text from TextEdit's menu bar). In other programs, check for options in the File→Save As window to make sure you're saving plain text.

8. **When you finish editing, close your text editor.**

   The next time you want to change your document, just fire up your text editor, choose File→Open, and then pick the file you want, or drag the file and drop it on an already-open text editor window.

> **TIP** Here's a trick that can help you open HTML files in a hurry. Find your file, and then right-click it (Control-click on a Mac) and choose "Open with." This pops open a list of programs you can use to open the file. Click Notepad (or TextEdit) in the list to launch a new text editor window and open your HTML file in one fell swoop.

   If you leave your web browser window open while you edit your HTML file in a text editor, the browser will hold on to the old version of your file. To see your recent changes, save your text file again (choose File→Save) and then refresh the page in your browser (usually, that's as easy as right-clicking the page and choosing Refresh or Reload).

Extra Practice: Opening HTML Files

As you learn the HTML language, you'll do lots of experimenting in your text editor, so you need to be completely comfortable opening and editing HTML files on your computer. Only later (in Chapter 5) will you try out heftier web editors, which do the same job but with more features.

If you want some extra practice, you can use the sample files for this chapter. You'll find them all on the companion site at *http://prosetech.com/web*. Once you download them to your computer, you can peek inside each one, just as you did with the HTML file you created yourself:

- Double-click a file to see its public face in a web browser.
- Load your text editor and choose File→Open to see its private HTML side.

Simple, right? If you have any doubts, take a minute to practice opening a few more HTML files before you forge on. We'll wait.

◾ Seeing the HTML of a Live Web Page

Most text editors don't let you open a web page that's on the Internet. However, web browsers *do* give you the chance to sneak a peek at the raw HTML that sits behind any web page.

If you're using Internet Explorer, Chrome, Firefox, or just about any browser other than Safari, you can use a shortcut. Once you navigate to the web page you want to examine, right-click anywhere on the page and choose View Source or View Page Source (the exact wording depends on the browser). A new window appears, showing you the raw HTML that underlies the page.

If you're using Safari on a Mac, you have to jump through an extra hoop to see a web page's HTML. First, switch on the Develop menu by choosing Safari→ Preferences→Advanced and then turning on the "Show Develop menu in menu bar" checkbox. Once you do, visit the page you want to dissect and choose Develop→Show Page Source.

TIP Firefox has a handy feature that lets you home in on just *part* of the HTML in a complex web page. Just select the text you're interested in on the page itself, right-click the text, and then choose View Selection Source.

Most web pages are considerably more complex than the *popsicles.htm* example shown in Figure 1-1, so you need to wade through many more HTML tags when you look at the web page markup. You're also likely to find a dense thicket of JavaScript code stuffed at the top of the page, stripped of all its spacing and almost impossible to read. But even if the markup looks like gibberish, don't panic. By the time you finish this book, you'll be able to scan through a jumble of HTML to find the bits that interest you. In fact, professional web developers often use the View Source technique to check their competitors' work.

■ A Closer Look at HTML Tags

Now that you know how to peer into existing HTML files and how to create your own, the next step is to understand what goes *inside* the average HTML file. It all revolves around a single concept—*tags*.

HTML tags are formatting instructions that tell a browser how to transform ordinary text into something visually appealing. If you were to take all the tags out of an HTML document, the resulting page would consist of nothing more than plain, unformatted text.

What's in a Tag

You can recognize a tag by looking for angle brackets, two special characters that look like this: < >. When creating a tag, you type HTML code between the brackets. This code is for the browser's eyes only; web visitors never see it (unless they use the View Source command to peek at the HTML). Essentially, the code is an instruction that conveys information to the browser about how to format the text that follows.

For example, one simple tag is the <b> tag, which stands for "bold" (by convention, tag names are usually written in lowercase). When a browser encounters this tag, it switches on boldface formatting, which affects all the text that follows the tag. Here's an example:

    This text isn't bold. <b>This text is bold.

On its own, the <b> tag isn't quite good enough; it's known as a *start tag*, which means it switches on some effect (in this case, bold lettering). You pair most start tags with a matching *end tag* that switches *off* the effect.

You can easily recognize an end tag. They look the same as start tags, except that they begin with a forward slash. That means they start like this </ instead of like this <. So the end tag for bold formatting is </b>. Here's an example:

    This isn't bold. <b>Pay attention!</b> Now we're back to normal.

Which a browser displays as:

    This isn't bold. **Pay attention!** Now we're back to normal.

This example reflects another important principle of browsers: They always process tags in the order in which you place them in your HTML. To get the bold formatting in the right place, you need to make sure you position the <b> and </b> tags appropriately.

As you can see, the browser has a fairly simple job. It scans an HTML document, looking for tags and switching on and off various formatting settings. It takes everything else (everything that isn't a tag) and displays it in the browser window.

> **NOTE** Adding tags to plain-vanilla text is known as *marking up* a document, and the tags themselves are known as HTML *markup*. When you look at raw HTML, you may be interested in looking at the content (the text nestled between the tags) or the markup (the tags themselves).

Understanding Elements

Most tags come in pairs. When you use a start tag (like <b>), you have to include the matching end tag (</b>). This combination of start and end tags, along with the text in between, makes up an HTML *element*.

Here's the basic idea: A pair of tags creates a container (see Figure 1-7). You place content (like text) inside that container. For example, when you use the <b> and </b> tags, you create a container that applies bold formatting to the text inside the container. As you create web pages, you'll use different containers to wrap different pieces of text. If you think about elements this way, you'll never forget to include an end tag.

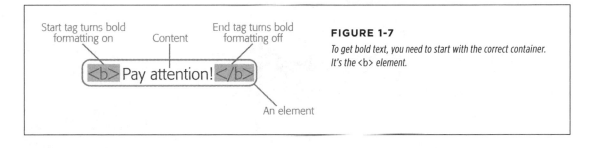

FIGURE 1-7

To get bold text, you need to start with the correct container. It's the <b> element.

NOTE When someone refers to the <b> *element*, she means the whole shebang—start tag, end tag, and the content in between. When someone refers to a <b> *tag*, she usually means the start tag that triggers the effect.

Of course, life wouldn't be much fun (and computer books wouldn't be nearly as thick) without exceptions. When you get right down to it, there are really *two* types of elements:

- **Container elements** are, by far, the most common type of element. They apply formatting to the content nestled between the start and end tags.

- **Standalone elements** don't turn formatting on or off. Instead, they *insert* something, like an image, into a page. One example is the <br> element, which inserts a line break in a web page. Standalone elements don't come in pairs, as container elements do, and you may hear them referred to as *empty* elements because you can't put any text inside them.

In this book, all standalone elements include a slash character before the closing >, sort of like an opening and closing tag all rolled into one. So you'll see a line break written as <br /> instead of <br>. This form, called the *empty element syntax*, is handy because it clearly distinguishes container elements from standalone elements. That way, you'll never get confused.

NOTE In the not-so-distant past, web developers were forced to use the empty element syntax—that is, tags that end with a forward slash—because it was an official part of the (now superseded) XHTML language. Today, the trailing slash is optional, so standalone elements can use the same syntax as start tags (which means you can use either `<br />` or `<br>` to insert a line break, for instance).

Figure 1-8 puts the two types of elements in perspective.

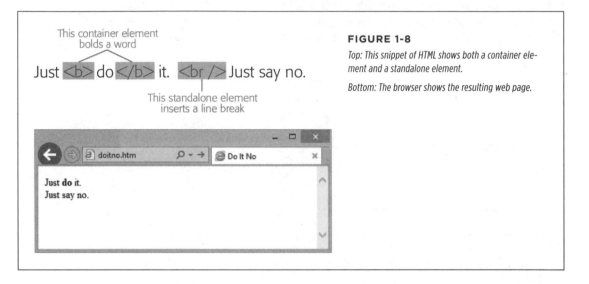

This container element bolds a word

Just `<b>` do `</b>` it. `<br />` Just say no.

This standalone element inserts a line break

FIGURE 1-8

Top: This snippet of HTML shows both a container element and a standalone element.

Bottom: The browser shows the resulting web page.

doitno.htm — Do It No

Just **do** it.
Just say no.

Nesting Elements

In the previous example, you applied a simple `<b>` element to get bold formatting. You put the text between the `<b>` and `</b>` tags. However, text isn't the only thing you can put between a start and an end tag. You can also nest one element *inside* another. In fact, *nesting* elements is common practice in building web pages. It lets you apply more detailed style instructions to text by combining all the formatting elements in the same set of instructions. You can also nest elements to create more complicated page components, like bulleted lists (see page 24).

To see nesting in action, you need another element to work with. For this example, consider what happens if you want to make a piece of text bold *and* italicized. HTML doesn't include a single element for this purpose, so you need to combine the familiar `<b>` element (to put your text in boldface) with the `<i>` element (to italicize it). Here's an example:

```
This <b><i>word</i></b> has bold and italic formatting.
```

When a browser chews through this scrap of HTML, it produces text that looks like this:

This ***word*** has bold and italic formatting.

Incidentally, it doesn't matter if you reverse the order of the <i> and <b> tags. The following HTML produces exactly the same result.

```
This <i><b>word</b></i> has italic and bold formatting.
```

However, you should always make sure that you close tags in the *reverse* order from which you opened them. In other words, if you apply italic formatting and then bold formatting, you should switch off bold formatting first, and then italic formatting. Here's an example that breaks this rule:

```
This <i><b>word</i></b> has italic and bold formatting.
```

Browsers can usually sort this out and make a good guess about what you really want, but it's a dangerous habit to get into as you write more complex HTML.

As you'll see in later chapters, HTML gives you many more ways to nest elements. For example, you can nest one element inside another, and then nest another element inside *that* one, and so on, indefinitely.

NOTE If you're a graphic-design type, you're probably itching to get your hands on more powerful HTML tags to change alignment, spacing, and fonts. Unfortunately, in the web world, you can't always control everything you want. Chapter 2 has the lowdown, and Chapter 3 introduces the best solution, called *style sheets*.

FREQUENTLY ASKED QUESTION

Telling a Browser to Ignore an Angle Bracket

What if I really do want the text "<b>" to appear on my web page?

The tag system works great until you actually want to use an angle bracket (< or >) in your text. Then you're in a difficult position.

Imagine you want to write the following bit of text as proof of your remarkable insight:

```
The expression 5 < 2 is clearly false,
because 5 is bigger than 2.
```

When a browser reaches the less-than symbol (<), it becomes utterly bewildered. Its first instinct is to assume you're starting a tag, and the text "2 is clearly false..." is part of a long tag name. Obviously, this isn't what you intended, and it's certain to confuse the browser.

To solve this problem, you need to replace angle brackets with the corresponding HTML *character entity*. Character entities stand in for letters and symbols that browsers would otherwise interpret as HTML. They always begin with an ampersand (&) and end with a semicolon (;). The character entity for the less-than symbol is < because the *lt* stands for "less than." Similarly, > is the character entity for the greater-than symbol.

Here's the corrected example:

```
The expression 5 &lt; 2 is clearly false,
because 5 is bigger than 2.
```

In your text editor, this doesn't look like what you want. But when a browser displays this document, it automatically changes the < into a < character, without confusing it with a tag. You'll learn more about character entities on page 63.

Incidentally, character replacement is one of the reasons you can get into trouble if you attempt to write your HTML documents in a word processor. When you save your word processor document as a text file, the program converts all the special characters (like angle brackets) into the corresponding character entities. When you open the page in a browser, you see ordinary text, not the formatting you expect.

■ Understanding HTML Documents

So far, you've considered snippets of HTML—portions of a complete HTML document. This gave you a taste of how HTML works, but you'll need to step up your game before you can conquer the Web. In this section, you'll learn about the structure that makes the difference between a scrap of HTML and an official HTML document.

The Document Type Definition

In the early days of the Internet, web browsers were riddled with quirks. When people designed web pages, they had to take these quirks into account. For example, browsers might calculate the margins around floating boxes of text in subtly different ways, causing pages to look right in one browser but appear odd in another.

Years later, the rules of HTML (and CSS, the style sheet standard you'll learn about in Chapter 3) were formalized. Using these new rules, every browser could display the same page in exactly the same way. But this change caused a serious headache for longstanding browsers, like Internet Explorer, that had lived through the dark ages of HTML. It had to somehow support the new standards while still being able to properly display existing web pages—including those that relied on old quirks.

The web community settled on a simple solution. When designing a new, modern web page, you indicate this fact by adding a code called a *document type definition* (DTD) or *doctype*, which goes at the very beginning of your HTML document (Figure 1-9).

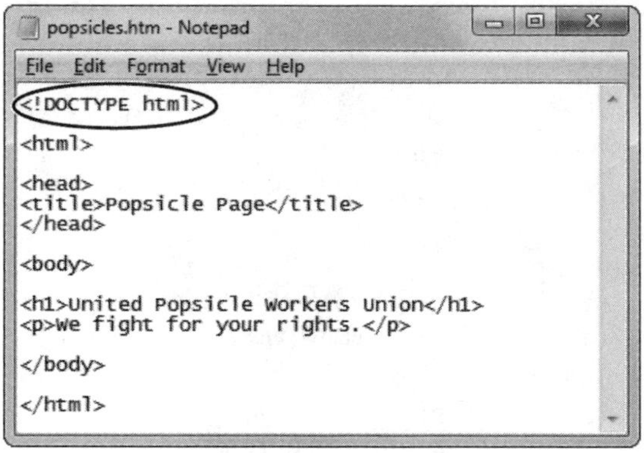

```
popsicles.htm - Notepad
File  Edit  Format  View  Help

<!DOCTYPE html>

<html>

<head>
<title>Popsicle Page</title>
</head>

<body>

<h1>United Popsicle Workers Union</h1>
<p>We fight for your rights.</p>

</body>

</html>
```

FIGURE 1-9

The document type definition (DTD) is the first piece of information in an HTML file. It tells the browser what markup standard you used to write the page.

When a browser encounters a doctype, it switches into *standards mode* and renders the page in the most consistent, standardized way possible. The end result is that the page looks virtually identical in every modern browser.

But when a browser encounters an HTML document that doesn't have a doctype, all bets are off. Internet Explorer, for example, switches into the dreaded *quirks mode*, where it attempts to behave the same way it did 10 years ago, quirks and all. This ensures that really old web pages retain the look they had when they were first created, even if they rely on ancient browser bugs that have long since been fixed. Unfortunately, different browsers behave differently when you view a page without a doctype. You're likely to get varying text sizes, inconsistent margins and borders, and improperly positioned content. For that reason, web pages without doctypes are bad news, and you should avoid creating them.

In the past, web designers used different doctypes to indicate different versions of HTML markup (for example, XHTML, HTML5, or truly old HTML 4.01). But today, web developers almost always use the simple, universal HTML5 doctype:

```
<!DOCTYPE html>
```

Even though this doctype was formalized as part of HTML5, every browser supports it—even old versions of IE that have never heard of HTML5. That's because the universal doctype doesn't indicate anything about the HTML version you prefer. Instead, it just indicates that the language *is* HTML. This one-line doctype simply reflects the true philosophy of HTML—to support documents old and new.

For comparison, here's the much wordier doctype for XHTML 1.0, which you may still stumble across in older web pages:

```
<!DOCTYPE html PUBLIC "-//W3C//DTD XHTML 1.0 Strict//EN"
"http://www.w3.org/TR/xhtml1/DTD/xhtml1-strict.dtd">
```

Even seasoned web developers had to copy the XHTML 1.0 doctype from an existing web page to avoid typing it in wrong.

In this book, all the examples use the HTML5 doctype not only because it's the current standard, but because it prepares your pages for the future, too. But just because you use this doctype doesn't mean you can use all of HTML5's features. In fact, you should avoid most of them for the time being, unless you're sure they're well supported by *all* the browsers that people use today.

NOTE In this book, you'll use only HTML5 features that work in all of today's browsers. But if you're interested in learning about the more experimental parts of the language that still have sketchy browser support, check out *HTML5: The Missing Manual* (O'Reilly).

The Basic Skeleton

Now you're ready to fill in the rest of your web page.

To create a true HTML document, you start with three container elements: <html>, <head>, and <body>. These three elements work together to describe the basic structure of your page:

<html>

    This element wraps everything (other than the doctype) in your web page.

`<head>`

> This element designates the *header* portion of your document, which includes some information about your web page. The first detail is the title—open your page in a browser, and this title shows up as the caption on the tab. Optionally, the `<head>` section can also include links to style sheets (which you'll learn about in Chapter 3) and JavaScript files (Chapter 14).

`<body>`

> This element holds the meat of your web page, including the actual content you want displayed to the world.

There's only one right way to use these three elements in a page. Here's their correct arrangement, with the HTML5 doctype at the beginning of the page:

```
<!DOCTYPE html>
<html>
<head>
...
</head>
<body>
...
</body>
</html>
```

Every web page uses this basic framework. The ellipses (...) show where you insert additional information. The spaces between the lines aren't required—they're just there to help you see the element structure more easily.

Once you have the HTML skeleton in place, you need to add two more container elements to the mix. Every web page requires a `<title>` element, which goes in the header section of the page, and you need to create a container for text in the `<body>` section of the page. One all-purpose text container is the `<p>` element, which represents a paragraph.

Here's a closer look at the elements you need to add:

`<title>`

> This element sets the title for your web page. The title plays several roles. First, web browsers display it in the browser tab or at the top of the browser window. Second, when a visitor bookmarks your page, the browser uses the title as the bookmark's label. Third, when your page turns up in a web search, the search engine usually displays this title as the first line in the results, followed by a snippet of content from the page.

`<p>`

> This indicates a paragraph. Web browsers don't indent paragraphs, but they do add a little space between consecutive paragraphs to keep them separated.

Here's the web page with these two new ingredients (in bold):

```
<!DOCTYPE html>
<html>
<head>
<title>Everything I Know About Web Design</title>
</head>
<body>
<p></p>
</body>
</html>
```

If you open this document in a web browser, you'll find that the page is blank, but the title appears (as shown in Figure 1-10).

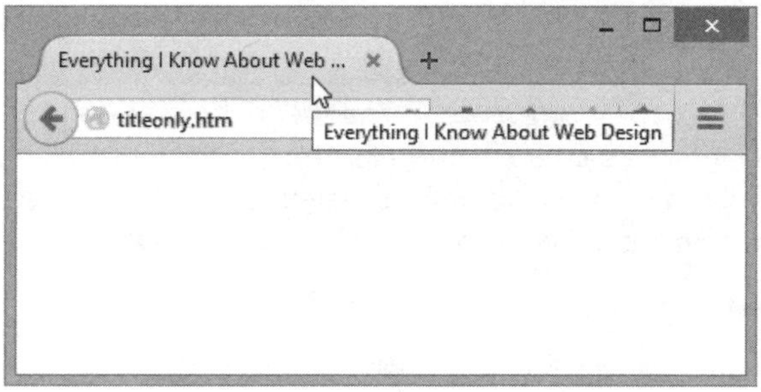

FIGURE 1-10

When a browser displays a web page, it shows the page's title on the browser's tab or at the top of the window. But be warned: the title won't always fit.

As it stands right now, this HTML document is a good template for future pages. The basic structure is in place; you simply need to change the title and add some text. That's the task you'll undertake next.

■ Tutorial: Building a Complete HTML Document

In this tutorial, you'll learn to assemble your first genuine web page. You'll be creating an online resumé (skip ahead to page 31 to see the final result), but the details apply to any page you create.

TIP Like all the tutorials in this book, you can find the solution for this exercise on the companion site at *http://prosetech.com/web*. Just look In the folder named *Tutorial-1-2* (short for "Chapter 1, second tutorial"). As you craft this page, adding a list, picture, and headings, it goes through several iterations. The tutorial files include a separate file for each stage of improvement.

Adding Your Content

No matter what sort of page you want to create, you always start out the same way:

1. **Launch your text editor.**

   That's Notepad or TextEdit.

2. **Type the HTML skeleton into a new file.**

   That's the doctype, the root <html> element, and the two major sections of every web page: <head> and <body>. It looks like this:

   ```
   <!DOCTYPE html>
   <html>
   <head>
   </head>
   <body>
   </body>
   </html>
   ```

   To save yourself some time in the future, save this page and then copy and paste this HTML skeleton each time you create a new file. The tutorial folder includes a file named *skeleton.htm* that helps you do just that—it contains the doctype and the three standard elements of an HTML page, but no content.

3. **Add a title to the <head> section.**

   Add the <title> element on a new line, between the opening <head> tag and the closing </head> tag:

   ```
   <title>Hire Me!</title>
   ```

4. **Add your content to the <body> section.**

   For example, suppose you want to write a simple resumé page. Here's a very basic first go at it:

   ```
   <!DOCTYPE html>
   <html>
   <head>
   <title>Hire Me!</title>
   </head>
   <body>
   <p>I am Lee Park. Hire me for your company, because my work is
   <b>off the hizzle</b>.</p>
   </body>
   </html>
   ```

   This example highlights (**in bold**) the modifications made to the basic HTML skeleton—a changed title and a single line of text. This example uses a single <b> element inside the paragraph, just to dress up the page a little.

5. **Save your HTML file as** *resume.htm*, **and open it in a web browser.**

If your page displays properly (see Figure 1-11), you can be reasonably certain you're off to a good start.

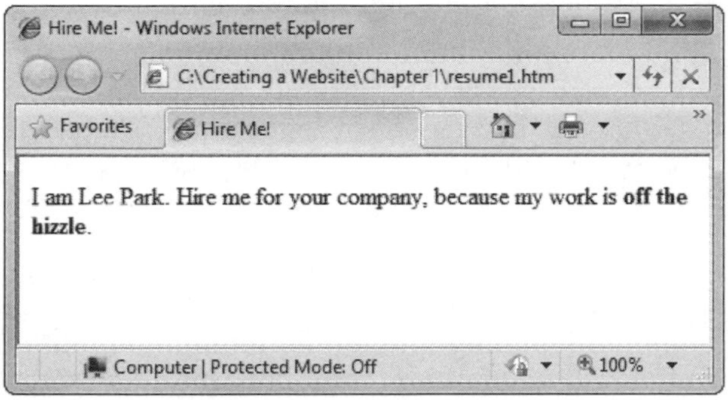

FIGURE 1-11

Welcome to the Web. This page doesn't have much in the way of HTML goodies (and it probably won't get Lee hired), but it does represent one of the simplest possible HTML pages you can create.

Using the HTML techniques described in the following sections, you can build on this example and give Lee a better resumé. Each time you make changes to your document in the text editor, refresh the page in your web browser to see if you're still on track.

Structuring Your Text

As you start to create more detailed web pages, you'll quickly discover that building a page isn't as straightforward as, say, creating a page in Microsoft Word. For example, you may decide to enhance the resumé page by creating a list of skills. Here's a reasonable first try:

```
<!DOCTYPE html>
<html>
<head>
<title>Hire Me!</title>
</head>
<body>
<p>I am Lee Park. Hire me for your company, because my work is <b>off the
hizzle</b>.
My skills include:
*Fast typing (nearly 12 words/minute).
*Extraordinary pencil sharpening.
*Inventive excuse making.
*Negotiating with officers of the peace.</p>
</body>
</html>
```

The trouble appears when you open this seemingly innocent document in your web browser (Figure 1-12).

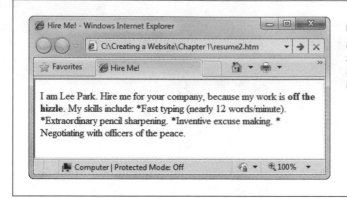

FIGURE 1-12

HTML disregards line breaks and consecutive spaces, so what appears as neatly organized text in your HTML file can turn into a jumble of text when you display it in a browser.

The problem is that HTML ignores extra white space. That includes tabs, line breaks, and extra spaces (anything more than one consecutive space). The first time this happens, you'll probably stare at your screen dumbfounded and wonder why web browsers are designed this way. But it actually makes sense when you consider that HTML needs to work as a *universal standard*.

Say you customize your hypothetical web page with the perfect spacing, indenting, and line width for *your* computer monitor. The hitch is, this page may not look as good on someone else's monitor. For example, some of the text may scroll off the right side of the page, making it difficult to read. And different monitors are only part of the problem. Today's web pages need to work on different types of *devices*. Lee Park's future boss might view Lee's resumé on anything from the latest widescreen laptop to a tablet computer or smartphone.

To deal with this range of display options, HTML uses elements to define the *structure* of your document. Instead of telling the browser, "Here's where you go to the next line and here's where you add four extra spaces," HTML tells the browser, "Here are two paragraphs and a bulleted list." It's up to the browser to display the page, using the instructions you include in your HTML.

To correct the resumé example, you need to use more paragraph elements and two new container elements:

`<ul>`

> Indicates the start of a bulleted list, called an unordered list in HTML lingo. A list is the perfect way to detail Lee's skills.

`<li>`

> Indicates an individual item in a bulleted list. Your browser indents each list item and, for sentences that go beyond a single line, properly indents subsequent lines so they align under the first one. In addition, it precedes each item with

a bullet (•). You can use a list item only inside a list element like `<ul>`. In other words, every list *item* (`<li>`) needs to sit within a list *element* (`<ul>`).

Here's the corrected web page (shown in Figure 1-13), with the structural elements highlighted in bold:

```
<!DOCTYPE html>
<html>
<head>
<title>Hire Me!</title>
</head>
<body>
<p>I am Lee Park. Hire me for your company, because my work is <b>off the
hizzle</b>.</p>
<p>My skills include:</p>
<ul>
  <li>Fast typing (nearly 12 words/minute).</li>
  <li>Extraordinary pencil sharpening.</li>
  <li>Inventive excuse making.</li>
  <li>Negotiating with officers of the peace.</li>
</ul>
</body>
</html>
```

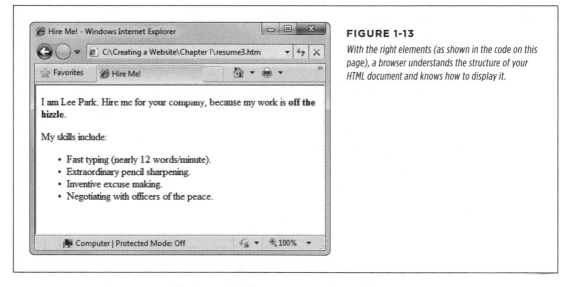

FIGURE 1-13

With the right elements (as shown in the code on this page), a browser understands the structure of your HTML document and knows how to display it.

You can turn a browser's habit of ignoring line breaks to your advantage. To help make your HTML documents more readable, add line breaks and spaces wherever you want. Web experts often use indentation to make the structure of nested elements easier to understand. In the resumé example, you can see this style in practice. Notice how the list items (the lines starting with the `<li>` element) are indented.

This has no effect on the browser, but it makes it easier for you to see the structure of the HTML document and to gauge how a browser will render it.

Figure 1-14 analyzes the HTML document using a *tree model*. The tree model is a handy way to get familiar with the anatomy of a web page, because it shows the page's overall structure at a glance. However, as your web pages get more complicated, they'll probably become too complex for a tree model to be useful.

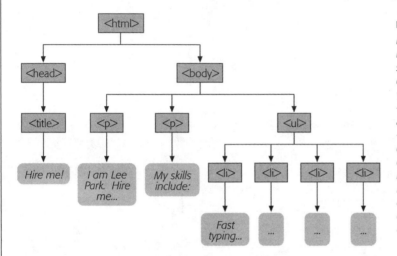

FIGURE 1-14

Here's another way to look at the HTML you created. The tree model shows you how you nested HTML elements. By following the arrows, you can see that the top-level <html> *element contains* <head> *and* <body> *elements. Inside the* <head> *element is the* <title> *element, and inside the* <body> *element are two paragraphs and a bulleted list with four items in it. If you stare at the tree model long enough, you'll understand why HTML calls all these elements "container elements."*

If you're a masochist, you don't need to use any spaces. The previous example is exactly equivalent to the following much-less-readable HTML document:

```
<!DOCTYPE html><html><head><title>Hire Me!</title></head><body><p>I am
Lee Park. Hire me for your company, because my work is <b>off the hizzle
</b>.</p><p>My skills include:</p><ul><li>Fast typing (nearly 12
words/minute).</li><li> Extraordinary pencil sharpening.</li><li>Inventive
excuse making.</li><li> Negotiating with officers of the peace.</li></ul>
</body></html>
```

Of course, it's nearly impossible for a human to write HTML like this without making a mistake.

Where Are All the Pictures?

Whether it's a stock chart, a logo for your underground garage band, or a doctored photo of your favorite celebrity, the Web would be pretty drab without pictures. So far, you've seen how to put text into an HTML document, but what happens when you need an image?

Have Something to Hide?

When you're working with a complex web page, you may want to temporarily remove an element or a section of content. This is a handy trick when you have a page that doesn't quite work right and you want to find out which element is causing the problem. You do so using the good ol' fashioned cut-and-paste feature in your text editor. Cut the section you think may be troublesome, save the file, and then load it up in your browser. If the section is innocent, paste it back in place, and then re-save the file. Repeat this process until you find the culprit.

But HTML gives you a simpler solution—*comments*. With comments, you can leave the entire page intact. When you "comment out" a section of the page, HTML ignores it.

You create an HTML comment using the character sequence `<!--` to mark the start of the comment, and the character sequence `-->` to mark its end. Browsers ignore everything in between, whether it's content or tags. You can comment out just a single line of HTML or an entire section of code.

However, don't try to nest one comment inside another, as that won't work.

Here's an example that hides two list items. When you open this document in your web browser, the list will show only the last two items ("Inventive excuse making" and "Negotiating with officers of the peace").

```
<ul>
<!--
<li>Fast typing (nearly 12 words/minute).
</li>
<li>Extraordinary pencil sharpening.</li>
-->
<li>Inventive excuse making.</li>
<li>Negotiating with officers of the
peace.</li>
</ul>
```

When you want to return the list to its original glory, just remove the comment markers.

Although it may seem surprising, you can't store a picture inside an HTML file. There are plenty of good reasons why you wouldn't want to anyway—your web page files would become really large, it would be hard to modify your pictures or do other things with them, and you'd have a fiendish time editing your pages in a text editor because the image data would make a mess. The solution is to store your pictures as separate files, and then *link* your HTML document to them. This way, your browser pulls up the pictures and positions them exactly where you want them on your page.

The linking tool that inserts pictures is the `<img>` element (short for "image"). It points to an image file, which the browser retrieves and inserts into the page. You can put the image file in the same folder as your web page (which is the easiest option), or you can put it on a completely different website.

Although you'll learn everything you ever wanted to know about web graphics in Chapter 4, it's worth considering a simple example now. To try this out, you need a web-ready image handy. (The most commonly supported image file types are JPEG, GIF, and PNG.) If you don't have an image handy, you can download the sample picture *leepark.jpg* from the Tutorial-1-2 folder. Here's an example of an `<img>` element that uses the *leepark.jpg* file:

```
<img src="leepark.jpg" alt="Lee Park Portrait" />
```

Like the <br> element discussed earlier, <img> is a standalone element with no content. For that reason, it makes sense to use the empty element syntax and add a forward slash before the closing angle bracket.

However, there's an obvious difference between the <br> element and the <img> element. Although <img> is a standalone element, it isn't self-sufficient. In order for the element to mean anything, you need to supply two more pieces of information: the name of the image file and some alternate text, which is used in cases where a browser can't download or display the picture (see page 116). To incorporate this extra information into the image element, HTML uses *attributes*, extra pieces of information that appear *after* an element name, but before the closing > character.

The <img> example includes two attributes, separated by a space. Each attribute has two parts—a name (which tells the browser what the attribute does) and a value (a piece of information you supply). The name of the first <img> attribute is src, which is shorthand for "source"; it tells the browser where to get the image you want. In this example, the value of the src attribute is *leepark.jpg*, which is the name of the file with Lee Park's headshot.

The name of the second <img> attribute is alt, which is shorthand for "alternate text." It tells a browser that you want it to show text if it can't display the image. Its value is the text you want to display, which is "Lee Park Portrait" in this case.

Once you understand the image element, you're ready to use it in an HTML document. Just place it wherever it makes sense, inside or after an existing paragraph:

```
<!DOCTYPE html>
<html>
<head>
<title>Hire Me!</title>
</head>
<body>
<p>I am Lee Park. Hire me for your company, because my work is <b>off the
hizzle</b>.
<img src="leepark.jpg" alt="Lee Park Portrait" />
</p>
<p>My skills include:</p>
<ul>
  <li>Fast typing (nearly 12 words/minute).</li>
  <li>Extraordinary pencil sharpening.</li>
  <li>Inventive excuse making.</li>
  <li>Negotiating with officers of the peace.</li>
</ul>
</body>
</html>
```

Figure 1-15 shows exactly where the picture ends up.

FIGURE 1-15

Here's a web page that embeds a picture, thanks to the linking power of the image element. To display this document, a web browser performs a separate request to retrieve the image file. As a result, your browser may display the text of the web page before it downloads the graphic, depending on how long the download takes (typically, that's a fraction of a second).

NOTE   You'll learn many more techniques for web graphics, including how to change their size and wrap text around them, in Chapter 4.

The 10 Most Important Elements (and a Few More)

You've now reached the point where you can create a basic HTML document, and you already have several elements under your belt. You know the fundamentals—all that's left is to expand your knowledge by learning how to use more elements.

HTML has a relatively small set of elements. You'll most likely use fewer than 25 on a regular basis. This is a key part of HTML's success, because it makes HTML a simple, shared language that anyone can understand.

NOTE   You can't define your own elements and use them in an HTML document, because web browsers won't know how to interpret them.

Some elements, like the <p> element that formats a paragraph, are important for setting out the overall structure of a page. These are called *block elements*. Block elements get extra space—when you add one to a page, the browser starts a new line (separating this block element from the preceding one). The browser also adds a new line at the end of the block element, separating it from the following element.

You can place block elements directly inside the <body> section of your web page or inside another block element. Table 1-1 provides a quick overview of some of the most fundamental block elements, several of which you've already seen. It also points out which of these are container elements and which are standalone elements. (As you learned on page 15, container elements require start and end tags, but standalone elements get by with just a single tag.) You'll study all of these elements more closely in Chapter 2.

TABLE 1-1 *Basic block elements.*

ELEMENT	NAME	TYPE OF ELEMENT	DESCRIPTION
<p>	Paragraph	Container	As your high school English teacher probably told you, the paragraph is the basic unit for organizing text. When you use more than one paragraph element in a row, a browser inserts space between the two paragraphs—just a bit more than a full blank line.
<h1>,<h2>,<h3>, <h4>,<h5>,<h6>	Heading	Container	Heading elements are a good way to add structure to your page and make titles stand out. They display text in large, boldfaced letters. The lower the number, the larger the text, so <h1> produces the largest heading. By the time you get to <h5>, the heading has dwindled to the same size as normal text, and <h6>, although bold, is actually smaller than normal text.
<hr>	Horizontal line (or horizontal rule in HTML-speak)	Standalone	A horizontal line can help you separate one section of your web page from another. The line automatically matches the width of the browser window. (Or, if you put the line inside another element, like a cell in a table, it takes on the width of its container.)
<ul>,<li>	Unordered list, list item	Container	These elements let you build basic bulleted lists. The browser automatically puts individual list items on separate lines and indents each one. For a quick change of pace, you can substitute <ul> with <ol> to get an automatically *numbered* list instead of a bulleted list (ol stands for "ordered list").

Other elements are designed to deal with smaller structural details—for example, snippets of bold or italicized text, line breaks, links that lead to other web pages, and images. These elements are called *inline elements*. You can put an inline element in a block element, but you should never put a block element inside an inline element. Table 1-2 lists the most useful inline elements.

TABLE 1-2 *Basic inline elements.*

ELEMENT	NAME	TYPE	DESCRIPTION
<b>, <i>	Bold and italic	Container	These two elements apply character styling—either bold or italic text. (Technically, <i> means "text in an alternate voice" and <b> means "stylistically offset text," and there are ways to change the formatting they apply, as you'll see in Chapter 3. But in the real world, almost all web developers expect that <i> means italics and <b> means bold.)
 	Line break	Standalone	Sometimes, all you want is text separated by simple line breaks, not separate paragraphs. This keeps subsequent lines of text closer together than when you use a paragraph.
<img>	Image	Standalone	To display an image inside a web page, use this element. Make sure you specify the src attribute to indicate the filename of the picture you want the browser to show.
<a>	Anchor	Container	The anchor element is the starting point for creating hyperlinks that let website visitors jump from one page to another. You'll learn about this indispensable element in Chapter 6.

To make the sample resumé look more respectable, you can use a few of the ingredients from Tables 1-1 and 1-2. Figure 1-16 shows a revised version of the web page that throws some new elements into the mix.

FIGURE 1-16

Featuring more headings, lists, and a horizontal line, this HTML document adds a little more style to the resumé.

Here's the pumped-up HTML, with the new headings and the horizontal rule high-lighted in bold:

```
<!DOCTYPE html>
<html>
<head>
  <title>Hire Me!</title>
</head>
<body>
  <h1>Hire Me!</h1>
  <p>I am Lee Park. Hire me for your company, because my work is <b>off the
hizzle</b>. As proof of my staggering computer skills and monumental work
ethic, please enjoy this electronic resume.</p>
  <h2>Indispensable Skills</h2>
  <p>My skills include:</p>
  <ul>
    <li>Fast typing (nearly 12 words/minute).</li>
    <li>Extraordinary pencil sharpening.</li>
    <li>Inventive excuse making.</li>
    <li>Negotiating with officers of the peace.</li>
  </ul>
  <p>And I also know HTML!</p>
  <h2>Previous Work Experience</h2>
  <p>I have had a long and illustrious career in a variety of trades.
    Here are some highlights:</p>
  <ul>
    <li>2008-2009 - Worked as a typist at <i>Flying Fingers</i></li>
    <li>2010-2013 - Performed cutting-edge web design at <i>Riverdale
    Farm</i></li>
    <li>2014-2015 - Starred in Chapter 1 of <i>Creating a Website: The
    Missing Manual</i></li>
  </ul>
  <hr />
</body>
</html>
```

Don't worry if this example has a bit too much markup for you to digest at once. In the next chapter, you'll get some more practice turning ordinary text into structured HTML.

■ Checking Your Pages for Errors

Even a web designer with the best intentions can write bad markup and break the rules of HTML. Although browsers really *should* catch these mistakes, virtually none of them do. Instead, they do their best to ignore mistakes and display flawed documents.

At first glance, this seems like a great design—after all, it smooths over any minor slip-ups you might make. But there's a dark side to tolerating mistakes. In particular, this behavior makes it all too easy for serious errors to lurk undetected in your web pages. What's a serious error? A problem that's harmless when you view the page in your favorite browser but makes an embarrassing appearance when someone views the page in another browser; a mistake that goes undetected until you edit the code, which inadvertently exposes the problem the next time your browser displays the page; or an error that has no effect on page display but prevents an automated tool (like a search engine) from reading the page.

Fortunately, there's a way to catch problems like these. You can use a *validation tool* that reads through your web page and checks its markup. If you use a professional web design tool like Dreamweaver, you can use its built-in error-checker (Chapter 5 has the details). If you create pages by hand in a text editor, you can use a free online validation tool (see below).

Here are some potential problems that a validator can catch:

- Missing mandatory elements (for example, the <title> element).

- A container start tag without a matching end tag.

- Incorrectly nested tags.

- Tags with missing attributes (for example, an <img> element without the src attribute).

- Elements or content in the wrong place (for example, text that's placed directly in the <head> section).

You can find plenty of validation tools online. The following steps show how to use the popular validator provided by the W3C standards organization (the official owners of the HTML language). Try it out with the *resume.htm* file you created in the second tutorial (page 21). Or give the validator something to complain about with the *popsicles.htm* file you created in the first tutorial (page 9). Because it's an HTML snippet, not a full HTML document, the validator is quick to complain about the missing bits, like the required <html>, <head>, and <body> elements.

Once you decide what you want to validate, here's what to do:

1. **Make sure your document has a doctype (page 18).**

   The doctype tells the validator what rules to use when validating your document. In this book, we stick with the universal HTML5 doctype (page 19).

2. **In your web browser, go to *http://validator.w3.org* (Figure 1-17).**

   The W3C validator gives you three choices, represented by three tabs: Validate by URI (for a page that's already online), Validate by File Upload (for a page that's stored on your computer), and Validate by Direct Input (for markup you type directly into the provided box).

FIGURE 1-17

The website http://valida-tor.w3.org *gives you three options for validating HTML. You can fill in the address of a page on the Web, you can upload a file of your own (shown here), or you can type the markup in directly.*

3. **Click the tab you want, and supply your HTML content.**

Validate by URI lets you validate an existing web page. Simply enter the URL (that's the full Internet address) for the page in the Address box (like *www. MySloppySite.com/FlawedPage.html*).

Validate by File Upload lets you upload any file from your computer. First, click the Browse button (called Choose File in Chrome) to see the standard Open dialog box. Browse to the location of your HTML file, select it, and then click Open. This is the easiest way to make sure you got everything right with the *resume.htm* page you built earlier.

Validate by Direct Input lets you validate any markup—you just need to type it into the large box provided. The easiest way to use this option is to copy the markup from your text editor and paste it into the box.

Before continuing, you can click More Options in any of the tabbed windows to set other options, but you probably won't. It's best to let the validator automatically detect the document type; that way, the validator will use the doctype specified in your web page. Similarly, leave the Character Encoding option set to "detect automatically" unless you wrote your page in something other than English and the validator has trouble determining the correct character set.

4. Click the Check button.

After a brief delay, the validator reports whether your document passed the validation check or, if it failed, what errors the validator detected (see Figure 1-18).

The validator also may offer a few harmless warnings for a perfectly valid HTML document, including a warning that the character encoding was determined automatically and a warning that the HTML5 validation service is considered to be an experimental, unfinished feature.

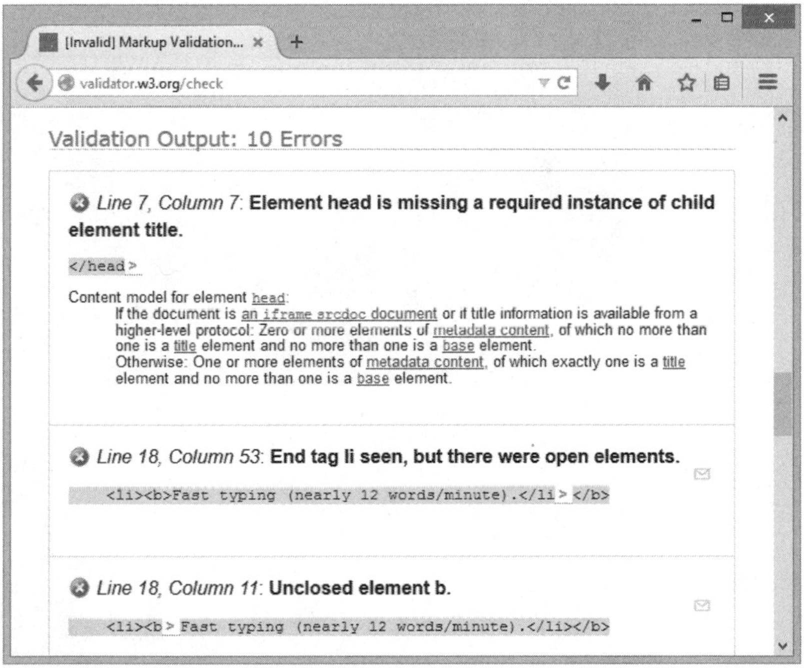

FIGURE 1-18

In this file, the validator has discovered 10 errors that stem from two mistakes. First, the page is missing the mandatory <title> element. Second, it closes the <li> element before closing the <b> element nested inside. (To solve this problem, you would replace </li></b> with </b></li>.) Incidentally, this file is still close enough to correct that browsers can display it correctly.

Putting More Pages under the Microscope

A validator is a good way to double-check the work you do for any of the tutorials in this book. But if you're keen to practice more validation right now, why not try the sample files from the companion site? This chapter includes a sample bad file, called *invalid_resume.htm*, that's chock-full of common mistakes. For a real challenge, peek inside the file and see if you can spot the problems before you hand it off to the W3C validator.

Becoming Fluent in HTML

G etting text into a web page is easy—you just open up an HTML file, drop in your content, and add the occasional HTML tag to format that content. But getting text to look *exactly* the way you want it to is a different story.

Before you can make your web pages look pretty, you need to organize their structure a bit. In this chapter, you'll learn about the first set of tools you need: the collection of HTML elements that let you break masses of text into neatly separated headings, paragraphs, lists, and more. You already put several of these elements to work in the Lee Park resumé tutorial in Chapter 1. In this chapter, you'll take a more detailed tour of *all* the HTML elements that let you structure text. Think of it as a condensed, one-chapter exploration of HTML's most important elements.

What you *won't* learn in this chapter is how to create the look of your pages. That's because HTML has virtually no formatting features. Instead, you need a separate standard—that's *CSS*, or Cascading Style Sheets—to change the way something looks on a web page. You'll tackle that subject in the next chapter. But for now, you'll focus on preparing properly structured HTML pages that you can pizzazz up later.

▓ Types of Elements

Before you dig in, it's time to review a couple of HTML essentials. As you learned in Chapter 1, you need to know two things about every new element you meet:

- Is it a container element or a standalone element?

- Is it a block element or an inline element?

The answer to the first question tells you something about the syntax you use when you add an element to a document. *Container elements* (like the <b> element that boldfaces text) require a start and end tag, with the content sandwiched in between. *Standalone elements* (like the <img> element that inserts an image into a page) use a single, all-in-one tag.

The answer to the second question tells you something about *where* you can place an element and how a browser will position your content. When you build a page, you build its HTML framework first, using *block elements*. Block elements (like the <p> element) go inside a page's main <body> element, or within another block element on the page. Each block element is a distinct chunk of content, and browsers automatically separate block elements from one another. *Inline elements* are for smaller bits of content, and they can slip seamlessly into another block element, with no extra spacing.

For example, consider this fragment of HTML:

```
<h1>Bread and Water</h1><p>This economical snack is really all you need to
sustain life.</p>
```

This snippet has a title in large, bold letters followed immediately by a paragraph of ordinary text. When a browser displays the page, you might expect to see both the heading and the text on the same line. However, the <h1> element is a block element. When you close it with the </h1> tag, the browser does a little housecleaning and adds a line break and some extra space before the next element. The paragraph of text starts on a new line, as you can see in Figure 2-1.

NOTE In an attempt to talk less about formatting and more about structure, HTML5 proposes some new terminology. It suggests that inline elements be called *phrasing elements* and block elements be called *flow elements*. The goal is to emphasize the difference in the way you can use and place these types of elements, while downplaying the way they affect formatting. (After all, the formatting details can be changed with style sheets, as you'll learn in the next chapter.) However, the terms "block element" and "inline element" are so common that it will be a while before new lingo replaces them—if the HTML5 jargon catches on at all.

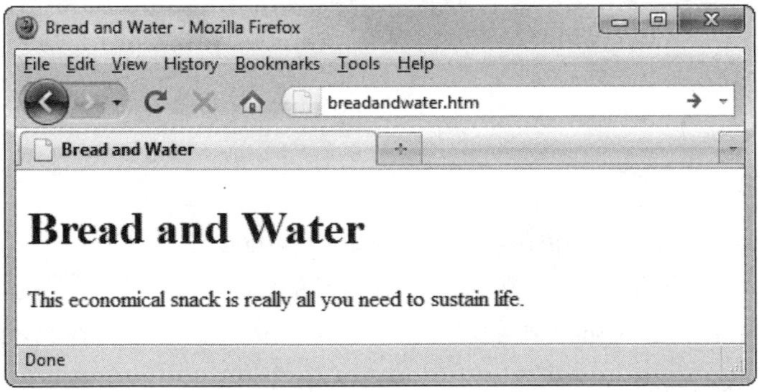

FIGURE 2-1

HTML separates block elements by a distance of approximately one and a half lines (in this figure, that's the space between "Bread and Water" and the sentence below it).

Browsers space out block elements to help ensure that one section of text doesn't run into another. However, in many cases, you won't be happy with this automatic spacing. For example, for dense, information-laden pages, the standard spacing looks far too generous. You can tighten up your text and shrink the spaces in between block elements using style sheets (page 91).

> **TIP** If you're ever in doubt about an element's status (container or standalone? block or inline?), just refer to the HTML reference in Appendix B, HTML Quick Reference.

HTML Elements for Basic Text

Now that you've reviewed element types, it's time to take a tour through your element toolkit. Once you learn all the text-structuring elements, you'll get a chance to put your skills to work with an exercise that invites you to mark up plain text with HTML tags (page 49).

But first, you'll start at the beginning, with the humble paragraph—the fundamental ingredient of many a web page.

Paragraphs

You've already seen the basic paragraph element, <p>. It's a block element that defines a paragraph of text.

```
<p>It was the best of times, it was the worst of times....</p>
```

You should get into the habit of thinking of the text in your web pages as a series of paragraphs. In other words, before you type in any text, add the <p> and </p> tags to serve as a container. Most of the time, paragraphs are the first level of structure you add to a page.

Figure 2-2 shows several paragraph elements in action.

> **NOTE** As you've no doubt noticed in your travels across the Internet, HTML paragraphs aren't indented as they often are in print. That's just the way of the Web, though you can change this with style sheets (page 91).

Web browsers don't pay attention to *hard returns* (the line breaks you create when you hit the Enter key). Consider, for example, this paragraph:

```
<p>
It looks
like
this text is spaced out. But really, the browser doesn't care about your extra
spaces, no matter how many you add.
</p>
```

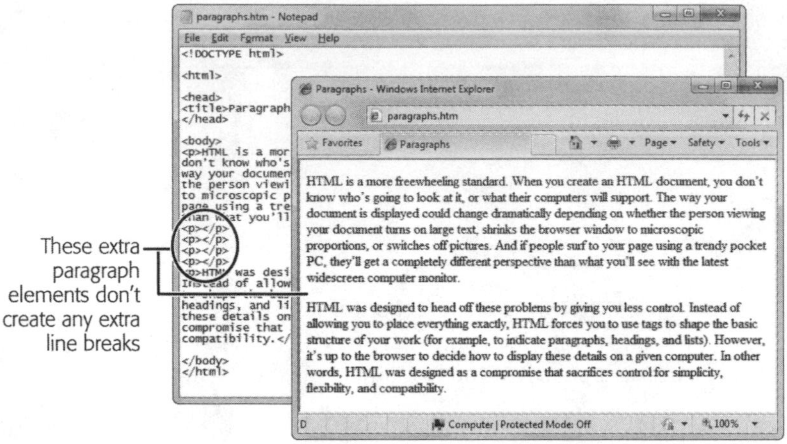

FIGURE 2-2

When you put several paragraphs of text in a row, a browser separates each one with a little over one line of space. Browsers ignore empty paragraph elements completely, however, and don't add any extra space for them.

These extra paragraph elements don't create any extra line breaks

Although this paragraph contains a few extra hard returns, the browser displays it as an unbroken paragraph, wrapping the text to fit the window, like this:

> It looks like this text is spaced out. But really, the browser doesn't care about your extra spaces, no matter how many you add.

This is the way browsers treat the text inside all elements (except the <pre> element, discussed on page 44). Web page writers often take advantage of this behavior, spacing out their HTML over several lines as they type it in. That makes the code easier to read and edit in a text editor, and the browser still wraps the content to fit the window. To insert a *real* break between your lines, check out the next section.

NOTE Technically, browsers don't ignore line breaks. They actually treat every line break as a single space. However, whenever a browser finds more than one space in a row, it ignores the extra ones. So, in the example above, the browser converts the two line breaks between "like" and "this" into two spaces, and then changes that to a single space. This behavior is called *collapsing the white space*.

Line Breaks

Sometimes you want to start a new line of text, but you don't want to use a paragraph element because browsers add extra space between paragraphs. This is the case, for example, when you want to include a business address on your site and you want it to appear in the standard single-spaced three-line format. In situations like this, the standalone line break element <br> comes in handy.

Line breaks are exceedingly simple: They tell a browser to move to the start of the following line (see Figure 2-3). They're inline elements, so you need to use them inside a block element, like a paragraph:

```
<p>This paragraph appears<br />
on two lines</p>
```

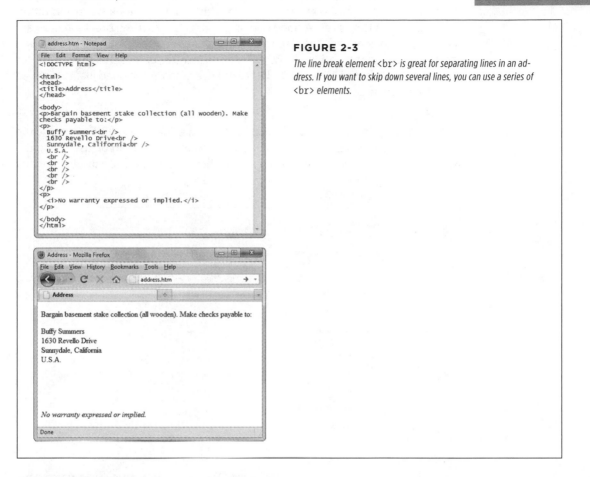

FIGURE 2-3

The line break element <br> is great for separating lines in an address. If you want to skip down several lines, you can use a series of <br> elements.

Getting More Space

The way that browsers ignore spaces can be exasperating. What if you really *do* want several spaces in a row? The trick is to use a special HTML *character entity* (see page 63) called the nonbreaking space, and written as . When a browser sees this entity, it interprets it as a space that it can't ignore. So if you create a paragraph by typing in this:

```
<p>Hello   Bye</p>
```

You end up with this:

```
Hello   Bye
```

Some web editors automatically add nonbreaking spaces when you press the space bar. This happens in Dreamweaver, for example, when you use the graphical preview of your web page and press the space bar.

Try not to use nonbreaking spaces more than necessary. And never, ever use spaces to align columns of text—that always ends badly, with the browser scrambling your attempts. Instead, use the layout features described in Chapter 8.

Don't overuse line breaks. Remember, when you resize a browser window, the browser reformats your text to fit the available space. If you try to perfect your paragraphs with line breaks, you'll end up with pages that look bizarre at different browser window sizes. A good rule of thumb is to avoid line breaks in ordinary paragraphs. Instead, use them to force breaks in addresses, outlines, poems, and other types of text whose spacing you want to tightly control. Don't use them for bulleted or numbered lists, either—HTML offers elements designed just for lists, as detailed on page 51.

In some cases, you want to *prevent* a line break, like when you want to keep the longish name of a company or a product on a single line. The solution is to use the HTML nonbreaking space code (which looks like) instead of just hitting the space bar. The browser still displays a space when it gets to the , but it won't wrap the words on either side of it (see Figure 2-4).

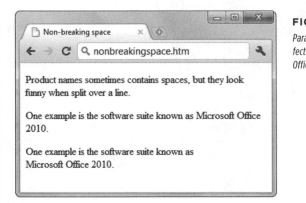

FIGURE 2-4

Paragraphs 2 and 3 in this figure show how the   code affects line breaks. Paragraph 3 is actually coded as Microsoft Office 2010. As a result, the browser won't split this term.

Headings

Headings are section titles, like the word "Headings" just above this paragraph. Browsers display them in boldface at various sizes, depending on the *heading level*. HTML supports six levels, starting at <h1> (the biggest) and dwindling down to <h6> (the smallest). Both <h5> and <h6> are smaller than regularly sized text.

Headings aren't just useful for formatting—they also help define the hierarchy of your document. Big headings identify important topics, while smaller ones denote lesser issues related to that larger topic. To make sure your document makes sense, start with the largest headings (level 1) and then work your way down. For instance, don't jump straight to a level-3 heading just because you like the way it looks.

NOTE It's probably occurred to you that if everyone uses the same heading levels in the same order, the Web will become as bland as a bagel in a chain supermarket. Don't panic—it's not as bad as it seems. When you add style sheets into the mix, you'll see that you can completely change the look of any and every heading you use. So for now stick to using the right heading levels in the correct order.

Webifying Your Text

You can't present text on the Web in the same way that you present it in print, but sometimes old habits are hard to shake. Here are some unwritten rules that can help you make good use of text in your web pages:

- **Split your text into small sections.** Web pages (and the viewers who read them) don't take kindly to long paragraphs.

- **Create short pages.** If a page goes on for more than two screens, split it into two pages. Not only does this make your pages easier to read, but it also gives you more web pages, which helps with the next point.

- **Divide your content into several pages.** The next step is to link these pages together (see Chapter 6). This gives

readers the flexibility to choose what they want to read, and in what order.

- **Put your most important information on the first screen.** The basic idea is to make sure there's something eye-catching or interesting for visitors to read without having to scroll down. This technique is called designing *above the fold*. Well-designed newspapers use the same strategy; it gives newsstand visitors something interesting to read without having to flip over the folded broadsheet, hence the term "above the fold."

- **Proofread, proofread, proofread.** Typos and bad grammar shatter your site's veneer of professionalism and web-coolness.

Horizontal Lines

Paragraphs and line breaks aren't the only way to separate sections of text. Another useful divider is the standalone <hr> element, which translates to "horizontal rule." A horizontal rule element adds a line that stretches from one side of its container to the other, separating everything above and below it.

> **NOTE** Usually, you position a horizontal break between paragraphs, which means it will stretch from one side of a page to the other. However, you can also put a horizontal rule in a narrower container, like a single cell in a table, in which case it won't turn out nearly as long.

Horizontal rules are block elements, so you can stick them between paragraphs (see Figure 2-5).

Obviously, the <hr> element is a design element, because it draws a line on your page. But the authors of the HTML5 specification want you to think of it as part of a page's structure by describing it not as a "horizontal rule" but as a "thematic break"—in other words, a basic way to separate different blocks of content, like scenes in a novel or topics in an academic paper. But it still looks like a line.

Preformatted Text

Preformatted text is a unique concept in HTML that breaks the rules you've read about so far. As you've seen, web browsers ignore multiple spaces and flow your text to fit the width of a browser window. Although you can change this to a certain extent using line breaks and nonbreaking spaces, some types of content are harder to deal with.

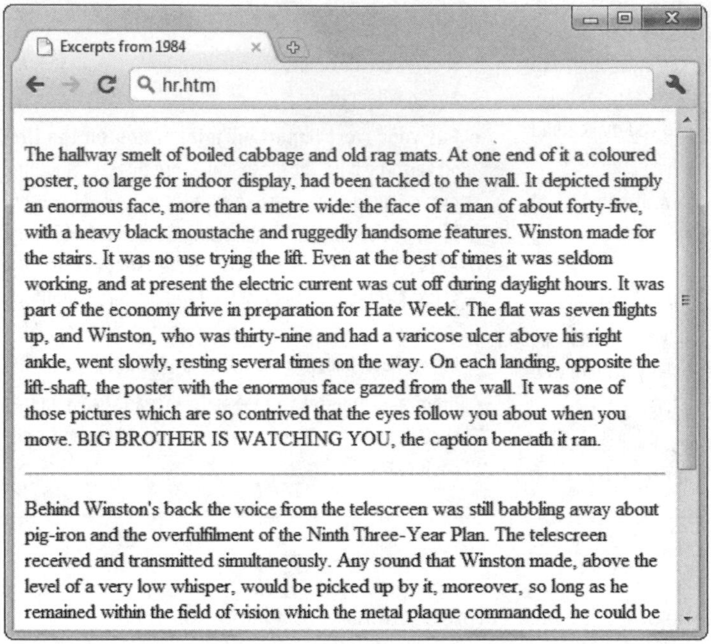

FIGURE 2-5

In this example, an `<hr>` element sits between the two paragraphs, inserting the solid line you see.

Imagine you want to display a bit of poetry. Using nonbreaking spaces to align the text is time-consuming and makes your HTML markup difficult to read. The `<pre>` element gives you a better option. It tells your browser to display the text just as you entered it, including every space and line break. Additionally, the browser puts all that text into a monospaced font (typically Courier), further setting this content off from the rest of the page. Figure 2-6 shows an example.

NOTE In a *monospaced* font, every letter occupies the same amount of space. HTML documents and books like this one use proportional fonts, where letters like W and M are much wider than I and i. Browsers use mono-spaced fonts for preformatted text because they let you line up rows of text exactly. The results, however, don't look as polished as when you use proportional fonts.

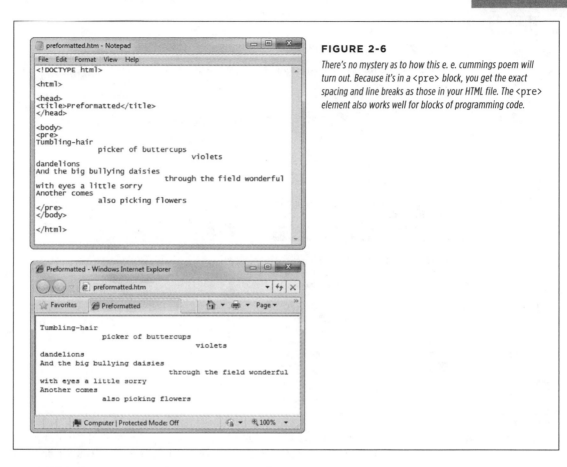

FIGURE 2-6

There's no mystery as to how this e. e. cummings poem will turn out. Because it's in a <pre> block, you get the exact spacing and line breaks as those in your HTML file. The <pre> element also works well for blocks of programming code.

Quotes

It may be a rare web page that spouts literary quotes, but the architects of HTML created a block element, named <blockquote>, especially for long quotations. When you use this element, your browser indents text on the left and right edges.

Here's an example:

```
<p>Some words of wisdom from "A Tale of Two Cities":</p>
<blockquote>
<p>It was the best of times, it was the worst of times, it was the age of
wisdom, it was the age of foolishness, it was the epoch of belief, it was
the epoch of incredulity, it was the season of Light, it was the season of
Darkness, it was the spring of hope, it was the winter of despair, we had
everything before us, we had nothing before us, we were all going direct to
Heaven, we were all going direct the other way-in short, the period was so
```

far like the present period, that some of its noisiest authorities insisted on its being received, for good or for evil, in the superlative degree of comparison only.</p>
</blockquote>
<p>It's amazing what you can fit into one sentence...</p>

Figure 2-7 shows how this appears in a browser.

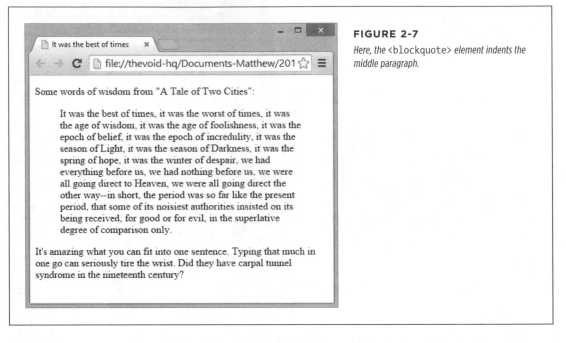

FIGURE 2-7

Here, the <blockquote> *element indents the middle paragraph.*

Occasionally, people use the <blockquote> element purely for its formatting capability—they like the way it sets off text. Of course, this compromises the spirit of the element, and you'd be better off using style sheets to achieve a similar effect.

As a block element, the <blockquote> element always appears independently of other block elements, like paragraphs and headings. It has one further restriction: It can hold only other block elements, which means that you need to put your content into paragraphs rather than simply type in free-form text between the blockquote start and end tags.

If, instead of using a quote that runs a paragraph or longer, you want to include a simple one-line quote, HTML's got you covered. It defines an inline element for short quotes that you can nest inside a block element. It's the <q> element, which stands for "quotation":

<p>As Charles Dickens once wrote, <q>It was the best of times, it was the worst of times</q>.</p>

Some browsers, like Firefox, add quotation marks around the text in a <q> element. Other browsers, like Internet Explorer, do nothing. If you want your quotation to stand out from the text around it in every browser, you might want to add some different formatting, like italics. You can do this by applying a style sheet rule (see Chapter 3).

And if you want to pack more information, you can add a URL that identifies the source of the quote (assuming it's on the Web) using the cite attribute:

```
<p>As Charles Dickens once wrote,
<q cite="http://www.literature.org/authors/dickens-charles/two-cities">It
was the best of times, it was the worst of times</q>.</p>
```

Looking at this example, you might expect this link to take readers to the referenced website (when they click the paragraph, for example). But that doesn't happen. In fact, the information in the cite attribute won't appear on your page at all. The *are* available to programs that analyze your page, like automated programs that scan pages and compile a list of references, or a search engine that uses this information to provide better search results. Most of the time, however, the reference has little benefit, except that it stores an extra piece of information that you, the website creator, might need later to double-check your sources.

If you do want to reference a source in your text, you might want to use the <cite> *element* (not the cite attribute mentioned above). It identifies the title of a work, like this:

```
<p>The quote <q>It was the best of times, it was the worst of times</q> is
from <cite>A Tale of Two Cities</cite>.</p>
```

In this case, a browser displays the text in the <cite> element in italics, just as if you had used the <i> element.

TIP Should you indeed want this paragraph to link to a reference, you need to investigate the <a> element described in Chapter 6.

Divisions and Spans

The last block element you'll learn about—<div>—is one of the least interesting, at least at first glance. On its own, it doesn't actually *do* anything.

You use <div> to group together one or more block elements. That means you could group together several paragraphs, or a paragraph and a heading, and so on. Here's an example:

```
<div>
    <h1>...</h1>
    <p>...</p>
    <p>...</p>
</div>
<p>...</p>
```

Given the fact that <div> doesn't do anything, you're probably wondering why it exists. The lowly <div> tag becomes a lot more interesting when you combine it with style sheets, because you can apply formatting commands directly to a <div> element, and therefore to all the other elements and their contents in the <div>. For example, if a <div> element contains three paragraphs, you can format all three paragraphs at once simply by formatting the <div> element.

> **TIP** As you'll see throughout this book, the <div> element is an indispensable, all-purpose container. You use it to shape the layout of your page, creating columns of text, navigation bars, floating figures, and more.

The <div> element has an important relative: the inline <span> element. Like its cousin, the <span> element doesn't do anything on its own, but when you place it *inside* a block element and define its properties in a style sheet, you can use it to format just a portion of a paragraph, which is very handy. Here's an example:

```
<p>In this paragraph, some of the text is wrapped in a span element. That
<span>gives you the ability</span> to format it in some fancy way later on.
</p>
```

You'll put the <div> and <span> elements to good use in later chapters.

POWER USERS' CLINIC

HTML5's Supercharged Structure

The <div> element is supremely flexible, but it doesn't say much about the real structure of your page. For example, one <div> element might represent a header that sits at the top of your page, while another might wrap a set of navigation links. For this reason, the <div> element isn't much help to anyone (or any program) trying to scan your markup and figure out what it all means. While this isn't a fatal flaw, it is a nagging shortcoming.

Part of the dream for the future of the Internet is to embed structural details into your pages, so that browsers, search engines, and automated tools can understand their structure and find important bits of information. To make the task easier, HTML5 offers several new elements that you can substitute for a plain-vanilla <div>, including <header>, <footer>, <article>, <section>, <aside>, and <nav>. Like the <div> element, these elements have no built-in formatting. They're simply containers where you can place content (and then position and format it with style sheets, as you'll learn

in Chapter 3). But unlike the <div> element, these elements have more meaning in your markup—they tell the person editing your page something about its structure. For that reason, HTML5 purists prefer to put a group of navigation links in a <nav> element rather than a generic <div> element, even though the final result in the browser looks the same.

Of course, because the HTML5 elements are relatively new, not all browsers can interpret them. This isn't a huge problem—after all, the <div>-replacement elements don't apply any formatting anyway, so it's perfectly fine if a browser chooses to ignore them. But there's a wrinkle with Internet Explorer, which doesn't let you use styles with elements it doesn't recognize. To fix this, you need to use a JavaScript workaround. Appendix B describes this workaround (page 578) and details the new elements that HTML5 adds. But people who don't need to be on the bleeding edge may prefer to wait for a while and stick to the tried-and-true <div>.

◼ Tutorial: Converting Raw Text to HTML

So far, you've considered a relatively small set of elements. But by combining these basic ingredients, you can create an endless number of different web pages. In this tutorial, you'll use just a few of these elements to transform plain, unremarkable text into a proper web page.

> **TIP** Like all the tutorials in this book, you can find the solution for this exercise on the companion site at *http://prosetech.com/web*. Just look in the folder named Tutorial-2-1 (which stands for "Chapter 2, first tutorial").

The starting point is the file *PessimistReviews_unformatted.htm*, which you can find in the Tutorial-2-1 folder. It contains the essential HTML elements that every web page requires: <html>, <head>, <title>, and <body>. But that's it—you'll find not a single formatting tag more:

```
<!DOCTYPE html>
<html>
<head>
<title>The Pessimist Reviews</title>
</head>
<body>
The Pessimist's Review Site

Here you'll learn about the greatest unpublished books ever (not) written.

The reviews on this Web site do not correspond to reality. Any correspondence
is purely coincidental.

How To Fail in Life
Chris Chu
Party Press, 1st edition
Tired of sabotaging yourself endlessly? With this book, the author Chris Chu
explains how to level the playing field and take on a challenge you can really
master. So throw away those old self-help books and start accomplishing
something!

Europe: Great Places to Miss
Antonio Cervantes<br>Focalio, 1st edition
Europe is brimming with world class attractions: glorious art galleries,
charming bed-and-breakfast inns, old school restaurants and much more. But who
can afford it? This book carefully documents some of the best attractions
across Europe, and provides detailed plans that explain how to miss them and
keep your last few paltry cents in your pocket.
</body>
</html>
```

Remember, browsers ignore line breaks and other white space in HTML, so if you open this unfinished file in a browser, all the text will flow in a single, unbroken paragraph (Figure 2-8).

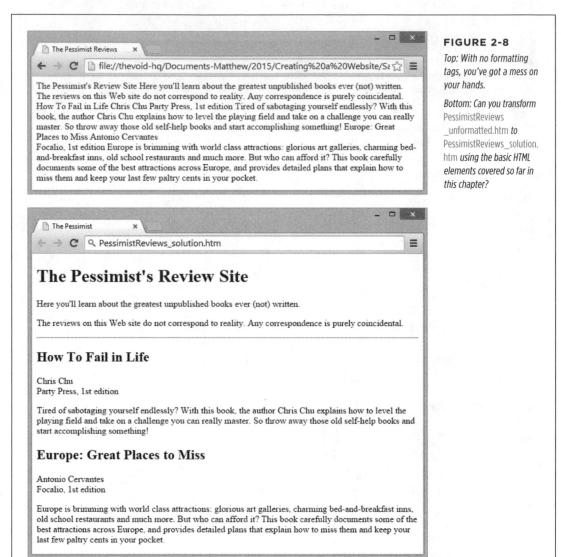

FIGURE 2-8

Top: With no formatting tags, you've got a mess on your hands.

Bottom: Can you transform PessimistReviews _unformatted.htm to PessimistReviews_solution. htm using the basic HTML elements covered so far in this chapter?

To conquer this challenge, begin by looking at the solution file (*PessimistReviews_solution.htm*) either on your own computer or in Figure 2-8. Identify each section of content, or block element, as best you can. You should be able to spot two levels of headings, some paragraphs, and a horizontal line, for starters.

Then add the corresponding elements to the unformatted file (*PessimistReviews_unformatted.htm*). The text is already split up on separate lines and waiting; all you need to do is fill in the missing start and end tags. For example, here's how you would mark up the title:

```
<h1>The Pessimist's Review Site</h1>
```

As you work, save your edits and check out the result in a browser. To double-check your finished effort, compare your work with *PessimistReviews_solution.htm*.

NOTE Earlier incarnations of HTML still have a number of useful elements you can use in an HTML5-built page. In the rest of this chapter, you'll look at the elements that let you build lists and tables, and the HTML codes you need to write special characters (like symbols and accented letters).

■ HTML Elements for Lists

Once you master HTML's basic text elements, you can tackle its list elements. HTML lets you create three types of lists:

- **Ordered lists** give each item in a list a sequential number (as in 1, 2, 3). They're handy when sequence is important, like when you list a series of steps that tell your relatives how to drive to your house.

- **Unordered lists** are also known as bulleted lists, because a bullet appears before each item. To some degree, you can control what the bullet looks like. You're reading a bulleted list right now.

- **Definition lists** are handy for displaying terms followed by definitions or descriptions. For example, the dictionary is one huge definition list. In a definition list on a web page, your browser left-aligns the terms and indents the definitions underneath them.

In the following sections, you'll learn how to create all three types of lists.

Ordered Lists

In an ordered list, HTML numbers each item consecutively, starting at some value (usually 1). The neat part about ordered lists in HTML is that you don't need to supply the numbers. Instead, the browser automatically adds the appropriate number next to each list item (sort of like the auto-number feature in Microsoft Word). This is handy for two reasons. First, it lets you insert and remove list items without screwing up your numbering. Second, HTML carefully aligns the numbers and list items, which isn't easy to do on your own.

To create an ordered list, use `<ol>` ("ordered list"), a block element. Then, inside the `<ol>` element, place an `<li>` element for each item in the list (`<li>` stands for "list item").

For example, here's an ordered list with three items:

```
<p>To wake up in the morning:</p>
<ol>
    <li>Rub eyes.</li>
    <li>Assume upright position.</li>
    <li>Turn on light.</li>
</ol>
```

In a browser, you'd see this:

To wake up in the morning:

1. Rub eyes.

2. Assume upright position.

3. Turn on light.

The browser inserts some space between the paragraph preceding the list and the list itself, as it does with all block elements. Next, it gives each list item a number.

Ordered lists get more interesting when you mix in the start and type attributes. The start attribute lets you start the list at a value other than 1. Here's an example that starts the counting at 5:

```
<p>To wake up in the morning:</p>
<ol start="5">
    <li>Rub eyes.</li>
    <li>Assume upright position.</li>
    <li>Turn on light.</li>
</ol>
```

Now you'll get the same list but with the items numbered 5, 6, 7 instead of 1, 2, 3.

HTML doesn't limit you to numbers in your ordered list. The type attribute lets you choose the numbering style. You can use sequential letters and Roman numerals, as described in Table 2-1. Figure 2-9 shows a few examples.

TABLE 2-1 *Types of ordered lists.*

TYPE ATTRIBUTE	DESCRIPTION	EXAMPLE
1	Numbers	1, 2, 3, 4...
a	Lowercase letters	a, b, c, d...
A	Uppercase letters	A, B, C, D...
i	Lowercase Roman numerals	i, ii, iii, iv...
I	Uppercase Roman numerals	I, II, III, IV...

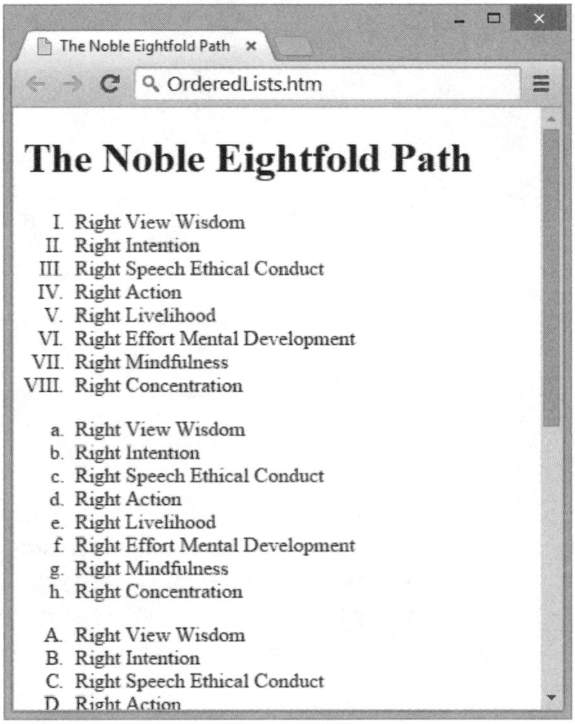

FIGURE 2-9

The type attribute in action. For example, the code to start off the first list is `<ol type="I">`.

Unordered Lists

Unordered lists are similar to ordered lists except that they aren't consecutively numbered or lettered. They do, however, use the same container element, `<ul>`, and you wrap each item inside an `<li>` element. The browser indents each item in the list and automatically draws the bullets.

The most interesting option that comes with unordered lists is the type attribute, which lets you change the style of bullet. You can use `disc` (a black dot, which is automatic), `circle` (an empty circle), or `square` (a filled-in square). Figure 2-10 shows the different styles.

Definition Lists

Definition lists are perfect for creating your own online glossary. Each list item consists of two parts, a term (which the browser doesn't indent) and a definition (which the browser indents underneath the term).

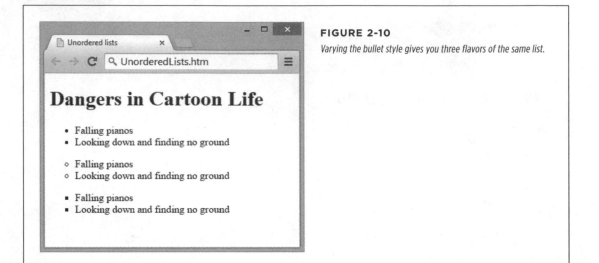

FIGURE 2-10

Varying the bullet style gives you three flavors of the same list.

Definition lists use a slightly different tagging system than ordered and unordered lists. First, you wrap the whole list in a dictionary list element (<dl>). Then you wrap each term in a <dt> element (dictionary term), and each definition in a <dd> element (dictionary definition). Here's an example:

```
<dl>
  <dt>eat</dt>
  <dd>To perform successively (and successfully) the functions of mastication,
  humectation, and deglutition.</dd>
  <dt>eavesdrop</dt>
  <dd>Secretly to overhear a catalog of the crimes and vices of another or
  yourself.</dd>
  <dt>economy</dt>
  <dd>Purchasing the barrel of whiskey that you do not need for the price of
  the cow that you cannot afford.</dd>
</dl>
```

In a browser you'd see this:

eat
> To perform successively (and successfully) the functions of mastication, humectation, and deglutition.

eavesdrop
> Secretly to overhear a catalog of the crimes and vices of another or yourself.

economy

Purchasing the barrel of whiskey that you do not need for the price of the cow that you cannot afford.

Nesting Lists

Lists work well on their own, but you can get even fancier by placing one complete list inside another. This technique is called *nesting* lists, and it lets you build multi-layered outlines and detailed sequences of instructions.

To nest a list, declare a new list inside an `<li>` element in an existing list. For example, the following daily to-do list has three levels. "Monday" is an example of an item at the first level, "Plan schedule for week" is at the second level, and "Wild Hypothesis" is at the third level. Figure 2-11 shows the result.

```
<ul>
  <li>Monday
    <ol>
      <li>Plan schedule for week</li>
      <li>Complete Project X
        <ul style="square">
          <li>Preliminary Interview</li>
          <li>Wild Hypothesis</li>
          <li>Final Report</li>
        </ul>
      </li>
      <li>Edit bucket list</li>
    </ol>
  </li>
  <li>Tuesday
    <ol>
      <li>Revise schedule</li>
      <li>Procrastinate (time permitting). If necessary, put off
      procrastination until another day.</li>
    </ol>
  </li>
  <li>Wednesday
  ...
</ul>
```

TIP When using nested lists, it's a good idea to use indents in your HTML so you can see the different levels of list elements at a glance. Otherwise, you'll find it difficult to determine where each list item belongs.

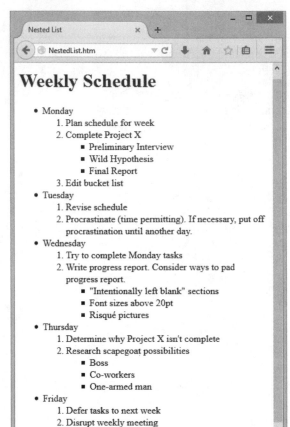

FIGURE 2-11

In nested lists, the different list styles really start to become useful for distinguishing each level. In this example, a bulleted list holds several numbered lists, and some of these numbered lists hold their own bulleted sub-lists. When you nest lists, browsers indent each subsequent list. Although you aren't limited in the number of levels you can use, you'll eventually run out of room in your browser window and force your text up against the right side of the page.

SHARPEN UP

Finish the Nested List

The example in Figure 2-11 covers five days of the week. However, the sample code shows the markup for just two days: Monday and Tuesday. If you understand the way HTML works with nested lists, you can fill in the rest—and it makes for excellent list-writing practice.

To try this out, start with the HTML document for the two-day list, which you can find in the Tutorial-2-2 folder on the companion site at *http://prosetech.com/web*. Then add the extra content to match what you see in Figure 2-11. You'll need to use the familiar suspects: the <ol>, <ul>, and <li> elements. When you finish, take a look in a browser, or check the solution in the Tutorial-2-2 folder to see if you got every detail.

■ HTML Elements for Tables

As with any table, an HTML table is a grid of cells built out of rows and columns using elements designed for the purpose. In the Bad Old Days of the Web, crafty web designers used invisible tables to line up pictures and arrange text into columns. Now style sheets fill that gap with top-notch layout features (as described in Chapter 8) and HTML tables are back to being just tables.

A Basic Table

You can whip up a table using these HTML elements:

- `<table>` wraps the whole shebang. It's the starting point for every table (and `</table>` is the end point).

- `<tr>` represents a single row in a table. Every table element (`<table>`) contains a series of one or more `<tr>` elements.

- `<td>` represents a table cell ("td" stands for "table data"). For each cell you want in a row, add one `<td>` element. Put the text you want to appear in the cell inside the `<td>` element. Browsers display it in the same font as ordinary body text.

- `<th>` is an optional table element designed for column headings. (Technically, you can use a `<th>` element instead of a `<td>` element at any time, although it usually makes the most sense in the first row of a table.) Browsers format the text inside the `<th>` element in almost the same way as text in a `<td>` element, except that they automatically boldface and center the text (unless you apply different formatting rules with a style sheet).

Figure 2-12 shows a table at its simplest. Here's a portion of the HTML used to create it:

```
<table>
  <tr>
    <th>Rank</th>
    <th>Name</th>
    <th>Population</th>
  </tr>
  <tr>
    <td>1</td>
    <td>Rome</td>
    <td>450,000</td>
  </tr>
  <tr>
    <td>2</td>
    <td>Luoyang (Honan), China</td>
    <td>420,000</td>
  </tr>
```

```
<tr>
  <td>3</td>
  <td>Seleucia (on the Tigris), Iraq</td>
  <td>250,000</td>
</tr>
  ...
</table>
```

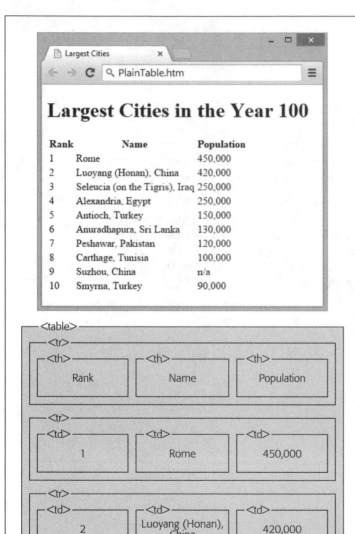

FIGURE 2-12

Top: This basic table doesn't have any borders (which is standard), but you can still spot the signature feature of a table: text lined up neatly in rows and columns.

Bottom: This behind-the-scenes look at the HTML powering the table above shows the <table>, <tr>, <th>, and <td> elements for the first three rows.

The markup for this table uses indented table elements to help you see the table's structure. Indenting table elements like this is always a good idea, as it helps you spot mismatched tags. In this example, the only content in the <td> elements is ordinary text. But you can put other HTML elements in cells, too, including images (the <img> element), numbers, and pretty much any other HTML you like.

NOTE   To add borders to tables or control the breadth of table columns, you need to use a style sheet. Page 111 shows you how to use CSS properties to create table borders.

Spanning Cells

Tables support *spanning*, a feature that lets a single cell stretch out over several columns or rows. Think of spanning as HTML's version of the Merge Cells feature in Microsoft Word and Excel.

Spanned cells let you tweak your tables in all kinds of funky ways. You can, for example, specify a *column span* to stretch a cell over two or more columns beside it. Just add a colspan attribute to the <td> element you want to extend, and specify the total number of columns you want to merge.

Here's an example that stretches a cell over two columns:

```
<table>
  <tr>
    <td>Column 1</td>
    <td>Column 2</td>
    <td>Column 3</td>
    <td>Column 4</td>
  </tr>
  <tr>
    <td> </td>
    <td colspan="2">Look out, this cell spans two columns!</td>
    <td> </td>
  </tr>
  ...
</table>
```

Figure 2-13 shows this column-spanning in action. To make sure your table doesn't get mangled, you need to keep track of the total number of columns you have to work with in each row. In the previous example, the first row starts off by defining four columns:

```
<tr>
  <td>Column 1</td>
  <td>Column 2</td>
  <td>Column 3</td>
  <td>Column 4</td>
</tr>
```

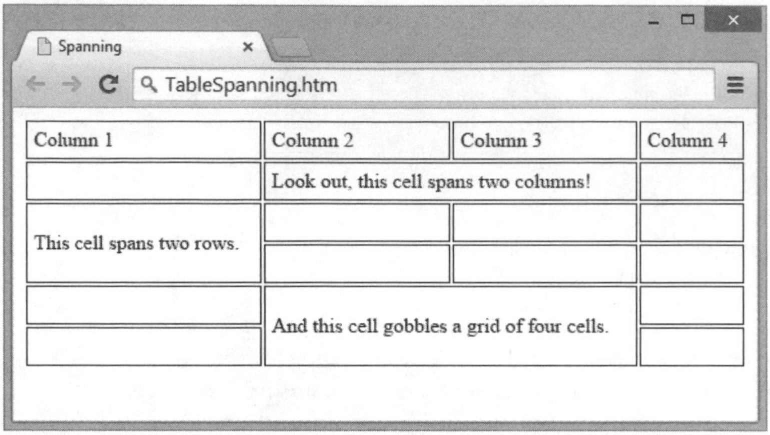

FIGURE 2-13

A table with row spanning and column spanning run amok. Here, the page creator turned on table borders (page 111) so you can see the outline of each cell.

In the next row, the second column extends over the third column, thanks to column spanning (see the markup below). As a result, the third `<td>` element actually represents the *fourth* column. That means you need only three `<td>` elements to fill up the full width of the table:

```
<tr>
  <!-- This fills column 1 -->
  <td> </td>
  <!-- This fills columns 2 and 3 -->
  <td colspan="2">Look out, this cell spans two columns!</td>
  <!-- This fills column 4 -->
  <td> </td>
</tr>
```

This same principle applies to *row spanning* and the rowspan attribute. In the following example, the first cell in the row actually takes up two rows:

```
<tr>
  <td rowspan="2">This cell spans two rows.</td>
  <td> </td>
  <td> </td>
  <td> </td>
</tr>
```

In the next row, the cell from above already occupies the first cell, so the first `<td>` element you declare actually applies to the *second* column. All in all, therefore, this row needs only three `<td>` elements:

```
<tr>
  <td> </td>
  <td> </td>
  <td> </td>
</tr>
```

If you miscount and add too many cells to a row, you end up with an extra column at the end of your table.

Inline Formatting

It's best not to format HTML too heavily. To get maximum control over your pages' appearance and to more easily update your website's look later on, you should head straight to style sheets (as described in the next chapter). However, a few basic HTML formatting elements are truly useful. You're certain to come across them, and you'll probably want to use them in your own pages. These elements are all *inline* elements, so you use them inside a block element, like a paragraph, a heading, or a list.

Formatting Text: Italics and Bold

You know the elements for bold (<b>) and italic (<i>) formatting from Chapter 1. They're staples in the HTML world, letting you quickly format snippets of text. Here's an example:

```
<p>
<b>Stop!</b> The mattress label says <i>do not remove under penalty
of law</i> and you <i>don't</i> want to mess with mattress companies.
</p>
```

A browser displays that HTML like this:

> **Stop!** The mattress label says *do not remove under penalty of law* and you *don't* want to mess with mattress companies.

To make life more interesting, HTML has a second set of elements that appear—at first glance—to do the same things. These are <em> (for emphasized text) and <strong>.

Here's the previous example rewritten to use the <em> and <strong> elements:

```
<p>
<strong>Stop!</strong> The mattress label says <em>do not remove under penalty
of law</em> and you <em>don't</em> want to mess with mattress companies.
</p>
```

Ordinarily, the <em> element italicizes text, just like the <i> element does. Similarly, the <strong> element bolds text, just as the <b> element does. The difference is philosophical.

Here's what the latest version of the HTML standard suggests:

- Use `<strong>` for words that are more important than the surrounding text. The word "Stop!" in the previous example is a good example.

- Use `<b>` for text that should be presented in bold but doesn't have greater importance than the rest of your text. This could include keywords, product names, and anything else that would be bold in print. For example, you might decide to bold the first three words of every paragraph in your document for stylistic reasons. It wouldn't be pretty, but `<b>` would be a better choice than `<strong>`.

- Use `<em>` for emphasized text, which would have a different inflection if read out loud. One example is the word "don't" in the previous example.

- Use `<i>` for text in an alternate voice, such as foreign words, technical terms, and anything else that you'd set in italics in print. The mattress warning in the previous example is a good model.

NOTE Truthfully, very few web designers haven't broken these guidelines at least a few times. The best advice is to be as consistent as possible in your own work. Also, remember that you can change the way you emphasize your text long after you apply your markup. For example, you might decide that you don't want `<strong>` text to be bold, but to have a different color, a different font, or a different size. As you'll see in Chapter 3, you can change the formatting of any element with style sheets.

A Few More Formatting Elements

A few more elements can change the appearance of small snippets of text (see Figure 2-14), although you won't use them much, if at all. Do take the time to learn them, however, so you can be ready, in the rare case that you need one.

First up are two elements that change the size and placement of your text. You can use the `<sub>` element for *subscripts*—text that's smaller than and placed at the bottom of the current line. The `<sup>` element stands for *superscript*—small text at the top of the current line.

Next is the `<del>` element, which generally represents deleted text in a revised document or text that doesn't apply anymore. The browser displays this text but crosses it out with a horizontal line. (HTML5 adds a complementary `<mark>` element for highlighting text, but it's still too new to get reliable browser support.)

Finally, the `<small>` element is the right way to format "small print," like the legalese at the bottom of a contract that a business is really hoping you'll overlook. In the past, the `<small>` element simply meant "small-looking text," and web designers rarely used it. HTML5, however, redefined it with a perfectly logical meaning, and with that gave it a new lease on life.

NOTE HTML also has a `<u>` element for underlining text, but webmasters consider it obsolete. If you really want to underline text, put it in a `<span>` element (which applies no formatting on its own), and then use the `text-decoration` style property to format the span using CSS (see page 96).

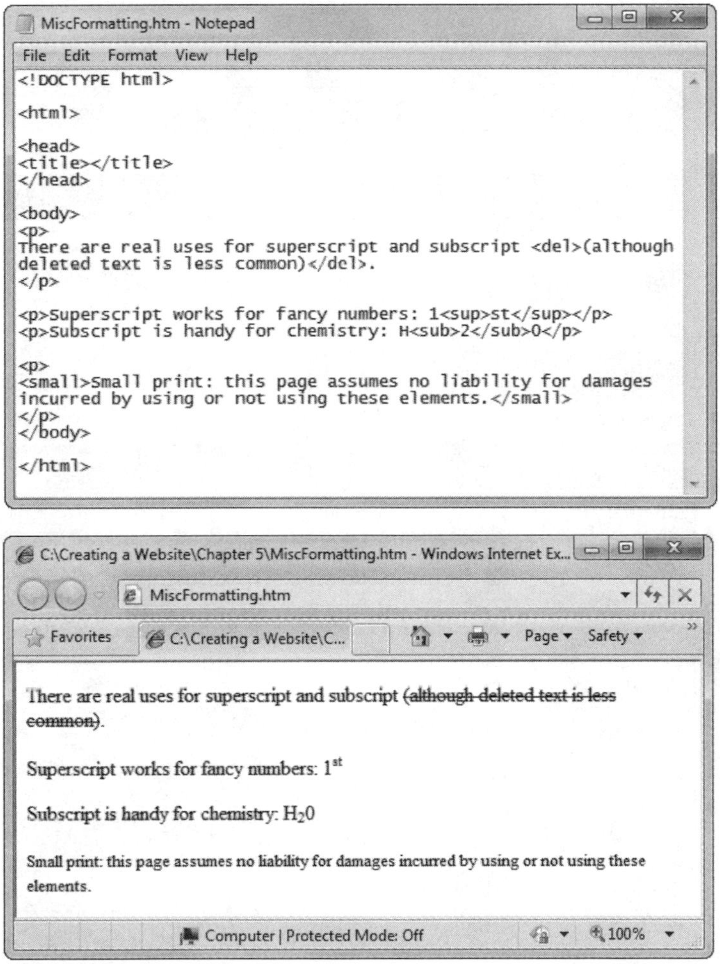

FIGURE 2-14

Deleted text, superscript, subscript, and small print in action.

Special Characters

Not all characters are available from your keyboard. For example, what if you want to add a copyright symbol (©), a paragraph mark (¶), or an accented e (é)? Good news: HTML supports them all, along with about 250 relatives, including mathematical symbols and Icelandic letters. To add them, however, you need to use some sleight of hand. The trick is to use *HTML character entities*—special codes that browsers recognize as requests for unusual characters. Table 2-2 has some common options, with a sprinkling of accent characters.

TABLE 2-2 *Common special characters.*

CHARACTER	NAME OF CHARACTER	WHAT TO TYPE
©	Copyright	&copy;
®	Registered trademark	&reg;
¢	Cent sign	&cent;
£	Pound sterling	&pound;
¥	Yen sign	&yen;
€	Euro sign	€ (but € is better supported)
°	Degree sign	&deg;
±	Plus or minus sign	&plusmn;
÷	Division sign	&divide;
×	Multiply sign	&times;
µ	Micro sign	&micro;
¼	One-fourth fraction	&frac14;
½	One-half fraction	&frac12;
¾	Three-fourths fraction	&frac34;
¶	Paragraph sign	&para;
§	Section sign	&sect;
«	Left angle quote, guillemot left	&laquo;
»	Right angle quote, guillemot right	&raquo;
¡	Inverted exclamation mark	&iexcl;
¿	Inverted question mark	&iquest;
æ	Small ae diphthong (ligature)	&aelig;
ç	Small c, cedilla	&ccedil;
è	Small e, grave accent	&egrave;
é	Small e, acute accent	&eacute;
ê	Small e, circumflex accent	&ecirc;
ë	Small e, dieresis or umlaut mark	&euml;
ö	Small o, dieresis or umlaut mark	&ouml;
É	Capital E, acute accent	&Eacute;

HTML character entities aren't just for non-English letters and exotic symbols. You also need them to deal with characters that have special meaning in HTML—namely angle brackets (< >) and the ampersand (&). You shouldn't enter these characters directly into a web page because a browser will assume you're trying to give it a super-special instruction. Instead, you need to use the equivalent character entity, as shown in Table 2-3.

TABLE 2-3 *HTML character entities.*

CHARACTER	NAME OF CHARACTER	WHAT TO TYPE
<	Left angle bracket	&lt;
>	Right angle bracket	&gt;
&	Ampersand	&amp;
"	Double quotation mark	&quot;

Strictly speaking, you don't need all these entities all the time. For example, it's safe to insert ordinary quotation marks into your web page text. However, you can't use quotation marks in attribute values, because there they have a special meaning (they indicate the beginning and ending of the value). If you need a quotation mark in an attribute value, you need to rely on the " character entity. On the other hand, the character entities for in-text angle brackets are always necessary, no matter where you plan to put them in a page.

Here's some flawed text that won't display correctly:

```
I love the greater than (>) and less than (<) symbols. Problem is, when I type
them my browser thinks I'm trying to use a tag.
```

And here's the corrected version, with HTML character entities. When a browser processes and displays this text, it replaces the entities with the characters you really want.

```
I love the greater than (&gt;) and less than (&lt;) symbols. Problem is, when
I type them my browser thinks I'm trying to use a tag.
```

TIP To get a more comprehensive list of special characters and see how they look in your browser, check out the reference on *http://tinyurl.com/special-chrs*, courtesy of the folks at Wired Webmonkey.

Taming Long URLs with TinyURL

Keen eyes will notice something unusual about the web address mentioned in the Tip box on page 65 (that's the URL *http://tinyurl.com/special-chrs*). Although the address leads to the Webmonkey site, the URL starts with the seemingly unrelated domain name *http://tinyurl.com*. That's because the full Webmonkey URL has been deliberately shortened using TinyURL, a free website redirection service. TinyURL is a handy tool you can use whenever you come across a URL that's so impractically long or convoluted that you'd ordinarily have no chance of jotting it down, typing it in, or shouting it over the phone.

Here's how to use TinyURL. First, copy your awkwardly long URL. Then, head to the website *http://tinyurl.com*, type or paste the URL into the text box on the front page, and click Make TinyURL. The site rewards you with a much shorter URL that starts with *http://tinyurl.com*. You can suggest some descriptive text for the URL (like *special-chrs* in the Webmonkey example) or you can let TinyURL pick an arbitrary address that includes random characters (like *http://tinyurl.com/ye8mf7k*).

Best of all, a TinyURL works just as well as the original one—type it into any browser and you'll get to the original site. So how does this system work? When you type a TinyURL, your browser takes you to the TinyURL website. TinyURL keeps a long list of all the whacked-out URLs people provide, as well as the new, shorter URLs it issues in their place. When you request a page, the site looks up the TinyURL in that list, finds the original URL, and redirects your browser to the site you really want. Here's the neat part: The whole process unfolds so quickly that you'd have no idea it was taking place if you hadn't read this box.

Non-English Languages

Although character entities work perfectly well, they can be a bit clumsy if you need to rely on them all the time. For example, consider the famous French phrase, "We were given speech to hide our thoughts," shown here:

> La parole nous a été donnée pour déguiser notre pensée.

Here's what it looks like with character entities replacing all the accented characters:

> La parole nous a été donnée pour déguiser notre pensée.

French-speaking web creators would be unlikely to put up with this for long. Fortunately, there's a solution called *Unicode encoding*. Essentially, Unicode is a system that converts characters into the bytes that computers understand and that display properly on your web page. By using Unicode encoding, you can create accented characters just as easily as if they were keys on your keyboard.

So how does it work? First, you need a way to get the accented characters into your web page. Here are some options:

- **Type it in.** Many non-English speakers will have the benefit of keyboards that include accented characters.

- **Use a utility.** In Windows, you can run a little utility called *charmap* (short for Character Map) that lets you pick from a range of special characters and copy your selected character to the Clipboard so it's ready for pasting into your text editor. To run charmap, click the Start button and then type *charmap* in the search box. Click the program name when it appears (Figure 2-15).

- **Use your web page editor.** Some web page editors include their own built-in symbol-pickers. In Dreamweaver, you can use Insert→HTML→Special Characters→Other. In Expression Web, choose Insert→Symbol. Usually, this process inserts character entities, not Unicode characters. Though the end result is the same, your HTML markup will still include a clutter of codes.

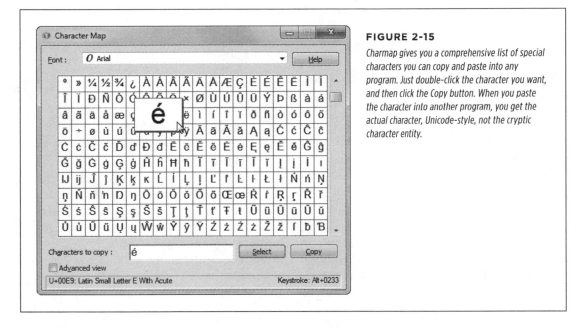

FIGURE 2-15

Charmap gives you a comprehensive list of special characters you can copy and paste into any program. Just double-click the character you want, and then click the Copy button. When you paste the character into another program, you get the actual character, Unicode-style, not the cryptic character entity.

When you use Unicode encoding, make sure you save your web page correctly. This isn't a problem if you use a professional web page editor, which is smart enough to get it right the first time, but Unicode can trip up text editors. For example, in Windows Notepad, you need to choose File→Save As, and then pick UTF-8 from the Encoding list (see Figure 2-16). For the Mac's TextEdit, go to TextEdit→Preferences. Choose the "Open and Save" tab and make sure you select "Unicode (UTF-8)" for the Encoding setting.

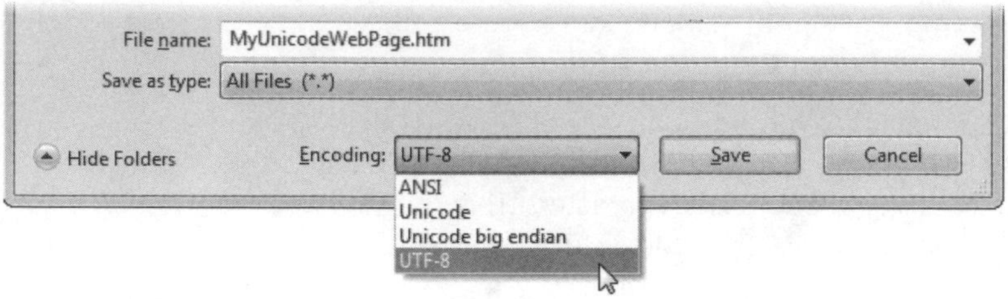

FIGURE 2-16

The overwhelming standard of the Web, UTF-8 is a slimmed-down version of Unicode. However, you need to explicitly tell Notepad to use UTF-8 encoding when you save a web page that includes special characters, like accented letters.

SHARPEN UP

Decode the Markup

Here's an excellent exercise that will force you to think like a web browser. In your text editor, open an HTML file that you've never seen before. Then read through the markup and try to piece together the document's structure, just by remembering what each element represents. When you finish, you can take a look at the page in a browser to see if you correctly interpreted all the tags.

Interested in giving it a shot? In the Tutorial-2-3 folder on the companion site, there's a small collection of sample web pages that feature the common text elements you explored in this chapter. However, there's a twist. Each web page uses

HTML comments (page 27) to hide the web page content. That means that you can't sneak a peek in your browser—if you do, all you'll see is a blank page.

Instead, you need to open the web page in a text editor, remove the two comment markers (that's the `<!--` code at the beginning of the content and the `-->` code at the end), and save the changes. Then you can open the page in your browser and see the result. But by this point, you'll have read through the markup, and you can make your prediction about what you'll see.

Building a Style Sheet

Last chapter, you learned HTML's dirty little secret: It doesn't have much format-ting muscle. As a result, if you want your web pages to look sharp, you need to add style sheets into the page-creation mix.

A *style sheet* is simply a document filled with formatting rules. Browsers read these rules and apply them when they display web pages. For example, a style sheet rule might say, "Make all the headings on this site bold and fuchsia, and draw a box around each one."

You want to put formatting instructions in a style sheet instead of embedding them in a web page for several reasons. The most obvious is *reusability*. Thanks to style sheets, for example, you can create a single rule to, say, format all level-3 headings a certain way. When you apply this rule to your site, it changes the appearance of *every* level-3 heading on *every* web page.

The second reason is that style sheets help you write tidy, readable, and manage-able HTML files. Because style sheets handle all your site's formatting, your HTML document doesn't need to do that work. All it needs to do is organize your pages into logical sections.

Finally, style sheets give you more extensive formatting choices than HTML does. Using style sheets, you can control colors, borders, margins, alignment, and fonts. These formatting features are either out of reach in HTML, or they require some seriously messy markup.

In this chapter, you'll learn how style sheets work, and how to attach one to a web page. Once you have these basics under control, you'll study the finer details of CSS, including how to get the colors, alignment, fonts, and borders you want in your pages.

NOTE You won't learn about every CSS feature in this chapter. For example, some properties apply primarily to pictures or to page layout. You'll learn about those properties as you work your way through different topics in later chapters.

Graphic Design on the Web

Sooner or later, every website creator discovers that designing for the Web is very different from designing for something that's going to be printed. Before you can unleash your inner web page graphic designer, you need to clear a few conceptual hurdles.

Consider the difference between an HTML page and a page created in a word processor. Word processing programs show you exactly how a document will look before you print it: You know how large your headlines will be, what font they're in, where your text wraps from one line to the next, and so on. If you see something you don't like, you change it using menus and formatting commands. Your word processor, in other words, gives you absolute control over every detail of your page.

The Web is a more freewheeling place. When you create an HTML document, you know some—but not all—of the details about how that page will appear on someone else's computer. While one person's browser may display large type instead of standard-size characters and stretch it to fill the full expanse of a 28-inch widescreen monitor, another's may be shrunk and tucked away in a corner of the desktop. And guests who visit your site with a smartphone, tablet computer, or web-enabled toaster will get yet another—and completely different—view. In short, you can't micromanage display details on the Web the way you can in print. But you *can* supply all the information a web browser needs to present your pages properly. You do this by structuring your pages so that browsers treat your page elements consistently, regardless of your visitors' browser settings.

Logical Structure vs. Physical Formatting

As you learned in the previous chapter, there's a sharp difference between *structuring* a document (dividing it into discrete chunks of content like headings, paragraphs, and lists) and *formatting* a document (making those chunks look pretty by applying italics, changing the text size, adding color, and so on). Novice webmasters who don't understand this difference often end up formatting when they should be structuring, which leads to messy and difficult-to-maintain HTML pages.

In the early days of the Web, HTML used two types of elements to emphasize the distinction between document structure and document formatting:

- **Semantic elements** define the individual components that make up your web page. They identify what in a page is a heading, a paragraph, a list, and so on. In other words, they tell you about the *structure* of your page.

• **Presentational elements** are all about formatting—what your content looks like onscreen. Examples include elements that apply italics, boldface, and underlining to text.

Over the years, the creators of HTML worked hard to strip the formatting details out of the HTML language. They made some presentational elements obsolete (like the clumsy <font> element) and redefined others. For example, <b> no longer means "bold text" (the standard presentational definition), but "stylistically offset text" (which is a more semantic definition). Similarly, <i> no longer means "italic text" but "text in an alternate voice, such as foreign words and technical terms." Of course, web browsers aren't affected. They still render <b> text in bold and <i> text in italics, unless you use a style sheet that tells them not to. But the change in wording emphasizes a fundamental shift in philosophy—namely, that HTML elements should describe the logical function of portions of text, not the typographic presentation of it.

CSS (Cascading Style Sheets)

If web pages are supposed to be clean and formatting-free, what's left to make those pages look good? The answer is found in another standard: Cascading Style Sheets, or CSS.

Here's how it works. First, you create a regular HTML document, like the one you learned to build in Chapter 1. Next, you create a separate document using the CSS standard. This document is called a *style sheet*, and it defines how browsers format the different elements in your HTML document. For example, a style sheet might contain instructions like "Make every heading bright red" or "Give all paragraphs a 12-pixel left margin."

The style sheet system offers many benefits. First, you can reuse the same style sheet for all your web pages. Because getting your formatting right can be a long and tedious chore, this is a major timesaver. Once you perfect your site's look and feel, you link your pages to this style sheet so they all take on that design (see Figure 3-1). Even better, when you're ready for a new look, you don't need to mess with your HTML documents—just tweak your style sheet and every linked page gets an instant face-lift.

■ Style Sheet Basics

Style sheets use a standard that's officially known as *CSS* (Cascading Style Sheets). CSS is a system for defining style *rules*. These rules change the appearance of the elements in your web pages, tweaking details like color, font, size, borders, and placement.

When you use CSS in a web page, a browser reads both the page's HTML file and its style sheet rules. The browser then uses those rules to format the page. Figure 3-2 shows the process.

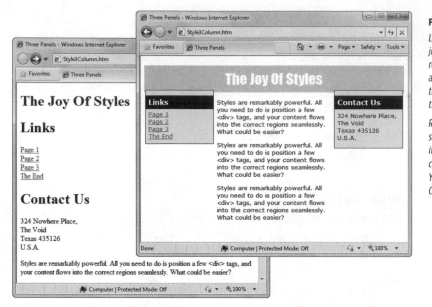

FIGURE 3-1

Left: This page displays just plain text, but it's ready for a style sheet: the author carefully separated the page into logical sections.

Right: When you apply a style sheet to the page, its formatting and layout change dramatically. You'll see this example in Chapter 8.

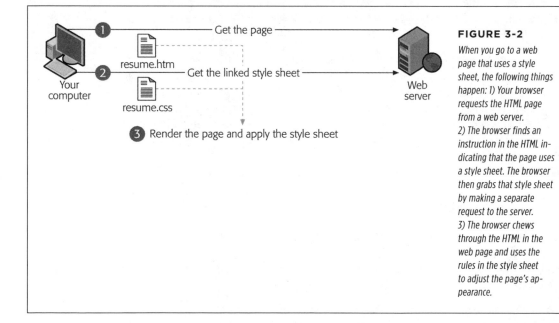

FIGURE 3-2

When you go to a web page that uses a style sheet, the following things happen: 1) Your browser requests the HTML page from a web server. 2) The browser finds an instruction in the HTML indicating that the page uses a style sheet. The browser then grabs that style sheet by making a separate request to the server. 3) The browser chews through the HTML in the web page and uses the rules in the style sheet to adjust the page's appearance.

Why HTML Is Not a Formatting Language

The keepers of the HTML standard chose to strip the formatting details out of HTML documents and stuff them into style sheets. Here are some of the reasons why:

- **To keep HTML simple.** If HTML handled formatting, your pages would get messy. That's because even a simple web page needs a lot of fine-tuned formatting. Put those details in a page along with your HTML, and you'd lose your content in a swamp of markup.

- **To make it easy to change your formatting.** If HTML had, say, an element to specify text color, you'd need to include that element every time you placed a heading on a page. Now imagine that you later decide to go with a more refined dark purple heading. To change your website, you'd have to open and edit each and every HTML page that had a heading—a time-consuming job, even for simple sites.

- **To make your pages more adaptable.** By taking the formatting out of your page, it becomes much more flexible. Using a style sheet, you can change the formatting of a page without editing the HTML. And if

you need to display the web page in a different way on a smartphone or another type of web-enabled device, you can do that, too, by adding another set of style instructions.

- **To make your pages more meaningful.** Semantic elements let external programs analyze a page's HTML. For example, someone could create an automated search program that scanned web pages and extracted just the top-level headings to produce a bare-bones outline of the page. Or a program could browse Amazon.com to find only book reviews. Or one could create a junk-mail list by reading <address> elements. A comparable program that looked at web page formatting would produce less interesting results. After all, who cares how much of eBay's text is in boldface?

- **To make HTML more accessible.** Screen-reading software and other automated tools work far better with logically structured pages. For example, a screen-reading program can guide a visually impaired person around your page by announcing only headings or links, rather than reading all the copy.

This system gives web weavers the best of both worlds—a rich way to format pages and a way to avoid mucking up your HTML beyond recognition. In an ideal world, the HTML document describes only the structure of your page (what's a header, what's a paragraph, what's a list, and so on), and the style sheet formats that page to give it its hot look.

The Three Types of Style Sheets

Before you learn how to write CSS rules, you first have to think about *where* you're going to place those instructions. CSS gives you three ways to apply a style sheet to a web page:

- You store an **external style sheet** as a separate file. This is the most powerful approach, because it completely separates formatting rules from your HTML pages. It also gives you an easy way to apply the same rules to many pages.

- You embed an **internal style sheet** inside an HTML document (it goes right inside the <head> section of your page). You still have the benefit of separating the style information from the HTML, and if you really want, you can cut and paste the embedded style sheet from one page to another (although it gets difficult to keep all those copies synchronized if you make changes later on). You use an internal style sheet if you want to give someone a complete web page, formatting instructions and all, in a single file—for example, if you email someone your home page. You might also use an internal style sheet if you know that you aren't going to use any of its style rules on another page.

- An **inline style** is a way to insert style sheet language directly inside the start tag of an HTML element. At first glance, this sounds suspicious. You've already learned to avoid embedding formatting instructions inside a web page, because formatting details tend to be long and unwieldy. That's true, but you might occasionally use the inline style approach to apply one-time formatting in a hurry, like italicizing the name of a book on the fly. It's not all that clean or structured, but it does work.

These choices give you the flexibility to either follow the CSS philosophy wholeheartedly (with external style sheets) or to use the occasional compromise (with internal style sheets or inline styles). Because style sheet language is always the same, even if you use a "lazier" approach like internal style sheets, you can always cut and paste your way to an external style sheet when you're ready to get more structured.

CSS Browser Compatibility

Before you embrace style sheets, you need to make sure they work on all the browsers your site visitors use. That's not as easy to figure out as it should be, because there's actually more than one version of the CSS standard—there's the original CSS1, the slightly improved CSS2, the corrected CSS2.1, and the latest-and-greatest CSS3. But the real problem is that browsers don't necessarily support the entire CSS standard, no matter what version it is.

In this book you'll focus on CSS properties known to be well-supported on all the major browsers. That said, don't forget to test your pages in a variety of browsers to be sure they look right. And if you're thinking of experimenting with one of the newer CSS3 features, you can learn more at *http://caniuse. com*. You'll find a list of advanced features in CSS3, HTML5, and related standards. Click the feature you're interested in, and the website details exactly which versions of the world's web browsers support it.

The Anatomy of a Rule

Style sheets contain just one thing: *rules*. Each rule is a formatting instruction that applies to a part of your page. A style sheet can contain a single rule, or it can hold dozens (or even hundreds) of them.

Here's a simple rule that tells a browser to display all <h1> headings in blue:

```
h1 { color: blue }
```

CSS rules don't look like anything you've seen in HTML markup, but you'll have no trouble with them once you realize that every rule uses only three ingredients: a *selector*, a *property*, and a *value*. Here's the format that every rule follows:

```
selector { property: value }
```

And here's what each part means:

- The **selector** identifies the type of content you want to format. A browser then hunts down all the parts of a web page that match the selector. For now, you'll concentrate on selectors that match every occurrence of a specific page element, like a heading. Later in this chapter (page 84), you'll learn to create more sophisticated selectors that act on only specific sections of your page.

- The **property** identifies the type of formatting you want to apply. Here's where you choose whether you want to change colors, fonts, alignment, or something else.

- The **value** sets a value for the property defined above. This is where you bring it all home. For example, if your property is color, the value could be light blue or a queasy green.

Of course, it's rarely enough to format just one property of an HTML element. Usually, you want to format several properties at the same time. You can do this with style sheets by creating a rule like this:

```
h1 {
  text-align: center;
  color: black;
}
```

This example changes the color of *and* centers the text inside an <h1> element. That's why style rules use the funny curly braces, { and }, so you can group as many formatting instructions inside them as you want. You separate one property from the next using a semicolon (;). It's up to you whether to include a semicolon at the end of the last property. Although it's not necessary, web-heads often do so to simplify adding additional properties onto the end of a rule.

> **TIP** CSS files let you use spacing and line breaks pretty much wherever you want, just as HTML files do. However, people often put each formatting instruction on a separate line (as in the example above) to make style sheets easy to read.

Conversely, you might want to create a single formatting instruction that affects several elements. For example, imagine you want to make sure that the first three heading levels, <h1> to <h3>, all have blue letters. Rather than write three separate rules, you can create a selector that includes all three elements, separated by commas. Here's an example:

```
h1, h2, h3 {
  color: blue;
}
```

Believe it or not, selectors, properties, and values are the essence of CSS. Once you understand these three ingredients, you're on your way to style sheet expertise.

Here are a few side effects of the style sheet system that you might not yet realize:

- A single rule can format a whole bunch of HTML. When you implement a rule for the kind of selectors listed above (called *type selectors*), that rule applies to every one of those elements. So when you specify blue <h1> headings as in the example above, every <h1> element in your page becomes blue.

- It's up to you to decide how much of your content you want to format. You can fine-tune every HTML element on your page, or you can write rules that affect only a single element, using the technique discussed on page 84.

- You can create two different rules for the same element. For example, you could create a rule that changes the font of every heading level (<h1>, <h2>, <h3>, and so on), and then add another rule that changes the color of <h1> elements only. Just make sure you don't try to set the same property multiple times with conflicting values, or the results will be difficult to predict.

- Some elements have built-in style rules. For example, browsers always display text that appears in a <b> element as boldfaced, even when the style sheet doesn't include a rule to do so. Similarly, browsers display text in an <h1> heading in a large font, with no style sheet rule necessary. But you can override any or all of these built-in rules using custom style rules. For example, you could explicitly set the font size of an <h1> heading so that it appears *smaller* than normal text. Similarly, you can take the underline off of a link, make the <b> element italicize text instead of bolding it, and so on.

Don't worry about memorizing the kinds of properties and values you can specify. Later in this chapter, after you see how style sheets work, you'll get acquainted with the formatting instructions you can use.

■ Tutorial: Attaching a Style Sheet to a Page

Now it's time to see style sheets in action. Before you go any further, dig up the *resume.htm* file you worked on in Chapter 1. If you don't have it handy, or if you're not sure which version to use, you can grab a copy from the companion site, in the Tutorial-3-1\Start folder.

> **TIP** Like all the tutorials in this book, you can find the solution for this exercise on the companion site at *http://prosetech.com/web*. Just look in the folder named Tutorial-3-1 (which stands for "Chapter 3, first tutorial"). Inside the Tutorial-3-1 folder is a Start folder that holds the files you start the exercise with and an End folder that holds the solution.

Right now the *resume.htm* file is a blank canvas, with content but not a lick of style (Figure 3-3, left). The goal is to apply a style sheet that will give it a face-lift (Figure 3-3, right), without touching a line of the original HTML markup.

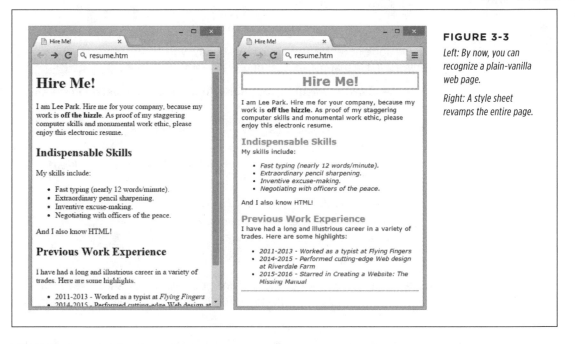

FIGURE 3-3

Left: By now, you can recognize a plain-vanilla web page.

Right: A style sheet revamps the entire page.

The following steps lead you through the process:

1. **First, you need to create your style sheet. To start, open your text editor.**

   You can use the same text editor you used to create HTML documents (Notepad or TextEdit). In fact, creating a style sheet is much the same as creating an HTML page—it's all plain text. But instead of HTML markup, your style sheet will contain style rules, like the one you considered in the previous section.

2. **Type the following rule into your style sheet:**

   ```
   h1 {
      color: fuchsia;
   }
   ```

   This rule instructs your browser to display all <h1> elements in bright fuchsia lettering.

3. **Save the newly created style sheet with the name *resume.css*. Make sure you place it in the same folder as the *resume.htm* file.**

   Like an HTML document, a style sheet can have just about any filename. As a matter of convention, however, style sheets almost always use the extension *.css*. For this example, make sure you save the style sheet in the same folder as your HTML page.

Now you have a style sheet you can use with a web page (or several web pages). However, you still need to *connect* your web page to your style sheet. That's the task you'll undertake next.

4. **Open the *resume.htm* file in your text editor.**

   If you don't have the *resume.htm* file handy, you can test this style sheet with any HTML file that has at least one <h1> element.

5. **Add the <link> element to your HTML file, somewhere between the <head> start tag and the </head> end tag.**

   The <link> element points your browser to the style sheet you wrote for your pages. You have to place it in the <head> section of your HTML page. Here's the revised <head> section of *resume.htm* with the <link> element added:

   ```
   <head>
     <title>Hire Me!</title>
     <link rel="stylesheet" href="resume.css" />
   </head>
   ```

   The link element includes two details:

   The rel attribute indicates that the link points to a style sheet (rel stands for *relationship*, because it indicates the relationship between the current page and the file you're linking to).

   The href attribute is the important bit, because it identifies the location of your style sheet (href stands for "hypertext reference"). If you put your style sheet in the same folder as your HTML file, the href attribute is simply the style sheet's filename, as it is in this example. If you put the style sheet in a different folder, you need to supply a relative file path (as explained on page 177).

6. **Save the HTML file, and then open it in a browser.**

   Here's what happens. Your browser begins processing the HTML document and finds the <link> element, which tells it to find an associated style sheet and apply all its rules. The browser then reads the first (and only, in this case) rule in the style sheet. To apply this rule, it starts by analyzing the selector, which targets all level-1 heading elements. Then it finds all the <h1> elements in the HTML and applies the fuchsia formatting.

The style sheet in this example isn't terribly impressive. In fact, it probably seems like a lot of work to simply get a pink heading. However, once you get this basic model in place, you can quickly take advantage of it. For example, you could edit the style sheet to change the font of your *resume.htm* headings. Or you could add rules to format other parts of the document. After you do, simply save the new style sheet, and then refresh the web page to see the effect of the changed or added rules.

In this chapter, you'll learn about plenty of useful settings for your style sheet rules. But to get a taste of how a few rules can change a web page, edit the *resume.css* style sheet so that it has these instructions:

```
body {
  font-family: Verdana,Arial,sans-serif;
  font-size: 83%;
}
h1 {
  border-style: double;
  color: fuchsia;
  text-align: center;
}
h2 {
  color: fuchsia;
  margin-bottom: 0px;
  font-size: 100%;
}
li {
  font-style: italic;
}
p {
   margin-top: 2px;
}
```

These rules change the font for the entire document (through the <body> element rule), tweak <h1> and <h2> headings, italicize list items, and shave off some of the spacing between paragraphs. Although you won't recognize all these rules at first, the basic idea stays the same—you put the content in the web page and the formatting in the style sheet. Figure 3-3 (right) shows the result. You can find this finished example in the Tutorial-3-1\End folder.

Using an Internal Style Sheet

In the previous example, you used an external style sheet. They're everybody's favorite way to use CSS because they let you link a single lovingly crafted style sheet to as many web pages as you want. But there are times when you're not working on an entire website, and you'd be happy with a solution that's a little less ambitious.

With an internal style sheet, you *embed* your style rules in the <head> area of your web page rather than link the page to an external style sheet. Yes, it bulks up your pages and forces you to give each page a separate style sheet. But sometimes the convenience of having just one file that contains your page *and* its style rules makes this approach worthwhile.

TIP   You should practice using all three types of styles: external, internal, and inline. Sooner or later, you'll need to use each technique in your own web pages.

To change the earlier example so that it uses an internal style sheet, follow these steps:

1. **Open the *resume.htm* file you created previously.**

2. **Remove the `<link>` element from your HTML markup.**

   This disconnects the page from the *resume.css* style sheet.

3. **Add a `<style>` element to the `<head>` section of the page.**

   You need both a `<style>` start tag and a `</style>` end tag. This is where you'll put all your style rules. It looks like this:

   ```
   <head>
     <title>Hire Me!</title>
     <style>
     </style>
   </head>
   ```

4. **Add your rules between the `<style>` start and end tags.**

   For example, to add a rule that makes `<h1>` headings fuchsia, you'd type this:

   ```
   <head>
     <title>Hire Me!</title>
     <style>
        h1 {
          color: fuchsia
        }
     </style>
   </head>
   ```

   As you can see, there's really no difference between the way you write an external and an internal style sheet rule. The syntax is the same—the only thing that changes is the place you put it.

   > **TIP** You can find the solution for this exercise on the companion site at *http://prosetech.com/web*. Just look in the folder named Tutorial-3-2.

Using Inline Styles

If you want to avoid writing a style sheet altogether, you can use yet another approach. Inline styles let you insert the property and value portion of a style sheet rule right into the start tag for an HTML element. You don't need to specify the selector because browsers understand that you want to format only the element where you add the rule.

Here's how you write an inline style that formats a single heading:

```
<h1 style="color: fuchsia">Hire Me!</h1>
```

The rule above affects only the <h1> element where you added it; any other <h1> headings on the page are unchanged.

Inline styles may seem appealing at first because they're clear and straightforward. You define the formatting information exactly where you want to use it. But if you try to format a whole page this way, you'll realize why web developers go easy on this technique. Quite simply, the average CSS formatting rule is long. If you need to put it alongside your content and copy it each time you use the element, you quickly end up with a web page that's mangled beyond all recognition. For example, consider a more complex heading that needs several style rules:

```
<h1 style="border-style: double; color: fuchsia; text-align: center">Hire
Me!</h1>
```

Even if this happens only once in a document, it's already becoming a loose and baggy monstrosity. So try to avoid inline styles if you can.

WORD TO THE WISE

Boosting Style Sheet Speed

External style sheets are a more efficient way to format websites than internal and inline styles because browsers use *caching*. Caching is a performance-improving technique in which browsers store a copy of some downloaded information on your computer so they don't need to download it again.

When a browser loads a web page that links to a style sheet, it makes a separate request for that style sheet, as shown back in Figure 3-2. If the browser opens another page that uses the *same* style sheet, it's intelligent enough to realize that it already has the right .css file on hand. As a result, it doesn't make the second request. Instead, it uses the cached copy of the style sheet, which makes the page load a little faster. (Of course, browsers only cache things for so long. If you go to the same site tomorrow, the browser will have to re-request the style sheet.)

If you embed the style sheet in each of your web pages, the browser always downloads the full page, including the style sheet rules. It has no way of knowing that you're using the same set of rules over and over again. Although this probably won't make a huge difference in page-download time, it could start to add up for a website with lots of pages. Speed is just one more reason web veterans prefer external style sheets.

When Styles Overlap

By now, you might be wondering what happens when styles disagree. For example, if an external style sheet indicates that <h1> headings should have blue letters, and then you apply bold formatting with an inline style, you'll end up with the sum of both changes: a blue-lettered, boldfaced heading. But what happens if the rules conflict? What if, for example, one rule specifies blue text while another mandates red? Which color setting wins?

The Cascade

To figure out the victor in a style conflict, you need to understand what the "cascading" part of "Cascading Style Sheets" means. It refers to the way browsers decide which property settings take precedence when you have multiple sets of rules.

When a browser formats a page according to your style sheet, it follows a specific sequence. It applies styles in this order:

1. The browser's standard settings

2. External style sheet

3. Internal style sheet (inside the <head> element)

4. Inline style (inside any HTML element)

The steps toward the bottom are the most powerful. The browser implements them after it applies the steps at the top, and they override any earlier formatting. So if an external style sheet conflicts with an internal style sheet, the setting in the internal style sheet wins.

> **NOTE** This sequence assumes that you place any <link> element (which invokes the external style sheet) before the <style> element (which defines the internal style sheet). This is the way most people like to arrange the content in their <head> section, but it's not mandatory. If you flip the order around and put the <style> element before the <link> element, the styles in the external style sheet will override the styles in the inline style sheet.

Based on this sequence, you might think that you can use this cascading behavior to your advantage by defining general rules in external style sheets and then overriding them with the occasional exception using inline styles. In fact you can, but there's a much better option. Rather than format individual elements with inline style properties, you can use *class selectors* to target and then format those elements, as you'll see shortly (page 84).

> **NOTE** The "cascading" in Cascading Style Sheets is a little misleading, because in most cases you won't use more than one type of style sheet (for the simple reason that it can quickly get confusing). Most web artistes favor external style sheets primarily and exclusively.

Inheritance

Along with the idea of cascading styles, there's another closely related concept—style *inheritance*. To understand inheritance, you need to recall that in HTML documents, one element can contain other elements. Remember the unordered list element (<ul>)? It contained list item elements (<li>). Similarly, a <p> paragraph element can contain character formatting elements like <b> and <i>, and the <body> element contains all the other elements that make up your web page.

Thanks to inheritance, when you apply formatting instructions to an element that contains *other* elements, that formatting rule applies to *every one of those other elements*. For example, if you set a <body> element to the font Verdana (as in the resumé style sheet shown earlier), every element inside that <body> element, including all the headings, paragraphs, lists, and so on, gets the Verdana font.

NOTE Elements inherit most, but not all, style properties. For example, elements never inherit margin settings from another element. Look for the "Can Be Inherited?" column in each table in this chapter to see whether CSS passes a property setting from one element to another through inheritance.

However, there's a trick. Sometimes, formatting rules may overlap. In such a case, the most specific rule—that is, the one hierarchically closest to the element—wins. For example, if you specify settings for an <h1> element, those settings will override the settings you specified for the <body> element for all level-1 headings. Or consider this style sheet:

```
body {
  color: black;
  text-align: center;
}
ul {
  color: fuschia;
  font-style: italic;
}
li {
  color: red;
  font-weight: bold;
}
```

These rules overlap. In a typical document (see Figure 3-4), you put an <li> (list item) inside a list element like <ul>, which in turn exists inside the <body> element. In this case, the text for each item in the list will be red, because the <li> rule overrides the <ul> and <body> rules that kick in first.

Crafty style sheet designers can use this behavior to their advantage. For example, you might apply a font to the <body> element so that everything in your web page—headings, paragraph text, lists, and so on—has the same font. Then you can judiciously override this font for a few elements by applying element-specific formatting rules.

NOTE Although you probably won't see cascading styles in action very often, you'll almost certainly use style inheritance.

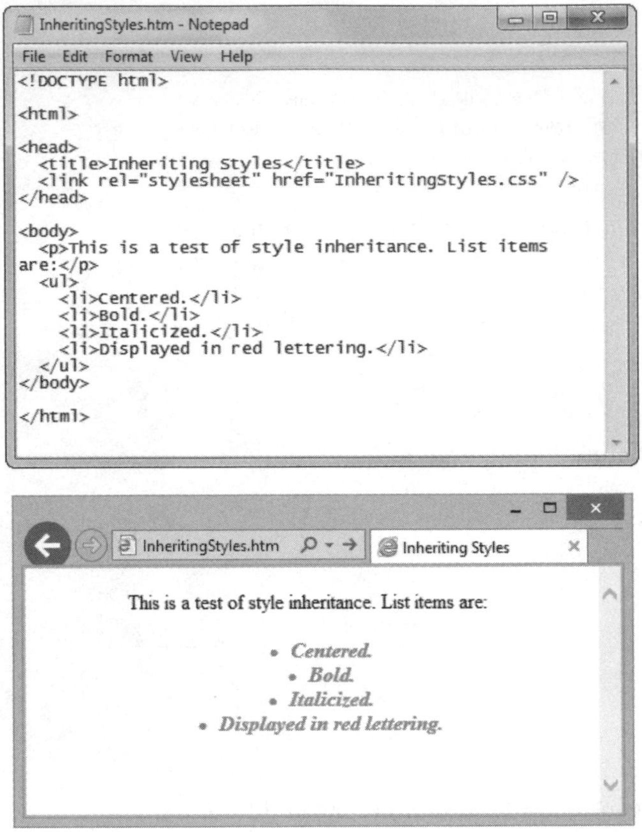

```
InheritingStyles.htm - Notepad                           □ ▣  X

File  Edit  Format  View  Help
<!DOCTYPE html>

<html>

<head>
  <title>Inheriting Styles</title>
  <link rel="stylesheet" href="InheritingStyles.css" />
</head>

<body>
  <p>This is a test of style inheritance. List items
are:</p>
  <ul>
    <li>Centered.</li>
    <li>Bold.</li>
    <li>Italicized.</li>
    <li>Displayed in red lettering.</li>
  </ul>
</body>

</html>
```

FIGURE 3-4

When rules collide, the most specific element wins. In this example, your browser displays the list items in red because the rule for the <li> element overrides the inherited properties from the <ul> and <body> elements (top). However, elements retain the style of an inherited rule if it doesn't conflict with another rule. In this example, that means the <li> element gets italics and center alignment through inheritance (bottom).

```
_ □ X
  ← →  🔍  InheritingStyles.htm  🔍 ▾ →   Inheriting Styles  X

This is a test of style inheritance. List items are:

                      •  Centered.
                       •  Bold.
                      •  Italicized.
              •  Displayed in red lettering.
```

■ Class Selectors

So far, you've seen style sheet rules that affect every occurrence of a specific HTML element. The selectors in these universal styles are known as *type selectors*.

Type selectors are powerful, but not that flexible. Sometimes you need a way to modify just one section of your HTML document or even just a single element. You could use inline styles, adding the formatting to the actual element tag itself, but that's messy. Fortunately, style sheets provide a practical solution to this problem: class selectors.

Class selectors are one of the best style sheet features around. First, you single out specific elements in your page by giving them the same *class name*. Then, you tell your browser to apply formatting to all the elements that carry that class name.

To try this out, begin by choosing a descriptive class name. You can pick whatever name you want, as long as you stick to letters, digits, and dashes and make sure that the first character is always a letter. The following example uses the class name *FancyTitle*.

Once you choose a class name, you need to define a rule for the class in your style sheet. This rule looks like any other, except that instead of using a tag name as the selector, you use the class name, preceded by a period (.):

```
.FancyTitle {
    color: red;
    font-weight: bolder;
}
```

You can put this rule in an external style sheet (like the *resume.css* file you created in the previous example) or directly inside an HTML file, as an internal style sheet.

So how does a browser know when to apply a rule that uses a class selector? Unlike type selectors, browsers never apply class rules automatically. Instead, you have to add the class name to the elements in your HTML markup that you want to format using the class attribute.

For example, if you want to apply the *FancyTitle* class to a heading in your HTML document, you would change its start tag like this:

```
<h3 class="FancyTitle">Learning to Embroider</p>
```

The class attribute makes the magic happen. When a browser discovers the instruction shown above, it looks for a class selector with the name *FancyTitle*, and then it applies the *FancyTitle* formatting to the heading, giving it red, bold lettering.

As long as the class name in the element matches a class name in the style sheet, the browser applies the formatting. If the browser can't find a style associated with that class name, nothing happens. So if you mistype a class name (say, writing "FancyTitel" instead of "FancyTitle"), you won't receive an error message, but your heading won't get the bold red formatting you expect, either.

> **NOTE** Class rules work *in addition* to any other rules. For example, if you create a rule for the <p> element, that rule applies to all paragraphs, including those that are part of a specialized class. However, if the class rule conflicts with any other rules, the class rule wins.

You can also create a rule that has a class name *and* specifies a type of element. For example, if you know that you want to use the *FancyTitle* class with the <h3> element only, you'd write the style rule like this:

```
h3.FancyTitle {
    color: red;
    font-weight: bolder;
}
```

Now, the *FancyTitle* formatting springs into action only if two conditions are met. First, you need to call it into action by adding the class attribute to an element (as you did before). Second, the element you use must be an <h3> heading. Apply the class somewhere else, and nothing will happen.

Most web designers use both element-specific class rules and more generic class rules (in other words, those that don't specify an element). Although you could stick with generic rules exclusively, if you know that you'll use a certain set of formatting options with only a specific type of element, it's good to clearly indicate that with an element-specific class rule. That way, you won't forget the purpose of the rule when you edit your style sheet later on.

id Selectors

Class selectors have a closely related cousin called *id selectors*. Like a class selector, an id selector lets you format just the elements you choose. And like a class selector, an id selector lets you assign it a descriptive name. But instead of using a period in front of the name, you use a number-sign character (#), as shown here:

```
#Menu {
   border-width: 2px;
   border-style: solid;
}
```

Right now, you can apply this Menu rule to any element. However, you can also limit your id selector to a specific type of element by putting the element name before the number sign, like this:

```
div#Menu {
   ...
}
```

Now you can apply the id selector named Menu only to <div> elements.

As with class rules, browsers don't apply id rules unless you specifically tell them to in your HTML. Instead of switching on the rules with a class attribute, however, you do so with the id attribute. For example, here's a <div> element that uses the Menu style:

```
<div id="Menu">...</div>
```

At this point, you're probably wondering why you would use an id selector—after all, it seems almost exactly the same as a class selector. But there's one difference: You can assign a given id to just *one* element in a page. In the current example, that means you can give the Menu style to just one <div>. This restriction doesn't apply to class names, which you can reuse as many times as you like.

The id selector is a good choice if you want to format a single, never-repeated element on your page. The advantage here is that the id selector clearly indicates the special importance of that element. For example, if a page has an id selector named Menu or NavigationBar, the web designer automatically knows that the page features only one menu or navigation bar. Of course, you never *need* to use an id selector. Some web designers use class selectors for everything, whether the section is unique or not. It's really just a matter of preference.

You've now learned the basics of building styles and calling them into action. Your next step is to explore the huge family of style properties that you can use to change the way things look. You'll start by learning how to add color to your pages.

Colors

Every web page starts out in stark black and white. A little color in your page—for example, a subtly shaded background, or dark red lettering that highlights important words—can add a touch of class. You want that. But too much will make your site look like a sunburned flamingo, so be judicious.

It isn't difficult to inject some color into your web pages. Style sheet rules have two color-related properties, listed in Table 3-1. You'll learn about the values you can use when setting colors (color names, color codes, and RGB values) in the following sections.

TABLE 3-1 *Color properties.*

PROPERTY	DESCRIPTION	COMMON VALUES	CAN BE INHERITED?
color	The color of the text. This is a handy way to make headings or emphasized text stand out.	A color name, color code, or RGB color value.	Yes
background-color	The color behind the text for just that element.	A color name, color code, or RGB color value. You can also use the value transparent, which lets the background of the containing element (or page) show through.	No*

* The background-color style property doesn't use inheritance (page 82). If you give the <body> section of a page a blue background and you then place a heading on the page, the heading doesn't inherit the blue background. However, there's a trick. If you don't explicitly assign a background color to an element, its color is transparent. This means the color of the containing element shows through, which has the same effect as inheritance. So the heading in this example still ends up with the appearance of a blue background.

The color property is easy to understand; it's the color of your text. The background-color property is a little more unusual.

If you apply a background color to the <body> element of a web page, the whole page adopts that color, as you might expect. However, if you specify a background color for an individual *element*, like a heading, the results are a bit stranger. That's because CSS treats each element as though it were enclosed in an invisible rectangle.

When you apply a background color to an element, CSS applies that color to just that rectangle.

For example, the following style sheet applies different background colors to a page, its headings, its paragraphs, and any bold text:

```
body {
  background-color: yellow;
}
h1 {
  color: white;
  background-color: blue;
}
p {
  background-color: lime;
}
b {
  background-color: white;
}
```

Figure 3-5 shows the result.

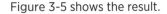

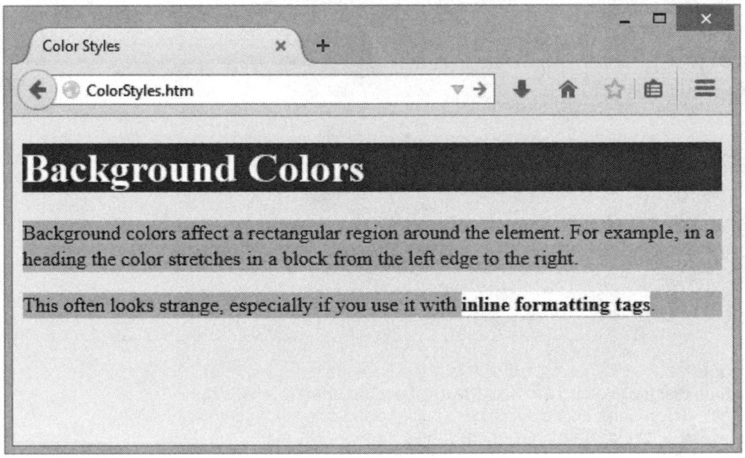

FIGURE 3-5

If you apply a background color to an element like <h1>, the CSS rule colors just that line. If you use a background color on an inline element like <b> or <span>, it affects only the words in that element. Both results look odd—it's a little like someone went wild with a bunch of highlighters. A better choice is to apply a background color to the whole page by specifying the color in the <body> element, or to tint just a large box-like portion of the page (like a sidebar), using a container element like <div>.

Specifying a Color

The trick to using color is finding the code that indicates the exact shade of electric blue you love. You can go about this several ways. First, you can use a plain English name ("lime"), as you've seen in the examples so far. This system limits you to a relatively small set of 140 colors, including the original standards: aqua, black, blue, fuchsia, gray, green, lime, maroon, navy, olive, purple, red, silver, teal, white, and yellow). For the full list, see *www.cssportal.com/css3-color-names*.

NOTE A set of 140 colors might seem like a lot, but it's actually pretty limited. For example, in typical design work you might start with two or three basic colors, and then flesh out a whole color palette with similar colors that have slightly different shades or intensities. (The color-picking tools on page 90 can help with this job.) But if you're stuck with a grab-bag of 140 colors, you won't have the variety you need.

Today's computers can display millions of colors. And even though CSS doesn't name these colors, you can add them to your web pages using two different color-specifying options: hexadecimal color values and RGB (or *red-green-blue*) values.

■ HEXADECIMAL COLOR VALUES

With *hexadecimal color values*, you use a strange-looking code that starts with a number sign (#). Technically, hexadecimal color values use three numbers to represent the amounts of red, green, and blue that go into creating a color. (You can create any color by combining various amounts of these three primary colors.) However, the hexadecimal color value combines these three ingredients into an arcane code that's perfectly understandable to computers but utterly baroque to normal people.

You'll find hexadecimal color notation kicking around the Web a lot, because it's the original format for specifying colors under HTML. However, it's about as intuitive as reading the 0s and 1s that power your computer.

Here's an example:

```
body {
   background-color: #E0E0E0
}
```

Even a computer nerd can't tell that #E0E0E0 applies a light-gray background. To figure out the code for your favorite color, check out the section "Finding the Right Color" below.

■ RGB COLOR VALUES

The other approach to specifying color is RGB values. According to this more logical approach, you simply specify how much red, green, and blue you want to "mix in" to create your final color. Each component takes a number from 0 to 255. For example, a color composed of red, green, and blue, each set to 255, appears white; on the other hand, all those values set to 0 generates black.

Here's an example of a nice lime color:

```
body {
   background-color: rgb(177,255,20)
}
```

Finding the Right Color

Style sheets can handle absolutely any color you can imagine. But how do you find the color code for the perfect shade of sunset orange (or dead salmon) you need?

Sadly, there's no way this black-and-white book can show you your choices. But there *are* a lot of excellent color-picking programs online. For example, try *www.colorpicker. com*, where all you need to do is drag your mouse around a color gradient to preview the color you want (and to see its hexadecimal code). Or try *www.colorschemer. com/online.html*, which groups complementary colors together, which is especially helpful for creating websites that look professionally designed. Some web design tools, like Dreamweaver, make life even easier with built-in color-picking (page 174).

> **NOTE** The RGB system lets you pick any of 16.7 million colors, which means that no color-picking website will show you every single possible RGB color code (if they do, make sure you don't hit the Print button; even with 10 colors per line, you'd wind up with thousands of pages). Instead, most sites limit you to a representative sampling of colors. This works, because many colors are so similar they're nearly impossible to distinguish.

The RGB color standard is also alive and well in many computer programs. For example, if you see a color you love in a professional graphics program like Photoshop (or even in a not-so-professional graphics program like Windows Paint), odds are there's a way to get the red, green, and blue values for that color. This gives you a great way to match the text in your web page with a color in a picture. Now that's a trick that will please even the strictest interior designer.

DESIGN TIME

Making Color Look Good

Nothing beats black text on a white background for creating crisp, clean, easy-to-read web pages with real presence. This black-and-white combination also works best for pages that have a lot of colorful pictures. It's no accident that almost every top website, from news sites (*www.cnn.com*) to search engines (*www.google.com*) to ecommerce shops (*www. amazon.com*) and auction houses (*www.ebay.com*), use the winning combination of black on white.

But what if you're just too colorful a person to leave your web page in plain black and white? The best advice is to follow the golden rule of color: *Use restraint.* Unless you're creating a sixties revival site or a Led Zeppelin tribute page, you don't want your pages to run wild with color. Here are some ways to inject a splash of color without letting it take over your web page:

- **Go monochrome.** That means use black, white, and one other dark color. Use the new color to emphasize an important design element, like subheadings in an article. For example, the *Time* magazine website uses its trademark red for some links and text.

- **Use lightly shaded backgrounds.** Sometimes, a faint wash of color in the background is all you need to perk up a site.

For example, a gentle tan or gold can suggest elegance or sophistication (see the Harvard library site at *http://lib. harvard.edu*). Or light pinks and yellows can get shoppers ready to buy sleepwear and other feminine accouterments at Victoria's Secret (*www.victoriassecret.com*).

- **Use color in a box.** Web designers frequently use shaded boxes to highlight important areas of a web page (check out the Wikipedia page at *http://en.wikipedia.org*). You'll learn how to create boxes later in this chapter.

- **Be careful about using white text.** White text on a black or dark blue background can be striking—and strikingly hard to read. The rule of thumb is to avoid it unless you're trying to make your website seem futuristic, alternative, or gloomy. (Even if you do fall into one of these categories, you might get a stronger effect with a white background and a few well-chosen graphics with splashy electric colors.)

Text Alignment and Spacing

At first, text alignment may seem like a boring subject. You can be forgiven for thinking that the way lines and paragraphs meet the borders of a page is a microscopically small detail. But the truth is that the flow of text shapes the feeling of your pages—and sets the first impression for new visitors. For example, crisp, crowded text might suggest a news magazine or a professional journal. By comparison, text with room to breathe may feel more casual, relaxed, or modern. Either way, choosing your text alignment and spacing is one of the ways that you establish the personality of your site.

CSS includes a great many properties that let you control how text appears on a web page. If you've ever wondered how to indent paragraphs, space out lines, or center a title, these are the tools you need.

Table 3-2 details your alignment options.

TABLE 3-2 *Alignment and spacing properties.*

PROPERTY	DESCRIPTION	COMMON VALUES	CAN BE INHERITED?
text-align	Lines up text on one or both edges of a page.	left, right, center, justify	Yes
text-indent	Indents the first line of text (typically in a paragraph).	A pixel value (indicating the amount to indent) or a percentage of the width of the containing element.	Yes
margin	Sets the spacing around the outside of a block element (page 30). To change the margin on just one edge, use the similar properties margin-bottom, margin-left, margin-right, and margin-top.	A pixel value or a percentage indicating the amount of space to add around the element.	No
padding	Sets the spacing around the inside of a block element. Has the same effect as margin, unless you have an element with a border or a background color.	A pixel value or a percentage indicating the amount of space to add around the element.	No
wordspacing	Sets the space between words.	A pixel value or a percentage.	Yes
letterspacing	Sets the space between letters.	A pixel value or a percentage.	Yes
line-height	Sets the vertical space between lines.	A pixel value or a percentage. You can also use a multiple (for example, use 2 for double spacing).	Yes
white-space	Tells the browser how to deal with spaces in your text.	normal, pre, nowrap	Yes

For example, if you want to create a page with indented paragraphs (like those in a novel or a newspaper), use this style sheet rule:

```
p {
   text-indent: 20px
}
```

In the following sections, you'll see examples that use the alignment and margin properties.

Alignment

Ordinarily, all the text on a web page lines up on the left side of the browser window. Using the text-align property, you can center that text, line it up on the right edge of the page, or justify it (that is, line it up along both edges). Figure 3-6 shows your options.

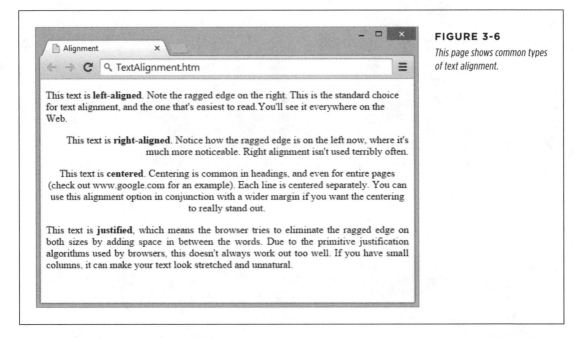

FIGURE 3-6

This page shows common types of text alignment.

The most interesting alignment choice is full justification, which formats text so that it appears flush with both the left and right margins of a page, like the text in this book. You specify full justification with the justify setting. Originally, printers preferred full justification because it crams more words onto each page, reducing a book's page count and, therefore, its printing cost. These days, it's a way of life. Many people feel that text with full justification looks neater and cleaner than text with a ragged edge, even though tests show plain, unjustified text is easier to read.

Justification doesn't work as well in the web world as it does in print. A key problem is a lack of rules that split long words into syllables, hyphenates them, and extends them over two lines. Browsers use a relatively simplistic method to justify text. Essentially, they add words to a line one at a time, until no more words can fit, at which point they add extra spacing between the words to pad the line to its full length. By comparison, the best page layout systems for print analyze an entire paragraph and find the justification strategy that best satisfies every line. In problematic cases, a skilled typesetter may need to step in and adjust line breaks manually. Compared to this approach, web browsers are irredeemably primitive, as you can see in Figure 3-7.

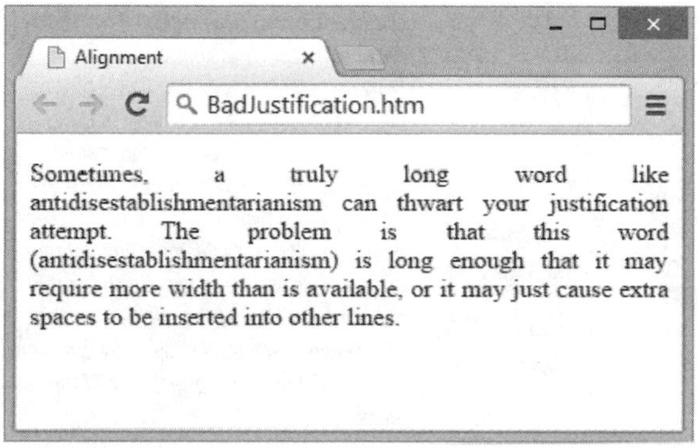

FIGURE 3-7

If you decide to use full justification on a web page, make sure you use fairly wide paragraphs. Otherwise, you'll quickly wind up with gaps and rivers of white space. Few websites use justification.

NOTE Right now, all the text flows through the middle of your page. Later, in Chapter 8, you'll learn to divide your content into multiple columns and use styles to create more complex layouts.

Spacing

To adjust the spacing around any element, use the margin property. For example, here's a rule that adds 8 pixels of space to all sides of a paragraph:

```
p {
  margin: 8px;
}
```

This particular rule doesn't have much effect, because web browsers already apply 8 pixels of margin around block elements on all sides to ensure a basic bit of breathing space. If you want to create dense pages of information, however, you might find this space allowance a bit too generous. Therefore, many website developers look for ways to slim down the margins a bit.

One common technique is to close the gap between headings and the text that follows them. Here's an example that puts this tightening into action using inline styles:

```
<h2 style="margin-bottom: 0px">This heading has no bottom margin</h2>
<p style="margin-top: 0px">This paragraph has no top margin.</p>
```

You'll notice that this style rule uses the more targeted `margin-top` and `margin-bottom` properties to home in on just one edge at a time. You can use `margin-left` and `margin-right` to set side margins. Figure 3-8 compares some different margin choices.

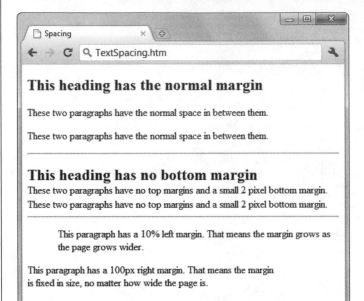

FIGURE 3-8

When you change the spacing between page elements like headers and paragraphs, consider both the element above and the element below. For example, if you stack two paragraphs on top of each other, two factors come into play—the bottom margin of the top paragraph and the top margin of the bottom paragraph. Browsers use the larger of these two values. That means there's no point in shrinking the top margin of the bottom element unless you also shrink the bottom margin of the top element. On the other hand, if you want more space, you need to increase the margin of only one of the two elements.

Many CSS properties support a shorthand syntax that can compress several properties into one setting. For example, instead of setting your four margin properties separately (`margin-top`, `margin-bottom`, `margin-left`, and `margin-right`), you can set them at once with a rule like this:

```
p {
    margin: 5px 10px 15px 20px;
}
```

This sets the top margin to 5 pixels, the right margin to 10 pixels, the bottom margin to 15 pixels, and the left margin to 20 pixels. The key is to make sure you separate each number by a space—don't add commas or extra semicolons.

If you're daring, you can even use *negative* margins. Taken to its extreme, this can cause two elements to overlap. However, a better approach for overlapping elements is absolute positioning, a style treatment you'll pick up on page 235.

NOTE Unlike most other CSS properties, elements never inherit margin settings. That means that if you change the margins of one element, other elements inside that element aren't affected.

White Space

As you learned in earlier chapters, HTML has a quirky way of dealing with spaces. If you put several blank spaces in a row, HTML treats the first one as a true space character but ignores the others. That makes it easy for you to write clear HTML markup, because you can add spaces wherever you like without worrying about it affecting your web page.

In the previous chapter, you learned two ways to change how browsers deal with spaces: the   character entity and the <pre> element. You can replace both of these workarounds with the white-space style sheet property.

First, consider the   character entity. It serves two purposes—it lets you insert spaces that a browser won't ignore, and it prevents a browser from wrapping a line in the middle of a company name or some other important term. Here's an example of the latter technique:

```
<p>You can trust the discretion of
Hush Hush Private Plumbers</p>
```

This works (the page displays the text "Hush Hush Private Plumbers" and doesn't wrap the company name to a second line), but it makes the markup hard to read. Here's the style-sheet equivalent with the white-space property set to nowrap:

```
<p>You can trust the discretion of
<span style="white-space: nowrap">Hush Hush Private Plumbers</span></p>
```

To make this work, your HTML needs to wrap the company name in a container that applies the formatting. The <span> element (page 48) is a good choice, because it doesn't apply any formatting except where you explicitly add it.

Now consider the <pre> element, which tells a browser to pay attention to every space in the content inside it. On page 45, you saw how you could use <pre> to apply the correct spacing to an e. e. cummings poem. You can get the same effect by setting the white-space property of an element (say, a <div>, <span>, or <p> element) to pre:

```
<p style="white-space: pre">Your browser won't    ignore    these
            s  p  a  c  e  s    .</p>
```

When you use the pre value for the white-space property, the browser displays all spaces, tabs, and hard returns (the line breaks you create when you press the Enter key). But unlike the <pre> element, the pre value of the white-space property doesn't change the text font. If you want to use a fixed-width font like Courier to space your letters and spaces proportionally, you need to add a font-family property (see the next section).

■ Basic Fonts

So far, your pages have been limited to the standard but somewhat old-fashioned Times font. Most sites use a different typeface, and many use more than one—for example, they might use one font for headings and another for the rest of their text.

Using the CSS font properties, you can choose a font family, font weight (its boldness setting), and font size (see Table 3-3). Be prepared, however, for a bit of web-style uncertainty, as this is one case where life isn't as easy as it seems.

TABLE 3-3 *Font properties.*

PROPERTY	DESCRIPTION	COMMON VALUES	CAN BE INHERITED?
font-family	A list of font names. The browser scans through the list until it finds a font that's on your visitor's computer. If it doesn't find a supported font, it uses the standard font the browser always uses.	A font name (like Verdana, Times, or Arial) or a generic font-family name: serif, sans-serif, monospace.	Yes
font-size	Sets the size of the font.	A specific size, or one of these values: xx-small, x-small, small, medium, large, x-large, xx-large, smaller, larger.	Yes
font-weight	Sets the weight of the font (how bold it appears).	normal, bold, bolder, lighter	Yes
font-style	Lets you apply italic formatting.	normal, italic	Yes
font-variant	Lets you apply small caps, which turns lowercase letters into smaller capitals (LIKE THIS).	normal, small-caps	Yes
text-decoration	Applies a few miscellaneous text changes, like underlining and strikeout. Technically speaking, these aren't part of the font (the browser adds these).	none, underline, overline, line-through	Yes
text-transform	Transforms text so that it's in all capital or all lowercase letters.	none, uppercase, lowercase	Yes

Finding the Right Font

Although most CSS font properties are straightforward, the font-family property has a nasty surprise—it doesn't work the way you probably expect. The problem you face is that no two computers have the same set of fonts installed, so the fonts you want to use for your web page won't necessarily exist on your visitors' machines. And if your visitor doesn't have a font you specify, his browser simply ignores your font-family setting and goes back to using ordinary Times text.

You can solve this problem in two ways:

- **Use a standard, *web-safe* font.** These are guaranteed to work on almost every computer and web-connected device there is. The tradeoff is that you're limited to a very small collection of typefaces.

- **Use a downloadable font (also known as a *web font*).** This is a newer option that was standardized with CSS3, though most browsers already supported it. It's a bit more complicated to set up (and you need to use a font that explicitly lets you share it with your guests). The great advantage is that you'll have thousands of distinctive typefaces to choose from.

In this chapter, you'll start with the easiest and least-risky approach, web-safe fonts. Then you'll delve into web typefaces using Google Fonts.

So what are the standard fonts that a web page can use? Unfortunately, web experts aren't always in consensus. If you want to be conservative, you won't go wrong with any of these fonts:

- Times
- Arial
- Helvetica
- Courier

Of course, all of them are insanely boring. If you want to take more risk, you can use one of the following fonts, found on almost all Windows and Mac computers (but not necessarily on other PCs running other operating systems, like Unix):

- Verdana
- Georgia
- Tahoma
- Comic Sans MS
- Arial Black
- Impact

As you'll see in the following section, you can create a whole list of font preferences, so if one font (like Georgia) isn't available, the visitor's browser goes to the next choice in the list (like Times). This gives you an ironclad safeguard, and it's the approach most websites use.

To compare these fonts, see Figure 3-9.

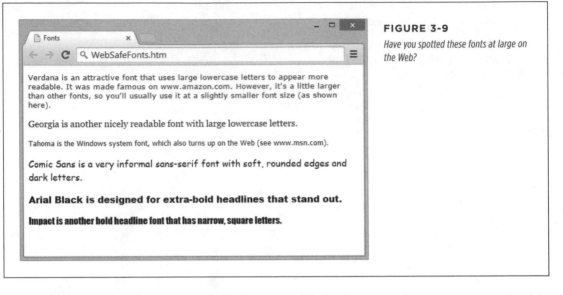

FIGURE 3-9

Have you spotted these fonts at large on the Web?

Verdana, Georgia, and Tahoma can all help give your web pages a more up-to-date look. However, the characters in Verdana and Tahoma start off a bit large, so you usually need to ratchet them down a notch using the font-size property (page 100).

For a good discussion of fonts, the platforms that reliably support them, and the pros and cons of each font family (some fonts look nice onscreen, for example, but lousy when you print them out) see *http://tinyurl.com/cr9oyx* and *http://tinyurl.com/325f9qs*.

Specifying a Font

You use the font-family property to assign a font. Here's an example that changes the font of an entire page:

```
body {
    font-family: Arial;
}
```

Arial is a *sans-serif* font found on just about every modern computer, including those running Windows, Mac OS, Unix, and Linux operating systems. (See Figure 3-10 for more about the difference between serif and sans-serif fonts.)

> **NOTE** When you set the font of the <body> element, it affects your whole page. That's because every other HTML element on the page is inside the <body> element, and so those other elements *inherit* the font-family setting from the <body> element (as described on page 82). Of course, you can change the font of a specific element by creating an additional style sheet rule that targets its font-family property.

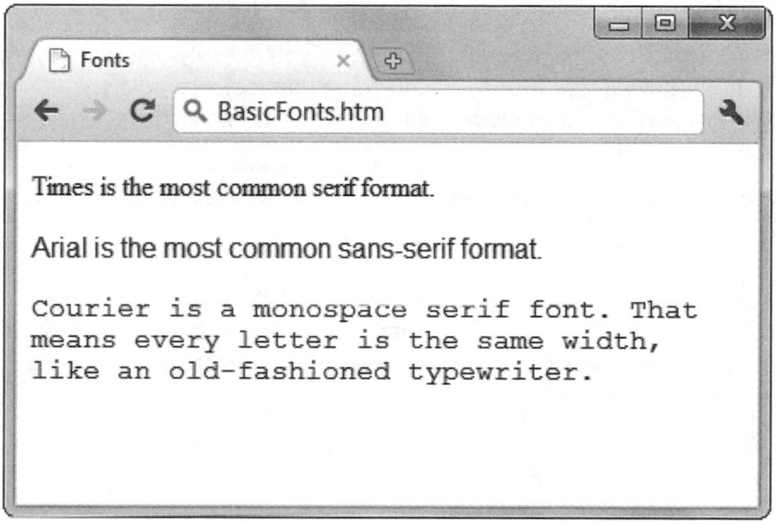

FIGURE 3-10

Serif fonts use adornments, or serifs, that make them easier to read in print. For example, if you look closely at the letter "T" that's at the beginning of the first line in this web page, you'll see tiny curlicues on the top-left, top-right, and bottom corners.

On the other hand, sans-serif fonts have a spare, streamlined look. They can make pages seem less bookish, less formal, more modern, and colder. Examples include the Arial font that appears in the second line of this web page, and the font that's used in the paragraph you're reading right now.

The font you specify with font-family is just a recommendation. If a computer doesn't have the font you request, the browser reverts to its standard font (Times). So instead of specifying a single font and blindly hoping that it's available to a browser, you should create a list of *font preferences* for your pages. That way, a browser tries to match your first choice and, if it fails, your second choice, and so on. At the end of this list, you should specify a generic font-family name. Every computer supports three generic fonts, named serif, sans-serif, and monospace.

Here's the modified style rule:

```
body {
    font-family: Arial, sans-serif;
}
```

At this point, you might be tempted to get a little creative by adding support for a less common sans-serif font. Here's an example:

```
body {
    font-family: Eras, Arial, sans-serif;
}
```

If Eras is relatively similar to Arial, this technique might not be a problem. But if the fonts are significantly different, it's a bad idea.

The first problem is that by using a nonstandard font, you're creating a page whose appearance may vary dramatically depending on the fonts installed on your visitor's computer. Whenever pages vary, it becomes more difficult to tweak them to perfection because you don't know exactly how they'll appear elsewhere. Different fonts take up different amounts of space, and if text grows or shrinks, the layout of other elements (like pictures) changes, too. And if you're really unlucky, a visitor's computer might have a font with the same name that looks completely different. Worst-case scenario: your lovingly crafted content turns into illegible text.

> **NOTE** To avoid this problem, stick to the standard fonts, or—if you really must have fancier lettering—use the web fonts discussed on page 103.

Lastly, if a font name has spaces or special characters, it's a good idea to wrap the whole thing in apostrophes or quotation marks so the browser reads the font name as a cohesive whole, rather than trying to interpret the spaces as something else. That means you should write:

```
body {
    font-family: "Comic Sans MS";
}
```

rather than:

```
body {
    font-family: Comic Sans MS;
}
```

Most browsers won't care, but this practice helps avoid potential problems.

Font Sizes

Once you sort out the thorny issue of choosing a font, you need to choose an appropriate font size. Here's where things get messy. Although the font-size property seems straightforward, you can set it using a dizzying range of units of measure, and these units don't behave the same when you use them in a densely nested page of elements. Some older browsers don't support the newer units, and even seasoned web designers can trip over the finer points.

In the following sections, you'll consider the simplest, most straightforward ways to size your text. You'll use three approaches that work on every browser and are almost impossible to mess up.

■ KEYWORD SIZING

The simplest way to specify the size of your text is to use one of the size values listed in Table 3-3 (page 96). For example, to create a really big heading and ridiculously small text, you can use these two rules:

```
body {
    font-size: xx-small;
}
h1 {
    font-size: xx-large;
}
```

These size keywords are often called *absolute sizes*, because they create text that's a precise size. Exactly what size, you ask? Well, that's where it gets a bit complicated. The basic rule of thumb is that the font size medium corresponds to a browser's standard text size, which is 12 points, and what it uses if a website doesn't specify a text size. Every time you go up a level, you add about 20 percent in size. (For math geeks, that means that every time you go down a level, you lose about 17 percent.)

The standard font size for most browsers is 12 points (although text at this size typically appears smaller on Macs than on Windows PCs). That means large text measures approximately 15 points, x-large text is 18 points, and xx-large text is 27 points.

Figure 3-11 shows the basic sizes you can choose from.

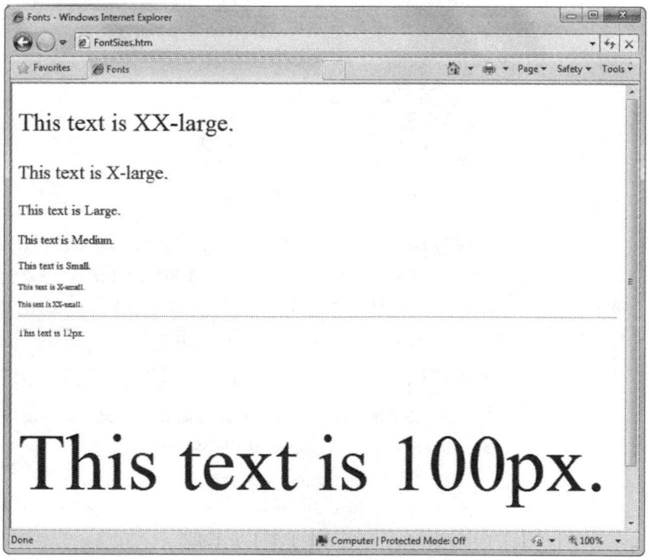

FIGURE 3-11

HTML offers seven standard text sizes, ranging from xx-large to xx-small. You can dictate font size by specifying a pixel measurement, too (see page 102).

NOTE When using size keywords, make sure your web page includes a doctype (page 18). If it doesn't, Internet Explorer renders your page in the dreaded "quirks" mode, which makes your text one size larger than it should be. As a result, your page won't look the same in Internet Explorer as it does in other browsers, like Firefox.

■ RELATIVE SIZING

Another approach for setting font size is to use one of two *relative size* values—larger or smaller. This takes the current text size of an element and bumps it up or down a bit.

The easiest way to understand how this works is to consider the following style sheet, which has two rules:

```
body {
    font-size: xx-small;
}
b {
    font-size: larger;
}
```

The first rule applies an absolute xx-small size to the whole page. If your page includes a boldfaced element (<b>), the text inside that <b> element *inherits* the xx-small size, and then the second style rule steps the text up one notch, to x-small.

Now consider what happens if you edit the <body> style in the example above to use a larger font, like this:

```
body {
    font-size: x-small;
}
b {
    font-size: larger;
}
```

Now all bold text will be one level up from x-small, which is small.

Relative sizes are a little trickier to get used to than absolute sizes. You might use them to write more flexible style rules. For example, you could use a relative size for bold text to make sure bold text is always a little bit bigger than the text around it. If you were to use an absolute size instead, the bold text would still appear larger than the small-sized paragraph text, but it wouldn't stand out in a large-sized heading.

> **TIP** When you use absolute or relative sizes, you create flexible pages. If a visitor ratchets up the text using his browser's preferences, the browser resizes all your other fonts proportionately.

■ PIXEL SIZING

For precise control over the size of your text, specify it using a *pixel size*. Pixel sizes can range wildly, with 12 or 14 pixels being about normal for body text. To specify a pixel size, use a number immediately followed by the letters *px*, as shown here:

```
body {
    font-size: 11px;
}
```

```
h1 {
   font-size: 24px;
}
```

NOTE Don't put a space between the number and the letters "px." If you do, your rule may work in Internet Explorer, but it will thoroughly confuse other browsers.

As always, you need to test, refine, and retest your font choice to get the sizes right. Some fonts look bigger than others, so you should specify smaller sizes for them. Other fonts work well at larger sizes but become less legible as you scale them down.

NOTE In the not-so-distant past, specifying a type size in pixels was discouraged. It caused problems with mobile browsers (the ones that run on smartphones and tablets), by locking the text in at a vanishingly small size. They also made it impossible (in some web browsers) for visually impaired people to scale up web pages and make the text larger and easier to read. But today, most of these problems have been solved. Modern mobile browsers deal with pixel sizes painlessly, and every web browser offers a zooming feature that magnifies the entire page, including pixel-sized text.

■ Web Fonts with Google

For most of the Web's history, page designers had to live with the limited capabilities of the font-family property. They learned to get the most out of the small set of standard fonts. But then CSS3 introduced a feature called @font-face, which provides a way for browsers to download the fonts for a web page on the fly (placing them in its temporary cache of pages and pictures). As a result, designers can use virtually any computer typeface.

At first glance, @font-face seems like the perfect solution to the font-family woes web designers face. Unfortunately, there are two significant challenges:

- **Font formats.** For each typeface you want to use, you need to have a normal, italic, and bold variation (so you can use bold and italic styling wherever you want). Then you need to have each of these variations in several formats, because different browsers require different formats. In the end, you need to juggle more than a dozen font files on your website, along with some fairly complex style sheet rules.

- **Font licensing.** Many fonts require a licensing fee. Even if you learn how to take a font from your computer and convert it into the right web font formats, you can't just slap it on your website without breaking a few dozen copyright laws. Instead, you're better off looking for a free (or cheap) web-optimized font.

You can solve both of these problems on your own, the do-it-yourself way. If that's the approach you want to take, start with the detailed Six Revisions article at *http://tinyurl.com/font-face-guide*, or try the comprehensive tutorial in *HTML5: The Missing*

Manual (O'Reilly). Both of these resources explain how to use the @font-face style rule on your own. But if you don't have an appetite for unnecessary extra challenges, there's an easier alternative: the Google Fonts service.

Google Fonts hosts free fonts that anyone can use. Their beauty lies in the fact that guests don't need to worry about font formats, because Google Fonts detects the kind of browser they use and automatically sends them the right font file. You don't even need to write the complex @font-face style rule, because Google provides the proper HTML, which you copy and paste into your style sheet.

To use a Google font in your pages, follow these steps:

1. **Go to** *www.google.com/fonts*.

    Google displays a long list of available fonts (Figure 3-12).

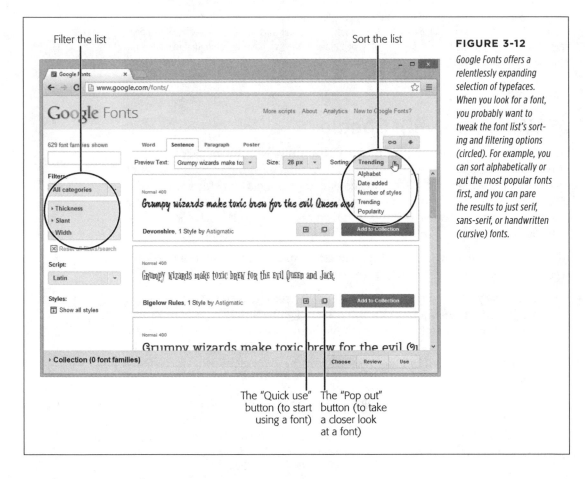

Filter the list

Sort the list

FIGURE 3-12

Google Fonts offers a relentlessly expanding selection of typefaces. When you look for a font, you probably want to tweak the font list's sorting and filtering options (circled). For example, you can sort alphabetically or put the most popular fonts first, and you can pare the results to just serif, sans-serif, or handwritten (cursive) fonts.

The "Quick use" button (to start using a font)

The "Pop out" button (to take a closer look at a font)

2. **At the top of the page, click a tab title (Word, Sentence, or Paragraph) to choose how you preview fonts.**

For example, if you're hunting for a font to use in a heading, you'll probably choose Word or Sentence to take a closeup look at a single word or line of text. But if you're looking for a font to use in your body text, you'll probably choose Paragraph to study a whole paragraph of text at once. No matter what option you choose, you can type in your own preview text and set an exact font size for it.

3. **Set your search options.**

If you have a specific font in mind, type its name into the search box. Otherwise, you'll need to scroll down, and that could take ages. To help you get what you want more quickly, start by setting a sort order (to list fonts by, for example, popularity, name, or date added) and perhaps some filtering options (to see serif fonts only, for example). Figure 3-12 shows you where to find these options.

4. **When you see a font you like, click the "Pop out" button (it looks like nested squares).**

Google opens an informative window that describes the font and shows each of its characters.

5. **If you like the font, click the "Quick-use" button to get the information you need to use it.**

Google gives you two bits of information. The first is the style sheet link, which you must add to your web page (so a browser knows where to find the font). The second is an example of a style sheet rule that uses the font.

6. **Add the Google Fonts link to your page.**

For example, if you picked the Metrophobic font, Google wants you to place the following link in the <head> section of your page:

```
<link href="http://fonts.googleapis.com/css?family=Metrophobic"
rel="stylesheet">
```

> **NOTE** Remember to put the link for the Google font style sheet before your other style sheet links. That way, your other style sheets can use the Google font.

7. **Use the font, by name, wherever you want.**

For example, here's how you could apply the newly registered Metrophobic font to the *resume.htm* example you formatted in the tutorial earlier in this chapter (page 76):

```
body {
  font-family: 'Metrophobic', arial, serif;
}
```

Figure 3-13 shows a revamped version of the resumé page with the Metrophobic font.

FIGURE 3-13

The Metrophobic font gives Lee Park's resumé a different, unique personality. Best of all, Google has hundreds more fonts you can use. And there's no limit to how many web fonts you can put in a page, so why not use one for headings and another for body text?

> **NOTE** Before continuing on, take the time to give Google web fonts a spin. Pick a font (any font that catches your fancy—it doesn't need to be Metrophobic) and alter the *resume.htm* file to use it. If you run into any trouble, double-check your work against the *resume_WebFont.htm* and *resume_WebFont.css* files, which provide a working solution and are found in the sample content on the companion site at *http://prosetech.com/web*.

Creating a Font Collection

These steps show you the fastest way to get the markup you need for a font. But if you have a bunch of fonts you like, you may want to create a *font collection*.

A font collection lets you tap all your favorite fonts using just a single line of HTML in your pages. To create one, start by clicking the "Add to Collection" button next to a font you like. As you add fonts to your collection, each one appears in the fat blue footer at the bottom of the page.

When you finish picking your fonts, click the Use button in the footer. Google displays a page that looks like the "Quick-use"

page, except that it gives you a single style-sheet reference that lets you use *any* of the fonts in your custom-picked collection.

Once you create a font collection, you might want to use two buttons at the top right of the Google Fonts page. Click the Bookmark button (which looks like a link in a chain) to create a browser bookmark that takes you to your collection so you can review and tweak it, and click the Download button (which looks like a down-pointing arrow) to save copies of the fonts to your computer, so you can install them and use them for print work.

Borders

The last group of style sheet properties you'll learn about in this chapter lets you add borders to your page (Figure 3-14). Borders are a great way to separate small pieces or entire blocks of content. You can add borders on one side of an element or all around it. You'll use borders throughout this book to separate content and delineate headings, columns, footers, and the other ingredients on your page (such as ads, pictures, or menu panels).

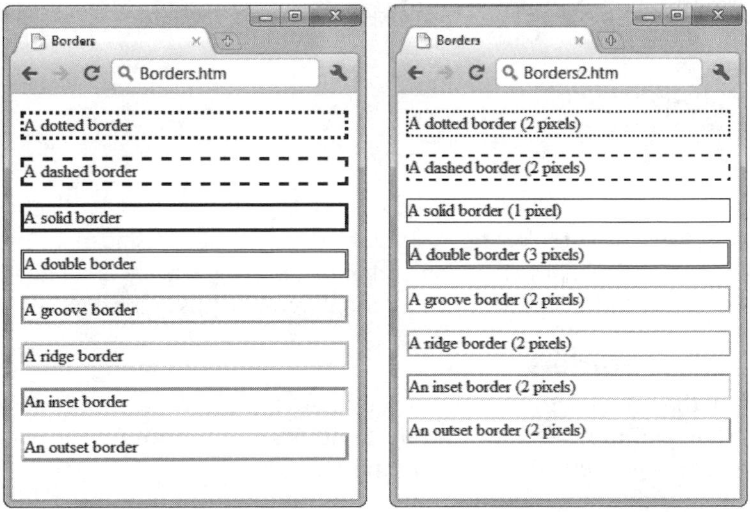

FIGURE 3-14

Left: The basic border styles look a bit old-fashioned in today's sleek websites.

Right: Shrink these borders down to 1 or 2 pixels, and they blend in much better.

Table 3-4 lists the three key border properties.

TABLE 3-4 *Border properties.*

PROPERTY	DESCRIPTION	COMMON VALUES	CAN BE INHERITED?
border-width	Sets the thickness of the border line. Usually, you want to pare this down.	A pixel width.	No
border-style	Browsers offer eight built-in styles for borders.	none, dotted, dashed, solid, double, groove, ridge, inset, outset	No
border-color	The color of the border.	A color name, hexadecimal color code, or RGB value (see page 88).	No

Basic Borders

The first choice you make when you create a border is the style you want it to have. You can use a dashed or dotted line, a groove or a ridge, or just a normal thin hairline (which often looks best). Here's a style rule that creates a dashed border:

```
.noteBox {
  border-style: dashed;
}
```

You don't want to apply the border to all <p> elements, because that would make for one cluttered page. Instead, use a class rule. To try these border settings, remember to apply the noteBox class to an element somewhere in your page, like this paragraph:

```
<p class="noteBox">There is a border around this text.</p>
```

The standard border width is almost always too clunky. To make a border look respectable, reduce the width to 1 or 2 pixels, depending on the border style:

```
.noteBox {
  border-style: dashed;
  border-width: 2px;
}
```

You can also use properties like border-top-style and border-left-width to set different styles, widths, and colors for every side of your element. Using many properties at once can occasionally create an odd effect, but you usually don't need to get this detailed. Instead, check out the border optimization tips in the next section.

Making Better Borders

In Figure 3-14, the actual borders look fine, but they're too close to the text inside. To remedy that, and to make your borders stand out, consider using the border property in conjunction with three other properties:

- background-color (page 87) applies a background hue to your element. Used in conjunction with a border, it makes your element look like a floating box, much like a sidebar in a magazine.

- margin (page 93) lets you set the spacing between your border box and the rest of your page. Increase the margin so that your boxes aren't crowded up against the rest of the page's content or the sides of a browser window.

- padding works like the margin property, but it sets spacing *inside* your element, between the edges of the box and the actual content within it. Increase the padding so that there's a good amount of space between a border and the text in the box. Figure 3-15 shows the difference between margin and padding.

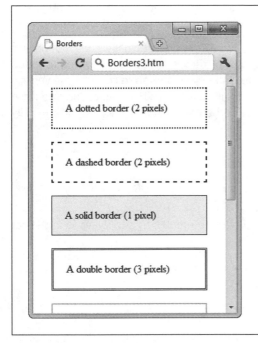

FIGURE 3-15

Usually, you can't tell the difference between margins and padding, because you can't see the edges of the element. For example, a <p> element displays a paragraph in an invisible box, but you won't see its sides. When you add a border, this changes. To get a good-looking box, you need to increase both the margin and the padding. For added effect, throw in a light background color (like the solid border box shown here).

Here's an example of a paragraph that looks like a shaded box:

```
.noteBox {
  background-color: #FDF5E6;
  margin: 20px;
  padding: 20px;
  border-style: solid;
  border-width: 1px;
}
```

The third box in Figure 3-15 shows how this combination of margin, padding, and background-color properties changes an ordinary paragraph into a shaded box.

Rounded Corners

In this book, we focus on style sheet properties that work everywhere, even in your granddad's browser. But every once in a while you can sneak in a newer setting because older browsers simply ignore style sheet properties they don't understand.

For example, consider the `border-radius` property, which rounds the corners of bordered boxes. Officially, it's a part of the relatively new CSS3 standard. If you're set up with Chrome, Firefox, or Safari, your browser almost certainly supports border-radius, because these browsers update themselves frequently and automatically. But if you come across a computer that's languishing in the past with Internet Explorer 8 (for example, a corporate computer saddled with this ancient but still-popular Windows XP operating system), it won't understand `border-radius`. The person using this computer will see ordinary square corners, which may not be as attractive but certainly won't hamper the overall visual effect or usability of your site.

When using the border radius property, you supply a size (usually in units of pixels). Technically, this is the length of the radius of the circle used to draw the rounded edge. However, you don't see the entire circle—just enough to connect the vertical and horizontal sides of the box. Set a bigger `border-radius` value, and you'll get a bigger curve and a more gently rounded corner. Finding the right size usually requires a bit of trial and error.

```
.noteBox {
  background: yellow;
  border-radius: 25px;
}
```

You can also round each of the four corners differently, by supplying four distinct values:

```
.noteBox {
  background: yellow;
  border-radius: 25px 50px 25px 85px;
}
```

But that's not all—you can also stretch the circle into an ellipse, creating a curve that stretches longer in one direction. To do this, you need to target each corner separately (using properties like `border-top-left-radius`) and then supply two numbers: one for the horizontal radius, the other for the vertical radius:

```
.noteBox {
  background: yellow;
  border-top-left-radius: 150px 30px;
  border-top-right-radius: 150px 30px;
}
```

Figure 3-16 shows some examples.

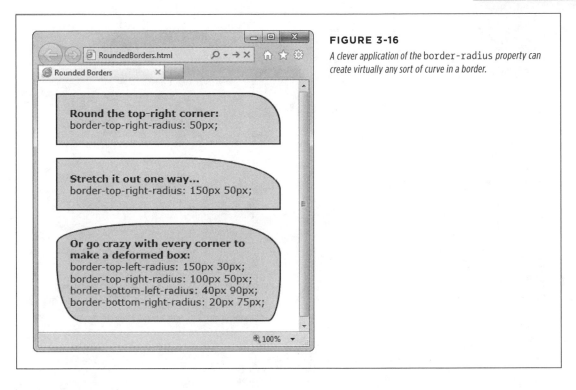

FIGURE 3-16

A clever application of the border-radius *property can create virtually any sort of curve in a border.*

Using Borders with Tables

As you learned in Chapter 2 (page 57), a table starts out as a borderless collection of cells. Using a style sheet, you can easily outfit your table with custom borders. You simply need to apply the border properties to some combination of the <tr>, <td>, <th>, and <table> elements.

For example, the following style sheet rules set a thin blue border around every cell and a thick blue border around the table itself:

```
table {
  border-width: 3px;
  border-style: solid;
  border-color: blue;
}
td, th {
  border-width: 1px;
  border-style: solid;
  border-color: blue;
}
```

Figure 3-17 shows the result.

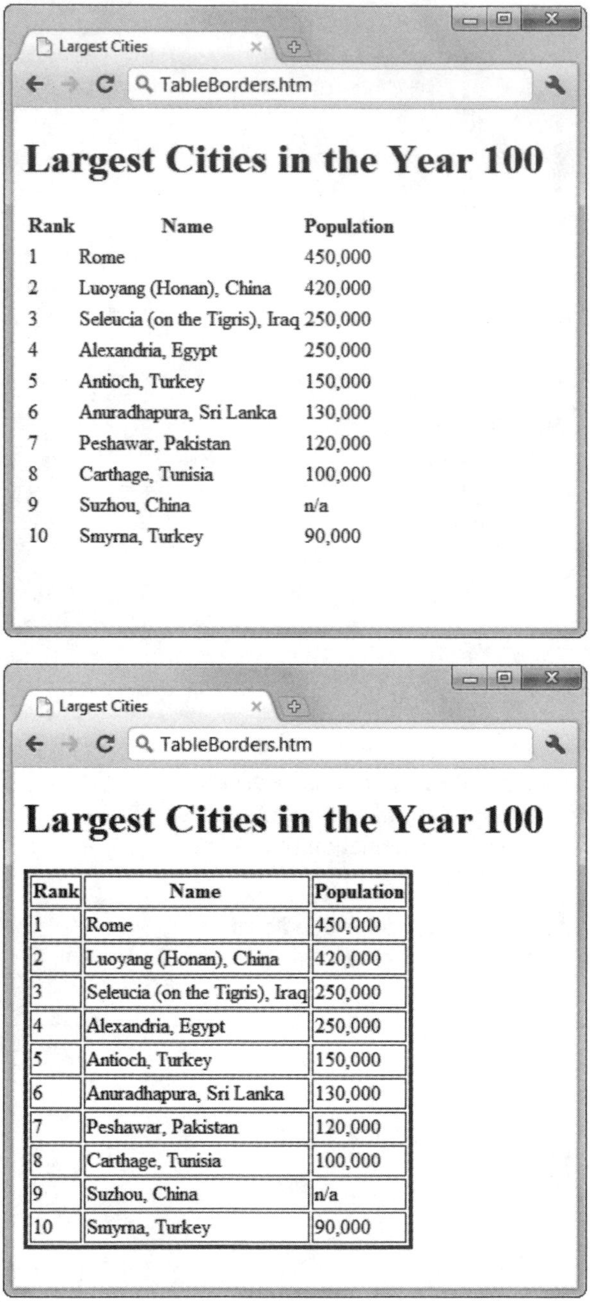

FIGURE 3-17
Compare a standard HTML table, which has no border (top), to the same table with a custom border added using style rules (bottom).

Good Design: The Art of Not Making Bad Sites

Now that you've completed this chapter, you know just enough CSS to be dangerous. To prevent your site from winding up on the dark side, you now need to master the critically important art of Not Making Bad Websites. Here are a few general principles that can help you out:

- **Keep it simple (and don't annoy your visitors).** We all have an impulse to play with color and texture. But unless your formatting frills serve a purpose, just say no. You'll find that exercising restraint can make a few fancy touches seem witty and sophisticated. Adding a *lot* of fancy touches can make your site seem heady and delusional. If you pare down the tricks, you'll make sure that your graphical glitz doesn't overshadow your site's content and drive your visitors away in annoyance.

- **Be consistent.** No matter how logical you think your website is, the majority of visitors probably won't think

the same way. To cut down on the confusion, organize your pages the same way, using similar headings, similar graphics and links, a single navigation bar, and so on. These touches help make visitors feel right at home. Best of all, a style sheet can help you stay consistent and codify the formatting rules you want to follow on all your pages. (You'll learn more about this way of thinking in Chapter 7.)

- **Know your audience.** Every type of site has its own unwritten conventions. You don't need to follow the same design in an ecommerce store as you do on a promotional page for an experimental electric harmonica band. To help you decide what is and isn't suitable, check out lots of other sites that deal with the same sort of material as yours.

Adding Graphics

I t's safe to say that the creators of the Internet never imagined that it would look the way it does today—thick with pictures, ads, videos, and animated graphics. They designed a meeting place for leading academic minds; we ended up with something closer to a Sri Lankan bazaar. But no one's complaining, because the Web would be an awfully drab place without pictures.

In this chapter, you'll master the art of web graphics. You'll learn how to add ordinary images to a web page and to position them perfectly. You'll also see how to use styles to jazz up your pictures with borders, captions, and background effects.

■ Introducing the <img> Element

Web page pictures don't live in HTML files. Instead, you store them as separate files, like *banana.jpg* and *photo01.jpg*. To display a picture in a web page, you use the <img> element.

For example, here's an <img> element that displays the picture *banana.jpg*:

```
<img src="banana.jpg" />
```

When a browser reads the <img> element above, it sends out a request for the *banana. jpg* file. After retrieving it, the browser inserts the picture into the page in place of the <img> element. If the image file is large or the Internet connection is very slow, you might actually see the web page text appear first, before the picture shows up.

Here's an example that puts a picture in the second paragraph of a typical (albeit somewhat boring) web page (Figure 4-1):

```
<!DOCTYPE html>
<html>
<head>
  <title>Two paragraphs, One picture</title>
</head>
<body>
  <p>In the next paragraph, you'll see a picture.</p>
  <p><img src="banana.jpg" /></p>
</body>
</html>
```

FIGURE 4-1

One <img> *element is all it takes to summon the* banana.jpg *picture and inject it into this* SimplePic.htm *web page.*

Alternate Text

The src attribute is the only detail an <img> element needs to function. But there's one other attribute you should supply—the alt attribute, which represents the alternate text a browser displays if it can't display the image itself.

Here's an example of an <img> element that includes alternate text:

```
<img src="matador.jpg" alt="There's no picture, so all you get is this
alternate text." />
```

Alternate text proves useful not only in the above circumstance, but in several other cases as well, including when:

- A viewing-impaired visitor uses a *screen-reading* program (a program that "speaks" text, including the words in an alt attribute).

- A search engine (like Google) analyzes a page and all its content so it can index the content in a search catalog.

- A browser requests a picture but can't find it. (Perhaps you forgot to copy it to your web server?)

- A web visitor switches off his browser's ability to display pictures to save page-download time (this isn't terribly common today).

- A browser doesn't support images (this is understandably rare these days, too, but the text-only Lynx browser is still kicking around on some old Unix systems).

The first two reasons are the most important. Web experts always use meaningful text when they write alt descriptions to ensure that screen readers and search engines interpret the corresponding pictures correctly.

Don't confuse alternate text with pop-up text, which is an optional message that appears when a website visitor points to an image (see Figure 4-2). To add pop-up text, use the title attribute:

```
<img src="matador.jpg" alt="A matador extends his cape in welcome."
title="Welcome to the ring." />
```

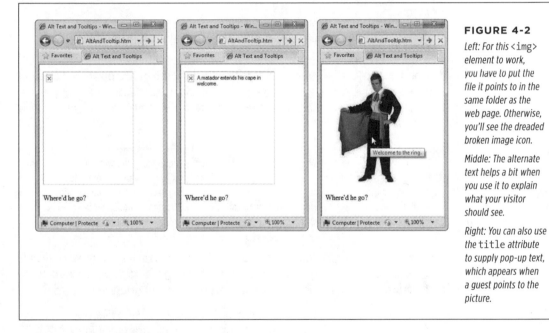

FIGURE 4-2

Left: For this <img> element to work, you have to put the file it points to in the same folder as the web page. Otherwise, you'll see the dreaded broken image icon.

Middle: The alternate text helps a bit when you use it to explain what your visitor should see.

Right: You can also use the title attribute to supply pop-up text, which appears when a guest points to the picture.

If an <img> element links to a picture that doesn't exist and you haven't supplied any alternate text, every browser reacts the same way—by showing a blank box with a broken-image icon (Figure 4-2, left). But if you have a missing picture *and* your <img> element includes alternate text, the result varies. Chrome continues to show a blank box. Internet Explorer shows a blank box but adds the alternate text inside it (see Figure 4-2, middle). And Firefox displays the alternate text as a paragraph of ordinary content on the page, with no picture box or missing picture icon to alert you of the problem.

Picture Size

When it comes to pictures, the word *size* has two meanings: it can refer to the dimensions of the picture (how much screen space it takes up on a web page), or it can signify the picture's file size (the number of bytes required to store it). To web page creators, both measures are important, but this section is all about the physical dimensions. (We'll talk about file sizes on page 123.)

Picture dimensions are noteworthy because they determine how much real estate an image occupies onscreen. Web weavers measure graphics in units called pixels. A pixel represents one tiny dot on a computer screen. The web world doesn't work with fixed units like inches and centimeters, because you never know how large your visitor's monitor is, and therefore how many pixels it can cram in.

Ordinarily, a picture gets its full resolution. So if your picture is a gigantic 2000 × 4000 pixels, that's what appears in your web page. However, the <img> element lets you resize a picture through its optional height and width attributes. Consider this example:

```
<img src="photo01.jpg" alt="An explicitly sized picture" width="100"
height="150" />
```

In this markup, the <img> element gives the picture a width of 100 pixels and a height of 150 pixels. If this is larger than the real dimensions of the *photo01.jpg* picture, the browser stretches and mangles the image to make it fit the size you set (see Figure 4-3).

NOTE Approach height and width attributes with caution. Sometimes, novice web authors use them to make *thumbnails*, small versions of large pictures. But using the height and width attributes to scale down a large picture comes with a performance penalty—namely, the browser still needs to download the original, larger image, even though it displays it at a smaller size. On the other hand, if you create thumbnails in a graphics editor like Photoshop, the file sizes are smaller, ensuring that your pages download much more quickly.

Many web page designers leave out image height and width attributes. However, experienced web developers sometimes add them using the *same* dimensions as the actual picture. As odd as this sounds, there are a couple of good reasons to do so.

First, when you include image size attributes, browsers know how large a picture is and can start laying out a page even as the graphic downloads (see Figure 4-2, left). On the other hand, if you don't include the height and width attributes, the browser won't know the dimensions of the picture until it's fully downloaded, at which point it has to rearrange the content. This is potentially distracting if your visitors have slow connections and they've already started reading the page.

The second reason is because the dimensions control the size of the picture box if a browser can't download the image (see Figure 4-2, middle). However, you shouldn't rely on this strategy, because it doesn't work in Firefox—that browser ignores the height and width attributes for missing pictures, and it doesn't display an image box. (To really prevent a missing picture from scrambling your layout, carve your pages into separate sections using <div> elements, and position them with style sheets, as described in Chapter 8.)

FIGURE 4-3

Never use HTML's height *and* width *attributes to resize a picture, because the results are almost always unsatisfying. Enlarged pictures are jagged, shrunken pictures are blurry, and if you change the ratio of height to width (as with the top-right and bottom images shown here), browsers squash pictures out of their normal proportions (top left).*

So should you use the height and width attributes? It's up to you, but they're probably more trouble than they're worth for the average website. If you use them, you need to make sure to update them if you change the size of your picture, a chore that can quickly get tedious.

Picture Placement

If you don't take any extra steps, a browser inserts each image into the flow of your text, right where you put the <img> element in your HTML. It lines up the bottom of the graphic with the baseline of the text that surrounds it. (The baseline is the imaginary line on which the text sits.) This is called an *inline* image, and you can see one in Figure 4-4.

You can change the vertical alignment of text using the vertical-align style sheet property. Specify a value of top, middle, or bottom, depending on whether you want the picture to line up with the top, middle, or bottom of the line of text.

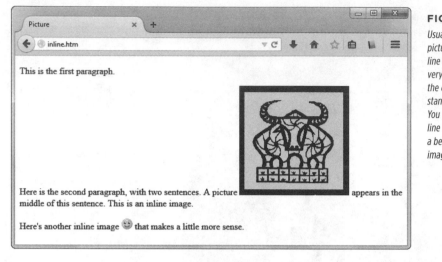

FIGURE 4-4

Usually, you don't want a picture inside an ordinary line of text (unless it's a very small emoticon, like the ones you find in instant message programs). You can use paragraphs, line breaks, or tables to do a better job of separating images from text.

Here's an example that adds an inline style (page 80) to the image that sets the vertical-align property. It lines the picture up with the top of the line of text.

```
<img src="happy.gif" alt="Happy Face" style="vertical-align: top" />
```

This technique is worthwhile if you're trying to line up a very small picture, like a fancy bullet. But it doesn't work very well with large images. That's because no matter which vertical-align option you choose, only one line of text can appear alongside an inline picture (as you can see in Figure 4-4).

If you don't want your picture to pop up in the middle of your text, you can separate it from the surrounding content using line breaks (<br>) or horizontal rules (<hr>). However, inline images never move on their own. If you want to create floating pictures with wrapped text, hold that thought—you'll see how on page 127.

■ Tutorial: Storing Images in a Subfolder

The previous examples kept things simple by assuming that your web pages and image files are all in the same folder. If, for example, you put the *SimplePic.htm* page (Figure 4-1) on your desktop, you also needed to put the *banana.jpg* file there as well, so the <img> element could find it.

This is all well and good, but sometimes you don't want to keep your web pages and pictures in the same place. In fact, if you have a large collection of pictures, it's a good idea to keep them in a separate subfolder. That way, you can better manage the clutter, so you can edit web pages without tripping over picture files. This setup also lets you browse and tweak the pictures without being distracted by the web pages. In the following tutorial, you'll set up this sort of arrangement.

TIP Like all the tutorials in this book, you can find the support files for this exercise on the companion site at *http://prosetech.com/web*. Just look in the folder named Tutorial-4-1 (which stands for "Chapter 4, first tutorial"). There you'll find the files you need to get started in the Start subfolder, and the solution to the exercise in the End subfolder.

Here's what you need to do:

1. **First, get the *SimplePic.htm* page and the *banana.jpg* image from the Tutorial-4-1\Start folder.**

   Put them both on your desktop, or copy them to the location you use to store web pages as you work on them.

2. **Create a subfolder named *images*.**

   You can name your image-holding subfolder whatever you want. The name "images" may not seem very descriptive, but it's a common choice, so it's the approach we'll take in this tutorial.

3. **Move the Image file (*banana.jpg*) into the *images* subfolder.**

   If you were to open the web page now, you'd find that your picture has gone missing from the <img> element. But fear not—a fix is at hand.

4. **Open the *SimplePic.htm* web page in your text editor.**

5. **Edit the src attribute of the <img> element so it includes the subfolder name.**

   In other words, you need to change this:

   ```
   <p><img src="banana.jpg" /></p>
   ```

   to this:

   ```
   <p><img src="images/banana.jpg" /></p>
   ```

   Notice that you use a forward slash (/) in relative addresses, not a backward slash (\). If you're used to file paths on Windows computers, this is a small but important change—ignore it, and your pictures might not appear when a browser opens your pages from a web server.

   NOTE Make sure you're consistent with capitalization. If you name a subfolder *images* but refer to it as *Images* in the <img> element, you can run into a serious headache. Your pictures may work when you test the web page on your own computer, but they'll fail to appear when you upload the page to a real website.

6. **Save your changes and then open your page in a browser (or refresh it, if it's already open).**

   Now the image appears in the page, exactly as it did before.

NOTE The technical term for the path that leads to the picture in this example (*images/banana.jpg*) is a *relative path*. Relative paths tell a browser where to go, starting from the current location (where the web page is located). Page 177 describes relative paths in more detail and has more examples.

■ File Formats for Web Graphics

So far, you've seen image examples that have the extension *.jpg*. However, web browsers actually support a small set of standard image formats:

- **The JPEG** (pronounced "jay-peg") format is suitable for photos and pictures that can tolerate some loss of quality. JPEG doesn't work as well if your picture contains text or line art, because the resulting image won't be as sharp.

- **The GIF** (pronounced "jif" or "gif") format is suitable for graphics with a very small number of colors (like simple logos or clip art). It gives lousy results if you use it to display photos.

- **The PNG** (pronounced "ping") format is suitable for all kinds of images, although it doesn't compress photos as well as JPEG. PNG is particularly good for small, sharp graphics (like logos) and today it's used as a more powerful replacement for the GIF standard.

- **SVG** (Scalable Vector Graphics) is an up-and-coming standard for *vector drawings* (for example, logos and figures that consist of text and shapes, rather than photographs). For the right type of art, SVG has a number of advantages, including its small size and flexibility. You can resize SVGs without losing detail or getting blurry images. However, Internet Explorer versions 8 and earlier don't display SVG images, which means it's still not a reliable choice for web graphics. For that reason, this chapter doesn't discuss it, although you can learn more about it (and some of the workarounds that make it work, sort of, in old versions of Internet Explorer) at *http://tinyurl.com/2gy2vyg*.

NOTE Some browsers give you a few more format options, but you're better off steering away from them to ensure widest browser compatibility. For example, Internet Explorer supports bitmaps (image files that end with the .bmp extension). Don't ever use them—not only will they confuse other browsers, but they're also ridiculously large because the standard doesn't include compression.

Graphics formats differ in how they use compression to squash down file sizes, and in how many colors they offer. You'll dive deeper into these considerations in the following sections. For now, Table 4-1 outlines how the different formats stack up, and Figure 4-5 compares them in a web page (see the box on page 124 for an explanation of compression types).

TABLE 4-1 *Image file formats for the Web.*

FORMAT	TYPE OF COMPRESSION	MAXIMUM COLORS	BEST SUITED FOR
JPEG	Lossy	24-bit (16.7 million colors)	Photos.
GIF	Lossless	8-bit color (256 colors)	Simple logos, graphical text, and diagrams with line art.
PNG	Lossless	24-bit (16.7 million colors)	Images that would normally be GIF files but need more colors.
SVG	Lossless (but it's optional, as SVG data is already quite small)	24-bit (16.7 million colors)	Art drawn in an illustration program. However, IE version 8 and earlier don't support it.

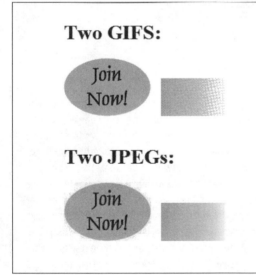

FIGURE 4-5

JPEGs and GIFs are the original image formats of the Web. You'll notice that GIFs produce clearer text, while JPEGs do a much better job of handling continuous bands of color. GIFs simulate extra colors through dithering, a process that mixes different colored dots to simulate a solid color. The results are unmistakably unprofessional. (You may not be able to see the reduced text quality in this black-and-white screen capture, but if you take a look at the file JPEGvsGIF.htm from the companion site, you'll see the difference up close.) For this reason, the PNG standard has largely replaced the GIF standard.

Compression

Once upon a time, web connections were slow and web designers spent hours agonizing over the size of every image on their sites. Today, image size is still a consideration (albeit a smaller one) because of mobile devices. People using smartphones, tablets, and other web-enabled devices are often forced to use slower connections (for example, the overtaxed WiFi at the local coffee shop). Phone companies also charge based on usage, so visit too many picture-clogged pages and it could cost you.

To keep your website as fast, lightweight, and efficient as possible, follow this advice:

- **Keep your pictures small.** If you really must fill the browser window, create a smaller version of the picture, put that on the page, and then make it a link (page 175). Then, when someone clicks the picture, you can open a new page with the full-sized image in it.

- **Use the right image format.** For large photos, that's JPEG.

- **Lower the quality.** To get better compression, you can lower the quality of your JPEGs (if your graphics program has this feature). But test out this approach first to make sure you can tolerate the loss in detail. As you compress a JPEG image, you introduce various problems collectively known as *compression artifacts*. The most common are blocky regions in an image, halos around edges, and a general blurriness. Some pictures exhibit these flaws more than others, depending on the image's amount of detail.

- **Use a picture-squishing tool.** There are plenty of free tools that can scan through a folder of image files and crush each one down to a smaller size. You'll probably need to go get coffee (because the process can take some time), but you'll be rewarded with files that are (on average) 15% to 40% smaller, with no reduction in quality. Try FileOptimizer (*http://tinyurl.com/FileOptimizer*) for Windows computers, and ImageOptim (*http://imageoptim.com*) for Macs.

UP TO SPEED

How Compression Works

All the standard web image formats use *compression* to shrink picture information. However, the type of compression you get with each format differs significantly.

The GIF and PNG formats use *lossless compression*, which means there's no *loss* of any information from your picture. Lossless compression uses a variety of techniques to perform its space-shrinking magic—for example, it might find a repeating pattern in a file and replace each occurrence of it with a short abbreviation. When the browser decompresses the file, it gets all the original image data back.

The JPEG format uses *lossy compression*, which means it discards (or *loses*) some information about your picture. As a

result, your picture's quality diminishes, and there's no way to get it back to its original tip-top shape. However, the JPEG format is crafty, and it tries to trick your eye by discarding information that doesn't harm the picture that much. For example, it might convert slightly different colors to the same color, or replace fine details with smoothed-out blobs, because the human eye isn't that sensitive to small changes in color and shape. Usually, the overall result is a picture that looks softer and (depending how much compression you use) more blurry. On the other hand, the size-shrinking results you get with lossy compression are more dramatic than those offered by lossless compression.

Choosing the Right Format

It's important to learn which format to use for a given task. To help you decide, walk through the following series of questions.

Is your picture a hefty photo?

Yes: JPEG is the best choice for cutting large, finely detailed pictures down to size. Depending on the graphics program you use, you may be able to choose how much compression you want to apply.

Does your picture have sharp edges and need more than 256 colors?

Yes: PNG is the best answer here. It supports full color and uses lossless compression, so you don't lose any detail. If your picture has a limited number of colors (256 or fewer), you can use GIF instead of PNG, but there's no reason to.

Does your picture include a transparent area?

Yes: Use PNG. As you'll learn on page 127, PNG permits partial transparency, which lets you stack transparent layers and blend them to create a more natural effect. GIF has a cruder all-or-nothing transparency feature, and JPEG doesn't support transparency at all.

NOTE You read earlier that HTML keeps page elements like headlines in rectangular boxes. The same holds true for images—even a picture of a beach ball is enclosed in a box. That's why transparency in images is so important. It lets you place an image on a page with that page's background showing through; the result is a page with a seamlessly integrated image.

FREQUENTLY ASKED QUESTION

Typical File Sizes for Images

How much disk space does a typical picture occupy?

There's no single answer because it depends on several factors, including the dimensions of the picture, the file format you use, the amount of compression you apply, and how well the picture responds to compression techniques. However, there are a few basic things to keep in mind.

The file size of a typical website logo is vanishingly small. For example, Google's signature logo clocks in at a mere 20 KB (it's a PNG file).

Photos can take up much more space. On the small side of the equation, a picture in an article on the *New York Times* website rarely uses more than 70 KB. On the larger side of things, a typical eBayer may include a product picture that's 300 KB. At this size, the picture usually takes up a larger portion of your browser window. However, that's nothing compared with the size the picture would be if you weren't using compression. For example, even an ancient 1-megapixel camera can take a raw, uncompressed picture that's about 3,000 KB in size. In a web page, you can compress this to 300 KB or less by using the JPEG file format, which uses a lower quality level.

Putting Pictures on Colored Backgrounds

No matter what format you use, graphics programs store your image files as rectangles, even if the image itself isn't rectangular. For example, if you create a smiley-face graphic, your graphics program saves that round illustration on a white, rectangular background.

If your page background is white as well, this doesn't pose a problem because the image's background blends in with the rest of your page. But if your page has a different background color (page 87), you'll run into the graphical clunkiness shown in Figure 4-6.

FIGURE 4-6

Top: When you place this smiley-face picture on a page with a white background, it blends right in.

Bottom: With a non-white background, the white box around your picture is glaringly obvious.

Web designers came up with two solutions. One is to use transparency, a feature common to both PNG and GIF graphics. The basic idea is that your image contains *transparent pixels*—pixels that don't have any color at all. When a browser comes across these, it doesn't paint anything. Instead, it lets the background of the page show through. To make part of an image see-through, you define a transparent color using your graphics program. In the example above, for instance, you'd set the white background of your smiley-face graphic as the transparent color.

Although transparency seems like a handy way to make sure your image always has the correct background, in practice, it rarely looks good. The problem you usually see is a jagged edge where the colored pixels of your picture end and the web page background begins (see Figure 4-7).

The easiest way to fix this problem is to use the correct background color when you create your web graphic, instead of using transparency. In other words, when you draw your smiley-face image, give it the same background color as your web page. Your graphics program can then perform antialiasing, a technology that smooths an image's jagged edges to make them look nice. That way, the image edges blend in well with the picture's background, and when you display the image on your web page, it fits right in. The only limitation with this approach is its lack of flexibility. If you change your page color, you need to edit all your graphics.

FIGURE 4-7

The picture at the bottom of this page uses transparency, but the result—a jagged edge around the smiley face—is less than stellar. To smooth this edge, graphics programs use a sophisticated technique called antialiasing, which blends the picture color with the background color. Browsers can't perform this feat, so the edges they make aren't nearly as smooth.

Another approach is to use blended transparency (also known as *alpha blending*, because the alpha value of an image is a number that represents how transparent a pixel is). For example, instead of creating an image that cuts abruptly between colored pixels and transparent pixels, use one that blends the edge out using a fringe of semitransparent pixels. This feature sounds great, and PNG graphics use it, but you need serious Photoshop skills to create this effect. (If you want to go this route, try starting with the bare-bones tutorial at *http://tinyurl.com/ypf78g*.) Sadly, this is the price of creating polished web graphics.

■ Tutorial: Wrapping Text Around an Image

When you put an ordinary, unadorned `<img>` in your web page, it becomes an inline image. As explained earlier, inline images are locked into place alongside your text. You can put text above an inline image and text below it, but that's about as fancy as your page can get.

While inline images serve their purpose, they aren't the most elegant solution. A more flexible approach—and one that almost every web page uses—is to wrap text *around* images, so that the page mixes text and pictures into a cohesive design. Images that have text wrapped on one side or the other are called *floating* images, because they float next to an expanse of text. To create a floating image, you rely once more on the power of style sheets.

UP TO SPEED

Graphics Programs

It's up to you to choose the format for your image files. Most good graphics programs (like Adobe Fireworks and Adobe Photoshop) save your documents in a specialized file format that lets you do some advanced editing. Photoshop, for example, saves files in the .psd format. When you're ready to put your picture on a web page, you save a copy of the .psd file in a *different* format, one specially designed for the Web, like JPEG, GIF, or PNG. Usually, you do so by choosing File→Save As from the program's menu (although sometimes it's something a little different, like File→Export or File→Save For Web).

As a rule of thumb, you always need at least two versions of every picture you create: one in your graphics program's original format, and a copy in the JPEG, GIF, or PNG format you use on your website. You need to keep the original file so you can make changes whenever necessary and to make sure the image quality for future versions of the picture are as high as possible.

Once you choose an image format, your graphics program gives you a number of other options that let you customize details, like the compression level. At higher compression levels, your image file is smaller but of lower quality. Some really simple image editors (like the Paint program that ships with Windows) don't let you tweak these settings, so you're stuck with the program's built-in settings.

Graphics programs usually come in two basic flavors—*image editors* like Adobe Photoshop that let you retouch pictures and apply funky effects to graphics, and *drawing programs* like Adobe Illustrator, which lets you create your own illustrations by assembling shapes and text. If you're editing pictures of the office party to cut out an embarrassing moment, an image editor makes sense. If you're creating a logo for your newly launched cookie company, you need a drawing program.

If you don't have the luxury of getting a professional graphics program, you can hunt for one on a shareware site like *www.download.com*. Two popular free image editors are GIMP (*www.gimp.org*), which works with all the major operating systems, and Paint.NET (*www.getpaint.net*), which is Windows-only.

TIP Like all the tutorials in this book, you can find the solution for this exercise on the companion site at *http://prosetech.com/web*. Just look in the folder named Tutorial-4-2 (which stands for "Chapter 4, second tutorial"). There you'll find the files that you need to get started in the Start subfolder, and the solution to the exercise in the End subfolder.

Here's how to get started:

1. **Get the ordinary version of the page from the Tutorial-4-2\Start folder.**

   Find the web page *TomatoSoupRecipe.htm* and an image named *TomatoSoup.jpg*. Right now, this page uses an inline image, so the picture of the steaming-hot bowl of soup sits in the middle of the content, between the recipe list and the recipe instructions. Figure 4-8 shows the page as it is now, and Figure 4-9 shows the result you're after.

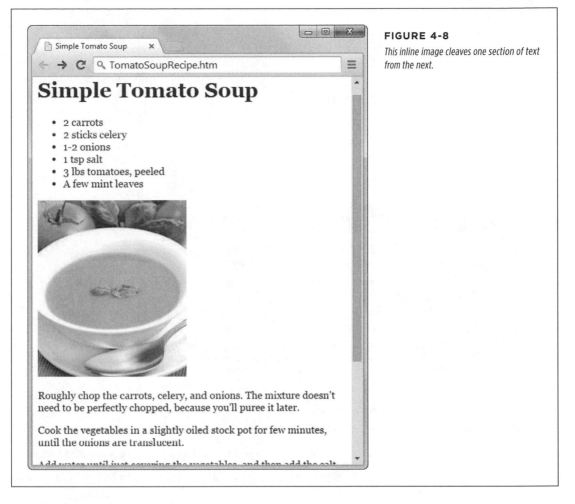

FIGURE 4-8

This inline image cleaves one section of text from the next.

2. **Decide what kind of style sheet you want to use.**

As always, you can apply style properties to the `<img>` element using an external style sheet, an internal style sheet, or an inline style (page 73 covers the differences).

In this example, the *TomatoSoupRecipe.htm* page already has an internal style sheet that sets the font. You can find the rules in the `<style>` element, which is in the `<head>` section at the top of the page.

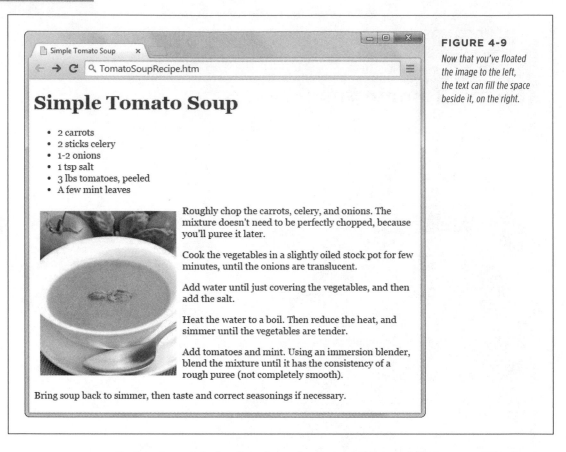

FIGURE 4-9

Now that you've floated the image to the left, the text can fill the space beside it, on the right.

3. **Create a style for the `<img>` element, and then add it to your style sheet.**

    This tutorial uses the following style, which you can add to the internal style sheet:

    ```
    <style>
      body {
        font-family: Georgia;
      }
      img.FloatLeft {
      }
    </style>
    ```

    This style has a two-part name. The first part, img, is the element name. It makes sure that the style can work only on images. The second part, FloatLeft, is the class name. It ensures that the rule targets images that have the *FloatLeft* class associated with them (because you probably don't want every picture on your page to float).

To apply the *FloatLeft* style, you have to add the class attribute to the target <img> element, like so:

```
<img src="TomatoSoup.jpg" alt="A bowl of tomato soup." class="FloatLeft" />
```

You now have a style sheet, a style rule for floating images, and an image that uses your rule. However, nothing has changed, because you haven't *defined* the *FloatLeft* style yet.

4. **Set the float property.**

   You create floating images using a CSS property named float. You set the value of the float property to either left or right, which lines up the image on either the left or right edge of the text.

   In this tutorial, you want to float your soup on the left, so you must add the two lines shown in bold:

```
<style>
  body {
    font-family: Georgia;
  }
  img.FloatLeft {
    float: left;
    margin: 10px;
  }
</style>
```

   When you set the float attribute, it makes sense to adjust the image's margin settings at the same time, so you have a little breathing room between your image and the surrounding text.

5. **Save your changes, and open (or refresh) the web page.**

   Now you can admire your handiwork (Figure 4-9).

To get floating text to work the way you want, always put the <img> element just *before* the text that should wrap around the image. In the soup recipe example, you placed it just after the recipe list and before the list of instructions.

NOTE Based on this example, you might think that the float property sends a picture to the left or right side of a page, but that's not exactly what happens. Remember, in CSS, HTML treats each element on a page as a container. When you create a floating image, the image actually goes to the left or right side of its *container*. If you put an image inside a smaller container—like a cell in a table or a <div> that creates a sidebar—you'll see that the image floats to the side of that element.

Figure 4-10 shows a few more image-wrapping examples, which demonstrate what happens if you move the image farther down into a paragraph of text or float it on the right.

If you place a floating image at the beginning of a paragraph, it floats in the top-left corner, with the text wrapped along the right edge. If the text extends beyond the end of the picture, it wraps underneath.

In this example, the floating image is inserted right after this sentence. It still floats in the top-left corner, but the text before it wraps above the picture. You still get the same wrapping after the image.

FIGURE 4-10

Remember, all image files are rectangles. When you wrap text around a floating image, the browser follows the contour of this invisible square, even if the image itself has a different shape, like a circle, or includes extra white space.

You can use the same technique to create a floating image on the right side of a paragraph. Just set the float property to right. Now it's lined up with the right side of the page.

TROUBLESHOOTING MOMENT

Floating with Lists

A strange thing happens if you try to float pictures around a bulleted or numbered list. Although the text sits next to the floating image, the bullets (if it's a bulleted list) or the numbers (if it's a numbered list) don't show up where you expect. Instead of sitting beside the picture, they're superimposed *on top* of it.

To solve this problem, simply add the following style sheet rules. One fixes bulleted lists (the <ul> element) and the other fixes numbered lists (the <ol> element).

```
ul { overflow: hidden; }
ol { overflow: hidden; }
```

The end result is that your lists fit perfectly next to any floating image, with no overlapped bullets or numbers.

Adding a Border

Right now, your picture is sitting pretty in the page. But maybe you want something else to divide the soup photo from its surrounding content. CSS has the perfect tool for you: a customizable border that you can draw around your picture in a close-fitting rectangle.

In Chapter 3, you learned to use the border-style and border-width properties to add borders around blocks of text. Happily, you can use these properties to add a border to an image just as easily.

In the tomato soup example, you simply add the border-style and border-width properties to the style rule you already created. Here's how you apply a thin, grooved border to all sides of the soup image:

```
img.FloatLeft {
  float: left;
  margin: 10px;
  border-style: groove;
  border-width: 3px;
}
```

Figure 4-11 shows the basic border styles. Remember, you can change the thickness and color of any border to get a very different look (page 108).

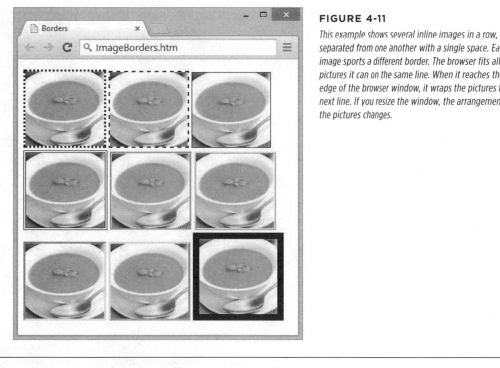

FIGURE 4-11

This example shows several inline images in a row, separated from one another with a single space. Each image sports a different border. The browser fits all the pictures it can on the same line. When it reaches the right edge of the browser window, it wraps the pictures to the next line. If you resize the window, the arrangement of the pictures changes.

Adding a Caption

Captions add a nice touch to photos, and you can put them above or below the image. For inline images, you just add a line of text immediately before or after the picture, separated by a line break. But that won't work with floated images, because the image *and* the caption have to float in tandem.

As it happens, the solution is simple. Just take the *FloatLeft* style rule shown earlier, and change the name from *img.FloatLeft* to *.FloatLeft*. That way, you can use the rule with *any* element:

```
.FloatLeft {
  float: left;
  margin: 10px;
}
```

Next, wrap the <img> element and your text in a <span> element, and then make the entire <span> element float using the *FloatLeft* style rule:

```
<span class="FloatLeft">
  <img src="TomatoSoup.jpg" alt=" A bowl of tomato soup." />
  <br />
  <i>A bowl of rustic tomato soup</i>
</span>
```

Figure 4-12 shows the result.

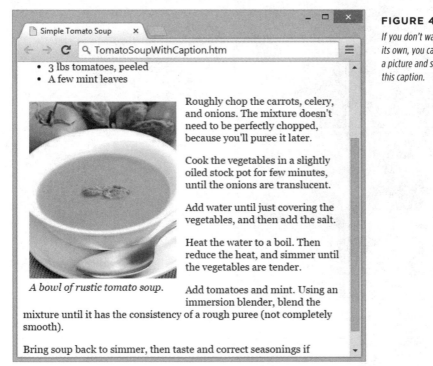

FIGURE 4-12

If you don't want to float a picture on its own, you can float a box that holds a picture and some other content, like this caption.

NOTE You use a `<span>` element in this example instead of a `<div>` element because you can put a `<span>` element *inside* other block elements, like a paragraph. In other words, by using a `<span>` element, you can easily put your floating picture-and-caption container inside one of your paragraphs.

POWER USERS' CLINIC

An Even Better Way to Float a Figure

Figure 4-12 shows how you can use a floating box to hold a figure and some related text. This is a popular technique in the web design world, but it isn't perfect. One shortcoming is that it muddies the structure of your web page. For example, it doesn't clearly indicate that the `<span>` is meant to represent a figure, or that the text has anything to do with the image.

This might not strike you as a serious problem (and it isn't), but high-minded markup purists are busy planning a world where web pages have more structure, which, in turn, helps programs better identify page elements—whether that program is a browser, a search engine, an accessibility tool, or something else altogether.

HTML5 adds two new elements that let you define a clear, well-structured figure: `<figure>` and `<figcaption>`. The `<figcaption>` element wraps the caption, and the `<figure>` element wraps the whole shebang: picture,

caption, and all. Here's how you'd use these two elements to clean up the previous example:

```
<figure class="FloatLeft">
  <img src="planetree.jpg"
    alt="Plane Tree" />
  <figcaption> The bark of a plane
  tree
  </figcaption>
</figure>
```

Neither new element applies any formatting, so you still need to use style sheet rules to get the appearance you want. But the real problem is that, like with some other new HTML5 elements, you can't use CSS to style the `<figure>` and `<figurecaption>` elements in any version of Internet Explorer before IE 9. So unless you're willing to use a JavaScript hack (described on page 578), it's probably best to wait.

Clearing a Float

Wrapping text can get a little tricky, because the results you get depend on the width of the browser window. For example, you might think that your text is long enough to wrap around a graphic, but in a wide window, it might take up just a few short lines, letting the rest of the page's content bump into your floating graphic. You might even end up with another floating picture bumping into your first floating picture.

To see this problem in action, it's time to look at another tutorial. In this tutorial, found in the Tutorial-4-3 folder, you're still dealing with the same content as the previous tutorial. However, there's a second picture added to the mix, which exposes a new problem.

Figure 4-13 demonstrates the issue, using the version of the *TomatoRecipe.htm* page from the Tutorial-4-3\Start folder. This page includes two pictures, both floating on the left edge. The effect works in a narrow window, but in a wide browser the two pictures get into a tangle.

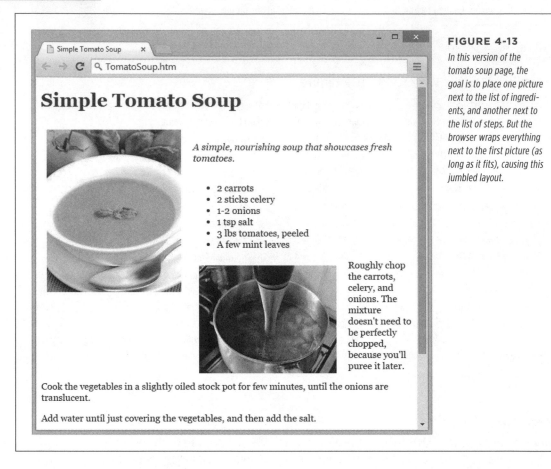

FIGURE 4-13

In this version of the tomato soup page, the goal is to place one picture next to the list of ingredients, and another next to the list of steps. But the browser wraps everything next to the first picture (as long as it fits), causing this jumbled layout.

To prevent this layout pileup, you use the `clear` property. It turns off any wrapping that's currently in effect on the page, forcing the browser to jump to the bottom of the floating content before it continues displaying the rest of the page.

You can add the clear property to any element. Common choices include the paragraph element (`<p>`) or the line break element (`<br>`). Here's an example:

```
<br style="clear: both;" />
```

To fix the problem in Figure 4-13, use the `clear` property after the list of ingredients ends and before the list of instructions starts. To try this out, open the starter version of the *TomatoRecipe.htm* page, insert the `<br>` element where you believe it should go, and then refresh the page to see the result. If you put the line break in the right place, you'll get the more organized version of the page featured in Figure 4-14.

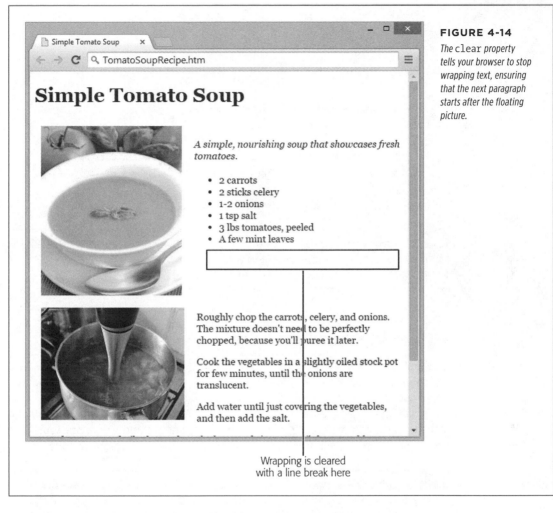

FIGURE 4-14

The clear *property tells your browser to stop wrapping text, ensuring that the next paragraph starts after the floating picture.*

Here's a shortened version of the solution, which shows where the pictures and line break fall in the markup. You can review the full markup by looking at the page in the Tutorial-4-3\End folder:

```
<h1>Simple Tomato Soup</h1>

<!-- Here's the first floating picture, next to the ingredients. -->
<img src="TomatoSoup.jpg" class="FloatLeft" alt="A bowl of tomato soup." />

<p class="Description">A simple, nourishing soup that showcases fresh
tomatoes.</p>
```

```
<ul>
<li>2 carrots</li>
<li>2 sticks celery</li>
<li>1-2 onions</li>
<li>1 tsp salt</li>
<li>3 lbs tomatoes, peeled</li>
<li>A few mint leaves</li>
</ul>

<!-- Now jump past the first floated picture. -->
<br style="clear: both;" />

<!-- Here's the second floating picture, next to the instructions. -->
<img src="BlendTheSoup.jpg" class="FloatLeft" alt="A bowl of tomato soup." />

<p>Roughly chop the carrots, celery, and onions. The mixture ...
```

NOTE In this example, the clear property is set to both, which tells the browser to turn off floating for both left-floated and right-floated content. Instead of using both, you can use left (skip past any left-floated content only) or right (skip past any right-floated content).

Background Images

CSS makes it possible to use an image as the background for a page, which is a neat but slightly old-fashioned way to add personality to your website. For example, you could use light parchment paper as a background for a literary site. A *Twilight* fan site might put a dark cemetery image to good use. Some people find the effect a little distracting, but it's worth considering if you want to add a dramatic touch and you can restrain yourself from going overboard. (Or if you straight-up love kitsch.)

TIP Although professional websites don't usually have a whole-page background, the CSS background image feature is still plenty useful. As you'll learn later in this section, you can use it to put a background behind any individual element, which makes it a useful way to add headers, panel borders, and other sorts of decoration to your pages.

Web designers almost always choose to *tile* background images, which means a browser copies a small picture over and over again until it fills the window (see Figure 4-15). You can't use a single image to fill a browser window because you have no way of knowing how wide and tall to make it, given people's variable browser settings. And if you *did* have visitors' exact screen measurements, you'd need to create an impractically large image that would take a long time to download.

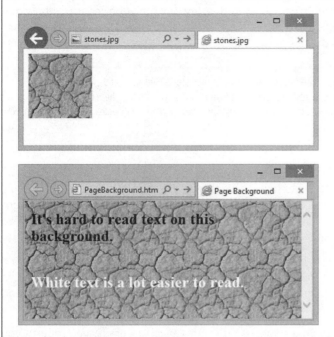

FIGURE 4-15

Top: Start with a small tile graphic with a stony pattern.

Bottom: Using style sheets, you can tile this graphic over the whole page. In a good tiled image, the edges line up to create the illusion of a seamless larger picture.

To create a tiled background, use the `background-image` style property. Your first step is to apply this property to the `<body>` element, so that you tile the whole page. Next, you need to provide the name of the image file using the form `url('filename')`, as shown here:

```
body {
   background-image: url('stones.jpg');
}
```

This tiles the image *stones.jpg* across a page to create your background.

Keep these points in mind when you create a tiled background:

• Make your background light, so the text displayed on top of it remains legible. (If you really have to go dark, you can use white, bold text so that it stands out. But don't do this unless you're creating a website for a trendy new band or opening a gothic clothing store.)

• Set the page's background color to match the color of the tiled image. For example, if you have a dark background picture and use white text for your content, make the background color black. That way, if a browser can't download the background image, visitors can still see your content.

- Use small tiles to reduce the amount of time your visitors need to wait before they can see the page.

- If your tiled image has an irregular pattern, make sure the edges line up. The left edge should continue the right edge, and the top edge should continue the bottom edge. Otherwise, when the browser tiles your image, you'll see lines where it stitches the tiles together.

> **TIP** The Web is full of common background images, like stars, blue skies and clouds, fabric and stone textures, fires, dizzying geometric patterns, borders, and much more. You can find these by searching Google for "backgrounds," or head straight to the somewhat dated sites that specialize in downloadable backgrounds, like *www.grsites.com/textures* and *www.backgroundsarchive.com*.

Background Watermarks

Most websites tile a picture to create a background image, but that's not your only option. You can also take a single image and place it at a specific position on your page. Think, for example, of a spy site whose background image faintly reads "Top Secret and Confidential."

An inconspicuous single-image background like this is called a *watermark*. (The name stems from the process used to place a translucent logo on paper saturated with water.) To make a good watermark, use a background picture that's pale and unobtrusive.

To add a watermark to your page, use the same background-image property you learned about above. But you need to add a few more style properties (see Table 4-2). First, you have to turn off tiling using the background-repeat property. At the same time, it makes sense to align your picture on the page to either side or centered, using the background-position property.

Here's an example that places a picture in the center of a web page:

```
body {
    background-image: url('smiley.jpg');
    background-repeat: no-repeat;
    background-position: center;
}
```

> **NOTE** The center of your document isn't necessarily the center of your browser window. If, for example, you position your image in the center of a long web page, you won't see it until you scroll down.

TABLE 4-2 *Background image properties.*

PROPERTY	DESCRIPTION	COMMON VALUES	CAN BE INHERITED?
background-image	The image file you use as your page background.	A URL pointing to the image file, as in url('mypig.jpg')	No*
background-repeat	Whether or not you tile the image to fill the page; you can turn off tiling altogether, or turn it off in one dimension (so that images tile vertically but not horizontally, for example).	repeat, repeat-x, repeat-y, no-repeat	No
background-position	Where you want to place the image. Use this only if you *aren't* tiling the image.	top left, top center, top right, center left, center, center right, bottom left, bottom center, bottom right	No
background-attachment	Whether you want to fix the image (or tiles) in place when a visitor scrolls the page.	scroll, fixed	No

* Background pictures aren't inherited. However, if you don't explicitly assign a background color to an element, it's given a transparent background, which means the background of the containing element will show through.

You can also turn off an image's ability to scroll along with the rest of a page to get the rather odd effect of an image that's fixed in place (see Figure 4-16). For example, this style creates a background image that always sits squarely in the center of a window:

```
body {
    background-image: url('smiley.gif');
    background-repeat: no-repeat;
    background-position: center;
    background-attachment: fixed;
}
```

Backgrounds for Other Elements

You don't need to apply a background to a whole page. Instead, you can bind a background to a single paragraph or, more usefully, to a `<div>` element. That way, you can create the same effect as a sidebar in a magazine. Usually, you want to add a border around this element to separate it from the rest of your web page. You might also need to change the color of the foreground text so it's legible (for example, white shows up better than black on dark backgrounds).

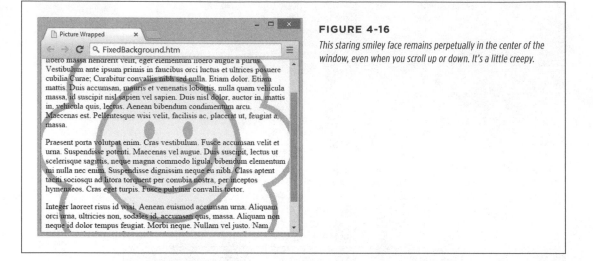

FIGURE 4-16

This staring smiley face remains perpetually in the center of the window, even when you scroll up or down. It's a little creepy.

Here's an example of a background image you can use with any container element:

```
.pie {
    background-image: url('pie.jpg');
    margin-top: 20px;
    margin-bottom: 10px;
    margin-left: 70px;
    margin-right: 70px;
    padding: 10px;
    border-style: double;
    border-width: 3px;
    color: white;
    background-color: black;
    font-size: large;
    font-weight: bold;
    font-family: Verdana,sans-serif;
}
```

This style specifies a background image, sets the margins and borders, and chooses background and foreground colors to match.

Here's a <div> that uses this style:

```
<div class="pie">
    <p>Hungry for some pie?</p>
</div>
```

Figure 4-17 shows the result.

FIGURE 4-17

Top: Using background images in small boxes is surprisingly slick.

Bottom: A particularly neat feature is the way the picture grows when you resize the page, thanks to tiling.

Graphical Bullets in a List

In Chapter 2, you learned how to use the <ul> element to create a bulleted list. However, you were limited to a small set of predefined bullet styles. If you look around
the Web, you'll see more interesting examples of bulleted lists, including some that
use tiny pictures as custom bullets.

You can add custom bullets by hand using the <img> element, but there's an easier
option. You can use the list-style-image property to set a bullet image. Here's an
example that uses a picture named *3Dball.gif*:

```
ul {
   list-style-image: url('3Dball.gif');
}
```

Once you create this style rule and put it in your style sheet, your browser automatically applies it to an ordinary bulleted list like this one:

```
<ul>
   <li>Are hard to miss</li>
   <li>Help compensate for feelings of inadequacy</li>
   <li>Look so darned cool</li>
   <li>Remind people of boring PowerPoint presentations</li>
</ul>
```

Figure 4-18 shows the result.

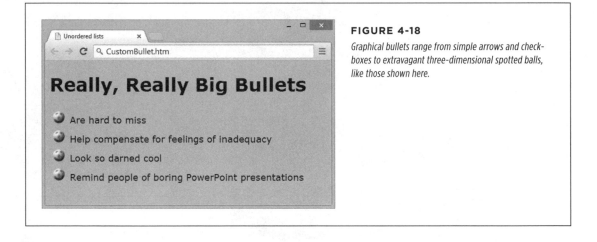

FIGURE 4-18

*Graphical bullets range from simple arrows and check-
boxes to extravagant three-dimensional spotted balls,
like those shown here.*

■ Finding Free Art

The Web is awash in graphics. In fact, finding a web page that isn't chock-full of
images is about as unusual as spotting Bill Gates in a dollar store. But how do you
generate all the pictures you need for a graphically rich site? Do you really need to
spend hours in a drawing program fine-tuning every picture you want? The answer

depends on exactly what type of pictures you need, of course, but you'll be happy to hear that the Web is a great resource for ready-to-use pictures.

It's not hard to find pictures on the Web. You can, for example, use a handy Google tool to search for graphics on a specific subject (type *http://images.google.com* into your browser and search away). Unfortunately, *finding* an image usually isn't good enough. To use it without worrying about a lawyer tracking you down, you also need the *rights* to use the picture. If you get lucky, a website owner might grant you permission to use a graphic after you send a quick email. But that's the exception rather than the rule.

Fortunately, photo enthusiasts have set up community sites where they post their pictures for the world to see—and on some of these sites, you can search for and reuse anything you want, for free. One of the best was Stock.XCHNG (pronounced "stock exchange," after *stock photography*, the name for the vast catalogs of reusable pictures that graphic designers collect). Recently, Getty Images purchased the Stock.XCHNG site and renamed it "Free Images." Sadly, there aren't many active contributors any more, but you can still access the same free catalog of pics at *http://sxc.hu* (Figure 4-19).

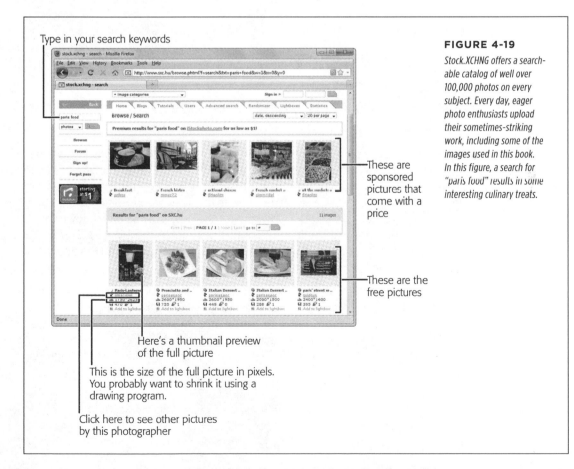

Type in your search keywords

These are sponsored pictures that come with a price

These are the free pictures

Here's a thumbnail preview of the full picture

This is the size of the full picture in pixels. You probably want to shrink it using a drawing program.

Click here to see other pictures by this photographer

FIGURE 4-19

Stock.XCHNG offers a searchable catalog of well over 100,000 photos on every subject. Every day, eager photo enthusiasts upload their sometimes-striking work, including some of the images used in this book. In this figure, a search for "paris food" results in some interesting culinary treats.

Another good place for digging up free photos is Flickr (*www.flickr.com*), though the site includes both images that are free to reuse and those that are not. The best way to find pictures you *can* use is with an advanced search at *www.flickr.com/search/advanced*. Enter your search keywords (as you would in a normal search), but check the "Only search within Creative Commons-licensed content" setting (Figure 4-20). That ensures that you find only files you can snatch.

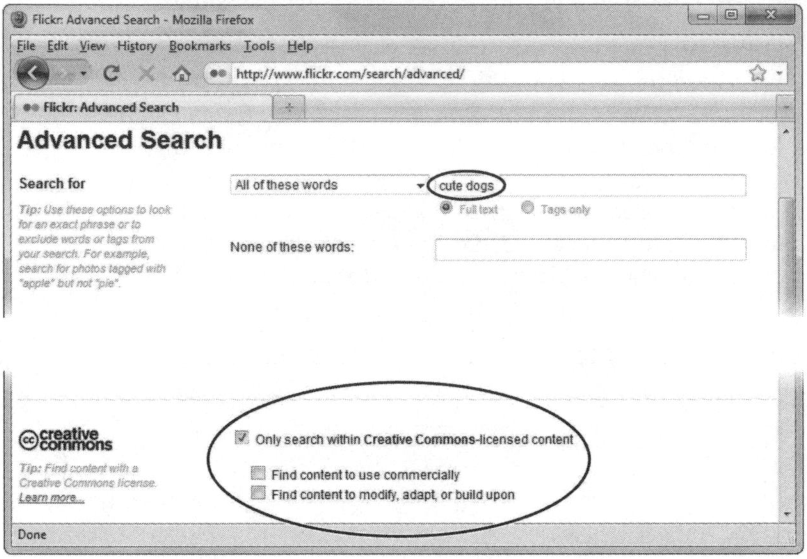

FIGURE 4-20

Here you've limited your Flickr search to figures you can use on your own website. However, the figures may still have restrictions that prevent you from using them on commercial sites or from modifying them.

Be aware, though, that content you use under a Creative Commons license may come with one or two restrictions. For example, it may stipulate that you can't use the picture on a commercial website (at least not without getting permission from the picture owner). It may also restrict you from changing or editing the picture. When you find a picture you like, you can get the details by scrolling down to the License box (which you'll find in the bottom-right corner of the page). Or you can explicitly search for pictures that don't have these restrictions, using the additional settings shown in Figure 4-20.

If you can't find the picture you want at Stock.XCHNG or Flickr, you may never find it—at least not without going to a commercial site, like iStockPhoto (*www.istock-photo.com*), Fotolia (*www.fotolia.com*), or Dreamstime (*www.dreamstime.com*), all of which charge a few dollars for royalty-free images. But if you'd like to look at some other no-pay alternatives, check out the article on finding free photographs at *http://tinyurl.com/49yquv3*.

Working with a Web Editor

I n Chapter 1, you built your first HTML page with nothing but a text editor and a lot of nerve—the same way all web page whiz kids begin their careers. To really understand HTML (and to establish your HTML street cred), you need to start from scratch.

However, very few web authors stick with plain-text editors or use them to create anything other than simple test pages. The average HTML page is filled with tedious detail. Try to write every paragraph, line break, and formatting tag by hand, and you'll probably make a mistake somewhere along the way. Even if you don't, it's hard to visualize a finished page when you spend all day staring at angle brackets. This is especially true when you tackle more complex pages, like those with graphics or multicolumn layouts.

The downside to outgrowing Notepad or TextEdit is the expense. Professional web design tools can cost hundreds of dollars. At one point, software companies planned to include basic web editors as part of operating systems like Windows and Mac OS. In fact, some older versions of Windows shipped with a scaled-down web editor called FrontPage Express (and some old Macs included a severely truncated editor called iWeb). But if you want a full-featured web page editor—one that catches your errors, helps you remember important HTML elements, and lets you manage your entire site—you have to find one on your own. Fortunately, there are free alternatives for even the most cash-strapped web weaver.

In this chapter, you'll learn how web page editors work and how to find the one that's right for you. You'll also discover some free web editors that can do the same work as their professional counterparts.

■ The Benefits of a Web Editor

Tools like Notepad and TextEdit aren't all that bad for starting out. They keep page development simple and don't mess with your HTML (as a word-processing program would). Seeing the result of your work is just a browser refresh away. So why might you outgrow a basic text editor? For a number of reasons, including these:

- **Nobody's perfect.** With a text editor, it's just a matter of time before you make a mistake, like typing <b> instead of </b>. Unfortunately, you might not realize your mistake even when you view your page in a browser. Browsers do their best to compensate for HTML inaccuracies, even if that means obscuring the real problems in your page. A good web page editor can highlight faulty HTML and help you correct it.

- **Edit-Save-Refresh. Repeat 1,000 times.** Text editors are convenient for small pages. But what if you're trying to size a picture perfectly or line up a table column? You need to jump back and forth between your text editor and your web browser, saving and refreshing your page each time, a process that can literally take hours. With a good web page editor, you get conveniences like drag-and-drop editing to fine-tune your pages—make a few adjustments, and your editor tweaks your HTML appropriately. Editors also have a preview mode that lets you immediately see the effect of your edits, no browser required.

- **Help, I'm drowning in HTML!** One of the nicest little frills of a web page editor is color-coded HTML. Color-coding makes those pesky tags stand out against a sea of text. Without this feature, you'd be cross-eyed in hours.

- **Just type <ul><li></li></ul>.** To create a bulleted list, of course. You haven't forgotten already, have you? The truth is, most web authors don't memorize every HTML element there is. With a web editor, you don't need to. If you forget something, there's usually a menu command, keyboard shortcut, or pop-up window to help you out.

Of course, using a graphical web page editor has its own risks. That's why you started out with a simple text editor and why you'll spend a good portion of this book learning more about HTML and CSS. If you don't understand these standards properly, you can fall into a number of traps. For example, you might unintentionally use non-web-safe fonts that won't show up on other computers (page 97), or include HTML5 elements that older browsers don't recognize. And no matter what editor you use, you still need to understand HTML, because you'll spend a significant amount of time looking at raw markup to see exactly what's going on, to clean up a mess, or to copy and paste useful bits to other pages.

Types of Web Page Editors

Although every web editor has its own personality, they generally fall into one of three broad categories:

- **Text-based** editors require you to work with the text and tags of raw HTML. The difference between an ordinary text editor (like Notepad) and a text-based

HTML editor is convenience. Unlike Notepad or TextEdit, text-based HTML editors usually include buttons that let you quickly insert common HTML elements or element combinations, and a one-click way to save your file and open it in a separate browser window. They often use color-coding to help you read your markup and highlighting to flag common problems (like missing or misspelled tags). Essentially, text-based HTML editors are text editors with some useful web-editing features stapled on top. The Brackets editor, which you'll meet in this chapter (page 169), is a good example.

- **WYSIWYG** (what you see is what you get) editors work like word processors. Instead of writing HTML tags, you type in a page's text, format it, and insert pictures just as you would in a word-processing program. Behind the scenes, the web editor writes your HTML markup. WYSIWYG web editors also give you the freedom to switch your view, so you can dart back and forth between the WYSIWYG rendition of your page and the HTML markup that creates it.

- **Split-window** editors combine the best of the text-based and WYSIWYG approaches. They use a split, two-paned window that puts your HTML markup beside a live, browser-style preview. The magic is that as you revise the HTML, the editor refreshes the preview. That way, you don't need to switch back and forth between text editor and browser to see what you've accomplished. The most advanced split-window editors also let you *edit* in the WYSIWYG view. Dreamweaver and Expression Web both provide this ability, as you'll see in this chapter.

Any of these editors make a good replacement for a simple text editor. The type you choose depends mainly on how many features you want, how you prefer to work, and how much money you're willing to shell out.

No matter which type of editor you use, you still need to know a fair bit about HTML to get the results you want. Even if you have a WYSIWYG editor, you'll almost always want to fine-tune your markup by hand. Understanding HTML's quirks lets you determine what you can and can't do—and the strategies you need to follow to get the most sophisticated results. Even in a WYSIWYG editor, you'll inevitably look at the HTML underbelly of your web pages.

◼ Choosing Your Web Editor

Getting the right web editor is a matter of taste, personal preference, and—perhaps most importantly—*money*. If you plan to embark on a new career as a junior web designer, you may not mind investing in a pricey commercial tool. But if your relationship with the Web begins and ends with a small hobby site that showcases your stamp collection, you'll be reluctant to part with any extra cash.

Here's the good news: These days, there's an excellent web editor for every budget, right down to free. The following sections outline your choices.

Save as HTML

My word-processing/page layout/spreadsheet program has a feature for saving documents as web pages. Should I use it?

Over the last decade, the Internet has become the hottest marketing buzzword around. Every computer program imaginable is desperate to boast about new web features. For example, virtually every modern word processor has a feature for exporting your documents to HTML. Don't use it.

HTML export features don't work very well. Often, the program tries to wedge a document designed for one medium (usually print) into another (the Web). But word processor documents just don't look like web pages. They tend to have larger margins, fancier fonts, more text, more generous spacing around that text, no links, and a radically different layout. When you export a document, your word processor tries to preserve these

details, in the process creating pages that aren't readable or attractive when viewed in a web browser.

Another problem with export features is that they often create wildly complex HTML markup. You end up with an ungainly web page that's nearly impossible to edit because it's choked with formatting details. (Dreamweaver even has a tool that aims to help you with the cleanup; look in the menu under Commands→Clean Up Word HTML.) And if you want to convert one of these pages into stricter, cleaner HTML, you need to do it by hand.

The lesson? If you can, steer clear of the "Save as HTML" command. You're better off copying and pasting the contents of your document into an HTML file as plain text, and then formatting it with HTML tags on your own.

Dreamweaver: The Best Choice if You're Not on a Budget

Adobe Dreamweaver is the favorite page-creation tool of graphic designers and hard-core HTML experts. Packed with features, it gives you fine-grained control of every HTML ingredient.

It's hard to go wrong with Dreamweaver. The program is chock-full of high-grade features, while relatively easy to use. It's also the de facto standard of web designers everywhere. So if you use Dreamweaver, you can talk shop with other Dreamweaver fanatics and professional web designers. The only possible drawback (other than price) is its complexity. You can't be the world's most advanced web editor without having a few overstuffed command menus. But as you'll see in this chapter, Dreamweaver is surprisingly unintimidating considering its status as the expert's tool of choice.

Now for that price. To use Dreamweaver, you need a Creative Cloud subscription from Adobe. That means that instead of forking over an eye-popping amount of money as a one-time payment, you're on the hook for a monthly fee. For Dreamweaver only, that's currently $20 per month. If you want to tap the complete catalog of Creative Cloud apps, which includes Dreamweaver, Photoshop, Illustrator, InDesign, and several more professional creative tools, you pay $50 per month (less if you're a student; alas, there is no student discount for the Dreamweaver-only plan).

To learn more or sign up for a Creative Cloud plan, visit *https://creative.adobe.com/plans*. To try the free 30-day trial, head to *http://tiny.cc/creativecloud*. You'll get a basic introduction to Dreamweaver on page 153.

Expression Web: A Solid Free Alternative (Windows Only)

Once upon a time, Microsoft mounted a challenge to Dreamweaver's dominance with a well-rounded editor called Expression Web. Expression Web attracted more than a little love, but it never acquired anywhere near the popularity or street cred of Dreamweaver. Many professional web designers still remembered the ugly markup generated by Microsoft's previous web editing tool, FrontPage, and they weren't ready to trust the company again.

Microsoft abandoned Expression Web at the end of 2012. At the same time, it decided to release the last version of the program online, and *for free*. That version is still available, and it continues to work with newer Windows operating systems. (At the time of this writing, it's been confirmed to work on computers running Windows XP right up to Windows 8.1.)

Of course, you won't get non-critical updates or new features with Expression Web, and Mac fans are completely out of luck. But even with these limitations, Expression Web remains a capable choice. It offers many of the same advanced features 4as Dreamweaver, including the ability to create style sheets and manage entire websites. It's far better than the crowd of modestly priced web editors you find on shareware sites like *www.download.com*.

> **NOTE** *Shareware* is software that's free to try, play with, and pass along to friends. If you like it, you're politely asked to pay for it, or not-so-politely locked out when the trial period ends. A typical shareware web editor (like CoffeeCup HTML Editor or HTML-Kit) costs $50 or $60. To make sure your shareware is virus- and spyware-free, download it from a reputable source like *www.download.com*. And if the setup program gives you the option to install additional software goodies (like anti-virus tools, registry cleaners, and browser search bars), *always say no*. At best, these programs will clog your computer; at worst, they'll snoop on your web travels and bother you with advertising.

So the bottom line is this: If you aren't out to impress a crowd of black-turtleneck-wearing web designers, and you don't mind living with the knowledge that someday, on some new system, your web editor will stop working, then Expression Web is a bargain that's almost too good to be true. (And if you're concerned about the editor's limited lifetime, check out the box on page 152 for a possible backup plan.)

To download Expression Web, visit *http://tinyurl.com/freeEW*. You'll get a chance to try it out in a tutorial on page 162.

Brackets: A Good Choice for Text Lovers and Techies

Looking for something simple, straightforward, and fast? The newest web editor you'll meet in this chapter is Brackets, a free tool from Adobe (the same company that owns Dreamweaver). Like Dreamweaver, Brackets works on Windows and Macs, so no one's left out.

What to Do When Expression Web Retires

Right now, Expression Web works great, and there's no reason to think that will change in the near future. But someday, you'll notice that Expression Web lacks something—maybe it won't recognize the yet-to-be invented details of a future edition of HTML, or perhaps it will come to a shuddering halt on a new version of the Windows operating system. If you're worried about that possibility, Microsoft has another professional-grade choice that shares the same zero-dollar price tag: It's called Visual Studio Express for Web.

Visual Studio Express for Web is one of the wildly popular Visual Studio tools designed for programmers who build applications for Windows computers, apps for Windows phones, and interactive websites fueled by the server software ASP.NET. (By writing web applications with ASP.NET, you can create highly interactive websites that query databases or place orders for ecommerce sites. The drawback is that you need to be a skilled

and patient programmer, and you need to run your website on a server that supports ASP.NET.)

But here's what non-techies often overlook: Visual Studio works just as well for plain-vanilla websites, although some might consider it overkill. Yes, there are plenty of developer features tucked into every nook and cranny, and the program just *feels* bigger and more complicated than Expression Web. But if you're not intimidated by Visual Studio's focus on programming, and you don't mind ignoring everything that doesn't apply to you, you can use it as an ordinary WYSIWYG web page editor, complete with the same sort of professional features you can find in Dreamweaver and Expression Web. Best of all, its high profile in the programming world means that you never need to worry about Microsoft abandoning it.

To try Visual Studio Express for Web, go to *www.asp.net/vwd*.

Brackets has a few characteristics that make it distinctly different from the web editors you've seen so far. First, it provides a no-nonsense editing environment that's like a supercharged, color-coded text editor. Unlike Dreamweaver, Expression Web, or Visual Studio, you can't preview your web pages in the Brackets window, but Brackets works closely with your browser, triggering an automatic refresh every time you change your markup.

Brackets is also unusual in that it's *open source*, meaning that it's in the public domain, so anyone can use it or explore the code that makes it work. It also means that the Brackets project relies on volunteer programmers, who contribute everything from new features to bug fixes.

Open-source projects have impressive benefits—as long as the project is thriving, the software is likely to get frequent updates, people are quick to spot and patch problems, and the team of developers listens closely to the comments and requests that come from the community of people who use the program. Brackets, for instance, gets new features and extensions every few weeks. But open-source projects can run into problems, too—most commonly, volunteer developers can get tired or move on, and if that happens, there's no authority to step in and force everyone to keep working.

Brackets was designed for web designers who like the simple, fast, uncluttered editing experience of a text editor. It's particularly well-suited to programmers, but it's an equally good tool for web-heads who want to keep things simple, and focus on the markup in their pages.

If you're interested, you can download Brackets at *http://brackets.io*. You'll see it in action on page 169.

GEM IN THE ROUGH

Other Fancy Text Editor Alternatives

If you aren't sold on Brackets but you still like the idea of a jacked-up text editor, there are other options.

For Windows computers, the free Notepad++ does an excellent job of replacing the classic Notepad editor with a tool that works similarly but offers much more. Among its best features are tag highlighting and a document map that gives you a bird's-eye view of long, sprawling text documents. Get it at *http://notepad-plus-plus.org*.

On Mac computers, TextWrangler is a similarly useful free text editor. It's not any more complicated than the standard TextEdit tool, but it offers the indispensable tag-highlighting feature so you can find your way through complex markup without headaches. Download it from *www.barebones.com/products/textwrangler*.

If you aren't concerned about price, you can splurge on Sublime Text, a really tricked-out text editor that runs on Windows or Macs but costs a princely $70. Among its many extra features are a way of opening files and jumping to a specific location in one go, the ability to select and change multiple bits of text at a time, and a ridiculous amount of customizability. Learn more at *www.sublimetext.com*.

Getting Started with Dreamweaver

Because Dreamweaver is part of Adobe's Creative Cloud program, it's a little harder to install than a standalone program, whether you're paying for a subscription or just starting a trial. The following steps take you through the process:

NOTE With a Creative Cloud subscription, you run the software on your computer, just as you do with a standard program. However, every time you launch a Creative Cloud application, it checks in with Adobe's web servers to make sure you have a valid license. When you stop paying your subscription, you can't use the software, even though it's still technically on your computer. This might seem harsh, and it has made more than a few enemies among cash-strapped graphics designers.

1. **In your browser, visit** *http://tiny.cc/creativecloud*.

2. **Click the Download button.**

   Adobe asks if you have an Adobe ID.

3. **Click the "Sign up for an Adobe ID" button.**

   You'll need to fill in some basic information about yourself, including your name, birthdate, and email address.

---

4. **When you finish, click Sign Up.**

   Your browser will begin downloading the setup program for the Creative Cloud system. This won't take long.

5. **Confirm your email address.**

   When you sign up for an Adobe ID, Adobe sends you a welcome email. In that email is a "Verify your email" link. At some point before you start using the Creative Cloud applications, you must click the verification link to confirm your email address.

6. **When you finish downloading the Çreative Cloud program, launch it.**

   The setup program has a name like *CreativeCloudSet-Up.exe*. The exact way you launch it depends on the browser you're using. You may see the setup program appear in a message bar at the bottom of the window (in which case you should click it), or your browser may ask you straight up if you're ready to run the program (click Yes).

   The Creative Cloud is a setup and management tool for all your Creative Cloud programs. It also includes some Adobe goodies, like free online storage. However, installing Creative Cloud doesn't actually get you any of the Creative Cloud applications. Instead, you need to opt in to each program you want, as you'll see shortly.

7. **Once you install Creative Cloud, launch it.**

   Usually, the Creative Cloud application launches automatically when you finish the setup. If not, you can use the shortcut on the desktop (on a Windows computer) or you can start it from the Launcher (on a Mac).

8. **In the Creative Cloud window, click "Install or update an application."**

   You'll see a list of Creative Cloud applications (Figure 5-1).

9. **Look for Dreamweaver CC, and then click the Try button next to it.**

   Now, at last, you're installing Dreamweaver. This will take a bit longer than the Creative Cloud setup, depending on the speed of your connection. To check how the process is unfolding, look at the progress bar in the Creative Cloud window.

When you finish the installation, you're ready to start experimenting with Dreamweaver. Remember, if you chose the trial version, you have just 30 days before the software becomes useless. If your trial period runs out and you want to stick with Dreamweaver, you can upgrade to a paid account at *https://creative.adobe.com/plans*.

Editing a Page

The first time you start Dreamweaver, you'll need to click your way through a number of messages. The program boasts about some of its new features, offers to give you a tour, and, if you're using the trial version, asks if you want to upgrade to the paid program. When you finally get to the Dreamweaver window, you may find some unnecessary panels crowding up the sides. Look for the tiny arrow buttons to shift them out of the way (Figure 5-2).

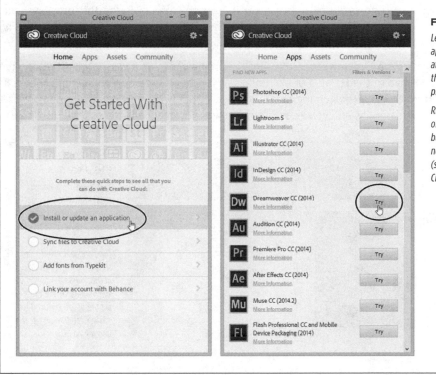

FIGURE 5-1

Left: The Creative Cloud application starts you out at the Home tab. Click the first link to install a program.

Right: You can try out any of the Creative Cloud apps, but the one you want right now is Dreamweaver CC (short for Dreamweaver Creative Cloud).

FIGURE 5-2

Here, a panel advertising one of Dreamweaver's newest fancy features (the ability to convert parts of a Photoshop file into images or styles that a web page can use) occupies the left side of the window. Since you don't need the panel, click the tiny "Collapse to Icons" arrows (circled) to hide it and reclaim the space for editing your pages.

To take Dreamweaver for a test spin, open one of the HTML sample files you worked on in the previous chapters (all of which are available on the companion site at *http://prosetech.com/web*), using the familiar File→Open command. Figure 5-3 shows Dreamweaver with the *resume4.htm* page from Chapter 1 open.

When you open a file in Dreamweaver, it gives you a split window that previews your page-in-progress on the top and shows the HTML markup on the bottom. Usually, you'll do your editing in the markup area.

As you type, Dreamweaver refreshes the preview to keep it in sync with the changes you make to the HTML. For example, say you open the Lee Park resumé shown in Figure 5-3 and replace the text "I am Lee Park" with "You can call me Mr. Park." Watch carefully, and you'll see Dreamweaver automatically refresh the preview.

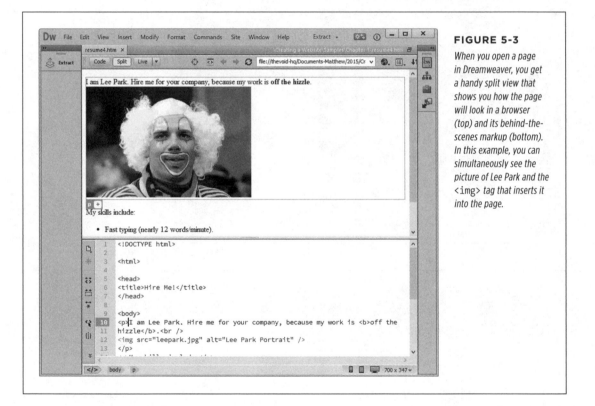

FIGURE 5-3

When you open a page in Dreamweaver, you get a handy split view that shows you how the page will look in a browser (top) and its behind-the-scenes markup (bottom). In this example, you can simultaneously see the picture of Lee Park and the <img> tag that inserts it into the page.

You can also use the preview area to jump to a specific location in your markup. For example, if you click a paragraph in the preview area, Dreamweaver selects the corresponding <p> element in the markup area. You can also double-click something in the preview area to make a quick edit. To try this out, double-click the last list item in the resumé example. This puts the preview area in edit mode so you can make changes. Now move to the end of the line, press Enter, and then type in a new entry. When you finish, click anywhere else in the page to make the change permanent.

Dreamweaver refreshes the markup below to match, adding a new `<li>` element with the text you just typed in.

Even if you're still a bit intimidated by angle brackets and HTML attributes, it shouldn't take you long to get comfortable in Dreamweaver's split window. Here are a few adjustments that let you customize the editing environment:

- You can move the splitter bar that divides the preview area from the markup area. For example, you can drag it up to get more space to review your markup.

- If you prefer to have the markup up top and the preview below, choose View→Live View on Top (which turns the "Live View on Top" setting off).

- If you have a large, widescreen monitor, you might prefer to put the preview and the markup side by side. Choose View→Spit Vertically.

- If you want to focus on the markup and ignore the preview for the time being, click the Code button at the top of the editing window (Figure 5-4). Click Split to go back to the split view, or Live to show just the preview.

NOTE If you're working with a complex page, or you need to make extreme changes, the live preview feature could slow you down. If it takes a long ti me for Dreamweaver to refresh the live preview, you can switch to the program's older design view, which works the same way but updates less often. To make the switch, choose View→Toggle Live view (or click the drop-down arrow next to the Live button at the top of the page, and then choose Design). Now Dreamweaver won't update the preview as you type in the markup area. Instead, it waits until you click the preview area, click a menu command, or switch to another program and then come back.

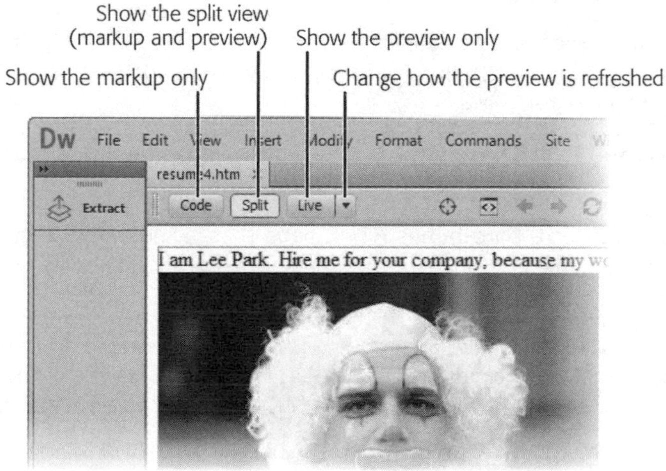

Show the split view
(markup and preview)   Show the preview only

Show the markup only   Change how the preview is refreshed

FIGURE 5-4

One of the best features of a professional web editor like Dreamweaver is the ability to look at a web page from several perspectives, depending on the task at hand.

Dreamweaver also has a neat way of dealing with style sheets. When you open a page that uses a linked style sheet, it adds the name of the style sheet (for example, *resume.css*) to the top of the editing window, just above the Code, Split, and Design buttons. Click the style sheet's name, and Dreamweaver shows the style sheet code in the markup window. Click Source Code to switch back to the HTML markup for your page. This handy feature lets you work with external style sheets as though they were a part of your web page, without opening a new window.

HOW'D THEY DO THAT?

The Mystery of Empty Paragraphs

In web authoring tools like Dreamweaver, if you're in Design view and you press Enter, the program creates a new paragraph. This seems a little counterintuitive, as you learned earlier in this book that browsers normally ignore line breaks and white space.

The trick is that when you hit the Enter key, both programs insert a paragraph that contains a special code. Here's what that creation looks like:

`<p> </p>`

This paragraph is still empty, but the browser won't ignore it because it includes the ` ` code. Therefore, the browser gives it the same space as a single-line paragraph and bumps down the content underneath.

Incidentally, Dreamweaver does let you use more ordinary line break elements (`<br>`) instead of empty paragraphs, even in Design view. To do this, press Shift+Enter instead of just Enter.

Creating a New Page

Now that you've taken a look at Dreamweaver's editing features, why not create a new page of your own? Here's how:

1. **Just as in a text editor, you start by picking File→New.**

   When you ask Dreamweaver to create a new file, it offers you an overwhelming panoply of choices (Figure 5-5). But right now, you want to stick with creating a plain-vanilla, blank HTML page.

2. **Make sure you select HTML5 from the DocType drop-down menu, and then click Create.**

   Dreamweaver produces a bare-bones HTML page that includes the doctype and the basic <html>, <head>, <title>, and <body> elements.

NOTE Later in this book, you'll learn how to create fancy layouts and pile on other web page frills. But if you let Dreamweaver add these details for you now, you'll end up with some markup and styles that you don't quite understand. And when you don't understand what's in your markup, you start to lose control of your page.

As a general rule of thumb, you should use a web editor for its convenience, not because it knows something you don't. And *never* let a web editor add something to your page that you don't fully understand.

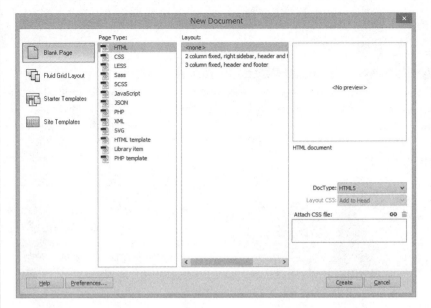

FIGURE 5-5

Dreamweaver lets you choose from a long list of file types in the Page Type list, including CSS style sheets and JavaScript code files. Choose HTML, and Dreamweaver gives you the choice of several ready-made page designs with multicolumn layouts (in the Layout list). To avoid confusion and keep things simple, stick with the first choice, <none>.

3. **Choose File→Save, pick a filename, and then save the HTML document to your hard drive.**

   Technically, you don't need to save your new web page right away, but doing so can avoid potential problems. For example, if you insert an image into an unsaved document, Dreamweaver writes a file path that points to the image on your hard drive. Later, when you put the page online, visitors will see the dreaded broken-image icon (page 117) because their browsers can't tap into your hard drive.

4. **Add some content.**

   If you want some good practice, try recreating one of the examples from Chapter 1. You can follow the instructions from the second tutorial, on page 21.

   As you type, you'll notice a few shortcuts. For example, when you start typing a tag name (by typing the initial angle bracket, <), Dreamweaver displays a pop-up menu with suggestions. You can choose a valid HTML tag from the list or just keep typing. And when you start typing an end tag with the </ characters, Dreamweaver figures out which element is currently open and fills in the rest (for example, </h1> if you're rounding off a heading).

5. **Preview your page in a browser.**

Dreamweaver does an excellent job of showing you what your page will look like once you put it on the Web. But to make sure the page works for all your guests, take a look at it in several web browsers. You can launch a browser and load up your page in one nifty step, right from inside Dreamweaver. Just choose File→"Preview in Browser," and then pick the browser you want to use.

Working with Several Pages at Once

Web editors like Dreamweaver have an elegant way of dealing with multiple pages. Each time you open another page or create a new document, Dreamweaver adds a tab at the top of the editing window (Figure 5-6). Switching from one page to another is as easy as clicking the tab you want. There's no need to juggle a dozen different windows.

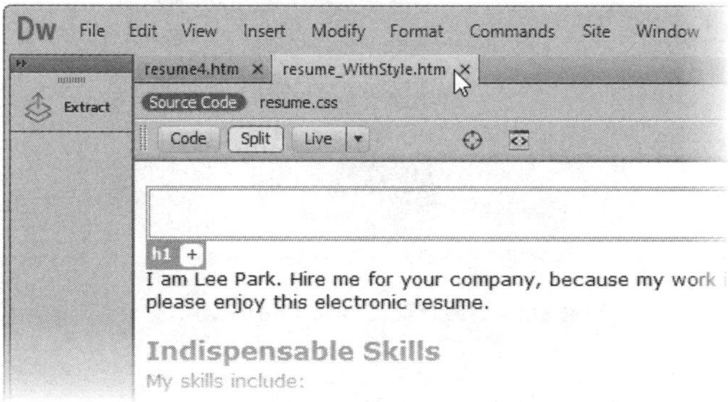

FIGURE 5-6

Here you have two web pages open in Dream- weaver. You switch between them using the tabs at the top of the editing window. The currently selected tab is for the page resume_WithStyle. htm (an example from Chapter 3). To close a tab, click the tiny X next to the filename.

If you're tired of opening all your site files one at a time, Dreamweaver has another feature that can help you out. You can browse your site files and folders using Dreamweaver's Files panel, which sticks to the side of the main Dreamweaver window (Figure 5-7). To summon it into existence, choose Window→Files, and then browse to the folder that holds your website. To open one of the files inside, give it a quick double-click.

TIP To keep the Files panel from popping out of sight whenever you stop using it, click the tiny Expand Panels arrows at the top of the skinny bar that sits against the right side of the Dreamweaver window (Figure 5-7).

Expand or collapse the side panels

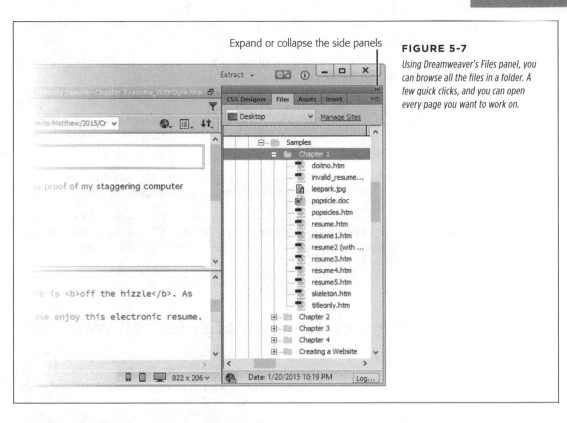

FIGURE 5-7

Using Dreamweaver's Files panel, you can browse all the files in a folder. A few quick clicks, and you can open every page you want to work on.

Defining a Dreamweaver Site

Dreamweaver also has a more formal *sites* feature. With it, you explicitly tell Dreamweaver what folder represents your website. You can also supply some other key details, such as the location of the web server where you want to upload your finished site. The sites feature is the gateway to a few other Dreamweaver site-management features, like link-checking (page 197).

Follow the next set of steps to tell Dreamweaver that a folder on your computer represents a work-in-progress website, one that you plan to upload to the Internet someday.

1. **Click the Manage Sites link in the Files panel, or just select Site→New Site.**

    Dreamweaver fires up a Site Setup window, where you fill in information about your new site.

2. **Enter a descriptive name in the Site Name box.**

The site name is just the one you use to keep track of your site, so use whatever name you want. This example uses LeeParkSite. The site name also appears in the Files panel.

3. **In the Local Site Folder box, fill in the full file path for your website folder (usually something like** *C:\Creating a Website\Chapter 1*).

If you aren't sure where your site folder is, you can click the folder icon next to the text box to browse for it. Or you can enter a path to a folder that doesn't exist yet; Dreamweaver creates a new, empty folder so you can start building your website.

Now that you've defined your site, you're only a small step away from putting your work online. You'll learn how to do that soon enough, in Chapter 9 (page 303).

TIP This walkthrough has only scratched the surface of Dreamweaver's many layers of web-building tools and frills. For an in-depth exploration of nearly every Dreamweaver feature, check out *Dreamweaver CC: The Missing Manual* (O'Reilly).

◼ Setting Up Shop with Expression Web

Expression Web is a middle-of-the-road web editor—not quite as hefty and feature-laden as Dreamweaver, but certainly not as streamlined as Brackets. You can download the straightforward setup program from *http://tinyurl.com/freeEW* and get started immediately.

When you open Expression Web, you start out with a black-bordered, multipaned window (Figure 5-8). Look past the clutter and focus on the large center region, which holds a new, blank web page.

The web page that Expression Web starts you out with isn't exactly right (it uses the older XHTML doctype instead of the HTML5 doctype you really want). You'll correct that on page 165, but don't worry about it just yet. For now, it's more important to try out the editor and figure out how it works.

Choosing Your View

Initially, Expression Web gives you a split-screen view that puts the HTML markup on top and a live preview on the bottom. To see how this works, try typing some content in the markup. For example, type, "This is my first day with Expression Web" between the <body> start tag that begins the page and the </body> end tag that finishes it off (Figure 5-9).

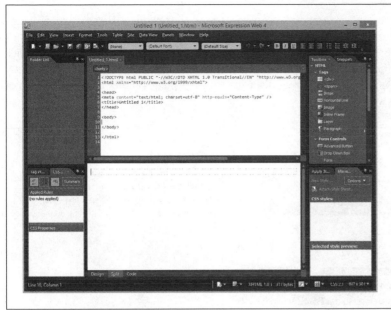

FIGURE 5-8

When you start Expression Web, it creates a new, empty web page with the working filename Untitled_1.html. *Although there's no content in the page yet, it already has a basic HTML skeleton, consisting of the* <html>, <head>, *and* <body> *elements.*

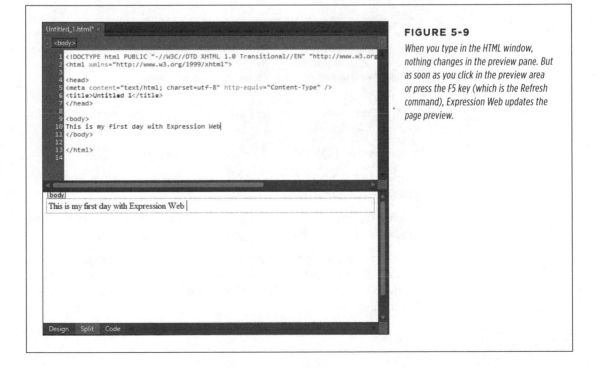

FIGURE 5-9

When you type in the HTML window, nothing changes in the preview pane. But as soon as you click in the preview area or press the F5 key (which is the Refresh command), Expression Web updates the page preview.

The preview isn't just a preview—it's also a fully editable WYSIWYG version of your page. Try it out—click in the preview area and edit your sentence. As you type, the changes appear in your markup above.

If you want more room to work, you don't need to stick with the split screen. Click one of the buttons in the bottom-left corner of the page to switch your view. Click Design to focus on the WYSIWYG rendition of the page and hide the markup, or click Code to fill the whole page with markup (Figure 5-10). Incidentally, this is exactly the same way Dreamweaver works, except that it places the buttons at the top of the editing window.

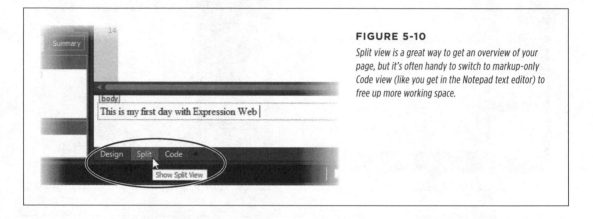

FIGURE 5-10

Split view is a great way to get an overview of your page, but it's often handy to switch to markup-only Code view (like you get in the Notepad text editor) to free up more working space.

TIP Do you want to stay in split view but see more of one view than the other? First, point to the bottom edge of the bar that separates the markup area from the preview area. If you're in the right spot, your mouse cursor will change into a line with an arrow pointing up and an arrow pointing down. Now just click and drag the dividing line up (to show a bigger preview area) or down (to show more markup).

Editing HTML in Code view is a breeze. Expression Web offers a number of useful features that can help you out:

- It color-codes your tags so they stand out from your text.

- When you type the left angle bracket (<), Expression Web pops up a handy list of elements that you can use.

- When you add a start tag (like <b> for bold lettering), Expression Web automatically adds the end tag (</b>), saving you a few keystrokes.

- If you make an obvious mistake (like deleting a tag you need, or misspelling a tag name), Expression Web points out the problem with a red squiggly underline or a yellow highlight. To get a description of exactly what you did wrong, just point to the mistake.

Expression Web also has plenty of features that are less useful for serious HTML writers. For example, you can drag an HTML tag from the Toolbox panel on the right side of the window and drop it on your page, but it's just as easy to type in the element you want by hand.

Similarly, you'll spot a fully stocked toolbar at the top of the Expression Web window. You might use the drop-down element-picker to create a heading or bulleted list, but most of the buttons are more trouble than they're worth. That's because they make a series of changes to your page that may not be exactly what you want.

For example, if you click the center-alignment button, Expression Web adds an internal style sheet to your page, creates a class-based new style rule (to which it assigns a rather useless name like auto-style1), and then adds the `class` attribute to your element to apply the style. This is all well and good, but it's even better if you decide exactly what effect you want, create a style with the name you want, put it in the place you want, and then give it the combination of style settings that you want.

Configuring Expression Web for HTML5

As you've already learned, Expression Web is a few years old, so its features set might not reflect the very latest and greatest developments in web design. One area where it shows its age is in the doctype it uses to adorn all new web pages. Ordinarily, Expression Web specifies the XHTML doctype for your pages, which was once the favorite of strict, standards-minded web developers. But now, every web designer uses the all-purpose HTML5 doctype instead.

If you don't want to edit the first line of every new web page you create, you need to tell Expression Web to use the HTML5 doctype all the time. Fortunately, that's easy to do:

1. **Choose Tools→Page Editor Options from the menu.**

   Expression Web opens a window with several tabs crammed full of options.

2. **Click the Authoring tab (Figure 5-11).**

3. **In the middle section ("Doctype and Secondary Schema"), change the "Document Type Declaration" setting to "HTML 5."**

4. **Click OK.**

From this point on, every new page you create gets the slimmed-down HTML5 doctype you've been using all along. To check, create a new page by choosing File→New→Page.

Opening Multiple Pages

To get a feel for Expression Web, you can experiment with a sample page from a previous chapter. For example, you can use one of the resumé pages from Chapter 1 or a style sheet from Chapter 3. Use the standard File→Open command to open the page you want.

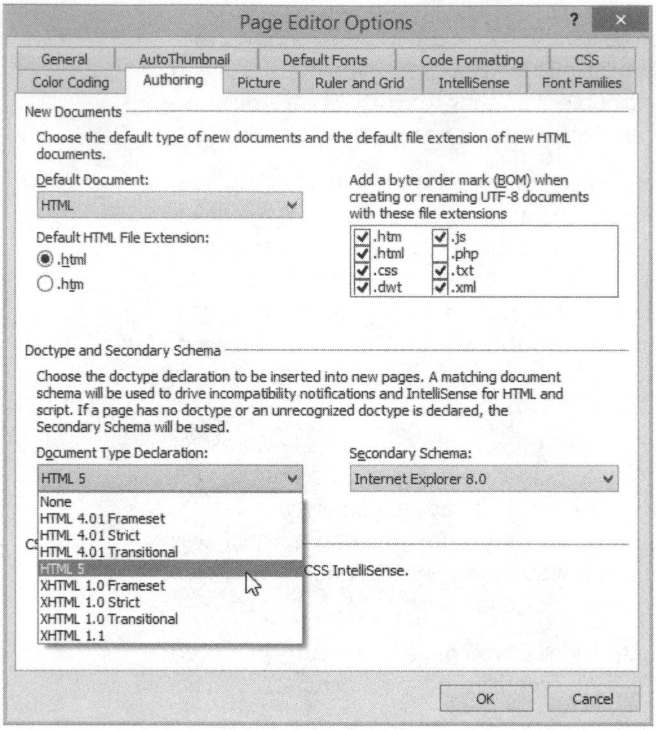

FIGURE 5-11

You need to tell Expression Web that you want to create official HTML5 pages. Ignore the minor mistake Expression Web makes by calling the standard "HTML 5" instead of using its true and official space-less name, "HTML5."

Expression Web lets you open as many pages as you want at a time. You use tabs to switch from one page to another (Figure 5-12), which is handy when you have to make changes to several pages in your site. To close a file, click the tiny X next to its name.

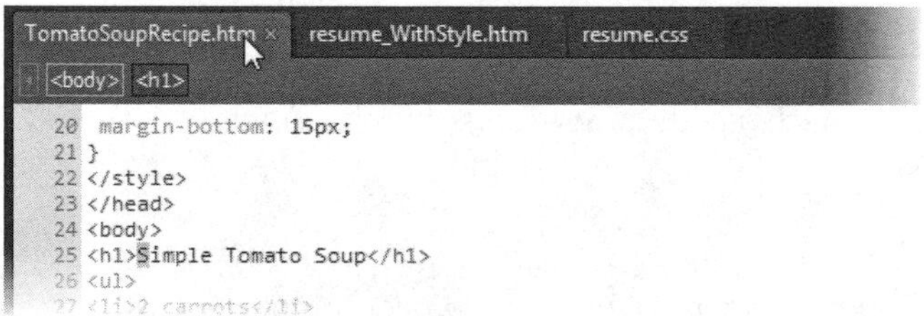

FIGURE 5-12

Here you have three documents open: the tomato soup recipe example from Chapter 4, the styled resumé from Chapter 3, and its linked style sheet. Click a tab to switch files.

Defining a Site in Expression Web

Like Dreamweaver, Expression Web provides a *site* feature that makes it easy to work with an entire folder of files. It also lets you tap other, advanced features, like link-checking and site-uploading (which you'll consider on page 307).

The basic idea is that an Expression Web site is a collection of web pages and other resources (like pictures and style sheets), stored in a folder on your computer (optionally with subfolders inside it). To open a site in Expression Web, you simply need to tell it where that website folder is. Here's how:

1. **Select Site→Open Site.**

   Expression Web opens the Open Site window, which lists all the sites you've opened before (Figure 5-13).

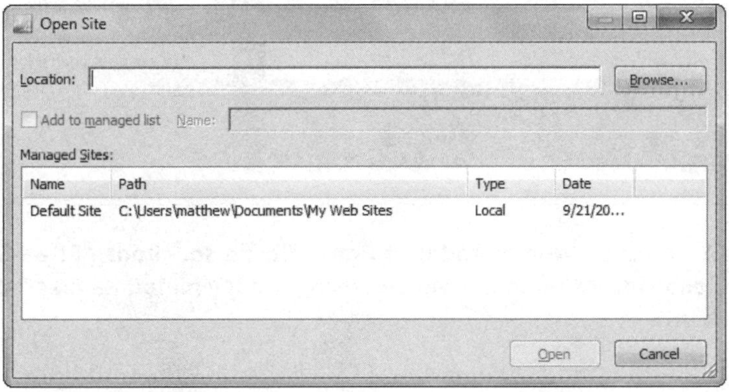

FIGURE 5-13

Expression Web's Open Site dialog box lists all the websites it knows about. When you open Expression Web for the first time, this list is empty (except for a nearly useless sample site that Expression Web creates when you install it). To hunt down one of your own sites, click Browse.

2. **Click Browse to search for your website folder.**

   Opening a website is just like browsing for a file, except that you'll see only folders listed, not filenames.

3. **Browse to the folder you want to open, select it, and then click Open.**

   For this example, pick the Chapter 1 folder from the companion site at *http://prosetech.com/web*.

   Clicking Open returns you to the Open Site dialog box. If you want to store the location of this website so you can open it more quickly next time, switch on the "Add to managed list" option. That way, Expression Web will add the folder to its Managed Sites list.

4. **Click Open to open your website in Expression Web.**

   After you click Open, the editor displays a Site View tab listing all the files in your site (see Figure 5-14).

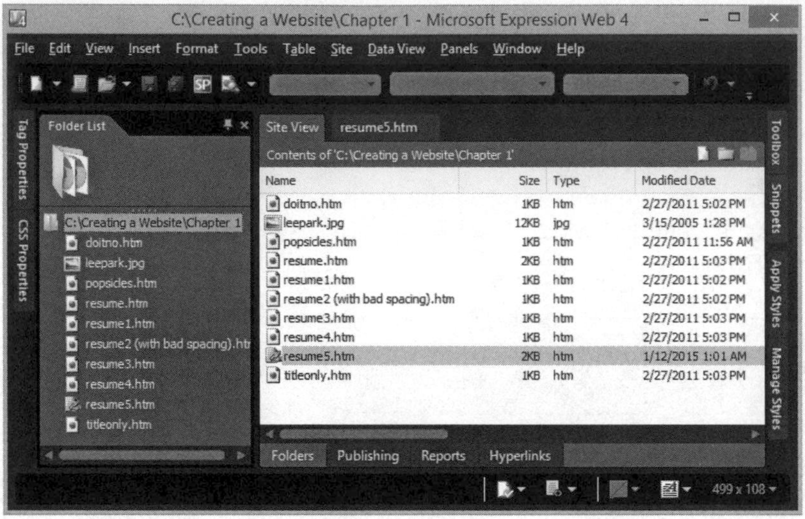

FIGURE 5-14

When you open a website folder (here it's a folder named C:\Creating a Website\Chapter 1), Expression Web adds a tab that displays all the files in that folder. You can do basic file management here—for example, you can right-click a file to pop open a menu with options to rename or delete the file. You can also double-click a page to open it for editing.

5. **Add the Expression Web metadata folders. To do so, choose Site→Site Settings, choose "Maintain the website using hidden metadata files," and then click OK.**

    Many of Expression Web's site-management features require tracking information, which Expression Web stores in hidden subfolders. However, Expression Web doesn't create these folders automatically; you need to opt in to get the program to produce them.

    The word *metadata* means "data *about* data." In other words, Expression Web's metadata folders store data *about* the data in your website. If you're curious, you can see these subfolders in Windows Explorer—they have names like _private, _vti_cnf, and _vti_pvt. (Web trivia: The VTI acronym stands for Vermeer Technologies Inc.—the company that originally created FrontPage and sold it to Microsoft.)

    These folders have several purposes. First, they keep track of what files you uploaded to your web server. This tracking makes it incredibly easy for you to update a website, because Expression Web transfers only changed files to your server, not the entire site. The folders also track information about your site's pages and resources, which Expression Web uses for handy features like reporting and link-checking (page 197).

TIP Treat the metadata folders as a bit of behind-the-scenes plumbing. You need to have them for certain features, but once you create the folders you don't need to think about them again.

When you finish working with a site, you can either close Expression Web or choose Site→Close to shut down the site view, close all the open web pages, and start working on something else.

Honing Your Expression Web Skills

Now that Microsoft has stopped developing Expression Web, it's difficult to find good help on the more complicated parts of the program. If you search the Web for "Expression Web tutorials," you'll turn up a few ad-heavy but low-information sites that may help you with some of the basics. But your best bet is to steer away from the more advanced and less commonly used features, some of which are linked to Microsoft-specific extensions that your web host might not support.

Instead, rely on the useful Expression Web features covered in this chapter, such as its HTML editing, its web page previews, and its site management. You'll round out your Expression Web knowledge in Chapter 9 when you learn how you can use it to upload your site to your web server (page 307).

◼ Trying Out Brackets

Not interested in old software and not willing to part with the big bucks? If Expression Web and Dreamweaver don't fit your style, you might find happiness with Brackets, the newest, slimmest, and most nerd-pleasing web development tool.

Getting Brackets onto your computer is easy. The setup program is just a download away at *http://brackets.io*. Once you install Brackets on your computer, open the program and keep reading.

Just like Dreamweaver and Expression Web, Brackets starts you out at its main window, where all your web editing work takes place. However, the Brackets window is simpler and more streamlined than what you get with those other web editors. In Brackets, there are no fancy toolbars and only a single side panel, on the left, which lists the files you're working on. The rest of the window shows the markup for the page you're currently editing (Figure 5-15). You get the markup only—there's no built-in preview or WYSIWYG view.

TIP You'll notice that Brackets helps you keep your spot in long files with line numbers in the left margin. Another nice feature is the ability to highlight the active line—the one you're currently working on—with a light-gray background. To switch that feature on, choose View→Highlight Active Line. Similarly, you can turn off the line numbers by choosing View→Line Numbers.

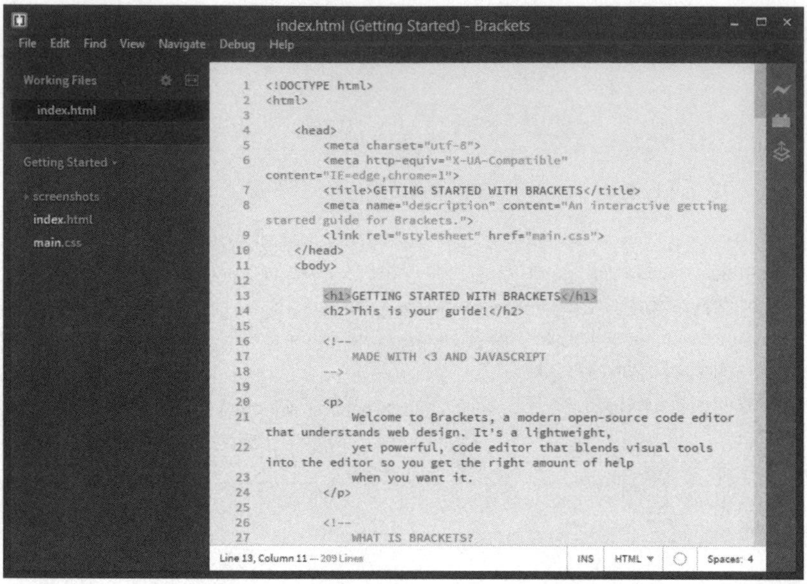

FIGURE 5-15

The first time you start Brackets, it displays a sample file named index. html *that tells you a bit about the program.*

The first bit of magic you get with Brackets is its live web browser integration. At the time of this writing, you need Google Chrome to use this feature. Assuming you have the browser, just click the lightning bolt icon on the right side of the Brackets window (or choose File→Live Preview) to open a new Chrome window with a preview of the page in it (Figure 5-16).

So far, this doesn't sound like anything special. But there's more going on than first meets the eye. When you start a live preview, Brackets wires itself into Chrome, breaking you out of the tedious edit-save-refresh cycle. In fact, as soon as you change a detail in the Brackets window, Chrome updates the linked window so that it reflects your edit. So even though the source code and preview aren't in the same window (as they are in Dreamweaver and Expression Web), the Brackets and Chrome windows work so well together that it's hardly a problem.

NOTE You only need to launch a live preview once. The Chrome window remains linked to the page you're editing in Brackets, until you close Brackets or Chrome.

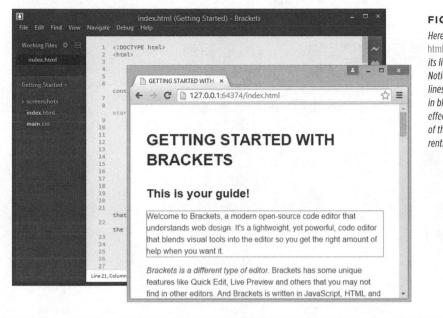

FIGURE 5-16

Here's the sample index.
html *page in Brackets and
its linked Chrome preview.
Notice how Brackets out-
lines the first paragraph
in blue. It uses this subtle
effect to indicate the part
of the page you're cur-
rently editing.*

Working with a Set of Files

Brackets has a curious way of dealing with files. Every time you open a page (by choosing File→Open) or create a new one (by choosing File→New), Brackets adds this file to the list of working files, which appears on the left side of the Brackets window. And there it stays. Brackets is so keen to keep your recent work at your fingertips that even if you close and then reopen the program, you'll see the same set of working files in the list on the left.

If this seems a bit awkward, don't worry—it all gets better when you take charge of the working file list. Here's how:

- To switch from one page to another, click the page's name in the list. (In other words, the working list replaces the tabs feature that you use to switch between pages in web editors like Dreamweaver and Expression Web.)

- If you finish working with a file and don't want it cluttering up your working files list, point to the filename and then click the tiny X that appears on the left (Figure 5-17).

- To rearrange the list of working files, click the tiny gear icon to pop open a menu of sorting options. You can order the list by filename (alphabetically), file type (to separate web pages from style sheets, code files, and so on), or the time you added it to the list (newest at the top).

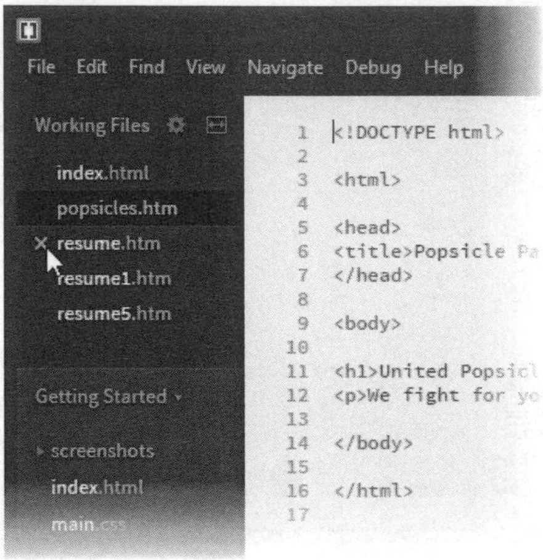

FIGURE 5-17

Brackets keeps track of the web pages you're editing in its working files list. To open one of the files, click it. To banish it from the list, click the X icon (shown here next to resume.htm*).*

The working files list is just one of two that appear in the Brackets window. Underneath it, Brackets displays the folder list; click a folder and you see all the files it contains. Initially, the list holds the Getting Started folder, which includes an example page that Brackets puts on your computer when you first install it. But it makes more sense for you to pick your website folder here. That way, you can quickly open all the web pages you need.

Start by choosing File→Open Folder. Then browse to your site folder, click it, and then click the Select Folder button. For example, you could pick the Chapter 1 folder from the companion site (*http://prosetech.com/web*), which holds all the examples from Chapter 1 (Figure 5-18).

Here's one more trick: Brackets remembers all the folders you open. So if tomorrow you want to return to the Chapter 1 website, just click the heading at the top of the folder list. You'll see a list of all the recent folders you've worked with. Pick the Chapter 1 folder, and you're on your way.

Brackets is stuffed with quirky tricks like this. To learn more, check out the video tutorials on the official Brackets YouTube channel at *www.youtube.com/user/ CodeBrackets*. You can also get the latest news from the official Brackets blog at *http://blog.brackets.io*.

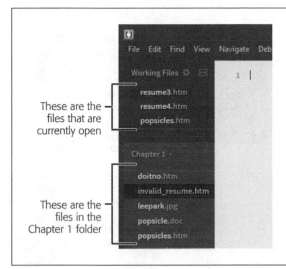

FIGURE 5-18

When you open a folder, Brackets displays a list of the files it contains. And when you open a file from the folder list, Brackets adds it to your working files list.

These are the files that are currently open

These are the files in the Chapter 1 folder

NOTE If Brackets suits your style, you're in luck. Unlike Expression Web and many other free web development tools, Brackets is under active development and has a community of enthusiastic web developers using it.

GEM IN THE ROUGH

Creating Style Sheets with Web Page Editors

The best web editors (including the three covered in this chapter: Dreamweaver, Expression Web, and Brackets) don't just help you write HTML; they also offer handy features for writing style sheets.

To try them out, start by opening an existing style sheet or creating a new one. To create a style sheet in Dreamweaver, choose File→New, pick CSS in the Page Type list, and then click Create. To create a style sheet in Expression Web, choose File→New→CSS. And in Brackets, choose File→New, and

then File→Save. (It's not until you save your file with the familiar *.css* extension that Brackets recognizes it as a style sheet.)

At first, you won't see anything to get excited about. But life gets interesting when you start to *edit* your style sheet. As you type, your web page editor pops up a list of possible style properties and values (see Figure 5-19). If you dig deeper in Dreamweaver or Expression Web, you'll find that both web editors have windows that let you build styles by pointing and clicking, as well as convenient shortcuts for applying styles to page elements.

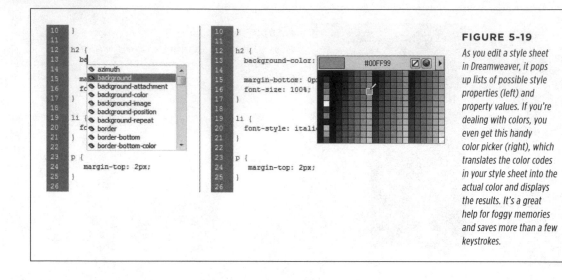

FIGURE 5-19

As you edit a style sheet in Dreamweaver, it pops up lists of possible style properties (left) and property values. If you're dealing with colors, you even get this handy color picker (right), which translates the color codes in your style sheet into the actual color and displays the results. It's a great help for foggy memories and saves more than a few keystrokes.

Linking Pages

So far in this book, you've worked on individual web pages. While creating a single page is a crucial first step in building a site, sooner or later you'll want to wire several pages together so a web trekker can easily jump from one page to another. After all, linking is what the Web is all about.

It's astoundingly easy to create links—officially called *hyperlinks*—between pages. In fact, all it takes is a single element, called the *anchor* element. Once you master this bit of HTML, you're ready to start organizing your pages into separate folders and transforming your humble collection of standalone documents into a full-fledged site.

◼ Understanding the Anchor

In HTML, you use the anchor element, `<a>`, to create a link. When a visitor clicks the link, her browser opens the associated page.

The anchor element is a straightforward container element. It looks like this:

```
<a>...</a>
```

You put the text a visitor clicks inside the anchor element:

```
<a>Click Me</a>
```

The problem with this link is that, as written above, it doesn't *point* anywhere. To turn it into a fully functioning link, you need to supply the address of the destination page using the href attribute (which stands for *hypertext reference*). For example, if you want a link to take a reader to a page named *LinkedPage.htm*, you create this link:

```
<a href="LinkedPage.htm">Click Me</a>
```

For this link to work, the *LinkedPage.htm* file has to reside in the same folder as the web page that contains the Click Me link. (You'll learn how to better organize your site by sorting pages into subfolders in the tutorial that starts on page 179.)

The anchor tag is an inline element—it fits inside any block element. That means that it's completely acceptable to make a link out of just a few words in an otherwise ordinary paragraph, like this:

```
<p>
  When you're alone and life is making you lonely<br />
  You can always go <a href="Downtown.htm">downtown</a>
</p>
```

Figure 6-1 shows this link in action.

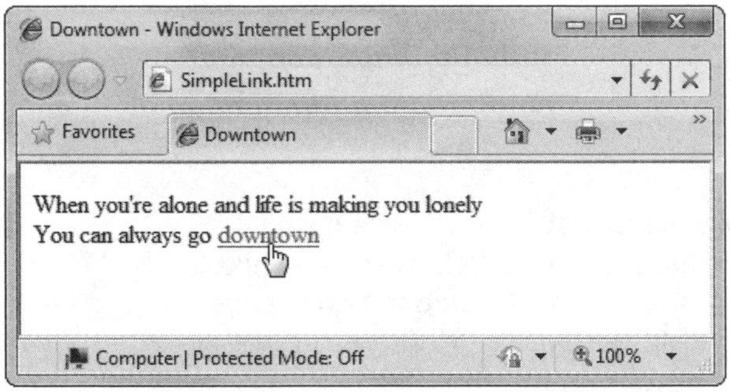

FIGURE 6-1

If you don't take any steps to customize an anchor element, its text appears in a browser with the familiar underline and blue lettering. When you point to a hyperlink, your cursor turns into a hand. You can't tell by looking at a link whether or not it works—if the link points to a non-existing page, you'll get an error message only after you click it.

It's worth noting that the label you give a link—that's the text inside the <a> element—is important. As you'll discover in Chapter 10, search engines pay extra attention to this label. Getting it right increases the odds that your website will turn up in a Web search and attract new visitors. Here are some examples of good, descriptive link text: "Products," "Register," "Our Policies," and "Contact Me." By comparison, unhelpful link labels usually consists of one or two vague words in a sentence, like "click," "here," "more," or "this link."

Internal and External Links

Links can shuttle you from one page to another within the same website, or they can transport you to a completely different site on a far-off web server. You use a specific type of link in each case:

- **Internal links** point to other pages on your site. They can also point to other types of resources on your site (like pictures or PDF files).

- **External links** point to pages (or resources) on other websites.

Linking to Other Types of Content

Most of the links you write will point to HTML web pages, but that's not your only option—you can link directly to other types of files as well. The only catch is that it's up to the browser to decide what to do when someone clicks a link that points to a different type of file.

Here are some common examples:

- **You can link to a JPEG, GIF, or PNG image file.** When visitors click a link like this, their browser displays the image in a new window without any other content. Websites often use this approach to let visitors take a closeup look at photos, like products in a catalog site. You'll use an image link in the tutorial on page 186.

- **You can link to a specialized type of file, like a PDF file, a Microsoft Office document, or an audio MP3 file.** These links rely on a browser having a plug-in (a mini-program that handles specific tasks) that recognizes the file type or on your visitor having a suitable program installed on his computer. If you use a less common file type and the computer doesn't have the right plug-in, the only thing your visitors will be able to do is download the file, where it will sit like an inert binary blob. However, if a browser has the right plug-in, a small miracle happens, and the file opens up right inside the browser window.

- **You can link to a file you want others to download.** If a link points to a file of a specialized type and the browser doesn't have the proper plug-in, visitors get a choice: They can ignore the content altogether, open it using another program on their computer, or save it on their computer. This is a handy way to distribute large files (like a ZIP file featuring your personal philosophy of planetary motion).

Say you have two files on your site, a biography page and an address page. If you want visitors to go from your bio page (*MyBio.htm*) to your address page (*ContactMe. htm*), you create an internal link. Whether you store both files in the same folder or in different folders, they're part of the same website on the same web server, so you'd use an internal link.

On the other hand, if you want visitors to go from your Favorite Books page (*Fav-Books.htm*) to a page on Amazon.com (*www.amazon.com*), you need an external link. Clicking an external link transports your guest from your website to a new site, located elsewhere on the Web.

So how do you create internal and external links? It's all in the way you write the web address, or URL. Internal links use something called relative URLs, while external links use absolute URLs. The following sections break down the differences between them.

■ RELATIVE URLS

When you create an internal link, you use a *relative URL*, which tells browsers the location of the target page *relative to the current folder*. In other words, it gives your browser instructions on how to find the page by telling it to move down into or up from the current folder. (Moving *down into* a folder means moving from the current folder into a subfolder. Moving *up from* a folder is the reverse—you travel from a subfolder up into the parent folder, the one that *contains* the current subfolder.) All the examples you've seen so far use relative URLs.

Imagine you visit a page named *Products.htm*, which has this address:

```
http://www.GothicGardenCenter.com/Sales/Products.htm
```

And say the text on the *Products.htm* page includes a sentence with this relative link to *Flowers.htm*:

```
Would you like to learn more about our purple
<a href="Flowers.htm">hydrangeas</a>?
```

If you click the word "hydrangeas," your browser attempts to send you to the *Flowers.htm* page. Because the <a> element in this example uses a relative link, your browser assumes that *Flowers.htm* is in the same location as *Products.htm*, and it fills in the rest of the URL. That means the browser actually requests this page:

```
http://www.GothicGardenCenter.com/Sales/Flowers.htm
```

One of the nicest parts about relative links is that you can test them on your own computer and they'll work exactly as they would online. For example, imagine you develop the site *www.GothicGardenCenter.com* on your computer and store it inside the folder *C:\MyWebsite* (that'd be *Macintosh HD/MyWebsite*, in Mac-ese). If you click the relative link that leads from *Products.htm* to *Flowers.htm*, the browser looks for the target page in the *C:\MyWebsite (Macintosh HD/MyWebsite)* folder.

Once you polish your work to perfection, you upload the site to your web server, which has the domain name *www.GothicGardenCenter.com*. Because you used relative links, you don't need to rewrite any of the links when you move your pages to the server. When a guest clicks a link, his browser requests the corresponding page from *www.GothicGardenCenter.com*. If you decide to buy a new, shorter domain name like *www.GGC.com* and move your website there, the links still work. For all these reasons, relative links are the best way to connect the different pages in your site.

NOTE Relative links can also travel into (and out of) subfolders. You'll learn how to write links that do that in the tutorial on page 179.

■ ABSOLUTE URLS

HTML gives you another linking option, called an *absolute URL*, which is an address that includes the target's domain name, full path, and page name. If you convert the previous relative URL to an absolute URL, it looks like this:

```
Would you like to learn more about our purple <a href=
"http://www.GothicGardenCenter.com/Sales/Flowers.htm">hydrangeas</a>?
```

This absolute link works just as well as the relative link did, but here's the catch: If you move the page to a different website or folder, the link stops working. Instead, when you click "hydrangeas," your browser tries to find the *Flowers.htm* page in the Sales folder, where it no longer exists.

For this reason, absolute URLs aren't a great way to connect the pages within your site. However, if you want to create an external link that travels to another site, they're essential. For example, imagine you want to link to the page *home.html* on Amazon's website. Here, a relative URL just won't work, because a browser assumes that *home.html* refers to a file of that name on *your* website.

FREQUENTLY ASKED QUESTION

Opening Pages in a New Window

How do I create a link that opens the requested page in a new browser window?

When visitors click external links, you might not want to let them leave your site. Web developers sometimes use a technique that opens external pages in separate browser windows (or in a new tab, depending on the browser's settings). This way, your site remains open in the visitor's original window, ensuring that she won't forget about you.

To make this work, you need to set another attribute in the `<a>` element—the `target` attribute. Here's how:

```
<a href="LinkedPage.htm"
target="_blank">Click Me</a>
```

The `target="_blank"` syntax tells a browser to open the link in a new window.

But before you start adding the `target` attribute to all your anchors, it's important to realize that it may not always work. Some browsers' vigilant *pop-up blockers* intercept this type of link and prevent the new window from opening. (Pop-up blockers are standalone programs or browser features designed to prevent annoying pop-up ads from appearing.)

Some people love the new-window feature, while others think it's an immensely annoying and disruptive act of website intervention. If you use it, apply it sparingly on the occasional link.

▨ Tutorial: Linking the Pages in a Site

Now that you've taken a good first look at the `<a>` element and learned the difference between relative and absolute URLs, you're ready to put this knowledge into practice. In the following tutorial, you'll begin with a small assortment of web pages that you'll transform into a tiny, interconnected site, all through the magic of links.

TIP Like all the tutorials in this book, you can find the solution for this exercise on the companion site at *http://prosetech.com/web*. Look inside the Tutorial-6-1 folder (which stands for "Chapter 6, first tutorial"). Inside you'll find two more folders: Start, which has the set of pages you begin the exercise with, and End, which holds the finished page.

The Starter Site

This tutorial is a bit different from those you've seen in previous chapters, because you start with a collection of pages that, taken together, represent a very small website. The only things that are missing from these pages are the links that let visitors jump from one page to another.

Figure 6-2 shows the website you're working with in its initial state. It holds four web pages, spread out in several subfolders for better organization. Connecting these pages requires internal links that use relative URLs.

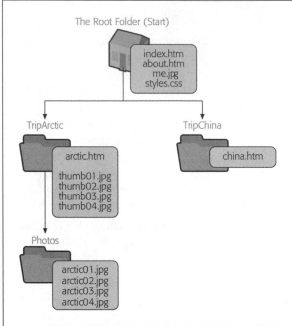

The Root Folder (Start)

index.htm
about.htm
me.jpg
styles.css

TripArctic

arctic.htm

thumb01.jpg
thumb02.jpg
thumb03.jpg
thumb04.jpg

Photos

arctic01.jpg
arctic02.jpg
arctic03.jpg
arctic04.jpg

TripChina

china.htm

FIGURE 6-2

This diagram maps the structure of a very small website featuring photos taken on a trip. The root folder contains a style sheet used across the entire site (styles.css), a picture (me.jpg), and two HTML pages. Two subfolders, TripChina and TripArctic, contain an additional page each. The TripArctic folder also contains several thumbnail images of pictures taken on one of the trips. For each thumbnail, there's a corresponding full-size picture in the Photos subfolder.

The root folder is the core of your website—it contains all your other site files and folders. The root folder of this website is named Start, but this is the least important detail. That's because when you put your website online, you copy all the files and subfolders from the root folder on your hard drive and transfer them to the root of your website. So it makes no difference whether you call your root folder Start, Root, TripSite, or Zingbobulous, because you don't use that name on your web server (or, by extension, in any of the links you write for your site).

If you're feeling a bit hazy on the relationship between folders and websites, check out the box on page 181. And if you're wondering how to get your site online, hold that thought—you'll explore this operation in detail in Chapter 9.

NOTE Most sites include a page with the name *index.htm* or *index.html* in the root folder. This is known as the *default page*. If a browser sends a request to your website without supplying a filename, the server sends back the default page. For example, requesting *www.TripToRemember.com* automatically returns the default page *www.TripToRemember.com/index.htm*. However, this feature only works once you put your website on the Web. Until then, using *index.htm* for your website home page is just a smart bit of preparation.

The Anatomy of a Site

A website is nothing more than a collection of pages and related resources, like images, style sheets, and JavaScript files. You can dump all these files into a single root folder, or you can split them into different subfolders inside the root folder.

So far in this book, you've kept your pages in a single folder, the root folder, with an optional subfolder for pictures. But now that you're creating a site with *many* pages, each of which may

have its own related resources, it's time to consider adding more subfolders to help keep your site organized.

There's no ironclad rule about whether a website should use subfolders (and, if it does, how many it should have). That's up to you to decide based on what you find easiest to manage. However, it's important to standardize the organization of your site now, because that arrangement determines how you'll write links.

Right now, everything works in the pages shown in Figure 6-2. They have some content, they all link to the same style sheet, and the *arctic.htm* page includes one `<img>` element for each thumbnail. But each page is a standalone creation—there's no way to get from one page to another without typing in the full page URL. You're about to fix that.

Linking to Pages Within the Same Folder

The easiest links to create are those where both the *source page* (the one that contains the link) and the *target page* (the one that opens when you click the link) are in the same folder. That's the kind of link you'll create to connect the *index.htm* page to the *about.htm* page, both of which sit in the root folder (Figure 6-3).

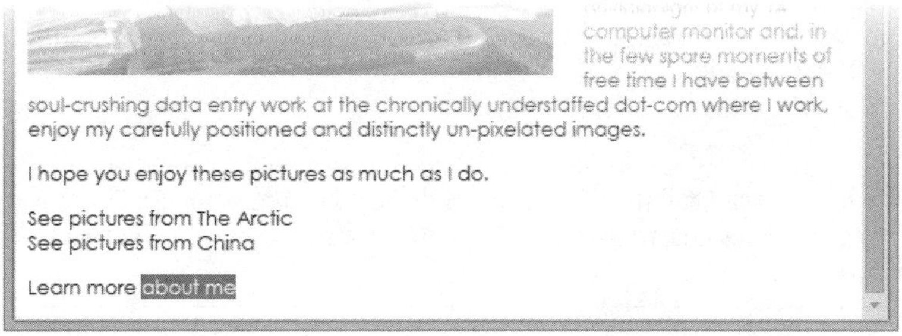

FIGURE 6-3

Your first task in creating a link is the easiest: Take this plain text at the bottom of the index. htm *page and wrap it with a link that, when clicked, opens the* about.htm *page.*

Here's what you need to do:

1. **Open *index.htm* in your editor.**

    You can use a garden-variety text editor or a professional tool like Dreamweaver; it doesn't matter.

2. **Find the paragraph that contains the text "About Me."**

   It looks like this:

   ```
   <p>About Me</p>
   ```

3. **Add an anchor element around the words "About Me."**

   All you need is an <a> tag at the beginning and an </a> tag at the end.

4. **Add and set the href attribute.**

   The href attribute uses a relative URL because both the source and target pages are in the same folder. The relative URL is simply the name of the destination page (that's *about.htm*).

5. **Save the page, open it in a browser, and try clicking your link.**

You probably found this exercise pretty easy. (Don't worry, you're just warming up.) But if you stumbled over an unexpected problem, here's what your final link should look like:

```
<p><a href="about.htm">About Me</a></p>
```

Moving Down into a Subfolder

The *index.htm* page also needs links that can take visitors to the two trip pages, *arctic.htm* and *china.htm*. Each of them is in its own subfolder (TripArctic and Trip-China, respectively).

To create a URL that leads into a subfolder, you simply add the name of the folder, followed by a slash (/), followed by the page name. Here's the link you need to add to the text "The Arctic" to jump from *index.htm* to *arctic.htm*:

```
See pictures from <a href="TripsArctic/arctic.htm">The Arctic</a>
```

This link gives a browser two instructions. First, it tells the browser to go into the subfolder TripArctic, and then it directs it to open the page *arctic.htm*. Figure 6-4 shows both sides of this equation.

NOTE You may remember this syntax, because you used it with the <img> element in Chapter 4 to grab an image from a subfolder. It also turns up when you link to an external style sheet with the <style> element and the <img> element.

Once you add the link to the *arctic.htm* page, add a similar link from the word "China" to the *china.htm* page.

There's no limit to how many levels of subfolders you can traverse with a relative URL. For example, imagine you want to add a link to the *index.htm* page that connects to the picture *arctic01.jpg*. This picture is two subfolders away, in a folder called Photos, which is inside the TripArctic folder. The URL you need looks like this:

```
Click to see a <a href="TripsArctic/Photos/arctic01.jpg">polar bear</a>
```

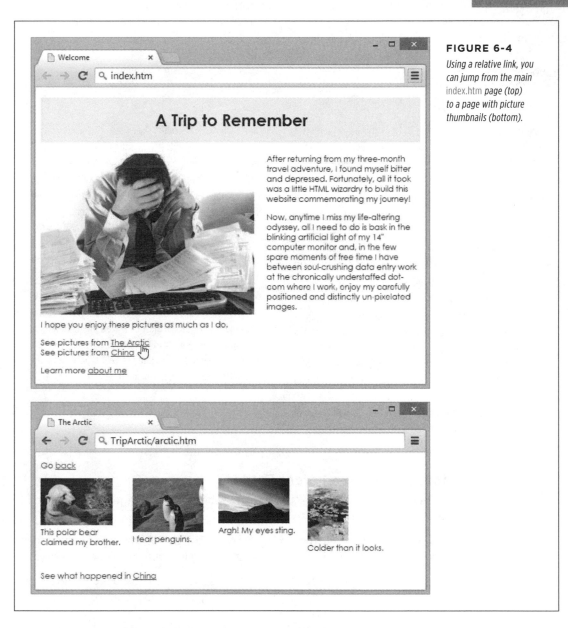

FIGURE 6-4

Using a relative link, you can jump from the main index.htm *page (top) to a page with picture thumbnails (bottom).*

Using relative URLs, you can dig even deeper, into subfolders of subfolders of subfolders. All you need to do is add the folder name and a slash character for each subfolder, in order.

TIP Once you start specifying subfolders in relative links, you shouldn't change any of the folder names or move them around because you may break a link. That said, web editors like Dreamweaver and Expression Web are crafty enough to adjust your relative links, provided you make any changes from within the program, and you define your website first.

UP TO SPEED

The Rules for URLs

The rules for correctly writing URLs in anchor elements are fairly strict, and a few common mistakes creep into even the best web pages. Here are some pointers to help you avoid these headaches:

- Don't mix up the backslash (\) and the ordinary forward slash (/). Windows uses the backslash in file paths (like *C:\Windows\win.ini*), but in the web world, the forward slash separates subfolders (as in *http://www.ebay.com/ Help/index.html*). Many web servers tolerate backslash confusion, but if you're unlucky, a stray slash can break your link.

- Don't use spaces or special characters in your file or folder names, even if these special characters are allowed. For example, it's perfectly acceptable to put a space in a filename (like *My Photos.htm*), but in order to request this page, the browser needs to translate that space into a special character code (*My%20 Photos. htm*). To prevent this confusion, steer clear of anything that isn't a number, letter, dash (-), or underscore (_).

- Don't ever use file paths (like *file:///C:/Temp/myPage. htm*) instead of a URL. It's possible to create a URL that points to a file on your computer using the *file* protocol, but this link won't work on anyone else's computer, because they won't have the same file on their hard drive. Sometimes, design tools like Dreamweaver or Expression Web may insert one of these so-called local URLs (for example, if you drag and drop a picture file into your web page). Be vigilant—check all your links to make sure this doesn't happen.

- When you create an absolute URL, you have to start with its protocol (usually *http://*). You don't need to follow this rule when typing a URL into a browser, however. For example, if you type *www.google.com*, most browsers are intelligent enough to assume the *http://* part. However, in an HTML document, it's mandatory.

Moving Up into a Parent Folder

You've now added all the links you need to the *index.htm* page. Now you need to add two links to the *arctic.htm* page.

The first link leads back to the *index.htm* page. To add it, put the <a> element around the word "back" at the top of the page, as shown in Figure 6-4 (bottom image).

To go *up* a folder level, you use the character sequence ../ (two periods and a slash). So to add a link in the *arctic.htm* page that brings the reader back to the *index.htm* page, you type this:

```
Go <a href="../index.htm">back</a>
```

If you like, you can add the same link to the *china.htm* page, so visitors can get back to your home page at any time.

You can use the "go up" command twice in a row to jump up two levels. For example, if you have a page in the Photos folder that leads to the home page, you'd use a link like this to get back:

```
Go <a href="../../index.htm">back</a>
```

For a more interesting feat, you can write a relative link that travels up one or more levels and then travels down a different path. That's how you create the second link in the *arctic.htm* page, which jumps straight to *china.htm*. To add this link, put the <a> element around the word "China" in the final line of the page, as shown in Figure 6-4 (bottom image):

```
See what happened in <a href="../TripChina/china.htm">China</a>
```

This link starts at the current folder (TripArctic), moves up one level to the root folder, and then down one level to the TripChina folder.

Moving to the Root Folder

The only problem with the relative links you've seen so far is that they're difficult to maintain if you ever reorganize your site.

For example, imagine you have a web page in the root directory. Say you want to feature an image on that page that's stored in the Images subfolder. You use this URL:

```
<img src="Images/flower.jpg" alt="A flower" />
```

But then, a little later on, you decide your page really belongs in *another* spot—a subfolder named Plant—so you move it there. The problem is that this relative link now points to *Plant/Images/flower.jpg*, which doesn't exist—the Images folder isn't a subfolder in Plants; it's a subfolder in your site's root folder. As a result, your browser displays a broken link icon.

There are a few workarounds. Programs like Dreamweaver and Expression Web automatically update all the relative links when you drag a file to a new location, saving you the hassle. You can also try to keep related files in the same folder, so you always move them as a unit. However, there's a third approach, called *root-relative* links.

So far, the relative links you've seen have been *document-relative*, because you specify the location of the target page relative to the current document. *Root-relative* links point to a target page *relative to your website's root folder*.

Root-relative links always start with the slash (/) character (which indicates the root folder). Here's the <img> element for *flower.jpg* with a root-relative link:

```
<img src="/Images/flower.jpg" alt="A flower" />
```

The remarkable thing about this link is that it works no matter where you put the web page that contains it. For example, if you copy this page to the Plant subfolder, the link still works, because the first slash tells your browser to start at the root folder.

The only catch to using root-relative folders is that you need to keep the real root of your website in mind. When using a root-relative link, the browser follows a simple procedure to figure out where to go. First, it strips all the path and filename information out of the current page address, so that only the domain name is left. Then it adds the root-relative link to the end of the domain name. So if the link to *flower.jpg* appears on this page:

```
http://www.jumboplants.com/horticulture/plants/annuals.htm
```

The browser strips away the */horticulture/plants/annuals.htm* portion, adds the relative link you supplied in the src attribute (*/Images/flower.jpg*), and looks for the picture here:

```
http://www.jumboplants.com/Images/flower.jpg
```

This makes perfect sense. But consider what happens if you don't have your own website domain name, and your web pages are stuck in some subfolder on a web server. Here's an example:

```
http://www.superISP.com/~user9212/horticulture/plants/annuals.htm
```

The domain name part of the URL is *www.superISP.com*, but for all practical purposes, the root of your website is your personal folder, *~user9212*. That means you need to add this detail to all your root-relative links. So, to get the result you want with the *flower.jpg* picture, you need to use this messier root-relative link:

```
<img src="/~user9212/Images/flower.jpg" alt="A flower" />
```

As before, the browser keeps the domain name part of the URL (*www.superISP.com*) and adds the relative part of the path. But in this case, the path starts with your personal folder (*/~user9212*).

Making Image Links

The links you've seen so far have acted on small bits of text, but you can turn images into links, too. This is a useful trick for the current website. You can use it to link each thumbnail on the *arctic.htm* page to the corresponding image file. That way, when a visitor clicks a thumbnail, his browser opens the full-size photo (Figure 6-5).

There's no secret to creating an image link. You just put an <img> element inside an anchor element (<a>). To try this out, take the <img> that holds the first thumbnail in the *arctic.htm* page:

```
<img src="thumb01.jpg" alt="Polar bear" /></a>
```

Now, wrap the entire thing in an anchor element:

```
<a href="Photos/arctic01.jpg"><img src="thumb01.jpg" alt="Polar bear" /></a>
```

When you point to a linked picture, the cursor changes to a hand, just like when you point to a text link.

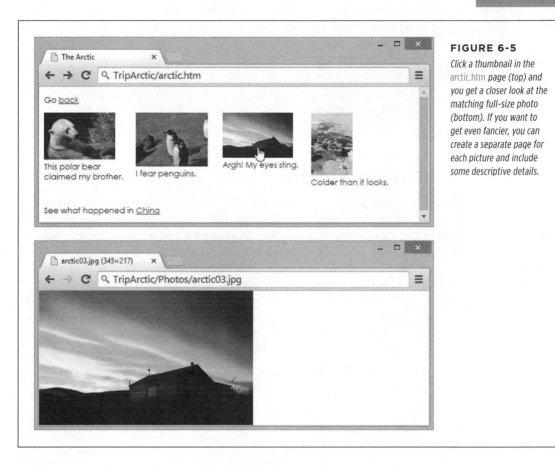

FIGURE 6-5

Click a thumbnail in the arctic.htm page (top) and you get a closer look at the matching full-size photo (bottom). If you want to get even fancier, you can create a separate page for each picture and include some descriptive details.

There's one quirk with linked images. If you view a page that has a linked image in it using Internet Explorer, you'll see an unsightly blue border around the picture, which is meant to indicate that visitors can click it. Usually, you want to turn this clunky-looking border off using the style sheet border properties (page 108). For example, here's a style rule that removes the border from all images, including linked ones:

```
img {
  border: none;
}
```

If you want to get a bit more sophisticated and remove the border from linked images *only*, you have two choices. You can use a class selector (page 84), and then apply that class to all the thumbnail <img> elements. Or you can create a contextual selector that acts only on <img> elements inside <a> elements (page 217).

Text and images aren't the only thing you can use as links. In fact, you can link any HTML, including entire paragraphs of text, bulleted lists, and so on. If you try this, you'll see that all the text inside becomes blue and underlined, and all the images sport blue borders. Web browsers have supported this bizarre behavior for years, but it's only HTML5 that makes it an official part of the HTML standard.

> **NOTE** Once you finish adding the four image links to the *arctic.htm* page, you've finished this tutorial. Congratulations—you should now be able to craft URLs that can walk up and down the folders of your site. To see the final site, with all these different types of links in place, check out the Tutorial-6-1\End folder.

More Tricks with Links

Using the knowledge you've picked up so far, you can get links to do 90% of everything you'll ever need them to do. But sometimes it's nice to have a few more tricks in your bag. In the following sections, you'll meet two unusual types of links, and you'll learn the easiest way to style the color of linked text.

"Mailto" Links

A *mailto* link is a special type of link that helps visitors send a message to you. When you click a mailto link, your browser opens your email program and begins creating a message. It's still up to you to actually send the message, but the mailto link can get the process started with a boilerplate subject line and body text.

To create a mailto link, specify a path that starts with the word "mailto," followed by a colon (:) and your email address. Here's an example:

```
<a href="mailto:me@myplace.com">Email Me</a>
```

> **NOTE** The mailto link doesn't work for every visitor, especially ones who use web-based email services (like Hotmail and Gmail). Clicking a mailto link in a message may open a desktop email program they never use or even give them an error message (depending on their browser and computer settings). To solve the problem or find a workaround on your computer, do a Google search for "mailto link" and your browser name.

Most browsers also let you supply text for the message's subject line and body. When someone clicks the mailto link, the new message includes this information, ready for sending (or editing).

To supply the subject line and body text, you have to use a slightly wonky syntax that follows these rules:

- Put a question mark after the email address.

- To include a subject line, add *subject=* followed by the subject text.

- To include body text, add the character sequence *&* after your subject text, and then type *body=* followed by the body text.

- Replace characters that could cause problems with specialized codes. Letters, numbers, and the period are all fine, but most other punctuation isn't. For example, you have to replace every space in the subject and body text with the character sequence *%20*. This gets quite tedious and makes your message hard to read after you compose it, but it ensures that the mailto link works in every browser. The easiest way to prepare your message text is to visit a page like *http://meyerweb.com/eric/tools/dencoder*, which adds the code sequences for you. Simply type your message text in the provided box, and then click Encode to replace potentially problematic characters with the appropriate codes.

Confused? The easiest way to grasp these rules is to take a look at a couple of examples. First, here's a mailto link that includes the subject text "Automatic Email":

```
<a href="mailto:me@myplace.com?subject=Automatic%20Email">
Email Me</a>
```

And here's a link that includes both subject text and body text:

```
<a href="mailto:me@myplace.com?subject=Automatic%20Email&body=
I%20love%20your%20site.">Email Me</a>
```

When a guest clicks this link, she'll probably see some sort of warning message informing her that the web page is about to open her email program and asking her permission (the exact message depends on her browser and operating system). If she agrees, she'll see an email form like the one in Figure 6-6 pop up.

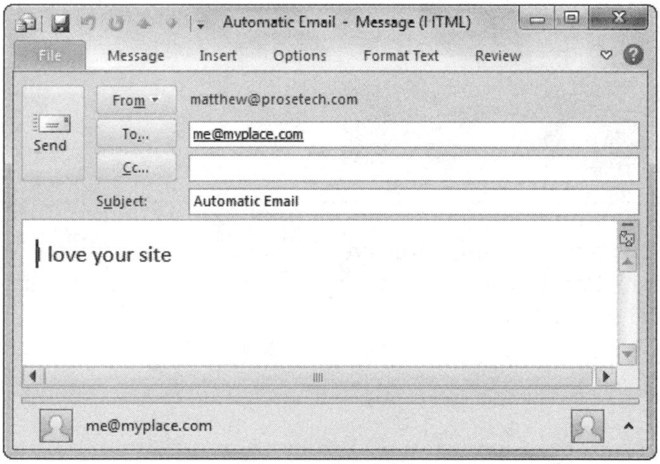

FIGURE 6-6

When you click a mailto link, your browser creates an email message (as shown here). It fills in the recipient, subject, and body text according to information in the link, although whoever clicked the link can change these details (or close the window without clicking Send). This example shows the message window from Microsoft Outlook, though the window your visitor sees may differ, depending on the email program installed on her computer.

Image Maps: Links Inside Pictures

You've already learned how to turn an ordinary picture into a clickable link (page 186). That's the most common way to link an image, but web developers who want to get fancier have other ways to turn a portion of a picture into a link. For example, they may use JavaScript code to intercept picture clicks and examine the coordinates. (This is the most popular approach for power users who aren't intimidated by the prospect of writing—and debugging—some code.) But HTML provides another option with its often-overlooked image map feature.

An image map lets you create distinct clickable regions, called hotspots, *inside* a picture. For example, consider Figure 6-7.

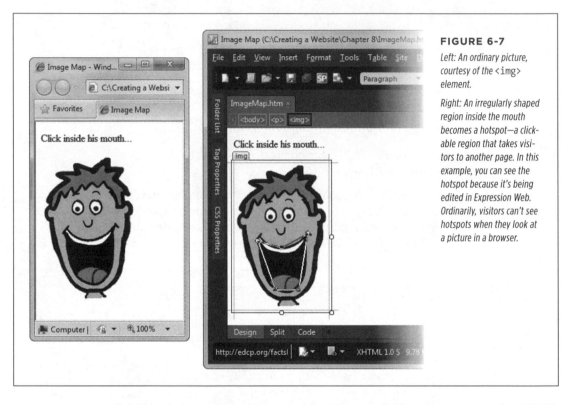

FIGURE 6-7

Left: An ordinary picture, courtesy of the <img> element.

Right: An irregularly shaped region inside the mouth becomes a hotspot—a clickable region that takes visitors to another page. In this example, you can see the hotspot because it's being edited in Expression Web. Ordinarily, visitors can't see hotspots when they look at a picture in a browser.

To add a hotspot to a picture, you start by creating an *image map* using HTML's <map> element. This part's easy—all you do is choose a unique name for your image map so you can refer to it later on:

```
<map id="FaceMap" name="FaceMap">
</map>
```

NOTE If you noticed that the <map> element uses two attributes that duplicate the same information (id and name), you're correct. Although in theory just the id attribute should do the trick, you need to keep the name attribute there to ensure compatibility with a wide range of browsers.

Then you need to define each hotspot, which you do between the start and end tags of the <map> element. You can add as many hotspots as you want, although they shouldn't overlap. (If they do, the one defined first takes precedence.)

To define each hotspot in an image, you add an <area> element, which identifies three important details: the target page a visitor goes to after clicking the hotspot (which you specify in the href attribute), the shape of the hotspot (the shape attribute), and the exact dimensions of the shape (the coords attribute, for "coordinates"). Much like an image element, the <area> element requires an alt attribute with alternate text that describes the image map to search engines, reader programs, and ancient text-only browsers.

Here's a sample <area> element:

```
<area href="Mouth.htm" shape="rect" coords="5,5,95,195"
alt="A clickable rectangle" />
```

This hotspot defines a rectangular region. When visitors click it, they go to *Mouth.htm*.

The shape attribute lets you define three types of shapes, each of which requires a different set of values for the attribute. You can specify a circle (circle), a rectangle (rect), or a multi-edged shape (poly). Once you choose your shape, you need to supply the coordinates for it. But to understand hotspot coordinates, you first need to understand how browsers measure pictures, as outlined in Figure 6-8.

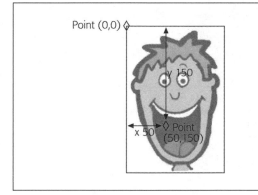

FIGURE 6-8

Browsers designate the top-left corner of a picture as point (0, 0). As you move down the picture, the y-coordinate (the second number) gets bigger. For example, the point (0, 100) is at the left edge of the picture, 100 pixels from the top. As you move to the right, the x-coordinate gets bigger. That means the point (100, 0) is at the top of a picture, 100 pixels from the left edge.

You indicate image map coordinates as a list of numbers separated by commas. For a circle, list the coordinates in this order: center point for the x-coordinate, center point for the y-coordinate, and radius. For any other shape, identify the corners, in order, as a series of x-y coordinates, like this: x1, y1, x2, y2, and so on. For a polygon, you supply every point. For a rectangle, you need only two points: the top-left corner and the bottom-right corner.

For example, you define the rectangle in the <area> element above by these two points: (5, 5) at the top left and (95, 195) at the bottom right. You define the more complex polygon that represents the mouth region in Figure 6-7 like this:

```
<area href="Mouth.htm" shape="poly" title="Smiling Mouth" alt="Mouth"
coords="38, 122, 76, 132, 116, 110, 102, 198, 65, 197" />
```

In other words, your browser creates this shape by drawing lines between these five points: (38, 122), (76, 132), (116, 110), (102, 198), and (65, 197).

NOTE Getting your coordinates right can be difficult. Many web page editors, like Dreamweaver and Expression Web, have built-in hotspot editors that let you create an image map by dragging shapes over your picture, which is a lot easier than trying to guess the correct coordinates. To use this tool in Dreamweaver, select a picture, and then look for the three hotspot icons (circle, square, and polygon) in the Properties panel. Expression Web offers similar icons in the Picture toolbar. (If you can't see the Picture toolbar, right-click the picture, and then select Show Picture Toolbar.)

Once you perfect all your hotspots, you need to apply them to the image by adding a usemap attribute to your <img> element. Use the same name for this attribute as you did for the image map itself, but precede it with the number-sign character (#), which tells browsers that you defined an image map for the picture:

```
<img src="face.gif" usemap="#FaceMap" alt="Smiling Face" />
```

Here's the complete HTML for the mouth hotspot example:

```
<!DOCTYPE html>
<html>
<head>
  <title>Image Map</title>
  <style type="text/css">
    img {
      border-style: none;
    }
  </style>
</head>
<body>
  <p>Click inside his mouth...</p>
  <p>
    <map id="FaceMap" name="FaceMap">
      <area href="Mouth.htm" shape="poly"
      coords="38, 122, 76, 132, 116, 110, 102, 198, 65, 197"
      alt="Smiling Mouth" />
    </map>
    <img src="face.gif" usemap="#FaceMap" alt="Smiling Face" />
  </p>
</body>
</html>
```

The hotspots you create are invisible (unless you draw lines on the picture to indicate where they are). When a visitor points to one, his cursor changes to a hand. Clicking a hotspot has the same effect as clicking an ordinary <a> link: Your visitor gets transported to a new page.

TIP It's tempting to use image maps to create links in all kinds of graphics, including buttons you may custom-design in an image editor, but hold off for a bit. You can create fancier menus and buttons with the JavaScript know-how you'll learn in Chapter 14.

Changing Link Colors and Underlining

Virtually everyone born since 1900 instinctively understands that blue underlined text is there to be clicked. But what if blue links are at odds with the overall look of your site? Thanks to style sheets, you don't need to play by the link-color rules.

Using CSS, you can quickly build a style sheet rule that changes the text color of all the link-producing anchor tags on your site. Here's an example:

```
a {
  color: fuchsia;
}
```

But watch out: custom link colors change the way the links behave. Ordinarily, when you click a link, it turns purplish red to show that you visited the page. Custom links, however, never change color—they retain their hue even after you click them.

A better way to create colorful links is to use another style sheet technique: *pseudo-classes*. Pseudo-classes are specialized versions of the CSS classes you learned about earlier (see page 84). They rely on details that a browser tracks behind the scenes. For example, ordinary classes apply rules indiscriminately to a given element, like an anchor. But pseudo-classes apply rules to elements that meet certain criteria, in this case links that are either clicked or unclicked.

Four pseudo-classes help you format links. They are `:link` for links that point to virgin ground; `:visited` for links a reader has already visited; `:active` for the color a link turns as a reader clicks it, before releasing the mouse button; and `:hover`, the color a link turns when a visitor points to it. As you can see, pseudo classes always start with a colon (:).

Here's a style rule that uses pseudo-classes to create a misleading page—one where visited links are blue and unvisited links are red:

```
a:link {
  color: red;
}
a:visited {
  color: blue;
}
```

If you want to apply these rules to some, but not all, of your links, add a class name to your rule:

```
a.BackwardLink:link {
  color: red;
}
```

```
a.BackwardLink:visited {
  color: blue;
}
```

Now an anchor element needs to specify the class name to display your new style, as shown here:

```
<a class="BackwardLink" href="...">...</a>
```

Finally, it's worth noting that you can use this technique with the `text-decoration` style sheet property to change whether browsers automatically underline links. Here's an example that removes the standard underlining:

```
a {
  text-decoration: none;
}
```

This technique is generally a bad idea with links you embed in the main content of a page, because it can make them hard to spot. However, it's useful if you have a panel that consists of nothing but links (like a menu sidebar) and you want to give it a cleaner look.

Links That Lead to Bookmarks

Most links lead from one page to another. When you make the jump to a new page, your browser plunks you down at the very top of the page. But you can also create links that lead to *specific parts* of a page, whether that's the current page (see Figure 6-9) or a newly opened one. This is particularly useful if you create long, scrolling pages and you want to direct your visitors' attention to a particular passage. The place you send your reader is technically called a *fragment*.

Creating a link that points to a fragment is a two-step process. First, you need to identify the fragment. You do this with the `id` attribute, which assigns a unique name to any HTML element on a page.

For example, imagine you want to send a visitor to the third level-3 heading in a web page named *sales.htm*. Initially, the markup looks like this:

```
...
<h3>Pet Canaries</h3>
<p>Pet canary sales have plummeted in the developed world, due in large part
to currency fluctuations and other macroeconomic forces.</p>
...
```

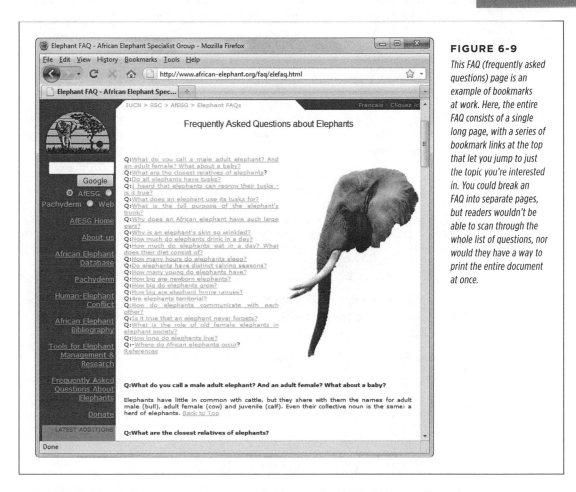

FIGURE 6-9

This FAQ (frequently asked questions) page is an example of bookmarks at work. Here, the entire FAQ consists of a single long page, with a series of bookmark links at the top that let you jump to just the topic you're interested in. You could break an FAQ into separate pages, but readers wouldn't be able to scan through the whole list of questions, nor would they have a way to print the entire document at once.

And here's the change that gives the Pet Canaries heading a unique name (in this case, the name is Canaries):

```
...
<h3 id="Canaries">Pet Canaries</h3>
<p>Pet canary sales have plummeted in the developed world, due in large part
to currency fluctuations and other macroeconomic forces.</p>
...
```

This doesn't affect the way the page looks; visitors never see the id attribute. However, it gives you a convenient way to drop visitors at the Pet Canaries heading. Essentially, you've created a bookmark that's locked onto this heading.

Once you create your bookmark, you can write a URL that points to it. The trick is to add the bookmark information to the end of the URL. To do this, you add the number-sign symbol (#) followed by the bookmark name.

For example, here's the link to send a reader to a bookmark named Canaries in the *sales.htm* page:

```
Learn about recent developments in <a href="sales.htm#Canaries">
canary sales</a>.
```

When you click this link, the browser heads to the *sales.htm* page and scrolls down until it encounters the Canaries bookmark. The browser then displays, at the very top of the browser window, the text that starts with the heading Pet Canaries.

TIP If your bookmark is near the bottom of a page, a browser might not be able to scroll the bookmarked section all the way to the top of the browser window. Instead, it appears somewhere in the middle of it. This happens because the browser hits the bottom of the page and can't scroll down any farther. If you suspect some potential for confusion (perhaps because you have several bookmarked sections close to one another at the bottom of a page), you can add a few <br> elements at the end of your document, which lets the browser scroll down.

Sometimes you want to create a link that points to a bookmark in your *current* page. In this case, you don't need to specify a page name at all. Just start with the number sign, followed by the bookmark name:

```
Jump to the <a href="#Canaries">canary</a> section.
```

Using bookmarks effectively is an art. Resist the urge to overcrowd your pages with links that direct readers to relatively small sections of content. Only use bookmarks to tame large pages that would otherwise take visitors a long time to scroll through.

■ When Good Links Go Bad

Now that you've learned all the ways to build links, it's a good time to consider what can go wrong. Links that go to pages on the same site can break when you rename or move files or folders. Links to other websites are particularly fragile; they can break at any time, without warning. You won't know that anything has gone wrong until you click the link and get a "Page Not Found" error message.

Broken links are so common that web developers have coined a term to describe how websites gradually lose their linking abilities: *link rot*. Sadly, you can upload a perfectly working website today and return a few months later to find that many of its external links have died off. They point to websites that no longer exist, have moved, or have been rearranged.

Link rot is an insidious problem because it reduces visitor confidence in your site. They see a link in a page that promises to lead to other interesting resources, but when they click it, they're disappointed. Experienced visitors won't stay long at a site that's suffering from an advanced case of link rot—they'll assume you haven't updated your site in a while and move on to a snazzier site somewhere else.

So how can you reduce the problem of broken links? First you should rigorously test your internal links—the ones that point to pages within your own site. Check for minor errors that can stop a link from working, and travel every path at least once. You can do this by hand, but leading web page editors include built-in tools that automate this drudgery. The next section explains how to use the link-checking features in Dreamweaver and Expression Web.

External links pose a different challenge. You can't create iron-clad external links, because link destinations are beyond your control and can change at any time. You could reduce the number of external links you include in your website to minimize the problem, but that isn't a very satisfying solution. Part of the beauty of the Web is the way a single click can take you from a comprehensive rock discography to a memorabilia site with hand-painted Elvis office supplies. As long as you want to connect your website to the rest of the world, you need to include external links. A better solution is to test your site regularly with an *online* link checker, which walks through every one of your pages and checks each link to make sure it still leads somewhere. Unlike the link checkers that you find in web-editing tools like Dreamweaver, online link checkers test both internal and external links. You'll learn how to use the most popular online link checker on page 198.

Checking Your Links in a Web Editor

Dreamweaver and Expression Web include their own tools to make sure internal links actually lead to a real page. They ignore external links, however.

NOTE To use the link-checking features in Dreamweaver and Expression Web, you must first define your folder as an official website (a process described on page 161 for Dreamweaver and page 167 for Expression Web).

In Dreamweaver, you scan links using the command Site→Check Links Sitewide. Dreamweaver pops open its Link Checker panel and reports any broken links as it works through your pages.

In Expression Web, you use a similar feature by following a three-step process. First, click the Site View tab. Then, click the Reports button at the bottom to see a list of all the reports you can run on your site. Finally, click Hyperlinks to investigate your links (Figure 6-10). Expression Web lists all the links in your site and puts a handy broken-link icon next to any that are problematic. You can also use the "Unlinked Files" link to find pages that don't have any links leading *to* them, and so can't be reached unless your visitors type the page name into their browsers.

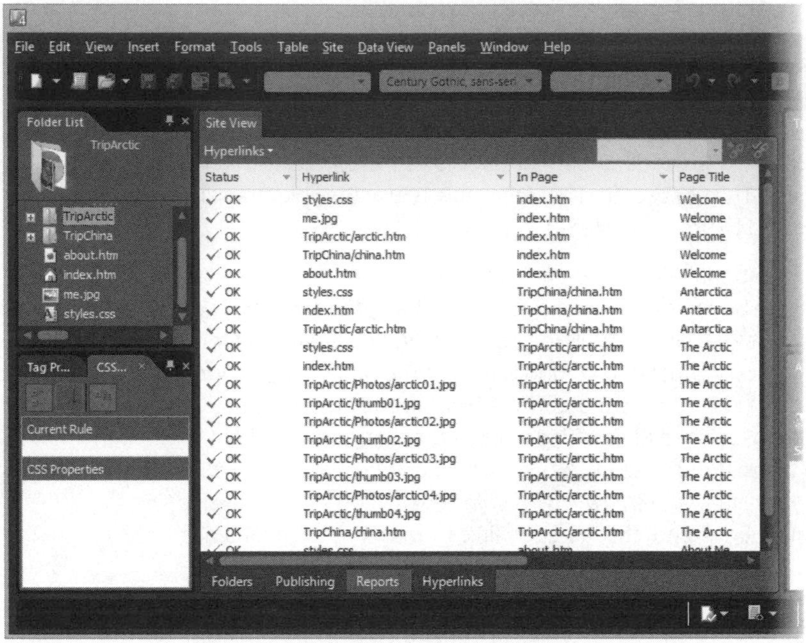

FIGURE 6-10

A quick scroll down the list of links reveals some good news: all this site's links are intact.

Checking Your Links Online

The link checkers built into these web page editors work on the copy of your website stored on your computer. That's the best way to keep watch for errors as you develop your site, but it's no help once your site is out in the wild. For example, it won't catch mistakes like a link to a file on your hard drive or to a file you forgot to upload to the web server.

To get the final word on your website's links, you might want to try a free online link checker. The World Wide Web Consortium provides a solid choice at *http://validator.w3.org/checklink*. Its link checker can scan any website that's currently online.

To start checking links, follow these steps:

1. **Go to** *http://validator.w3.org/checklink*.

   This takes you to the W3C Link Checker utility.

2. **In the text box, type in the full URL of the page you want to check.**

   It should point to the home page of your site on the Web (like *http://PoniesAreMagic.org/Ponies.htm*). If your website has a default page like *index.*

htm (see the note on page 180), you don't need to supply the filename, you can type in just the domain name (like *http://PoniesAreMagic.org*).

3. **Choose the options you want to apply (Figure 6-11).**

Select "Summary only" if you want the checker to omit the detailed list of steps it takes as it examines each page. It's best to leave this option turned off so you can better understand exactly what pages the link checker examines.

Select "Hide redirects" if you want the checker to ignore instructions that would redirect it to a web page other than the target page specified in the link (see page 200 for more). Usually, redirects indicate that your link still works, but also that you should update it to point to a new destination page.

The "Don't send the Accept-header" option prevents a link checker from telling a website its language preferences. This setting matters only if you're creating a multilingual website, which is beyond the scope of this book.

The "Check linked documents recursively" option validates links using recursion. If you don't use this option, the validator simply checks every link in the page you specify and makes sure it points to a live web page. If you use recursion, the validator checks all the links in the current page, and then *follows* each internal link on your site. For example, if a link points to a page named *info.htm*, the link checker first verifies that *info.htm* exists. Then it finds all the internal links in *info.htm* and starts testing *them*. In fact, if *info.htm* links to yet another internal page (like *contact.htm*), the link checker branches out to that page and starts checking its links as well. The link checker is smart enough to avoid checking the same page twice, so it doesn't waste time checking links it has already validated.

NOTE   Link checkers don't use recursion on external links. That means that if you start your link checker on the home page of your website, it follows the links to get to every other page on your site but won't go any further. Still, recursion is a great way to drill through all the links in your site in one go.

If you want to limit recursion (perhaps because you have a lot of pages and don't need to check them all), you can supply a "recursion depth," which specifies the maximum number of levels the checker digs down. For example, with a recursion depth of 1, the checker follows only the first set of links it encounters. If you don't supply a recursion depth, the checker checks everything.

4. **Select "Save options in a cookie" if you want your browser to remember your link-checker settings.**

If you use this option, the next time you use the link checker, your browser fills in the checkboxes using your previous settings.

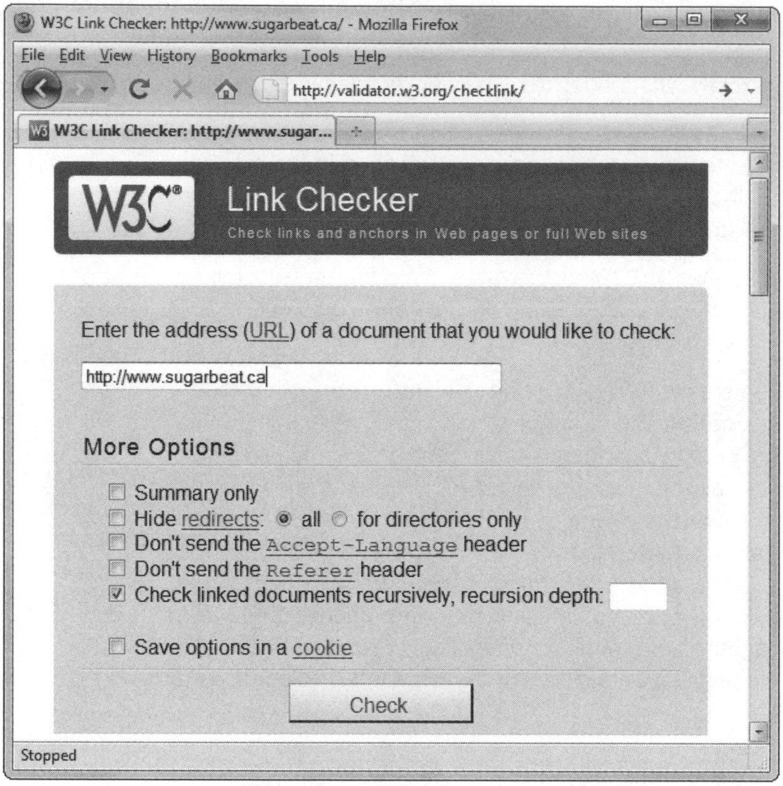

FIGURE 6-11

When you use a link checker, specify the web page you want to check and whether or not you want to use recursion, as in this example. (For the inside scoop on recursion and how it works, see the description in step 3 on the previous page.) Then click Check to get started.

5. **Click the Check button to start checking links.**

   The link checker lists each link it checks (Figure 6-12), updating the list as it goes along. If you use recursion, you'll see the link checker branch out from one page to another. The report adds a separate section for each page.

Using Redirects

To be a good web citizen, you need to respect people who link to your site. That means that once you create your site and it becomes popular, try to avoid tinkering with page and folder names. Making a minor change could disrupt someone else's link, making it difficult for return visitors to get back to your site.

FIGURE 6-12
The link checker's final report shows a list of links found in anchors and images. The checker highlights links that lead to dead ends in red and flags those that may need attention in yellow. One example of potential problem links are redirected links. Although they still work, they may be out of date and might not last for long.

Some web experts handle this problem using *redirects*. When they rearrange their sites, they keep all the old files, removing the content from them and replacing the old pages with a *redirect*—a special instruction that tells browsers to automatically navigate to a new page. The advantages of redirects are twofold: they prevent broken links, and they don't lock you into the old structure of your site if you decide to make a change.

To create a redirect, you add a special <meta> element to the <head> portion of your web page. This element indicates the new destination using an absolute URL and lists the number of seconds a browser should wait before performing the redirect. Here's an example:

```
<!DOCTYPE html>
<html>
<head>
  <meta http-equiv="REFRESH"
   content="10; URL=http://www.mysite.com/homepage.htm" />
  <title>Redirect</title>
</head>
<body>
  <h1>The page you want has moved</h1>
```

```
<p>
   Please update your bookmarks. The new home page is
   <a href="http://www.mysite.com/homepage.htm">
   http://www.mysite.com/homepage.htm</a>.
</p>
<p>
   You should be redirected to the new site in 10 seconds. Click
   <a href="http://www.mysite.com/homepage.htm">
   here</a> to visit the new page immediately.
</p>
</body>
</html>
```

To adapt this page for your own purposes, change the number of seconds (currently at 10) and the redirect URL. When a browser tries to open this page, it shows the temporary page for the indicated number of seconds and then automatically requests the new page.

> **NOTE** Although redirects are designed for live pages on the Web, you can test them on your own computer. For example, if you put the page shown above on your hard drive and open it, your browser will wait 10 seconds and then follow the URL to the new location.

Redirected pages really serve two purposes: They keep your pages working when you change your site's structure, and they inform visitors that the link is obsolete. That's where the time delay comes in—it provides a few seconds to notify visitors that they're entering the site the wrong way. Many sites keep their redirect pages around for a relatively short amount of time (for example, a year), after which they remove the page altogether.

Designing Better Style Sheets

Y ou've covered a lot of ground with CSS. You've used it to set colors, fonts, borders, and more, and you've applied your settings with carefully targeted class rules. But CSS isn't just a way to make stylish web pages; it's also a way to apply a consistent design to your entire site.

In this chapter, you'll lay the groundwork you need to build a modern, CSS-powered website. You'll deepen your understanding of style selectors, and create a properly organized style sheet that suits a whole site's worth of pages, not just a single document.

All this hard work has significant rewards. If you structure your pages and organize your styles with care, you can create a flexible, adaptable site. You won't break a sweat when it comes time to change something—whether you need to move a sidebar, change the size of a heading, or revamp everything, extreme-makeover style.

■ Planning a Style Sheet

You've already picked up the basic skills of style-sheet writing. You know how to create an external style sheet and attach it to as many web pages as you want with the `<style>` element. You've also had plenty of practice writing style rules—the formatting instructions that make things happen. But even though you know what style sheets can do, you're probably less sure about building a practical one—one that condenses complex formatting down to a simple set of rules but remains flexible enough to grow with your website.

That's OK. Creating style sheets is an art and takes a fair bit of practice. The examples in this chapter will help get your mind in gear. You begin with a single unformatted page in a simple site. First you'll learn how to pick out the elements in this page and write logical, well-organized rules to format them. Then you'll expand your rules to cover your entire site.

Figure 7-1 shows your starting canvas—a properly structured HTML page without any style-sheet formatting. Right now, it doesn't look like much, but it's always better to start with an ugly but properly designed page than a half-decent-looking page that uses inconsistent markup. (That's because you can always fix the ugly page with a new style sheet, but you'd need to rewrite its markup before you can give it a face-lift.)

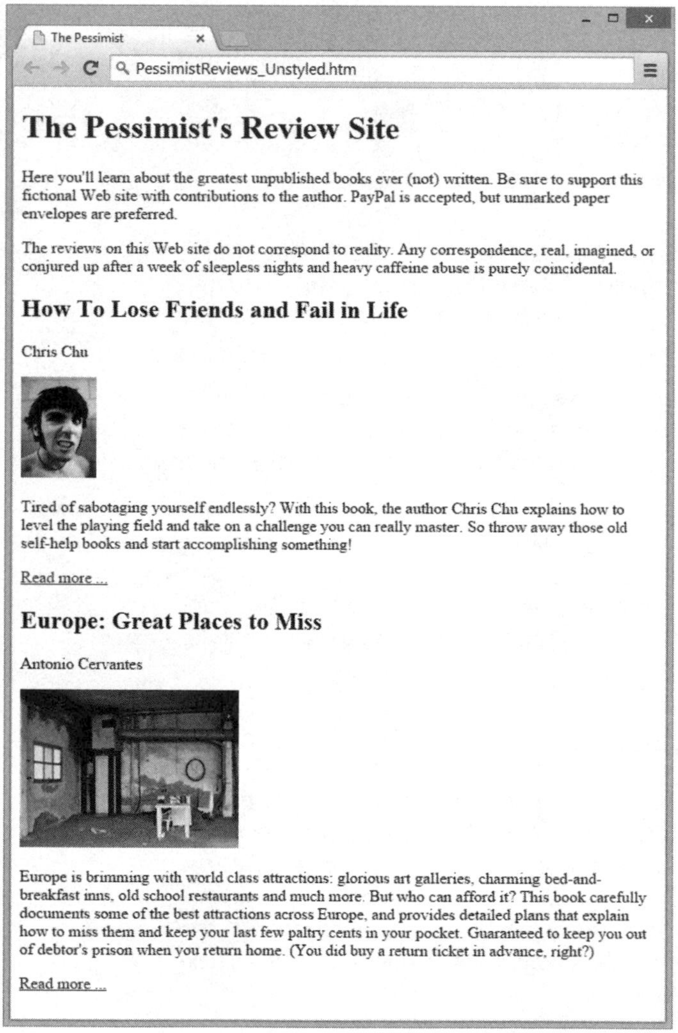

FIGURE 7-1

This page is pretty straightforward: it holds a general introduction followed by a list of book review summaries, with a link after each one to a full review on a separate page. Right now, the only formatting in the page is the built-in styling that HTML applies to headings, which sets the text in large, bold letters.

Before you get going, it's a good idea to look at the markup for this page. You can find it on the companion site (*http://prosetech.com/web*)—look for the file *PessimistReviews_Unstyled.htm*. Here's the markup, slightly condensed by leaving out some of the text:

```
<!DOCTYPE html>
<html>
<head>
  <title>The Pessimist</title>
</head>
<body>
  <h1>The Pessimist's Review Site</h1>
  <p>Here you'll learn about the greatest unpublished books ever ...</p>
  <p>The reviews on this Web site do not correspond to reality. Any ... </p>

  <h2>How To Lose Friends and Fail in Life</h2>
  <p>Chris Chu</p>
  <img src="scowl_small.jpg" alt="Face">
  <p>Tired of sabotaging yourself endlessly? With this book, the author ...
  </p>
  <p><a href="LoseFriends.htm">Read more ...</a></p>

  <h2>Europe: Great Places to Miss</h2>
  <p>Antonio Cervantes</p>
  <img src="house_small.jpg" alt="House">
  <p>Europe is brimming with world class attractions: glorious art ... </p>
  <p><a href="Europe.htm">Read more ...</a></p>
</body>
</html>
```

Identifying the Main Ingredients

Before you can write any style sheet rules, you need to think hard about your web page and how it's structured. Here's a good exercise: make a printout of your page, and then highlight each design element with a pen or marker (Figure 7-2). Your goal is to divide the page into its logical components and then format those different types of content in distinct ways.

For example, your style sheet should distinguish between the paragraph of text in the introduction and the paragraphs of text in the book reviews. And these differences should be clear and obvious, so you (or someone else) can look at the style sheet 12 months from now and still understand what's going on—and what rules to edit when you want to change the formatting.

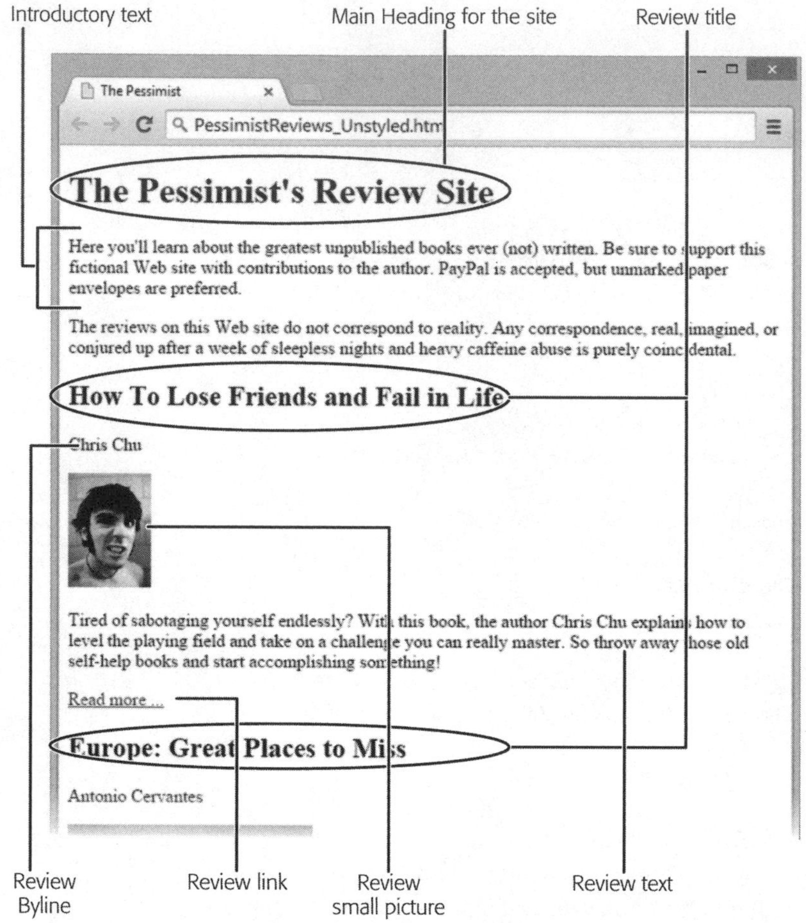

Introductory text   Main Heading for the site   Review title

FIGURE 7-2

In the average HTML document, you have a sea of similar elements—even a complex page often boils down to just headings and paragraph elements. In this example, the general introduction, the author byline, and the book summaries all use <p> elements. However, you should format these elements differently, because they represent different types of content. You'll tackle that task below.

Review Byline   Review link   Review small picture   Review text

▇ Building a Complete Style Sheet

When crafting a style sheet, you should begin by writing the most general, wide-reaching style rules first. These include instructions that set the background and typeface for the entire page and rules that target certain types of elements (like paragraphs and headings). Once you finish this job, you can target smaller and more specific design elements using rules that act on specific classes (for example, the author byline and the "Read more" link in Figure 7-1).

Figure 7-3 shows the first version of the review site style sheet. It's not the finished product—you'll improve on it as you work through this chapter—but it's a decent first step on the journey.

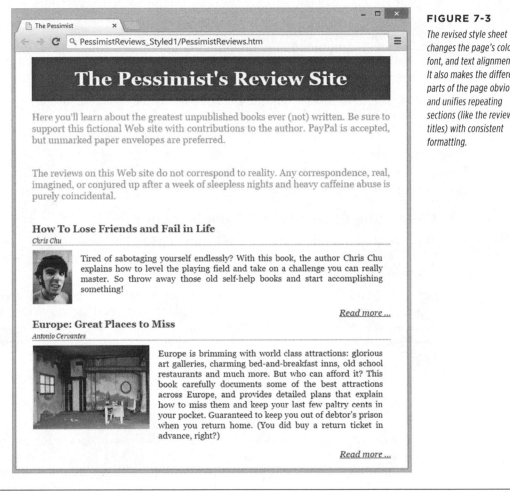

FIGURE 7-3

The revised style sheet changes the page's colors, font, and text alignment. It also makes the different parts of the page obvious and unifies repeating sections (like the review titles) with consistent formatting.

Setting the Ground Rules

Your first step is to lock down the basic design for your page, and the best way to do that is by applying a style rule to the most general of HTML elements: <body>.

As you know, the <body> element wraps the rest of your HTML markup. That means that any formatting you apply to it becomes the norm for the entire page. That makes the <body> element a good place to set the following styles:

- **Font.** Set the typeface and initial type size here.

- **Margins.** Every web page starts with a thin margin along the edges. This space interferes with certain style effects, like positioning a header that fits snugly against the top and sides of the page (an effect you'll try out on page 214). Set the margin to 0 if you want your content to stretch out and fill the whole display area, with no space between the edge of the page and the frame of the browser window.

- **Background.** If you want a background color (page 87) or a background picture (page 138) for the entire page, here's the spot to set it.

In the first version of the review site, the style rule for the <body> element is pretty simple. It sets the Georgia font as the standard typeface for the page:

```
body {
    font-family: Georgia,serif;
    font-size: 18px;
}
```

Formatting Elements with Type Selectors

Your next job is to write style rules that target specific elements. You use these rules to establish the overall formatting of your site, by specifying some of the basic details that apply *everywhere* in your page.

For example, the review site uses justified text that fills the space between the left and right margins (page 92), rather than the standard left-aligned, ragged-right text. It makes sense to apply this alignment to all the paragraphs in the page, but not to other elements, like headings or lists. You can do that easily by creating a rule that targets all paragraphs, like this:

```
p {
    text-align: justify;
}
```

It also makes sense to apply consistent formatting to all the images in the site. In the review site, every image is floated on the left (page 127), given a wider right margin, and outlined with a thin white border. Here's the style rule that does all that:

```
img {
    float: left;
    margin-top: 3px;
    margin-right: 15px;
    margin-bottom: 7px;
    border-style: solid;
    border-color: white;
    border-width: 1px;
}
```

NOTE You don't need any black magic to figure out the dimensions you should use to put margins around your elements. Instead, it's a matter of trial and error. Because the review site floats images to the left, you know you'll probably need to add extra margin space on the right side of the picture to leave some breathing room between the picture and the surrounding text. However, it takes a few edit-save-refresh cycles before you find the settings that look just right.

When you start building a style sheet for your site, you'll find that it fills up fast. If you can keep your rules lean and concise, your style sheet becomes a bit more manageable and a bit more readable. One way to do that is to use CSS *shorthand syntax* wherever you can. That means that instead of using style sheet properties like border-style, border-color, and border-width, consider the all-in-one border property that lets you set these three details in a single line of HTML.

You can also condense the margin and padding properties. If you supply a single number, the browser uses that value for all sides of an element. If you supply two numbers, the first one sets the top and bottom margins (or padding), while the second one sets the margins on the side. And if you supply *four* numbers, they set the margins in this order: top, right, bottom, left.

Here's a revised version of the <img> rule that applies the same formatting as earlier but uses the CSS shorthand syntax:

```
img {
  float: left;
  margin: 3px 15px 7px 0px;
  border: solid white 1px;
}
```

Now you face a few decisions. You have a page filled with content you need to format, but element-based style rules aren't always the right choice.

For example, most of the page's content lives inside <p> elements, but you want to format these paragraphs differently, depending on their logical role. This makes them a good candidate for the class-based rules you'll apply in the next section. However, the two types of headings *are* consistent. The <h1> heading announces the title of the site, while each <h2> heading represents a review title.

Here's the style rule that formats the <h1> heading. It sets a background color, so the heading becomes a shaded red banner. The style rule also changes the text to white lettering and centers it:

```
h1 {
  background-color: #761C00;
  margin: 0px;
  padding: 20px;
  color: white;
  text-align: center;
}
```

You don't need to set the font, because the headline inherits it from the style you applied to the <body> element. However, you *can* set the font-size property if the standard <h1> size is too big or too small.

Choosing Harmonious Colors

Picking the right colors for your site can take time. If you have a logo or graphic prominently featured in your site, you can use a graphics tool (for example, one of the paint programs described on page 128) to pick out the most important colors. You can then use those colors in your style sheet. But if you aren't trying to match an already established color scheme, you can benefit from an online color-picking tool.

For example, visit *http://paletton.com* for a graphical color picker that's both highly advanced and surprisingly easy to use. You choose the type of color scheme you want (monochromatic, adjacent three-color, coordinated four-color, and so on) and then spend some time clicking and dragging dots on an interactive color wheel. As you do, Paletton updates a carefully shaded palette of harmonious color choices. Once you see what you like, copy the color codes so you can use them in your style sheet—just as we did when building the red-and-gray color scheme for the review site.

The last element you might decide to target with a type selector is the <h2> element, which holds the review headings.

Here's where good web developers can disagree. Although every <h2> element in the page is a review title, this design might not hold true forever. It's easy to imagine adding <h2> elements that aren't review titles, either for other sections of this page or in other pages. For that reason, it's probably better to distinguish the review headings with their own dedicated *class*, as you'll do in the next section.

Creating Classes

With the basic rules out of the way, it's time to move on to the real work of style sheet creation—writing class rules. As you learned on page 84, class rules let you apply style sheet formatting to a single, specific element or group of elements. They also help you think in a more logical, structured way about your web pages. Instead of focusing on the HTML tags you're using, classes help you focus on styling the different types of information you present.

For example, the review site includes plenty of paragraphs, but they don't share the same formatting. With class rules, you can format the same element (in this case, <p>) in different ways, depending on whether that paragraph represents a review heading, a review byline, or the actual review text.

Once you mentally divide your page into sections (see Figure 7-2), you're ready to add the class rules that format them. For example, you can format the review heading with a class selector like this:

```
h2.reviewTitle {
  margin-top: 0px;
  font-size: 16px;
  color: #761C00;
  margin-bottom: 0px;
}
```

This rule applies to <h2> elements only, and only <h2> elements with the class name *reviewTitle*. You need to edit the page to put it into effect:

```
<h2 class="reviewTitle">How To Lose Friends and Fail in Life</h2>
```

This technique makes sense because at some point the website may include other level-2 headings that don't correspond to review titles, and so need different formatting.

TIP Remember, the best class names provide a succinct description of the type of content you want to format. In this example, the class name is *reviewTitle*, because you're going to apply this style to the book-review headings. Good class names describe the *function* of the class rather than its appearance. For example, *WarningNote* is a good class name, while *BoldRedArialBox* isn't. The problem with the latter is that it won't make sense if you decide to change the formatting of your warning note box (for example, by giving it red lettering). And two years from now, when you edit your style sheet, you may not remember what element *BoldRedArialBox* is supposed to format.

Class selectors really show their value when you start formatting the paragraphs in your page. The review site uses <p> elements to hold several different types of content, and each one needs its own class with distinct formatting.

```
/* The introduction text */
p.intro {
  color: #9C9C9C;
}

/* The review byline */
p.byline {
  font-size: 12px;
  font-style: italic;
  border-style: outset;
  border-width: 0 0 1px 0;
  margin: 5px 0 5px 0;
}

/* The review summary text */
p.review {
  font-size: 16px;
  margin: 15px;
}
```

```
/* The link at the end of the review summary */
p.reviewEnd {
  font-size: 16px;
  font-style: italic;
  text-align: right;
  margin-bottom: 0px;
  clear: both;
}
```

> **NOTE** This example introduces another feature—CSS comments. CSS comments look a little different from HTML comments. They always start with the characters /* and end with the characters */. Comments let you document what each class selector does. Without them, it's all too easy to forget what each style rule does in a complicated style sheet, particularly when you use class selectors.

Practice your style-decoding skills by figuring out what these styles do. Most of the properties apply the usual tweaks to font size and margin space. However, there are a couple of interesting tricks. The byline class, for example, puts a thin border under the author's name to separate it from the review text. And the *reviewEnd* class uses the clear property to turn off text wrapping and skip to the bottom of the floated image. This ensures that the next review doesn't end up beside the floating image from the previous review, which can happen when you have floating images displayed in wide browser windows. (Page 136 shows what this blunder looks like.)

To put these styles into action, you need to add your newly chosen class names to various parts of your page. Here's the modified markup for the review page, incorporating these class names. (To save space, most of the text is left out, but the essential structure is here.)

```
<h1>The Pessimist's Review Site</h1>
<p class="intro">Here you'll learn about the greatest unpublished books ever
...</p>
<p class="intro">The reviews on this Web site do not correspond to reality.
Any ... </p>

<h2 class="reviewTitle">How To Lose Friends and Fail in Life</h2>
<p class="byline">Chris Chu</p>
<img src="scowl_small.jpg" alt="Face">
<p class="review">Tired of sabotaging yourself endlessly? With this book, the
...</p>
<p class="reviewEnd"><a href="LoseFriends.htm">Read more ...</a></p>

<h2 class="reviewTitle">Europe: Great Places to Miss</h2>
<p class="byline">Antonio Cervantes</p>
<img src="house_small.jpg" alt="House">
<p class="review">Europe is brimming with world class attractions: glorious
...</p>
<p class="reviewEnd"><a href="Europe.htm">Read more ...</a></p>
```

This isn't too shabby, but you can streamline your markup with smarter selectors, as you'll see shortly. But for now, this completes the first version of your style sheet. Fire the page up in your browser, and you'll get the cleaned-up appearance shown in Figure 7-3. You can see the complete style sheet on the companion site (*http://prosetech.com/web*), in the PessimistReviews_Styled1 folder.

Keeping Your Style Sheet Organized

To make your style sheet's rules hierarchy as clear as possible, add the styles that use type selectors (those that target a specific type of element) first. In this example, those are the rules that format the <body> and <p> elements. Then add the class rules, putting related rules together (for example, grouping the styles for the different parts of a review).

Remember, your elements can (and often will) inherit style properties from more than one rule. For example, in the review site, the review text gets its justification setting from the <p> rule. The *review* class can then extend this style with additional style properties or override the style (for example, change the alignment) if necessary. Of course, extending is better than overriding, because life gets confusing when you have overlapping rules. (In the situation described here, the class selector wins over the type selector, because CSS deems it to be more specific. However, figuring out which rule is the most specific isn't as straightforward in every situation, as you'll see on page 219.)

Improving Your Style Sheet

The missing ingredient in the previous style sheet is the always-useful <div>.

You probably remember the <div> element from previous chapters. It's an all-purpose container that lets you group various sections of your web page. You can corral as many elements with the <div> tag as you want, including headings, paragraphs, and lists.

The <div> element plays several important roles in a well-designed style sheet:

- **It groups logically related sections.** For example, you can wrap the review title, review byline, and review text in a <div>, making it clear that these components belong together.

- **It adds boxes where you need them.** Wouldn't it be nice to wrap each review in a shaded and bordered box? With a <div>, that's easy (Figure 7-4).

- **It simplifies your markup.** Thanks to style sheet inheritance, the styles you apply to a <div> trickle down to the elements inside. You're about to see how that can help you trim the number of style rules in your style sheet.

Grouping Content with the <div> Element

A properly applied <div> element can do wonders for your page. It's the secret weapon that transforms a page from merely functional to flexible.

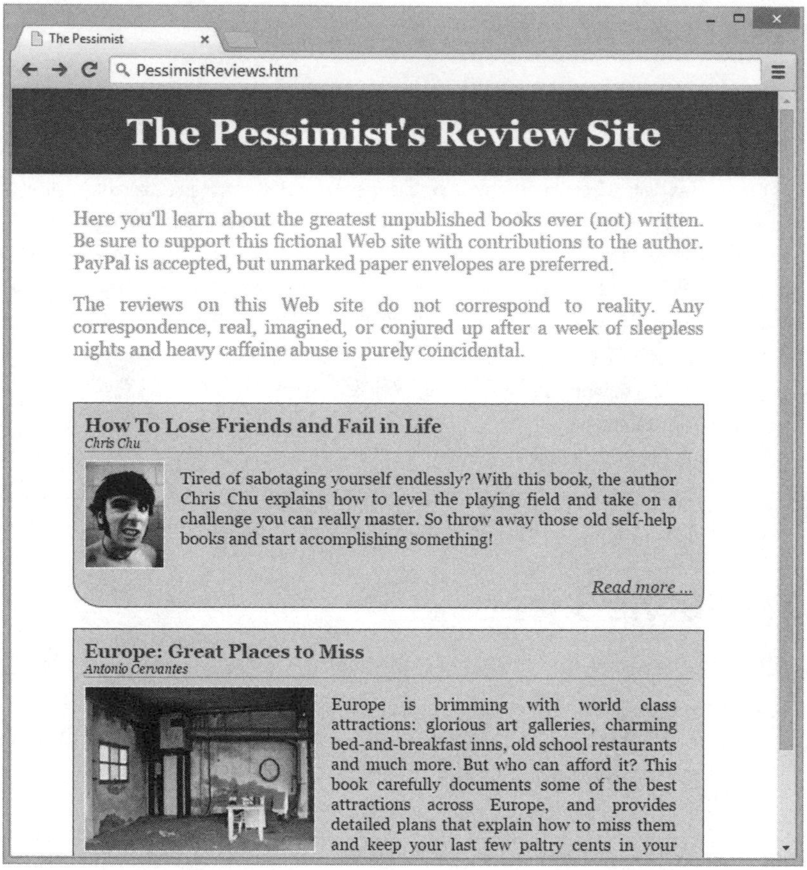

FIGURE 7-4

This version of the review site adds a number of refinements. Most obviously, the site's header now sits flush against the top and sides of the page, and each review has its own bordered, shaded box.

You'll first use a <div> to create the boxes that wrap the reviews. To do that, you need to add a separate <div> element around each review:

```
<div class="review">
  <h2 class="reviewTitle">How To Lose Friends and Fail in Life</h2>
  <p class="byline">Chris Chu</p>
  <img src="scowl_small.jpg" alt="Face">
  <p class="review">Tired of sabotaging yourself endlessly? With this book,
  the ...</p>
  <p class="reviewEnd"><a href="LoseFriends.htm">Read more ...</a></p>
</div>
```

```
<div class="review">
  <h2 class="reviewTitle">Europe: Great Places to Miss</h2>
  <p class="byline">Antonio Cervantes</p>
  <img src="house_small.jpg" alt="House">
  <p class="review">Europe is brimming with world class attractions: glorious
  ...</p>
  <p class="reviewEnd"><a href="Europe.htm">Read more ...</a></p>
</div>
```

Then you simply add a rule that styles the review <div>s:

```
/* The review box. */
div.review {
    background-color: #E4E4E4;
    margin: 20px 0 20px 0;
    padding: 10px;

    border: 1px #8A2700 solid;
    border-bottom-left-radius: 28px 26px;
    border-bottom-right-radius: 7px 14px;
}
```

These properties shade the review's background, add a border, and set the margin (the space between the border and the surrounding content), and padding (the space between the border and the *inside* content, which is the review text in this example). The style gets a little bit fancy with the border-bottom-left-radius and border-bottom-right-radius properties, which use slightly different curves to smooth out the bottom-left and bottom-right corners of the box.

But the review copy isn't the only place the revised review site uses a <div>. You also need a <div> for the header bar shown in Figure 7-4. Creating this bar takes two steps. First, you strip out the standard margin around the page using a style for the <body> element:

```
body {
    margin: 0px;
    padding: 0px;
    font-family: Georgia,serif;
    font-size: 18px;
}
```

Second, you add another <div> to hold all the content of the page *except* the header. This <div>'s job is to add the margin space *back* to the page, so your pictures and text don't end up scrunched along the side.

```
/* The page content, not including the header */
div.main {
    margin: 30px 70px 0 60px;
}
```

You put the start tag for this `<div>` just after the header, and the closing `</div>` tag at the end of the page, just before the footer (or in this case, just before the `</body>` tag that ends the page, because there is no footer). Here's the basic structure:

```
<!DOCTYPE html>
<html>
<head>
  ...
</head>
<body>
<h1>The Pessimist's Review Site</h1>
<div class="main">
  <!-- The rest of the page goes here, including everything. -->
</div>
</body>
</html>
```

NOTE There's no shame in having a `<div>` hold other `<div>` elements. In fact, it's a rare page that doesn't have `<div>` elements nested this way. For example, in the review site, the main `<div>` holds all the `<div>` elements for the reviews.

Figure 7-5 dissects the second version of the review site, showing you where the hidden `<div>` elements lie.

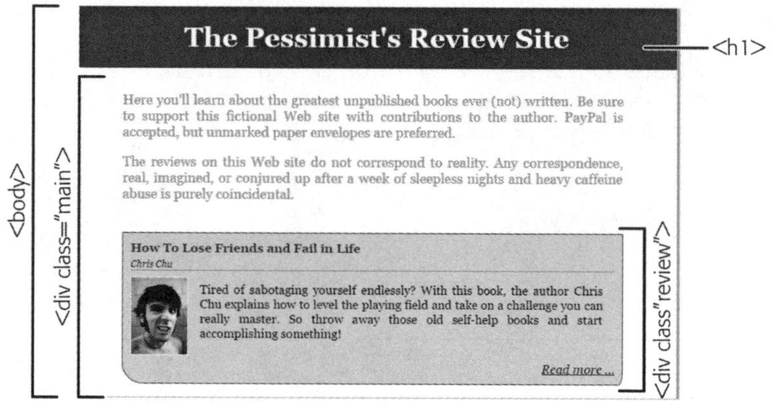

FIGURE 7-5

In this example, the HTML markup wraps each review in a `<div>` element, which applies a background color and borders to visually set off the reviews from the rest of the page. Techniques like these can help organize dense pages that have lots of information.

NOTE The `<div>` element is also the key to page layout. Once you put a distinct chunk of content into a `<div>`, not only can you style it as a single unit, but you can also place the whole block wherever you need it on your page. This makes the `<div>` a perfect container for things like headers, menus, footers, ad bars, and any sort of panel or box. You'll learn more about `<div>`-powered layouts in the next chapter.

Saving Work with the `<div>` Element

Thanks to style sheet inheritance (page 82), elements within a `<div>` inherit many of their properties from the parent `<div>`. Font size and margin settings are two good examples. If you set the `font-size` property in a `<div>` that contains paragraphs of review text, all those paragraphs get that formatting for free.

NOTE Although there are some style properties (like `margin` and `padding`) that don't support inheritance, most do. The style property tables in Chapter 3 indicate which properties use inheritance.

Once you add review boxes to your page, you can use inheritance to your advantage. For example, instead of assigning a 16-pixel font size to the *p.review* and *p.reviewEnd* classes, you can set the type size once in the *div.review* class (and still override it in the *p.byline* class).

You can save even more markup by adding a *div.intro* class to hold the two introductory paragraphs at the beginning of the page. There you can set the text color:

```
/* The introduction section. */
div.intro {
  color: #9C9C9C;
  margin-bottom: 40px;
}
```

Now you don't need the *p.intro* class at all. You can delete it from your style sheet and remove the `class` attribute from the two introductory paragraphs.

If these changes seem small, remember that a typical style sheet is stuffed with dozens or hundreds of rules. A few modest savings like these can reduce the complexity of your style sheet quite a bit.

The `<div>` element is a great way to save loads of time, and web experts use it regularly. But the next technique can help you improve your markup even more.

Saving Work with Contextual Selectors

Applying a class attribute to every element you want to format can get tedious fast. In the example above, you need to add the `class="review"` attribute to every paragraph after the byline. Fortunately, you can use another great shortcut, courtesy of the `<div>` element and a new type of selector, called a *contextual selector*.

A *contextual selector* targets an element *inside another element*. To understand what that means, take a look at this type selector:

```
b {
  color: red;
}
```

It formats all bold text in red. But what if you want it to work only on bold text that appears inside a bulleted list? You can do that using the following contextual type selector, which finds unordered list elements (<ul>) and then hunts for bold elements inside them. If it finds any, it makes the bold text red:

```
ul b {
  color: red;
}
```

To create a contextual type selector, you simply put a space between the two elements.

Contextual selectors are useful, but figuring out how to write one in a style sheet full of nested elements can get a little dizzying. You'll see the real benefit of a contextual selector when you use one to target a specific type of element inside a specific type of *class*. For example, consider what happens if you take this style sheet rule:

```
h2.review {
```

and change the selector to this:

```
div.review h2 {
```

The first part of this selector finds all the <div> elements in your page. The second part limits those matches to <div> elements that have the class name *review* applied to them. The third and final part of the selector locates the <h2> elements inside the <div>. The end result is that every level-2 review heading gets the appropriate formatting, while headings in the rest of the page are left alone.

Best of all, you can remove the class attribute from the <h2> element, leaving the following, simpler markup:

```
<div class="review">
  <h2>...</h2>
```

You can repeat this trick to format the <img> or <a> elements in a review without using class names.

You can even target the ordinary paragraphs inside your <div>, but here you have to be careful. That's because CSS considers contextual selectors to be more specific than type or class selectors. For example, imagine that you want to create a paragraph-formatting rule that uses a contextual selector like this:

```
div.review p {
```

You want this rule to apply to all the review paragraphs except the byline at the beginning and the link at the end. Ideally, you want to use just three classes in the review markup, like this:

```
<div class="review">
  <h2>...</h2>
  <p class="byline">...</p>
  <p>...</p>
  <p>...</p>
  <p>...</p>
  <p class="reviewEnd">...</p>
</div>
```

Here's where you run into a problem, because the browser ignores the formatting in the byline and *reviewEnd* classes. That's because the browser decides that these class rules are less specific than the new paragraph rule that uses the contextual selector.

NOTE Confused? CSS has a quirky and often overlooked system of *precedence*, which decides which rules are more specific than others (and so win out in a formatting clash). The rule of thumb is that a contextual selector always beats a class selector. But if you want the full, gory details, which spell out the winners when different types of style rules conflict, check out the Smashing Magazine article at *http://tinyurl.com/css-specific*.

To correct this problem, you need to change the byline and *reviewEnd* classes. The easiest way to make them more specific is to modify them to use a contextual selector as well. In other words, instead of creating a rule that applies to any paragraph that uses the byline class, you need to create a rule that applies to any paragraph that uses the byline class *and* is located inside a review:

```
div.review p.byline {
```

This corrects the problem. Best of all, it lets you simplify your markup. Now you need to apply classes to each review in just three places: in the <div> container for the review itself, in the byline, and in the link at the end. You no longer need to add a class to the regular paragraphs or the heading.

NOTE When using classes and contextual selectors, most web designers don't bother specifying the element names. That's because this selector is a bit clunky:

```
div.review p.byline
```

Instead, this works just as well and is more readable: *.review .byline*

This selector grabs the elements that use the *byline* class, provided they're inside an element the uses the *review* class. The end result is the same.

Contextual selectors are a wildly popular way to define formatting rules for different sections of a page. If you look at other people's style sheets (and you should, to learn new tricks and practice your CSS skills), you'll see plenty of <div> elements and contextual selectors at work.

If you've lost track of what style rules are still in the style sheet and which ones you don't need anymore, check out the following outline, which lists all the rules in the revised version of review-site style sheet.

```
/* Remove the margin and set the font for the whole page */
body { ... }

/* Set the justification for all paragraphs */
p { ... }

/* Float and style all images */
img { ... }

/* The shaded site header */
h1 { ... }

/* The page content, not including the header */
div.main { ... }

/* The introduction section. */
div.intro { ... }

/* The entire review box. */
div.review { ... }

/* The review title */
.review h2 { ... }

/* The review summary text */
.review p { ... }

/* The review byline */
.review .byline { ... }

/* The link at the end of the review summary */
.review .reviewEnd { ... }
```

You can see this style sheet, complete with all its formatting glory, on the companion site (*http://prosetech.com/web*) in the PessimistReviews_Styled2 folder.

Practice Styling a Page

You may understand the style sheet techniques covered in this chapter, but there's no substitute for trying them out yourself. If you're ready to apply some CSS mojo, here's a good exercise: First, get the *PessimistReviews_Unstyled.htm* page from the companion site. That's the unformatted version of the review page you saw back in Figure 7-1. Next, grab the latest and greatest style sheet, *PessimistReviews.css*, from the PessimistReviews_Styled2 folder.

Your challenge is to apply the styles from the *PessimistReviews. css* style sheet to the *PessimistReviews_Unstyled.htm* page. To do that, you first need to add the missing `<div>` elements. You need one that wraps all the content in the page (the main content), one for the introduction, and one for each review. Then you must add the `class` attributes to the elements that need them. If you rework the page correctly, you'll see the page shown in Figure 7-4. If you run into trouble, check out the correct solution—the *PessimistReviews.htm* page in the PessimistReviews_Styled2 folder.

Creating a Style Sheet for an Entire Site

Class rules aren't just useful for separating different types of content. They're also handy if you want to define rules for your whole site in a single style sheet.

Consider the review site you've been working on. As you add more pages to it, it's reasonable to assume that you'll use some of the same formatting rules on the new pages. For example, you're likely to keep the site header, the Georgia font, and the text-justification settings for other pages in your site. But you'll probably need to supplement the style sheet you've built so far with additional rules that deal with different types of content.

Figure 7-6 shows an example of a new page that could benefit from some extra fine-tuning. It displays the full text of a single review. This is the page visitors see if they click the "Read more" link in the review summary on the main page.

You can adapt the existing style sheet to suit this new page several ways. One is to create a whole new set of rules for full-review pages. For example, you could wrap the review summaries in a `<div>` and apply a class named *reviewSummary* to them, and you could wrap the full reviews in a `<div>` and use the class name *reviewFull* for them. The *reviewSummary* class would get the border and smaller heading, while the *reviewFull* class would get a similar page, but with no border and larger text.

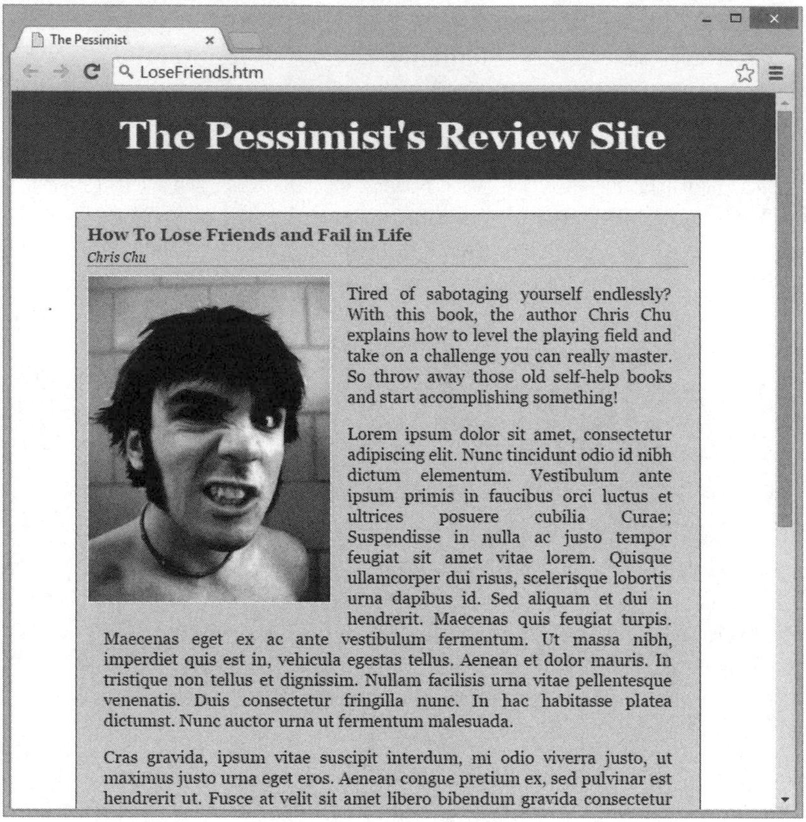

FIGURE 7-6

The full review gets the same formatting as the review summary on the main page. However, some of the styling doesn't seem to fit as well here, including the bordered box that surrounds the entire review and the small-seeming review title.

Here's an outline of the style rules you need:

```
/* ********************************************** */
/* Styles for the review summaries on the main page. */
/* ********************************************** */

/* The entire review box. */
div.reviewSummary { ... }

/* The review title */
.reviewSummary h2 { ... }

/* The review summary text */
.reviewSummary p { ... }
```

```
/* The review byline */
.reviewSummary .byline { ... }

/* The link at the end of the review summary */
.reviewSummary .reviewEnd { ... }

/* ************************************************** */
/* Styles for the full review on the single-review page. */
/* ************************************************** */

/* The whole review section. */
div.reviewFull { ... }

/* The review title */
.reviewFull h2 { ... }

/* The review text */
.reviewFull p { ... }

/* The review byline */
.reviewFull .byline { ... }
```

Another approach is to continue using the same class names. After all, in both cases you're formatting a review. The only difference is the context of that review—the fact that it now has the whole page to itself. To capture the change in this context, you can add another <div> container around the <div> that holds the review. For example, on the single review page you could use markup like this:

```
<div class="singlePageReview">

<div class="review">
<h2>How To Lose Friends and Fail in Life</h2>
<p class="byline">Chris Chu</p>
<img src="scowl_big.jpg" alt="Face">
<p>Tired of sabotaging yourself endlessly? With this book, the author Chris
Chu explains how to level the ...
```

Now you need to write contextual selectors that alter a few details for reviews on the single-review page. For this task, you'll need more elaborate contextual selectors. Instead of simply specifying the *byline* class (the author byline) in the *review* class (the <div> container that holds the review), as you did earlier, now you need to target the *byline* class in the *review* class *in the singlePageReview class*. Here's the selector that does the job:

```
.singlePageReview .review .byline {
```

If you're making just a few changes, this add-on approach is surprisingly elegant. For example, by adding the three rules shown below, you can give the single-review page a more suitable appearance (Figure 7-7).

FIGURE 7-7

Using contextual selectors, full-page reviews like this one look different from review summaries. But thanks to the many shared details in coloring, type, and alignment, both pages stay consistent and look like they belong in the same site.

```css
.singlePageReview .review {
  border: none;
  background: transparent;
}

.singlePageReview .review .byline {
  font-size: 14px;
  text-align:right;
  margin-right: 15px;
}
```

```
.singlePageReview .review h2 {
  font-size: 24px;
  text-align:right;
  color: #E4E4E4;
  background: #D46A6A;
  border-radius: 30px 0;
  padding: 20px;
}
```

Tutorial: Becoming a Style Detective

In this chapter, you accomplished some serious styling work. But no matter how carefully you organize your styles, something will eventually go wrong. You'll tweak the properties in a rule, refresh the page, and find that the element you're attempting to change has stubbornly ignored your commands.

You could have altered the wrong rule. Or mistyped a class name. Or added a rule that another setting in a different rule canceled out. Finding the root of a style problem isn't always easy, because the more complex your style sheet, the more difficult it is to identify the rules that format a specific part of your page.

Consider one of the review paragraphs in the previous example. It acquires a combination of styles from no fewer than *four* places:

- It inherits <body> element settings, like the font family.
- It gets the paragraph-specific formatting you set in the <p> style rule.
- It inherits the settings from the <div> that holds the review.
- It gets the formatting you specified for all review paragraphs through the contextual .review .p selector.

So what do you do if an element on your page doesn't have the formatting you think it should, based on the styles you set? You could fumble around in the dark, making random changes to the style sheet in an attempt to fix the problem. But a better idea is to call in the reinforcements and use a *CSS inspection tool*.

A CSS inspection tool is a browser feature or plug-in that analyzes what's happening in your web page. It tells you what style properties are in effect on every element, and where the element gets these settings *from*. Using a CSS inspection tool is like performing an x-ray on your page to see the CSS logic hiding underneath.

In the not-so-distant past, you needed to install (and maybe even buy) some sort of specialized tool to get this CSS wizardry. But today, every modern browser provides this feature—and, surprisingly, each browser implements it in pretty much the same way. The following steps walk you through the process of using CSS inspection:

1. **First, grab yourself a page you want to analyze.**

   A good starting point is the final review in the *PessimistReviews.htm* page, which you can find in the PessimistReviews_Styled2 folder on the companion site (*http://prosetech.com/web*).

2. **Open the page in your favorite browser.**

   Google Chrome is a superb choice for CSS inspection, but Firefox and Opera offer CSS tools that are nearly as good. Internet Explorer can perform the same magic, but it works best in IE 11 or later.

   If you're using Safari, you need to make a quick trip to the menu to turn on the developer tools before you go any further. Choose Safari→Preferences→Advanced and make sure the "Show Develop menu in menu bar" checkbox is turned on.

3. **Choose an element you want to study.**

   For example, in the *PessimistReview.htm* page, you might decide to zero in on one of the review bylines.

4. **On the web page, right-click the element you want to examine, and then choose Inspect Element.**

   A multi-tabbed panel of web developer tools appears at the bottom of your web page (Figure 7-8).

The element you're inspecting

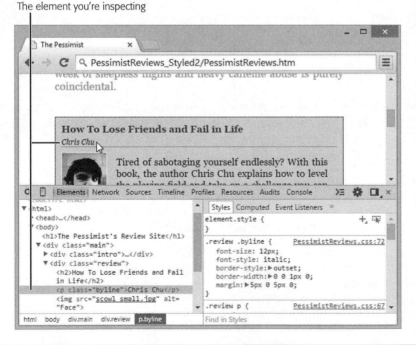

FIGURE 7-8

There are plenty of goodies packed into the inspection-tool tabs you see here. On the left, you'll see the HTML markup for the page, nicely formatted and color coded. You can collapse or expand parts of the listing to focus on the part that interests you (just click the tiny arrows in the left margin). On the right side is something even more interesting—a list of all the styles that affect the element you picked.

5. **Expand the developer panel so you can see most of the CSS styles listed.**

The developer panel starts out small, but you can make it bigger by dragging the bar that separates the developer panel from the web page up.

Figure 7-9 shows a closeup view of the style list in Chrome.

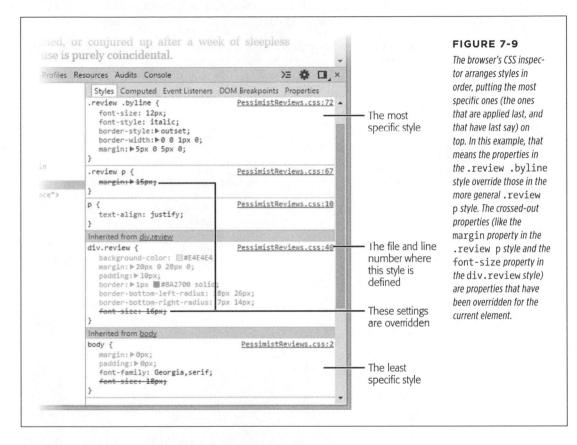

FIGURE 7-9

The browser's CSS inspector arranges styles in order, putting the most specific ones (the ones that are applied last, and that have last say) on top. In this example, that means the properties in the .review .byline style override those in the more general .review p style. The crossed-out properties (like the margin property in the .review p style and the font-size property in the div.review style) are properties that have been overridden for the current element.

The most specific style

The file and line number where this style is defined

These settings are overridden

The least specific style

6. **When you finish, pick a new element to study.**

You can choose an element two ways. You can right-click something on the page and choose Inspect Element again, or you can click the element you want in the HTML outline on the left side of the developer panel.

If you're prepared to dig deeper, most browsers add a few more CSS analyzing goodies. You can do any of the following:

• **See the computed style settings.** You may see a Computed button or tab above the style list. Click it to see the combined effect of your styles—in other words, to see a single list that shows all the properties in effect on the chosen element.

- **Turn off a style property.** Most browsers also let you turn off specific style settings to better understand how they affect the page. To do this, clear the checkbox next to the property you want to turn off. (In some browsers, including Chrome and Firefox, you need to point to the property before the checkbox appears.) Keep in mind that this style-switching is just a temporary testing tool—it doesn't change your style sheet, nor does it affect what your page looks like the next time you open it in a browser.

- **Edit a style property.** Want to quickly test a change? Double-click one of the style properties in the list and then type in a new value. Your browser applies the new style setting immediately (Figure 7-10). If this solves the problem or improves the page, you can make the same edit to your style sheet.

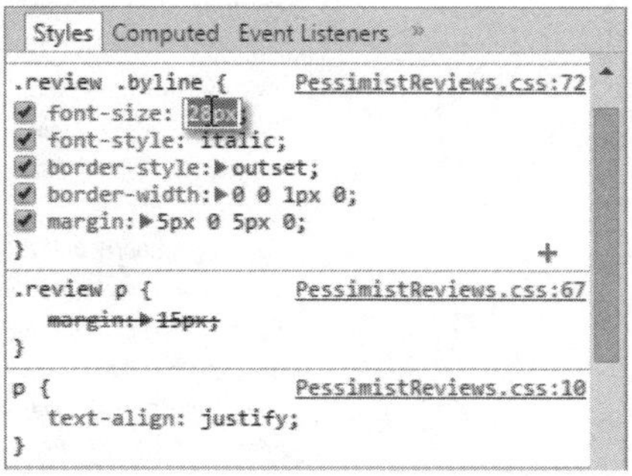

FIGURE 7-10

Curious about what would happen if you gave the byline class a 28-pixel font? You can find out by double-clicking the font-size *property and making this quick edit. You can clear the checkmark next to any property to temporarily turn that setting off.*

From Web Page to Website

Page Layout

I n this book, you've covered some serious ground with CSS. In Chapter 3, you used styles to polish up drab web pages. And in Chapter 7, you learned to build larger, more ambitious style sheets to standardize the design of an entire website. In this chapter, you'll extend your style sheet skills to deal with page layout.

Up to now, your pages have been locked into fixed layouts based on the order of their HTML elements. So if you put a heading at the beginning of your markup, that heading shows up at the top of your page. This behavior makes perfect sense, but it doesn't suit more complicated layouts. For example, a typical modern website uses headers, fat footers, and sidebars (often on both sides of a page) to place major elements like headers, menus, advertisements, links, galleries, social media plug-ins, and more. If you lock each ingredient to a specific spot in your page, you'll have a hard time replicating the layout on every page and a heck of a time changing your site's layout in the future.

Once again, you've met a problem that styles can solve. With a well-organized style sheet—like the kind you built in the previous chapter—you can carve your page into logical sections, and then use CSS to slip those sections into the right arrangement.

In this chapter, you'll see exactly how CSS-based layouts work. You'll learn to use modern layout techniques like floating boxes, side-by-side columns, and overlapping pictures and text. But first, you'll consider the challenges of layout on the Web and learn why online viewing isn't as straightforward as it seems.

◼ Understanding Style-Based Layout

In the early, lawless days of the Web, designers had to improvise their layout tools. One of their favorites was the invisible table, which uses the <table> element you learned about in Chapter 2 to position rows and columns of content. Although ghost tables worked well enough, they left a tangled mess of markup in their wake. Today, web developers have given up on table-based layouts in favor of a cleaner, more powerful approach: style-based layout.

You've already taken your first tentative steps toward style-sheet nirvana by learning about borders and boxes (Chapter 3), floating images (Chapter 4), and logical containers (Chapter 7). With these tools, you have almost everything you need to lay out a full page. So before you go any further, it's a good idea to review these basics.

Structuring Pages with the <div> Element

Before you start placing elements in specific positions on a page, you need a way to bundle related content together, into a single, neat package. In an old-fashioned table-based layout, that package was the table cell. When you use style-based layout, that package is the <div> element—the all-purpose container you learned about on page 47.

Imagine you want to create a box with several links in it on the left side of your page. Positioning each link in that column is as much fun as peeling grapes. By using the <div> element, you can group all those links together and manipulate them as a single unit:

```
<div class="Menu">
  <a href="...">Home Page</a>
  <a href="...">Buy Our Products</a>
  <a href="...">File a Lawsuit</a>
  ...
</div>
```

Whenever you create a <div> element, you should choose a class name that describes the type of content it contains (like *Menu*, *Header*, *AdBar*, and so on). Using that class name, you can create a style rule that positions this <div> element and sets its font, colors, and borders.

Remember, a <div> element doesn't have any built-in formatting. In fact, on its own, it doesn't do anything at all. The magic happens when you combine a <div> element with a style sheet rule.

Floating Boxes

Ordinarily, HTML pages use a "flow" layout model. The elements in your web page flow from the top of the browser window to the bottom, appearing in the same order as they appear in your HTML markup. But when you use CSS layout properties, you take selected elements out of this system and arrange them according to different rules—the rules that you define in your style sheet.

One of the simplest ways to lay out a web page is to take a small portion of content and *float* it outside of the main layout of your page (see Figure 8-1). That way, the floating box sits wherever you place it, and the rest of the content flows around that box. In fact, you already used this technique in Chapter 4, to make pictures float using the style sheet property, float. A floating layout works just as readily with <div> elements as it did with those <img> elements, with one exception: You need to supply a width for the <div> element.

NOTE When you float an image, browsers automatically make the floating box as wide as the image. When you float a <div> element with text inside, *you* must specify how wide it should be.

FIGURE 8-1

Here are three examples of floating layouts.

Top: A standard floating box.

Bottom left: You can stack place more than one float-ing box at a time. Your browser adds each new box to the left of the one before it.

Bottom right: To stack the boxes, add the clear: both *style sheet property (page 136) to force the second floating box to appear under the first.*

Here's a style that defines a class and floats an element on the right side of some text:

```
.FloatingBox {
    float: right;
    width: 150px;
    background-color: red;
    border-width: 2px;
    border-style: solid;
    border-color: black;
    padding: 10px;
    margin: 8px;
    font-weight: bold;
    color: white;
}
```

And here's the `<div>` that uses that style:

```
<div class="FloatingBox">
    <h1>Buy now!</h1>
    <p>...</p>
</div>
```

You'll notice that the *FloatingBox* class sets the width of the box but not its height. Browsers handle the latter task, making the box just tall enough to fit the content inside. You could specify a fixed height using the *height* property, but you might truncate the end of your text (if you make the box too small) or leave extra white space at the bottom (if it's too big).

Fixed Boxes

The examples in Figure 8-1 are called floating boxes because they "float" around the page to different positions. When a browser encounters a `<div>` element that uses the `float` property, it positions that element on the side of the page (left or right) you specify in your style sheet. It positions the top of the `<div>` at the point in the page where it encounters the `<div>` element in the HTML. So if a browser finds a `<div>` halfway down the HTML for a page, it puts the floating box halfway down that page.

Style sheets give you another option: You can place an element in a set, unchanging position. To do that, you use the `position` property (set to absolute in this case) in conjunction with the properties `top`, `left`, `bottom`, and `right`. Here's an example:

```
.FixedBox {
    position: absolute;
    top: 20px;
    left: 0px;
    width: 150px;
    background-color: orange;
    border-width: 2px;
    border-style: solid;
    border-color: black;
    padding: 10px;
    margin: 8px;
    font-weight: bold;
    color: white;
}
```

Unlike floating boxes (which float at the sides of a page), fixed boxes can go any-where. When you specify the location of an element using absolute positioning, you remove that element from the normal "flow" of the page. As a result, the rest of your content won't wrap around a fixed box. Instead, the box sits on top of the content, as you can see in Figure 8-2.

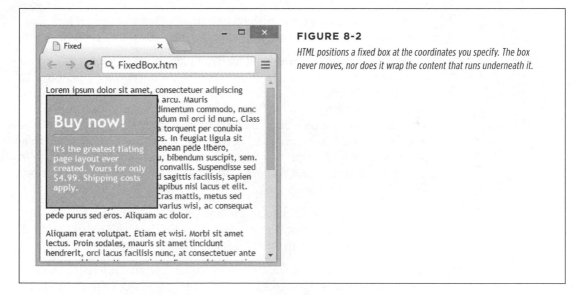

FIGURE 8-2

HTML positions a fixed box at the coordinates you specify. The box never moves, nor does it wrap the content that runs underneath it.

At first glance, fixed boxes seem like a problem. After all, who wants to deal with a jumble of overlapping content? But if you're careful, you can carve the page into distinct sections that don't clash. The most common way to do this is by creating columns, as you'll see shortly.

■ Choosing Your Layout

When you design a page for print, you take into account the physical size of your final document. You'd use much larger text on a poster than you would on a business card, for example. But in the world of the Web, this system breaks down, because your website visitors can resize their browser windows (as well as the text itself) to all sorts of different dimensions, and they may view your site with tablets and smartphones that have small screens. These details affect how much display space your web pages have. The higher the resolution and the bigger the browser window, the more of your content fits onscreen. This raises a dilemma—how do you make sure your pages look their best when you don't know your visitors' screen settings?

You deal with variable screen sizes using one of two basic layout strategies:

- **Go for flexibility with proportional sizing.** With proportional sizing, your layout expands or shrinks to fit the available space in a browser window. For example, if you create a proportionally sized web page with a fixed-size menu panel (on the left) and a variable content area (on the right), the menu section always stays at the same width, while the content area grows or contracts to fit the browser window, no matter how big or small your guest makes that window. If you're in doubt, proportional sizing is the way to go, because it ensures that your web pages will conform to any size browser window. However, you might want to impose a maximum or minimum width to prevent your pages from being scrambled beyond recognition. You'll learn how to do that in this chapter.

- **Pick a reasonable fixed width.** Sometimes, too much flexibility can cause its own problems. For example, if you shrink a proportionally sized page to extremely small dimensions, some page elements might get bumped into odd positions. If you have a complex layout with lots of graphics and floating elements, the result can be a bit of a mess. On the other hand, extremely large windows can cause problems, too. For example, if you stretch a proportionally sized page to the full width of a widescreen monitor, you might end up with extremely long lines of text that are hard to read. One solution is to use fixed-width pages that look good at a range of common browser settings.

Both approaches make sense, but in different scenarios. For a typical site that presents ordinary text, like a blog post or news story, fixed-width sizing works best. Figure 8-3 shows it at work on the Wall Street Journal's website (*www.wsj.com*).

On other websites, proportional sizing works better, because it lets the website make the best use of whatever screen space a visitor's got. For example, perform a text search on Google and you'll get a page of results that uses a fixed layout. But perform an image search on Google, and you'll notice that the image results stretch to fill the whole width of the browser window, even on the widest widescreen monitor (Figure 8-4).

FIGURE 8-3

Top: To read the text of this article without scrolling side to side, you need a window that's around 600 pixels wide. Just about every computer screen can accommodate that.

Bottom: Widen the window to about 1,000 pixels and you see frills like videos, ads, a search box, and a list of popular articles. If you make the window any wider, all you'll get is extra blank space.

These days, some sites get even fancier by creating *multiple* layouts that they swap in and out as needed, depending on destination device. For example, people viewing this sort of site on a widescreen monitor will see one version of the site, while people viewing it on a smartphone get a different view, governed by different style sheet rules. This approach is more complex, and it requires the latest version of the style sheet language, CSS3. You'll learn more in the box on page 250.

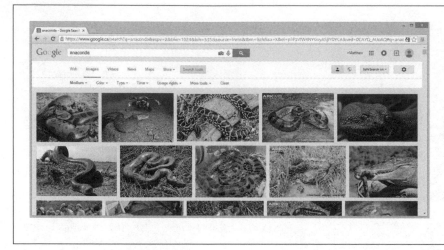

FIGURE 8-4

*Proportional sizing has the
potential to adapt to the
needs of your web visitors.
Although it makes sense
to fill a browser window
with images, the same
approach wouldn't work
well with text, because
very long lines become
difficult to follow. For this
reason, you may want to
cap the maximum width of
a proportional web page,
as described on page 248.*

No matter which layout strategy you choose, you should test your pages at a variety of browser sizes to make sure your visitors see the best side of your work. In this chapter, you'll learn to build a couple of multiple-column layouts, one of which uses fixed widths, and one that uses proportional sizing.

The 1,000-Pixel Rule of Thumb

If you opt to create a standard fixed-width layout, you need to figure out how wide that layout should be. Of course, you have no way of knowing the size of a visitor's browser window, which is the most important factor in page layout. Fortunately, there's a good rule of thumb to help you out: Make sure your pages look great at a width of 1,000 pixels. (Pixels are the tiny dots on your computer screen. For a deeper explanation, see the box on page 239.) The Wall Street Journal example in Figure 8-3 meets this guideline.

The 1,000-pixel mark is an arbitrary number, but it works surprisingly well for everyone. Very old computers may have monitors that top out near that range, which means people using those computers can see everything on a 1,000-pixel-wide page, as long as they enlarge their browser window to fill the whole screen. The 1,000-pixel rule also works for folks with wider displays. Even though they have more room to spare, they're less likely to stretch their browser windows to the full possible width (if they did, wider columns lead to extremely long lines of text, which are difficult to read).

Understanding Resolution

A pixel is the smallest unit of measure on a monitor, and is otherwise known as a "dot." For example, a resolution of 1366 x 768 means that a monitor displays a grid of pixels that's 1,366 pixels wide and 768 pixels high (for a total of just over 1 million pixels). The smallest resolution you're likely to find on a desktop or laptop computer today is 1024 x 600, which are the dimensions of a teeny netbook screen (a netbook is a tiny and somewhat underpowered laptop). But remember, people with large monitors won't necessarily size their browser windows to fill up the entire screen. For that reason, 1,000 pixels is a good lower-limit assumption you can make for the width of a browser window.

To get some perspective, you might want to figure out what screen resolution you're using—or even change it. To do so on a Windows PC, right-click the desktop, choose Personalize, click Display Settings, and then adjust the resolution using the handy slider. In earlier versions of Windows, you can find the same settings when you right-click the desktop and then select Properties→Settings. In Mac OS X, click System Preferences→Displays, and then select from the list of resolutions.

A 1,000-pixel-wide display works on tiny smartphone screens, too, sort of. However, even though your page will technically fit on a smartphone display (because smartphones cram plenty of pixels into their super-sharp screens), the text on your page will be too small to read without squinting. That means visitors with mobile devices are in for a bit of zooming and scrolling. You can avoid this using a technology called media queries, but it takes a bit of work (see the box on page 248).

TIP Some web page editors let you open pages in a range of browser window sizes. For example, in Expression Web you can choose File→"Preview in Browser," which has options for a few standard, but old, window sizes. And some web browsers have add-ons that do the same thing. For example, Chrome and Firefox fans can use the Web Developer extension (*http://chrispederick.com/work/web-developer*), which adds a toolbar packed full of handy web design tools, including an option to quickly change the size of the browser window.

The best way to understand the difference between fixed and proportional layouts, and to see the 1,000-pixel rule in action, is to put these techniques into practice. And that's exactly what you'll do in the next section.

▮ Tutorial: Creating a Layout with Multiple Columns

One of the most common web page layouts is a two- or three-column design. The column on the left typically holds navigation buttons or other links. The column in the middle includes the main content for the page, and it takes up the most space. The column on the right, if present, displays additional information, like an advertisement or another set of links.

In the following tutorial, you'll take a basic web page and create a classic three-column layout. You'll make it a fixed-width layout first, then you'll try out a resizable layout, and finally you'll add a few more refinements. By the time you finish, you'll know exactly how to arrange your site with styles.

TIP You get the practice files for this tutorial from the Missing CD (available at *www.missingmanuals.com/cds/caw4*). Look for the Tutorial-8-1 folder (which stands for "Chapter 8, first tutorial"). Inside is the Start folder, which has the set of pages you begin the exercise with, and the End folder, which shows the solution. This tutorial has *two* solutions, and each one is in a separate subfolder inside the End folder. For example, the first page you'll develop has a fixed layout, and you can check the finished page at Tutorial-8-1\End\FixedWidth. The second has a resizable layout, with the final page at Tutorial-8-1\End\Resizable.

Laying the Groundwork

Before you write any style rules, you need to plan your layout.

As you've already seen, you can use style rules to place elements in precise locations on a page. To create a multicolumn layout, for example, you need to create a box for each column and then put each box in a separate location on the page. If you arrange the columns properly, you'll end up with a page divided into a tightly interlocked grid of <div> elements, each with its own content (Figure 8-5).

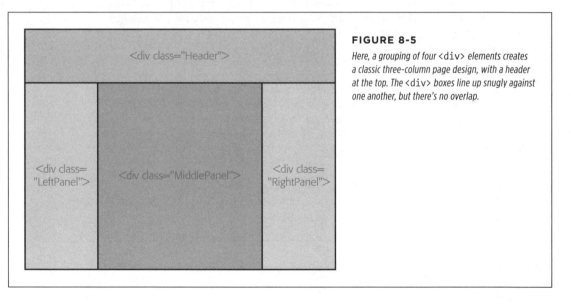

FIGURE 8-5

Here, a grouping of four <div> elements creates a classic three-column page design, with a header at the top. The <div> boxes line up snugly against one another, but there's no overlap.

You don't need to map out the exact dimensions of your layout just yet. First, you need to decide how many sections you want and what each section will contain. Once you do that, you'll know everything you need to write your HTML.

Figure 8-6 shows a page that uses the three-column layout outlined in Figure 8-5. You can find this page, named *ThreeColumns.htm*, in the Start folder for this tutorial.

Initially, the page has all its content but none of the organization (Figure 8-6). It's up to you to enclose each section in a <div> element.

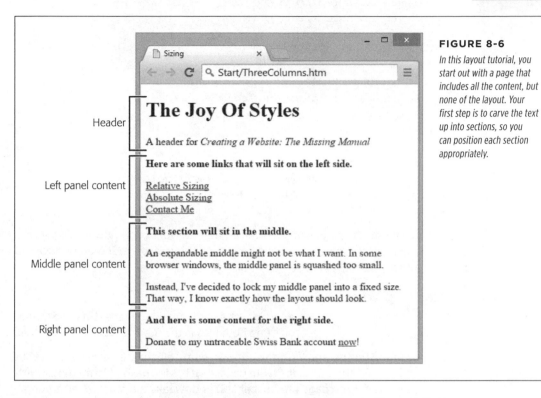

FIGURE 8-6

In this layout tutorial, you start out with a page that includes all the content, but none of the layout. Your first step is to carve the text up into sections, so you can position each section appropriately.

Give each <div> a class name that corresponds to its position in Figure 8-5. For example, the page begins with this content, which represents the header:

```
<h1>The Joy Of Styles</h1>
<p>A header for <i>Creating a Website: The Missing Manual</i></p>
```

Here's how you wrap that header in a <div> element:

```
<div class="Header">
  <h1>The Joy Of Styles</h1>
  <p>A header for <i>Creating a Website: The Missing Manual</i></p>
</div>
```

Repeat this process to add <div> elements for each of the three columns. Altogether, you have to add four <div> elements. Here's what the final HTML should look like:

```
<div class="Header">
  <h1>The Joy Of Styles</h1>
  <p>A header for <i>Creating a Website: The Missing Manual</i></p>
</div>
```

```
<div class="LeftPanel">
  <p><b>Here are some links that will sit on the left side.</b></p>
  <a href="...">Page 1</a><br />
  <a href="...">Page 2</a><br />
  ...
</div>

<div class="MiddlePanel">
  <p><b>This section will sit in the middle.</b></p>
  <p>An expandable middle might not be ...</p>
</div>

<div class="RightPanel">
  <p><b>And here is some content for the right side.</b></p>
  <p>Donate to my untraceable Swiss Bank account ...</p>
</div>
```

When you finish, the page won't look any different—your content will still have the boring, column-less layout shown in Figure 8-6, but you've laid the groundwork to apply your styles and layout settings.

Attaching Your Style Sheet

The *ThreeColumns.htm* example comes with a ready-made style sheet, named (rather logically) *ThreeColumns.css*. You'll find both files in the Start folder for this tutorial.

You need to add two details. First, the *ThreeColumns.css* style sheet lacks the layout instructions necessary to structure your page. All it has is a dash of formatting, which sets a nicer font for the page (Trebuchet MS) and tweaks the font size all around.

Second, the *ThreeColumns.htm* page doesn't actually use the *ThreeColumns.css* style sheet. You can rectify that by opening *ThreeColumns.htm* and adding a <link> element in the <head> section of the page, like so:

```
<head>
  <title>Sizing</title>
  <link rel="stylesheet" href="ThreeColumns.css" />
</head>
```

By this point in the book, attaching a style sheet is nothing new. Now you're ready to move on to the real work, writing the layout rules.

Building a Fixed-Width Layout

Before you can position the <div> elements that shape your page, you need to decide whether you want a fixed-width or a resizable layout. (Flip back to page 236 for a summary of the differences.) In the following sections, you'll learn to create both, but you'll start with a classic fixed-width layout.

To set up a fixed-width layout, you need to decide on the exact pixel width of each `<div>` element. Here are some good starting widths for this example:

- 100 pixels for the left panel
- 450 pixels for the middle panel
- 150 pixels for the right panel

This adds up (with a bit of margin space in between), to a total of about 700 pixels.

TIP If you go with a fixed layout, follow the 1,000-pixel guideline to make sure visitors don't need to do any side-to-side scrolling. It's also a good idea to restrict any individual column of text to a maximum width of 600 to 700 pixels. Any wider and you run into the problem of long lines of text, where readers can lose their place as they skip to a new line and have to scan back across the page to the left edge.

Once you decide how to allocate your space, you simply need to create three style rules, one for each column. As in the examples you saw earlier, you control the horizontal placement of a column by setting its `left` coordinate, and you let the content determine its total height.

The following style rule defines a panel that's 100 pixels wide and positioned along the left side of a page:

```
.LeftPanel {
  position: absolute;
  left: 0px;
  width: 100px;
  padding: 15px;
}
```

The middle panel starts at the 120-pixel mark and takes up another 450 pixels. That leaves 20 pixels of blank space between the right side of the left panel and the left side of the middle panel. The middle panel also separates itself from the content on the left side using border properties.

```
.MiddlePanel {
  position: absolute;
  left: 120px;
  width: 450px;
  border-left-width: 1px;
  border-right-width: 1px;
  border-top-width: 0px;
  border-bottom-width: 0px;
  border-style: solid;
  border-color: blue;
  padding: 15px;
}
```

Finally, the panel on the right side starts at the 605-pixel mark and takes up 150 pixels.

```
.RightPanel {
    position: absolute;
    left: 605px;
    width: 150px;
    padding: 15px;
}
```

Although you could use absolute positioning for the <div> that holds the header at the top of the page, you don't need to, because the header comes first in the HTML. As a result, a browser displays the header and then starts adding the other <div> elements at the locations you specified, so that the top of each panel starts just underneath the header. (Another option is to manually set the height property for the header and the top property for the two side panels, to explicitly set the horizontal placement of each section.)

You can see the result in Figure 8-7. And if you run into trouble, you can double-check your changes against the official solution in the Tutorial-8-1\End\FixedWidth folder.

The remarkable thing about this example is that your HTML document is free of messy formatting details. Instead, it's a small miracle of clarity, with content divided into several easy-to-understand sections. And because all the style rules are in an external style sheet, you can build a second page using the same HTML and without spending any time puzzling out the correct formatting.

DESIGN TIME

Centering a Fixed-Width Layout

Sometimes, webmasters center fixed-width layouts horizontally. That way, their content always appears in the center of a browser window rather than smushed up against the left edge.

Implementing this design is fairly easy in theory, but it can be a bit tricky in practice. First, you need to wrap your entire layout in another <div> element. In this example, it's named *BodyContainer*:

```
<div class="BodyContainer">
    <div class="Header">...</div>
    <div class="Left">...</div>
    <div class="Middle">...</div>
    <div class="Right">...</div>
</div>
```

Then you need to set the width of this <div> to the total width of your full layout, and you need to set the right and left margins to auto:

```
.BodyContainer {
    width: 750px;
    margin-left: auto;
    margin-right: auto;
}
```

When you set auto margins on both sides, the browser automatically makes them equal. The result is that your <body> element ends up centered in the middle of the browser window.

But using this technique presents another problem: you can't absolutely position any of the <div> elements for the columns. The workaround is to float all the <div> columns on the left, one after the other. As long as you set a fixed width for each column and add them in the right order, this technique works without a hitch. To see it in practice, check out the *AbsoluteSizing_Centered.htm* file with the examples for this chapter on the companion site (*http://prosetech.com/web*).

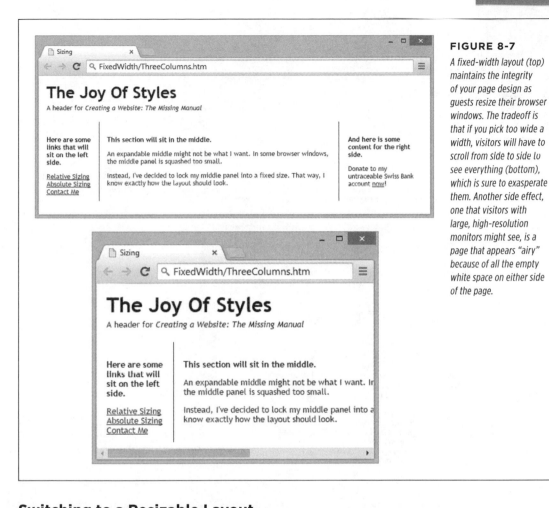

FIGURE 8-7

A fixed-width layout (top) maintains the integrity of your page design as guests resize their browser windows. The tradeoff is that if you pick too wide a width, visitors will have to scroll from side to side to see everything (bottom), which is sure to exasperate them. Another side effect, one that visitors with large, high-resolution monitors might see, is a page that appears "airy" because of all the empty white space on either side of the page.

Switching to a Resizable Layout

A resizable layout is one in which the middle column—the one with the main content of your page—expands to take advantage of the available browser space. Figure 8-8 shows the difference.

One of the great joys of style-based layout is the fact that you can change your page design without changing the structure of your HTML. For example, the easiest way to create the resizable layout shown in Figure 8-8 is to adapt the fixed-width style sheet you built in the previous section. (If you're starting from scratch, just grab it from the folder Tutorial-8-1\End\FixedWidth.) You can convert it into a resizable layout by making a few small changes to the style rules that govern the three columns.

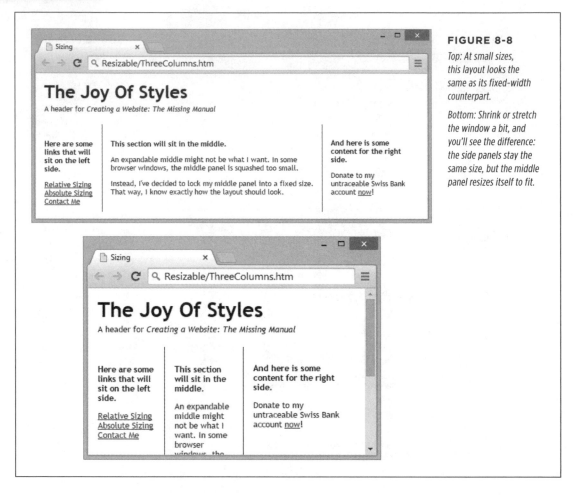

FIGURE 8-8

Top: At small sizes, this layout looks the same as its fixed-width counterpart.

Bottom: Shrink or stretch the window a bit, and you'll see the difference: the side panels stay the same size, but the middle panel resizes itself to fit.

First, consider the rule for the left panel. Interestingly, you don't need to change this style at all. It can still use absolute positioning to lock onto the side of the page:

```
.LeftPanel {
  position: absolute;
  left: 0px;
  width: 100px;
  padding: 15px;
}
```

The panel on the right is slightly different. Because you don't know how wide the middle section will be, you don't know what its left coordinate should be. You get around this in an interesting way: by using the right position property. This places the <div> for the right panel in relation to the *right* side of the browser window, so

0px is smack up against the right edge, 100px is 100 pixels to the left, and so on. In this example, you give the panel 10 pixels of extra space to make sure its content doesn't rub up against the right border of the browser window. Here's the new style rule with the changed line highlighted in bold:

```
.RightPanel {
    position: absolute;
    right: 10px;
    width: 150px;
    padding: 15px;
}
```

The final step is to define the content section that sits between these two panels. You can't use absolute positioning for this, because you don't know how wide your guest's browser will be. Fortunately, there's another trick you can use—margin space. To make this work, you pretend that your middle panel has the full run of the browser window, like any normal piece of content. However, you pad the left and right margins with enough space to leave room for the side panels.

In this example, the left panel measures 100 pixels wide. Add 20 pixels of space in between, and that means your center panel needs a left margin of 120 pixels. The right margin is 190 pixels, because you need 150 pixels to accommodate the width of the right panel, plus 30 pixels of margin space for both sides of the center panel, and 10 extra pixels to compensate for the space you left between the right panel and the right edge of the browser window. Here's the final style sheet rule:

```
.MiddlePanel {
    margin-left: 120px;
    margin-right: 190px;
    border-left-width: 1px;
    border-right-width: 1px;
    border-top-width: 0px;
    border-bottom-width: 0px;
    border-style: solid;
    border-color: blue;
    padding: 15px;
}
```

Notice that the middle panel no longer has the position: absolute setting.

This solution presents a problem, however. Because the middle panel no longer uses absolute positioning, the right panel gets bumped down the page, so that the top of the right panel aligns with the bottom of the middle panel. To fix this, you *could* reshuffle your markup, putting the <div> elements for the left and right panels *before* the <div> for the middle panel. But it's always better if you can make layout changes without touching your markup. In this case, the problem is more easily solved by explicitly moving the right panel up the page, back to its proper position, with the help of the top property. Here's the style rule, which assumes a header that's 90 pixels high:

```
.RightPanel {
    position: absolute;
    top: 90px;
    right: 10px;
    width: 150px;
    padding: 15px;
}
```

Now, just five small style sheet changes later, you've replaced the layout of your page. And you don't need to stop there—with a few more edits, you can change the panel widths, swap the panels from one side to the other, or even transform a panel into a footer.

UP TO SPEED

Super-Flexible Sites: The Zen of Web Design

Style sheets not only let you apply formatting and layout to a page, they also let you *change* the formatting and layout in one (immensely gratifying) step. This is the holy grail of web design—a simple, efficient way to update, revamp, and customize an entire site as your needs change. Figure 8-9 shows the CSS Zen Garden example website, which demonstrates this vision.

Here's a quick recap of the design steps you need to follow to make flexible design work on your website:

1. Plan your pages before you write a single HTML tag. Divide your page into distinct regions.

2. Put each region into a separate `<div>` element.

3. Give each `<div>` element a unique class name that reflects its purpose, not its format. Do this for every section of a page, even if you don't intend to apply style sheet rules to it right now.

4. Finally, write the style sheet rules that position and format each `<div>` element. This is the most time-consuming part of your markup to write, but it's time well spent—you can tweak your formatting rules at any time, without disturbing your content.

Maximum Width: The Safety Net

When you create a resizable layout, you can run into two types of trouble. The first problem occurs if your visitor shrinks her browser window to ridiculously narrow dimensions. Space becomes so constricted that even a single word can't fit in the middle column, and the separate sections begin to overlap. This isn't a huge problem—after all, most people don't expect a website to keep looking pretty when squashed paper-thin—but it's still a bit short of a professional page.

The second issue rears its head if a visitor expands his browser window to fill all the space on a widescreen, high-resolution monitor. In that case, the middle panel is so wide that the text fits on just two or three lines. Besides looking odd, it's extraordinarily difficult to read.

FIGURE 8-9

One page, dozens of looks. The website www.css zengarden.com *shows you how you can thoroughly reformat and reorganize an ordinary page (top left) just by switching the style sheet it uses. Best of all, you can download the HTML and dozens of sample style sheets for this page so you can see the power of style sheets for yourself.*

You can prevent both these problems using two more CSS properties: max-width and min-width. The max-width property sets a maximum width beyond which an element will not expand, and the min-width property sets a minimum width beyond which an element will not shrink. Essentially, when you hit these limits, your page turns into a fixed layout. Expand the page further than the maximum, and you get extra white space. Shrink it smaller than the minimum, and the browser gives you scroll bars.

You might think that you can put this technique into practice by applying max-width and min-width to the middle panel only. And you can—but the result won't be exactly what you want. If you limit the growth of the middle panel, the right panel will still follow the right edge of the browser and will gradually move farther and farther away from the center panel's content. The solution is to wrap the entire page, with all its panels, in *another* <div> container, as shown here:

```
<!DOCTYPE html>
<html>
<head>
  ...
</head>
<body>
  <div class="BodyContainer">
    <div class="Header">...</div>
```

```
        <div class="LeftPanel">...</div>
        <div class="RightPanel">...</div>
        <div class="MiddlePanel">...</div>
      </div>
    </body>
  </html>
```

Then you can set maximum and minimum size rules for this <div>:

```
.BodyContainer {
  position: absolute;
  max-width: 1000px;
  min-width: 100px;
}
```

This creates a perfect compromise between flexible and fixed-width sizing. Now the middle column adapts to the best possible width within reasonable constraints, and the page looks professional no matter the size of the browser window. You can find the final solution for this exercise in the Tutorial-8-1\End\Resizable folder.

POWER USERS' CLINIC

Switching Between Layouts Using a Media Query

The hottest new trend in website design is a CSS3 feature called *media queries*, which let you switch between different layouts.

Using media queries, you can create one layout that works for wide windows (usually a fixed layout), and then switch to another one for narrower windows, and maybe even a third one for *really* tiny screens, like those on smartphones. The advantage to this approach is that it lets you create a site that gracefully adapts itself to a range of devices. The disadvantage is that it's significantly more complicated to pull off, because you need to juggle another layer of overlapping style rules that extend or override your original rules. And because media queries are a relatively new part of CSS, not all browsers support them.

If you're interested in experimenting with media queries, you'll find an entire chapter on the subject in *HTML5: The Missing Manual*. Or you can jump into the deep end with a Smashing Magazine article on the subject at *http://tinyurl.com/mq-for-mobile*. And if you simply want to take a peek and tinker, you can find a version of the three-column layout example that uses media queries in the MediaQueries folder, found with the example files for this chapter. It uses media queries to rearrange the layout for very narrow pages, putting the left panel at the top, above the content, and the right panel at the bottom, after the content. Expand the browser window and the panels spring back to their proper positions, at the side of the main content.

■ A Few More Layout Techniques

Now that you've taken your first steps to becoming a style sheet layout guru, it's time to cover a few more techniques you might need to know. You won't use all of them, but they're good to keep in your back pocket.

Stretching Column Height

So far, you've focused on making columns the correct width, but you haven't worried much about height. After all, a browser takes care of that by making an element just big enough to fit its content, along with any extra padding you specified with the padding property (page 91).

But there are several situations in which you need to size a column based on the height of the browser window, rather than on the content it contains. For example, you might need to apply a background color that fills an entire column, not just the portion with text in it. Or you might want to use borders that stretch to the bottom of the window (unlike the borders in the examples you've seen so far, which end with the text). Figure 8-8 shows this effect in practice.

Fortunately, you can dictate height using the min-height property. The trick is to use a *percentage* size instead of a pixel size. For example, if you set min-height to 100 percent, the column will stretch to fill the browser window, even if you have only a small amount of content.

Here's the formatting rule for the side panels in Figure 8-10:

```
.LeftPanel {
  position: fixed;
  top: 0px;
  left: 0px;
  left-padding: 10px;
  width: 150px;
  min-height: 100%;
  background-color:#eee;
  border-right-width: 1px;
  border-right-style: solid;
  border-right-color: black;
  padding-bottom: 8px;
}

.RightPanel {
  position: fixed;
  top: 0px;
  right: 0px;
  width: 150px;
  min-height: 100%;
  background-color:#eee;
  border-left-width: 1px;
  border-left-style: solid;
  border-left-color: black;
}
```

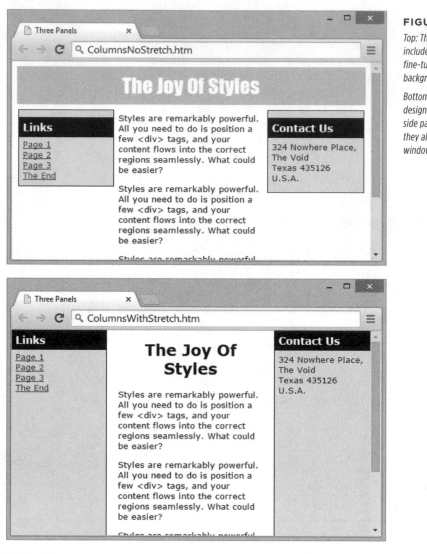

FIGURE 8-10

Top: This three-panel layout includes a few refinements, like fine-tuned borders, fonts, and background colors.

Bottom: A variation of the same design sets the height of the side panels to 100 percent, so they always fill up a browser window.

It's important to note that this example includes a slight change to the position property. Before, you set it to absolute, which placed an element on a page using absolute coordinates. A value of fixed places the element using absolute coordinates, too, but it positions the element *relative to the viewport*—that's the window of content your browser displays on a single screen. In many cases, absolute and fixed have the same effect, but in this situation the distinction is important. That's because you want to size the panels relative to the size of the browser window, not relative to the size of the entire web page. If you use absolute positioning, the side panels might grow larger than necessary, forcing the browser to show scroll bars.

Sticky Headers

Fixed positioning is also the kernel of another neat trick: sticky headers. A sticky header is a bar that sticks to the top of the window and stays there, even when you scroll down. Usually, the point of a sticky header is to keep a small set of navigation links or buttons handy even as guests move through a lengthy page. The fanciest sticky headers incorporate JavaScript code that shrinks the header to just the essentials (like navigation buttons) and keeps it at the top of the screen as guests scroll down. It's particularly common on blogs and news sites (see the news and gossip site *www.salon.com* for an example).

To create a sticky header, you add two <div> elements, one for the header, and one for everything else. Here's the basic arrangement:

```
<body>
  <div class="Header">
    <h1>The Joy Of Styles</h1>
    <p>A sticky header for <i>Creating a Website: The Missing Manual</i></p>
  </div>

  <div class="BodyContainer">
    ...
  </div>
</body>
```

For the header, set the position property to fixed, the top property to 0 (to put the header at the top of the page), and the width property to 100% (so the bar stretches from side to side). You must also set the background property to give the bar a background color, so the rest of your content won't show through the bar when a visitor scrolls the page. You can also optionally add a border to separate the header from the rest of the page.

```
.Header {
  position: fixed;
  top: 0px;
  width: 100%;
  background: #6F4D8F;
  color: white;
  border-bottom: 3px solid #351456;
  padding: 15px 15px 0px 15px;
}
```

For the <div> that holds the content underneath, you simply need to set the margin-top property to the approximate height of the header. That way your content won't bump into the header.

```
.BodyContainer {
    margin-top: 80px;
    padding: 20px 70px;
}
```

You put the rest of your layout inside the second `<div>`. You can even use one of the multicolumn layouts you just studied. Figure 8-11 shows a sticky header in action.

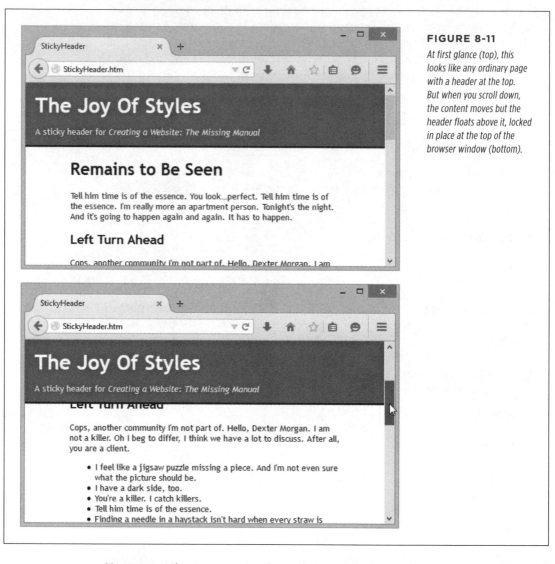

FIGURE 8-11

At first glance (top), this looks like any ordinary page with a header at the top. But when you scroll down, the content moves but the header floats above it, locked in place at the top of the browser window (bottom).

You can use the same approach to create a sticky footer that's locked to the bottom of the browser window. In this case, you set the `bottom` property instead of the `top` property, because you want to position the footer relative to the bottom edge of the browser window.

Layered Elements

Remember how you need to position elements carefully when you use absolute positioning to make sure you don't overlap one element with another? Interestingly, advanced web pages sometimes *deliberately* overlap elements to create dramatic effects. For example, you might create a logo by overlapping two words or create a heading by partially overlapping a picture. These designs use overlapping *layers*.

To use overlapping layers, you need to tell your browser which element goes on top. You do this through a simple number called the *z-index*. Browsers put elements with a high z-index in front of elements with a lower one.

For example, here are two elements positioned absolutely so that they overlap:

```
.Back {
  z-index: 0;
  position: absolute;
  top: 10px;
  left: 10px;
  width: 150px;
  height: 100px;
  background-color: orange;
  border-style: dotted;
  border-width: 1px;
}
.Front {
  z-index: 1;
  position: absolute;
  top: 50px;
  left: 50px;
  width: 230px;
  height: 180px;
  font: xx-large;
  border-style: dotted;
  border-width: 1px;
}
```

The first class (*Back*) defines an orange background square. The second class (*Front*) defines a large font for text. You set the z-index property of both elements so that the browser superimposes the Front box (which has a z-index of 1) over the Back box (which has a z-index of 0). In the example above, the HTML adds a dotted border around both elements to make it easier to see how the boxes overlap on a page.

> **NOTE**   The actual value for the z-index isn't important, but the *relative* value—how one z-index value compares to others—is. For example, if you have two elements with z-index settings of 48 and 100, you'll get the same effect as two elements with values of 0 and 1: The second element overlaps the first. If two or more elements have the same z-index value, the one that's first in the HTML gets shoved underneath those that come later.

In your HTML, you need to create both boxes using <div> elements. It also makes sense to supply some text for the Front box:

```html
<div class="Back">
</div>

<div class="Front">
  This text is on top.
</div>
```

Load this page in a browser and you'll see a block of text that stretches over part of the orange box and out into empty space (see Figure 8-12, left).

You can swap the z-index values to change the example (Figure 8-12, right):

```css
.Back {
  z-index: 1;
  ...
}
.Front {
  z-index: 0;
  ...
}
```

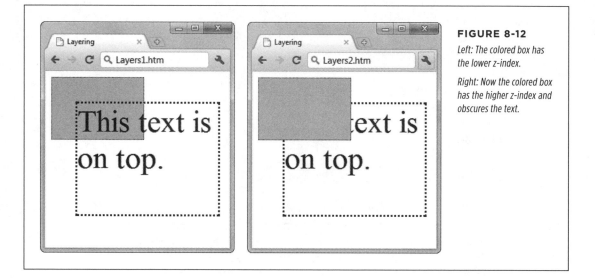

FIGURE 8-12

Left: The colored box has the lower z-index.

Right: Now the colored box has the higher z-index and obscures the text.

Combining Absolute and Relative Positioning

Style sheet experts know that they don't need to stick to just absolute or relative positioning. They can get the best of both worlds with a little careful planning.

To understand how this works, you need to know the following style-sheet secret: When you use absolute positioning, your browser interprets the coordinates *relative to the container*. As you saw in several examples earlier, when you put a <div> element in the <body> section of a page, your browser positions that element in relation to the page. Set the <div> element's left coordinate to 10 pixels, and your browser positions the element 10 pixels from the left edge of the page. But here's a nifty experiment: Try placing the same <div> element inside another element, like a table cell. Now your browser positions the <div> element 10 pixels from the left edge of the table cell, *no matter where you place that table cell on the page*. It's as if the <div> element exists in its own private world—and that's the world of the container that it lives in, not in the world of the main page.

So how can you use this understanding to your advantage? One technique is to use absolute positioning to create a special effect, like text superimposed on a photo. To try this out, create a page with several <div> elements. But don't use absolute positioning—instead, let these <div> elements fit themselves into the page one after the other, the normal web way. In the first and last <div> elements, add ordinary content (text, pictures, and whatever else you like). But in the middle <div>, let loose with absolute positioning.

Figure 8-13 shows an example. Here, the first <div> element holds an ordinary paragraph, as does the third <div> element. But the middle <div> element uses absolute positioning to add white text over the picture of a tombstone.

FIGURE 8-13

On this page, the middle section uses absolute positioning to place text over a picture. The neat part is that the rest of the page is perfectly normal, and even if you shrink the browser window, thereby bumping the picture down the page, the text and picture stay locked together.

```
<div>
  <p>Here is some ordinary content. Whatever you put here
  bumps the grave stone box further down the page.</p>
</div>

<div class="GraveContainer">
  <img alt="Tombstone" src="tombstone.jpg" />
  <p class="GraveText">Fatal error.<br />Please reboot.</p>
</div>

<div>
  <p>Here is some more ordinary content.</p>
</div>
```

The middle <div> element uses two rules to apply all the style properties this example needs. The *GraveText* rule turns on the absolute positioning:

```
p.GraveText {
  position: absolute;
  top: 60px;
  left: 115px;
  color: white;
  font-size: x-large;
  font-weight: bold;
  text-align: center;
}
```

And the *GraveContainer* rule sizes the <div> element. Ordinarily, a <div> element enlarges itself to fit its contents. But when you use absolute positioning, the <div> element no longer knows how big it should be, and it shrinks itself down to nothing. Here's the rule that gives the <div> element the correct height and ensures that the subsequent content on the page (the third <div> element, with the final paragraph in it) appears in the correct place:

```
div.GraveContainer {
  position: relative;
  height: 250px;
}
```

You'll notice that the *GraveContainer* rule uses relative positioning. This allows it to fit into the flow of your web page, without any hassle.

As a general rule, use relative positioning to make sure a page's layout is as flexible and adaptable as possible. But as you see in this example, it's perfectly reasonable to use a <div> element and absolute positioning to style smaller regions—in fact, doing so gives you the chance to add some nifty effects.

Sizing Tables

The time when tables were used to shape the layout of a page is distant history. However, tables still play a role in web pages as an easy way to show grids of information (like the population statistics in Figure 8-14).

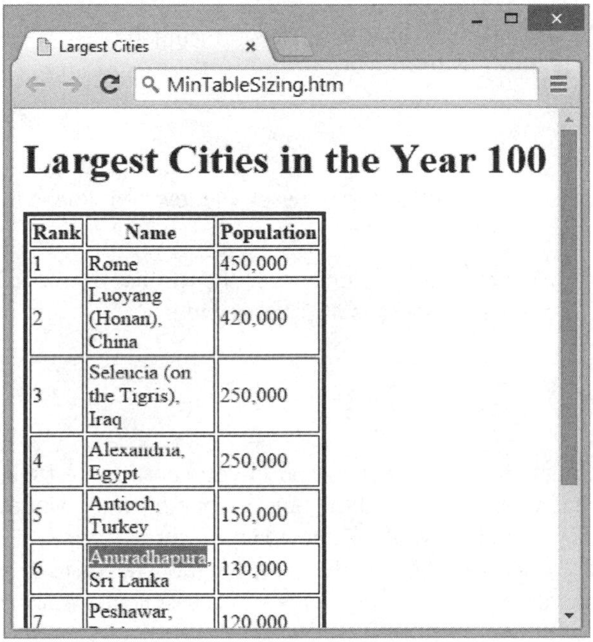

FIGURE 8-14

In this example, the style sheet calls for a table width of 1 pixel. But the browser doesn't shrink the table down that far because the content influences the table's minimum size. The city name Anuradhapura is the longest unsplittable value, so the browser uses that name to determine the width of the column. If you really want to ratchet the size down another notch, try shrinking the text by applying a smaller font size.

Ordinarily, HTML makes a table as wide as necessary to display all its columns, and each column grows just wide enough to fit the longest line of text (or to accommodate other content, like a picture). However, there's one additional rule: The table can't grow wider than the browser window. Once a table reaches the full width of the current window, the browser starts wrapping the text inside each column, so that the table grows taller as you pile in more content.

Of course, there are some circumstances when you need to take control of table sizing. For example, you might want to give more space to one column than another. In such a situation, you use the same width and height properties you used to size <div> elements when you organized a page into columns (see page 239).

▮ SIZING AN ENTIRE TABLE

In most cases, you want to explicitly set the width of your table and its individual columns. When you do, the table respects those dimensions and wraps text to accommodate those widths.

When sizing a table, you can use a pixel width or a percentage width. For example, the following rule limits the table to half the width of its current container (which, in an ordinary page, makes it half the width of the page):

```
table.Cities {
  width: 50%;
}
```

To display the table, you cite the table class in your HTML document:

```
<table class="Cities">
    ...
</table>
```

The table dynamically resizes as you resize the browser window so it keeps to its half-window width.

If you use exact pixel widths, the table dimensions never change. For example, the following rule creates a table that's a generous 500 pixels wide:

```
table.Cities {
  width: 500px;
}
```

There's one important caveat to table sizing: Although you can make a table as large as you want (even if it stretches beyond the borders of a browser window if you used absolute sizing), you don't have the same ability to shrink a table. If you specify a table size that's smaller than the minimum size the table needs to display your content, the table ignores your settings and appears at this minimum size (see Figure 8-14).

■ SIZING A COLUMN

Now that you know how to size a table, you probably want to know what your browser does if a table has more than enough space for its content. Once a table reaches its minimum size (just large enough to fit all its content), your browser distributes any extra space proportionately, so that every column increases in width by the same amount.

Of course, this isn't necessarily what you want. You might want a wide descriptive column paired with a narrow column of densely packed text. Or you might want to set columns to a specific size so that all your pages look uniform, even if the content differs.

To set a column's size, you use the width property in conjunction with the <td> and <th> elements. Once again, you can do this proportionately, using a percentage, or exactly, using a pixel width. However, proportional sizing has a slightly different effect when you use it with columns. Earlier, when you used a percentage value for table width, you sized the entire table relative to the width of the page. In that example, you had a table width of 50 percent, which means the table occupied 50 percent of the full width of the page. But when you use a percentage value to set a *column* width, you're defining the percentage of the *table* width that the column should occupy. So when you set a column width of 50%, the column takes up 50 percent of the *table*.

When you specify the width for columns, you need to create a style rule and unique class name for each one, unless you want them all to have exactly the same width.

The following style rules set different widths for each column in the table you saw in Figure 8-14.

```
th.Rank {
  width: 10%;
}
th.Name {
  width: 80%;
}
th.Population {
  width: 10%;
}
```

In this example, the class names match the column titles, which makes it easy to keep track of which rule applies to which column.

NOTE   When you use percentage widths for columns, you don't need to specify values for all three columns. If you leave one out, the browser sizes that column to fill the rest of the space in the table. If you do decide to include percentage widths for each column (as in the previous example), make sure that they add up to 100 percent; otherwise, the browser will override one of your settings, and you won't know how your table will actually appear.

For these rules to take effect, you need to apply them to the corresponding cells:

```
<table class="Cities">
  <tr>
    <th class="Rank">Rank</th>
    <th class="Name">Name</th>
    <th class="Population">Population</th>
  </tr>
  <tr>
    <td>1</td>
    <td>Rome</td>
    <td>450,000</td>
  </tr>
  ...
</table>
```

Notice that you specify widths only for the column elements in the first row (the ones that contain the cell headers in this example). You could apply the rule to every row, but there's really no point. When the browser builds a table, it scans the whole table structure to determine the required size, based on the cell content and any explicit width settings. If you apply a different width to more than one cell in the same column, the browser simply uses the largest value.

SIZING A ROW

You can size a row just as easily as you size a column. The best approach is to use the height property in the `<tr>` attribute, as shown here:

```
tr.TallRow {
  height: 100px;
}
```

When you resize a row, you affect every cell in every column of that row. However, you're free to make each row a different height.

TIP   Need more space inside your table? Style rules make it easy. To add more space between the cell content and its borders, increase the *padding* property for the `<td>` and `<tr>` elements. To add more space between the cell borders and any adjacent cells, up the margin width for the `<td>` and `<tr>` elements.

Putting the Same Content on Multiple Pages

As you start building bigger and more elaborate websites, you'll no doubt discover one of the royal pains of website design: making a common ingredient appear on every page.

For example, you might decide to add a menu of links that lets visitors jump from one section of your site to another. You can place these links in a `<div>` element, and you can use a style rule to put this `<div>` in the correct position on your page. Add that style rule to your external style sheet, and the menu shows up in the right spot across your entire website.

But style sheets have their limits. They can't help you put the same *content* in more than one page. So if you want a menu on every page, you're stuck copying the big block of HTML that has all the links in it and pasting it into each page. If you're not careful—say you inadvertently place the menu in a slightly different spot in a page—one page can end up with a slightly different version of the same menu. And when you decide to make a change to the menu, you face the nightmare of updating every one of your pages. Website creators who try this approach don't get out much on the weekend.

So how do web designers create site-wide chunks of content? Big websites use content management systems or custom web applications that assemble HTML pages on the fly (see the box on page 264). But if you aren't relying on one of these tools, you need a different approach.

You can choose from three potential solutions:

- **Server-side includes.** A server-side include is a command that injects the contents of one HTML file inside another. This lets you create a block of HTML content (for example, a menu) and reuse it in multiple pages. However, there's a caveat: Server-side includes aren't part of the HTML standard. Instead, they're an extension to HTML that work only if your web server supports them. Fortunately, almost all web servers do.

- **Seamless frames.** This is a new HTML5 feature that lets you inject the contents of one page into another using the `<iframe>` element (page 565). It's like a server-side include, except that the *browser* makes the magic happen, not the web server. Seamless frames sound like a great solution, but hands off for now—at present, not a single browser supports them.

- **Web templates.** Some high-powered web page editors (namely, Dreamweaver and Expression Web) include a template feature. You begin by creating a template that defines the structure of your web pages and includes the repeating content you want to appear on every page (like a menu or header). Your web editor then generates the final pages. But don't get too excited, because this technique has a few hidden deal-breakers. The most significant problem is that minor changes (like adding a link to a menu) force your editor to open, update, and upload *every page* in your entire site. Another serious problem is that web templates aren't standardized in any way, which means that once you start using web templates, you're locked in—you can't switch to another web editor without rewriting your entire site.

The best way for the average web developer to solve the problem is with server-side includes, and you'll learn how to do that in the next section. Seamless frames are best ignored—the feature has gotten little attention in the web world, meaning its future prospects are doubtful. Web templates may make sense for some people, if they're developing tiny sites and don't mind limiting their editing options in the future. You'll find templates covered on page 267.

Using Server-Side Includes

Even though you can't write a web application on your own, you *can* borrow a few tricks from the web application model—if your web host supports it. The simplest example is a technology called *server-side includes* (SSIs), which is a scaled-down version of the HTML-assembling technique used on sites like Amazon and Expedia.

Essentially, a server-side include is an instruction that tells a web server to insert the contents of one HTML file into another. For example, imagine you want to use the same menu on several pages. You would begin by saving the menu as a separate file, which you could name *menu.htm*. Here are its contents:

```
<h1>Menu</h1>
<a href="...">Page 1</a><br />
<a href="...">Page 2</a><br />
<a href="...">Page 3</a><br />
<a href="...">The End</a>
```

Multipart Pages on Big Websites

Popular websites don't seem to have a problem dealing with repeating content. No matter what product you view on Amazon, for example, you see the familiar tabbed search bar at the top. No matter what vacation you check out in Expedia, you keep the same set of navigation tabs. That's because Amazon and Expedia, like almost all of the Web's hugest and most popular sites, are actually *web applications*. When you request a page from one of these sites, a custom-tuned piece of software actually creates the HTML page.

For example, when you view a product on Amazon, a web application reads the product information out of a gargantuan database, transforms it into an HTML page, and tops it off with the latest version of the search bar. Your browser displays the end result as a single page. This technique lets Amazon assemble any pieces of content into a slick web page, without forcing the site designers to maintain thousands (or even millions) of HTML files. The web application approach is a bit like the server-side include approach described below (in both cases, the process involves assembling a whole page out of pieces on the web server), but it's more elaborate.

This sort of custom web application is beyond the reach of an average person. Ordinary people can use a content-management system like WordPress (*http://wordpress.org*), but this involves giving up on the dream of designing everything yourself. If that doesn't suit your vision, you need to use the techniques described in this chapter.

Notice that *menu.htm* isn't a complete HTML document. It lacks elements like <html>, <head>, and <body>. That's because *menu.htm* is a building block that you embed in other, full-fledged HTML pages.

Now you're ready to use the menu in a web page. To do that, you need to add a special instruction to your page where you want the menu to appear. It looks like this:

```
<!--#include file="menu.htm" -->
```

The #include command disguises itself as an HTML comment (page 27) using the <!-- characters at the beginning of the line and the --> characters at the end. But its core tells the real story. The number sign (#) indicates that this command is actually an instruction for the web server, and the *file* attribute points to the file you want to use. In this case, that's the snippet of HTML that holds the menu.

Here's the #include command at work in a complete web page:

```
<!DOCTYPE html>
<html>

<head>
  <title>Server-Side Include Test</title>
  <link rel="stylesheet" href="styles.css" />
</head>
<body>
  <div class="Header">
    <h1>Templates Rule!</h1>
```

```
    </div>
    <div class="MenuPanel">
      <!--#include file="menu.htm" -->
    </div>
    <div class="Content">
      <p>This is the welcome page. Just above this text is the handy menu
      for this site.</p>
    </div>
  </body>
</html>
```

When you request this page, the web server scans through it, looking for instructions. When it finds the #include command, it retrieves the specified file and inserts its contents into that position on the page. It then sends the final, processed file to you. In the current example, that means your web browser receives a web page that actually looks like this:

```
<!DOCTYPE html>
<html>
<head>
  <title>Server-Side Include Test</title>
  <link rel="stylesheet" href="styles.css" />
</head>
<body>
  <div class="Header">
    <h1>Welcome to a Multipart Page</h1>
  </div>
  <div class="MenuPanel">
    <h1>Menu</h1>
    <a href="...">Page 1</a><br />
    <a href="...">Page 2</a><br />
    <a href="...">Page 3</a><br />
    <a href="...">The End</a>
  </div>
  <div class="ContentPanel">
    <p>This is the welcome page. Just to the left of this text is the
    handy menu for this site.</p>
  </div>
</body>
</html>
```

Figure 8-15 shows the final page as it appears in your browser.

The advantage to this technique is obvious. You can add the #include command to as many pages as you want and still keep just one copy of your menu. That lets you edit your menu easily and ensures that all your pages will have the same version of it.

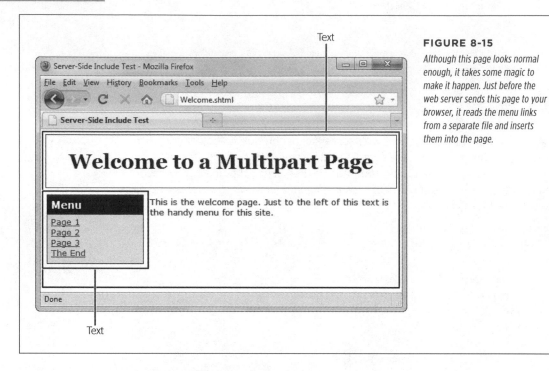

Text

FIGURE 8-15

*Although this page looks normal
enough, it takes some magic to
make it happen. Just before the
web server sends this page to your
browser, it reads the menu links
from a separate file and inserts
them into the page.*

If this discussion sounds a bit too good to be true—well, it is. You may face a number of complications:

- **Web server support.** Not all web servers support server-side includes. To get the lowdown, contact your web hosting company.

- **Page types.** For a server-side include to work, the web server has to process your page and scan for server-side includes. This process happens automatically, but only if you use the right page type. Usually, you need to use the extension *.shtml* instead of *.htm* or *.html*, but you'll need to check with your web hosting company.

> **NOTE** Don't worry about changing the extension of your pages. The HTML markup inside them will continue to work exactly the same as it did before.

- **Design difficulties.** Server-side includes come into effect only when there's a web server at work. If you open a web page stored on your hard drive, your browser ignores the Include instruction, and you won't see the menu at all. That makes it difficult to test your site without uploading it to a live web server. Dreamweaver gives you partial relief—if you open a web page that uses server-side includes, you'll see the contents of the included files in Dreamweaver's design window while you edit the page.

If you know that your web host supports server-side includes and you aren't fazed by the design difficulties, why not give them a whirl?

PHP Includes

Server-side includes are nearly as old as the Web itself. These days, web weavers more commonly use the `include` command in PHP, which is a popular server-side programming language. The PHP include command works in almost exactly the same way as the #include command you saw in the previous section, but it looks like this:

```
<?php include "menu.htm"; ?>
```

Here, the <?php tag designates the start of a PHP script block, and the ?> marks the ending. Inside the block, you put as many lines of PHP as you want. In this case, the script block has just a single line, which injects the contents of the *menu.htm* file into the page.

There's one more difference with the PHP `include` command. As you just learned, pages that use includes need a different file extension than the ordinary *.htm* or *.html*. If you use server-side includes, you probably need the extension *.shtml*. If you use PHP includes, you definitely need the extension *.php* (as in *Welcome.php*). But don't worry: if you rename a page to reflect a newly added PHP `include` command, you can still keep editing it in your favorite web editor and keep viewing it in your favorite browser.

At this point, you're probably wondering, "If server-side includes and PHP includes are almost identical, why would you prefer one over the other?" The reason is that PHP is commonly used for all sorts of programming tasks, like validating forms and reading from giant databases of information. So if there's a chance your site might use PHP, you may as well use PHP's `include` command. And if you aren't using PHP—which describes you, as a beginning website builder—there's no harm in getting yourself ready for the future.

NOTE If the *.php* extension really bothers you, it's possible to change the configuration on your web server so that it checks all your HTML pages for PHP code. That way, you can use the `include` command in ordinary *.html* or *.htm* files. Making this change is usually as simple as adding a single line to a configuration file on your website (see *http://tinyurl.com/php-in-html*). However, this is one configuration task you don't want to mess up, so talk to your web host first.

Web Templates

So far, you've seen how you can put the same content on a whole batch of pages using server-side includes. This approach is great—if you don't mind the design challenges. After all, the alternative (making a separate copy of the repeated content on each page) is a surefire way to fry the last few neurons of your overworked brain.

However, web designers who own Adobe Dreamweaver have one more option: They can create a web template that sets out the structure of their site pages, and then reuse that template relentlessly. The technique is similar to server-side includes, but instead of having a web server do the work, you give the task to your web page editing program (Figure 8-16).

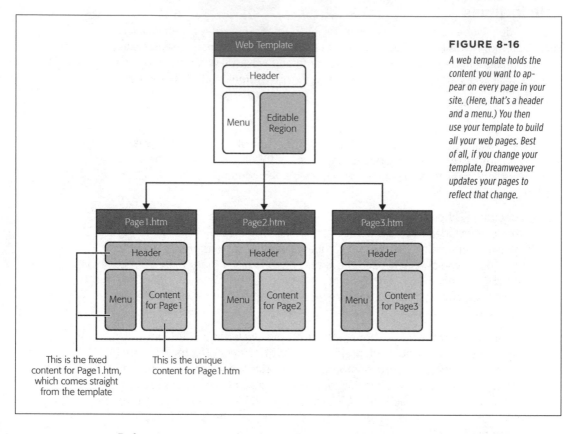

FIGURE 8-16

A web template holds the content you want to appear on every page in your site. (Here, that's a header and a menu.) You then use your template to build all your web pages. Best of all, if you change your template, Dreamweaver updates your pages to reflect that change.

This is the fixed content for Page1.htm, which comes straight from the template

This is the unique content for Page1.htm

Before you get started with templates, it's time to face a few drawbacks:

- **More time.** Every time you change a template, your web design tool needs to update all the pages that use the template. For this reason, web templates aren't a great idea for huge websites, because the updating process takes too long.

- **More fragile.** As you'll see, the template system is based on a few secret comments you bury in your HTML pages. Unfortunately, it's all too easy to accidentally delete or move one of these comments and break the link between a page and its template. When using templates, you need to edit your pages with extra caution.

- **Nonstandard.** Web templates work differently in different web editors. If you use templates to craft the perfect website in Expression Web, you can't switch your site over to Dreamweaver (or vice versa)—at least not without a painstaking conversion process that you have to carry out by hand.

If you're willing to put up with these shortcomings to create true multipart pages, keep reading.

> **NOTE** Expression Web's template system is similar to Dreamweaver's. But, as you learned in Chapter 5, Expression Web is nearing the end of its life, and its template system will die with it. For that reason, we don't recommend building a site with Expression Web templates—the risk is just too great that you'll need to switch editors and you'll have no way to take your carefully crafted template file with you.

■ CREATING A WEB TEMPLATE

To use Dreamweaver's template system, you need to create a *.dwt* file, which stands for Dreamweaver Web Template. In a typical website, you create one template that standardizes your layout. Then you use that template to create all the HTML pages on your site.

To create a new, empty template in Dreamweaver, follow these steps:

1. **Before getting started, make sure you define your website, as described on page 161.**

   Dreamweaver always puts templates in the Templates subfolder of your website folder. If you don't define a website, you'll still be able to create a template, but you won't be able to apply it to other pages, which makes it relatively useless.

2. **Choose File→New.**

   Dreamweaver's New Document window appears.

3. **On the left, choose Blank Page. In the Page Type list, choose HTML Template.**

   In the Layout list, keep the standard option ("<none>") highlighted. You can use other layouts, but this example assumes you're creating the entire template from scratch.

   This is also a good time to pick the doctype you want from the DocType list, so you don't need to change it by hand after you create the template.

4. **Click Create.**

   This creates a new template, with the bare minimum of markup. In the following sections, you'll learn how to customize the template.

After you finish perfecting your template, choose File→Save; the Save As Template dialog box opens. From the Site list, pick the defined site where you want to store the template. It starts out with a name like *Untitled_1.dwt*, but you can type in a better name, and then click Save to make it official. Dreamweaver stores the template in the Templates subfolder of your website folder.

You now have a brand-new web template. But right now your template is little more than a basic HTML skeleton. To turn it into something useful, you need to understand a bit more about how templates work.

Surprisingly, a web template looks a whole lot like an ordinary web page. In fact, you can edit your template in Dreamweaver in the same way you edit any other HTML file. However, there's a difference: Any HTML markup that you put in a template becomes *fixed content*.

Dreamweaver uses fixed content as the basis for every page you create with the template. For example, if you pop a menu bar and a bunch of <div> elements into the template, every page gets that same menu bar and those same <div> elements. And you can modify this fixed content only in the page template itself; you can't edit fixed content in the pages the template creates. To be able to edit any part of a page created from a template, you need to include one or more editable regions.

■ ADDING EDITABLE REGIONS TO YOUR TEMPLATE

The trick to designing a good template is to add *editable regions* wherever you need them, in the midst of your fixed content. Editable regions are areas where you insert each page's unique content.

To create an editable region, Dreamweaver uses specialized comments. Although these look like ordinary HTML comments, they actually identify the editable sections of a page. These comments come in pairs, so the first one defines the start of an editable region, while the second one demarcates its end:

```
<!-- TemplateBeginEditable name="body" -->
...
<!-- TemplateEndEditable -->
```

There are two things to notice here. First, comments begin with the standard comment indicator <!--followed by a specific command (like TemplateBeginEditable). That's how Dreamweaver recognizes that the comment is actually a template instruction. Second, you can see that the comments give your editable region a name. In this example, the region is named "body."

To really understand how editable regions work, you need to see them in the context of a complete example. Figure 8-17 shows a suitable candidate—a simple multipart page with a header and a menu. It closely resembles the server-side include example you saw earlier (page 263).

In this example, the header and navigation bar are fixed, unchangeable elements. The editable content region is the portion that appears under the header and just to the right of the menu bar.

The most straightforward way to create an editable region is to type the magic comments into Code view on your own (Figure 8-18). Alternatively, you can choose Insert→Template Objects→Editable Region. Web designers in a hurry can press the shortcut key combination Alt+Ctrl+V.

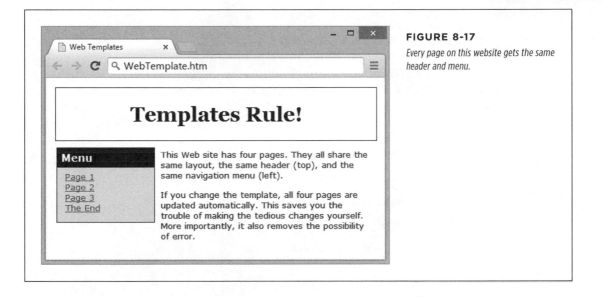

FIGURE 8-17

Every page on this website gets the same header and menu.

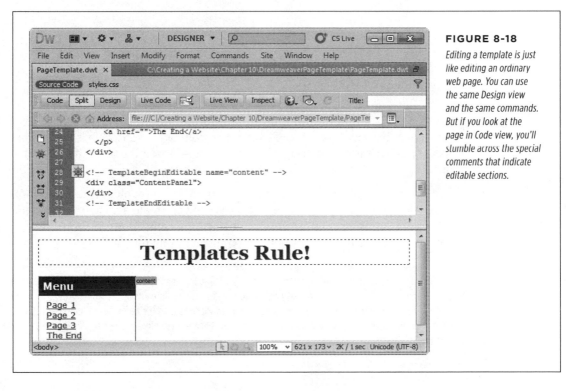

FIGURE 8-18

Editing a template is just like editing an ordinary web page. You can use the same Design view and the same commands. But if you look at the page in Code view, you'll stumble across the special comments that indicate editable sections.

Here's the finished template for the page in Figure 8-17:

```
<!DOCTYPE html>
<html>
<head>
  <!-- TemplateBeginEditable name="title" -->
  <title></title>
  <!-- TemplateEndEditable -->
  <link rel="stylesheet" href="styles.css" />
</head>
<body>
  <div class="Header">
    <h1>Templates Rule!</h1>
  </div>
  <div class="MenuPanel">
    <h1>Menu</h1>
    <p>
      <a href="">Page 1</a><br />
      <a href="">Page 2</a><br />
      <a href="">Page 3</a><br />
      <a href="">The End</a>
    </p>
  </div>
  <!-- TemplateBeginEditable name="content" -->
  <div class="ContentPanel">
  </div>
  <!-- TemplateEndEditable -->
</body>
</html>
```

Notice that this example actually creates two editable regions. One is the content that appears to the right of the menu panel, and the other is the title at the top of the browser window. Thanks to this latter detail, you can give all your pages a unique title.

You'll also notice that both editable regions include some content (like the tags for the <title> element or a <div> element). When you create a page from this template, the editable regions always include these elements. However, you're free to change or replace them with something completely different.

NOTE Because templates use comments, they're a bit fragile. Seemingly minor changes, like deleting one of the comments in a pair, changing a section name, or rearranging comments in the wrong order, can cause problems. At worst, Dreamweaver will become so confused that updating the template will erase part of your page. To avoid issues like these, always make a backup of your website before you begin editing it, especially when templates are involved.

■ USING YOUR WEB TEMPLATE

Once you finish your template, you're ready to use it to create some pages. Here's how it goes down:

1. **Choose File→New.**

   Dreamweaver's New Document window opens.

2. **On the left of the New Document window, choose "Page from Template." Then, in the Site list, choose your website.**

   You'll see all the templates in your website's Templates folder listed.

3. **Select the template you want, and then click Create.**

   You'll see the markup for both fixed and editable content in your new page. You won't be able to change the fixed content, which comes directly from the template. Dreamweaver displays the fixed content in light gray to remind you that it's off limits.

   Make sure you keep the "Update page when template changes" checkbox selected. This way, when you change your template, Dreamweaver updates all the pages that use it.

To create the page shown in Figure 8-17, you simply add a title and a couple of paragraphs of text in the editable content region. Here's the finished page in Dreamweaver:

```
<!DOCTYPE html>
<html>
<!-- InstanceBegin template="/Templates/PageTemplate.dwt"
codeOutsideHTMLIsLocked="false" -->
<head>
  <!-- InstanceBeginEditable name="title" -->
  <title>Web Templates</title>
  <!-- InstanceEndEditable -->
  <link rel="stylesheet" href="styles.css" />
</head>
<body>
  <div class="Header">
    <h1>Templates Rule!</h1>
  </div>
  <div class="MenuPanel">
    <h1>Menu</h1>
    <p>
      <a href="">Page 1</a><br />
      <a href="">Page 2</a><br />
      <a href="">Page 3</a><br />
      <a href="">The End</a>
    </p>
  </div>
```

```
<!-- InstanceBeginEditable name="content" -->
<div class="ContentPanel">
  <p> This website has four pages. They all share the same layout,
  the same header (top), and the same navigation menu (left).</p>
  ...
</div>
<!-- InstanceEndEditable -->
</body>
<!-- InstanceEnd --></html>
```

When you use a template to build a page in Dreamweaver, the new page's comments are slightly different from those in the original page. For example, Dreamweaver replaces the TemplateBeginEditable instruction with an InstanceBeginEditable command.

NOTE When it's time to upload your website to a server, remember that you want to upload your web pages, not your templates. The templates are for your design convenience, and you use them only on your computer.

This example shows just a single page. You see the real advantages of a template when you create dozens of pages based on it. In every case, to create a new page, you need do nothing more than set a title and add a bit of content.

But you'll see the biggest benefit when you change the original template. For example, imagine you modify the template to use a spiffy new graphic for its header:

```
<div class="Header">
  <img src="TemplatesRule.jpeg" alt="Templates Rule!" />
</div>
```

Once you save your changes, your web page editor asks if you want to apply those changes to all the linked pages in the current website. Say Yes, and the editor quickly and quietly opens all the pages that use the template and updates them with the new content. The result is an instant face-lift for your site (see Figure 8-19).

NOTE Although this chapter gives you a basic introduction to the template system, you may need to consider other subtleties. For example, you may make changes to a template so dramatic that the edited template becomes incompatible with the pages that currently use it. Or you might want to rewire an existing page to use a different template. To learn about the finer points of web templates, consult a dedicated Dreamweaver resource, such as *Dreamweaver CC: The Missing Manual* (O'Reilly).

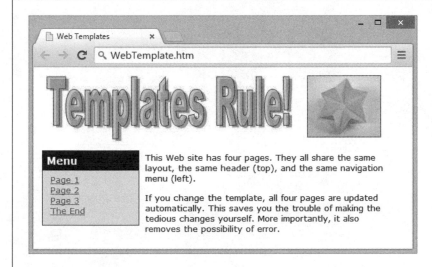

FIGURE 8-19

This header graphic really makes your web pages stand out. But the best part is that you never cracked open Page1.htm to add this graphic. Instead, your web page editor did the updating for you.

Getting Your Site Online

B y this point, you know how to build a complete, basic website. You've written HTML pages, formatted them with style sheets, incorporated some pictures, and linked everything together. But all this work is for naught if you don't put your page online so your legions of fans (or your uncle Dan in Fresno) can visit it on the Web.

In this chapter, you'll learn how web servers work and how to put them to work for you. Armed with these high-tech nerd credentials, you'll be ready to search for your own *web host*, a company that lets you park your site on its web server. All you need to do is figure out your requirements, see which hosts offer what you need, and start comparison-shopping.

■ How Web Hosting Works

As you learned in Chapter 1, the Web isn't stored on any single computer, and no company owns it. Instead, the individual pieces (websites) are scattered across millions of computers known as web servers. And while it may seem like all these sites are part of a single environment, in reality, the Internet is just a set of standards that let independent computers talk to one another.

Understanding Web Servers

Web servers are the computers that store HTML pages. When you type a web address into your browser, the browser sends your request to the web server that hosts the site. When the server receives the request, it carries out a simple and essential task—it *serves* the corresponding page to the person who wants it.

For a busy website, this basic task can add up to a lot of work. As a result, web servers tend to be industrial-strength computers. Even though the average Windows PC with the right setup can host a website, it's rarely worth the effort (see the box on page 310). Instead, most people get a commercial company, called a *web host*, to rent them a little space on one of their servers for a small monthly fee. In other words, to put your site online, you need to lease some space on the Web.

Sometimes, you can rent this space from the same company you use to get online in the first place, called an Internet service provider, or ISP; it may even include server space as part of your Internet connection package. But the most straightforward way to get your site online is to use a web hosting company. Either way, you're going to copy your newly built website to some far-off computer that will make sure a worldwide audience can enjoy your talents.

Understanding URLs

Now that you know where you're going to put your site (on a web server), it's time to answer another question—how does a browser know which of the thousands of web servers to call when someone requests one of your pages? The process involves a bit of traffic direction, and it starts with the *URL* (Uniform Resource Locator), which is simply the website address a web surfer types into his browser.

A URL consists of several pieces. Some are optional, because a browser or web server can fill in those blanks automatically. Others are required. Figure 9-1 dissects the URL *http://www.SellMyJunkForMillions.com/Buyers/listings.htm*.

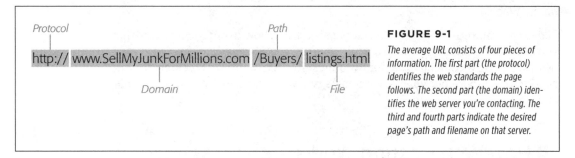

FIGURE 9-1

The average URL consists of four pieces of information. The first part (the protocol) identifies the web standards the page follows. The second part (the domain) identifies the web server you're contacting. The third and fourth parts indicate the desired page's path and filename on that server.

Web addresses pack a lot of detail into a single line of text:

- **The protocol** reflects the standard your browser uses to communicate with web servers. Websites always use the HTTP (HyperText Transfer Protocol) standard, which means the protocol portion of a website URL is always *http://* or *https://*. (The latter establishes a super-secure connection to the Web that encrypts sensitive information you submit, like credit card numbers or passwords.) In most browsers, you can get away without typing in this part of the URL. For example, when you type *www.google.com*, your browser automatically converts it to the full URL, *http://www.google.com*.

NOTE Although *http://* is the way to go when browsing the Web, depending on your browser, you may use other protocols for other tasks. Common examples include *ftp://* (FIle Transfer Protocol) for uploading and downloading files and *file:///* for retrieving a file directly from your own computer's hard drive.

- **The domain name** identifies the server that hosts the site you want to see. By convention, server names usually start with *www* to identify them as World Wide Web servers. In addition, as you'll discover later in this chapter, friendly domain names like *www.google.com* or *www.microsoft.com* are really just stand-ins for what your browser really needs in order to locate a server—namely, its numeric address (see page 281).

- **The path** identifies the folder where the server stores the web page you're looking for. This part of the URL can have as many levels as needed. For example, the path */MyFiles/Sales/2011/* refers to a MyFiles folder that contains a Sales folder that, in turn, contains a folder named 2011. Windows fans, take note—the slashes in the path portion of a URL are ordinary forward slashes, not the backward slashes used in Windows file paths (like *c:\MyFiles\Current*). This convention matches the file paths Unix-based computers use, which were the first machines to host websites. It's also the convention used in modern Macintosh operating systems.

NOTE Many browsers are smart enough to correct the common mistake of typing in the wrong type of slash. However, you shouldn't rely on this because similar laziness can break the web pages you create. For example, if you use the `<img>` element to link to an image and use the wrong type of slash, your picture won't appear.

- **The filename** is the last part of the path, and it identifies the specific web page you're requesting. Often, you can recognize it by the file extension *.htm* or *.html*, both of which stand for HTML.

NOTE While web pages often end with *.htm* or *.html*, they don't need to. For example, if you look at a URL and see the strange extension *.blackpudding*, odds are you're still looking at an HTML document. In most cases, browsers ignore an extension as long as the file contains information that a browser can interpret. However, just to keep yourself sane, this is one convention you shouldn't break.

- **The fragment** is an optional part of a URL that identifies a specific position within a web page. You can recognize a fragment because it always starts with the number-sign character (#) and appears after a filename. For example, the URL *http://www.LousyDeals.com/index.html#New* includes the fragment *#New*. When you click the URL, it takes you to the section of the *index.html* page where the webmaster placed the New bookmark. (You can learn about bookmarks on page 196.)

- **The query string** is an optional part of a URL that some websites use to send extra information from one web page to another. You can identify one because it starts with a question mark (?) and appears after a filename. To see a query string in action, go to Microsoft's search engine *www.bing.com* and search for "pet platypus." When you click the Search button, Bing creates a URL like *http://www.bing.com/search?q=pet+platypus&form=QBLH&filt=all&qs=n*. This address is a little tricky to analyze, but if you hunt for the question mark and look to the left of it, you'll discover that you're on a page named "search." The information to the right of the question mark indicates that you're executing an English-language search for pages that match both the "pet" and "platypus" keywords. When you request this URL, a specialized Microsoft web program analyzes the query string to determine what to search for.

> **NOTE** You won't use a query string for your own web pages, because it's designed for heavy-duty web programs like the one that powers Bing (or Google). By understanding the query string, however, you gain a bit of insight into how other websites work.

How Browsers Analyze a URL

Clearly, URLs include a lot of detail. But how does a browser actually use one to fetch the web page you want? To understand that, take a peek behind the scenes (see Figure 9-2).

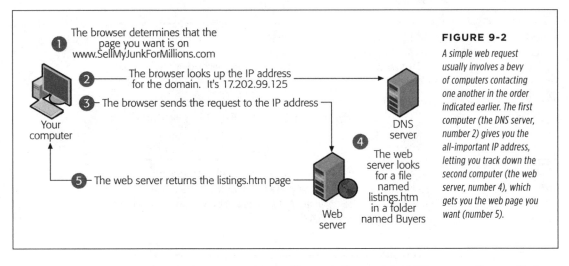

FIGURE 9-2

A simple web request usually involves a bevy of computers contacting one another in the order indicated earlier. The first computer (the DNS server, number 2) gives you the all-important IP address, letting you track down the second computer (the web server, number 4), which gets you the web page you want (number 5).

For example, after you type *http://www.SellMyJunkForMillions.com/Buyers/listings. htm* into a browser's address bar and press Enter, here's what happens:

1. **The browser figures out what web server to contact by extracting the domain name from the URL.**

   In this example, the domain name is *www.SellMyJunkForMillions.com*.

2. **To find the server that hosts** *www.SellMyJunkForMillions.com* **, the browser converts the domain name into a computer-friendly number called the** *IP address***.**

   Every computer on the Web—from web servers to your own machine—has its own unique IP address. To find the IP address for a server, the browser looks up the server's domain name in a giant online catalog called the DNS (Domain Name System). An IP address looks like a set of four numbers separated by periods (or, in techie speak, dots). For example, the *www.SellMyJunkForMillions. com* website may lead to a web server that has the IP address 17.202.99.125.

NOTE The DNS catalog isn't stored on your computer—your browser gets this information from the Internet. You can see the advantage of this approach. Under ordinary circumstances, the domain name for an online business never changes; it's the public face customers use and remember. Behind the scenes, however, its IP address may change, because the business moved its website from one server to another. As long as the business updates the DNS, the move won't cause any disruption. Fortunately, you won't need to worry about managing the DNS yourself if your web host moves to a new server, because the host automatically handles the change for you.

---

3. **The browser sends the page request to the web server's now-retrieved IP address.**

   The actual route the message takes is difficult to predict. It may cross through a number of other servers on the way.

4. **The server receives the request and looks at the path and filename in the URL.**

   In this case, the server sees that the request is for a file named *listings.htm* in a folder called *Buyers*. The server looks up that file and sends it back to the browser. If the file doesn't exist, the server sends back an error message.

5. **The browser receives the HTML page it's been waiting for (***listings.htm***) and then displays it for your viewing pleasure.**

The URL *http://www.SellMyJunkForMillions.com/Buyers/listings.htm* is a typical web address. In the wild, however, you'll sometimes come across URLs that seem a lot simpler. For instance, consider *http://www.amazon.com*. It clearly specifies the domain name (*www.amazon.com*), but it doesn't include any path or filename for a page. So what's a web server to do? It sees that you aren't requesting a specific file, so it sends you the site's fallback page—its *default* page, in geekspeak, which is often named *index.htm* or *index.html*, and is what you know as the site's home page. (However, a web administrator can configure any page as the default.)

Internet vs. Intranet

As you already know, the Internet is a huge network of computers that spans the globe. An *intranet* is a lot smaller; it's a network that exists within a specific company, organization, or home that joins together a much smaller number of computers. In fact, an intranet could have as few as two computers.

An intranet makes sense anytime you need a website available to only a small number of people in one location. For example, a company could use an intranet to share marketing information (or the latest office gossip). In your own home, you could let your housemates browse your web creations from their own computers. The only limitation is that a website on an intranet is accessible to the computers on that network only. Other web visitors won't be able to see it.

Setting up a website for an intranet is easier than setting one up for the Internet because you don't need to register a domain name. Instead, you can use the network computer's name. For example, if your computer has the network name SuperServer, you could visit a web page with a URL like *http://SuperServer/MySite/MyPage.htm*. Of course, this works only if you've set up a home network (easy) and some web server software (a little more complicated). For example, on a Windows computer, you might use the IIS (Internet Information Services) server software, which most versions of Windows include, but you need to explicitly enable and configure the program. These tasks are outside the scope of this book. To learn more, consult a good networking resource.

Domain Names

Before you sign up for a web hosting plan, put some serious thought into the first part of your website address, the domain. It's hard to find a domain name that's both catchy and available. The solution is to brainstorm some ideas and find out what's on the market before you sign up for a hosting plan. That way, you can buy the domain and sign up for a plan at the same time, from the same company. The following sections help you get started.

Choosing the Right Domain Name

Shakespeare may have famously written "What's in a name? That which we call a rose/By any other name would smell as sweet." But he may have seen things differently if he had to type *www.thesweetsmellingredflowerwiththorns.biz* into his browser instead of *www.rose.com*. Short, snappy domain names attract attention and are easy to remember.

Unfortunately, most short, clever word combinations have already been claimed as domain names. Even if they aren't in use, *domain squatters*—people who buy and hold popular names in hopes of selling them to desperate high bidders later—have long since laid claim to common names. Give up on *www.worldsbestchocolate.com*—it's gone. However, you may find success with names that are a little longer or more specific (*www.worldsbestmilkchocolate.com*), use locations or the names of people (*www.bestvermontchocolate.com* or *www.anniesbestchocolate.com*), or introduce made-up words (*www.chocolatech.com*). All these domain names were available at the time of this writing.

NOTE   Valid domain names can include only letters, numbers, and dashes.

Choosing a good domain name isn't an exact science, but you can find plenty of anecdotal evidence on names that don't work. Here are some mistakes to avoid:

- **Too-many-dashes.** It may be tempting to get exactly the domain name you want by adding extra characters, like dashes, between words. For example, you have no chance of getting *www.popularbusiness.com*, but *www.popular-business.com* is still there for the taking. Think carefully. Dashes can confuse some people, and others may overlook them. Some webmasters believe that a domain name with a single dash is perfectly reasonable, but one with several dashes looks like a spam site and should be avoided.

- **Phrases that look confusing in lowercase.** Domain names aren't case-sensitive, and when you type a poly-case domain name into a browser, the browser converts everything to lowercase. The problem is that some phrases can blend together in lowercase, particularly if you have words that start with vowels. Take a look at what happens when the documentation company Prose Xact puts its business name into a lowercase domain name: *www.prosexact.com*. You get the picture. (Incidentally, this is one situation where you might want to resort to a dash.)

TIP   Even though domain names don't distinguish case, that doesn't stop businesses from using capital letters in business cards, promotions, and marketing material to make the domain name more readable. Whether customers type *www.google.com* or *wWw.gOOgLE.cOm* into their browsers, they get to the same site.

- **Names that don't match your business.** It's a classic business mistake. You set up a flower shop in New York called Roses are Red, only to find out that the domain *www.rosesarered.com* is already taken. So you go for the next-best choice, *www.newyorkflorist.com*. Huh? Now you've created two separate business names, and a somewhat schizophrenic identity for your company. If you're starting a new business, try to choose your business name and your domain name at the same time so they match. If you already have a business name, settle on a URL that has an extra word or two, like *www.rosesareredflorist.com*. This name may not be as snappy as *www.newyorkflorist.com*, but it avoids the inevitable confusion caused by creating a whole new identity.

In the time since the first edition of this book was published, it's become much, much harder to get a decent domain name. In the past, your only competition was other people planning to set up a website and unscrupulous domain name resellers looking to buy a hot name and flip it for a big profit. But now, nefarious people buy just about any domain name at the drop of a hat, build a fly-by-night web page filled with ads, and wait a few months to see how much unsuspecting web traffic stumbles their way. This practice, called *domain tasting*, is surprisingly profitable. The bottom line? It's possible to cook up a decent domain name that's still available, but you'll need a dash of compromise and all the creativity you've got.

More Choices for Top-Level Domains

The *top-level domain* is the part of the domain name after the last period, like *.com*. While you can choose whatever you want for the first part of your domain name (so long as you stick to letters, numbers, and dashes), you're restricted to a set of predefined choices for the top-level domain.

Everyone wants a *.com* address for their business, and as a result they're the hardest top-level domain to get. But you might want to compromise by choosing a less popular top-level domain (like *.net*) to get what you want for the rest of the domain name (say, *www.WhenPigsCanFly.net*). Is the tradeoff worth it? It depends on the sort of site you're building. The following sections lay out your options.

■ THE ORIGINALS

There's a small set of general-purpose domains that are nearly as old as the Internet itself. They include *.com*, *.net*, *.org*, and a few more that are limited to specific uses (such as *.edu* for educational institutions and *.gov* for government organizations). A few more that are nearly as old are *.biz*, *.info,* and *.name*.

You'll find that it's easier to get the domain name you want if you use one of the less popular top-level domains. The problem is, most web visitors expect a *.com*. If you have the domain name *www.SuperShop.biz*, odds are someone will type in *www. SuperShop.com* while trying to find your site. That mistake can easily lead your fans to a competitor (or to a vastly inferior website). You need to weigh whether this tradeoff is acceptable for your site. If you're a local business and you think that a significant portion of your visitors will get to your site by typing the domain name straight into their browsers (rather than following a link), you might not want to risk confusion with a less common top-level domain.

One exception is the top-level domain *.org*, which was originally intended for nonprofit organizations. It's now available for anyone to use and abuse. However, if you're setting up a nonprofit of your own, the *.org* domain makes more sense than *.com* and is just as recognizable.

■ COUNTRY-SPECIFIC DOMAINS

These are domains that are (or were) reserved for a specific country. Examples include *.us* (USA), *.ca* (Canada), and *.co.uk* (United Kingdom, which looks like two domains, but just go with it). You might use these because you live in that country, or—in some exceptional cases—because the domain name sounds cool and has been made available to everyone.

For example, if you offer piano lessons in England, *www.pianolessons.co.uk* isn't a bad choice. If you plan to sell products to an international audience, however, *www. HotRetroRecords.co.uk* could frighten away otherwise interested buyers, who may assume dealing with a British seller is too much trouble.

Special rules apply regarding who can register country-specific names. For example, some are available only to people who live in the corresponding country or who have a registered business there. Due to these restrictions, some web hosting companies can't sell certain country-specific domains. If you have trouble registering the country-specific name you want, you can use Google to find a registrar that supports your choice. For example, to find a registrar for Australian domains, search for "Australian domain names."

Each country in the world has its own unique top-level domain, but some are now available for people to use in more creative ways. For example, the top-level domain *.tv* was created for the tiny country of Tuvalu, but it's now available for anyone who wants to create a television-focused website (with the Tuvaluan government getting a small cut of the domain registrar's profits). Similarly repurposed domains include *.me*, *.cd*, *.tm*, and *.ws*. You can find more information about these odder domain name choices on Wikipedia, at *http://tinyurl.com/rnlmf*.

■ **THE NEW KIDS ON THE BLOCK**
Recently, longer and more exotic top-level domains have started to appear. Examples include *.club*, *.church*, *.consulting*, *.directory*, *.fitness*, *.estate*, *.global*, *.guru*, *.services*, and *.training*, to name just a few. At the time of this writing, there are nearly 100 top-level domains in existence. But you can't find them all in one place, because different domain registrars have rights to different top-level domains.

Experts are divided about whether these domain names will help organize the Web or just encourage spammers to buy up more addresses. And because they're so new and unfamiliar, these new options might trip up people trying to visit your site. Right now, most seasoned web experts would prefer the domain *pacysgrillrestaurant.com* to *pacysgrill.restaurant*, even though the latter is shorter and perfectly clear. The problem is that the *.restaurant* domain hasn't caught on yet, and so the address doesn't instantly look like a URL to the average web visitor.

There's another risk with the new top-level domains. Certain browsers, operating systems, web servers, and programs don't recognize them yet. That's especially true for mobile devices, like phones and tablets that run the Android operating system or older versions of Apple's iOS. Their browsers don't recognize the new top-level domains. If you type one in, the browser performs a *search* for that text, rather than taking you to the corresponding site.

This situation will probably change in a couple of years. But if even a small fraction of your audience is locked out of your site because they're using old devices, that's a serious problem. So for now, your best bet is to avoid the new top-level domains and stick with the tried, true, and less glamorous domains described in the previous sections.

Searching for a Name

With a few domain name ideas in hand, you're ready to start checking their availability. Every web hosting company has a domain searching tool, and you can use any one of them. (Google "domain names" to find hundreds.) It doesn't matter where you go to perform your search, and you don't need to be ready to commit to hosting with that particular company. For now, you're just conducting some web domain research.

> **TIP** Domain name searches are an essential bit of prep work. Try to come up with as many variations and unusual name combinations as possible. Aim to find at least a dozen available names to give yourself lots of choice. Once you compile the list, why not make a few late-night phone calls to pester friends and relatives for their first reactions?

Just about every web hosting company provides its own version of a domain name search tool. Figure 9-3 shows one from *www.instantdomainsearch.com*. To get started, type in the domain you want most and then click Search. (In most cases, you don't have to type the *www* at the start of the name or the *.com* at the end, because the search tool adds them behind the scenes.)

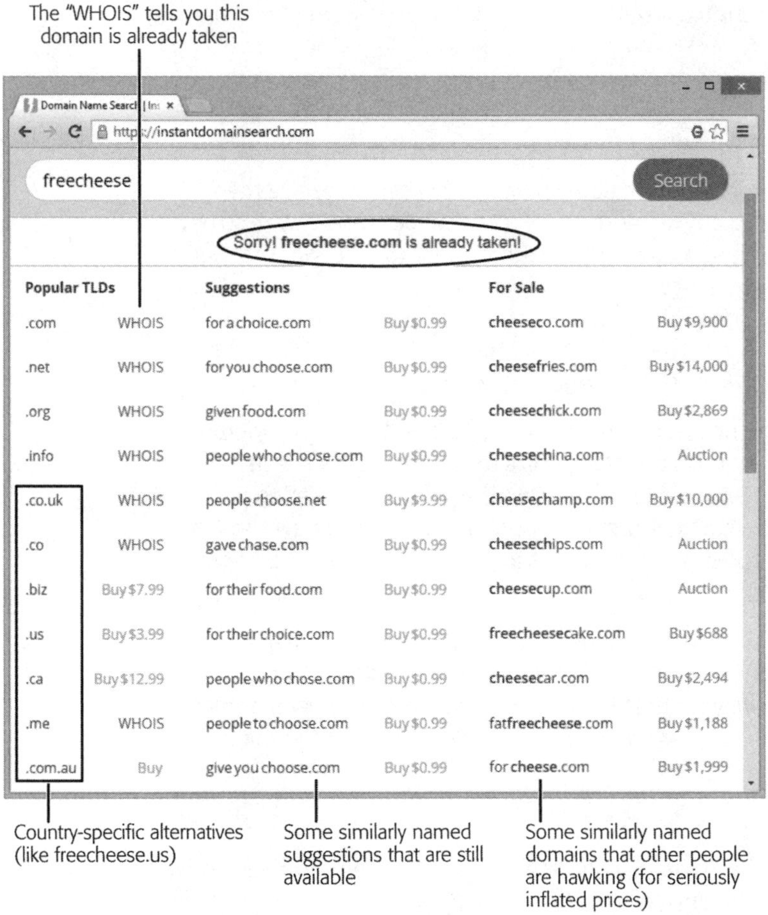

The "WHOIS" tells you this
domain is already taken

FIGURE 9-3

This search reveals that your first choice, www.freecheese.com, *is gone. All that's left are the less-catchy* www.freecheese.biz *and country-specific domains (left). Some domain registrars will suggest similar domain names that are still available (middle), or list already registered domains that you can buy from their owners (right). This is rarely worthwhile, however, because domain resellers usually expect you to shell out some serious bank (like $9,900 for* cheeseco.com).

Popular TLDs		**Suggestions**		**For Sale**	
.com	WHOIS	for a choice.com	Buy $0.99	cheeseco.com	Buy $9,900
.net	WHOIS	for you choose.com	Buy $0.99	cheesefries.com	Buy $14,000
.org	WHOIS	given food.com	Buy $0.99	cheesechick.com	Buy $2,869
.info	WHOIS	people who choose.com	Buy $0.99	cheesechina.com	Auction
.co.uk	WHOIS	people choose.net	Buy $9.99	cheesechamp.com	Buy $10,000
.co	WHOIS	gave chase.com	Buy $0.99	cheesechips.com	Auction
.biz	Buy $7.99	for their food.com	Buy $0.99	cheesecup.com	Auction
.us	Buy $3.99	for their choice.com	Buy $0.99	freecheesecake.com	Buy $688
.ca	Buy $12.99	people who chose.com	Buy $0.99	cheesecar.com	Buy $2,494
.me	WHOIS	people to choose.com	Buy $0.99	fatfreecheese.com	Buy $1,188
.com.au	Buy	give you choose.com	Buy $0.99	for cheese.com	Buy $1,999

Sorry! **freecheese.com** is already taken!

Country-specific alternatives
(like freecheese.us)

Some similarly named
suggestions that are still
available

Some similarly named
domains that other people
are hawking (for seriously
inflated prices)

When you find an available domain name, the hosting company gives you the option to buy it. But don't do anything yet, because you still need to do some comparison-shopping to find the best host.

> **NOTE** You may think you could see if a domain is free just by typing it into your web browser. But this method of checking takes more time, and it doesn't give you a definitive result. Someone can buy a domain name without setting up a website, so even if your domain-fishing doesn't hit on a live site, the domain may not be available.

Registering Your Name

After you find an available name, you probably want to wait to register it until you're ready to sign up for a web hosting plan (which you'll read about in the next section). Most web hosts offer free or discounted domain name registration when you rent space from them. In addition, doing both at once is the easiest way to set up your domain name, because the process automatically establishes a relationship between your domain name and your website.

In a few cases, however, you may want to register a domain name separately from your web hosting package. Here are some examples:

- You don't want to create a website right now, but you do want to register a name so no one else can grab it—a tactic known as *domain parking* (see the box on page 288). Sometime in the future, you may develop a website that uses that name.

- You already have web space, possibly through your ISP (Internet service provider), and all you need to make your website seem more professional is a personalized domain name. It takes more work to set up this sort of arrangement, but you can learn how to get started in the box on page 296.

- Your hosting company can't register the type of domain you want. This can happen if you need a domain name with a country-specific top-level domain or one of the new top-level domains (page 284) and your web host isn't authorized to register them.

If you decide to register a domain name separately, remember that you won't be able to use it until you get a web hosting plan. Either way, the next section will help you get properly set up with the right web host.

> **NOTE** All web hosting companies let you register more than one domain for the same website. That means you can register both *www.FancyPants.com* and *www.FancyPants.biz*, and specify that both these addresses point to the same website. Of course, you'll need to pay an extra domain name registration fee. (Really big web companies use this strategy to accommodate typos. For instance, see where *http://amzn.com* and *http://googel.com* take you.)

Buying a Domain for the Future

Domain parking means you've registered a domain name but haven't yet purchased any other services, like renting web space.

Most people use domain parking to put a domain name away on reserve. In the increasingly crowded world of the Web, many people use it to protect their own names (for example, *www.samanthamalone.com*). Domain parking is also useful if you want to secure several potential business names you may use in the future.

If you do reserve a domain name, do your research and pick a company that you'd also like to use to host your website. You can switch domain names from one web host to another, but it's a bit of a pain. Contact the host you're currently working with for specific instructions.

The real appeal of domain parking is that it's cheap. You pay a nominal domain-name registration fee (as little as $5 a year), and get to keep the name for as long as you're willing to pay for it.

Getting Web Space

All you need to achieve web superstardom is a domain name and a small amount of space on a web server. There's no one-size-fits-all solution when it comes to finding a web host. Instead, you choose a hosting company based on your budget, what you want your website to do, and your own capricious whims (let's face it—some hosting companies just have way cooler names than others).

What you *don't* want is a web host that offers some sort of special software that promises to help you create a website in two or three easy steps. These tools range from mediocre to terrible. After all, if you were content to create the same cookie-cutter website as everyone else, you probably wouldn't be interested in learning HTML, and you wouldn't have picked up this book.

Instead, you want standard website hosting, where you're given a slot of space on a server to manage as you see fit. You create your pages on your own computer and then copy those files to the web server so others can view them. This type of web hosting is all you need to use this book.

Web hosts usually charge a monthly fee. For basic hosting, it starts at the reasonable sum of $5 to $10 per month. Of course, that cost can escalate quickly, depending on the features you want your host to provide.

Assessing Your Needs

Before you decide on a host, ask yourself one important question—what features do you need? Web hosts are quick to swamp their ads and websites with techie jargon, which doesn't tell you which services are truly useful. Here's a quick overview that describes what hosts sell and what you need to know about each offering.

- **Web space** is how much server space you rent to store your website. Although HTML pages are extremely small, you may need more space for images or files you want others to download, like a video of your wedding. A modest site can easily survive with a measly 100 MB (that's megabytes, not gigabytes) of space, unless you're stuffing it full of pictures or videos. Most web hosts throw in 10 or 100 times more server space, knowing you'll probably never use it.

> **NOTE** For the numerically challenged, a gigabyte (GB) is the same as 1,024 megabytes (MB). To put that in perspective, today's hard drives can have 500 GB of space or more, enough room for tens of thousands of websites.

- **Bandwidth** (or web traffic, as it's sometimes called) is the maximum amount of information you can deliver to visitors in a month. Usually, you can make do with the lowest bandwidth your hosting company offers. For more information, see the box on page 291.

- **A domain name** is a custom website address, as in *www.HenryTheFriendly.com*. If you decide to get a personalized domain name, you don't necessarily need to get it from the same company that hosts your site. However, getting both from the same source makes life easier, and hosting companies often throw in one or more domain names at a discounted price when you sign up for a hosting plan.

- **Email addresses.** Odds are, you already have some of these. But you may want an email address that matches your website address, especially if you're paying for a customized domain name. For example, if you own *www.HenryTheFriendly.com*, you'd probably like to use an email address like *Hank@HenryTheFriendly.com*. Most hosting companies let you create dozens or hundreds of email addresses for your domain (which is good if you're running a small company), and most also let you read your email in your browser or send it to a desktop program like Microsoft Outlook.

- **Upload-ability.** The ease of transferring files to your server is another important detail. As you saw in the previous chapter, you can perfect your web pages on your own computer before you upload them. But once your website is ready for prime time, you need a convenient way to copy all the files to your server. The vast majority of commercial web hosts offer something called FTP (File Transfer Protocol), which lets you easily copy a number of files at once (for details, see page 301).

- **Programming support.** Today, most web hosts support at least some of the dozens of server-side programming languages available. When shopping for a web host, you'll come across their names—ASP, PHP, CGI, Perl, Python, Ruby, and so on. Although server programming is too complex for most ordinary people, this feature gives you some room to grow. To take advantage of a server-side programming technology, you could conceivably use someone else's script in your web pages to carry out an advanced task, like collecting visitor information with a form.

NOTE Although this book doesn't cover server-side programs in depth, you'll learn about *client-side scripts* in Chapter 14. Client-side scripts are based on JavaScript, and they run right inside visitors' browsers. They're more limited in ability than server-side programs, and you'll commonly see them used for special effects like animated buttons. The nice thing about client-side scripts is that even programming novices can drop a simple script into a web page and enjoy the benefits. But you don't need to worry about any of this right now, because unlike server-side programming, client-side scripts don't require any special support from your web hosting company.

- **Tech support.** The best companies provide 24-hour tech support, ideally through a toll-free number or a live chat feature that lets you ask questions using your browser.

- **Frills.** In an effort to woo you to their side, web hosts often pack a slew of frills into their plans. For example, they'll sometimes boast about their amazing, quick-and-easy website creation tools. Translation: They'll let you use a clumsy piece of software on their website to build yours. You'll end up with a cookie-cutter site and not much opportunity to express yourself. Steer clear of these pointless features. More usefully, a web hosting company can provide site *statistics*—detailed information about how many visitors flock to your site daily or monthly. (In Chapter 10, you'll find out about a free visitor-tracking tool that runs circles around what most hosts provide.)

- **Private domain registration.** Ordinarily, when you register a domain, your contact information—which includes your email address, full name, and mailing address—appears in the official domain records. These records are public, which means spammers may send you junk and mail you fake domain renewal letters. To avoid the hassle, you can ask your web host to hide your contact information for a small fee (usually about $10 per year). But if you're setting up a site for a business, you're probably already publishing your contact details publicly, so there's no reason to hide anything.

Choosing Your Host

With your requirements in mind, you're ready to shop for a web host. You're looking for a plan that's often called *shared hosting*, because your website *shares* a web server with hundreds of other websites.

If you have heftier hosting needs, you can opt for a *dedicated* hosting plan. This super-premium option gives you an entire web server to yourself. Big companies use this type of hosting to get rock-solid stability, but few people want to pay the extra cost, which can run well over $100 a month.

A similar but somewhat cheaper choice is a VPS, or *virtual private server* hosting. With VPS hosting, you don't get the entire web server computer to yourself, but your website gets its own private "environment," so there's no chance that someone else's malfunctioning website can trample on its toes. VPS hosting also gives advanced webmasters the ability to customize the software that runs on the web server. VPS hosting is cheaper than dedicated hosting but still significantly more expensive than shared hosting.

The Riddle of Bandwidth

Most web hosting companies base their prices, at least in part, on how much web space and bandwidth you need. This can be a problem, because the average website creator has no idea how to calculate those numbers to come up with a realistic estimate.

Fortunately, you can save a lot of time and effort by taking advantage of a dirty little secret: For the average personal or small-business site, you don't need much disk space or bandwidth. You can probably take the smallest amounts on offer from any web hosting company and live quite happily.

If you still insist on calculating bandwidth, here's how it works. Suppose you create a relatively modest website of 50 pages, a pile of small web-optimized graphics, and a few downloadable documents (say, PDF files or Word documents). Altogether, this website occupies 10 MB of space.

Suppose your site is doing well, and receives about 30 visitors a day. If each guest visits every page (in other words, downloads your *entire website*), your daily bandwidth requirement is 300 MB (30 visitors x 10 MB), and your monthly bandwidth consumption weighs in at 9 GB (30 days x 300 MB). That's far less than what the typical startup web hosting package offers, which often includes 100 GB or more per month.

As a result, most people can ignore the bandwidth limits offered by their web host. The only exceptions are if your website is absurdly popular; if you want to store extremely large files and let visitors download them; or if you're showcasing a huge catalog of digital photos, music, or video, and you don't want to use a third-party service like Flickr or YouTube. If you're in the small minority of people who need huge amounts of bandwidth, look for a web host that promises unlimited bandwidth. That way, you don't need to worry about exceeding your limit.

NOTE The bottom line is this: If you don't know what type of hosting plan you want, the best choice for you is shared hosting. Dedicated and VPS hosting plans are for sites with special requirements or huge amounts of traffic.

Every web host offers shared hosting, and there's no shortage of choices. Table 9-1 lists just a few hosts (ordered alphabetically) so you can get started comparison-shopping.

TABLE 9-1 *A few of the Internet's many web hosting firms.*

NAME	URL
DreamHost	www.dreamhost.com
Hawkhost	www.hawkhost.com
HostGo	www.hostgo.com
Insider Hosting	www.insiderhosting.com
MDDHosting	www.mddhosting.com
OCS Solutions	www.ocssolutions.com
Pair Networks	www.pair.com
SpeedySparrow	http://speedysparrow.com
StableHost	www.stablehost.com

It's not easy finding honest web host reviews on the Web. Most websites that claim to review and rank hosts are simply advertising a few companies that pay for a recommendation. Popular tech sites haven't reviewed web hosts in years, because a thorough analysis of even a fraction of them would require a massive amount of manpower. And old reviews aren't much help either, because the quality of a hosting company can change quickly.

However, the Web isn't completely useless in your hunt. You can get information about hosting companies from a web discussion board, where people like you chat with more experienced hosts and customers. One of the best is WebHostingTalk, which you'll find at *http://tinyurl.com/5zffwp*. Its discussion board is particularly useful if you've narrowed your options to just a few companies, and you'd like to ask a question or hear about other people's experiences.

As you consider different hosts, you'll need to sort through a dizzying array of options. In the next two sections, you'll practice digging through some marketing haze to find the important information in the offerings of two example hosting companies.

FREQUENTLY ASKED QUESTION

Becoming a Web Host

Can I run a web server?

In theory, you definitely can. The Web was designed to be an open community, and no one is out to stop you. In practice, however, it's not at all easy—no matter how many computer-savvy relatives you have.

Several monumental challenges prevent all but the most ambitious people from running their own servers. The first is that you need to have a reliable computer that runs 24 hours a day. That computer also needs to run special web-hosting software that can serve up web pages.

The next problem is that your computer requires a special type of connection to the Internet, called a *fixed IP address*. An IP

address is a number that identifies your computer on the Web. (*IP* stands for Internet Protocol, which governs how different devices communicate on a network.)

Most ISPs (Internet service providers) randomly assign IP addresses to customers like you as needed, and change them on a whim. For your computer to run a website and make sure others can find it, you need to lock down your IP address so that it's not constantly changing. That means that most people can't use their computers to host a permanent website, at least not without special software. If you're still interested, you can call your ISP and ask if it provides a fixed IP address service, and at what cost.

A Web Host Walkthrough

Figure 9-4 shows the home page for the popular web hosting company Aplus.net. The company offers dedicated servers, standard hosting, domain name registration, and web design services. All four options are designed to help you get online, but you're really interested in the one for web hosting.

The top of the Aplus home page includes several tabbed buttons. The Domain Registration tab gives you the option to transfer an existing domain name or park a domain for future use. The Website Hosting tab lets you see Aplus's hosting plans (see Figure 9-5), which is what you really want. The "Build a Website" tab is mainly of interest to HTML-phobes. It lets you pay a web design team to craft all the HTML pages and graphics for your website. But where's the fun in that?

FIGURE 9-4

This page packs a lot of information. Click the Website Hosting tab to find out about Aplus's hosting plans. At the top of the page, Aplus lists a toll-free number for sales or support. Click the Live Chat link and a chat window opens. Type your question there, and an Aplus technician gives you an immediate answer. If you're serious about signing up with Aplus, give both these options a try so you can evaluate its technical support.

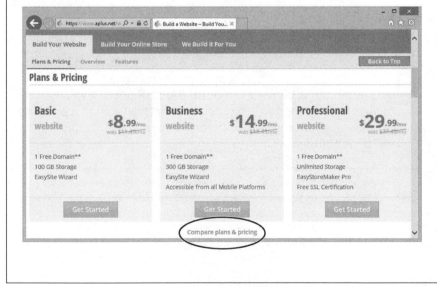

FIGURE 9-5

Aplus offers three web hosting packages. The Basic package has everything you need right now. Some of the features in the other packages are red herrings—for example, only novices would consider using the EasySite Wizard, and you don't actually need a special plan to make your site "Accessible from All Mobile Platforms." To get a deeper comparison of these plans, click the "Compare plans & pricing" link underneath (Figure 9-6).

To continue, click the Website Hosting tab. Aplus shows you its basic web hosting package. To compare that with its other offerings, click the See All button (Figure 9-5). And to get even more details about the plans, click the "Compare plans & pricing" link (Figure 9-6).

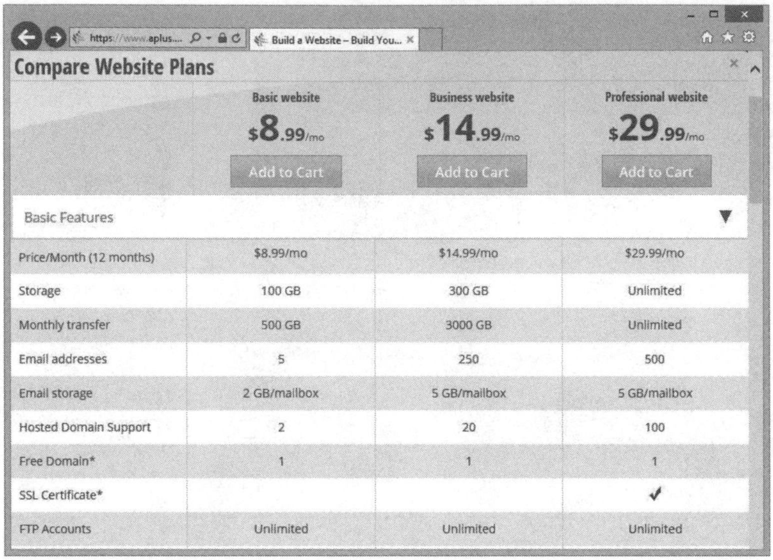

FIGURE 9-6

Here's a breakdown that spells out the details of Aplus's three hosting plans, including how much bandwidth you'll get (described as "Monthly transfer"), how much space you'll have for your email inboxes, and so on. Some of these details are immediately important (you want FTP support, as explained on page 289), while some are more advanced features for web programs that use server-side scripts (like databases).

At the end of your search, you'll discover that the cheapest option is $9 per month for a free domain name and 100 GB of storage space for your website. Aplus throws in a free domain name and five email addresses for good measure, along with FTP support.

Overall, the Aplus.net search turned up a solid offer at a fair price. However, discerning web shoppers may hope to save a few dollars or get a little more space. Before you sign up, browse several other web hosts, and then research your first choice in greater detail at WebHostingTalk.

NOTE If your web host is letting you down, don't panic. It's not too hard to upgrade your hosting plan or even switch hosts altogether. The key thing to remember is when you change hosts, you're essentially abandoning one server and setting up shop on another. It's up to you to copy your web pages to the new server—no one will do it for you. As long as you have a copy of your website on your personal computer (and you always should), this part is easy. If you're still a little skeptical about what company to choose, look for a 30-day, money-back guarantee.

What to Expect after You Sign Up

Once you decide on a web host, you don't need anything more than a credit card. Along the way, you'll need to choose your domain name. Then sit back and wait—you'll be online in only a few hours.

First, you'll get an email or two from your web host (Figure 9-7). They include a receipt for your payment and the login information you need to get to your account page. Log in to open the page to manage your hosting plan, pay for renewal, buy additional domain names, and change your contact information.

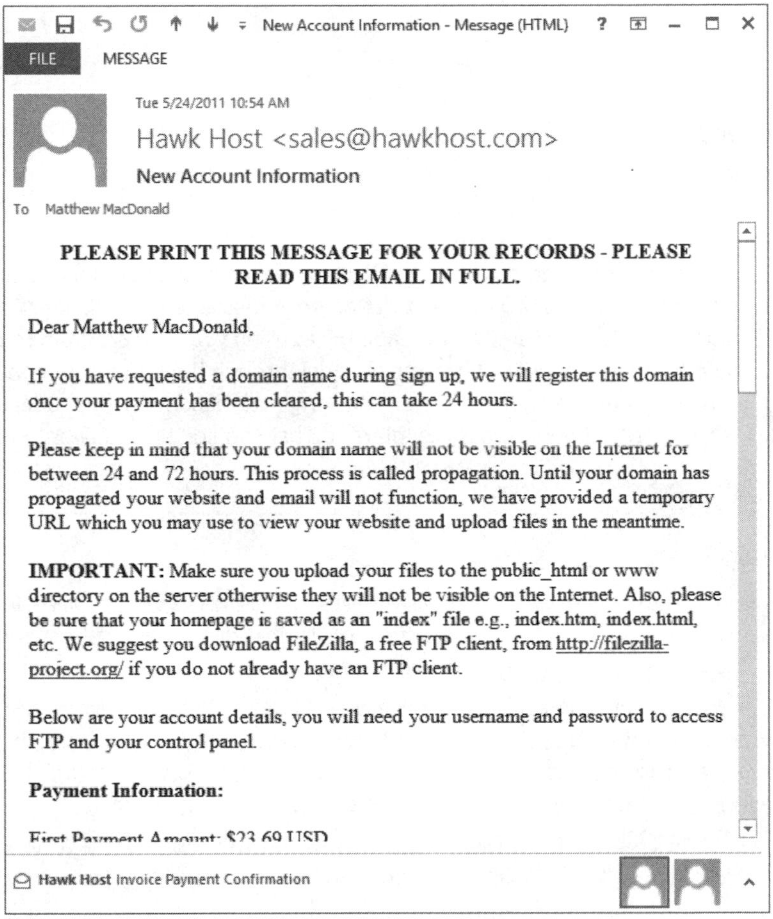

FIGURE 9-7

After signing up with a web host, you'll receive an email like this one. Scroll down and you'll see the payment details and the login information for your account. You'll also find instructions about how to configure your FTP program (page 301) and set up an email account.

You'll also get a web address that points to your site's control panel, where you can tap a dizzying array of tools. Most handle features beyond the scope of this book (for example, you won't start using databases or installing new software packages on your site in this book), but you'll explore your site's traffic statistics in Chapter 10.

Finally, you'll get the address for your website. Usually, you'll get *two* addresses: the real website domain that you picked (say, *www.reboot-me.com*), and a temporary numeric address (like *http://174.37.162.41/~rebootme*). Here's an example of what this part of the message might look like:

Temporarily, you may use one of the addresses given below to manage your website:

Temporary FTP Hostname: 174.37.162.41

FTP Port: 21

Temporary Webpage URL: http://174.37.162.41/~rebootme/

Temporary Control Panel: http://174.37.162.41/cpanel

Once your domain has propagated:

FTP Hostname: www.reboot-me.com

FTP Port: 21

Webpage URL: http://www.reboot-me.com

Control Panel: http://www.reboot-me.com/cpanel

You can use the temporary address right now. Of course, you haven't uploaded anything yet, so if you visit your site, you'll just get an error message or an "Under Construction" page. However, you can start uploading files using your FTP program (page 301), and you can get to your website's control panel through the temporary control panel URL. The real website address takes a bit longer to become active, because it has to spread to DNS servers across the Internet. That should take a day or two.

FREQUENTLY ASKED QUESTION

A Host Here, a Domain There

Can I buy my domain name and web space from different companies and still make them work together?

The simplest approach is to get both from the same company, but that's not always possible. Maybe you bought your domain name before you set up your site and you don't want to pay to transfer the domain. Or maybe you have a country-specific domain name (like *www.CunningPets.co.uk*) that your web host can't register. Or maybe you just want the flexibility to change hosts frequently, so you can get the best service or cheapest rates.

To make this multiple-company tango work, you need some technical support from your web hosting company. Contact its help desk and let the staff know what you plan to do. They can give you specific instructions, and they'll set up their name servers (more on what those are in a moment) with the right information for your domain.

The next task is to change the registration information for your domain. Follow these steps:

1. Find out the name of the *domain name servers (DNS servers)* at your web hosting company. These are the computers that convert domain names into numeric IP addresses (page 281). The technical support staff can give you this information.

2. Go to the company where you registered the domain name and update your domain registration settings. Change the name server setting to match the name servers you found out about in step 1 (as shown in Figure 9-8).

Due to the way DNS servers work, the change can take 24 hours or more to take effect.

When you make this change, you're essentially saying that your web host is now responsible for giving out the IP address of your website. When someone types your domain name into a browser, the browser contacts the name server at your hosting company to get the IP address. From that point on, it's smooth sailing.

Once you modify your domain name registration, you still have the same two bills to pay. You'll pay your hosting fees to the web hosting company and the yearly domain name registration fee to the company where you registered your domain name.

FIGURE 9-8

Here, the website owner has registered his domain (sugarbeat.ca) with www.hover.com, *but hosts his content through* www.brinkster.com. *To make this work, he transfers control of his domain name to the name servers* ns1.brinkster.com (http://ns1.brinkster.com) *and* ns2.brinkster.com (http://ns2.brinkster.com).

Free Web Hosts: Just Say No

As you no doubt know, the Web is a great place for frugal shoppers. Not only can you score a great deal on a sporty iPod and a used sofa bed, you can also pick up a bit of web space storage for the princely sum of zero dollars. Sound attractive? Think again.

Free hosts give you a small parcel of web space without charging you anything. Sometimes it's because they hope to get you to upgrade to a cost-based service if you outgrow the strict limitations of the free package. Other times, free hosts force you to include an obnoxious ad banner at the top of your web pages.

Although free hosts don't set out to scam people (at least most of them don't), they aren't worth the risk and aggravation. Here are some of the headaches you can face:

- **Ad banners.** The worst free hosts force you to display their advertisements on your pages. If you'd like to crowd out your content with obnoxious credit card commercials, this is the way to go. Otherwise, move on to somewhere new. It's finally possible to find free hosts that don't impose the Curse of the Blinking Banner Ad, so don't settle for one that does.

- **Unreliability.** Free web hosts may experience more downtime, which means your website may periodically disappear from the Web. Or the web servers the host uses may be bogged down by poor maintenance or other people's websites, causing your site to slow to a crawl.

- **Unpredictability.** Free hosts aren't the most stable companies. It's not unheard of for a host to go out of business, taking your site with it and forcing you to look for a new web home in a hurry. Similarly, free hosts can change their requirements overnight, sometimes shifting from an ad-free web haven to a blinking-banner extravaganza without warning.

- **Usage limits.** Some free hosts force you to agree to a policy that limits the type of content you can put on your site. For example, you may be forbidden from running a business, selling ad space, or uploading certain types of files (like music, movies, or large downloads).

- **Limited tech support.** Many professional website operators say that what makes a good host isn't a huge expanse of free space or a ginormous bandwidth limit—it's the ability to get another human being on the phone at any hour to solve unexpected problems. Free web hosts can't afford to hire a platoon of techies for customer service, so you'll be forced to wait for help—if you get it at all.

- **Awkward uploads.** Many free hosts lack support for easy FTP uploading (see the next section). Without this convenience, you'll be forced to use a time-consuming upload page.

If you absolutely must try a free web host—perhaps you have the time to experiment, and your site doesn't need rock-solid reliability—you can learn more at *www. free-webhosts.com*. The site provides a huge catalog of free hosts, which painstakingly details the space they give you and the conditions they impose. You'll also find thousands of user reviews. However, keep in mind that unscrupulous web hosts may pad the rankings with their own reviews, and any free host can abruptly change its offerings.

■ Transferring Files to Your Site

Once you sign up with a web host, you're ready to transfer files to your web space. As long as your host supports FTP (and all the good ones do), this task is almost as easy as copying files from one spot to another on your computer. You just need to pick your tool:

- **Windows Explorer.** If you're using a Windows computer, you can do the job using the same tool that you use to manage your computer's files.

- **An FTP program.** You can transfer files using one of the many free FTP programs you can find online.

- **A professional web editor.** If you're using a professional web editor like Dreamweaver or Expression Web, you get all the FTP smarts you need right in the program.

The following sections outline these approaches. But before you can upload files using FTP, you need to collect a few details. These include the address of the FTP server, as well as the user name and password you use to log onto that server. The FTP login information may match the login information you use for your web hosting account, or it may be different.

You also need to decide what you want to upload. To run a simple test, you can upload a standalone web page, like one of the resumé examples from Chapter 1. For a more ambitious test, you can upload an entire *site*—in other words, a collection of web pages and the resources they use, like style sheets and pictures. For example, you can transfer the trip website from the tutorial in Chapter 6 (page 181). In this case, you need to copy all the files in the website folder (in this example, that's Tutorial-6-1\End), along with all its subfolders (if there are any).

After you upload a file, you can check your work. Type in your domain name followed by the web page name. For example, if you upload the *resume4.htm* example to your website *www.supersavvyworker.com*, try requesting *www.supersavvyworker.com/resume4.htm*. You don't need to wait. Once you upload the file to your server, it's available almost instantly to any browser that requests it.

Uploading with Windows Explorer

In these modern times, you don't need a standalone FTP editor. Windows includes its own built-in FTP features that handle the task comfortably. Here's how it works:

1. **Open Windows Explorer.**

   One quick way to do this is by right-clicking the Start button and then choosing Explore (in older versions of Windows) or File Explorer (in Windows 8 and up).

2. **Type the FTP address into the Windows Explorer address bar (Figure 9-9).**

   Make sure the URL starts with *ftp://*. In other words, if you want to visit *ftp.myhost.com*, enter the URL *ftp://ftp.myhost.com*, not *http://ftp.myhost.com*, which incorrectly sends your computer off looking for web pages.

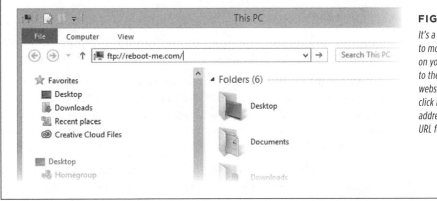

FIGURE 9-9

It's a surprisingly small jump to move from the file system on your Windows computer to the file system on your website. It all starts when you click in the Windows Explorer address box and type in the URL for your FTP server.

3. Enter your login information (see Figure 9-10).

Once you log in, you'll see your site's folders and files on the web server; you can copy, delete, rename, and move them in much the same way you do local folders and files. Since you haven't uploaded anything yet, the folder may be empty, or it may contain a generic *index.htm* file that displays an "Under Construction" message if someone happens to browse to the page.

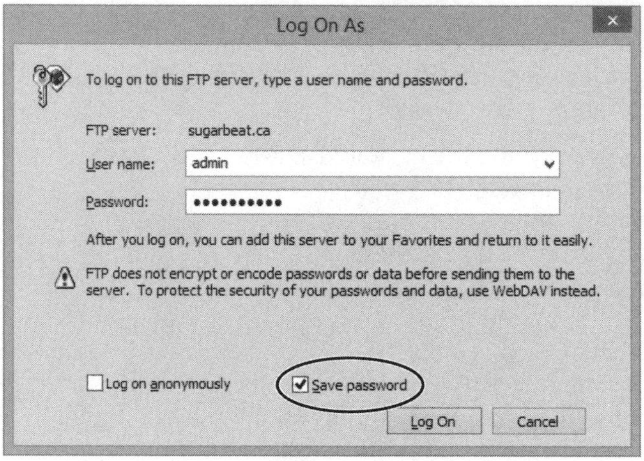

FIGURE 9-10

When you first type in an FTP address, Windows Explorer may try to log you in anonymously and fail. It may then prompt you for your user ID and password (as shown here), or it may display an error message. If you get an error message, click OK and then right-click the file display area (on the right), and choose Login As. If you turn on the "Save password" checkbox (circled), you don't need to repeat this process on subsequent visits.

4. Browse to the folder that holds your website.

You need to copy your files to the right place—the root folder that holds the content of your website. Depending on your web host, you may start out in this folder, or you may need to browse to it.

Often this is a folder named *public_html*. However, it could be something else, like *www* or *webroot*. Your web host can give you the correct name—in fact, you're likely to find the details in your welcome email (page 296).

5. Copy your files to the server.

The easiest way to do this is to open a second Windows Explorer window. Then you can drag the files from that window and drop them in the FTP window.

Figure 9-11 shows the steps to upload the resumé example from Chapter 1. Make sure you upload both the *resume4.htm* file and the linked picture, *leepark.jpg*, to the same folder on your site. You can drag these files one at a time or as a group (hold down the Ctrl [⌘] key as you click each filename), and then pull them over en masse.

If you want to transfer an entire website, browse to the root website folder on your computer. Select everything, and then drag all the files and subfolders to your FTP folder. For example, to copy the trip files from the first tutorial in

Chapter 6, browse to the Tutorial-6-1\End folder and select everything, including all the pages and the TripArctic and TripChina folders. You can then drag all the selected files in one step.

TIP Drag-and-drop isn't the only way to transfer files. You can use all the familiar Windows shortcuts, including the Cut, Copy, and Paste commands in the Edit menu, and the Ctrl+C (copy) and Ctrl+V (paste) keyboard shortcuts.

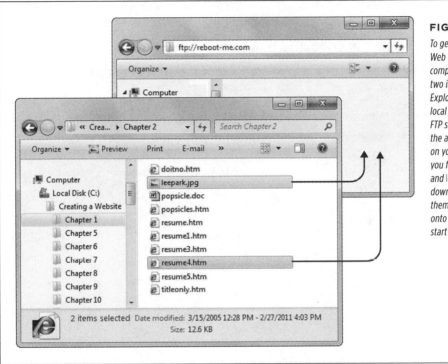

FIGURE 9-11

To get Lee Park onto the Web from a Windows computer, start by opening two instances of Windows Explorer. Use one for your local files and one for your FTP site. Then browse to the appropriate folder on your computer. When you find the resume4.htm and leepark.jpg files you downloaded earlier, select them, and then drag them onto the FTP window to start uploading files.

Uploading with an FTP Program

There are plenty of FTP programs that can help you transfer files from your computer to your website. Some come equipped with bells and whistles, like the ability to set up automated transfers that follow your preset rules. But if you don't want any of these exotic features, you can get plenty of basic FTP programs for free, for any operating system.

Two good, popular, and free FTP programs are Cyberduck (*http://cyberduck.io*) and FileZilla (*http://filezilla-project.org*). Both offer Windows and Mac versions, and both work more or less the way you'd expect—like a glorified file browser that shows you the contents of your web server.

NOTE The Mac operating system does include an FTP feature, but it's read-only. That means you can use the built-in FTP feature to copy files from a web location to your computer, but you can't use it to transfer your work to your web server, which makes this feature useless for website development.

To use Cyberduck, follow these steps:

1. **Begin by visiting** *http://cyberduck.io* **to download Cyberduck and install it on your computer.**

2. **Once you install Cyberduck, fire it up.**

   The main window appears. Right now, it's empty.

3. **Click the plus (+) button in the bottom-left corner (Figure 9-12).**

   This brings up a window where you tell Cyberduck how to connect to your FTP server.

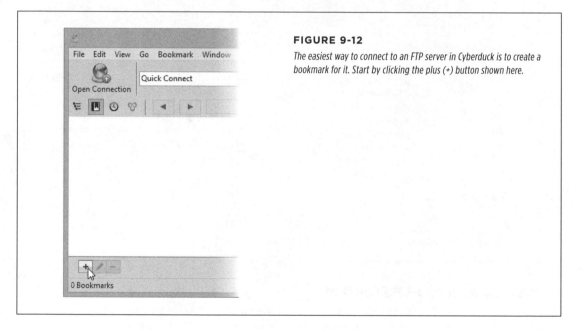

FIGURE 9-12

The easiest way to connect to an FTP server in Cyberduck is to create a bookmark for it. Start by clicking the plus (+) button shown here.

4. **Fill in your account details (Figure 9-13).**

   You need to supply the standard information, including the FTP server address and your user name. You also need to pick a nickname, because you're creating a link to the server and you need to label it. (Cyberduck calls these links "bookmarks.")

5. **When you finish, click the red X icon in the top-right corner of the box to close it.**

   Now you'll see your bookmark in the main Cyberduck window.

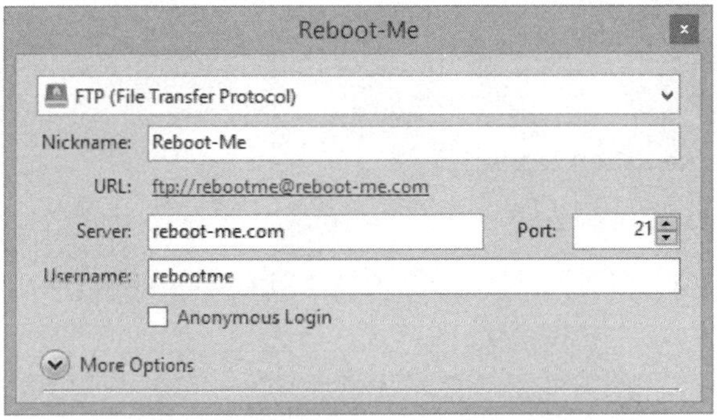

FIGURE 9-13

Cyberduck saves the connection information for your FTP site and calls it a bookmark. Cyberduck lists all the bookmarks you've created in the main window.

6. **Double-click your new bookmark to connect to the FTP server.**

7. **Enter your password.**

   If you turned on the "Save password" checkbox, Cyberduck remembers the password for this site, so you won't need to enter it the next time you connect.

   Once Cyberduck connects, you'll see a list of the folders and files on your web hosting account.

8. **Browse to the root folder for your site.**

   Often, it's named *public_html*, but not always. Check with your web host if you can't find the right spot.

9. **Start transferring your files.**

   To upload something to your website, simply drag your files and folders from Windows Explorer (on Windows) or Finder (on Mac) and drop them onto the Cyberduck window.

Uploading in Dreamweaver

If you're fortunate enough to be working with Dreamweaver, you don't need to fiddle around with Windows Explorer or another FTP program. Instead, you can do all your uploading from the comfort of the Dreamweaver window. Even better, Dreamweaver's uploading feature is intelligent. For example, with a single click, it lets you copy just the files you changed since the last time you uploaded files to your site.

■ ADDING YOUR FTP INFORMATION

Before you can use Dreamweaver's FTP features, you need to "define" your website, a process first described on page 161. However, merely defining a site isn't enough. You also need to make sure you've added the FTP connection information to your site. Here's how:

1. **Go to the Site Setup window.**

   If you're creating a new site, start by choosing Site→New Site. Then fill in a descriptive name and pick the folder on your computer where you store your site's files, as described on page 162.

   If you've already created a site, choose Site→Manage Site. Then, double-click the site you want to edit.

2. **Now click Servers in the list on the left.**

   This takes you to the Servers section of the Site Setup window.

3. **Click the tiny plus icon in the bottom-left corner of the empty server list (Figure 9-14).**

   Dreamweaver displays a dialog box where you fill in your connection information (see Figure 9-15).

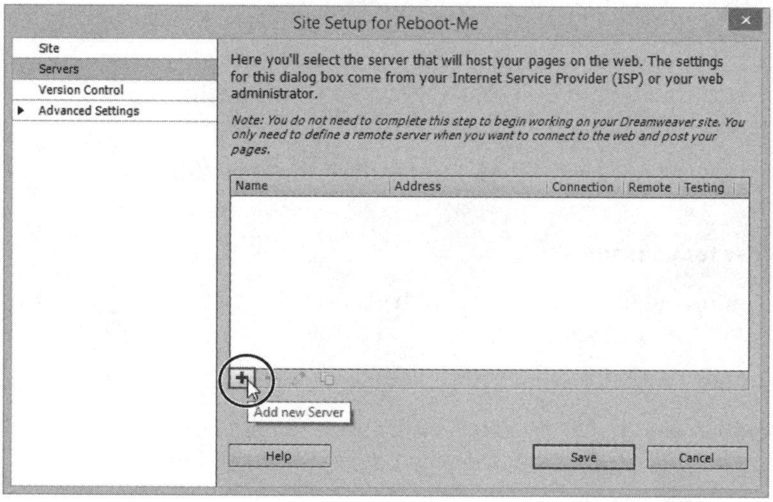

FIGURE 9-14

Initially, Dreamweaver's list of web servers is empty. You need to fill in the information for your web server.

NOTE Don't forget to fill in the Root Directory setting. This is the folder on your web hosting account that holds your site (usually it's something like *public_html*). Dreamweaver is going to do the uploading for you, and if this detail isn't in place, it won't put your files in the correct location.

---

4. **When you finish entering your server information, click Save.**

   Dreamweaver stores your connection information so you won't need to enter it again and returns you to the Site Setup window.

5. **Click Save again to close the Site Setup window.**

   You return to the Manage Sites dialog box.

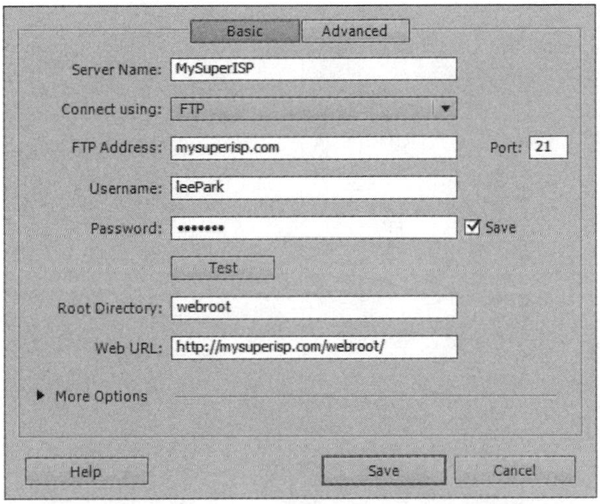

FIGURE 9-15

*Your web host can supply all the connection information
you need. Key details include the address of your FTP
server, your user name and password, and the root directory (folder name) of your website on the server.*

6. **Click Done.**

   You return to Dreamweaver's main window.

Once you finish adding the FTP information to your site, you'll be able to take a peek
at the contents of it using Dreamweaver's Files panel (Figure 9-16). In the location
drop-down list at the top right of the panel, choose "Remote server" to see what's on
the web server. Choose "Local view" to switch back to the folder on your computer.

The Files panel includes a strip of buttons that let you transfer files back and forth
from your computer to the server. The following sections explain how to use them.

■ COPYING FILES TO YOUR WEBSITE

To transfer files from your local computer to your server, you use an operation called
a *put* in FTP jargon. It works like this:

1. **In the Files panel, choose your website from the drop-down menu at the
   top left.**

2. **Choose "Local view" from the drop-down menu at the top right.**

   The Files panel lists the files on your computer (see Figure 9-16).

TIP Initially, Dreamweaver crams the file view into a small corner of the Dreamweaver window. To expand
it to fill the entire window and simultaneously display both the files on your local hard drive *and* those on the
web server, click the Expand button shown in Figure 9-16. This gives you a view that's similar to the Site View tab
in Expression Web.

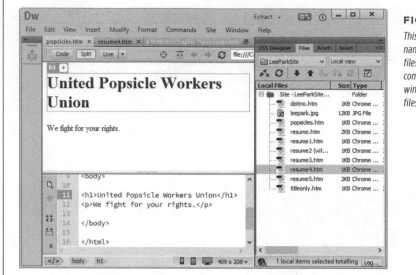

FIGURE 9-16

This is the local view of a website named LeeParkSite. It lists all the files in the site folder on your computer. Using the icons in this window, you can quickly transfer files to and from your server.

3. **Select the files you want to transfer to the server.**

   You can select multiple files by holding down Ctrl (⌘) while you click each file's icon.

4. **Click the Put arrow (the one that points up), or right-click the selected files, and choose Put.**

   Dreamweaver asks if you want to copy dependent files.

5. **Choose Yes to copy all the files that make up your site.**

   For example, if you upload a page that uses <img> elements to display graphics, click Yes to make sure Dreamweaver uploads the graphics files as well as the pages themselves. If you don't have any dependent files, your choice has no effect.

   Once you make your choice, Dreamweaver connects to your web server and transfers the files.

■ COPYING FILES TO YOUR COMPUTER

To do the reverse and transfer files from your server to your computer, you use a *get* operation. Follow these steps:

1. **In the Files panel, choose your website from the drop-down menu at the top left.**

2. **Choose "Remote server" from the drop-down menu at the top right (see Figure 9-16).**

   Dreamweaver doesn't automatically display the list of files on your server, because getting that list could take a little time. So you need to specifically ask Dreamweaver for an updated view of the files on the server, which you'll do in the next step.

3. **Click the Refresh button, which looks like a circular arrow icon.**

   Dreamweaver connects to the web server and displays the list of site files.

4. **Select the files you want to transfer to your computer.**

   You can select multiple files by holding down Ctrl (⌘) while you click each file's name.

5. **Click the Get arrow (the down-pointing arrow icon), or right-click the selected files, and choose Get.**

   Dreamweaver asks if you want to copy dependent files.

6. **Choose Yes if you want to copy linked files.**

   For example, if you download a page that uses <img> elements to display graphics, click Yes to make sure Dreamweaver downloads the graphics, too. If your page doesn't have any dependent files, your choice has no effect.

   Now Dreamweaver connects to your web server and copies the files to the site folder on your computer.

> **TIP** Once you're comfortable transferring small batches of files, you can try out Dreamweaver's Synchronize button. It works like the website publishing feature in Expression Web. When you click it, Dreamweaver examines the web page files on your computer, determines which ones you updated, and transfers just those to your server.

Uploading in Expression Web

Uploading a site in Expression Web is just as convenient as it is in Dreamweaver. Not only does it save you the effort of switching to a separate program, but it also keeps track of pages that have changed and lets you update just those files in a single, speedy operation.

Before you can take advantage of Expression Web's FTP features, however, you need to define your local website by following the site definition process explained on page 167. Make sure you choose to add the metadata folders, because Expression Web needs them to keep track of the files you change.

Once you define a site and switch on the metadata folders, you're ready to press on. Here's how to upload your site:

1. **Choose Site→Publishing (or click Publishing at the bottom of the Site View tab).**

   You can't publish your website until you fill in some basic information about your web hosting company.

2. **Click the big "Add a publishing destination" link in the middle of the Site View tab.**

   Expression Web displays the Connection Settings window (see Figure 9-17).

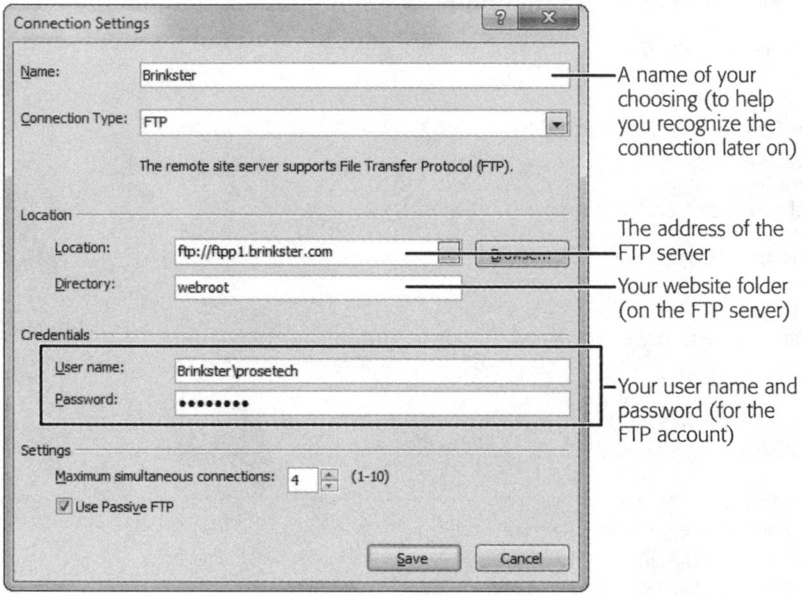

FIGURE 9-17

Your web hosting company should tell you the exact choices to make in the Connection Settings window. Typically, you need to supply the address of your host's FTP server, the directory (folder name) of your website on the server, and your user name and password. You need to complete this form only once. If you're successful, Expression Web uses this information the next time you publish your site (although you have to type in your password each time).

A name of your choosing (to help you recognize the connection later on)

The address of the FTP server

Your website folder (on the FTP server)

Your user name and password (for the FTP account)

3. **Fill in the information that tells Expression Web how to connect to your server, and then click Add.**

   Expression Web saves the info and connects to your web host. The next time you upload files, you'll see a "Connect to publishing destination" link instead of the "Add a publishing destination" link. Just click once to connect, with no extra work.

   Once you're connected, Expression Web shows you a side-by-side file list that compares the contents of the website stored on your computer with that on the server, so you can tell at a glance which files have changed (Figure 9-18).

4. **To bring your web server up to date, choose Site→Publish Changed Files.**

   This choice starts the publishing process (see Figure 9-19).

You can also transfer individual files using the arrows that appear between the two file lists. To transfer files from your computer to the server, select them on the left list and then click the right-facing arrow. To download a file from your server, select it from the right list and then click the left-facing arrow. The two-way arrow underneath ("Synchronize files") is like both operations rolled into one; it examines each file you select and makes sure it updates any old versions on either your computer or web server.

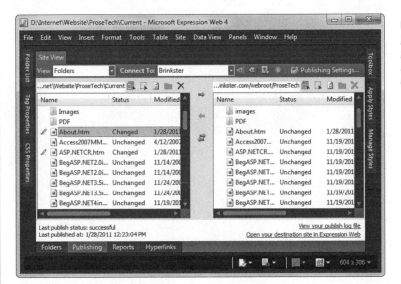

FIGURE 9-18

Here, Expression Web uses a pencil icon to highlight two files that you updated on your computer but not on the web server.

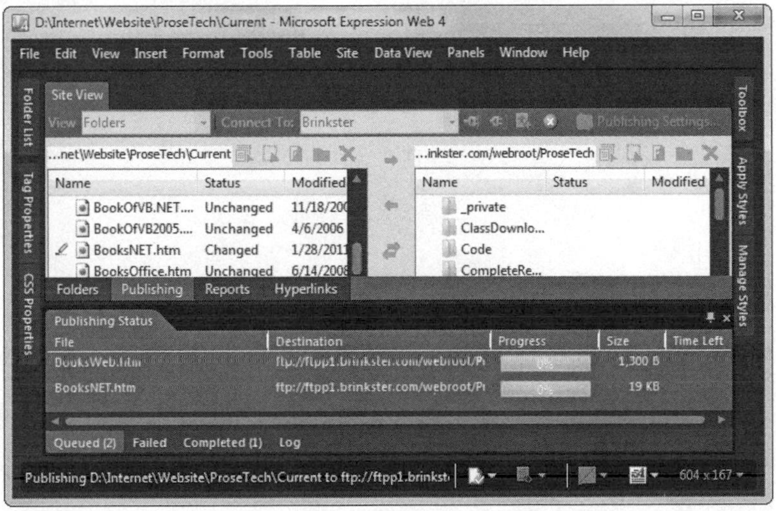

FIGURE 9-19

When you publish a website, Expression Web scans your files and copies only the ones you added or changed since the last time you published the site. A progress indicator identifies the file being copied and estimates how long the operation will take.

Connecting with Your Audience

Introducing Your Site to the World

So far, you've polished your website-design mettle and learned how to build sleek and sophisticated pages. Now it's time to shift to an entirely different role, that of website *promoter*.

One of the best ways to attract new visitors to your site is to turn up as a result in a web search. For that to happen, the leading search engines (that's Google, Yahoo, and Bing) need to know about your site, and they need to think it's important enough to rank as a search result. For example, if you're hawking fried delicacies at *www. sweetsaltysweets.com*, you want your website to turn up when someone searches for "chocolate-covered potato chips." And ideally, that result will be among the first few listed, or at least on the first page of results, which greatly increases your odds of getting noticed.

In this chapter, you'll see how search engines work. You'll learn how to make sure they regularly index your site, capture the right information, and expose your brilliance to the world. (Later, in Chapter 11, you'll continue this journey and learn more promotion strategies, all of which can help you work your way up the search results rankings.)

Lastly, you'll learn to gauge the success of your site with *visitor tracking*. You'll use a powerful, free service called Google Analytics to discover some of your visitors' deepest secrets—like where they live, what browsers they use, and which of your web pages they find absolutely unbearable. With this information, you'll have all the tools you need to improve your content and fine-tune the organization of your website. Before you know it, you'll be more popular than chocolate ice cream.

■ Your Website Promotion Plan

Before you plunge into the world of website promotion, you need a plan. Grab a pencil and plenty of paper, and get ready to jot down your ideas for global website domination (fiendish cackling is optional).

Although all webmasters have their own tactics, web mavens generally agree that the best way to market a site is to follow these steps:

1. **Build a truly great site.**

   If you start promoting your site before there's anything to see, you're wasting your effort (and probably burning a few bridges). Nothing says "Never come back" like a website that consists of an "Under Construction" message.

2. **See step 1.**

   If in doubt, keep polishing and perfecting your site. Fancy graphics aren't the key concern here. The most important detail is whether you have some genuinely useful content. Ask yourself—if you were browsing the Web, would you stop to take a look at this site? Make sure you take the time to add the kinds of features that keep visitors coming back. One great option: include a discussion forum (see the next chapter for details on that).

3. **Make your site search-engine friendly.**

   There are a number of ways to tweak and optimize your site to help search engines understand the nature of your content. Small details like page titles, alternate text, and meta elements (page 317) are easy to overlook when you start building a site but become more important when you need to popularize it.

4. **Submit your site to Internet search engines.**

   Now you're ready for the big time. Once you submit your site to search heavyweights like Google and Yahoo, it officially enters the public eye. However, it takes time to climb up the rankings and get spotted.

5. **Tweak your website's public profile with the free Google Webmaster Tools.**

   These handy tools let you adjust how Google sees your site and reveal some valuable information about it. For example, it lets you specify the geographic region you want associated with your site and lets you discover whether Google's having trouble indexing some of your pages.

6. **Figure out what happened.**

   To assess the successes and failures of your promotion strategies, you need to measure some vital statistics, like how many people visit your site, how long they stay, and how many visitors come back for more. To take stock, you need to crack open tools like hit counters and server logs.

You'll tackle all these steps in this chapter.

■ Making Your Site Search-Engine Friendly

A "search-engine friendly" website is one that search engines understand. As explained in the box on this page (below), a search engine needs to be able to pull some essential information from your web pages. Then it analyzes those details every minute and decides how useful your site is to millions of web searchers.

Modern search engines handle this task quickly and quietly, without revealing how much effort it really is. But behind the scenes, search engines use a lot of messy logic and number-crunching to analyze raw website data. If you can simplify the engines' work and make the content, quality, and relevance of your site stand out, you just might be rewarded with higher placement in search results.

UP TO SPEED

How Web Search Engines Work

A web search engine like Google consists of three parts. The first is an automated program that roams the Web, downloading everything it finds. This program (often known by more picturesque names like *spider*, *robot*, *bot*, or *crawler*) eventually stumbles across your site and copies its contents.

The second part is an indexer that chews through web pages and extracts a bunch of meaningful information, including the page's title, description, and keywords. The indexer also records a great deal more esoteric data, like tracking the words that crop up most often on your page, what other sites link to your page, and so on. The indexer inserts all this digested information into a giant catalog (technically, a *database*).

The search engine's final task is the part you're probably most familiar with—the search home page. You enter the keywords you're hunting for, and the search engine scans its catalog looking for suitable pages. Different engines have different ways of choosing pages, but the basic idea is to make sure the best and most relevant pages turn up early in the search results. (The *best* pages are those that the search engine ranks as highly popular and well-linked. The *most relevant* pages are those that most closely match your search keywords.) Due to the complex algorithms search engines use, a slightly different search (say, "green tea health" instead of just "green tea") can get you a completely different set of results.

Choose Meaningful Page Titles

Remember that short snippet of content that goes in the `<title>` element in your web page (page 20)? It's easy to overlook but vitally important, because the title text becomes the key piece of identifying information people see in a search result (Figure 10-1).

A common newbie mistake is to give every page the same title—for example, a company name. This is appropriate on your home page, but not anywhere else on your site. Instead, a good page title describes the function of your page. For example, a music school named Cacophony Studios might have page titles like this: Our Teachers, The Cacophony Studios Difference, Signing Up for Music Class, Payments and Policies, and so on. (If you really must have the company name in a page title, place it after the descriptive text, as in "Our Teachers - Cacophony Studios.")

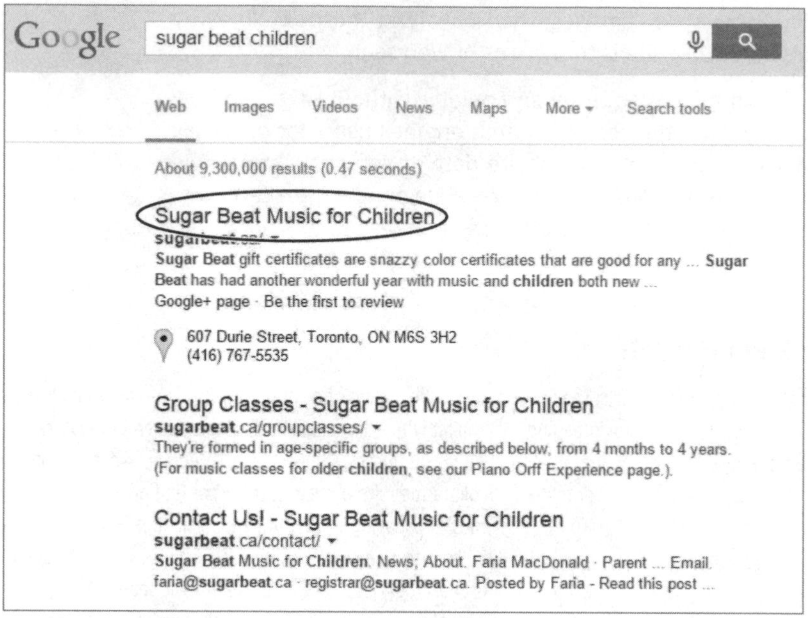

FIGURE 10-1

Ever wondered where the information you see in search listings comes from? The link in this example ("Sugar Beat Music for Children") is the title of the target page, as set in the <title> element.

> **TIP** If a visitor bookmarks your page, the text in the bookmark label comes from the <title> element in your page. Keep that in mind, and refrain from adding long slogans. "Ketchup Crusaders – Because ketchup isn't just for making food tasty" is about the longest you can stretch a title, and even that's iffy. On the other hand, your titles should include essential information; titles like Welcome or Untitled 1 (a favorite in Expression Web) aren't very helpful.

Title text is also important because search engines look for it. In fact, they give it more weight than the text inside your page. So if someone's search keywords match words in your title, odds are your page will get better placement in the search results. (But don't try to game the system with ridiculously long page titles, because search engines may compensate by ignoring them.)

Include a Page Description

Along with the title, every web page should have one other basic piece of information: a description that briefly summarizes the page. Once again, the description text plays two roles. First, search engines give it extra weight in a search, and second, they often display the description on the search results page, as shown in Figure 10-2.

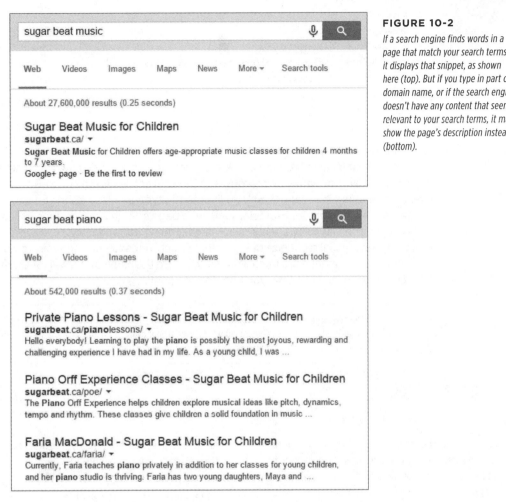

FIGURE 10-2

If a search engine finds words in a page that match your search terms, it displays that snippet, as shown here (top). But if you type in part of a domain name, or if the search engine doesn't have any content that seems relevant to your search terms, it may show the page's description instead (bottom).

To add a description, you need to supply something called a *meta element* (also known as a *meta tag*). Technically, meta elements contain hidden information—information that doesn't appear in a visitor's browser but may convey important information about your site's content to something else, like an automated search-bot.

NOTE Fun fact for etymologists and geeks alike: the term "meta element" means "elements *about*," as in "elements that provide information *about* your web page."

You put all meta elements in the <head> section of a page. Here's a sample meta element that assigns a description to a web page:

```
<!DOCTYPE html>
<html>
<head>
  <meta name="description"
    content="Noodletastic offers custom noodle dishes made to order." />
  <title>Noodletastic</title>
</head>
<body>...</body>
</html>
```

All meta elements look more or less the same. The element name is <meta>, the name attribute indicates the type of meta element it is (a page description, a set of keywords, an author name, and so on), and the content attribute supplies the relevant information. In theory, there's no limit to the type of information you can put inside a meta element. For example, some web page editing programs insert meta elements that say its software built your pages (don't worry; once you understand meta elements, you'll recognize this harmless fingerprint and you can easily remove it). Another page might use a meta element to record the name of the web designers who created it, or the last time you updated the page.

> **TIP** Although you can stuff a lot of information into your description, it's a good idea to limit it to a couple of focused sentences that total no more than around 50 words. Even if your description appears on a search results page, readers see only the first part of it, followed by an ellipsis (...) where it gets cut off.

NOSTALGIA CORNER

The Keyword Meta Element

Long ago, when life was far simpler and Nigerian gentlemen never needed help transferring large sums of money, search engines had an easy task. Many ignored most of a web page but paid close attention to the *keywords* meta element. Then, when someone went searching, the search engine simply checked for pages that had the search terms in their keyword list and put those in the search results.

Here's an example of a typical keywords list. It includes about 25 words or phrases that best represent the website, with each entry separated by a comma.

```
<meta name="keywords"
content="Noodletastic, noodles, noodle,
```

```
pasta, delicious, Italian food, fantastic
noodles, ramen, custom, made-to-order,
dishes, organic, whole-wheat, spelt" />
```

Today, most search engines ignore the keyword list. That's because it was notorious for abuses (many a webmaster stuffed her keyword list full of hundreds of words, some only tangentially related to the site's content). Search engines like Google take a more direct approach—they look at all the words on your web page and pay special attention to words that appear most often, appear in headings, and so on. Most web experts argue that the keyword list has outlived its usefulness, and many don't bother adding it to their pages at all.

Supply Alternate Text for All Your Images

A search engine draws information from many parts of your page. One easily overlooked detail is alternate text—the text a browser displays if it can't retrieve an image. As you learned on page 116, you specify this text using the `alt` attribute in the `<img>` element:

```
<img src="fish0123.jpg" alt="rainbow trout" />
```

Search engines pay attention to alternate text. If a web search uses keywords that match your alternate text, there's a greater chance of your page turning up in the results. The odds increase even more if the searcher is looking for a picture. For example, Google uses alternate text as the basis for its image search tool at *http:// images.google.com*. If you don't have alternate text, Google has to guess what the picture is about by looking at nearby text, which is less reliable.

Use Descriptive Link Text

The famous anchor tag can wrap any piece of text. Search engines like Google give that piece of text—the clickable bit that's underlined in blue—extra weight. But that's not much help if you waste it with a link like this:

```
To learn more about elephants, <a href-"ElephantStories.htm">click here</a>.
```

A better-designed link like this tells search engines more about your site:

```
To learn more about elephants, visit our
<a href="ElephantStories.htm">Elephant Stories</a> page.
```

It's also worth your while to make sure that the web page you link to (in this case, that's *ElephantStories.htm*), has a good, recognizable name.

Don't Try to Cheat

There are quite a few unwholesome tricks that crafty web weavers have used to game the search engine system (or at least try). For example, they might add a huge number of keywords but hide the text so that it isn't visible on the page (white text on a white background is one oddball option, but there are other style-sheet cheats, too). Another technique is to create pages that aren't really part of your website but that you store on your server. You can fill these pages with repeating keywords. To implement this trick, you use a little JavaScript code to make sure real people who accidentally arrive at the page are directed to the entry point of your site, while search engines get to feast on the keywords.

As seductive as some of these strategies may seem to lonely websites (and their owners), the best advice is to avoid them altogether. The first problem is that they pose a new set of headaches and technical challenges, which can waste hours of your day. But more significantly, search engines learn about these cheats almost as fast as web developers invent them. If a search engine catches you using them, it penalizes your site (so it ranks lower in the search results) or bans it completely, relegating it to the dustbin of the Web. (It even happens to the heavyweights. For example, JCPenney was given a hefty search demotion for using a few dirty search-engine optimization tricks during the Christmas 2010 season.)

If you're still tempted, keep this in mind: Many of these tricks just don't work. In the early days of the Web, primitive search engines gave a site more weight based on the number of times a keyword cropped up, but modern search engines like Google use much more sophisticated page-ranking systems. A huge load of hidden keywords won't move you up the search list one iota.

■ Registering with Search Engines

For most people, search engines are the one and only tool for finding information on the Web. If you want the average person to find your site, you need to make sure it appears in the most popular search engine catalogs and turns up as one of the results in relevant searches. This task is harder than it seems, because millions of sites jockey for position in search-engine rankings. To get noticed, you need to spend time developing your site and enhancing its visibility. You also need to understand how search engines rank pages (see the box on page 321 for more on that).

But every website needs to start somewhere. In the following sections you'll learn how to formally introduce yourself to Google, Bing, Yahoo, and an online directory of sites called the ODP.

Submitting Your Site to Google

The undisputed king of web search engines is Google (*www.google.com*). It's far and away the Web's most popular search tool, with a commanding share of over 70 percent of all search traffic.

Second place currently goes to Yahoo, and third place to Microsoft's Bing. But behind the scenes, Yahoo quietly uses Bing to power its search results. This means that just two search engines (Google and Bing) are responsible for at least 95 percent of the web searches in the Western world. Other countries, particularly those with web censorship practices, like China, have their own search engines.

It's not too difficult to get Google and other search engines to notice your site. By the time it's about a month old, Google will probably have stumbled across it at least once, usually by following a link from another site. As described in the box on page 321, Google takes outside links into consideration when sizing up a site, so the more sites that link to you, the more likely you are to turn up in someone's search results.

If you're impatient or you think Google is passing you by, you can introduce yourself directly using the submission form at *www.google.com/addurl* (see Figure 10-3). To get Bing's attention, go to *www.bing.com/toolbox/submit-site-url*. Most search engines include a submission form like this. Just make sure you keep track of where you apply, so you don't inadvertently submit your site to the same search engine more than once.

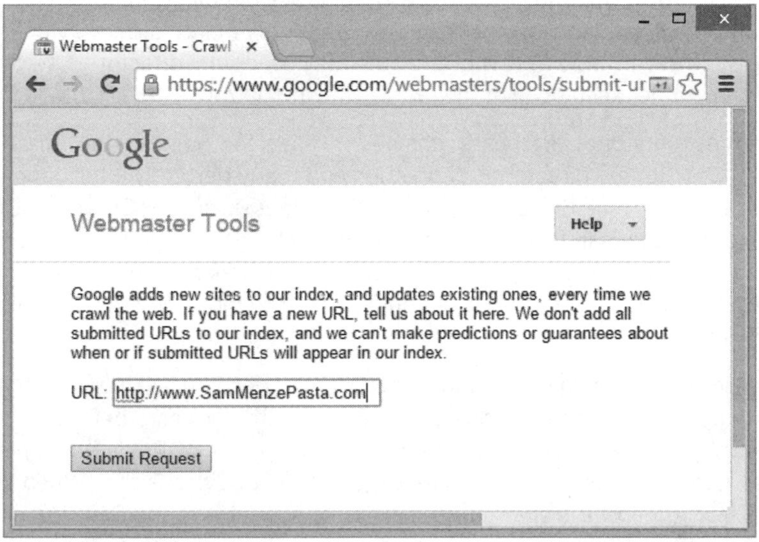

FIGURE 10-3

Google's stripped-down submission form requires just one detail: the URL that points to your site's home page. Make sure you include the http:// prefix at the start.

Webmaster Tools - Crawl

https://www.google.com/webmasters/tools/submit-ur

Google

Webmaster Tools   Help ▾

Google adds new sites to our index, and updates existing ones, every time we crawl the web. If you have a new URL, tell us about it here. We don't add all submitted URLs to our index, and we can't make predictions or guarantees about when or if submitted URLs will appear in our index.

URL: http://www.SamMenzePasta.com

Submit Request

How Google's PageRank Works

Google uses a rating system called *PageRank* to size up different web pages. It doesn't use PageRank to *find* search results; it uses it to *order* them. When you execute a search with Google, it pulls out all the sites that match your search keywords. Then it orders the results according to the PageRank of each page.

The basic idea behind the PageRank system is that it determines the value of your site by the community of other websites that link to it. There are a few golden rules:

- The more sites that link to you, the better.
- A link from a more popular site is more valuable than a link from a less popular site.
- The more links a site has, the less each link is worth. In other words, if someone links to your site and just a

handful of other sites, that link is valuable. If someone links to your site and *hundreds* of other sites, the link's value is diluted.

Although Google regularly fine-tunes its secret PageRank recipe, web experts spend hours trying to deconstruct it. For some fascinating reading, you can learn more about how PageRank works (loosely) at *www.markhorrell.com/seo/pagerank.html*. For a more technical look at the math behind PageRank, check out *http://en.wikipedia.org/wiki/PageRank*.

Submitting Your Site to the Open Directory Project

Directories are searchable site listings with a difference: humans, not programs, create them. The idea made a lot of sense in the early days of the Internet, and it turned Yahoo, the creator of the most popular early Internet directory, into a tech titan. But over the years, directories have become increasingly marginalized. Companies like Google and even Yahoo have shuttered their once-popular directories, because they could no longer keep up with the rapidly changing Web.

So, given that directories are nearly obsolete, what's the point of talking about them? You *could* ignore directories altogether, and many perfectly intelligent web designers do exactly that. However, some search engines (including Google) still pay attention to the listings in the Open Directory Project (ODP) at *http://dmoz.org*, a long-standing website directory staffed entirely by thousands of volunteer editors. If you get a spot in the ODP, it can help your site start to move up the results list in a full-text search.

However, there's a catch. In recent years, the ODP has become swamped with registration requests. In some categories, it may be months or years before a site is considered. And there's been more than one sordid story of ODP editors demanding bribes to get a website into the directory. The best advice is this: When your website is ready, follow the steps in this section to submit it to the ODP. But don't panic if your site doesn't get listed, as search engines have plenty of other ways to find and rank your pages.

Before submitting to the ODP, take the time to make sure you do it right. An incorrect submission could result in your website not getting listed at all. You can find a complete description of the rules at *http://dmoz.org/add.html*, but here are the key requirements:

- Don't submit your site more than once.

- Don't submit your site for consideration in more than one subject category.

- Don't submit more than one page or section of your site (unless you have a really good reason, like that the separate sections are notably different).

- Don't submit sites that contain "illegal" content. By the ODP's definition, that's more accurately described as unsavory material like pornography, libelous content, or material that advocates illegal activity—you know who you are.

- Clean up any broken links, outdated information, or other red flags that might suggest that your site isn't here for the long term.

- When you submit your site, describe it carefully and accurately. Don't promote it. In other words, "Ketchup Masters manufactures gourmet ketchup" is acceptable. "Ketchup Masters is the best food-oriented site on the Web—the Louisville Times says you can't miss it!" isn't.

- Don't submit an incomplete site. Your "Under Construction" page won't get listed.

The next step is to spend some time at the ODP site until you find the single best category for your website (see Figure 10-4).

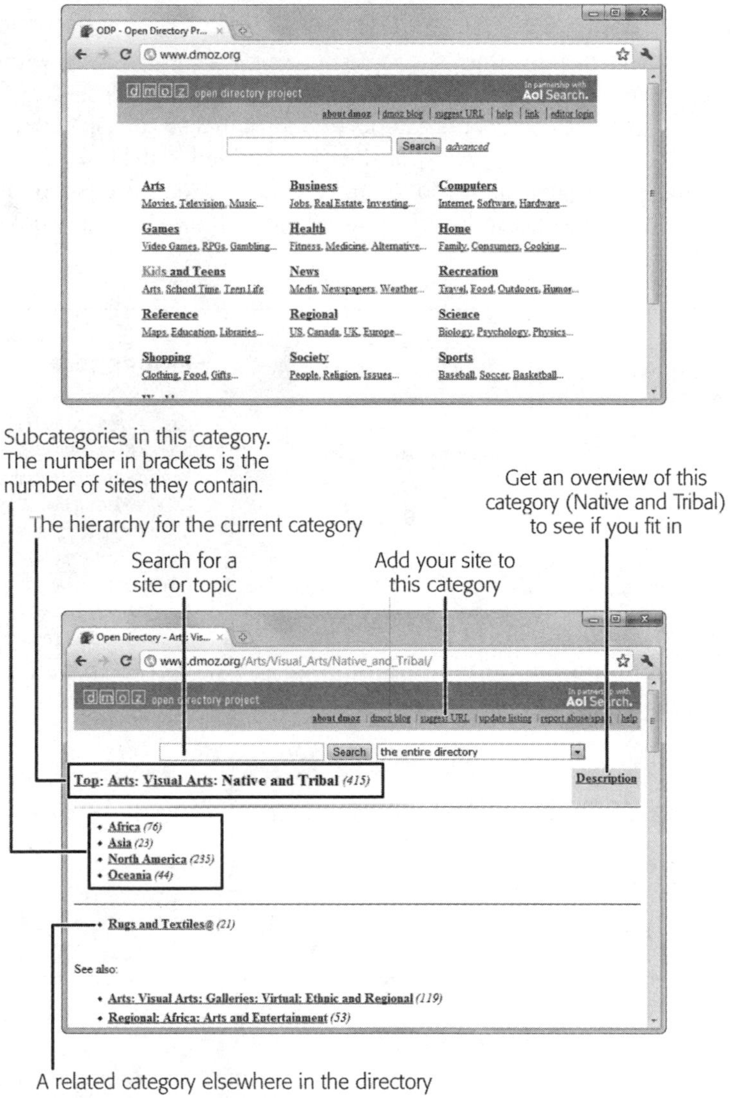

FIGURE 10-4

Top: When you arrive at the ODP site, you see a group of general, top-level categories.

Bottom: As you click your way deeper into the topic hierarchies, you'll eventually find a specific subcategory that would make a good home for your site, such as the Arts→Visual Arts→"Native and Tribal" category. There are several subcategories (like Asia, with 23 sites). Categories with an @ after their names link to related categories in a different place in the directory.

Subcategories in this category. The number in brackets is the number of sites they contain.

The hierarchy for the current category

Search for a site or topic

Get an overview of this category (Native and Tribal) to see if you fit in

Add your site to this category

A related category elsewhere in the directory

Once you find the perfect category, click the "suggest URL" link at the top of the page and fill out the submission form. It asks for your URL, the title of your site, a brief description, and your email address.

Once you submit your site, there's nothing to do but wait. If a month passes without your site appearing in the listing and you haven't received an email describing any problems with it, it's time to contact the category editor. If that still doesn't work, it's time to write a polite email asking why your site wasn't added to the listings, being sure to include the date of your submission(s) and the name, URL, and description of your site. You can find the email address for the category editor at the very bottom of the category page (see Figure 10-5).

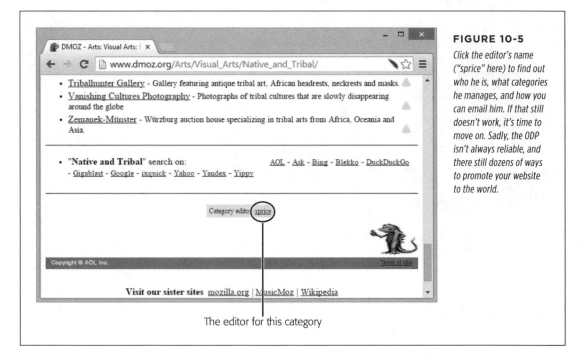

FIGURE 10-5

Click the editor's name ("sprice" here) to find out who he is, what categories he manages, and how you can email him. If that still doesn't work, it's time to move on. Sadly, the ODP isn't always reliable, and there still dozens of ways to promote your website to the world.

The editor for this category

Rising Up in the Search Rankings

You'll soon discover that it's not difficult to get into Google's index, but you might find it exceedingly hard to get noticed. For example, suppose you submit the site *www.SamMenzesHomemadePasta.com*. To see if you're in Google, try an extremely specific search that targets just your site, like "Sam Menzes Homemade Pasta." This should definitely lead to your doorstep. Now try searching for just "Homemade Pasta." Odds are you won't turn up in the top 10, or even the top 100.

So how do you create a site that the casual searcher is likely to find? There's no easy answer. Just remember that the secret to getting a good search ranking is having a good PageRank, and getting a good PageRank is all about connections. To stand out, your website needs to share links with other leading sites in your category. It also helps to have people talking about your site online, whether that's on Twitter, Facebook, or a personal blog. In the next chapter, you'll get plenty of tips for website promotion.

Google won't tell you the PageRank of your website. (In fact, it suggests you concentrate on building a fantastic website rather than getting fixated on a number.) However, most webmasters want to know how they rank, if only so they can gauge how the site's standing changes over time. Although you can't get the exact Page-Rank that Google uses in its search calculations, you *can* get a simplified PageRank score that gives you a general idea of your website's performance. This simplified PageRank is based on the real PageRank, but it's updated just twice a year, and it provides only a value from 1 to 10. (All things being equal, a website ranked 10 will turn up much earlier in someone's search results than a page ranked 1.)

There are two ways to find your website's simplified PageRank. First, you can use the free Google Toolbar (*www.google.com/toolbar*), which snaps on to your browser window and provides a PageRank button. However, you need to explicitly enable this feature, as described at *http://tinyurl.com/64bjmtd*. A simpler approach is to use an unofficial PageRank-checking website, like the one shown in Figure 10-6. You simply type in your URL and click a button to get your simplified PageRank score.

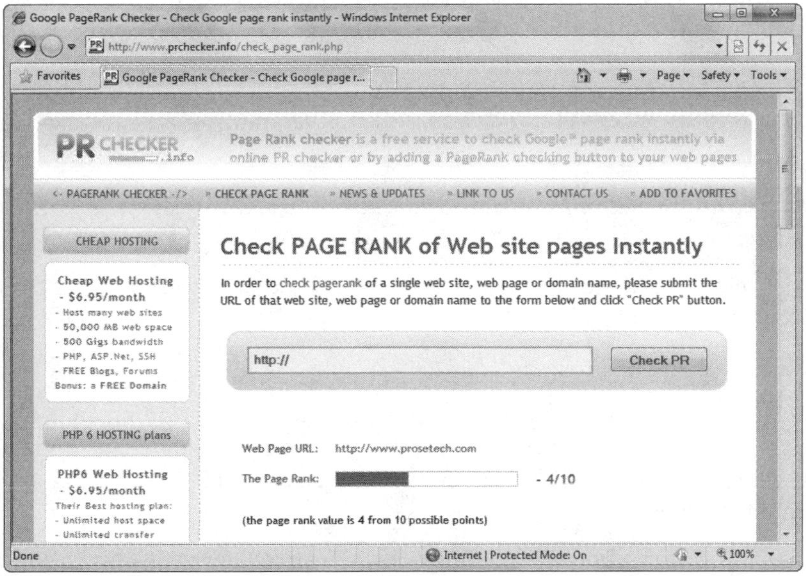

FIGURE 10-6

Use www.prchecker.info *(or search Google for a different PageRank checker) to quickly rank any website. Here, it reports that* www.prosetech.com *scores a middle-of-the-road 4 out of 10.*

If you want to delve into the nitty-gritty of *search engine optimization* (known to webmasters as SEO), consider becoming a regular reader of *www.webmasterworld. com* and *www.searchengineland.com*. You'll find articles and forums where webmasters discuss the good, bad, and downright seedy tricks you can try to get noticed.

TIP It's possible to get too obsessed with search engine rankings. Here's a good rule of thumb: Don't spend more time trying to improve your search engine rank than you do improving your website. In the long term, the only way to gain real popularity is to become one of the best sites on the block.

Hiding from Search Engines

In rare situations, you might create a page that you *don't* want to turn up in a search result. The most common reason is because you posted some information, like the latest Amazon e-coupons, that you want to share only with a few friends. If Google indexes your site, thousands of visitors could come your way, expecting to find a discount coupon and sucking up your bandwidth for the rest of the month. Another reason may be that you're posting something semi-private that you don't want other people to stumble across, like a story about how you stole a dozen staplers from your boss. If you fall into the latter category, be very cautious. Keeping search engines away is the least of your problems—once a site is on the Web, it *will* be discovered. And once it's discovered, it won't ever go away (see the box on page 328).

But you can do at least one thing to minimize your site's visibility or, possibly, hide it from search engines altogether. To understand how this procedure works, recall that search engines do their work in several stages. In the first one, a robot program crawls across the Web, downloading sites. You can tell this robot not to index your site, or to ignore a portion of it, in several ways.

To keep a robot away from a single page, add the *robots* meta element to the page. Set the content attribute to noindex, as shown here:

```
<meta name="robots" content="noindex" />
```

Remember, like all meta elements, you place this one in the <head> section of your HTML document.

Alternatively, you can use nofollow to tell robots to index the current page but not to follow any of its links:

```
<meta name="robots" content="nofollow" />
```

If you want to block larger portions of your site, you're better off creating a specialized file called *robots.txt*, and placing it in the top-level folder of your site. The robot will check this file before it goes any further. The content inside the *robots. txt* file sets the rules.

If you want to stop a robot from indexing any part of your site, add this to the *robots.txt* file:

```
User-Agent: *
Disallow: /
```

The User-Agent part identifies the type of robot you're addressing, and an asterisk represents all robots. The Disallow part indicates what part of the website is off limits; a single forward slash represents the whole site.

To rope off just the Photos subfolder on your site, use this (making sure to match the capitalization of the folder name exactly):

```
User-Agent: *
Disallow: /Photos
```

To stop a robot from indexing certain types of content (like images), use this:

```
User-Agent: *
Disallow: /*.gif
Disallow: /*.jpeg
```

As this example shows, you can put as many Disallow rules as you want in the *robots.txt* file, one after the other.

Remember, the *robots.txt* file is just a set of *guidelines* for search engine robots; it's not a form of access control. In other words, it's similar to posting a "No Flyers" sign on your mailbox: It works only as long as advertisers choose to heed it.

> **TIP** You can learn much more about robots, including how to tell when they visit your site and how to restrict robots from specific search engines, at *www.robotstxt.org*.

The Google Webmaster Tools

If you're feeling a bit in the dark about your website's relationship with Google, you'll be happy to know that the company has a service that can help you out. It's called the Google Webmaster Tools, and it serves two purposes. First, it provides information that clarifies how Google indexes your pages. Second, it lets you tweak a few settings that govern how Google treats your site.

To use the Google Webmaster Tools, follow these steps:

1. **Go to *www.google.com/webmasters/tools* and sign in with your Google account. If you don't have one (it's free), click "Create an account now."**

   A Google account lets you use a number of indispensable Google services, like Google Analytics (page 332), Gmail (Google's web-based email service), Google AdSense (Chapter 13), and Blogger (Chapter 12). Every webmaster has one.

Web Permanence

You've probably heard a lot of talk about the ever-changing nature of the Web. Maybe you're worried that the links you create today will lead to dead sites or missing pages tomorrow. Well, there's actually a much different issue taking shape—copies of old sites that just won't go away.

Once you put your work on the Web, you've lost control of it. The corollary to this sobering thought is: Always make sure you aren't posting something that's illegal, infringes on a copyright, is personally embarrassing, or could get you fired. Because once you put this material out on the Web, you can assume it will be there forever.

For example, imagine you accidentally reveal your company's trade secret for carrot-flavored chewing gum. A few weeks later, an excited customer links to your site. You realize your mistake and pull the pages off your web server. But have you really contained the problem?

Assuming the Google robot has visited your site recently (which is more than likely), Google now has a copy of your old site. Even worse, people can get this *cached* (saved) copy from Google if they know about the *cache* keyword.

For example, if the offending page's URL is *www.GumLover. com/newProduct.htm*, a savvy Googler can get the old copy of your page by typing in the search term *cache:www.GumLover. com/newProduct.htm*. (Less savvy visitors might still stumble onto a cached page by clicking the Cached link that appears after each search result in Google's listings.) Believe it or not, this trick has been used to resurrect accidentally leaked information, ranging from gossip to software license keys.

You can try to get your page out of Google's cache as quickly as possible using the remove URL feature at *www.google.com/ webmasters/tools/removals*. But even if this works, you're probably starting to see the problem: You have no way to know how many search engines made copies of your work. Interested (or nosy) people who notice that you pulled information off of your site may hit these search engines and copy the details to their own sites, making it pretty near impossible to eliminate the lingering traces of your mistake. There are even catalogs dedicated to preserving old websites for posterity (see the Wayback Machine at *www.archive.org*).

2. **Once you sign in, you need to register your website. Click the "Add a site" button, type in the full URL of your site (like *www.supermagicalpotatoes. co.uk*), and then click Continue.**

    This associates your website with your Google account. However, before you can actually view data for your site or manage its Google-related search settings, you need to prove that you're the legitimate owner of the site.

3. **Choose how you want to prove website ownership (see Figure 10-7).**

    Google asks you to prove ownership by uploading a Google-supplied file to your website folder. In some situations, however, you might need to take a slightly more awkward approach. For example, if you use domain forward to direct the visitor to another site, Google will check for the uploaded file on the website that does the forwarding, which isn't the website that holds your content. In this case, you can verify your website by adding a DNS record (click "Alternate methods," choose "Domain name provider," and then follow the instructions from there).

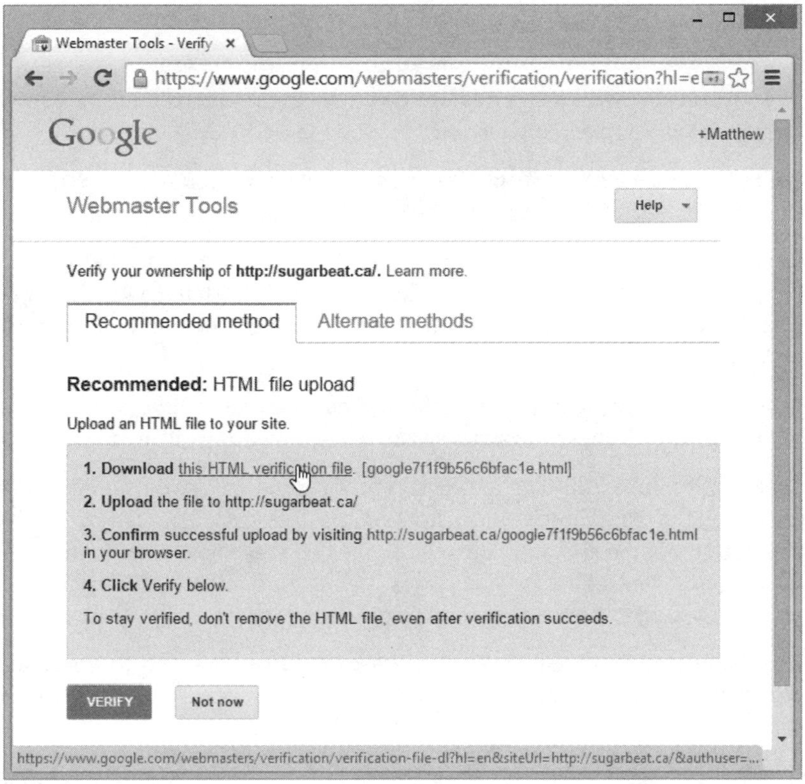

FIGURE 10-7

To verify that you own a site, download the Google-supplied verification file, and then upload it to your site's root folder.

NOTE Rest assured, no matter what verification method you use, it won't affect the way your website works. In fact, Google recommends that you don't remove the meta element you added (or delete the verification file you uploaded). That way you won't need to verify your ownership to Google again.

4. **Once you upload the confirmation file, click Verify.**

   Usually, Google verifies your site mere seconds after you make the appropriate change. Once the company knows that you're the real owner, it brings you to the Webmaster Tools' site-management page and adds a pile of management links to the left side of it (see Figure 10-8). From this point on, whenever you log into the Google Webmaster Tools and click your site's name, you'll be able to use all of Google's tools to review and manage it.

The Google Webmaster Tools let you look at your website through the eyes of Google. You choose what you want to do by clicking one of the links in the Dashboard section on the left side of the page. Here are some of the possibilities:

- **Search Appearance→Sitelinks.** Sitelinks are the quick-access links that appear underneath some search listings and let visitors jump straight to a specific page in the website. Unfortunately, only Google can decide to reward your website with sitelinks (based on the popularity and structure of your site). If Google does give you sitelinks, however, you can use this section to remove any that aren't appropriate.

- **Search Traffic→Search Queries.** Here you get information about the searches that have led Googlers to your website (see Figure 10-8).

- **Search Traffic→Links to Your Site.** This option shows you which websites link to yours. It's a useful way to see who's paying attention to your content.

- **Crawl→Crawl Errors.** This section warns you about any problems Google encounters as it indexes your site, like incorrect metadata (page 317), pages that it couldn't access (and therefore couldn't index), or evil malware lurking on your server.

- **Crawl→robots.txt Tester.** This section helps you create a *robots.txt* file, which hides a portion of your site from nosy search engines, as explained on page 326.

- **Crawl→Sitemaps.** This section helps you build a *sitemap*—a special file that describes the structure of your site and the files in it. You can submit your sitemap to Google and other search engines so they know what to index. This is particularly useful if you have pages that Google might ordinarily miss, like standalone pages (those not linked to other pages).

- **Gear icon (top-right corner)→Change of Address.** Moving to a new URL? This section helps you redirect Google to your new home, so you can take your web traffic with you.

Most serious web designers eventually check out their sites with Google Webmaster Tools. If nothing else, you can use it to make sure everything is running smoothly—in other words, that Google can get to your pages, that its automated robot returns frequently to check for new content, and that the robot reviews all the pages you have to offer.

■ Tracking Visitors

As a website owner, you'll try a lot of tactics to promote your site. Naturally, some will work while others won't. You want to keep the good strategies and prune those that fail. To do this successfully, you need a way to assess how your site performs.

Almost every web hosting company (except free web hosts) gives you some way to track the number of visitors to your site (see Figure 10-9). Ask your host how to use these tools. Usually, you need to log onto a "Control Panel" or "My Account" section of your host's site. You'll see a variety of options there; look for an icon labeled "Site Counters" or "Web Traffic."

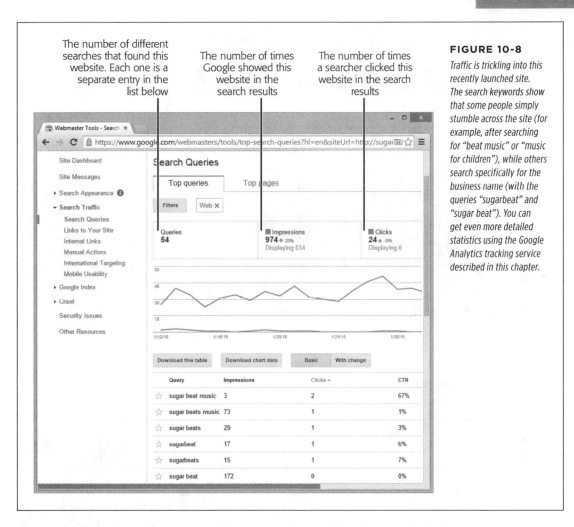

The number of different searches that found this website. Each one is a separate entry in the list below

The number of times Google showed this website in the search results

The number of times a searcher clicked this website in the search results

FIGURE 10-8

Traffic is trickling into this recently launched site. The search keywords show that some people simply stumble across the site (for example, after searching for "beat music" or "music for children"), while others search specifically for the business name (with the queries "sugarbeat" and "sugar beat"). You can get even more detailed statistics using the Google Analytics tracking service described in this chapter.

With more high-end hosting services, you often have more options for viewing your site's traffic statistics. Some hosts provide the raw *web server logs*, which store detailed, blow-by-blow information about every one of your visitors. This information includes the times visitors came to your site, their IP addresses (page 281), their browser types, what sites referred them to you, whether they ran into an error, what pages they ignored, what pages they loved, and so on. To make sense of this information, you need to feed these raw numbers into a high-powered program that performs *log analysis*. These programs are often complex and expensive. An equally powerful but much more convenient approach is the Google Analytics tracking service, described next.

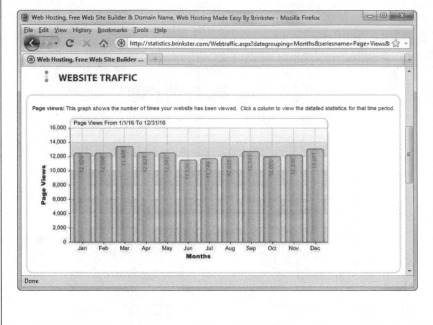

FIGURE 10-9

This Brinkster Page View Summary shows the number of hits (page requests) received on a given day. The chart below the summary (not shown) details the total number of bytes of information downloaded from your site. It's important to realize that a "hit" is defined as a request for a page. If a single visitor travels around your website, requesting several pages, she generates several hits. To find out how many unique visitors you have, you need to use a separate log analysis program, described below.

Understanding Google Analytics

In 2005, Google purchased Urchin, one of the premium web tracking companies. It transformed Urchin into *Google Analytics* and abolished its hefty $500-a-month price tag, making it free for everyone. Today, Google Analytics just might be the best way to see what's happening on any website, whether you're building a three-page site about dancing hamsters or a massive compendium of movie reviews.

Google Analytics is refreshingly simple. Unlike other log analysis tools, it doesn't ask you to provide server logs or other low-level information. Instead, it tracks all the information you need *on its own*. It stores this information indefinitely and lets you analyze it anytime with a range of snazzy web reports.

To use Google Analytics, you need to add a snippet of JavaScript code to every web page you want to track (usually, that's every page on your site). Once you get the code in place, everything works seamlessly. When a visitor heads to one of your pages, the browser sends a record of the request to Google's army of monster web servers, which store it for later analysis. The visitor doesn't see the Google Analytics stuff. Figure 10-10 shows you how it works.

> **NOTE** Remember, JavaScript is a type of mini-program that runs inside virtually every browser in existence. Chapter 14 provides an introduction to JavaScript.

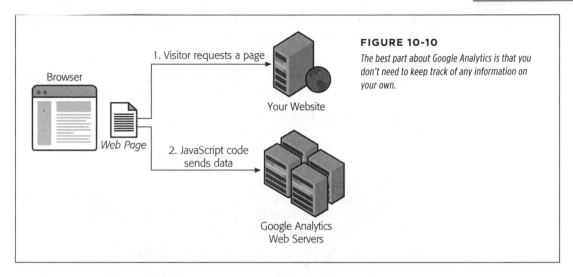

FIGURE 10-10

The best part about Google Analytics is that you don't need to keep track of any information on your own.

Using this system, Google Analytics collects two kinds of information:

- **Information about your visitors' browsers and computers.** Whenever a browser requests a page, it supplies a basic set of information. This includes the type of browser it is, the features it supports, and the IP address of the computer it connects through (an *IP address* is a numeric code that uniquely identifies a computer on the Internet). These details don't include the information you really want—for example, there's no way to find out personal details like names or addresses. However, Google uses other browser information to infer additional details. For example, using the IP address, it makes an educated guess about your visitor's geographic location.

- **Visitor tracking.** Thanks to its sophisticated tracking system, Google Analytics can determine more interesting information about a visitor's patterns. Ordinarily, if a visitor requests two separate pages from the same site, there's no way to establish whether those requests came from the same person. However, Google uses a *cookie* (a small packet of data stored on a visitor's computer) to uniquely identify each visitor. As a result, when visitors click links and move from page to page, Google can determine their navigation paths, the amount of time they spend on each page, and whether they return later.

Google Analytics wouldn't be nearly as useful if it were up to you to make sense of all this information. But as you'll see, Google not only tracks these details, but it also provides reports that help you figure out what the data really means. You generate the reports using a handy web screen menu, and you can print them out or download them for use in another program, like Excel, to do further analysis.

Signing Up for Google Analytics

Signing up for Google Analytics is easy:

1. **Head over to** *www.google.com/analytics*. **If you're not logged into your Google account, click the "Sign in" link.**

   Google Analytics is yet another of many services you can use with a single Google account. If you don't have a Google account, click "Create an account," supply the standard personal details, and then continue on.

2. **Click the "Sign up" button, and then fill in the information about your website.**

   You need to supply several pieces of information, including the following:

   - A descriptive name for your account and your website. It doesn't matter what you pick (but using your business name or your website's domain name makes good sense). These names are just there so you can tell your sites apart if you add more than one.

   - The URL for the site you want to track (for example, *www.supermagical potatoes.co.uk*). A Google Analytics account can track as many sites as you like, but for now start with just one.

   - The industry category, which characterizes the type of site you're tracking. You pick from a list that includes entries such as "Arts and Entertainment" and "Politics."

   - Your time zone. This lets Google Analytics synchronize its clock with yours.

3. **Click the "Get Tracking ID" button.**

   After you sign in, Google gives you the JavaScript code you need to add to your pages to start tracking visitors (see Figure 10-11). The next section tells you how.

4. **Add the tracking code to your web pages.**

   When you add Google's code to a page, put it at the very end of the <head> section, just before the closing </head> tag. Here's an example of where it fits in a typical web page:

   ```
   <!DOCTYPE>
   <html>
   <head>
     <title>Welcome</title>
     <!-- Put the analytics code here. -->
   </head>
   <body>
     ...
   </body>
   </html>
   ```

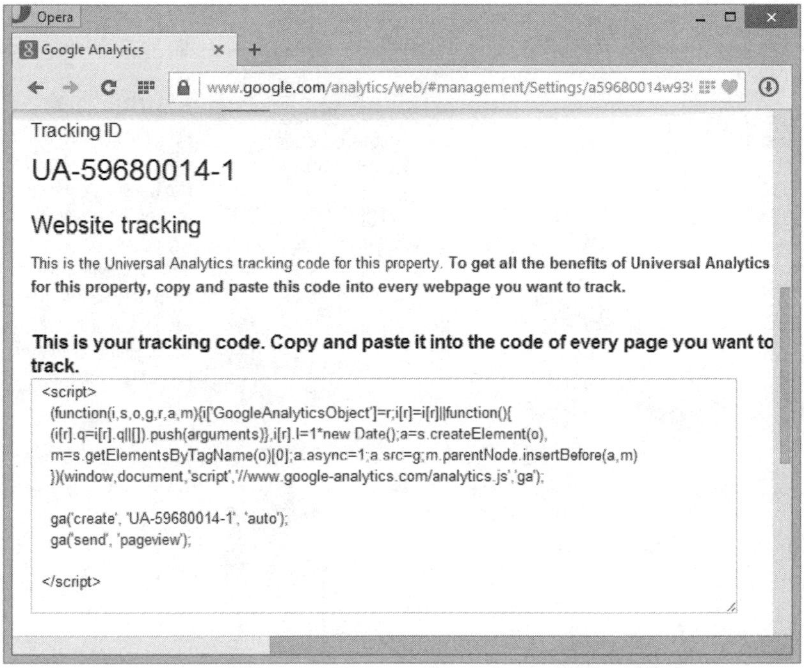

FIGURE 10-11

The Google Analytics code is lean and concise, requiring just a few lines of JavaScript. It links to a file on Google's web servers to get the real tracking code. Select all the code displayed, and then copy it to your Clipboard (you do this in most browsers by selecting the text, right-clicking it, and then choosing Copy).

Be advised, however, that Google Analytics used to use a different approach for several years, which put a slightly different tracking code after the </body> tag. So if you look at another page that uses Google Analytics, you might find the tracking code in a different place.

TIP For best results, copy the tracking code to every page in your site.

5. **Upload the new version of your web pages.**

   Once you change all your pages, make sure to upload them to your server. Only then can Google Analytics start tracking visitors. The tracking features won't work when you run the pages from your own computer's hard drive.

Now it's a waiting game. Within 24 hours, Google Analytics has enough information about recent visitors to provide its detailed reports.

The Google Analytics Dashboard

Once you set up your site, log into Google Analytics. You start at the Home tab shown in Figure 10-12, where you'll see a list of all the sites you're tracking and a few key details about each one.

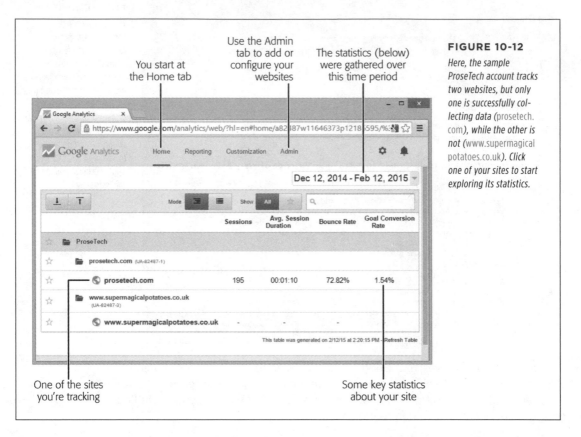

You start at
the Home tab

Use the Admin
tab to add or
configure your
websites

The statistics (below)
were gathered over
this time period

FIGURE 10-12

*Here, the sample
ProseTech account tracks
two websites, but only
one is successfully col-
lecting data (prosetech.
com), while the other is
not (www.supermagical
potatoes.co.uk). Click
one of your sites to start
exploring its statistics.*

One of the sites
you're tracking

Some key statistics
about your site

For example, in Figure 10-12 you can see that the *prosetech.com* site had 195 separate visits, with people lingering an average of just over a minute. But the bounce
rate, which tells you how many visitors left the site after viewing just a single page,
reports the bad news: 72% of your guests quickly moved on.

If you've waited 24 hours and Google still hasn't collected any statistics for your
site (as with the *www.supermagicalpotatoes.co.uk* site in Figure 10-12), it's time to
investigate the problem. Here's how to check your site's status:

1. **Click the Admin link at the top of the page.**

   Google takes you to a multicolumn management page.

2. **At the top of the Property column, choose the site that has the problem.**

   The column lists all the sites you track. If you track only one site, it's already
   picked.

3. **In the same column, click Tracking Info→Tracking Code.**

Google displays a box with the Analytics tracking code (just like in Figure 10-11). This is handy if you somehow made a mistake copying the code or if you need to add it to more pages. Just above the tracking code is the tracking *status*, which tells you whether the tracking code is working (Figure 10-13). You could see three values:

• **Receiving Data** indicates that all is well. Your visitors are going from page to page under the watchful eye of Google Analytics.

• **Waiting For Data** indicates that Google's JavaScript code is running on your pages, but the information needed for a report isn't available yet. Usually, you see this for the first 6 to 12 hours after you register a new site, but it could take a full day.

• **Tracking Not Installed** indicates that Google isn't collecting any information. This could be because you need to wait for visitors to hit your site, or it could suggest you haven't inserted the correct JavaScript tracking code.

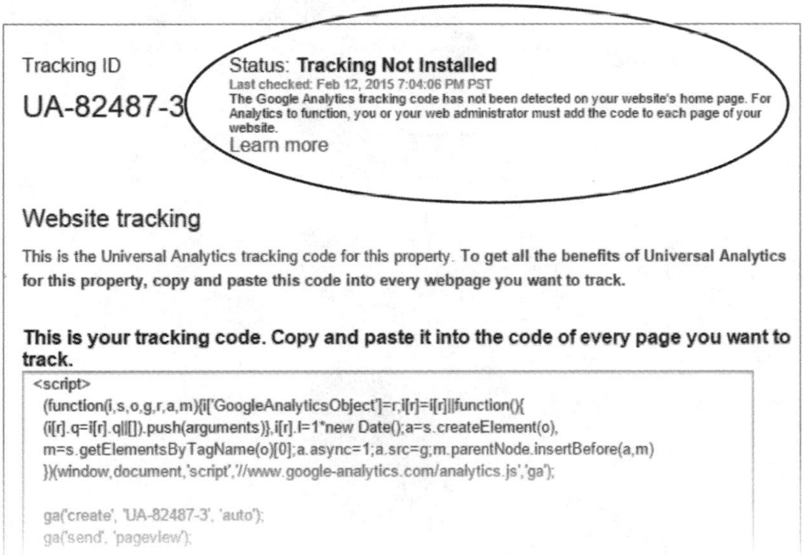

FIGURE 10-13

"Tracking Not Installed" means the Google Analytics code isn't running on your pages. Perhaps you forgot to copy the JavaScript code, put it in the wrong spot, left part of it out, or somehow introduced a mistake.

You start tracking new sites from the Admin tab, too. To do that, click the drop-down list of websites in the Property column, and then choose Create New Property. You'll need to supply a descriptive website name, website URL, industry category, and reporting time zone, just like you did when you added your first site.

Examining Your Web Traffic

The Home tab (Figure 10-12) gives you just the tiniest bit of information. It lets you see, at a glance, how many people are visiting your site and how they like it. You can focus on any time period you like, from a single day to several years. To change the date range, click the arrow next to the current range (just above the top-right corner of the website list) and pick new start and end dates.

It won't take you long to tire of the Home page. When you're ready to take a deeper look at your statistics, click the website you want to study. Google Analytics switches to the Reporting tab, which contains dozens of customizable tracking reports. Pick the report you want using the links on the left, but you'll start out with the Audience Overview graph (Figure 10-14).

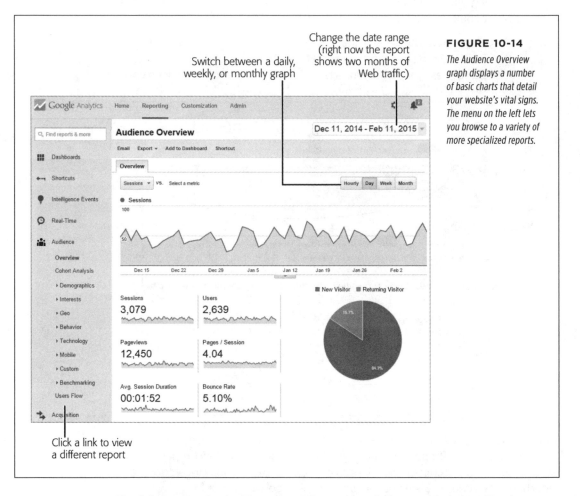

Change the date range
(right now the report
shows two months of
Web traffic)

Switch between a daily,
weekly, or monthly graph

Click a link to view
a different report

FIGURE 10-14

The Audience Overview graph displays a number of basic charts that detail your website's vital signs. The menu on the left lets you browse to a variety of more specialized reports.

The information in the Reporting tab can be a little overwhelming. To give you a better sense of what's going on, the following sections take you through some of the most interesting statistics, one chart at a time.

◼ SESSIONS GRAPH

At the top of the page, the Sessions graph (Figure 10-15) shows the day-by-day popularity of your site over the last month. This count doesn't say anything about how many pages the average visitor browsed or how long she lingered. It simply records how many different people visited your site. Using this chart, you can get a quick sense of the overall uptrend or downtrend of your web traffic, and you can see if it rises on certain days of the week or around specific dates.

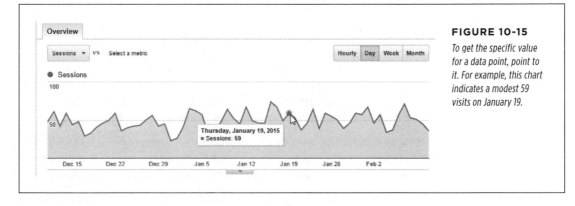

FIGURE 10-15

To get the specific value for a data point, point to it. For example, this chart indicates a modest 59 visits on January 19.

With a few clicks, you can change this chart to show *pageviews*, the count of how many web pages your visitors viewed. For example, if an eager shopper visits your Banana Painting ecommerce store, checks out several enticing products, and completes a purchase, Google Analytics might record close to a dozen pageviews but only a single session. The number of pageviews is always equal to or greater than the number of sessions; after all, each session includes at least one pageview. To see pageviews, click the down arrow next to the word "Sessions" in the top-left corner of the chart, and then choose Pageviews.

> **TIP** Remember, you can look at the data Google Analytics collects over a different range of dates using the date box in the top-right corner of the Reporting page, as identified in Figure 10-14. Initially, Google sets the date range to a single month, ending yesterday.

◼ SITE USAGE

The Site Usage section is crammed with key statistics (Figure 10-16). Details include:

- **Sessions.** The total number of separate visits to your site for the selected date range.

- **Users.** The total number of unique visitors. The number of users will always be less than the number of sessions, because some people will stop by your site more than once.

- **Pageviews.** The total number of viewed pages. This adds up every page that every visitor browsed.

NOTE   There are some types of repeat visitors that Google won't correctly identify. For example, if a repeat visitor uses a different computer, a different browser, or logs into his computer with a different user name, he'll appear to be a new visitor. For these reasons, the number of repeat visitors may be slightly underreported.

- **Pages/Session.** The average number of pages a visitor reads before leaving your site.

- **Avg. Session Duration.** The average time a visitor spends on your site before browsing elsewhere.

- **Bounce Rate.** A *bounce* occurs when a visitor views only one page—in other words, she gets to your site through a specific page and then departs without browsing any further. A bounce rate of 5 percent tells you that 5 percent of your visitors leave immediately after they arrive. Bounces are keenly important to webmasters because they indicate potential lost visitors. If you can identify what's causing a big bounce rate, you can capture a few more visitors.

- **% New Sessions.** The percentage of new visits. For example, a rate of 81 percent indicates that 19 percent of your traffic is repeat business, and 81 percent are new visitors. Both types of visitors are important to your website's health.

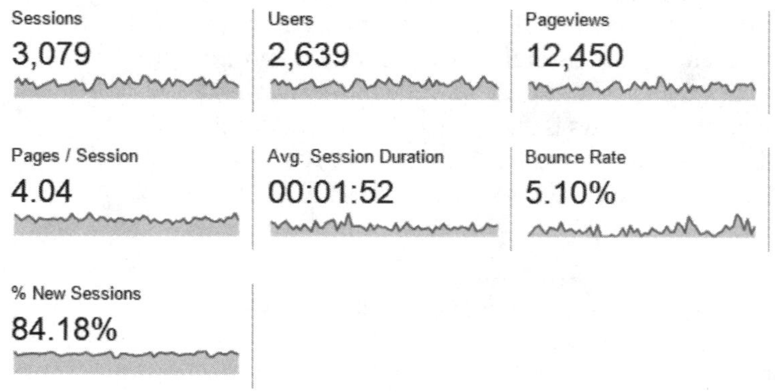

Sessions	Users	Pageviews
3,079	2,639	12,450

Pages / Session	Avg. Session Duration	Bounce Rate
4.04	00:01:52	5.10%

% New Sessions
84.18%

FIGURE 10-16

These statistics show you the most important indicators of your site's overall web health. Click one of them to see a separate report with more detail.

◼ MAP OVERLAY

If you scroll down the Audience Overview report, you'll find an interesting chart at the bottom of the page. It displays your visitor count by country and tallies up the countries with the largest number of guests. However, you don't need to stop there. You can get an even more interesting look using the Map Overlay, which gives you a graphical picture of where your visitors are located on the globe.

To see the Map Overlay, choose Audience→Geo→Location from the menu of reports on the left. Google shows you a map of the world, divided into countries and color-coded. The darker the shade, the more popular your website is in that country. Underneath the map is a table with the exact numbers.

The Map Overlay gets even more interesting if you use the City view, shown in Figure 10-17. To see it, click the City link under the map.

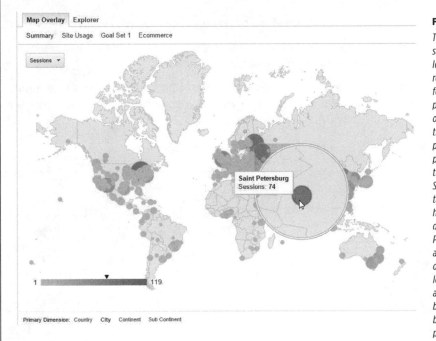

FIGURE 10-17

The City view adds a small circle next to every location where a visitor resides, using larger circles for areas that funneled a particularly large amount of traffic your way. To see the city-by-city details, point to individual data points. Here, 74 visits in the month originated in St. Petersburg, Russia. The table below (not shown here) adds a few more details—for example, St. Petersburg visitors viewed an average of 3.6 pages on each visit (slightly lower than usual), spent a surprising 13 minutes browsing (on average), but accounted for only 20 percent of new visitors.

FREQUENTLY ASKED QUESTION

Does Google Really Know Where I Live?

How accurate is the location data Google supplies?

Being able to determine the location of your visitors is a powerful tool. After all, if you know your Graceland Vacation site is absurdly popular in Japan, you might consider accepting payments in yen, translating a few pages, or adding some new pictures. But Google's geographic locating service isn't perfect. In fact, it has two weaknesses:

- The location service is based on a visitor's ISP (Internet service provider), not the actual visitor herself. In many cases, the ISP is located in a different area from the visitor's own computer.

- ISPs economize by pooling their traffic together and dumping it onto the Internet at a central location. This means that even if your visitor and her web server are in a specific city, the computer that connects that visitor to the Internet might be somewhere else.

As a general rule of thumb, the geographic information that Google uses is likely to be close to reality, but not exact. It's highly likely that the country is correct, but the specific city may not match that of your visitor.

■ TRAFFIC SOURCES OVERVIEW

One key piece of information every webmaster needs to know is how visitors find your website. Are they typing it in by hand, following a link from another site, or stumbling across it in a Google search? The Traffic Source Overview chart can help answer that question. To take a look, choose Acquisition→Overview.

The Traffic Sources Overview chart has three slices:

- **Referral.** This slice counts visitors who arrive through websites that link to yours.

- **Direct.** This slice counts visitors who type your URL directly into a browser or use a bookmark to make a return visit.

- **Organic Search.** This slice counts visitors who come to your site through a search engine. If this percentage is small, you might want to spend more time on search engine optimization (page 324).

Figure 10-18 shows a closer look.

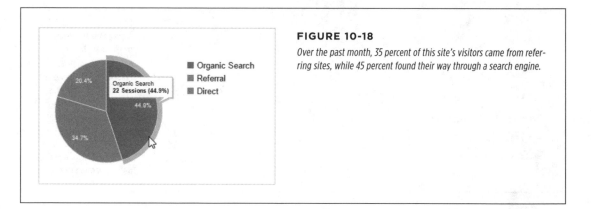

FIGURE 10-18

Over the past month, 35 percent of this site's visitors came from referring sites, while 45 percent found their way through a search engine.

The Traffic Sources Overview chart provides a good high-level look at how your visitors get to your site, but there are plenty more details to explore.

To learn what sites lead visitors to your site, choose the Acquisition→All Traffic→ Referrals report. It shows a chart of referring sites, sorted by the amount of traffic they've sent your way. This is a great tool for quickly identifying your most successful web partnerships.

To learn what searches send people to your site, choose the Acquisition→Search Engine Optimization→Queries report. It shows the search keywords that people typed in to find your site, which lets you determine what your visitors are looking for (and possibly diagnose why they left unhappy).

> **NOTE** Before you can use the search query report, you need to have your site set up and verified with the Google Webmaster Tools (page 327). The first time you try to view the search query report, you'll see a "Set up Webmaster Tools data sharing" button. Click it and follow the steps to get your site's Google Webmaster Tools profile affiliated with your Google Analytics account.

■ CONTENT OVERVIEW

As every webmaster knows, all pages aren't created equal. Some might command tremendous interest while others languish, ignored. To get a snapshot of how your pages are performing, check out the Behavior→Site Content→All Pages report (Figure 10-19).

> **NOTE** The Behavior group of reports is so named because it includes analyses that help you figure out the behavior of your visitors—for example, where they go first, what pages they look at last, and how they travel through your site in between.

Page	Pageviews ↓	Unique Pageviews	Avg. Time on Page	Entrances	Bounce Rat
	63,300 % of Total: 100.00% (63,300)	**45,177** % of Total: 100.00% (45,177)	**00:00:57** Avg for View: 00:00:57 (0.00%)	**15,620** % of Total: 100.00% (15,620)	8.98 Avg for 8.98% (0
1. /BooksNET.htm	**14,028** (22.16%)	9,655 (21.37%)	00:00:45	176 (1.13%)	25.
2. /	**12,179** (19.24%)	9,711 (21.50%)	00:00:03	9,570 (61.27%)	1
3. /Classes.htm	**7,200** (11.37%)	4,186 (9.27%)	00:04:02	57 (0.36%)	12
4. /prosetech/	**6,501** (10.27%)	4,228 (9.38%)	00:00:03	4,176 (26.73%)	0
5. /ProWPF.htm	**3,190** (5.04%)	2,151 (4.76%)	00:00:51	54 (0.35%)	31.
6. /ProWPFinC.htm	**2,774** (4.38%)	2,188 (4.84%)	00:01:40	75 (0.48%)	70.
7. /BegASP.NET4inC.htm	**1,634** (2.58%)	1,134 (2.51%)	00:01:23	27 (0.17%)	74
8. /About.htm	1,584 (2.50%)	1,282 (2.84%)	00:00:24	16 (0.10%)	25

FIGURE 10-19

For this site, BooksNET.htm *is the clear winner of the Most Popular Page award, with 22 percent of the total website traffic. It's not the page that entices visitors to linger the longest, however—that honor goes to* Classes.htm.

Simply determining which pages your visitors view the most isn't enough to determine how useful they are to your site. Some pages are extra important because of their ability to *attract* visitors. For example, the page of Member Photos on your International Nudist site might attract large volumes of visitors who then stick around to check out your personalized coffee cups, clothing, and memorabilia. To figure out where visitors *enter* your site, so you know what pages are attention-getters that lure traffic, see the Behavior→Site Content→Landing Pages report.

Almost as important are the pages that mark the end of a visit. They may indicate a problem, like a page that's slow to download, doesn't work correctly in some browsers, or just plain irritates people. To get this detailed information, take a look at the Behavior→Site Content→Exit Pages report.

> **NOTE** You can explore many more reports in Google Analytics, and find many more ways to slice and dice the info there to come up with some conclusions about your web traffic. In fact, entire books have been written about the fine art of analyzing website performance. However, the five charts explained above get you started with great insight into how your site is doing.

Website Promotion

T he best website in the world won't do you much good if it's sitting out there all by its lonesome self. For your site to flourish, you need to attract new visitors and then keep them flocking back for more.

You started on this path in the previous chapter. You learned how to get your site noticed in a web search and how to track the number of visitors who stop by. But a search listing, on its own, isn't enough to grow a brand-new site into a thriving web destination. For that, you need a range of promotional tactics, from sharing links to buying ad space. Contrary to what you might expect, this sort of grassroots promotion might bring more traffic to your site than high-powered search engines like Google.

In this chapter, you'll learn some of the best techniques for website promotion. You'll also see how to build a *sticky* site—one that not only attracts new faces, but also encourages repeat visitors. To pull this off, you need to transform your site into a web *community* by giving visitors a way to interact with you and with one another. You make that happen using newsletters, blogs, Twitter, Facebook, and special-interest social media groups.

> **NOTE** The tasks in most of this book—crafting web pages, formatting them with style sheets, uploading your finished site—are relatively straightforward. They might take some time and effort, but when you're done, you *know* you're done. The tasks you'll tackle in this chapter—promoting your website and building a community around it—aren't so well-defined. They require continuous work, and it may take a lot of thankless slogging before your site traffic starts to grow.

■ Spreading the Word

To promote your website well, you need to master many skills. Good site promotion ranges from old-fashioned advertising to search-engine magic.

In the following sections, you'll pick up several fundamental techniques. You'll start thinking about how to promote yourself in the right places, take a quick look at services like Google Places and Google AdWords, and plan a strategy that encourages repeat visits.

Shameless Self-Promotion

Some of the best advertising doesn't cost anything. The secret is to look for sites where you can promote yourself *and* contribute at the same time.

For example, if you create the website *www.HotComputerTricks.com*, why not answer a few questions in a computing newsgroup, discussion board, or on a Facebook page? Openly promoting your site is considered tactless, but there's nothing wrong with dispensing some handy advice and following it up with a signature that includes your URL.

Here's an example of how you can answer a poster's question and put in a good word for yourself at the same time:

> Jim,
>
> The problem is that most hard drives will fail when submerged in water. Hence, your fishing computer idea won't work.
>
> Sasha Mednick
>
> *www.HotComputerTricks.com*

On a popular site, hundreds of computer aficionados with the same question could read this post. If even a few decide to check out Sasha's site, he's made great progress.

If you're very careful, you might even get away with something that's a little more explicit:

> Jim,
>
> The problem is that most hard drives will fail when submerged in water. Hence, your fishing computer idea won't work. However, you might want to check out my homemade hard-drive vacuum enclosure (*www.HotComputerTricks.com*), which I developed to solve the same problem.
>
> Sasha Mednick
>
> *www.HotComputerTricks.com*

WARNING This maneuver requires a very light touch. The rule of thumb is that your message should be well-intentioned. Direct someone to your site only if it really does have content that addresses the poster's question.

If you're unsure of how much promotion is too much, consider the popular website *www.reddit.com*, which has thousands of discussion groups (called *subreddits*) covering every conceivable topic. Reddit's rule of thumb is that 10% or fewer of your posts should link to your own content or talk about your business. For more detailed guidelines on how to share the good news about your site without being a spammer, check out *www.reddit.com/wiki/selfpromotion*—it includes good advice for contributing to any site. Violate these good-taste guidelines, and you'll find yourself ignored, insulted, and even banned from a group altogether.

You don't have to limit your posts to comments and discussion groups. You can also seek out sites that let you post tips, reviews, or articles. There you can use a variation of the technique shown above. Remember, dispense useful advice, and then follow it up with a signature at the end of your message. For example, if you submit a free article that describes how to create your groundbreaking vacuum enclosure, end it with this:

> Sasha Mednick is a computer genius who runs the first-rate computing site www. HotComputerTricks.com.

Promotion always works best if you believe in your product, so make sure your site has relevant, high-quality content before you boast about it. Don't ever send someone to your site based on content you plan to add (someday).

TIP If you're a business trying to promote a product, you'll get further if you recruit other people to help you spread the word. One excellent idea is to look for influential *bloggers*—people who create websites with the personal posting format you'll learn about in Chapter 12. For example, if you're trying to sell a new type of fluffy toddler towel pajamas, hunt down popular blogs about parenting. Then offer the blogger some free pajamas if she'll offer her thoughts in a blog review (with full disclosure, of course). This sort of word-of-mouth promotion can be dramatically more successful in the wide-reaching communities of the Web than it is in the offline world.

Cultivating Links

Even better than linking to yourself is getting other people to link to your site. Links from high-quality websites not only drive traffic, but they also increase your street cred in the eyes of Google, encouraging it to rank your site higher in its search results. Finding people who will link to your site takes time and research. Here's some good advice:

- **Help others.** Your best bet is to reach out to people who can benefit from your content, and then provide something useful. Writing emails and asking for links has a low rate of success, but it does occasionally have success.

- **Network.** If you're a business, consider the people and organizations you interact with in real life. They may have sites that can link up with yours.

- **Never pay for a link.** The world is full of business registries that exist for no other purpose than to collect links for certain types of services (like children's programs, medical establishments, restaurant listings, and so on). They make money by charging for "enhanced" listings, even though few people actually use these registries. In most cases, the only link worth having is one that's freely given.

- **Research the competition.** One way to identify good link prospects is to find out who's linking to other sites like yours. One tool that can help you out is the Open Site Explorer (*http://moz.com/researchtools/ose*). Enter a URL there, and the Explorer finds other pages on the Web that link to the site. These are places where you might want to get your own site mentioned.

- **Study your most valuable links.** By analyzing your inbound links using Google Analytics (page 332), you can figure out what links do the best job directing traffic to your site. You need as many of these types of links as you can get.

Google Places

In the previous chapter, you learned how your site can show up in a web search result. That's a critical way to reel in new people, and many webmasters spend their late-night hours obsessing about page rank and search keywords.

But if you're running a business or organization that has a physical presence in the real world (not just the virtual one), you can improve your search listing for free. In fact, you've probably seen this sort of enhanced listing before, if you've ever used Google to hunt down a local business (Figure 11-1).

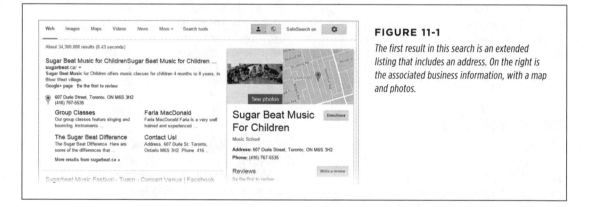

FIGURE 11-1

The first result in this search is an extended listing that includes an address. On the right is the associated business information, with a map and photos.

Clearly, this listing has more presence than the average search listing. It takes up more space, provides more information, and makes the business seem more professional. When visitors see a listing like this, they feel that they've come across a real, established business.

The service that makes this happen is called Google Places, which is a part of the Google+ social networking service. Happily, you can sign up for Google Places and have your own beefed-up search listing for free. There are just two things to keep in mind:

- **You need to provide your location's mailing address.** To verify that your business exists at the location you say it does, Google will mail you a confirmation code. Once you enter that code, your Google Places listing becomes active. If you don't have a physical mailing address (even if it's your home), or you don't want it to appear on Google, then the Google Places service isn't for you.

- **The enhanced listing appears only for certain searches.** Google's goal is to show the enhanced listing when a web searcher specifically looks for your business. So if someone types your business name or street address into Google, he's likely to get the enhanced page. But if someone simply enters a few keywords that match the content on your website, Google displays only an ordinary search listing.

To create your own Google Places listing, head to *http://places.google.com/business*. If you have a Google account (used for other services, like Gmail and Google Webmaster Tools), sign in. Otherwise, click "Sign up now" to create one.

After you log in, you can add your business listing. You need to fill out a single-page form of business information that includes your address, phone number, website address, a short description, and a category. Optionally, you can upload pictures (which is always a good idea, because people will see them on your Google Places page), add YouTube videos, and specify operating hours. When you finish, submit the form. Remember, your listing won't appear automatically, because Google sends you a confirmation code by mail. When you get it, type in the code to activate your Google Places page. Then it's just a matter of time before your enhanced listing starts showing up in web searches and in Google Maps.

Google AdWords

As a traveler on the World Wide Web, you've no doubt seen several lifetimes' worth of flashing messages, gaudy banners, and invasive pop-ups, all trying to sell you some awful products. It probably comes as no surprise that these types of ads aren't the way to promote your site—in fact, they're more likely to alienate people rather than entice them. However, there are respectable paid placements that can get your site in front of the right readers, at the right time, and with the right amount of tact. One of the best is AdWords (*http://adwords.google.com*), Google's insanely flexible advertising system.

The idea behind AdWords is that you create text ads that Google shows alongside its regular search results (see Figure 11-2). The neat part is that Google doesn't show the ads indiscriminately. Instead, you choose the search keywords you want your ad associated with.

The nice (and slightly confusing) part about AdWords is that you *bid* for the keywords you want to use. For example, you might tell Google you're willing to pay 25 cents for the keyword "food." Google takes this into consideration with everyone else's bids and displays the higher bidders' ads more often. But Google isn't out to rip anyone off, and it charges you only the going rate for your keyword, regardless of how much you told Google you're willing to pay. And Google doesn't charge you anything to simply display your ad on a search results page. It charges you only when someone clicks your ad to get to your site.

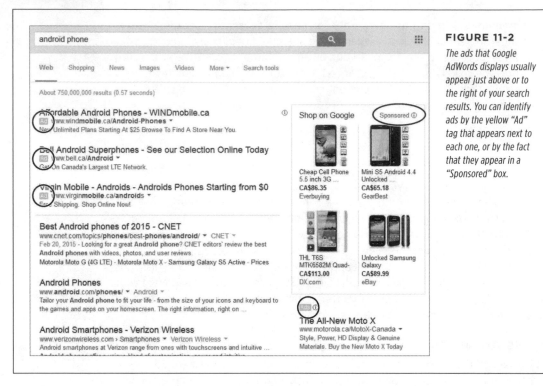

FIGURE 11-2

The ads that Google AdWords displays usually appear just above or to the right of your search results. You can identify ads by the yellow "Ad" tag that appears next to each one, or by the fact that they appear in a "Sponsored" box.

By this point, you might be getting a little nervous. Given the fact that Google handles hundreds of millions of searches a day, isn't it possible for a measly 1-cent bid to quickly put you and your site into bankruptcy? Fortunately, Google has a solution for this, too. You just tell the company the maximum you're willing to pay per day. Once you hit your limit, Google stops showing your ad.

Interestingly, the bid amount isn't the only factor that determines how often your ad appears. Popularity is also important. If Google shows your ad over and over again and it never gets a click, Google realizes that your ad just isn't working and lets you know with an automated email message. Google may then start showing your ad significantly less often or stop showing it altogether, until you improve it.

You can also limit your ads to people in certain geographic regions (like a specific country or city) so you don't waste money showing ads for your kiddie hair salon to people in Tunisia. This sort of geographic targeting makes AdWords equally effective for both local and global promotions.

Bidding for AdWords can be competitive. To have a chance against all the AdWords sharks, you need to know how much a click is worth to your site. For example, if you sell monogrammed socks, you need to know what percentage of visitors actually *buy* something (the *conversion rate*) and how much they're likely to spend. A typical cost-per-click hovers around $1, but there's a wide range, depending on the word you choose and your campaign settings (how many clicks you want to buy, whether you're limiting your ad to a specific region, and so on). If you're willing to compete for a prime-time word like *lawyer*, you can easily spend $10 for a click. But you can steal an unlikely keyword combination like *llama care* for a few cents. (And in recent history, law firms have bid "mesothelioma"—an asbestos-related cancer that could become the basis of a class-action lawsuit—up over $100.) Before you sign up with AdWords, it's a good idea to conduct some serious research to find out the recent prices of the keywords you want to use.

NOTE You can learn more about AdWords from Google's AdWords site (*http://adwords.google.com*). For a change of pace, go to *www.iterature.com/adwords* for a story about an artist's attempt to use AdWords to distribute poetry, and why it failed.

Return Visitors

Attracting fresh faces is a critical part of visitors, website promotion, but novice webmasters often forget something equally important: return visitors. For a website to become truly popular, it needs to attract visitors who return again and again. Many a website creator would do better to spend less time trying to attract new visitors and more time trying to keep the current flock.

If you're a marketer, you know that a customer who comes back to the same store three or four times is a lot more likely to make a purchase than someone who's there on a first visit. These regulars are also more likely to get excited and recruit their friends to come and take a look. This infectious enthusiasm can lead more and more people to your site's virtual doorstep. The phenomenon is so common that it has a name: the *traffic virus*.

NOTE Return visitors are the ultimate yardstick of a website success. If you can't interest someone enough to come back again, your website is just not fulfilling its destiny.

So how does your website become a favorite stopping point for web travelers? The old Internet adage says it all—*content is king*. Your site needs to be chock-full of fascinating, must-read information. Just as important, this information needs to change regularly and noticeably. If you update information once a month, your website barely has a pulse. But if you update it two or more times a week, you're ready to flourish.

Never underestimate the importance of regular updates. It takes weeks and months of up-to-date information to create a return visitor. However, one dry spell—say, three months without changing anything more than the color of your buttons—doesn't just stop attracting newcomers; it can kill off your current roster of return visitors. Savvy visitors immediately realize when a website has gone stale. They have much the same sensation you feel when you pull out a once-attractive pastry from the fridge and find it's as hard as igneous rock. You know what happens next: Toss the pastry away, clear out the website bookmarks, and move on.

Keepin' It Fresh

Creating a website is hard enough, and keeping its content fresh is even more taxing. Here are a few guidelines that can help you out:

- **Think in stages.** When you put your first website online, it won't be complete. Instead, think of it as version 1, and start planning a few changes for the next version. Bit by bit, and stage by stage, you can add everything you want your site to have.

- **Select the parts you can modify regularly, and leave the rest alone.** There's no way you can review and revise an entire website every week. Instead, your best strategy is to identify sections you want to change regularly. On a personal site, for example, you might put news on a separate page and update just that page. On a small-

business website, you might concentrate on the home page so you can advertise new products and upcoming specials.

- **Design a website that's easy to change.** This is the hardest principle to follow, because it requires not only planning, but a dash of hard-won experience. As you become a more experienced web author, you'll learn how to simplify your life by making your pages easier to update. One method is to separate information into several pages, so you can add new content without reorganizing your entire site. Another is to use style sheets to separate page formatting from your content (see Chapter 3). That way, you can easily insert new material without having to format the content from scratch to match the rest of your site.

The other way to encourage return visitors is to build a community. Discussion forums, promotional events, and newsletters are like glue. They encourage visitors to feel as though they're participating in your site and sharing your web space. If you get this right, hordes of visitors will move in and never want to leave.

Bookmark Icons

One of your first challenges in promoting your site is getting visitors to add your site to their browser bookmarks. Bookmarking, however, isn't enough to guarantee a return visit. Your site also needs to be fascinating enough to beckon from the bookmark menu, tempting visitors to come back. If you're a typical web traveler, you regularly visit only about 5 percent of the sites you bookmark.

One way to make your site stand out from the crowd is to change the icon that appears in visitors' bookmarks or favorites menu, an icon technically called a *favicon* (Figure 11-3). This technique works in any modern browser.

To create a favicon, add an icon file to the top-level folder of your website, and make sure you name it *favicon.ico*. The best approach is to use a dedicated icon editor, because it lets you create both a 16-pixel x 16-pixel icon and a larger 32-pixel x 32-pixel icon in the same file. Browsers use the smaller icon in their bookmark menus, and computers display the larger version when visitors drag the favicon to their desktop. If you don't have an icon editor, create a bitmap (a .bmp file) that's exactly 16 pixels wide and 16 pixels high. To get an icon editor, visit a shareware site like *www.download.com*.

NOTE Signs of a stale site include old-fashioned formatting, broken links, and references to old events (like a Spice Girls CD release party or a technical analysis of why Enron stock is an ironclad investment).

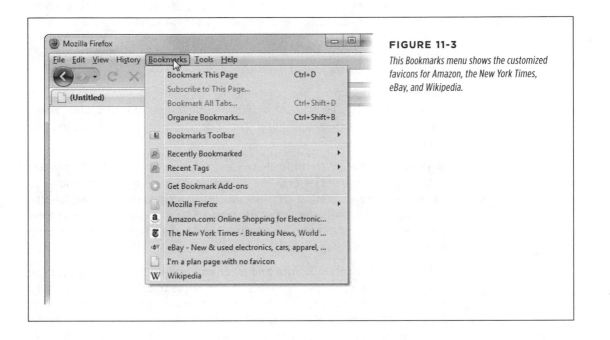

FIGURE 11-3

This Bookmarks menu shows the customized favicons for Amazon, the New York Times, eBay, and Wikipedia.

Transforming a Site into a Community

The Web is the crowded home of many millions of site owners, so when you put your website online, it doesn't just drop into a vacuum. Instead, it takes center stage in front of an audience that's always interested and often opinionated.

For your site to really fit in with the rest of the Web, you need to interact with your visitors. The idea of dialogue—back-and-forth communication among peers—is hard-wired into the Internet's DNA. Get it right and people won't just be talking about you—they'll be promoting you to friends, getting to know you better, and putting you in the public eye.

To make this magic happen, you need a bit of planning, a willingness to promote yourself (almost to the point of embarrassment), and a smattering of social media skills. In the following sections, you'll learn how to do all this.

Fostering a Web Community

How do you start transforming your website into a web community? The first thing to do is change your perspective, so that you plan your website as a meeting place instead of just a place to vent your (admittedly brilliant) thoughts. Here are a few tips to help you get in the right frame of mind:

- **Clearly define the purpose of your site.** For example, the description "*www. BronteRevival.com* is dedicated to bringing Charlotte Bronte fans together to discuss and promote her work" is more community-oriented than "*www.Bronte Revival.com* contains information and criticism of Charlotte Bronte's work." The first sentence describes what the site aims to do, while the second reflects what it contains, thereby limiting its scope. Once you define a single-sentence description, you can use it in your description meta element (page 318) or in a mission statement on your home page.

- **Build gathering places.** No one wants to hang around a collection of links and static text. Jazz up your site with discussion forums or chat boards, where your visitors can kick up their heels. You'll learn how to put these bits in place later in this chapter.

- **Give your visitors different roles.** Successful community sites recognize noteworthy contributors—some use gold stars (or some other sort of icon) to recognize frequent posters. Others give certain visitors more power, like the ability to manage members in a group (page 371). The right people can grow into leadership roles and even coordinate events, newsletters, discussion groups, or portions of your site.

- **Advertise new content before and after you add it.** To get visitors coming back again and again, you need lots of new content. But new content on its own isn't enough—you need to build visitors' expectation of new content so they know enough to return, and you need to clearly highlight the new material so guests can find it once they do come back. To help this work smoothly, try adding links on your home page that lead to newly added content, along with a quick line or two about upcoming content you plan to add and concrete information about when it'll be there.

- **Introduce regular events.** It's hard to force yourself to update your site regularly. Even when you do, visitors have no way of knowing when there's something that makes a return visit worthwhile. Why not help everyone keep track of what's going on by promoting regular events (like a news section you update weekly or a promotional drawing that happens on a set date)?

- **Create feedback loops.** It's a law of the Web—good sites keep getting better, while bad ones magnify their mistakes. To help your site get on the right track, make sure there's a way for visitors to tell you what they like. Then spend the bulk of your time strengthening what works and tossing out what doesn't.

Now that you have your website good-citizenship philosophy straight, it's time to learn how to build the ingredients every web community needs.

Website Community Tools

On its own, an ordinary website is a one-way medium, like cable television or a newspaper. A visitor surfs to your site, reads a few pages, and leaves. At that point, the conversation ends.

But community-oriented websites deepen and extend this interaction using strategies that remind fickle viewers that you exist. If you're a big business, this approach is part of a branding strategy that establishes the value of your products in the minds of potential customers. If you're a small business, it could be part of the long courting process that leads up to a sale. And even if you're not selling or promoting anything, keeping visitors engaged with your website is the best way to boost traffic, reach new people, and remain the center of attention.

Websites differ in how deeply they focus on community. Some add just a touch of it (for example, the product review system on an ecommerce site), while others go all the way with fan-run Facebook pages and discussion forums. Table 11-1 lists some of the ways a website can build a community.

TABLE 11-1 *Different ways to reach your visitors.*

APPROACH	DESCRIPTION	LEVEL OF COMMUNITY	LEARN MORE ON/IN
Email newsletters	Readers sign up, and you contact them with the latest news whenever you want. It's a good way to keep your community up to date without forcing people to make a repeat visit.	Low. Newsletters are still a one-way conversation, and there's no opportunity for readers to respond.	Page 356
Blogs	You write regular, informal posts. Readers can keep up to date using a feed reader and talk back by adding comments.	Medium. Blogs feel more conversational, and popular blogs attract piles of comments.	Chapter 12
Twitter	You send out brief snippets of text to the world with news, commentary, or random thoughts. Other people can pick up your theme and tweet (send out a message) to their fans.	High. At first, Twitter feeds look like a one-way conversation. But in reality, Twitter is part of a large, overlapping discussion that never ends.	Page 358
Facebook	You create a page where you can post news, start discussions, and let other people chat about you. In some ways, the page is a hybrid of a newsletter and a group, with Facebook gluing it all together.	High. Like groups, but any one of the hundreds of millions of registered Facebookers can post.	Page 363
Groups	Readers join a forum where they can post messages and talk to one another. Usually, the discussion is limited to a pool of registered members.	High. Not only can you talk back to your visitors, but they can also talk to one another.	Page 371

The rest of this chapter outlines how you can use these community-building practices with your own site.

NOTE This chart includes two of the biggest names in social media (Facebook and Twitter), but there are many more sites that can help you connect with the world and attract attention. Examples include snap-share site Instagram, business network site LinkedIn, and the all-in-one Facebook competitor Google+, just to name a few.

Email Newsletters

The idea behind email newsletters is simple: When visitors stop by your website, you offer them the chance to subscribe to your newsletter. With a little luck, visitors type in their email addresses, click a button, and open up their inboxes to you.

After that, you send subscribers periodic emails with news or special offers. Usually you do that no more than once a month. After all, you don't want an exasperated recipient blocking your address and sending your messages straight to the junk mail bin.

Even in today's world of blogs, Facebook, and social media, email newsletters are wildly popular. However, they introduce a few new challenges.

First, you need a small box somewhere on your website where people can type in an email address and sign up for your newsletter (see Figure 11-4). Creating this chunk of HTML is easy. Technically, it's called a *contact form*, and it uses a set of elements called *HTML forms* (page 487). The difficult part is controlling what happens when someone clicks the sign-up button.

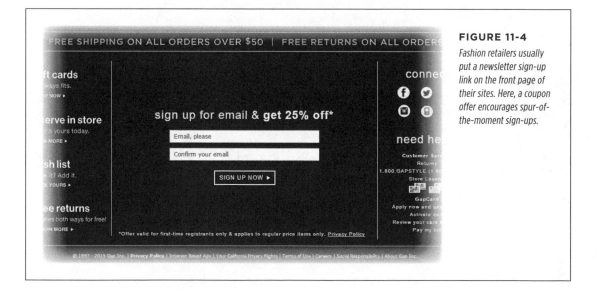

FIGURE 11-4

Fashion retailers usually put a newsletter sign-up link on the front page of their sites. Here, a coupon offer encourages spur-of-the-moment sign-ups.

If you're a web coder working with a high-powered programming platform, contact forms are easy. When a visitor clicks a button, the browser sends her email address to a web application running on the web server, and that program stores the address in a database. But mere mortals need a different approach. Essentially, you have three choices: use your web host's form-processing program, borrow someone else's server-side script (a tiny scrap of code that runs on a web server), or use a form submission service. Here are the details:

- **Ask your web host.** First, check with your web host to see if they have any ready-made scripts you can use to create a basic contact form. Typically, you'll use a small snippet of prewritten PHP or ASP code, which will extract the visitor's email address and send it to you in an email. You simply need to paste that code into your web page and tweak a few details.

- **Search the Web.** If you can't find a ready-made script, check with your web host again—this time to find out if it supports a server scripting language, and what that language is. (The code for the script differs depending on the server-side programming technology it uses.) Then you can use Google to hunt down a suitable script on the Web. For example, *www.freecontactform.com/free.php* has the bare-bones HTML and script you need to collect email addresses on a web server that supports PHP.

- **Form submission services.** Finally, if your web host doesn't support server scripts, or you just don't want to wrestle with the headaches a programmer would normally handle, you can use a free *form submission service*. Essentially, this service runs your form on its web servers but emails you the data. To create your form, you simply choose the data you want to collect. The form submission company gives you a block of HTML that you plop into your page. You can find free form-creation services at *www.emailmeform.com* and *www.123contactform. com*. However, free services may put a tiny note at the bottom of the form (that says something like "This form powered by TheSuperCoolFormCreationCompany"); if that bothers you, you can pay to have it left out.

> **NOTE** Contact forms are just the simplest example of data-collection forms. Using a form-submission service, you can create a form that collects a whole whack of information. For example, you might want to get a mailing address so you can send out product samples. But be wary of asking for too much. The longer the form, the less chance that a guest will fill it out and submit it.

Just because your website has a working sign-up box doesn't mean anyone will use it. People are justifiably paranoid about spammers and junk mail, and they only give up their email addresses if they think it benefits them. To get sign-ups, make the process easy—that means one box for an email address and a button that says "Sign Up" or "Subscribe." You don't need names, phone numbers, birth dates, or any other information that might make a potential subscriber bail out. Then sell the benefits of signing up with a simple, one-sentence description. These benefits could include hot deals, coupons, notifications about special events, or opportunities that aren't available through the website.

Once you get guests' email addresses, use them. Web marketing research suggests that the average person looks at an email newsletter for just 51 seconds, so include something compelling that captures a reader's interest in that brief moment. Most newsletters are formatted in HTML, but it's best to compose them in an email program, because some mail programs don't properly handle HTML features (like external or embedded style sheets). Use pictures sparingly and always add alternate text (page 116), because many email programs block images if they don't recognize the sender. Don't forget to include links that let readers jump from the email to the relevant page on your website, so they can follow up on breaking news or a hot new offer.

■ Twitter

Twitter is sometimes called a "micro-blogging" system. It lets anyone talk to the world by sending out text messages of 140 or fewer characters (hence the "micro" moniker). Of course, the success of your Twitter messages—called *tweets*—depends on whether anyone pays attention to what you say. Top tweeters have a huge crowd of followers that hang on every word. And followers can bring you more attention by retweeting your messages—that is, sending *your* message to *their* followers.

You can follow a tweeter that you like in a number of ways. You could just read their messages on an ordinary web page (Figure 11-5), but more serious tweeters keep up with a huge crowd of people using a third-party program or by having tweets delivered to their smartphones. (Similarly, tweeters can *send* tweets in a variety of ways, from typing them in on Twitter's web page to using a smartphone app.)

Paradoxically, Twitter's greatest strength is also its greatest limitation: the 140-character limit that constrains Twitter messages to a sentence or two. When it works, the limit forces tweeters to stick to concise, complete thoughts. For example, a tweet might announce a new product, link to a useful website, comment on current news, or reply to another tweet.

Another great thing about Twitter is the breadth of people using it. You can follow tweets by everyone from the Dalai Lama to Kim Kardashian. To sign up for your own Twitter account, go to *http://twitter.com*.

Twitter can be a tricky medium. It takes time—perhaps a few weeks—to absorb the rhythm and flow of messages. The biggest mistake new tweeters make is to launch a feed, use it as a place to vent random or low-content thoughts (examples include "School sucks," "I've lost my socks," and "Am eating a piece of gristly chicken, right now!"), and then wonder why no one is paying attention. But if you tweet useful, insightful messages, you can gradually attract more attention to yourself, your brand, and your website.

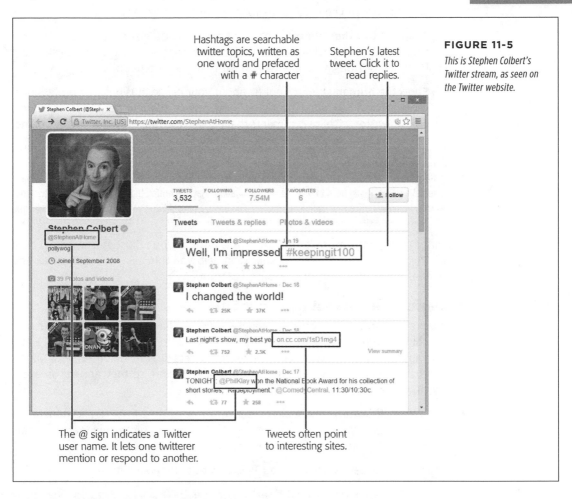

Hashtags are searchable
twitter topics, written as
one word and prefaced
with a # character

Stephen's latest
tweet. Click it to
read replies.

FIGURE 11-5

*This is Stephen Colbert's
Twitter stream, as seen on
the Twitter website.*

The @ sign indicates a Twitter
user name. It lets one twitterer
mention or respond to another.

Tweets often point
to interesting sites.

Here are good guidelines for any new tweeter:

- **Take it slow.** Don't start tweeting madly until you have a good feel for what works and what doesn't. To do that, follow other tweeters. Use the Twitter search tool (*http://twitter.com*) to find tweets relevant to you (your business name, your area of expertise, your website topic), and see what other people are saying.

- **Share useful things.** Point out neat tools, recommend web links, and pass out snippets of advice. Don't use your Twitter account for relentless selling or self-promotion, because that turns everyone off.

- **Solicit opinions.** Ask others to interact with you. Here are examples of how top companies get attention: offer advance copies of a book to review, ask about problems with current products, or run a promotion where people chime in with stories or suggestions. The key is to contribute to the Twitter community *before* you have something to sell. They'll appreciate the gesture, give good feedback, and maybe even help publicize your site when the time is right.

- **Respond to other people.** Comment on someone else's tweet, or retweet a comment made about your site's subject area. That way, you're not just shouting from the rooftops, you're engaging with like-minded people.

- **Show the human side.** It's not all about your cause, business, or professional aspirations. When people follow a tweeter, they expect to get a personal touch. So use Twitter to share comments that explain the real-life side of what you do.

> **TIP** You can achieve Twitter success two ways. First, you can start off being such an important, wonderful, and famous person that no one wants to miss what you text from your mobile phone at 3:00 a.m. But assuming you're not a celebrity, you need to take the second approach: Say something that's relevant to other tweeters. That way, they may notice your comments, follow up on them, and help bring your words to a wider audience.

Twitter mastery is outside the scope of this book. If you're just starting out, check out *The Twitter Book* (O'Reilly), which can help you think like a true tweeter, and provides great advice for Twitter-based promotion.

Sharing Your Tweets on Your Site

If you're a seasoned tweeter, you probably want to share your tweets on your site. You could take the simple path, and just add a link to your Twitter stream. But a niftier idea is to put a snapshot of your recent tweets directly on one of your pages. Even better, you can stick your tweets in a side column, so they appear on every page in your site.

Pulling this off is surprisingly easy. You simply need to ask Twitter to generate a widget according to your specifications. Technically, a Twitter widget is a short snippet of HTML markup.

Here's how to create a personalized Twitter widget for your site:

1. **Go to the Twitter account settings page (*https://twitter.com/settings/ account*) and log in with your email address and password.**

   The settings page lets you configure a set of options.

2. **In the panel on the left, click Widgets.**

   You see a list of all the Twitter widgets you've created. (Chances are, that will be exactly none.)

3. **To create your first widget, click Create New.**

   Twitter takes you to the widget-creation page shown in Figure 11-6.

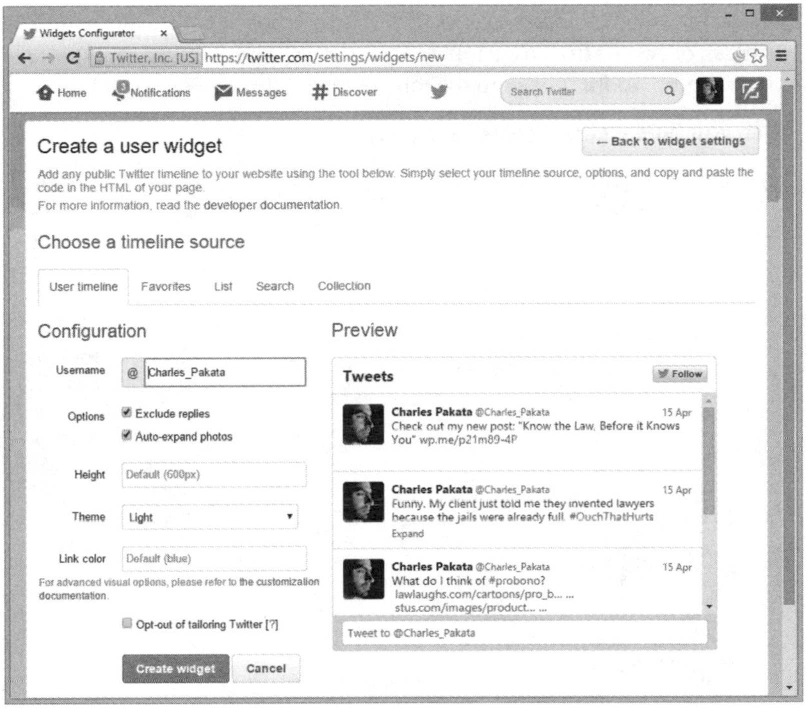

FIGURE 11-6

As you set options for your timeline (on the left), Twitter shows a preview of what it will look like (on the right).

4. **Configure your widget.**

   You don't need to change anything if you don't want to. Twitter automatically creates a timeline (Twitter's name for a reverse-chronological list of tweets) that shows just your tweets. However, here are some details you might want to change:

   - **Exclude replies** hides a tweet if it's just a reply to someone else's tweet (which readers can find confusing because it's out of context).

   - **Auto-expand photos** displays the pictures you link to in your tweets right in your timeline (no extra click required).

   - **Height** sets the vertical size of the timeline, and therefore determines how many tweets readers can see at once. Choose a height that fits nicely alongside the content in your page (or, if your tweets are going site-wide, choose a height that fits nicely in a side column). Don't worry about the width—the timeline will automatically size itself to fit the space in your layout.

   - **Theme** lets you change the color scheme from light (the standard) to dark. The dark option blends in better with dark page backgrounds.

Alternatively, you can create a different type of Twitter timeline by picking a different tab (just under "Choose a timeline source"). Ordinarily, Twitter assumes you want the "user timeline" option, which shows the tweets you've made. Alternatively, you can show favorite tweets, tweets from a list you create, tweets that match a search keyword (for example, tweets about you or your business), or tweets from a custom timeline you created. Twitter provides plenty of information about these more exotic choices.

5. **When you finish, click Create Widget.**

   The markup for your widget appears in a text box just underneath the widget preview (Figure 11-7).

FIGURE 11-7

The quickest way to copy your Twitter widget is to right-click the teeny text box with the markup in it, choose "Select all" to highlight all the HTML, and then press Ctrl+C.

6. **Copy the widget markup and paste it into one of your web pages. Then save the page, load it up in your browser, and watch the magic happen.**

   You don't need to upload your page to a web server before you try it out. The `<script>` code works even if you launch the page right from your desktop (Figure 11-8).

   To have your tweets appear on every page of your site, you need to use the layout and content-sharing techniques from Chapter 8. First, carve out a section of a page where you want the Twitter timeline to appear—usually, that's a separate column on the right side of your page. Create a `<div>` for that column and use the normal CSS rules to set its position and width (see page 240 to recap your options). Then put the Twitter script in your `<div>`. To save effort and reduce the likelihood of mistakes, you can put the Twitter script in a separate file, and inject it into your pages using a server-side include, as explained on page 263.

> **NOTE** If you're using a web editor, make sure you don't paste the markup in design view. If you do, your editor will convert your HTML into ordinary text, which isn't what you want. For the widget to work, you need to put the `<script>` element in your HTML markup.

JavaScript powers the Twitter script. It talks to the Twitter web server, grabs a chunk of HTML with your most recent tweets, and inserts it into your page. Although you won't learn how to talk to web servers in this book, you will learn the other half of this equation—how to dynamically insert new content into a page—when you explore JavaScript in Chapter 14.

FIGURE 11-8

Here's the now-embedded Twitter feed you created in Figure 11-7, scaled down to fit the column where you placed it. In the feed, each tweet becomes a link that, if you click it, takes you to Twitter to read the whole conversation.

Facebook

It can be tough to build an audience from scratch. That's why an increasing number of web dwellers don't try to do it alone. Instead, they bring their audience to an existing community—one set up around a social networking site. And when it comes to social networking, no company is better known than Facebook.

Facebook began as a way for college students to keep in touch with one another. In only a few years, it mushroomed into a social site where hundreds of millions of ordinary people track down everyone from long-lost loves to faintly remembered high-school acquaintances. Thanks to Facebook Pages (the feature you'll learn about in this section), Facebook has even become a branding tool for businesses and nonprofit organizations—one with unique advantages and limitations.

Creating a Facebook Page

A *Facebook page* (formerly known as a Facebook *fan page*) is a public meeting spot you create on Facebook. You use it to promote something—say, a company, a cause, a product, a television show, or a band. You might already have a Facebook Page to promote your business or yourself (for instance, musicians, comedians, and journalists often do). Any Facebook member can create one. For example, *www.facebook.com/kristof* is the Facebook Page for *New York Times* columnist Nicholas D. Kristof. He uses it to comment on current affairs and discuss the issues of the day with readers. On an entirely different but more delicious note, *www.facebook.com/benjerry* is a Facebook Page for Ben & Jerry's ice cream. It's a chattier, less formal version of its website, complete with whimsical discussions about now-abandoned ice cream flavors.

A Facebook Page is similar to a personal Facebook profile, but it's better suited to promotion. That's because anyone can visit a Facebook Page and read its content, even if she doesn't have a Facebook account. Those who do have accounts can do the usual Facebook things—click Like to follow the page, post on the page's timeline, and join in any of its discussions.

> **NOTE** A personal Facebook page (known as a *profile page*) is more restrictive than a Facebook Page. It's better suited to talking to your friends or networking with business contacts. But a Facebook Page is a better way to promote yourself, your business, or your cause to the masses of people you don't know.

Here's how to create a Facebook Page:

1. **Go to** *www.facebook.com/pages/create.php*.

   If you haven't already signed into Facebook, do so now. (Or, if you don't have a Facebook account, click the "Sign up" link to create one, and provide the usual details about yourself.)

   Once you reach the Facebook Page creator, you'll see a few big, tiled buttons with labels like "Company, Organization, or Institution" and "Brand or Product." Each button represents a different type of page.

2. **Click the button that represents the type of page you want.**

   For example, you can create a page for your local business, a big company, a band, a product, a public figure, or a cause.

Facebook then asks you for more information (Figure 11-9). The most important detail is the *name*, which will appear prominently on your page. Depending on the type of page you're creating, you'll use your name, the store's name, your band's name, or something else. Good examples include "Larry S. Tindleman" or "Larry's Polka Band" or "Tindleman World-o-Shoes," depending on what you want to promote.

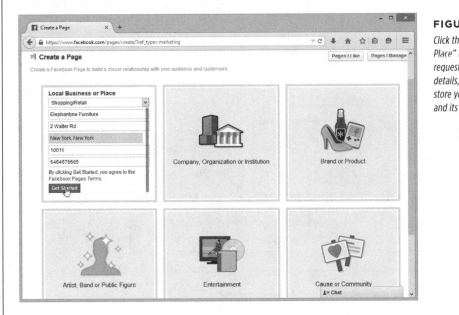

FIGURE 11-9

Click the "Local Business or Place" tile and Facebook requests some additional details, such as the type of store you have, its name, and its address.

3. **Once you fill in the details, click Get Started.**

   Facebook sends you to a new page to gather a bit more information (Figure 11-10).

4. **Choose a category for your page and type in a brief description.**

   After you create your page, Facebook submits it to search engines like Google on your behalf. The category and description help search engines figure out what your page is all about, so it can place your page in its search results.

   As you type a category, you'll see a list of choices appear in a pop-up list. Choose the best fit for your site. You can specify more than one category (the site in Figure 11-10 has two), but make sure you always choose from the list of suggestions—your site won't rank as well if you make up a category of your own.

   Make your description as concise as possible. Facebook doesn't let you type more than 155 characters, which is the length of the description in Figure 11-10.

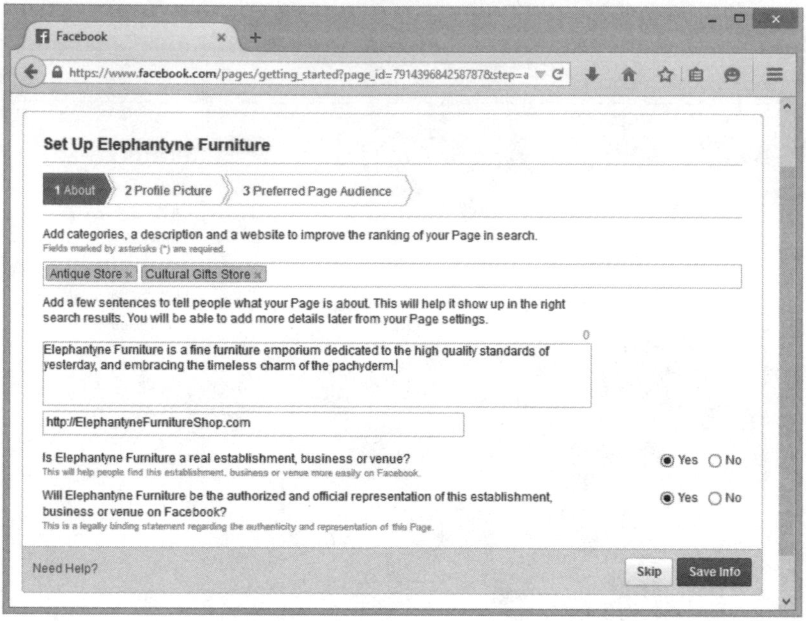

FIGURE 11-10

Facebook leads new-page creators through three steps, represented by the buttons at the top of the page. In the first and most important step, About, you describe your page and pick an official page address.

5. **Optionally, add a link to your website.**

   Some people or businesses create a Facebook Page but no website of their own, but the best way to promote yourself is to have both. Usually, it's best to put the most important content on your built-from-scratch website, and then *promote* your site with a Facebook Page. In essence, your Facebook Page extends the reach of your site into the social world.

6. **Tell Facebook if your page is for a real establishment, and if it's an official page.**

   Facebook lets you create pages for fictional places (say, the Hogwarts School of Witchcraft & Wizardry). It also lets you create a page for something you like but don't own (like a fan club for your favorite sports team). But Facebook needs to know if what you're doing is real and if it's official, so it knows how to describe your site to the world.

7. **Click Save Info to continue.**

   Facebook takes you to the second step, where you supply your profile picture.

8. **Click Upload From Computer, pick your picture, and then click OK to upload it.**

   The profile picture will sit in the top-right corner of your page. This detail is critically important, because it's the first thing viewers see, and it establishes your identity.

9. **Click Next to continue.**

   Facebook takes you to the final step, where you describe the types of people you want to reach.

   Depending on your page, Facebook may ask about your audience's location (for example, a local store may target people in a specific city), their age range, and their interests. All this information is optional, but it can help Facebook get your site in front of the right people.

10. **Once you enter your audience information, click Save.**

    Now Facebook creates your page and takes you to its Timeline (Figure 11-11).

    A new Facebook Page starts with several tabs, much as an ordinary Facebook page does (which Facebook nerds call a personal profile). The most obvious difference between the two is the fact that a Facebook Page includes a Reviews tab, which lets fellow Facebookers weigh in on the person or business with a *review*—a short post that includes a one- to five-star ranking.

FIGURE 11-11

Here's the freshly created Elephantyne Furniture page. It includes a timeline where you can add posts, the store's contact information, a map, a tiled view of pictures, and a count of the Page's likes.

11. **Take note of the URL for your Facebook Page.**

    The quickest way to get your page's URL is to look at the web browser's address bar. Your URL is everything up until the question mark. It includes the Facebook site, page name, and a series of numbers.

    For example if you see this in the address bar:

    ```
    https://www.facebook.com/pages/Elephantyne-Furniture/791439684258787?sk=timeline
    ```

    Your Facebook Page URL is this:

    ```
    https://www.facebook.com/pages/Elephantyne-Furniture/791439684258787
    ```

    You can send this URL to other people so they can find your page.

Although you might not feel like you've done very much, your Facebook Page is now live and accessible to anyone on the social network. People outside of Facebook can see it too, but it will take awhile before it turns up in Google's search results.

In the meantime, here are some good ideas for what to do next:

- **Give your page its first like.** Start your page out right by clicking the Like button.

- **Post on the timeline.** The timeline is where you and your fans post messages. People read your timeline to take the pulse of your page. If it's full of lively chatter, news, and events, it's a good sign that your page is thriving.

- **Flesh out the About tab.** The About tab holds the basic information you supplied when you created the page. In this case, that's the description and address for the business. Depending on the type of page, the About tab will give you the option of adding other details. In the store example, you can add your operating hours (click Add Hours), and the price range of your goods (click Add Price Range).

- **Invite your Facebook friends.** Eventually, your page will get attention by word of mouth, but you need to start somewhere. The easiest approach is to get your circle of friends or colleagues to take note. To do that, click the three-dot button (...), which appears at the top of your page right next to the Message button, and choose Invite Friends. You'll see a list of all your Facebook friends; click the Invite button next to each person you want to recruit. Facebook contacts these people on your behalf, inviting them to check out your new page and give it a Like. If they do, they'll be connected to your page (Figure 11-12).

> **TIP** Remember, Facebook is all about community. You don't need to reply to every comment, but you should talk back often. Offer thanks when praised and apologies when criticized.

- **Reach out to more people by email.** You can use Facebook's email feature to invite people from your contact list using any popular email program (click the three-dot button, and then click Suggest Page to get started). Or, if you want to craft your own message so it sounds less spammy, make a note of your page's URL and send it to your peeps. For a better response, let them know about some pictures or content that might interest them, or ask them to give your page a review.

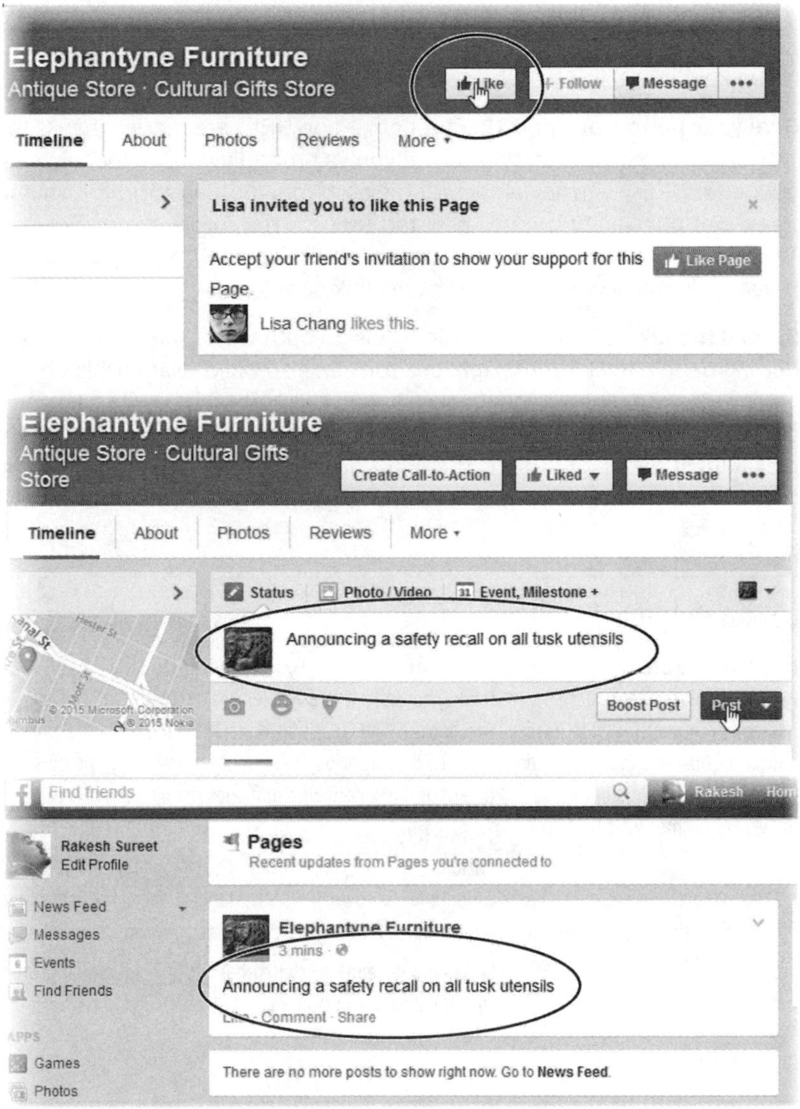

FIGURE 11-12

One of a Facebook Page's most important jobs is delivering your posts to fans. It all starts when someone clicks Like on your page (top). Now, when you post a message on your Timeline (middle), the information shows up on your fan's page (bottom).

- **Add pictures on the Photos tab.** Facebookers expect to be able to see you, so photos are a must. Often, Facebook pictures are informal and focus on people (for example, a business might upload pictures of its employees or a social event).

- **Choose whether other people can post.** It's up to you whether you want to be the sole picture uploader or let your fans in on the action, too. Initially, your timeline and Photos tab are open to all, which encourages people to get involved and form a relationship with you. But if you need to clamp down on these permissions, click the Settings button (it appears in a bar just above your page, on the right side). On the Settings page, choose the General tab and then, under Posting Ability, edit the options.

- **Give your page a better URL.** Facebook Page URLs are messy, thanks to the long series of numbers at the end. But you've probably noticed that big players get better URLs, with no numbers at the end. You, too, can apply for a number-free Facebook vanity URL. To get started, click the About tab on your page. Then, click Page Info in the column on the left. Finally, look for the setting named "Facebook Web Address," and click the link next to it.

- **Spread the Likes.** Facebook relationships go both ways. Your main focus is on getting people to like your page, but you can also build relationships by liking other pages and other people. For example, a children's store might Like a nearby daycare center, a baby-themed event, or a children's entertainer. The trick is to make sure it's your page doing the liking, not your personal Facebook account. (See the box below to make sure you're using the right identity.)

Becoming Your Facebook Page

In the past, Facebook Page creators had to use their personal Facebook accounts to manage their professional pages. This wasn't always perfect. For example, it made it hard to keep some distance between you and your business or brand, and you had to take on the role of official spokesperson for your organization, even though the page really may have belonged to a whole team of people.

All this changed when the makers of Facebook introduced a feature that lets you explicitly take on the identity of your Facebook Page. Once you assume the identity of your page, you can leave messages on other people's Timelines, track the activity on your page, add comments to ongoing discussions, and Like other businesses (which gives you a great avenue

for cross-promotion). For example, Elephantyne Furniture might choose to Like a wholesaler, marketer, or supplier. On Facebook, it will clearly indicate that Elephantyne Furniture likes the person or business, without revealing the personal details of the person who manages the page.

To switch to your Facebook Page account, click the Account button in the top-right corner of your Facebook profile page (it looks like a down-pointing triangle). Facebook lists all the pages you've created. Click the page you want to become.

When you're ready to switch back to your personal profile, click the Account button again and choose your name in the "Use Facebook as" list.

Promoting Your Facebook Page on Your Website

Now that you've crafted the perfect Facebook Page, it's time to promote it on your website. You have several options, including the following:

- **Facebook badge.** This small box advertises your Facebook Page on a web page. When someone clicks the box, they move from your website to your Facebook Page. To create a badge, go to *www.facebook.com/badges* and then click Profile Badge. Optionally, click the "Edit this badge" link to customize your icon's look. Then click the Other button and get the relevant HTML, which you can copy into any of your web pages.

- **Like button.** You can slap this Facebook-styled Like button on any of your web pages. If a Facebooker visits your page and clicks the button, it's the same as clicking Like on your actual Facebook Page: It establishes a relationship that boosts your ranking and allows information to flow from your page to your fan's Facebook page. To get a Like button, go to *http://tinyurl.com/get-like-button*. Fill in your Facebook Page URL, tweak the other options if you want to change the button's appearance, and then click Get Code.

- **Like box.** This panel includes a summary of what's happening with your Facebook page—for example, recent Timeline and note postings. It also includes the ever-important Like button. To get a Like box, go to *http://tinyurl.com/get-like-box*. Fill in your Facebook Page URL, tweak the other options if you want to change what the Like box looks like, and then click Get Code (Figure 11-13).

Typically, you'll position a Like box or a Facebook badge in a separate column on your page, using the CSS positioning properties you learned about in Chapter 8.

◼ Groups

A group is a small community of people who share the same online space. They interact by posting messages to the group, just like you do on a social network like Facebook. The difference is that a group has a more formalized arrangement. Usually, it focuses on a certain topic or limits its membership to members of a certain organization. Whereas people use Facebook casually, to share the experiences and gossip of everyday life, they use groups to pursue specific interests or get work done.

Before you create a group, you need to understand where it works and where it doesn't. Groups are *not* a good way to strike up a conversation with people who don't really know you and who don't have a vested interest in your website. Potential customers, curious web tourists, and people who stumble across your site aren't going to go through the trouble of joining a group to talk to you. You'll have a better chance luring them in with Facebook.

On the other hand, there are some situations where groups work better than loose-knit social media sites like Facebook. Here are some examples:

- **You have a niche topic**, one that attracts highly dedicated fans, but isn't already discussed somewhere else. This isn't easy, because the Web already has *Glee* forums, forums for people to complain about bosses, vampire fan forums, and so on.

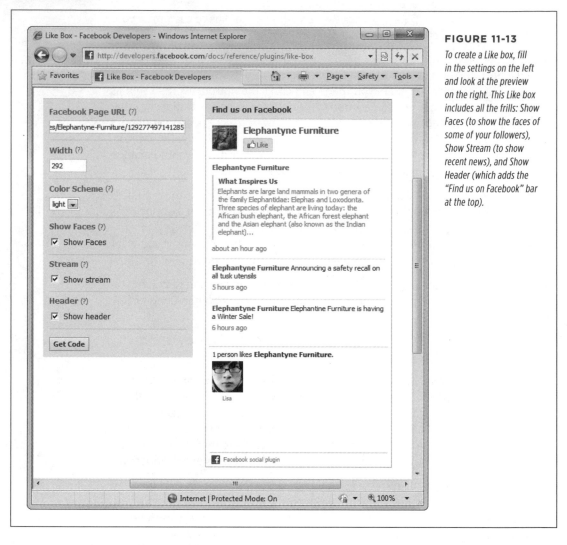

FIGURE 11-13

To create a Like box, fill in the settings on the left and look at the preview on the right. This Like box includes all the frills: Show Faces (to show the faces of some of your followers), Show Stream (to show recent news), and Show Header (which adds the "Find us on Facebook" bar at the top).

- **You provide product support.** If you run a business, it makes sense to answer common questions in a forum so all your fans can find the answers they need, rather than repeating yourself over and over again in email messages.

- **Your group is an extension of the real world.** In this case, the people in the group already know one another, and already have a reason to band together. For instance, a group could be a convenient way for you to chat with the members in your knitting circle.

- **Your group wants privacy.** For example, if you run a support group for recovering addicts, you might want to shut out the Internet riffraff. In this case, you can create a group and limit its membership.

The best forums drive themselves. Once you get the right ingredients in place, a forum can succeed without you having to intervene. Think of forums as a dinner party that you host, and all you need to do is get the conversation started before making a polite retreat. And if you use forums to answer technical questions, you can reduce your workload immensely. For example, in many forums, the emphasis is on customers or experts helping one another. That means forum members share information, advice, and answers, and you need to step in only to clear up a long-running debate.

Creating a Google+ Community

Many sites let you create your own group, and they're all free. Examples include Facebook Groups (which work well with groups that are casual or social), LinkedIn Groups (which tend to focus on business networking), Google Groups (which are fantastic, but a bit dated), and Google+ Communities (which are the modern successors to the long-lived Google Groups).

Before you dive into Google+ Communities, take a step back and consider Google+, which is Google's social networking service. People sometimes think of it as a Facebook competitor, although it really isn't—Facebook is far more popular, and nobody jumps ship for a new social site without their friends. Instead, Google+ is better understood as a suite of social networking services, some of which are useful to anyone. Most people already have a Google account, whether it's for YouTube, Gmail, or one of Google's indispensable web developer services (like the Google Webmaster Tools or Google Analytics). Or maybe you use it to synchronize your bookmarks in Chrome, back up your Android phone, or create a blog on Blogger. The point is that most web fans pick up a Google account at some point. And when you have a Google account, you can use all the Google+ services. That means you can join a Google+ community without the usual rigmarole of entering your personal details, thinking up a new password, and clicking a link in a confirmation email.

To create a new Google+ group (known to Google as a *community*), follow these steps:

1. **Go to** *http://plus.google.com.*

   That's the hub for Google+. If you're not yet signed in, Google asks you to do so before you continue.

2. **Click the drop-down menu in the top-left corner (right now it says Home) and choose Communities.**

   Google shows you a list of communities you can join. But right now, you want to establish one of your own.

3. **At the top of the list of communities, click the "Create community" button.**

   Google asks you what type of community you're creating (Figure 11-14).

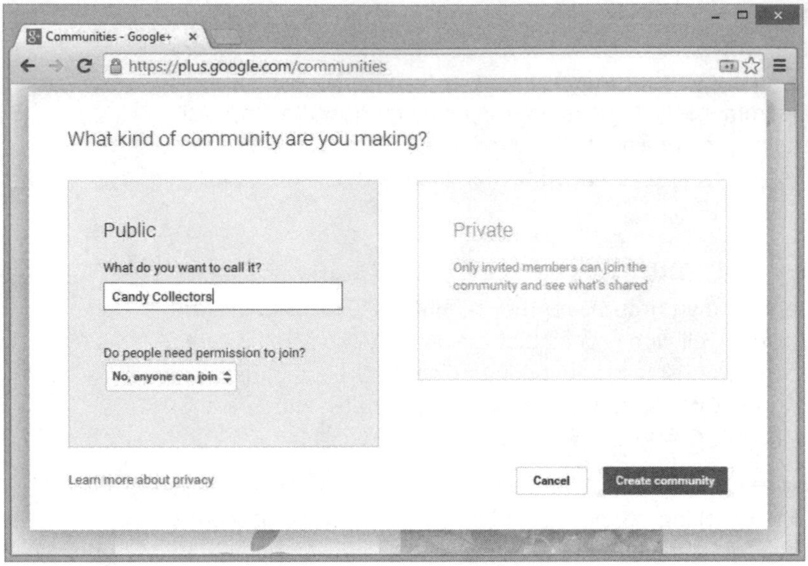

FIGURE 11-14

If you click the Public tile on the left, you can create a group that's open to everyone on the Web. The next step is to pick a community name (here, that's "Candy Collectors"), and decide if people need to ask for your approval before they can join.

4. **Choose either a public or a private community.**

   - **Public communities** are open to friends, strangers, and random Internet visitors. Everyone can find your group and read its posts. This approach is most in keeping with the spirit of the Web. If you don't have a good reason to lock down your community, make it open.

   - **Private communities** are hidden from view. Members of the group can read its posts, but other people can't. In fact, they might not even be aware that the group exists at all.

   TIP It's important to get the privacy settings right, because you can't change them later on.

5. **Enter a name for your community in the "What do you want to call it?" text box.**

   A good, descriptive name is essential. It tells people the purpose of your community. If your community is public, the name tells newbies what the group is all about.

   Community names don't need to be unique, because Google+ identifies them using a numeric ID that it generates automatically, That means it doesn't matter if someone else already has a community that uses the name you want for your own community.

NOTE You can change the name of your community after you create it, as long as it has fewer than 500 members. If your community expands beyond that, its identity becomes fixed, and Google won't let you rename it.

6. **If you're creating a public community, choose whether people need permission to join.**

   • **Choose "No, anyone can join"** to let people sign up to your group at will, without your intervention. This really lowers the barrier of entry to your community. It means that someone can discover your group, sign up, and start posting without any delays.

   • **Choose "Yes, anyone can ask to join"** to micromanage who joins your group. Visitors who want to join must send a request, and it's up to you to approve it. No matter how carefully you watch your email, there will be an inevitable delay between the moment someone makes a request and the time you approve it. Although this setting prevents spammers, it also hampers requests, because many prospective members will wander away without bothering to ask for membership.

FREQUENTLY ASKED QUESTION

Putting a Lock on Your Community

Should I restrict people from joining my community?

It's tempting to force members to apply to your group, but resist the ego trip. On the Web, people are impatient and easily distracted. If you place barriers in the way of potential group members, they may just walk away.

On the other hand, there are some cases where restricted membership makes a lot of sense. Two examples are when you want to discuss semi-secret information, like company strategies, or you're afraid your topic might attract the wrong kind of crowd. For example, if you set up a group called Software-Piracy to discuss the social implications of software piracy, you might find yourself deluged with requests for the latest versions of

stolen software. As a general rule, restrictions make sense only if you use them to control the quality of your group.

The same holds true for message moderation. Most healthy online communities are self-regulating. If a member inadvertently offends the general community, others will correct him; if it's deliberate, most will eventually ignore the provocation. You might need to step in occasionally to ban a member, but screening every message is overkill. It also requires a huge amount of extra work from you and severely cramps the dynamic of your group, because a new message won't appear until you review it, which will usually be several hours after the poster wrote it. For fans of the Web who expect instant gratification, that's not good news.

7. **If you're creating a private community, choose whether people can find it in a search.**

   • **Choose "No, hide it from searches"** if you want your group to go completely underground. No one will know it exists, except the people you invite.

- **Choose "Yes, people can find it and ask to join"** if you want your group to hide its posts, but you're willing to consider new members. Visitors can find your community, visit its page on Google+, and make a request to join. But unless you grant them membership, they won't see any of your group's content.

8. **Click the "Create community" button.**

   Google creates your community and opens the page (Figure 11-15).

TIP   Check the address bar in your browser and you'll see the URL for your community page. It doesn't include the community name, just a unique number that Google assigned it. Here's an example: *https://plus.google.com/communities/101390776243635376950.*

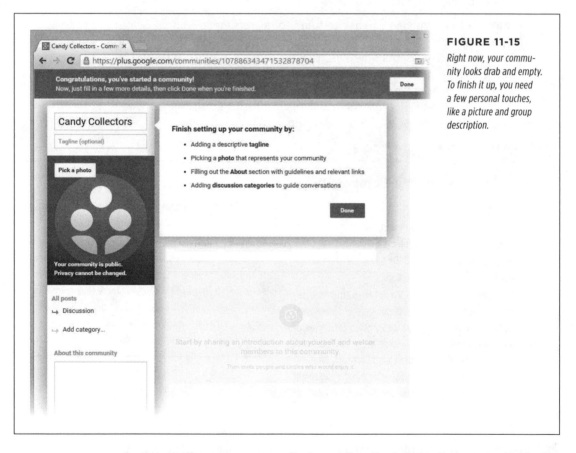

FIGURE 11-15

Right now, your community looks drab and empty. To finish it up, you need a few personal touches, like a picture and group description.

9. **Personalize your community by adding the information requested in the sidebar on the left.**

   Every self-respecting community needs the following:

- **Tagline.** The tagline appears just under the community name. Think of it as a catchphrase for your site, like "Candy lovers unite!"

- **Photo.** Click the "Pick a photo" button and choose an image for your community. It'll appear in the sidebar on the left, giving your group an instant identity.

- **Description.** Type a longer description in the "About this community" text box, which appears farther down the page. Think of this as a one-paragraph description that sums up the purpose of your community.

- **Discussion categories.** If you don't add any categories, everyone's postings will land in the general Discussion category. If you expect plenty of conversation, you can impose some order by subdividing the discussions into separate sections. For example, the Candy Collector community uses the custom categories Candy Facts and Your Favorite Candies. Every other posting winds up in the Discussion category. To add a category, click the "Add category" link and then type a short category name of your choosing.

10. **When you finish, click Done.**

    Your community is ready for action. Google may prompt you to invite potential members. For now, just click Cancel so you can survey your community (Figure 11-16).

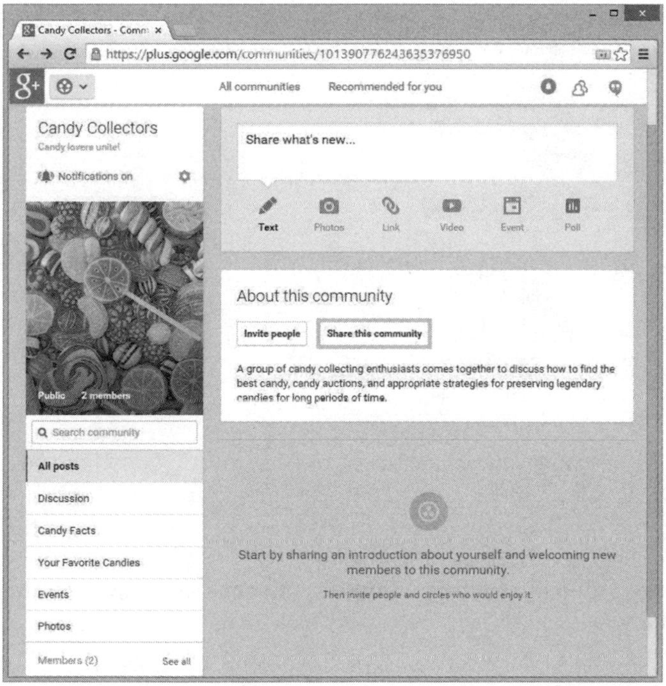

FIGURE 11-16

The Candy Collectors community is quiet but ready for action.

11. Invite some company.

There are two ways to recruit members for a public community. You can *invite* them, which means you specifically ask someone to join, or you can *share* your group with them, which means you're simply telling them about the group and suggesting they stop by for a look. But if you have a private community, inviting is the only action that makes sense.

To send some invites, click the "Invite people" button (Figure 11-17). To share your group, click "Share this community." Either way, the effect is almost the same. Google sends an email to the people you specify, describing your community and inviting them to click a button to join (if you sent an invitation) or to visit (if you opted to share).

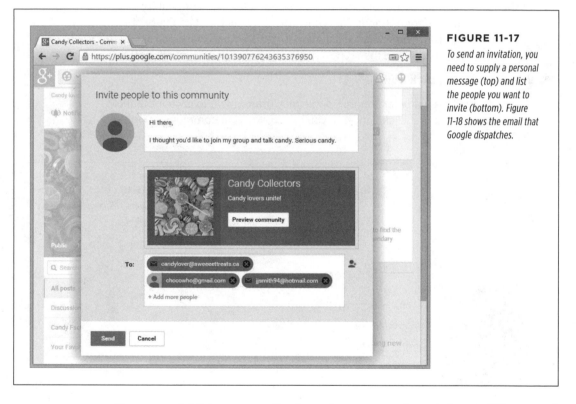

FIGURE 11-17

To send an invitation, you need to supply a personal message (top) and list the people you want to invite (bottom). Figure 11-18 shows the email that Google dispatches.

Once you establish a community of people, your group is ready to get off the ground. Members can visit the group, write posts, comment on other people's posts, add events to the Events section, upload photos to the Photos section, and see the list of other members. From this point on, the challenge isn't in setting up the group, it's in attracting enough interesting people so that it becomes a lively community.

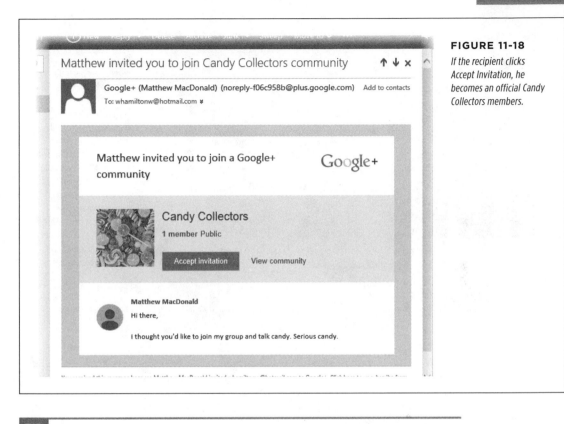

FIGURE 11-18

If the recipient clicks Accept Invitation, he becomes an official Candy Collectors members.

TIP Google communities are chatty places. Every time someone adds a post, you (and other members) will get an email notification. You can turn this off by clicking the alarm bell icon, which sits at the top of the sidebar on the left, just under the community name.

POWER USERS' CLINIC

Managing Your Members

As your community expands, you'll accumulate more and more members. You can see who's in your group by visiting your community, scrolling to the bottom of the left-hand sidebar until you see the Members section, and then clicking the "See all" link.

You, the group creator, have extra powers. Not only can you review the list of members, but you can also explicitly remove a member, ban her (so the person can't rejoin the group), or promote her to the role of a moderator. To do either, click the

Options button (the down-pointing arrow in the top-right corner of the box for that member). You'll see a short menu of options, including "Remove from community," "Ban from community," and "Promote from member to moderator."

Moderators gain the same post-management powers you have (Figure 11-19). They aren't limited to writing posts and comments—they can also delete posts and comments, pin important posts so they stick to the top of the community page, and ban troublemakers. However, they can't delete your posts.

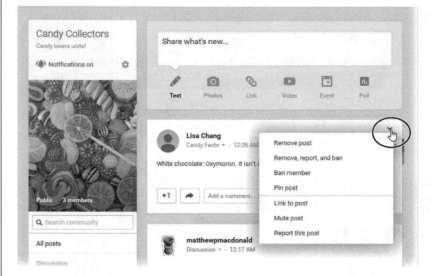

FIGURE 11-19

Moderators have super-powers over posts. To see your choices, click the Options button in the corner of a post or comment. Everyone has the ability to mute a post (to stop getting notifications about it) or report it (essentially, to send a complaint to the group owner when you discover spam or inappropriate content). But only moderators can pin posts, delete posts, and ban malicious posters.

Adding a Blog

A traditional website is the gold standard of the web world. It's infinitely flex-ible—able to chronicle a personal trip to Machu Picchu just as well as it powers an ecommerce storefront.

However, there's something distinctly unspontaneous about a website. For example, imagine you want to post a piece of gossip about a celebrity sighting in your home-town. Before you can share your thoughts with the rest of the word, you need to pick a web page filename, decide what HTML elements you'll use, determine how you'll link your page to other pages, and so on. None of these tasks is really that difficult, but taken together, they're enough to discourage casual web authors from writing anything that doesn't seem worth the trouble.

That's where blogs fit into the picture. Blogs are a self-publishing format that gets your thoughts online quickly and easily, while avoiding the headaches of website management. They're a fresh, straightforward, and slightly chaotic way to communi-cate on the Web. To maintain a blog, you publish short entries whenever the impulse hits you. High-powered blogging software collects, chronologically organizes, and presents your posts on web pages. That means that if you don't want to fuss with the fine details of website management, you don't need to. All you need to worry about is posting your thoughts—and with some blogging software, that's as easy as firing off an email.

In this chapter you'll learn how blogs work, and you'll see how to create your own blog with Google's Blogger, one of the Web's most popular blogging services.

■ Understanding Blogs

The word "blog" is an combination of the words *web* and *log*, which makes sense because blogs are logs of a sort—regular, dated blurbs, like a cross between a diary entry and a posting in a discussion forum. "Blog" is also a verb, as in "I just ate at a terrible restaurant; when I get home I'm going to blog about it." Figure 12-1 dissects the anatomy of a basic blog.

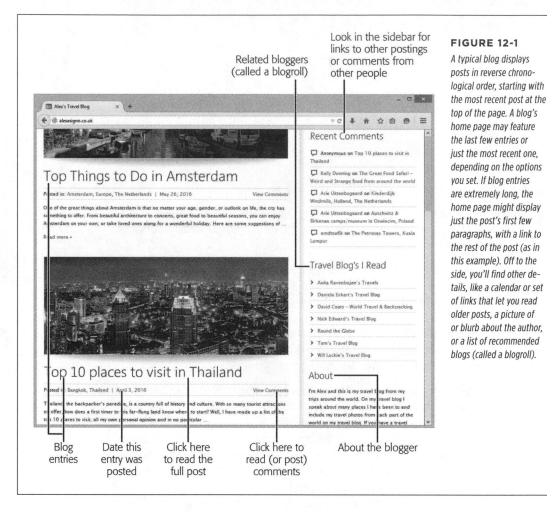

Related bloggers
(called a blogroll)

Look in the sidebar for
links to other postings
or comments from
other people

Blog
entries

Date this
entry was
posted

Click here
to read the
full post

Click here to
read (or post)
comments

About the blogger

FIGURE 12-1

A typical blog displays posts in reverse chronological order, starting with the most recent post at the top of the page. A blog's home page may feature the last few entries or just the most recent one, depending on the options you set. If blog entries are extremely long, the home page might display just the post's first few paragraphs, with a link to the rest of the post (as in this example). Off to the side, you'll find other details, like a calendar or set of links that let you read older posts, a picture of or blurb about the author, or a list of recommended blogs (called a blogroll).

Although blogs make it easy to post your thoughts on the Web, it's unfair to say that they're just a simplified way to publish online. Rather, blogs are a wholly different form of online communication. And although there's no definitive test to determine what is or isn't a blog, most blogs share several characteristics:

- **Blogs are often personal.** You can find topic-based blogs, work-based blogs, political blogs, and great numbers of blogs filled with random, offbeat musings. No matter their mission, however, blogs usually emphasize the author's point of view. They rarely attempt to be objective—instead, they're unapologetically idiosyncratic *opinions*.

- **Blogs are organized chronologically.** When you design a website, you spend a lot of time deciding how best to organize your material, often using menus or links to guide visitors through an assortment of topics. Blogs take a radically different approach. They have no organization other than ordering your posts chronologically. Anything else would just slow down restless bloggers.

- **Blogs are updated regularly.** Blogs emphasize fast, freewheeling communication rather than painstakingly crafted web pages. Bloggers are known to add content obsessively, often several times a week. Because blog entries are dated, it's glaringly obvious if you don't keep your blog up to date. If you can't commit to blogging regularly, don't start a blog—set up a simple web page instead.

- **Blogs are flexible.** There's a bit of blog wisdom that says no thought is too small for a blog. And it's true—a blog post communicates equally well whether you write a detailed discussion on the viability of peanut-butter Oreos or a three-sentence summary of an uneventful day.

- **Blogs create a broader conversation.** Blogs form communities more readily than websites do. Not only are blogs more conversational in nature, but they also support comments and links that can tie different blogs together in a conversation. If someone posts an interesting item on a blog, a legion of fellow bloggers follow up with replies, blog posts, Twitter messages, and Facebook Likes. Scandalous blog gossip can rocket around the globe in a heartbeat.

Blogs occupy a specialized web niche, distinct from a lot of the other types of sites you've seen. For example, you can't effectively sell a line of trench coats for dogs on a personal blog. But many people start blogs *in addition* to ordinary websites. This is a great combination. Visitors love blogs because they crave a glimpse behind the scenes. They're also sure to visit again and again if they can count on a regularly updated blog that offers a steady stream of news, gossip, and insight.

NOTE A significant number of big businesses have found that they can make their companies seem friendlier and more open by adding a blog from a senior executive, manager, designer—or even the CEO.

Syndication

One neat feature that many blogs provide is *syndication*, which lets avid readers monitor their favorite blogs using a program called a *feed reader*. To use a feed reader, you provide links to all your favorite blogs and then keep an eye out for updates. The reader periodically checks these blogs and alerts you to new posts, saving you from having to check every blog 94 times a day to see if there's fresh content. If you follow blogs regularly, feed readers are the most practical way to stay current with your friends in the blogosphere.

WORD TO THE WISE

The Hazards of Blogging

There's something about the first-person nature of a blog that sometimes lures people into revealing much more information than they should. Thanks to reckless moments of blogging, lovers have discovered their cheating spouses, grandmothers have read memorable accounts of their granddaughters' nights on the town, and well-meaning employees have lost their jobs.

The dangers of impulse blogging are particularly great in the workplace. In most countries, companies can fire employees who make damaging claims about a business (even if they're true). Even famously open-minded Google ditched Mark Jen after he blogged a few choice words about a Google sales conference that he claimed resembled a drunken frat party. The notable part of his story is that he didn't set out to undermine Google or publicize his blog. In fact, only his close friends and family even knew he had a blog. Unfortunately, a few Google-watching sites picked up on the post and sent the link around the Internet.

There are many more stories like this, where employees have lost their jobs after revealing trade secrets, admitting

to inappropriate on-the-job conduct (for example, posting risqué at-work photos or bragging about time-wasting games of computer solitaire), or just complaining about the boss.

To protect yourself from the hazards of blogging, remember these rules:

- "Anonymous" never is.
- If you plan to hide your identity, adopt a pseudonym, or conceal personal details, remember the first rule.
- Funny is in the mind of the beholder. Your humorous work-related stories will be seen in a different light when read by high-powered executives who lack your finely developed sense of irony.
- Think before you write. There's a fine line between company secrets and information in the public domain.
- There's no going back. Although many blogging tools let you edit or remove old posts, the original versions can stick around in search-engine caches for eternity (see page 328).

Although most blogs work with feed readers, some don't. To work with a reader, blogs need to provide a *feed* (Figure 12-2), a computer-friendly format of recent blog posts. Readers interpret the feeds and cull important information from them, like the post's title, description, date, and text. They display that information for your reading pleasure, without forcing you to make a separate trip to the blog itself.

If you click a feed link or icon (like the one shown in Figure 12-2), you'll see the feed itself, with its list of recent posts (Figure 12-3).

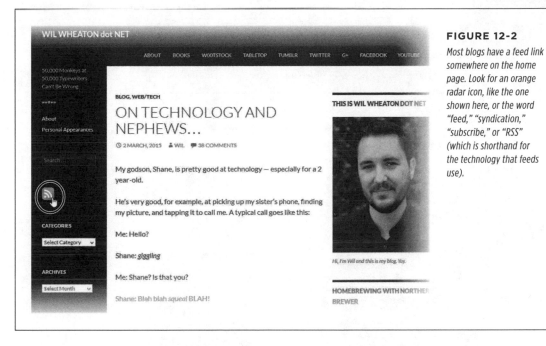

FIGURE 12-2

Most blogs have a feed link somewhere on the home page. Look for an orange radar icon, like the one shown here, or the word "feed," "syndication," "subscribe," or "RSS" (which is shorthand for the technology that feeds use).

You can subscribe to a feed by right-clicking the feed icon and copying the URL (choose "Copy link address" or "Copy shortcut"—the exact wording depends on your browser). Then, open your feed-reading program, select "Add a new feed" (here again, the wording might differ depending on your reader), and paste the link.

If you don't have a feed reader of your own, there's no shortage to choose from. Here are three of the most popular:

- Feedly (*http://feedly.com*)
- The Old Reader (*http://theoldreader.com*)
- NewsBlur (*http://newsblur.com*)

The best readers let you keep up with your favorite blogs on multiple platforms. For example, they let you browse the blogs you follow by visiting a website (on your desktop computer) or using an app (on your mobile phone or tablet). They also keep track of what you read, no matter where you read it.

NOTE Most feed readers start out free but charge a monthly fee for premium features like better blog searching and the ability to add more than a hundred feeds.

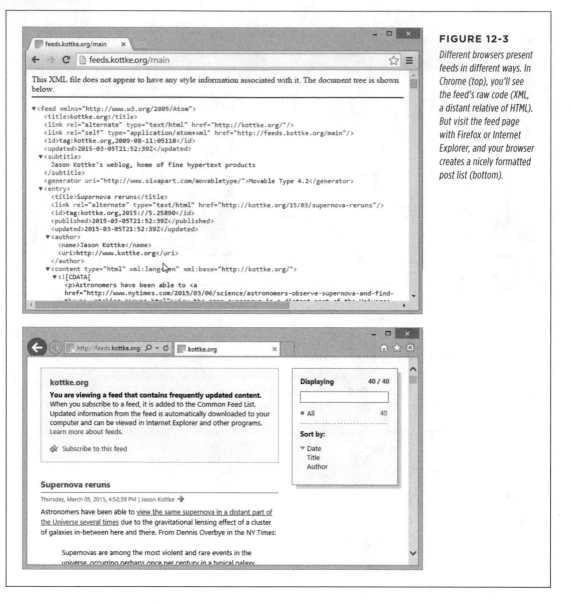

FIGURE 12-3

Different browsers present feeds in different ways. In Chrome (top), you'll see the feed's raw code (XML, a distant relative of HTML). But visit the feed page with Firefox or Internet Explorer, and your browser creates a nicely formatted post list (bottom).

Some web browsers include their own built-in feed readers. Although they're far less powerful than dedicated readers, they might be enough to satisfy a casual blog-browser:

- **Internet Explorer** lets you subscribe to a feed in much the same way you bookmark a site. First, visit a blog's feed page (Figure 12-3, bottom) by clicking the feed icon or link on a blog. Then click the "Subscribe to this feed" link at the top of the page. Now you can get a list of recent posts quickly and at any time from the Favorites Center (click the Favorites star in the top-right corner of the browser window).

- **Chrome** doesn't have a feed reader, but you can easily get a plug-in that offers basic feed-reading features. Try the one at *http://tinyurl.com/chromefeeds*.

- **Firefox** has a *live bookmarks* feature that tracks feeds. Figure 12-4 shows how it works.

- **Safari** once had feed-reading features, but Apple tossed them out in recent years. It now recommends a separate feed reader service instead.

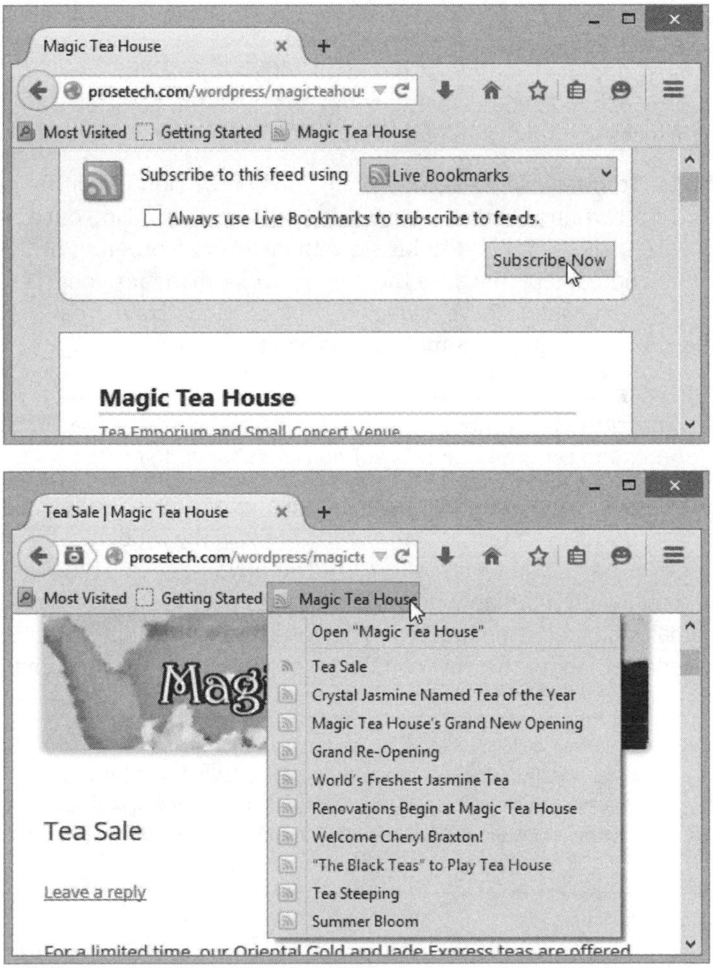

FIGURE 12-4

Top: Firefox asks you how you want to store your feed bookmark. You can use its Live Bookmarks feature or a separate feed-reading program, if you've in- stalled it (just pick it from the list). Click the "Always use" setting if you don't want to see this options page again, and then click the Subscribe Now button.

Bottom: You can't tell a live bookmark from an ordinary one on the Bookmarks toolbar, but click it and you'll see a menu of current blog posts, which Firefox updates automatically. You still need to check the live bookmark to see if there's a new post, but you don't need to visit the original site.

Blog Hosting Options

Before you set up your own blog, it helps to understand the different kinds of blog-making options out there. There are really two types of blogs:

- **Self-hosted blogs.** If you want the greatest amount of control over your blog, you might be interested in hosting it entirely on your own. To do this, you need to pick the blogging program you want to use, find a web host that supports it, and then configure everything. This approach gives you unlimited flexibility (and possibly better performance), but it also requires a bit more work to get off the ground.

  By far the most popular example of blogging software is WordPress (*http://wordpress.org*), although you can also experiment with the CMS software described in the note at the bottom of this page.

- **Hosted blogs.** To post using a hosted blog, you simply sign up with a blog provider and start writing. Adding a blog entry is as simple as filling out a form in your browser. You never need to hassle with installing a program or figure out how to upload content, because the blog provider manages your files for you. You don't even need to have a website. Hosted blogs are a great bet for new bloggers, because they're completely painless.

  Examples of hosted blog providers include Blogger (*www.blogger.com*), WordPress (*http://wordpress.com*, not *http://wordpress.org*, which is where you get the free blog-hosting program), and TypePad (*www.typepad.com*).

In this chapter, you'll spend your time using one blogging tool, called Blogger. Blogger is tremendously popular—in fact, it consistently ranks in the list of most-visited websites (*http://mostpopularwebsites.net/1-50*). The advantages to Blogger are that it's simple to use yet remarkably powerful, with support for group blogging, personalized domain names, customized templates, and a variety of add-on features. These attributes make Blogger the best candidate for all-around blogging champ.

NOTE A number of website-creation tools called *content management systems* (CMSes) let you build ordinary blogs *and* other types of websites. Two popular examples are Drupal (*http://drupal.org*) and Joomla (*www.joomla.org*). Typically, these products suit businesspeople who need to set up complex web applications—say, a sprawling ecommerce store or a web magazine with a team of contributors—without building everything from scratch.

Why You Might Want to Self-Host

Some die-hard blogging fanatics prefer self-hosted blogs, which offer a few unique advantages that Blogger can't match. Here are some examples:

- **Censorship-proof.** When you use a free blogging service like Blogger, Google is in control of your content. If other users complain that your blog has offensive content or pornography, Google can force prospective readers to click through a warning page before they reach your posts. And if Google decides that you're breaking copyright laws or encouraging criminal activity, it can vaporize your blog without warning. Furthermore, some censorship-crazy countries like China block Blogger's sites, which means that no one in those countries can see your blog (unless you pay for a custom domain name, as described in the box on page 408).

- **Linked websites.** Thanks to HTML's linking power, it's easy enough to send readers from your website to your blog and back again. They don't even need to know that they're changing web servers. However, if you host both your website and blog on the same server, you gain some unique advantages. They can use the same domain name, they can share content (like pictures), and they can benefit each other in the search engine rankings because Google sees them as part of the same site.

- **Complete control.** Some blogs involve multiple authors and huge amounts of traffic. Their scope and popularity rival traditional newspapers. (Two popular examples are the news and gossip sites Gawker Media, at *www.gawker.com*, and the Huffington Post, at *www.huffingtonpost.com*.) The creators of this sort of site need complete control over every fine detail to craft search engine campaigns and advertising strategies. Clearly, in this echelon, a free blog service just won't do.

These features don't come without a cost. Self-hosted blogs are more complicated to set up and manage, and you need to pay a monthly hosting fee. But if you're still interested, start out with WordPress (*http://wordpress.org*), the favorite of hard-core technogeeks everywhere. (You can read a whole book's worth of WordPress coverage in *WordPress: The Missing Manual*.) And if you're still not sure, don't be afraid to embrace Blogger—or any blogging service. Your choice won't limit your success, as there are mind-blowingly popular blogs on all the blogging platforms mentioned in this chapter.

Getting Started with Blogger

Blogger is one of the most commonly used blogging services. It provides the easiest way to start a blog, and it's chock-full of nifty blog management tools. Once upon a time, Blogger's premium features required a small yearly contribution. But all that changed when Google bought Blogger. Now all of Blogger's features are free.

Setting up a blog on Blogger is ridiculously easy. In the following sections, you'll learn how to create a blog, add posts, and take charge of a few neat features.

TIP You can also check out the official catalog of Blogger help at *http://help.blogger.com* and the discussion boards at *http//productforums.google.com/forum*, where bloggers share tips, ask questions, and vent their frustrations.

Creating a Blog

Before you create your blog, it's a good idea to assess your goals and decide exactly what type of content you plan to showcase. Although you can create a blog with random thoughts or a chronicle of daily life, the most successful blogs have a clear voice and purpose. They attract a loyal audience with targeted, topic-specific posts.

Once you know how you want to position your blog, you'll be able to choose a snappy name and suitable URL. Start with these steps:

1. **Go to** *www.blogger.com*.

   This is the home page for the Blogger service.

2. **If you have a Google account, enter your login information and click Sign In. If not, click "Get started" to create an account.**

   By this point, you almost certainly have a Google account. In this book, you've used it for Google Analytics, the Google Webmaster Tools, and Google+ Communities. Even if you've ignored all these useful services, you may have picked up a Google account to keep track of videos on YouTube or to write emails on Gmail.

> **NOTE** You need to create an account only once. However, you can create multiple blogs for the same account.

Once you log in, Google takes you to the Blogger dashboard (Figure 12-5).

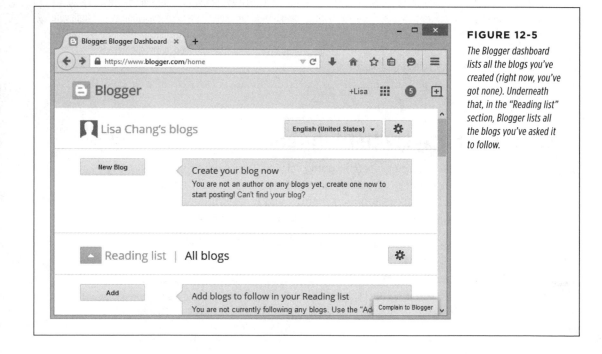

FIGURE 12-5

The Blogger dashboard lists all the blogs you've created (right now, you've got none). Underneath that, in the "Reading list" section, Blogger lists all the blogs you've asked it to follow.

NOTE When you follow a blog in Blogger, it shows you a list of new posts every time you log in, and it keeps track of which ones you've read. However, people rarely use this feature anymore, because dedicated feed readers (page 385) work so much better.

3. **Click New Blog.**

   Google asks for three key pieces of information (Figure 12-6).

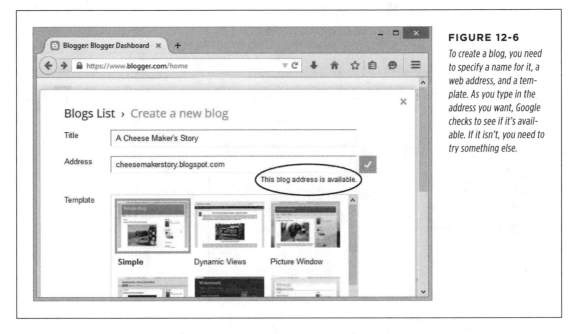

FIGURE 12-6

To create a blog, you need to specify a name for it, a web address, and a template. As you type in the address you want, Google checks to see if it's available. If it isn't, you need to try something else.

4. **Supply the title and URL you want your blog to have.**

   A blog title is just like a web page title—it's the descriptive bit of text that appears in a browser title bar.

   The URL is the really important part, because you don't want to change this later on and risk losing your loyal readers. It's the address that eager web followers use to find your blog. Google lets you use just about any URL, so long as it ends with *.blogspot.com*. Although other bloggers have already taken some of the most obvious names, it's still reasonably easy to create short-and-sweet blog names like *http://secretsandchocolate.blogspot.com* or *http://wildrichman.blogspot.com*.

   If you want to use a custom domain name for your blog, which lets you use your own URL, you first need to create a blog with an ordinary *.blogspot* address. The box on page 408 explains the process.

5. **Choose a template for your blog.**

When you create a blog, you choose a preset template, and Blogger formats your posts using that template's color, graphics, and layout. If you change your template later on, Blogger adjusts all your posts to match the new style.

Blogger gives you just a few starter templates to choose from. But fear not—once you create your blog, you can modify your template's formatting or swap in something completely different.

6. **Click the "Create blog!" button.**

Blogger displays a congratulatory message and brings you back to the dashboard (Figure 12-7).

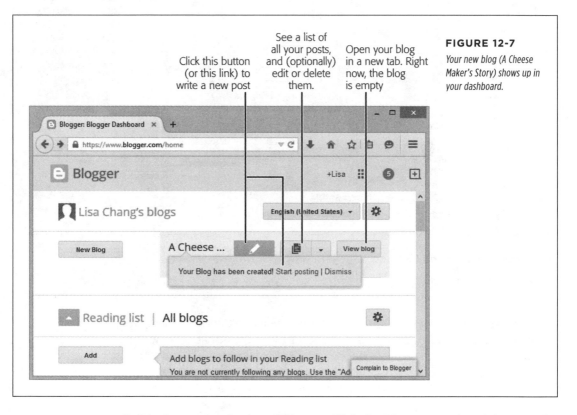

FIGURE 12-7

Your new blog (A Cheese Maker's Story) shows up in your dashboard.

Click this button (or this link) to write a new post

See a list of all your posts, and (optionally) edit or delete them.

Open your blog in a new tab. Right now, the blog is empty

7. **It's time to create your first post. Click the "Create new post" button (the one with the pencil icon) or the "Start posting" link.**

You can return to manage your blog any time by going to *www.blogger.com*. For now, continue with the next step to create your first blog entry.

8. **Enter the title for your blog post, and then type the content of your post into the large text box (see Figure 12-8).**

   Don't worry about all the fancy frills in the editing window just yet—you'll learn about those in the next section.

> **NOTE** A blog entry can be as long or as short as you want. Some people blog lengthy stories, while others post one or two sentences that simply provide a link to an interesting news item (or, more commonly, to a post from another blogger).

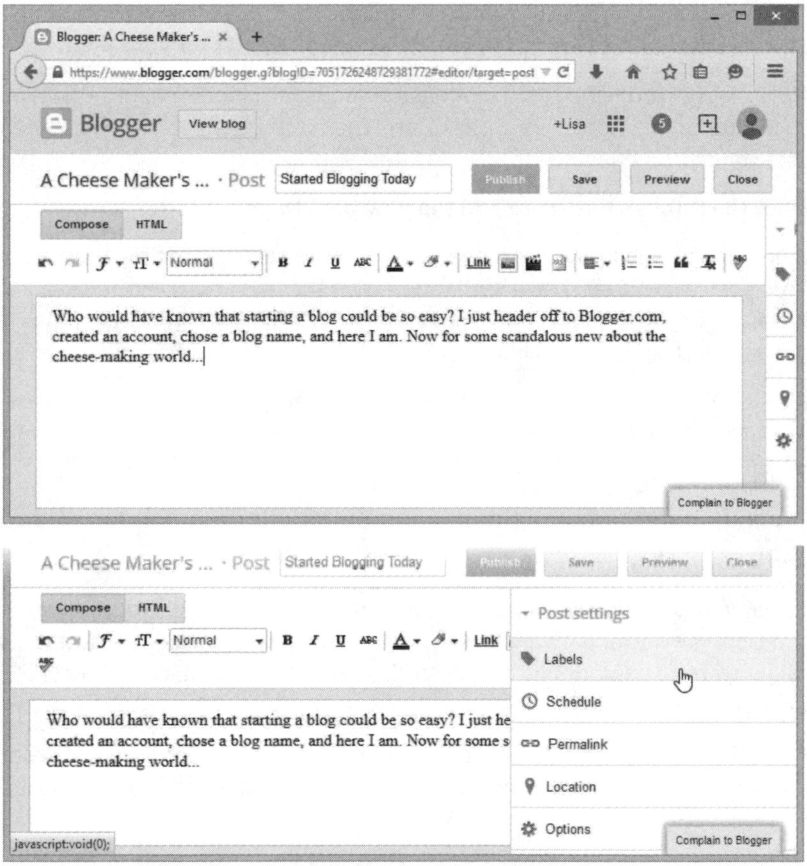

FIGURE 12-8

Blogger's post editor is like a mini word processor (top). A bar on the right holds extra options. To see them, point to the side of the page (bottom).

9. **Categorize your posts with one or more keywords.**

   People search your blog by keyword. For best results, always use the same keywords to identify the same types of posts. For example, every time you talk about your pet hogs, add the label *pig*.

To supply a keyword, point to the sidebar on the right (see Figure 12-8), click Labels, and then type your keyword into the text box. To supply more than one keyword, separate them with commas.

> **NOTE** Keywords can have spaces. So "American Idol" is a valid keyword. But for best results, keep your keywords as short and simple as possible.

10. **Optionally, decide to defer your post's publication.**

    If you don't want your post to appear right away, click Schedule, choose "Set date and time," and then pick a date in the future. Blogger waits until then to add your post to the blog.

11. **Decide whether you want people to make comments on your post.**

    Normally, you do—and that's Blogger's standard setting. But if you don't, point to the bar on the right, click Options, and then change the "Reader comments" setting to "Don't allow."

12. **Click the Publish button to add the new post to your blog.**

    If, instead of publishing right away, you want to take some time to think over your post, click Save. That way, Blogger saves the text you just typed and keeps it waiting for you the next time you return to your blog. (Page 398 explains how you can find an unposted entry and edit it.)

> **TIP** Blogger automatically saves a draft of your post as you type, just in case you run into Internet troubles (or you accidentally close the browser window). However, it saves your entry only every few minutes. Clicking Save stores your current draft immediately.

13. **Optionally, share your work on Google+.**

    When you publish a new post, Google invites you to publicize your work on the Google+ social network. If you have a thriving network of followers, you might want to explore this option (click Share). Otherwise, click Cancel to get on with your blogging.

    Next, Google takes you to the blog management page, which lists your recently written posts. Right now, there's just one entry in the list: the new post you just finished.

14. **Click the "View blog" button to take a look at your handiwork.**

    Now is a great time to check out what your post looks like. Figure 12-9 shows an example of what you'll see.

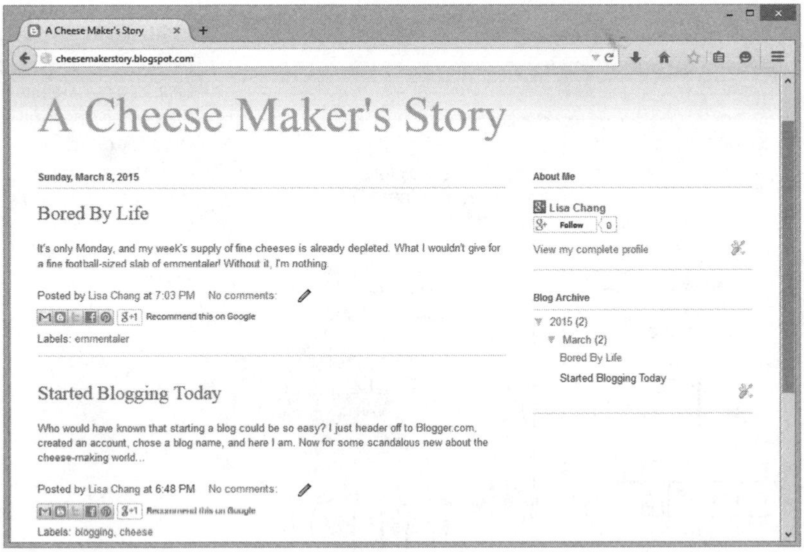

FIGURE 12-9

This blog shows two recent posts (in reverse chronological order, so the most recent one appears first). On the right, a sidebar provides information about the author, along with links to recent posts.

Formatting Your Posts

So far, you've seen how to post text on a blog. But Blogger is pretty flexible when it comes to customizing your blog. You can add all sorts of fancy design elements, from highlighted text to graphics. Best of all, Blogger lets you run rampant with the HTML markup. You just need to know your way around the Blogger editor.

To do some customizing, start a new post by clicking the "Create new post" pencil button. Choose your post title and type in some content. Next, select some text and try out some of the buttons in the toolbar above the text box (see Figure 12-10). Behind the scenes, Blogger uses inline styles (page 80) to format your post.

Blogger's editor, called the *visual composer*, is designed to mimic a word processor. However, if you're itching for some HTML action, click the HTML button above the toolbar over the edit window. Now you can add elements and other HTML goodies directly. Click the Compose button to switch back to the WYSIWYG view.

> **TIP** To get a glimpse of what your post will look like once it's on your blog, you don't need to publish it. Instead, click the Preview button to open a new tab that shows what you'll see based on the formatting you've applied so far.

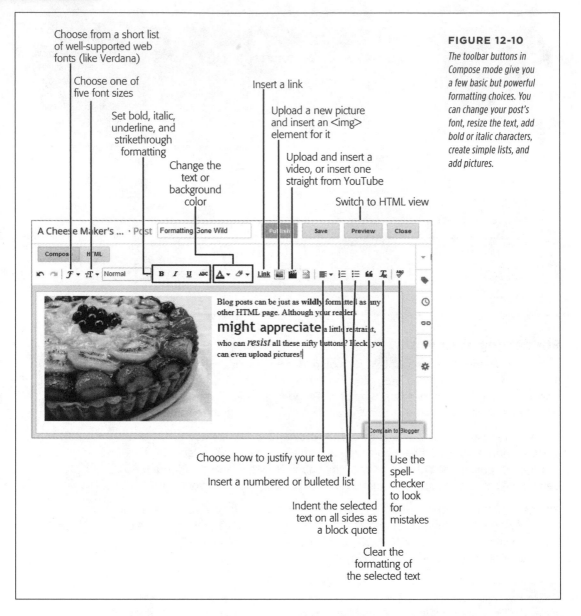

Choose from a short list
of well-supported web
fonts (like Verdana)

Choose one of
five font sizes

Set bold, italic,
underline, and
strikethrough
formatting

Change the
text or
background
color

Insert a link

Upload a new picture
and insert an <img>
element for it

Upload and insert a
video, or insert one
straight from YouTube

Switch to HTML view

FIGURE 12-10

*The toolbar buttons in
Compose mode give you
a few basic but powerful
formatting choices. You
can change your post's
font, resize the text, add
bold or italic characters,
create simple lists, and
add pictures.*

A Cheese Maker's ... · Post | Formatting Gone Wild | Publish | Save | Preview | Close

Compose | HTML

Normal | **B** *I* U ABC A ▼ ✎ ▼ | Link | 🖼 | 🎬 | 📷 | ▦ ▼ | ≣ | ≣ | 66 | T͟ₓ | ✓

Blog posts can be just as **wildly** formatted as any
other HTML page. Although your reader

might appreciate a little restraint,

who can *resist* all these nifty buttons? Heck, you
can even upload pictures!

Complain to Blogger

Choose how to justify your text

Insert a numbered or bulleted list

Indent the selected
text on all sides as
a block quote

Use the
spell-
checker
to look
for
mistakes

Clear the
formatting of
the selected text

Remember, this sort of formatting is a one-off. To consistently change the way common elements appear in your posts (like post titles, the blog text, the author byline, and so on), you need to modify your blog's template (page 401). This approach is akin to using a style sheet on a large website: By editing your template, you create a set of formatting rules that customizes the look of your blog.

■ Blog Management

Once you create your blog, you can perform any of the following tasks:

- Add new posts.

- Edit existing posts.

- Review comments left by other people.

- Change your blog settings.

You do most of this work on the blog management page (Figure 12-11). To get there, head to *www.blogger.com*, find the blog you want to work with in the list, and then click the adjacent "Go to post list" button (it appears next to the pencil button, and its icon looks like a page of paper).

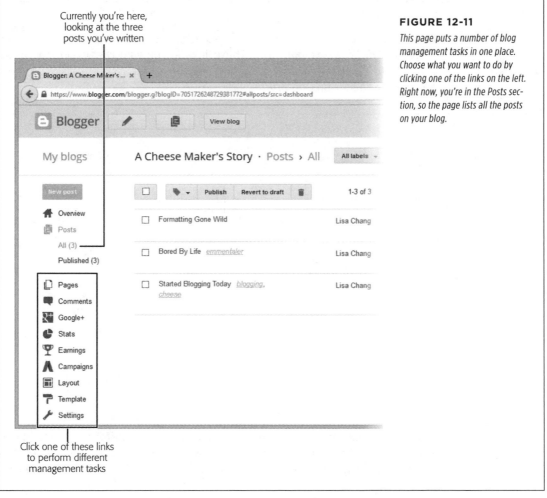

FIGURE 12-11

This page puts a number of blog management tasks in one place. Choose what you want to do by clicking one of the links on the left. Right now, you're in the Posts section, so the page lists all the posts on your blog.

NOTE After you publish a new post, Blogger takes you to the blog management page.

There's a lot of stuff packed into this page. In the following sections, you'll explore its nooks and crannies.

Managing Posts

The post list is one of the most useful parts of the blog management page. (If you aren't there already, click Posts in the sidebar.)

You don't see the actual content of your posts in the list, but you can see some key details, including each post's title, its keywords, its author, and the number of views and comments it's collected so far (Figure 12-12). You can also check on a post's *status*—whether it's live on your site or saved for the future. The word "Draft" appears next to posts you've saved but not yet published. The word "Scheduled" appears next to posts set for upcoming publication, using the scheduling feature described on page 394.

If you point to a post, Blogger displays some useful links, as you can see in the "Bored By Life" post in Figure 12-12. These links let you quickly edit, view, or delete any post. If it's a published post, you'll also see a Share link you can click to promote your post to friends on Google+.

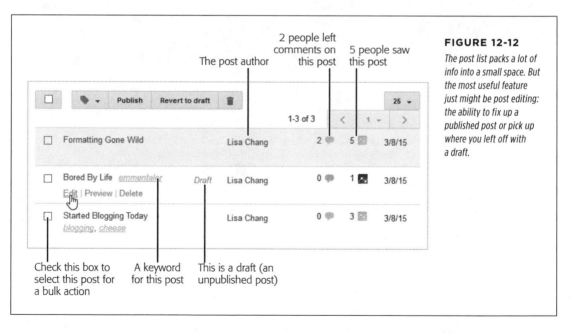

FIGURE 12-12

The post list packs a lot of info into a small space. But the most useful feature just might be post editing: the ability to fix up a published post or pick up where you left off with a draft.

Want to be a blog-editing whiz? Using the post list, you can perform *bulk* operations, which are tasks that act on several posts at a time. Start by clicking the checkbox next to each post you want to change (it appears in the first column on the left), and then specify an action. Here are three quick bulk operations you can apply once you select at least one post:

- **Publish the posts.** Click the Publish button on draft or scheduled posts to make them live now.

- **Unpublish the posts.** If you have second thoughts about one or more posts, click the "Revert to draft" button to turn them into drafts. Blogger stores the content so you can work on it later, but it won't show up on your blog.

- **Add or remove a keyword.** Click the "Label selected posts" button, which has a tiny picture of a tag on it. This opens a list of keywords you use on your blog. Click a keyword to apply it to the selected posts. Click it again to remove it from the selected posts.

- **Delete the posts.** To clear out the garbage, click the trash can icon.

Tweaking Common Settings

Now that your blog is up and running, take some time to fine-tune a few settings. In the following steps, you'll add a description for your blog, choose how many posts you want to display on your home page, and set the time zone to make sure your posts get the right date stamp. Along the way, you'll get a look at some of the many Blogger settings under your control.

1. **On the management page, in the sidebar on the left, click the Settings link.**

   You'll see several submenus, each of which has its own group of settings. Initially, Blogger displays the Basic section, which includes some of the most commonly tweaked options.

2. **Find the Description setting and then click Edit. Type in a description for your blog.**

   This text appears on your home page, usually just under your blog title, though the exact spot depends on your template. Try to keep the description to a sentence or two that hints at the flavor of your blog. Two good descriptions are "The sober confessions of an unlicensed meat handler," and "An on-again, off-again look at my life and adventures."

3. **Click the "Save changes" button at the bottom of the page.**

   When you save your settings, your changes take effect immediately. But before you check out your blog, there's more work to do.

4. **Take another look at the Settings section in the bar on the left. Click the "Post and comments" submenu.**

   Blogger displays a hodgepodge of settings for posts and comments.

5. **In the "Show at most" box at the top, choose how many posts you want to appear on your blog's home page (Figure 12-13).**

You can ask Blogger to show a certain number of posts, or the posts for a specific number of days. For example, you could tell Blogger to display your 12 most recent posts, no matter when you published them (type *12* in the "Show at most" box). Or you could ask Blogger to show your last 30 days' worth of posts (type *30* in the "Show at most" box), and then choose "days" instead of "posts."

For best results, don't crowd your front page with too many entries. If you post daily, stick to a small number of posts or to topics from the current week. Ordinarily, Blogger shows just your seven most recent posts.

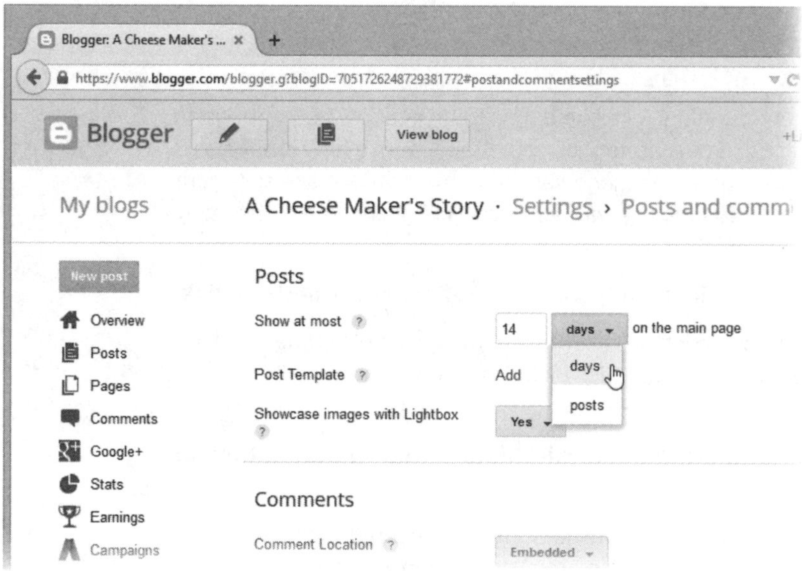

FIGURE 12-13

Here's how to configure your blog to show two weeks' worth of posts.

6. **Click the "Save settings" button at the top of the page.**

You're not quite finished.

7. **Under the Settings section (in the bar on the left), click the "Language and formatting" submenu item.**

Choose your language and a time format.

8. **Specify your time zone in the Time Zone list, and pick a date format from the Date Header Format list.**

Blogger dates every post at the beginning or end of your entry, depending on your template. By setting the time zone, you won't need to manually set the date every time you create a post.

9. **Click Save Settings.**

To see how these changes look, click the "View blog" button.

GEM IN THE ROUGH

Group Blogging

Having trouble keeping your blog up to date? If you want to be part of the blogosphere but just can't manage to post more than once a month, consider sharing the effort with some friends. Look for a natural reason to band together—for example, colleagues can create a blog to discuss a specific work project, and families can use one to keep in touch (if they're not already addicted to Facebook). On a larger scale, group blogging lets like-minded people create a blog that's greater than the sum of its parts. Two wildly popular, trend-setting group blogs are Lifehacker (*http://lifehacker.com*), which posts do-it-yourself productivity tips you can apply to real life, and the Daily Kos (*www.dailykos.com*), which provides left-leaning political news and analysis.

Creating a team blog in Blogger is easy. First, go to your blog management page, click the Settings link on the left, and then click Basic. Scroll down to the "Permissions" section, find the Blog Authors box, which lists all the people who are authorized to contribute to your blog, and then click the "Add authors" link to add your collaborators.

You need to supply just one piece of information—the email address of the blogger you want to enlist. Blogger sends an invitation to each potential blogger. To accept the invitation, the recipient clicks a link in the email message (and creates a Google account, if the blogger-to-be doesn't have one).

All blog authors have the ability to post entries on your blog. Additionally, you can give some bloggers administrator status, which means they can add more bloggers themselves (and delete existing ones).

Customizing Your Template

Templates are keenly important in Blogger. They not only reflect your blog's visual style (irreverent, serious, technical, breezy, and so on), but they also determine its ingredients and how those ingredients appear on the page. Fortunately, Blogger lets you change many of your template's components. For example, you can move the About Me box to a new position, modify its appearance, or remove it entirely.

You can also add new sections, like a set of links that point to your favorite fellow bloggers, or a sidebar of targeted Google ads (page 415). You can even get more radical and replace your template entirely, even if you've been posting for years. Blogger retrofits all your old posts to the new template, so your thoughts, both old and new, remain available for eager readers.

To control these details, click the Template link in the bar on the left side of the blog management page (Figure 12-11). Blogger shows a thumbnail-sized preview of your blog's template, along with its mobile view (the simplified template that kicks into action if a visitor browses your site on a smartphone). You also get options that let you customize your template or choose a new one.

To change your template to something completely different, scroll down. You'll find many more template choices, with odd names like Awesome and Ethereal. Most templates come in several different color schemes. If you see something you want to try out on your blog, click the template thumbnail for a preview. If you like what you see, click the "Apply to Blog" button to make it the face of your blog.

To really get the look you want, you need to customize your template. There are three ways to do that:

- **Change the formatting settings.** These choices let you pick fonts, text colors, and column widths.

- **Change the layout.** You can rearrange your blog, remove parts you don't want, or add new types of content. For example, you can quickly throw in a list of links, a poll for your readers, a slideshow, or a Facebook sharing link.

- **Edit your template's HTML.** Use this approach to customize the raw HTML in your template. If you aren't afraid to muck around in the markup, you can do anything.

You'll see how to use all these features in the following sections.

■ REFORMATTING A TEMPLATE

When you choose a template, it applies a combination of formatting settings. But if you peek under the hood, you can tweak most of them to get exactly what you want. Here's how:

1. **If you aren't already looking at the template settings, click the Template link on the left side of the blog management page.**

2. **Click Customize.**

    Blogger opens a two-part page, with a pile of formatting tools at the top and a preview of your blog at the bottom (see Figure 12-14).

    Blogger splits the formatting tools into several categories:

    - **Templates** lets you pick a whole new template, though it limits you to the same few templates you saw when you created your blog, so there's not much point to this option.

    - **Background** lets you choose a set of themed background colors and a background picture. For the background picture, you can upload your own creation, or you can pick from a wide selection of premade backgrounds organized into categories like "Abstract," "Food & Drink," and "Travel."

    - **Adjust Widths** lets you set the maximum width (in pixels) of your blog's main column and sidebars. Blogs use adjustable layouts that shrink to fit a browser window, along with a maximum-width limit that keeps page components from growing ridiculously big. Page 248 describes this type of layout.

    - **Layout** lets you switch between a few basic layouts. You can have a simple, single column of content, add a sidebar on either or both sides, or pump up the footer with room for extra widgets (like your blog archive and author information).

- **Advanced** has the most interesting formatting controls. Start by using Blogger's scrolling list to pick the detail you want to format (Page Text, Links, Blog Title, Post, and so on), and then use the controls on the right to change its font and colors. The font options are particularly impressive. Not only do they support common web fonts like Arial, Verdana, and Georgia, but they also include a library of free Google fonts, implemented using CSS's hot new embedded fonts feature (page 103).

Choose an editing task

Give it a new font here

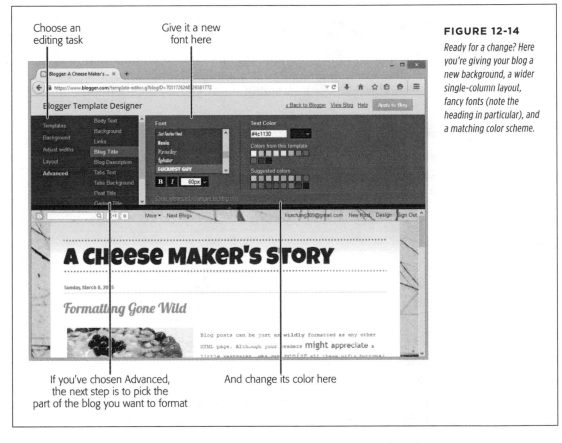

FIGURE 12-14

Ready for a change? Here you're giving your blog a new background, a wider single-column layout, fancy fonts (note the heading in particular), and a matching color scheme.

If you've chosen Advanced, the next step is to pick the part of the blog you want to format

And change its color here

3. **Click the "Apply to Blog" button to make your changes permanent (at least until you need your next formatting fix).**

   Or, if you don't like the changes you made, click "Back to Blogger" to abandon them.

■ ADDING, DELETING, AND REARRANGING GADGETS

The focus of your blog is the series of posts that runs down the middle of the page. However, every blog includes extra blocks of content, positioned in a sidebar next to your posts or in a footer at the bottom of the page. Examples include an About Me box, a Blog Archive box (which lists your most recent posts, organized in a tree diagram by month), and the Google Friends list (which lists the Google+ people fol-lowing your blog). Blogger calls these ingredients *gadgets*, and it gives you complete control to move them, add new ones, or remove existing ones. Here's how:

1. **On the blog management page, click the Layout link on the left.**

   Blogger displays an outline of your blog's current structure, showing you the location of your current gadgets (Figure 12-15).

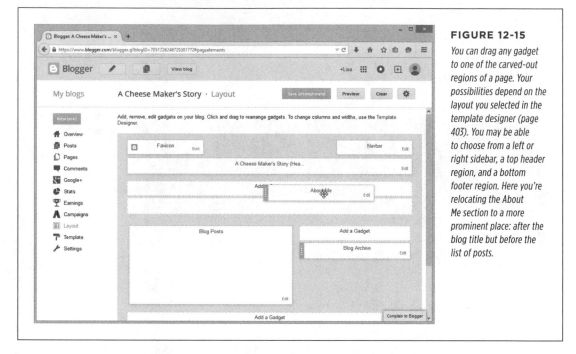

FIGURE 12-15

You can drag any gadget to one of the carved-out regions of a page. Your possibilities depend on the layout you selected in the template designer (page 403). You may be able to choose from a left or right sidebar, a top header region, and a bottom footer region. Here you're relocating the About Me section to a more prominent place: after the blog title but before the list of posts.

2. **Move your gadgets around.**

   Initially, your page displays whatever content blocks your template defines. However, you have plenty of ways to mix things up. The easiest change you can make is to move a gadget. Simply drag it to a new place (Figure 12-15).

3. **Add new gadgets.**

   If you want to add a gadget, click one of the "Add a Gadget" links in the preview. Blogger displays a pop-up list with a wide choice of handy add-ons. Click one, and Blogger previews it for you. If you like what you see, click the plus-sign button (+) to pop it into your page, and then drag it to any spot you want.

   Some gadgets are plain—blocks of ordinary text, lists, pictures, and links, for example (see Figure 12-16). But others are more interesting. Here are some examples:

- **Blog List** catalogs the blogs you follow or admire, complete with links. **Link List** does the same thing, but for websites rather than blogs.

- **Search Box** adds a Google search box that visitors can use to search the posts in your blog.

- **Popular Posts** lists the most visited posts on your blog, so new readers can find them quickly and check them out. This feature is wildly popular on news sites. **Recent Comments** is similar, but it displays the most recently left comments for any post. It lets readers quickly see what others are saying.

- **AdSense** displays the money-making Google ads described on page 415.

- **Slideshow** shows a rotating gallery of your pictures, culled from a photo service like Picasa, Flickr, or Photobucket.

- **Poll** lets you survey your readers and tally their votes.

FIGURE 12-16

This blog has three new gadgets on the right: an ad box, a list of links, and a list of popular posts.

4. **Configure or remove your existing gadgets.**

   To change a gadget's settings, point to it and then click Edit in the gadget box. Your options depend on the gadget. For example, the Blog Archive gadget displays a calendar of previous blog entries. You can change the order of the entries, the way Blogger groups the posts, or the way it formats the dates. If you edit the Blog List gadget, you can add or remove the blogs you link to.

To remove a gadget, click the Edit link, and then click Remove. One detail you can't remove is the *NavBar*, the thin strip that appears at the top of your blog. Visitors who view your blog can use it to travel from one blog to another, sign up for their own blog, or (most usefully) search your blog for keywords. The good news is that, although you can't remove the NavBar, you can assign it a color so that it matches your template and blends in with the scenery.

5. **When you finish adding and arranging gadgets, click the "Save arrangement" button.**

   Alternatively, you can click Preview to see what your blog will look like when you commit to the changes, or click Clear Edits to abandon your changes and go back to the way things were.

■ EDITING THE HTML IN A TEMPLATE

The tools you've used so far give you a lot of control over your blog's appearance, but there's one more frontier for die-hard bloggers who want unrestricted control over their pages: your template's HTML markup. Using the skills you've learned throughout this book, you can change virtually any element there.

This is obviously more work than using Blogger's template designer, so why take this extra step? There are a few good reasons:

- **You want to use an entirely new template.** Blogger includes only a small set of templates for you to choose from. You can find more online (search for "blogger template").

- **You want to use advanced CSS formatting.** Blogger doesn't give you much design control beyond fonts and colors. If you want to change something else—tweak margins and padding, for example, or add borders or set a background picture—you need to dig into the template and modify its style sheet.

- **You want no-holds-barred customization.** Adding gadgets is a powerful system, but it doesn't give you the complete, fine-grained control that editing the HTML does. Of course, sometimes too much control makes life unnecessarily complicated.

Blogger's templates are really just HTML documents that define the look of your blog pages. At first glance, this seems a little unusual—after all, a modest blog has dozens of pages, and you have only a relatively simple template! The trick is that the template defines special replaceable regions. When a visitor requests a page in your blog, Blogger starts with your template and fills in the appropriate content wherever it finds special codes.

For example, if Blogger finds this odd-looking code:

```
<title><data:blog.pageTitle /></title>
```

It replaces the highlighted element above with your blog's title. The final HTML file it creates for your home page actually contains this text:

```
<title>A Cheese Maker's Story</title>
```

To change the HTML in your template, follow these steps:

1. **If you aren't already looking at the template settings, click the Template link on the left side of the blog management page.**

2. **Click Edit HTML.**

   You see a text box with the full HTML for your template, codes and all. You can change some details right away, like the formatting rules in the inline style sheet. But if you want to add new content or rearrange the page, you need to understand Blogger's template codes. You can get that information at *http://tinyurl.com/295vg5*.

3. **When you finish making changes, click Save Template.**

   Blogger updates your blog to use the new template immediately.

4. **If you like the results, consider making a backup of your work.**

   Once you alter your template, you should back it up before you make any more changes. Otherwise, you could muck up your template and have no way to get back to the version you like.

   To make a backup, click the Template link on the left side of the blog-management page, and then click the Backup/Restore button in the top-right corner of the page. Finally, click the "Download full template" button, and then pick a safe storage location on your computer.

   If you need to restore a backup you've made previously, the process is similar. First, click Template, and then click the Backup/Restore button. Next, click the Browse button or the Choose File button (the wording depends on your browser) to find the backup file on your computer. Once you select the right file, click Upload to transfer it back to Blogger.

■ Reviewing Comments

Ordinarily, Blogger lets visitors comment on your posts. That means your readers can add their own thoughts and follow-ups, and Blogger displays them along with your posts.

To leave a comment, a visitor must have a Google account or an OpenID account (a standard that many blogging services and websites use). Blogger imposes this restriction to reduce *comment spam*—distracting comments, usually posted by automated programs, that advertise the spammer's products. Fortunately, Blogger has your back. It intercepts comments that look like spam and moves them to a special holding zone. It's then up to you to review these comments and decide whether to let them through. To do that, go to the blog management page, click Comments (on the left), and then click Spam underneath. Blogger lists the quarantined comments from all your blog posts. If you find a valid comment, select it and click Not Spam. And if you're drowning in junk comments, click Select All, and then click Delete to clear away the clutter.

POWER USERS' CLINIC

Giving Your Blog a Custom Domain Name

Even though there's nothing wrong with a *.blogspot.com* URL, there's a good reason to get a custom domain name for your blog. No matter how much you love Blogger right now, someday you might move on to a different service. It's always easier to make this transition if you don't need to tell all your readers to update their bookmarks and head to a completely new web address.

To use a custom domain name with Blogger, you first need to buy one from a domain seller, as you learned to do in Chapter 9. Then you can configure your domain name to point to Blogger's web servers.

Of course, you probably don't want Blogger to take over your entire domain, because you want room for a traditional website, too. One good solution is to add a *subdomain* to a domain you own. For example, if you have a website at *www.deviousweevils.org*, you might want to host your blog at the subdomain *blog.deviousweevils.org*. This you can do. Unfortunately, it's not possible to connect a sub*folder* of your website to Blogger, so give up your dreams of having your blog appear at *www.deviousweevils.org/blog*. For that, you need a self-hosted blog, like WordPress (page 389).

Even after you configure your custom domain, your blog's *.blogspot.com* address will remain in service, and all your files will stay on Blogger's web servers. You're just creating a new way for fans to find your blog.

To make this change, follow Blogger's instructions at *http://tinyurl.com/n2zsbl*. You'll need the help of your web host, but the instructions cover all the technical issues you need to know.

The comment spam feature isn't as good at catching objectionable comments left by real-life people. If your blog discusses controversial topics, you might want to impose stricter regulations to prevent unhinged commenters from attacking one another. You can wrangle comments in two ways: by deleting them or by moderating them.

Deleting the Junk

The first approach is to delete objectionable comments after the fact. To do this, go to the blog management page and click the Comments link in the sidebar on the left. Blogger lists all the comments left on all your posts, in reverse chronological order (so new comments top the list, no matter how old the post is). If you find a comment you don't like, you have three ways to dispatch it, as shown in Figure 12-17.

- **Delete** removes the comment immediately.

- **Spam** deletes it immediately and alerts Blogger that a spammer is at work (which may get the commenter's ID blacklisted)

- **Remove content** deletes the text of the comment but leaves the record of the comment on the blog post, with the user's ID and the message "This post has been removed by the author." Sometimes, this approach can shame unruly commenters into better behavior, and it prevents people from criticizing you for sneaky censorship.

> **TIP** Just as you can edit multiple posts at once with a bulk action, so you can delete an entire batch of troublemaking comments. To do so, tick the checkbox next to each one, and then click the Delete, Spam, or "Remove content" button above the list (see Figure 12-17).

FIGURE 12-17

When you point to a comment, Blogger displays a set of relevant links.

The only problem with deleting comments is that you have to log on regularly, and your edits take place after the fact. If you don't have the time to keep checking or you want to make sure no one gets a chance to post inflammatory remarks (even briefly), you need a different approach.

Moderating Comments

Your other option is to *moderate* the comments, allowing them on your blog only after you give them your personal thumbs-up. Moderating comments imposes extra work, but in some situations it's the only way to lock out undesirable comments—particularly if you have a popular blog on a hot topic. Here's how you moderate comments:

1. **On the blog management page, click the Settings link on the left.**

2. **Click "Posts and comments." Scroll down to the section of comment settings.**

   Blogger gives you a surprisingly thorough set of options to control comments. For example, you can control whether anonymous readers can post comments (ordinarily they can't), or you can switch off comments entirely. But the most interesting option is the one that controls moderation.

NOTE Regardless of whether you allow anonymous readers or use comment moderation, you should always keep the "Show word verification" option switched on. This forces readers to type in a word from a picture before they can post their comments. Annoying as it sometimes is, this technique cripples automated comment-posting software that leaves the worst comment spam.

3. **Change the "Comment moderation" setting from Never to Always (or, optionally, to Sometimes).**

If you pick Always, there's no chance of a bad comment making it onto your blog. You need to approve everything. This is the safest choice, but it can make for a lot of work.

The Sometimes option is an interesting compromise. It lets readers post comments freely when your blog entry is new, which is when most comments come in, but it switches to moderated comments after a certain number of days. This model works well because spammers are far more likely to comment on old postings than your readers are. The standard setting is two weeks, but you can choose a different number of days. Reduce the number to fight comment spam more aggressively, or increase it to give your readers more time to speak their mind without hassle.

If you choose Always or Sometimes, the "Email moderation requests to" box appears. Optionally, type your email address here if you want Blogger to notify you whenever someone posts a comment.

4. **Click the "Save settings" button.**

Now you're ready to try the system out. First, log out of Blogger. To test the moderating system, sign back in with a different Google account or as an anonymous visitor (if your blog lets anonymous readers leave comments). You could leave a comment while you're logged in as the blog owner, but Blogger will assume you don't need to second-guess yourself and skips the moderation step.

5. **Post a new comment.**

To leave a comment, click the Comment link at the end of a blog entry. Add a comment and your account information, and then click Publish to make it official. Blogger is smart enough to know that the blog uses moderation, so it displays a message explaining that the comment won't appear until the blog's owner (that's you) approves it.

6. **Review your comments.**

To look at new comments, log in as the blog owner again, head to the blog management page, click the Comments link, and then click the "Awaiting moderation" link underneath. You'll see just the comments that await your approval.

Promoting Your Blog

You need to promote your blog just as you do any other website. Although you can use all the techniques you learned in Chapter 11, there are some others that are unique to the blogosphere. Here are some important tips to get you started:

- **Add a blogroll to your site.** A blogroll is really just a set of links to blogs you like. But blogrolls also make a statement. They say, "These are the people I like" or "This is the crowd I want to be associated with." To use a blogroll, add a Blog List gadget.

- **Participate with others.** Bloggers are an open-minded bunch. If you leave an insightful comment in response to someone else's blog entry, odds are good that at least some readers will head over to your blog to see what else you have to say.

- **Make it easy for people to share your post.** You need to capitalize on the enthusiasm of your visitors. If you blog about a truly fascinating piece of gossip or news, readers might just decide to tell all their friends about it—if you make it easy enough. To encourage this impulse, add the Share It gadget, which adds links that visitors can use to quickly recommend your post on Facebook or Twitter.

- **Promote your feed.** Feeds, discussed on page 384, work with feed readers. True blog aficionados love them because they can track dozens or even hundreds of blogs at a time. Blogger's software lets you create a feed, and it's worth promoting your feed to your regular readers. To see your feed, click the "Subscribe to Posts (Atom)" link on your home page. To add the familiar orange radar icon, which makes this option more obvious, add the Feed gadget to your blog.

- **Use BlogThis.** A huge number of blog posts simply call attention to interesting news stories, scandalous gossip, or funny pictures that appear online. If you're an infrequent blogger, linking to these stories is a great way to beef up your blog. Using a nifty tool called *BlogThis*, you can create a new blog entry that links to an existing web page with a single click. You can do this two ways—add the Google Toolbar to your browser, which has a button for just this purpose, or add a link to your Bookmarks or Favorites menu that does the same thing. For the full details, check out *http://tinyurl.com/3n4hvu*.

Making Money with Your Site

I f it's not for sale on the Web, it's probably not for sale at all. It's no secret that the Internet is a global bazaar with more merchandise than a decade's worth of garage sales. Web surfers generate huge amounts of traffic hunting for travel discounts, discussing hot deals, and scouring eBay for bargains. So how can you get your share of web capital?

One obvious option is to sell a real, tangible product. The Internet abounds with specialty shops hawking art, jewelry, and handmade goods. But even if you have a product ready to sell, you need a few specialized tools to transform your corner of the Web into a bustling ecommerce storefront. For example, you'll probably want a virtual *shopping cart*, which lets visitors collect items they want to buy as they browse. And when they check out, you need a secure way to accept their cash—usually by way of a credit card transaction. In this chapter, you'll learn how to implement both of these features on your site using PayPal's merchant tools.

Even if you aren't looking for a place to unload your hand-crafted fishbone pencils, your website can still help fatten your wallet. In fact, just about any website can become profitable, either by selling ad space or by recommending other companies' products. In this chapter, you'll use two of the Web's most popular *affiliate programs*—Google AdSense and Amazon Associates—to collect some spare cash.

> **NOTE** Not a U.S. citizen? Don't worry—all the money-making ideas in this chapter use companies that provide services worldwide. Google, Amazon, and PayPal let you rake in the cash no matter where you live.

Money-Making the Web Way

The Web offers many paths to fiduciary gain. Here are some of the most popular:

- **Donations.** It sounds crazy, but some websites badger visitors for spare change. Donations might work if your site provides some truly valuable and unique content (see Figure 13-1). Otherwise, save yourself the bother. Don't be seduced by logic like "If 1,000 visitors come to my site and every one pays just 10 cents...." They won't.

> **TIP** If you think that your website offers some unique, practical information, and you think your visitors might be tempted to cough up a few cents in appreciation, you can add a Donate button to your page using PayPal (page 442). Consider including a message like "Buy me a beer/cup of coffee" above the Donate button to make the virtual transaction feel like a real-world tip (and to emphasize that you're hoping to collect spare change, not the next payment on your car loan).

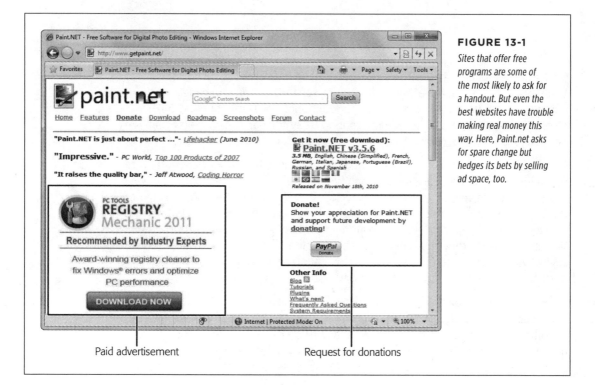

Paid advertisement   Request for donations

FIGURE 13-1

Sites that offer free programs are some of the most likely to ask for a handout. But even the best websites have trouble making real money this way. Here, Paint.net asks for spare change but hedges its bets by selling ad space, too.

- **Advertisements.** The most popular way to make money on the Web is by selling small pieces of web page real estate. Unfortunately, it's also a great way to exasperate your visitors, especially if the ads are distracting, unrelated to your site, or simply take up too much space. Not long ago, ads were the worst thing you could do to web pages. Fortunately, in the 21st century, monitors are bigger, and companies like Google provide targeted, unobtrusive ads that fit right in with the rest of your page.

- **Affiliate programs.** Rather than plaster ads across your site, why not put in a good word for a company you really believe in? Many affiliate programs give you a commission for referring customers to their sites. For example, if you review gourmet cookbooks, why not include links to those books on Amazon's website? If an interested reader buys a book, Amazon's associate program forks over a few dollars.

- **Sell stuff.** If you have your own products to sell, the Web is the perfect medium, since the cost to set up shop online is much smaller than it is in the real world. You can build a slick store, complete with product pictures and a shopping cart, with surprisingly little work. (And if you don't have your own products to sell, you can whip up some simple customized goods at CafePress, as described in the box on page 442.)

- **Pay-for-content.** If you have really great content, you can ask for cash *before* letting your visitors into your site. Warning: This is even harder to pull off than asking for donations, because visitors need to take a huge leap of faith. It's a technique used by established media companies like the *Wall Street Journal* and by hucksters promising secret ways to conquer the real estate market or get free camcorders.

> **NOTE** Pay-for-content is the only money-making scheme you won't learn to pull off in this chapter. That's because in order for it to work, you need a way to *authenticate* visitors—in other words, you need to be able to identify visitors to tell whether they've paid you or not. This requires some heavy-duty programming (or the ability to pay a company for the service).

■ Google AdSense

Even if you don't have a product to sell, you still have one valuable asset: the attention of your visitors. The good news is that a huge number of companies are ready to pay for those eyes.

Some of these companies pay you a minuscule fee every time someone visits a page that carries their ad, while others pay you only when a reader actually clicks an ad, or when a visitor both clicks an ad *and* buys something. Fortunately, you don't need to waste hours checking out all these options, because Google has an advertising program that handily beats just about every other system out there. It's called Google AdSense.

The AdSense program requires you to display small text, image, or video advertisements on your pages. You sign up, set aside some space on one or more pages, and paste in some Google-supplied HTML (see Figure 13-2). Google takes care of the rest, filling that space with one or more ads every time someone requests your page.

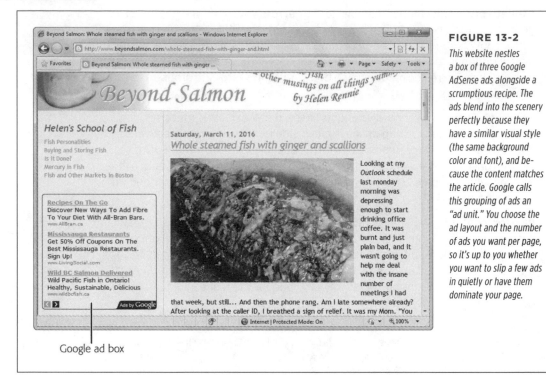

FIGURE 13-2

This website nestles a box of three Google AdSense ads alongside a scrumptious recipe. The ads blend into the scenery perfectly because they have a similar visual style (the same background color and font), and because the content matches the article. Google calls this grouping of ads an "ad unit." You choose the ad layout and the number of ads you want per page, so it's up to you whether you want to slip a few ads in quietly or have them dominate your page.

Google ad box

Just displaying Google AdSense ads doesn't get you anything, but whenever a visitor *clicks* one of those ads (and travels to the advertiser's website), you earn a few cents. When your total reaches $100, Google mails you a check or sends the cash straight to your bank account.

There's no way to know for sure how much money an individual AdSense click is worth. That's because Google advertisers compete for keywords by bidding on them, and keyword prices can fluctuate over time. Google *does* let you know how much your clicks were worth (in total) when it pays you. A typical click nets you about 10 cents, but per-click prices often range from a few pennies to several dollars.

Before you become an AdSense devotee, you should know what makes AdSense different from other ad programs. Here are some of its top advantages:

- **AdSense ads are relevant.** Google automatically scans your site and picks ads based on your content. So if you have a site devoted to SpongeBob SquarePants, Google provides ads hawking SpongeBob DVDs, inflatable dolls, and birthday gear. Using content-based ads is far, far better than aggravating your visitors with offers for completely unrelated products, like high-tech spy cameras. Even better from a profit perspective, these "targeted" ads dramatically increase the chance that a visitor will click an ad, netting you a click-through fee. And if you're worried about a competitor's site turning up in an advertisement, you can tell Google to filter it out (see page 421).

- **AdSense ads blend in with the scenery.** Google gives you a range of layout and color options for its ads, so you can match the design and slick color scheme of your site.

- **Google provides fair payment.** Google charges advertisers different amounts of money for different keywords. Some advertising providers pay their members the same amount for any click-through and swallow the extra money. Not Google. It pays you according to the current value of the keyword, which guarantees that you always get a competitive rate.

- **There are no startup charges.** The AdSense program is free.

> **TIP** Don't try to cheat AdSense. Devious web developers have tried to game the system by clicking their own ads over and over again, or even firing up automated programs to do that for them. The problem is that Google uses various techniques to spot suspicious usage patterns. If it sees a ridiculous number of clicks over a short period of time, all originating from the same computer, it's likely to spot the deception and ban your site outright.

Signing Up for AdSense

When you're ready to get started with AdSense, follow these steps:

1. **Go to the AdSense home page (*www.google.com/adsense*).**

   If you're not already logged in with your Google Account, click "Sign in." Use the same account you use for other Google services, including Gmail, the Webmaster Tools, and Google Analytics. After you sign into your Google account, you still need to explicitly sign up for the AdSense program.

2. **Click the "Sign up" link or the "Get Started Now" button to join up with AdSense.**

   Clicking either one starts the AdSense enrollment process. Next, Google starts gathering account information.

3. **Enter your site URL and identify its language (Figure 13-3). Then click Continue.**

   Google insists on checking out your site before it places ads there. If your website is still in the planning stage and you haven't picked a domain yet, you'll need to sign up for AdSense later. (However, Google will let you add more websites to your AdSense account after you create it.)

> **TIP** You can learn much more about the specifics of Google's ad program by visiting *www.google.com/ adsense*. There's also a great, not-too-detailed walkthrough at *www.google.com/services/adsense_tour*.

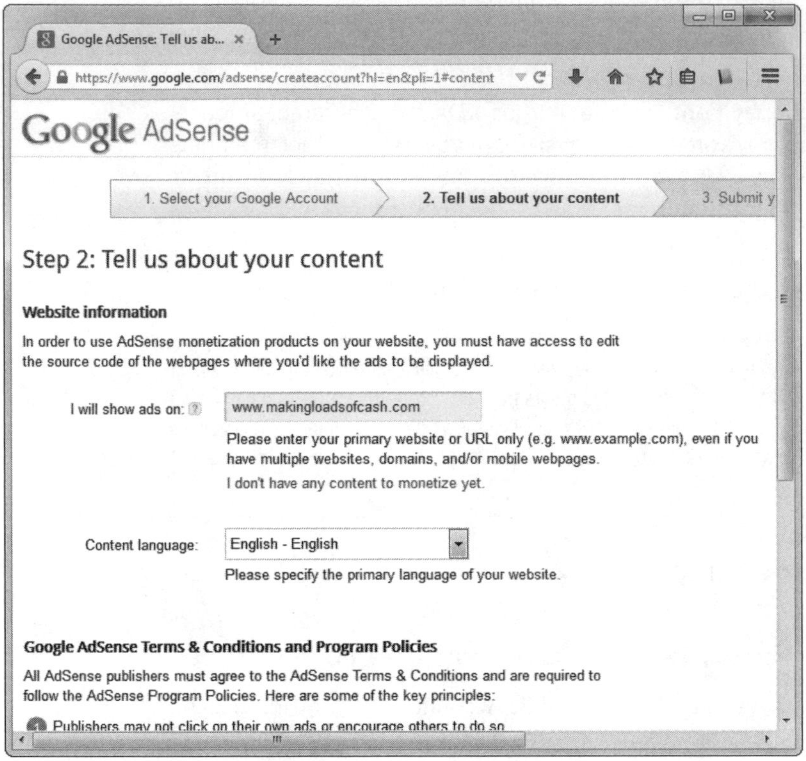

FIGURE 13-3

Google asks you to fill out two pages of information before you can sign up for AdSense. The bottom of this page includes a long list of rules about how you can use AdSense and the types of sites Google allows into the program (see the box on page 420 for a recap).

4. **Fill in your contact details (Figure 13-4).**

When applying for AdSense, you need to indicate whether your account is for an individual (you, personally) or a business (your registered business). This determines the kind of tax information Google needs to collect. Registered businesses based in the U.S. need an EIN (Employer Identification Number). U.S. citizens applying as individuals need to give Google a Social Security number. Citizens of other countries may need to apply for a U.S. Taxpayer Identification Number—see *www.google.com/adsense/taxinfo* for the lowdown.

Finally, fill in your name, address, and phone number.

NOTE Google won't pay you until it gets your tax details. To help make the process less painful, it guides you to the correct tax form and lets you submit it online. However, Google won't prompt you for tax information until you collect at least $10 in advertising revenue.

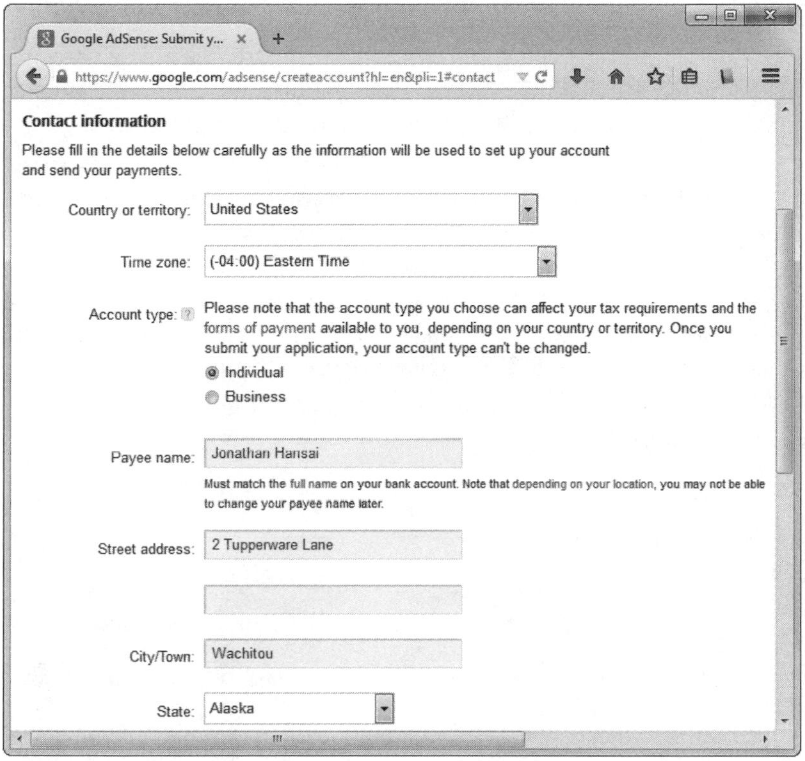

FIGURE 13-4

In the final step, Google needs to know exactly who you are. Get this info right, because you can't change it later on.

5. **Once you finish, click "Submit my application."**

Now you need to wait for Google to approve your application. This usually takes a couple of days, during which someone at Google takes a quick look at your site to confirm that it exists and that it isn't promoting illegal activity (for example, offering pirated copies of Windows 10). Once this is done, you'll get a message confirming that Google has activated your AdSense account.

The AdSense Window

Now that you have an AdSense account, you're ready to design some ads and put them on your site. Go to *www.google.com/adsense* and log in with your email address and password. Google opens the AdSense page, which displays a summary of your recent earnings. You can switch to a different AdSense page using the tabs at the top of the window (see Figure 13-5).

AdSense Rules

Google enforces a handful of rules that your website has to follow. Many are common sense, but it's still worth taking a quick look at them.

- You can't put the Google ads in email messages or pop-up windows; the temptation for spammers to abuse the system that way is just too great.

- You can't put ads on pages that don't feature any "real" content. This includes error, login, registration, welcome, and under-construction pages. You definitely can't create pages that include nothing but ads.

- You can't try to obscure parts of an ad (for example, by placing other elements over them using a style sheet rule). The entire content of an ad needs to be visible.

- You can't click your own ads, or use automated programs to do that for you. Finally, you can't entice your visitors to click your links using threats or incentives.

- Your website can't include excessive profanity, copyrighted material, pornography, content about hacking high-tech security systems, advocacy for illegal drugs, hate speech, or anything related to gambling.

To read the full AdSense policy, visit www.google.com/adsense/policies.

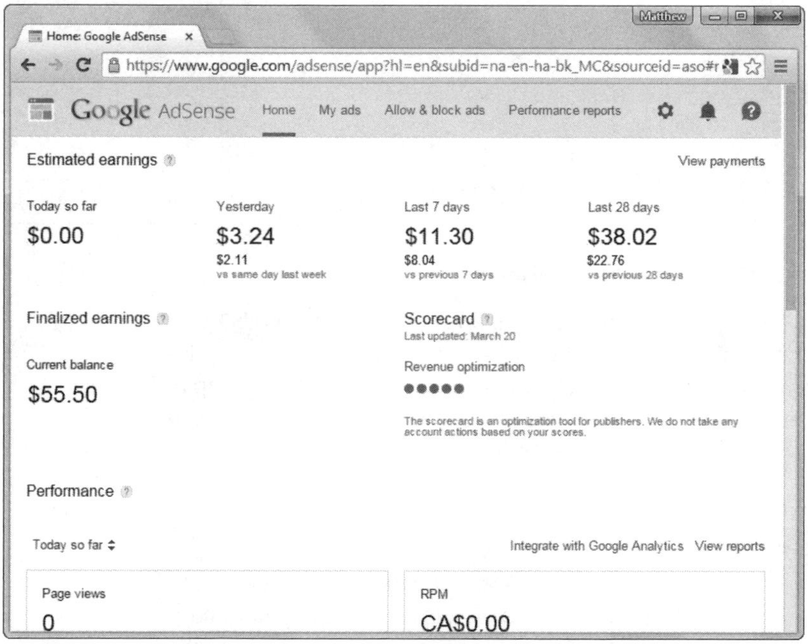

FIGURE 13-5

Use the tabs at the top of the AdSense window to switch to another page. Initially, you begin on the Home tab, where you configure your AdSense account and review the money you've made so far.

These pages include the following:

- **Home.** This page gives you some critical summary information, including the amount of money you've made today, and notifications about any problems that prevent your ads from running (called *alerts*).

  You'll also see some additional links in the panel on the left. For example, you can view your payment history, which lists each check Google mailed you (click Payments), and you can update the account information you supplied when you registered, such as your mailing address and tax information (click "Account settings"). Or click Resources to browse the AdSense blog, chat with others in AdSense's help forum, and watch some inspiring success stories on video.

- **My ads.** This is your starting point for creating AdSense ads—it's where you specify your ads' display format and get the code you need to insert into your web pages.

- **Allow & block ads.** Here you manage one of AdSense's most advanced features: filtering out the ads you don't want. For example, you can tell Google to refrain from showing ads in certain categories or from specific websites. The idea here is twofold: to bar your competition and to ensure that your visitors see ads relevant to them. (If the ads aren't useful, your visitors are less likely to click, and your earnings will plummet.)

- **Performance reports.** These reports help you assess the success of your ads. You start out with a graph that charts how much money you made over the last week. You can customize this graph by changing options and playing with filters until you find exactly the data you need. And if you want to do some heavy-duty analysis, you can download the numbers in an Excel-friendly CSV format in a single click.

NOTE No matter which report you run, Google won't tell you what each individual click was worth or which particular ad caught a reader's eye. Instead, it gives you an estimate of the click value on a given day (what Google calls the CPC, or *cost-per-click*). Google displays other useful information, too, like the percentage of times your visitors clicked your ads (called the CTR, or *click-through rate*). For example, a click-through rate of 2 percent means that if your page was requested 100 times, an ad on the page was clicked just twice.

Creating an Ad

Google provides different types of ads, from plain two- or three-word text links to video boxes. However, most ads are of two types:

- **Text ads.** These are brief, text-only pitches, like the ones you saw in Figure 13-2. They typically include a title (which is also a link), followed by a line or two of text, and may include the advertiser's website name at the bottom.

NOTE Text ads are still the most popular type of Google ad. They're particularly adept at blending into page backgrounds, which means less irritation for your visitors (which is good) but fewer clicks (which is not so good).

- **Display ads.** These ads are actually images that range in size from banner strips to large squares. Image ads are more obtrusive than text ads, but they're steadily gaining in popularity. If your web page already has plenty of pictures, image ads look particularly good—for example, you'll often see them blending in at the side of a news article.

Before you can create the right ads, you need a basic idea of where you plan to put them. Consider whether you want a vertical or horizontal strip of ads, and how wide or long that bar should be. Figure 13-6 previews just a few of your layout options.

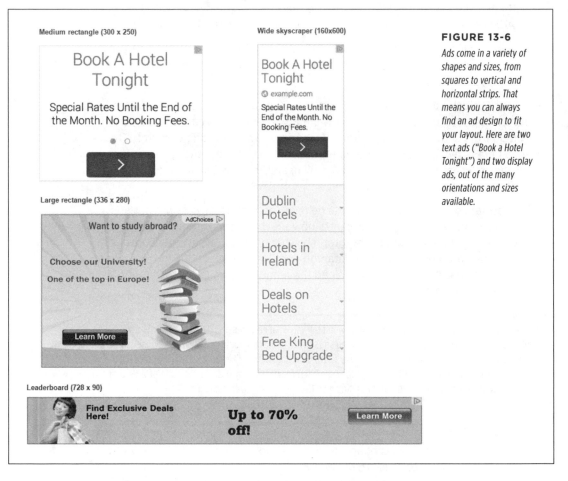

Medium rectangle (300 x 250)

Wide skyscraper (160x600)

Large rectangle (336 x 280)

Leaderboard (728 x 90)

FIGURE 13-6

Ads come in a variety of shapes and sizes, from squares to vertical and horizontal strips. That means you can always find an ad design to fit your layout. Here are two text ads ("Book a Hotel Tonight") and two display ads, out of the many orientations and sizes available.

When you're ready to dive in and build your first ad (which Google calls an *ad unit*), follow these steps:

1. **Click the "My ads" tab at the top of the page.**

   This opens the "My ads" section, which lists all the ads you've created. Right now, the list is empty.

2. **Click the "New ad unit" button, which appears under the Content→"Ad units" heading.**

Now it's time to fill in the information for your ad.

3. **Choose a name for your ad.**

This name doesn't actually appear in the ad; it just makes your life easier as you manage ads. After you create your ad, you can call it up by name (for example, Travel Page Ad) and modify it. This saves you the trouble of rebuilding your ad from scratch.

4. **Choose the size of the ad box from the "Ad size" list (Figure 13-7).**

Google always packages AdSense ads in boxes. A box can include one or several ads. The format you choose determines whether you'll get a vertical stack of ads or a horizontal row. It also determines how many ads you see at once (from one to five).

TIP To get a closer look at a specific ad size, click its Preview link. Google opens a window that shows a sample ad at that size.

Google provides one special size option, called Responsive. Choose this, and Google supplies just enough ads to fill the width of the containing element. For example, say you create a <div> that's 140 pixels wide. Choose the Responsive ad size, and Google might give you a block of ads that's 120 pixels wide (because that fits inside the 140-pixel width) and 240 pixels tall (because that's a standard height for an ad block with that width). But the real reason to use Responsive ad sizes is if you're creating a layout that *changes* based on the size of the browser window, such as the proportional layouts discussed on page 245.

Say, for example, you have a column that has a proportional width of 30% of the browser window. If you use the Responsive ad size and a viewer makes the window wider, Google fetches a bigger ad block to match. If you have a fixed layout (page 242), on the other hand, you already know exactly how much space is available for your ad, so you don't need to use the Responsive ad size.

5. **Select a type of ad from the "Ad type" list.**

Choose whether you want to use text ads, display ads, or a mix of the two (the preselected choice). Generally, image ads stand out more than text ads, but you need to balance two conflicting goals: your desire to make money by attracting clicks with eye-catching ads and your desire to minimize distraction by choosing less obtrusive ads.

Choose a category

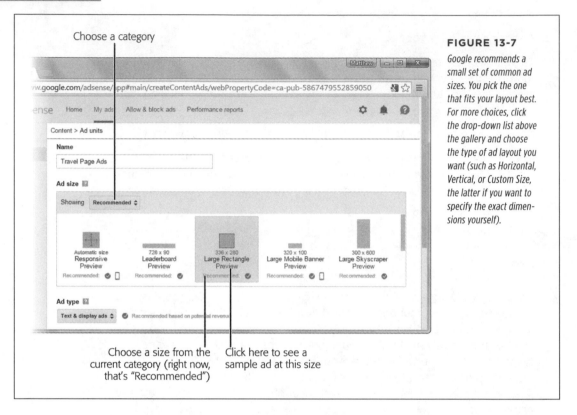

FIGURE 13-7

Google recommends a small set of common ad sizes. You pick the one that fits your layout best. For more choices, click the drop-down list above the gallery and choose the type of ad layout you want (such as Horizontal, Vertical, or Custom Size, the latter if you want to specify the exact dimensions yourself).

Choose a size from the current category (right now, that's "Recommended")

Click here to see a sample ad at this size

6. **Customize your ad's colors, borders, and fonts in the "Text ad style" section (optional).**

You can choose from a ready-made color palette, like Minimalist (black and gray text on white) or Neon (purple on black). But if you want to make the colors in your buttons match the colors on your site, click the "Create ad style" button (Figure 13-8). For example, you might want the ad box's border or background color to blend in with the background on your page.

To change the colors of an ad, modify the color codes in the boxes underneath the list of color palettes. You can also choose a font family (from a very limited list) and font size. When you finish, make sure your custom style has a name and then click Save.

NOTE The color and font settings apply to text ads. If you choose to use display ads only, you can skip this section because the settings won't have any effect.

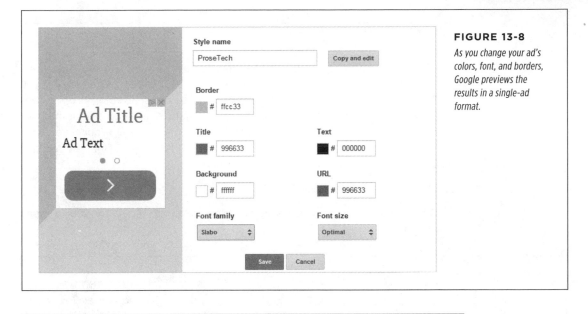

FIGURE 13-8

As you change your ad's colors, font, and borders, Google previews the results in a single-ad format.

TIP If you don't change Google's standard ad colors, your ad box will have the same background color as your web page (because it's transparent) and no border. For advice on how to choose custom HTML colors, see page 90.

---

7. **Choose a channel in the "Custom channels" section (optional).**

    If you create a half-dozen ads and scatter them on different pages throughout your site, you don't know which ones are making you money. Google's ad sales report shows you only the *total* number of clicks for all the pages on your site. Many site owners want more detail about which ads are working. Enter Google's *channels* feature.

    To track the performance of individual ads, you place each ad in a separate, virtual "channel," which tallies ad clicks. Google lets you create reports that compare channels so you can tell which ads perform best.

    To create a new channel, click "Create new custom channel," which opens a window asking you to name the channel.

    Once you create a channel, you can assign an ad to it by clicking the tiny "include" link next to the channel name. (Click it again to stop tracking an ad.)

TIP Channels are a great way to try out different ad strategies and see which ad format and placement work best. You can add multiple ads to the same channel to track them as a group, or you can create a separate channel for each ad.

8. **Choose a backup ad.**

   When you first put an ad on a page, Google doesn't yet know what ads are a good match for your content, so it temporarily keeps that space blank. If you don't like that, you have two options. You can choose a solid color, in which case Google fills the ad with that color only. The idea is to use a color that matches the background of your page, so the "ad" disappears entirely. Your second option is to specify a URL for a page you want to place there. Until the real ads are ready, that content appears on your page.

9. **Click "Save and get code."**

   Once you do, a window pops up with the JavaScript code for your ad (see Figure 13-9).

FIGURE 13-9

You'll notice that the Ad-Sense code doesn't include HTML. Instead, it's a script that uses the JavaScript programming language (which you'll learn about in Chapter 14). Every time a visitor views a page that contains an AdSense ad, the script runs. It fetches a relevant ad from Google's web servers and inserts the ad's HTML into the page, in the same spot as the script block.

10. **Copy your ad code, and then click Close.**

    Select all the code in the text box, right-click the markup, and then choose Copy. You can now paste the code into one or more pages, as described in the next section.

> **NOTE** If you need to modify your ad later, log back into Google AdSense, click the "My ads" tab, and find your ad in the list. When you click the ad, Google displays its details and lets you edit them. Most changes—say, altering the ad box color scheme—take effect immediately. However, if you want to change the format of your ad box, you need to get new code and paste it into your pages, because the size of your ad will change.

Placing Ads in Your Web Pages

After Google creates your ad script, you're ready to pop it into your web page. Horizontal strips are the easiest to position; you simply paste the entire script right where you want the ad to appear.

Here's an example that places ads at the bottom of a page:

```
<!DOCTYPE html>
<html>
<head>...</head>
<body>
  <h1>A Trip to Remember</h1>
  <p><img src="me.jpg" alt="Me" class="floatLeft" />
  After returning from my three-month travel adventure ...</p>
  <p>I hope you enjoy these pictures as much as I do.</p>
  <p>See pictures from ...</p>

<script async src="//pagead2.googlesyndication.com/pagead/js/adsbygoogle.js">
</script>
<!-- Travel Page Ads -->
<ins class="adsbygoogle"
     style="display:inline-block;width:300px;height:250px"
     data-ad-client="ca-pub-5867479552859050"
     data-ad-slot="1245776735"></ins>
<script>
(adsbygoogle = window.adsbygoogle || []).push({});
</script>

</body>
</html>
```

Figure 13-10 shows the result.

Positioning vertical ads requires a little more work, but it's easy once you learn the trick. The challenge is flowing the rest of your page content *beside* the vertical ad. As you learned in Chapter 8, you can use style sheet rules to float content on the side of a page.

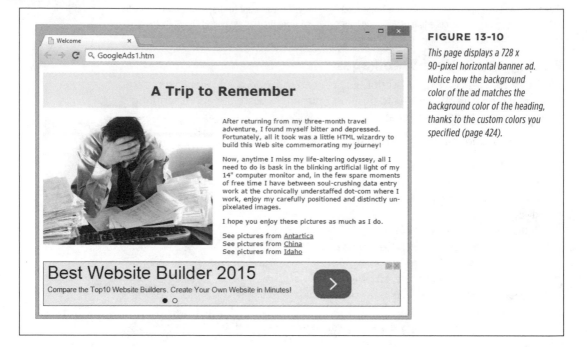

FIGURE 13-10

*This page displays a 728 x
90-pixel horizontal banner ad.
Notice how the background
color of the ad matches the
background color of the heading,
thanks to the custom colors you
specified (page 424).*

To use the style sheet approach, begin by wrapping your ad script in a <div> element. Here's an example featuring the content you saw in Figure 13-10:

```
<!DOCTYPE html>
<html>
<head>...</head>
<body>
  <h1>A Trip to Remember</h1>
  <img src="me.jpg" alt="Me" class="floatLeft" />

  <div class="floatRight">
    <script async src="//pagead2.googlesyndication.com/pagead/js/adsbygoogle.js">
    </script>
    <!-- Travel Page Ads -->
    <ins class="adsbygoogle"
        style="display:inline-block;width:300px;height:250px"
        data-ad-client="ca-pub-5867479552859050"
        data-ad-slot="1245776735"></ins>
    <script>
     (adsbygoogle = window.adsbygoogle || []).push({});
    </script>
  </div>
```

```
    <p>After returning from my three-month travel adventure ...</p>
    <p>I hope you enjoy these pictures as much as I do.</p>
    <p>See pictures from ...</p>
  </body>
</html>
```

Notice that the <div> element (which has no formatting on its own), uses the style sheet class *floatRight*. In your style sheet, use the rule below to make the <div> section float using the float attribute (see page 232):

```
.floatRight {
  float: right;
  margin-left: 20px;
}
```

Figure 13-11 shows the result.

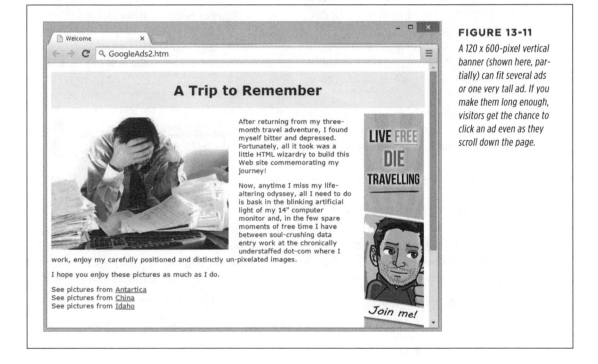

FIGURE 13-11

A 120 x 600-pixel vertical banner (shown here, partially) can fit several ads or one very tall ad. If you make them long enough, visitors get the chance to click an ad even as they scroll down the page.

How AdSense Creates Targeted Ads

Every time you serve up a web page that contains Google ads, the AdSense script sends a message to Google's web server asking for ads. This message includes your ad preference information and your unique client ID. (Your client ID is something like *pub-5876479552359052*; you can see it in the script Google produces.)

The first time Google receives this request, it realizes that it hasn't examined your page yet, and it doesn't know what types of ads are best suited for it. So it sends you a block of generic ads (or your alternate content, if you chose that feature, as described on page 426). Google also adds your page to a list of pages it needs to visit. Sometime in the next couple of days, the Google bot heads over to your site and analyzes its content. From that point forward, you'll see ads based on the content of your page.

If 48 hours pass and you still aren't getting targeted ads, there could be a problem. One of the most common mistakes is putting ads on pages that don't have much text, in which case Google can't figure out what your site is really all about. Remember, AdSense considers only a single page—the one with the ad in it—when it checks out your site. You can run into another potential problem if you put your ad on an inaccessible page. For example, the Google bot can't get to any page that's not on the Internet—pages on your desktop computer or local network just won't cut it. Likewise with password-protected pages. Some websites block robots through exclusion rules (see page 326), which stops the Google bot cold.

Finally, remember that Google may create ads that aren't appropriate for your site. For example, you might be discussing the pros and cons of the programming language Python, and Google might respond with a promotional ad for a pet store. Often, Google will figure out this sort of problem on its own, both by analyzing your pages and by discarding ads that don't generate many clicks. But you may be able to help it rule out some inappropriate options using the ad-blocking feature. To get started, log into AdSense and click the "Allow & block ads" tab.

Google-Powered Searches

Google gives you another way to please your visitors (and earn some cash in the process). You can add a search box to your pages, letting visitors launch Google queries right from your site. Even better, you get the earnings for any ads they click in the search results—a feature Google calls (rather unimaginatively) AdSense for Search.

From your AdSense account, you can easily add a Google search box to your site:

1. **Log into your AdSense account, and then click the "My ads" link.**

   This is the same place you create ads, but you want to go to a different subsection to build your search box.

2. **In the panel on the left, click Search to see its subcategories. Click the "Custom search engines" link, and then click the "New custom search engine" button.**

   Now you can fill in the information for your search box.

3. **Name the search.**

The name lets you retrieve your customized search box, tweak your settings, and get new code, without starting from scratch.

4. **Choose the search type.**

Choose "The entire web" to create a search box that uses the familiar Google search engine we all know and love.

Choose "Only sites I select" to restrict the search to a limited set of sites. You can use this feature to limit searches to your site only.

5. **If you choose to limit the search, fill in a list of searchable sites in the "Selected sites" box (Figure 13-12).**

You can enter individual pages (as in *http://www.NewTravelDiaries.com/trip_arctic.html*), an entire folder (*http://www.NewTravelDiaries.com/trips*), or your whole site (as in *http://www. NewTravelDiaries.com*), which is the most common choice. If you need to enter multiple URLs, put them on separate lines in the box.

NOTE Even when you limit searches to your website, Google polls its standard, centralized catalog of web pages—it just limits the results it displays to the pages from your site. If Google doesn't have your pages in its catalog (either because you just created the site or because Google doesn't know your site exists), these pages won't turn up in any searches, no matter how you customize the search box. For a refresher about getting Google to notice you, see page 320.

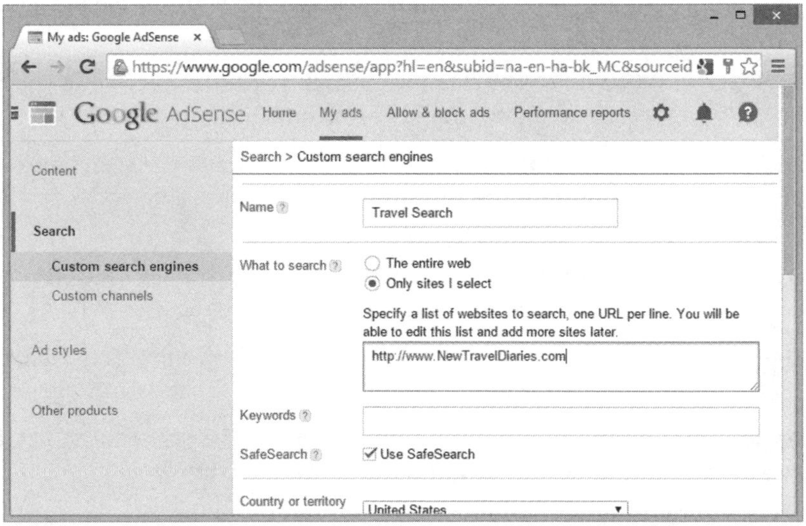

FIGURE 13-12

Usually, when you pick "Only sites I select," you enter just one site in the "Selected sites" box—yours. That way, visitors can search your pages without being tempted to go to another site on the Web. For example, if you have dozens of pages of travel stories, a visitor could home in on the page she wants by searching for "funny story about rubber chicken in Peru."

6. **Fill in the Keywords box (optional).**

   Google automatically adds any keywords you include here to your visitors' searches. This gives you a way to design a search box that's targeted to certain types of content. For example, if your site is all about golf, you might include the keyword *golf*. That way, if a visitor searches for *tiger*, the search returns pages about Tiger Woods, not the African savanna.

7. **Check the SafeSearch box, if you want to switch it on.**

   SafeSearch filters profanity and sexual content from search results. You'll find SafeSearch useful in three situations: First, it's de rigueur for children's sites. Second, it's useful if you want to shield your guests from possibly offensive search results. And finally, it's handy if your website deals with a topic that shares some keywords with adult-only sites. For example, if you create a breast cancer awareness page, you don't want someone to type "breast exam" into your web search box and dig up the wrong goods.

8. **Tweak the country and language settings on the page, if they apply to you.**

   These settings identify your website's language and geographic location. As you probably know, Google has country-specific pages that can tweak search results, providing them in different languages or giving priority to local sites.

9. **Optionally, click the plus-sign (+) box next to the "Custom channels" section, and pick a custom channel.**

   You can place your search box in a specific channel, just as you can an ad. This technique is useful if you have a Google search box on more than one website, and you want to track ad clicks separately for each domain. See page 425 for more about channels.

10. **Click the plus-sign (+) box next to the "Search box style" section so you can tailor the appearance of the Google search box (optional).**

    There's not a lot to change here. You can alter the size of the search box and the placement of Google's logo, and choose between a white, black, and dark-gray background.

11. **Optionally, click the plus-sign (+) box next to the "Ad style" section so you can customize how Google displays ads in its search results.**

    This way, the ads can blend in with your site's color scheme. This feature is almost the same as the color palettes for AdSense ads (page 424).

12. **Optionally, click the plus-sign (+) box next to the "Search results" section so you can customize how Google shows its search results.**

    Google gives you a few minor options for tweaking the placement of its logo. But more important, you can choose where Google puts the search results with the "Display results" setting. You have three choices:

- **Choose "on a Google page in the same window"** to replace the current page with Google's standard search results page.

- **Choose "on a Google page in a new window"** to have the browser open a new window with the search results in it. Visitors usually find pop-up windows annoying, but this technique is handy if you want to make sure your visitor doesn't leave your website.

- **Choose "on my website using an iframe"** to keep your visitors on your website, and show the search results alongside your content. This is everyone's favorite option, but it requires slightly more work because you need to create two pages: one with the search box, and one that holds the search results. Google gives you some markup to place on each page.

  To use this option, you need to supply the URL for your search results page (for example, *http://www.NewTravelDiaries.com/searchresults.html*). Don't worry if you haven't created this page yet—you can create and upload it when you finish with the search box. You also need to tell Google how wide the search results should be. The standard option is 800 pixels, which is a good choice if you don't plan to pad the sides of your search page with extra content (like ads or a menu bar). Google will inject the search results into your page *dynamically*, in the same way that it inserts an ad every time you view an AdSense page. If you have other content you want to show on the page, you can place it above the search results.

13. **Click the "Save and get code" button.**

    The final setup page includes the markup for your complete, customized search box (see Figure 13-13) in a `<form>` element. (Page 487 has more about forms in HTML.) As with the AdSense code, you can paste this HTML into any web page.

    If you chose to use a search results page on your own site, you'll get a second box with the markup you need to create that page. It consists of a `<div>` element and some JavaScript code, and works in much the same way as the AdSense code. You simply place the `<div>` element where you want the search results to appear.

■ Amazon Associates

As popular as ads are with website owners, they have one serious drawback: They clutter up your pages. Once you perfect a design with carefully chosen pictures and style sheets, you might not want to insert someone else's ad. And although Google ads aren't as visually distracting as other ads can be, like animated banners or pop-up windows, they still chew up valuable screen space. If you can't bear to disturb your web page masterpieces, you might be interested in a subtler option.

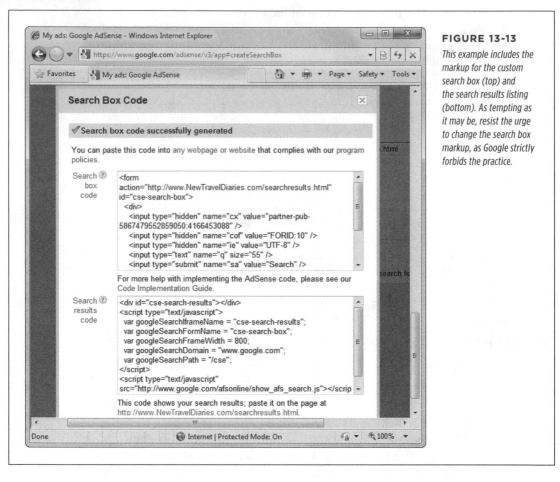

FIGURE 13-13

This example includes the markup for the custom search box (top) and the search results listing (bottom). As tempting as it may be, resist the urge to change the search box markup, as Google strictly forbids the practice.

Amazon Associates is the Web's longest-running affiliate program. If you have a personal site with a "favorite books" page, or if you just refer to the odd book here and there, you might be able to make some extra money by signing up as an affiliate.

The basic idea is that you provide links to book pages and other product pages on Amazon's website. For example, if you write a blurb about a great recipe, you could add a link to the Amazon page that sells the cookbook you're quoting. The link itself is a nice feature for your site, because it lets visitors branch out and possibly get more information about the topic at hand. But the best part is what happens if a visitor decides to buy the book. You wind up making a healthy commission of 4 percent of the book's sale price.

NOTE Amazon commissions aren't just for books. You can provide links to pretty much everything for sale on Amazon (except items that other retailers, like Target and Office Depot, sell). But Amazon Associates limits how much you can make on non-book items. For example, with personal computers, you're capped at a maximum $25 commission per item. You can also earn more than 4 percent for some category types (like MP3 downloads) or if you sell a certain number of items per month. These rules change from time to time, so make sure you scour the Amazon Associates website carefully to get the lowdown.

Signing Up as an Associate

Signing up for the Amazon Associates program is even easier than joining AdSense. Just follow these steps:

1. **Go to** *http://affiliate-program.amazon.com*, **click the "Join now" button, and then log in with your Amazon email and password.**

   To join the associates program, you need an Amazon account. If you don't have one, click "I am a new customer" to create one.

2. **Enter your personal information, and then click Next**

   Amazon needs your name, address, and telephone number.

3. **Enter your website information and then click Next.**

   You need to supply a website name, URL, and brief description (see Figure 13-14). You also need to answer a long list of questions about how many visitors you get, how you attract traffic, how you heard about Amazon Associates, how you make money from your site (if you do), and so on.

4. **Use your phone number to confirm your identity.**

   Enter your phone number and then click "Call me now." An Amazon robot will call you and recite a unique number. You must then type this number into the box on the signup page to prove it's really your phone number.

5. **Tick the box that confirms you agree to Amazon's terms, and then click Finish to submit your application.**

   Shortly afterward, you'll get a confirmation message saying that you're approved on a trial basis. This email includes your unique associate ID. This number is important, because it's the single piece of information you need to add to all your Amazon links to start earning commissions. You can now use the associate tools at *http://associates.amazon.com* (see the next section).

   In a couple of days, after someone at Amazon verifies your site and confirms that it doesn't run afoul of the law, you'll get a second message confirming that you're in for good.

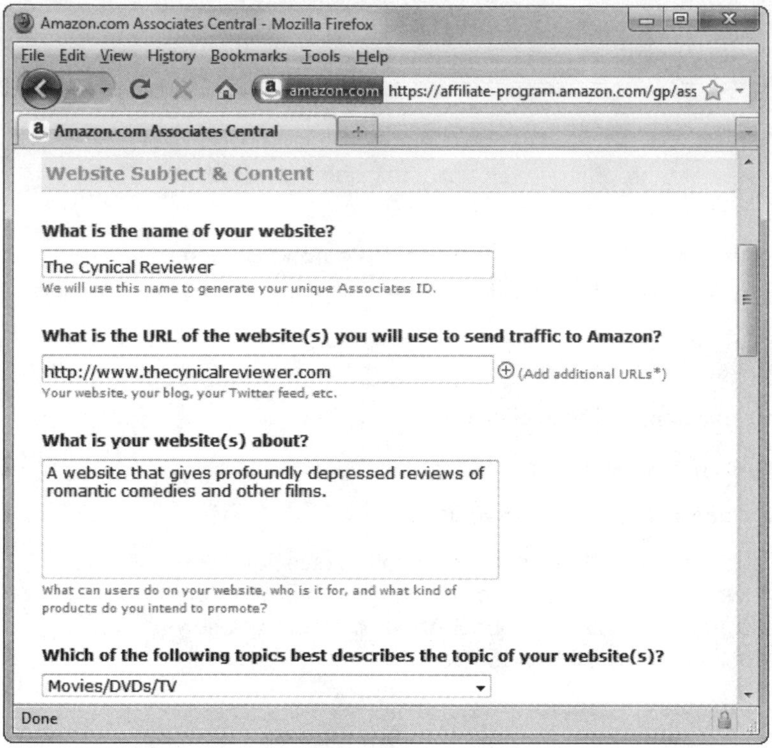

FIGURE 13-14

To become an Amazon associate, you need to supply some basic information about your site. Don't skip this step, because someone from Amazon will take a quick look at your site before she approves you for the program.

6. **If you'd like to tell Amazon how to pay you right now, click Specify Payment Method Now.**

    You can choose your preferred form of payment even before Amazon officially accepts you into its program. Your choices include payment by check, Amazon gift certificate, or direct deposit to a U.S. bank account. Amazon doesn't send checks until you make at least $100, and it charges you a $15 processing fee. Other payment types kick in once you reach $10, and they don't involve any fees.

Generating Associate Links

Once you have your associate ID, you can create *associate links*, the hyperlinks that send your visitors to Amazon. The trick is formatting the URLs the right way.

You add your associate ID to the very end of the associate link. For example, the first email Amazon sends includes an example of the associate link to its home page. It looks like this:

```
http://www.amazon.com?tag=prosetech-22
```

In this example, the associate ID is *prosetech-22*. (Replace it with your own ID to create a link for your website.) If someone follows this link and buys something, you earn a 4 percent commission.

Here's how you link to the Amazon page using an anchor element:

```
Visit <a href="http://www.amazon.com?tag=prosetech-22">Amazon</a> and
help me save up to buy a Ferrari.
```

■ PRODUCT LINKS

You get better commissions with links that lead directly to a specific product. Amazon offers several associate link formats, and here's one of the simplest:

```
http://www.amazon.com/dp/ASIN/?tag=AssociateID
```

And here's a specific example:

```
http://www.amazon.com/dp/0141181265/?tag=prosetech-22
```

You customized two details in this link, the ASIN (Amazon Standard Item Number) and the associate ID. The ASIN is 0141181265 (which leads to the book *Finnegans Wake*) and the associate ID is *prosetech-22*. Figure 13-15 shows you where to find an ASIN.

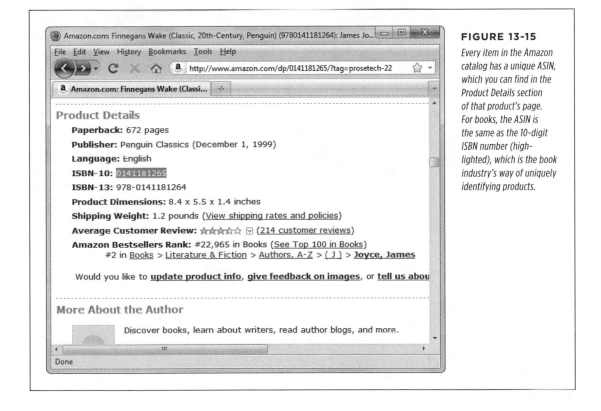

FIGURE 13-15

Every item in the Amazon catalog has a unique ASIN, which you can find in the Product Details section of that product's page. For books, the ASIN is the same as the 10-digit ISBN number (highlighted), which is the book industry's way of uniquely identifying products.

Here's an example of a complete link:

```
The development of the modern personal computer was first presaged in Joyce's
<a href="http://www.amazon.com/dp/0141181265/?tag=prosetech-22">
Finnegans Wake</a>.
```

That's all you need.

> **NOTE** If a visitor follows a link to a specific Amazon product but goes on to buy something completely different, it's all good—you still get the same 4 percent commission.

■ ADVANCED LINKS

Amazon has a set of specialized tools that help you generate links. Using them, you can create a range of snazzy links. Your options include:

- Links with thumbnail pictures
- Links to product categories (like *equestrian magazines* or *bestselling kitchen gadgets*)
- Ad banners that advertise a specific Amazon department
- Amazon search boxes that let visitors perform their own queries

Even if you don't want these fancier links (and if your life isn't dedicated to selling books, you probably don't), there's still good reason to build links with the tools Amazon provides: its links have built-in tracking, so you can determine how many people see each link.

> **NOTE** Amazon tracking is very clever. Essentially, it embeds an <a> element within the link that requests a tiny 1-pixel image from Amazon's servers. When someone requests a page that contains one of these links, the browser automatically fetches the invisible picture from Amazon. When Amazon sees the request for the invisible picture, it knows someone saw the link, and it records a single *impression* (page view) in its tracking database.

Here's how you use Amazon's link-building tools:

1. **Go to** *http://affiliate-program.amazon.com* **and log in.**

   This takes you to the Amazon Associates home page, which offers a variety of reports for checking your sales progress to date, as well as tools for building links.

> **TIP** For detailed information about the more ambitious things you can do with Amazon Associates, click the Get Started Now button. You can also get invaluable advice from other associates by visiting the discussion forums—look for the Discussion Boards link at the bottom of the menu bar on the left.

2. **Click the "Links & Banners" tab. Then, in the pop-up menu, choose Product Links.**

   Amazon lets you build many types of links. Product links point to individual items on Amazon's site. They're generally the most useful. But if you plan to go Amazon-crazy, feel free to explore all the other types of links.

3. **In the search box, type the ASIN for your product, and then click Go.**

   If you don't know the ASIN, select what you think is the most appropriate category, and then type in the product name. When you click Go, Amazon searches for the product and lists the results (see Figure 13-16).

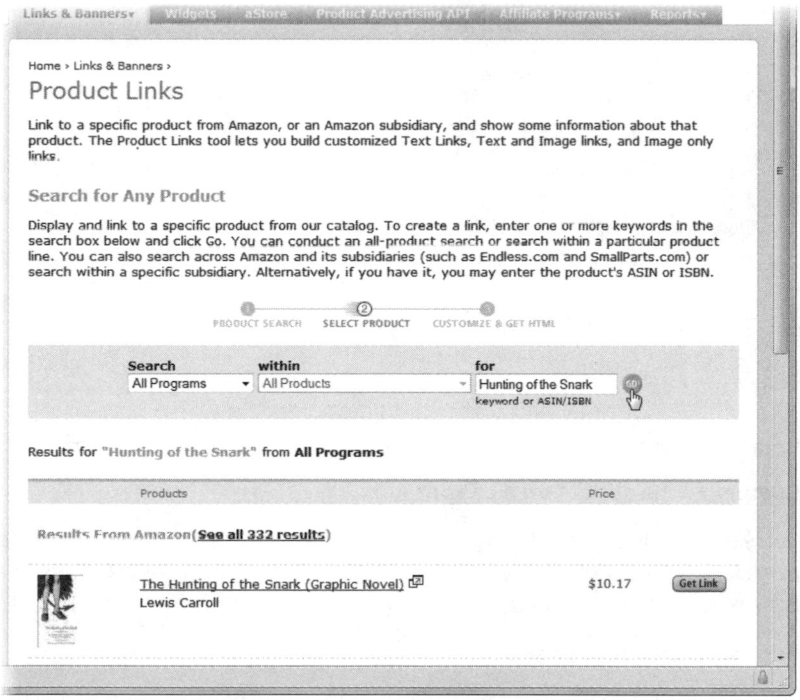

FIGURE 13-16

When you build a link, you can search for the specific product you want. This search works in more or less the same way as a search from Amazon's home page.

4. **Click the Get Link button next to the product you want to link to.**

   You'll see a page that shows you the product and previews the link you're about to create.

5. **Choose the type of link you want by clicking one of the tabs on top (Figure 13-17).**

   You start out at the "Text and Image" tab, which creates a detailed box that includes a product picture and price. To create a plain text link, click the Text Only tab. To create a clickable book cover image, click the Image Only tab.

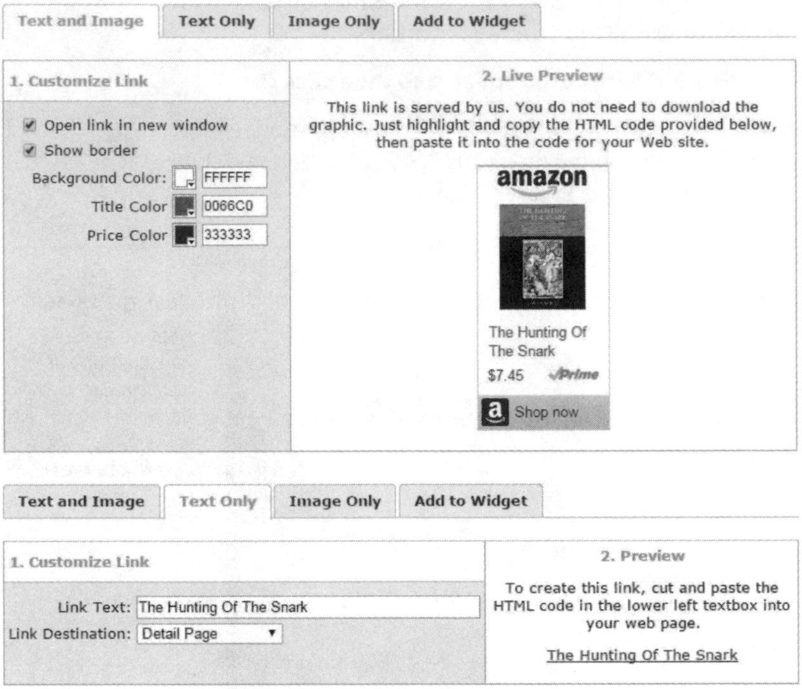

FIGURE 13-17

As you choose your link options, Amazon previews the result. You can choose to make a text-and-image link (top) or a plainer, easier-to-integrate text-only link (bottom).

6. **Customize the appearance of your link.**

   You can pick the text and background colors. You can also choose whether your page opens the product-page link in a new browser window, how big the image is, what price information the product box includes, and what colors it uses.

7. **Put the link on your page.**

   As you configure your link, Amazon puts the matching HTML in a text box underneath. When you perfect your link's appearance, copy that HTML and paste it in one of your web pages.

When you create a text link, Amazon creates an anchor element that looks fairly complex. (As described earlier, the anchor element contains an invisible <img> element that lets Amazon track how many times it displays the link.)

However, like all anchor elements, it's relatively easy to put this element where you want it. Just pop it into an existing paragraph, like this:

```
<p>Lewis Carroll's work as a mathematician may have driven him insane,
as his famous book
<a href="http://www.amazon.com/exec/obidos/...">The Hunting of the Snark</a>
<img src="http://www.assoc-amazon.com/..." width="1" height="1" />
attests.</p>
```

NOTE   Amazon puts the full title of the book inside the anchor element. This might make your link a little longer than you intend, because it might include information about the edition or a byline. If that happens, just edit the title down.

Amazon sends you monthly emails to let you know how much you're earning, but if you can't stand the suspense, you can log into Amazon Associates any time. Click the Reports tab (Figure 13-18) to get detailed information on how much you're earning per day, week, month, or quarter.

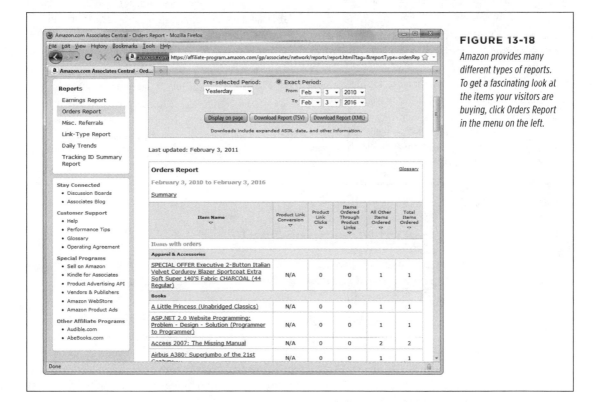

FIGURE 13-18

Amazon provides many different types of reports. To get a fascinating look at the items your visitors are buying, click Orders Report in the menu on the left.

Sell Your Custom Designs

It's no secret that the Web is full of small-scale businesses selling handmade and custom goods. You can expand your product offerings beyond those from Amazon, but it might take some effort. Depending on what you want to sell, you might need to search out the right wholesalers or craftspeople, or just build a woodworking shop in your basement. But if you have something a bit simpler in mind, like customized clothes, mugs, hats, magnets, posters, buttons, iPhone cases, or yoga mats, then CafePress (*www.cafepress.com*) and Zazzle (*www.zazzle.com*) are your new best friends.

Both sites let you design your own goods and offer them for sale on a personalized section of the website (no HTML coding required). The genius of CafePress and Zazzle is that they let you use your own artwork. If, for example, you want to create a custom beer mug, you aren't limited to typing in a cheesy message and picking a preset font. Instead, you can upload your own graphics file (whether it's a digital picture or a Photoshop masterpiece), and slap that on the side of your product. Of course, life isn't perfect.

On many products, CafePress and Zazzle limit where you can place your pictures. For example, you can put graphics on the front and back of most clothes, but you can't fill the whole surface or wrap around the sides. (Zazzle's shoes are an eye-catching exception. They let you wrap graphics along the entire outer surface.)

Once you create a design, you can order one for yourself or peddle it to an audience of millions by sending your visitors to an automatically generated store page on the CafePress or Zazzle site. If someone buys an item, you get a small cut of the price, and CafePress or Zazzle processes the payment, prints the item, and ships it to your customer.

If you're interested in the idea but still in search of some inspiration, head to Zazzle and click the Search button without typing in a product name. You'll see a list of everything they offer, organized so that the bestsellers come first. Timely t-shirts with corny graphics, sophomoric slogans, or a reference to politics or current events are always among the most popular items.

PayPal Merchant Tools

Unless your website is wildly popular, ads and other affiliate programs will net you only spare change. If you have all-consuming dreams of web riches, you need to actually sell something.

You don't need to go far to run into self-made Internet commerce kingpins. A surprisingly large number of people have made their living with creative products. Examples include t-shirts with political catchphrases, empty bottles of wine with R.M.S. Titanic labels, and collectable toys from a relative's basement. Your path to a thriving e-business might involve little more than buying tin spoons from Honest Ed's and decorating them with macramé.

No matter how good your goods, you need a way to sell vast quantities of them easily and conveniently. Very few people will go through the hassle of mailing you a personal check. But if they can make an impulse purchase with a credit card, your odds of making a sale improve significantly.

Accepting credit cards isn't the easiest thing in the world to do. You can do so two ways:

- **Open a merchant account with a bank.** This is the traditional way businesses accept credit cards. Requirements vary from country to country, but you may need a business plan, an accountant, and some up-front capital.

- **Use a third-party service.** A number of companies accept credit card payments on your behalf in exchange for a flat fee or a percentage of the sale. In this chapter, you'll learn how to use one of the best—PayPal.

Unless you have a large business, the second option is always better because of the additional risks that accompany web-based sales.

First of all, the Internet is an open place. Even if you have a merchant account, you need a *secure* way to accept credit card information from your customers. That means the credit card number needs to be *encrypted* (scrambled using a secret key) so that Internet eavesdroppers can't get at it. Most webmasters don't have a secure server sitting in their basement, and many web hosts charge extra for the privilege of using theirs.

Another problem is that when you conduct a sale over the Web, you don't have any way to collect a signature from the e-shopper. This makes you vulnerable to *chargebacks* (see the box on page 444).

NOTE PayPal is a staggeringly large Internet company that offers its payment services in nearly 200 countries. If you were to rank banks by the sheer number of accounts they hold, PayPal (with roughly 150 million account members) would be one of the largest banks in the world.

Signing Up with PayPal

Once you sign up with PayPal, you can accept payments from customers across the globe. Here's how you go about it:

1. **Head to the PayPal website (***www.paypal.com***) and click the Sign Up link on the home page.**

   This takes you to PayPal's Sign Up page.

2. **Choose your country and language.**

3. **Choose the type of account you want to create (Personal, Premier, or Business), and then click the Get Started button in the corresponding box.**

   A *personal account* is ideal if you want to use PayPal to buy items on sites like eBay using your credit card or with funds from your bank account. You can also *accept* money transfers from other PayPal members without having to pay any fees. However, there's a significant catch: Personal accounts can't accept credit card payments. As a result, customers who want to do business with you need to have money in their PayPal accounts (which they get by selling something and receiving a PayPal payment, or by transferring money into their account from a linked bank account).

Understanding Chargebacks

What's a chargeback?

Credit card companies issue a chargeback when a cardholder asks them to remove a charge from their account. The buyer may claim that he never made the purchase in the first place or that the seller didn't live up to his end of the agreement. A chargeback can occur weeks or months after someone buys an item.

From the buyer's point of view, a chargeback is relatively easy. He simply phones the credit card company and reverses the transaction. The money you made is deducted from your account, even though you already shipped the product. If you want to dispute the buyer's claim, you're in the unenviable position of trying to persuade a monolithic credit card company to take your side. Many small businesses don't dispute chargebacks at all, because the process is too difficult, expensive, and unsuccessful.

However, when you use a third-party service, the odds tilt in your favor. If the buyer asks for a chargeback, the chargeback is made against the third-party company that accepted the payment (like PayPal), not you. And even though PayPal isn't as large as the average multinational bank, it's still a major customer of most credit card companies, which means it has significant clout to fight a chargeback.

The end result is that buyers are less likely to charge back items when they pay through PayPal. And if they do, PayPal gives you the chance to dispute the chargeback. It even lets you contact the buyer to see if there's a simple misunderstanding (for example, to check whether you sent the item to the wrong address). And if you're really paranoid, you can use PayPal's Seller Protection policy, which, if you take a few additional steps (like retaining proof of delivery), insures you for up to a $5,000 loss. For more information about how PayPal handles chargebacks, check out *www.paypal.com/chargeback*. To learn about PayPal's Seller Protection program, refer to *www.paypal.com/SellerProtection*.

A *premier account* is the best way to run a small business. You can send money (great if you crave a rare movie poster on eBay) and accept any type of payment that PayPal accepts, including both credit and debit cards. You also get to use PayPal's ecommerce tools. However, PayPal charges you a fee for every payment you receive, an amount that varies by sales volume but ranges from 1.9 percent to 2.9 percent of the payment's total value (with a minimum fee of 30 cents). That means that on a $25 sale, PayPal takes about $1 off the top. If you accept payments in another currency, you surrender an extra 2.5 percent. To get the full scoop on fees and to see the most current rates, refer to *www.paypal.com/fees*.

A *business account* is almost identical to a premier account, except that it allows multiple logins. This is the best choice if you have a large business with employees who need to use your PayPal account to help you manage your site.

4. **Enter your email address and choose a password, and then fill in your name, address, and phone number.**

   Make your password complex; you don't want a malicious hacker guessing it and using your PayPal account to go on an electronic buying binge.

> **TIP** As a general rule, guard your PayPal account information the same way you guard your bank PIN. If you're really paranoid, don't use your PayPal account to buy items on other websites. Don't use your credit card to do so either—electronic eavesdroppers can snag your info and then head out on a first-class cruise to Ibiza.

5. **Finally, click "Agree and Create Account" to complete the process.**

    PayPal sends you an email confirmation immediately. Click the link in the message to activate your account, and then you can start creating PayPal buttons and shopping carts to collect payments (see below for details).

Accepting Payments

PayPal makes creating ecommerce web pages ridiculously easy. One way is to add a Buy Now button to any page on your site:

1. **Go to** *www.paypal.com* **and sign in.**

    You start out on a page that summarizes your account history, including recent purchases and credits.

2. **Scroll down until you see the "Selling tools" link near the bottom of the sidebar on the left. Click it.**

    You'll see a variety of tools for collecting money, as explained in Figure 13-19.

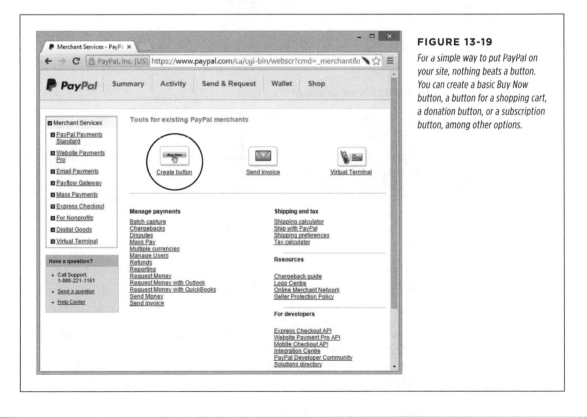

FIGURE 13-19

For a simple way to put PayPal on your site, nothing beats a button. You can create a basic Buy Now button, a button for a shopping cart, a donation button, or a subscription button, among other options.

3. **Click the Create Button link.**

PayPal displays the page where you configure your button's appearance and set the price of your product (Figure 13-20).

4. **Choose Buy Now as the button type.**

PayPal has plenty more types of buttons. You'll create a shopping cart button on page 449.

5. **Give your item a name and, if you want to keep track of it, a product code. Then supply the price and currency.**

Don't worry about locking out international visitors when you set your currency. Credit card companies are happy to charge Canadian customers in U.S. dollars, U.S. customers in euros, and European customers in rupees. Just choose the currency you think your buyers expect to see.

6. **If you want to let customers specify options for the products they buy, fill in the information in the "Customize button" box.**

You can collect extra buying information from your buyers in three nifty ways:

- **"Add drop-down menu with price/option"** lets you give buyers a list of options for your product, each with a different price (see Figure 13-21). For example, you could let a buyer choose between a plain, premium, or organic tin of hamster food.

- **"Add drop-down menu"** gives your buyers a list of options, but without changing the product's price. For example, you could use a list like this to let buyers choose the color of the embroidered undergarments they're about to buy.

- **"Add text field"** adds a text box where buyers can type in anything. Use this if you need to collect information that varies, like the name your buyer wants engraved on a magnetic screwdriver.

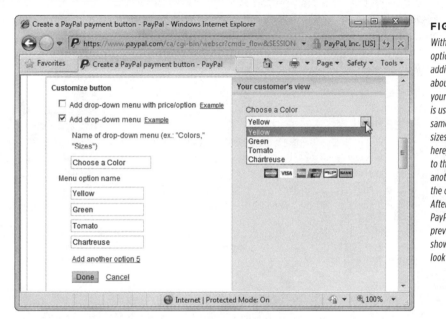

FIGURE 13-21

With a drop-down list of options, you can collect additional information about the type of product your visitor wants. This is useful if you offer the same item in multiple sizes or colors (as shown here). To add another color to the list, click the "Add another option" link under the current set of options. After you click Done, PayPal updates the button preview on the right to show you what the list will look like.

7. **To change the appearance of a button, click "Customize appearance."**

   PayPal gives you limited options for the button's size and text.

   The standard Buy Now button is perfectly usable but a little plain. If you created a nicer button picture, upload it to your site, and then supply the URL for it here. (You can always change the HTML that PayPal generates if you want to use a different button later on.)

8. **Scroll down and fill in any additional options you want.**

   PayPal gives you a heap of extra payment possibilities. You can add a flat fee for shipping and a percentage for sales tax. You can instruct PayPal to track how many items you have in stock and to stop selling your product when it's sold out—all you do is fill in the number of items you currently have.

   And PayPal has an entire section of advanced possibilities, like whether you need a buyer's address (PayPal assumes you do), if you want your customers to fill in additional comments with their payments (ordinarily they can't), and where PayPal should send visitors after they complete or cancel a payment (you can send shoppers to a specific URL on your site, rather than to PayPal's generic pages).

9. **Click Create Button.**

PayPal displays a text box with the markup for your customized Buy Now button. Copy and paste the markup into your web page.

When you create a Buy Now button, PayPal puts everything inside a `<form>` element (explained on page 489). Here's an example of a button for a pair of handmade origami socks:

```
<form action="https://www.paypal.com/cgi-bin/webscr" method="post">
  <input type="hidden" name="cmd" value="_s-xclick" />
  <input type="hidden" name="hosted_button_id" value="633788" />
  <table>
    <tr><td>
      <input type="hidden" name="on0" value="Choose a Color" />
       Choose a Color</td></tr><tr><td>
      <select name="os0">
        <option value="Yellow">Yellow</option>
        <option value="Green">Green</option>
        <option value="Tomato">Tomato</option>
        <option value="Chartreuse">Chartreuse</option>
      </select>
    </td></tr>
  </table>
  <input type="image" border="0" name="submit" alt=""
   src="https://www.paypal.com/en_US/i/btn/btn_buynowCC_LG.gif" />
  <img src="https://www.paypal.com/en_US/i/scr/pixel.gif" alt=""
   width="1" height="1" />
</form>
```

If you added any options, you'll see `<select>` and `<option>` elements in the HTML that define the relevant list boxes (page 490). The form also includes the Buy Now button. Clicking it sends the form to PayPal. You can change the button's `src` attribute (bolded in the listing above) to point to a different image file. PayPal inserts the invisible tracking image (*pixel.gif* in the example above) after the code for the Buy Now button. (This tracking technique is the same one Amazon uses.)

TIP As long as you don't tamper with the `<input>` fields and you keep everything inside the `<form>` tags, you can tweak the markup PayPal creates for you. For example, you can add other elements to the form or gussy it up with a style sheet. Or you might want to change the layout by removing the invisible table (represented by the `<table>`, `<tr>`, and `<td>` elements) that PayPal uses to organize your button and your options.

So what happens when a shopper clicks the Buy Now button and submits this form? The action attribute in the very first line of the code above tells the story: The browser sends the buyer's information to PayPal using the action URL (which is *https://www.paypal.com/cgi-bin/webscr*). As it does, it uses a secure channel to prevent Internet eavesdroppers—that's why the URL starts with "https" instead of "http."

Notice that this form doesn't include key pieces of information, like the product name or price. That's a safety measure designed to prevent troublemakers from tampering with the markup in your web page and paying you less than your products are worth. When PayPal receives the form data, it retrieves the hidden ID value (633788 in the example above), and looks it up in its giant, private database of products to identify the relevant product, price, and seller (you).

In fact, the PayPal markup doesn't provide any information about the item you're selling. You put the item name, picture, description, and price into your web page (probably before the Buy Now button). Here's an example:

```
<!DOCTYPE html>
<html>
<head>...</head>
<body>
  <h1>Handmade Origami Socks</h1>
  <p><img src="origami.jpg" alt="Handmade Origami Socks" class="float">
  You've waited and they're finally here. Order your own
  pair of origami socks for only $26.95 and get them in time
  for the holidays. What better way to show your loved ones how
  poor your gift giving judgement really is?</p>
  <form action="https://www.paypal.com/cgi-bin/webscr" method="post">
    ...
  </form>
</body>
</html>
```

Figure 13-22 shows the result. This example displays the standard PayPal ordering page, but you can customize it with your own logo (see the next section).

Building a Shopping Cart

PayPal's Buy Now button gives you a great way to make a quick sale. But if you dream about an ecommerce empire, you need to create a store where visitors can collect several items at once and pay for them all at the same time.

To give your buyers this kind of convenience, you need a shopping cart, which is a staple of ecommerce websites. The good news is that you don't need to program your own cart—you can use a prebuilt one from PayPal, which integrates smoothly into your website.

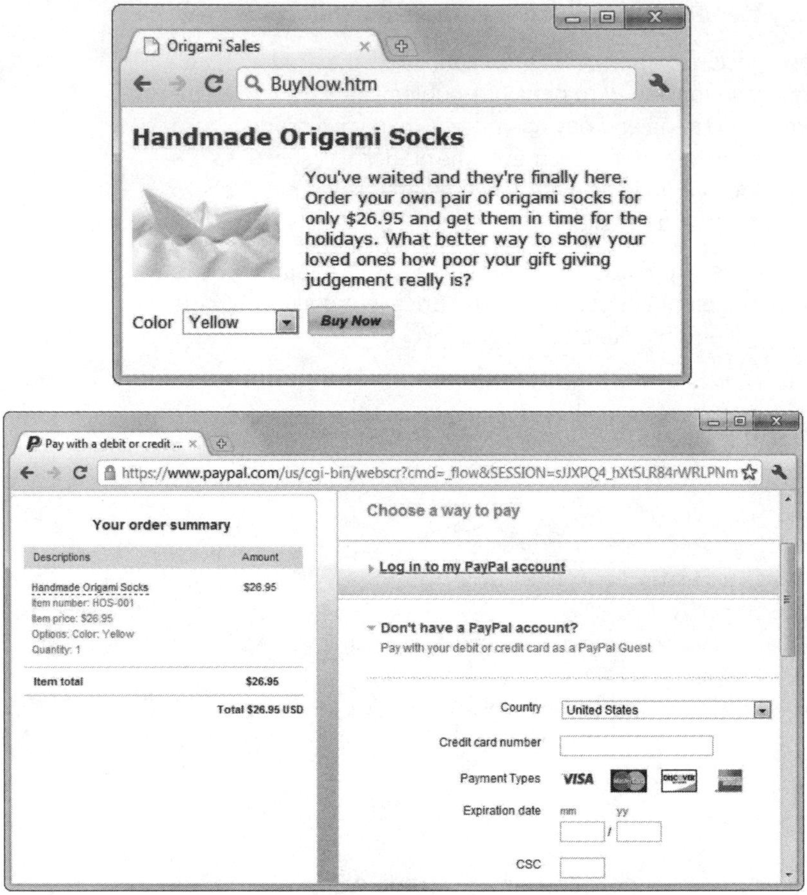

FIGURE 13-22

Top: The Buy Now button waits patiently on your page.

Bottom: Clicking the Buy Now button starts a secure checkout process using PayPal. Your visitor can pay for an item by credit card, and you both get an email confirming the transaction. Then it's up to you to fulfill your end of the deal.

Creating a PayPal shopping cart is remarkably similar to creating a Buy Now button (so if you haven't tried that, you might want to play around with it before you go any further). The basic idea is that you create a separate "Add to Cart" button for each item you sell. You get many of the same options you did with the Buy Now button. For example, you can set a price, product code, shipping charges, and so on. The difference is that when visitors click an "Add to Cart" button, PayPal doesn't send them straight to a checkout page; it displays a shopping cart page in a new window. Visitors can keep shopping until they have everything they want. Then they click a Checkout button to complete their purchase.

To show you how this works, the following example uses the page pictured in Figure 13-23 as a starting point. This example also shows a great use of style-based layout. Check out the downloadable samples—available from the companion site at *http://prosetech.com/web*—to try it out for yourself.

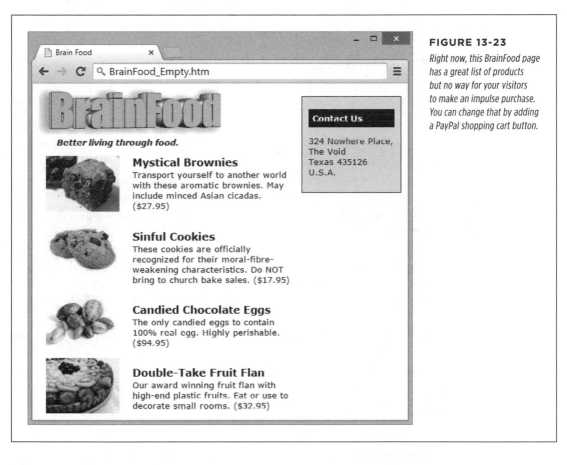

FIGURE 13-23

Right now, this BrainFood page has a great list of products but no way for your visitors to make an impulse purchase. You can change that by adding a PayPal shopping cart button.

■ CREATING A CUSTOM PAGE STYLE

Before you create your shopping cart, you can take an extra step to really personalize your payment page. If you're happy with the PayPal standard, feel free to skip to the next section. But if you'd like to have your company logo appear on the shopping cart pages, keep reading.

1. **If you're not already there, head to *www.paypal.com* and sign in.**

2. **Scroll down and click the "Seller preferences" link at the bottom of the panel on the left.**

   This brings you to a page with a pile of information about your preferences. In this case, you're interested in the "Selling online" section.

3. **In the "Selling online" section, find the "Custom payment pages" setting, and click the Update link next to it.**

This takes you to a page that lists all the page styles you've created. At first, you start off with only a single style—the PayPal standard, which sports a basic PayPal logo.

4. **Click Add to create a new page style.**

PayPal displays a set of options that let you define how your page looks and functions.

5. **Fill in whatever information you want to customize on your payment page.**

First, type a descriptive title into the Page Style Name box to help you remember which style is which.

Next, use the Header Image URL to point to the picture you want to appear in the top-left corner of the shopping cart page. You can use an image that's up to 750 pixels wide and 90 pixels high, and you need to upload it to your web server. Optionally, you can supply a Logo Image URL to set a similar picture for the order summary page (make this one 190 x 60 pixels).

> **NOTE** Because PayPal's shopping cart is a secure page, when you use a custom logo, the shopper may get a message informing her that there are some insecure items on the page (namely, your picture). To prevent that from happening, talk to your web hosting company about putting your picture on a secure (HTTPS) server.

You can specify color codes for the Header Background Color, Header Border Color, and Background Color settings. This part is optional; leave it out if you're happy with the standard white.

6. **Click Save to store your page style.**

Before you commit, you can click Preview to take a sneak peek at what the payment page looks like.

7. **Select your new page style, and then click Make Primary.**

All your visitors will see your customized page when they check out.

■ BUILDING THE SHOPPING CART BUTTONS

Now you're ready to build the buttons that add items to your customer's cart. Here's how:

1. **If you're not already there, head to *www.paypal.com* and sign in.**

2. **Scroll down and click the "Selling tools" link on the left.**

You've been here before.

3. **Click the "Create button" link.**

A shopping cart functions a bit differently from the Buy Now button you built before, but you still need to supply the same product and price information.

4. **For the button type, choose "Shopping cart."**

PayPal displays a page where you configure the "Add to Cart" button for a single item.

5. **Give your item a name and, if you want to keep track of it, a product code. Then supply the price, currency, and any other relevant information.**

These settings are exactly the same as those for a Buy Now button.

6. **Click Create Button.**

You'll see a text box with the markup for your customized "Add to Cart" button. Copy the markup and paste it into your web page. But remember, this "Add to Cart" code applies to a single, specific product. If you have more than one item on a page (as in the BrainFood example), you need to create multiple buttons. To do so, click "Create similar button" and return to step 3. When you finish building all the buttons and copying them into your page, continue with the next step.

7. **Create a View Cart button.**

Your shopping cart wouldn't be complete without a button that lets shoppers see what's in their carts (and then head to the virtual checkout counter). To create one, click the "Create a View Cart button" link.

You have virtually no options for the View Cart button, as its purpose is pretty straightforward. You can use the standard View Cart button or supply a URL that points to a button of your own design. Once you make your selection, click Create Button, and then copy the markup into your page along with all the other buttons. Figure 13-24 shows the result.

Withdrawing Your Money

PayPal safely stashes all your payments in your PayPal account (which is like a virtual bank account). You can see the balance at any time. Just log in and click the My Account tab.

If you earn a small amount of money, you may be happy leaving it with PayPal so you can buy other stuff on a variety of websites, from eBay to Etsy. But if you're raking in significant dough, you'll want to transfer some of it to the real world.

The most common approach is to send the money to your bank account. To do this, you need to give PayPal your bank account information. PayPal waives its transfer fee as long as your withdrawal meets a certain minimum (like $150). However, your *bank* may apply an electronic transaction fee. Depending on the country you live in, PayPal may offer other withdrawal options, too. For example, it may let you transfer money to a debit card or a credit card.

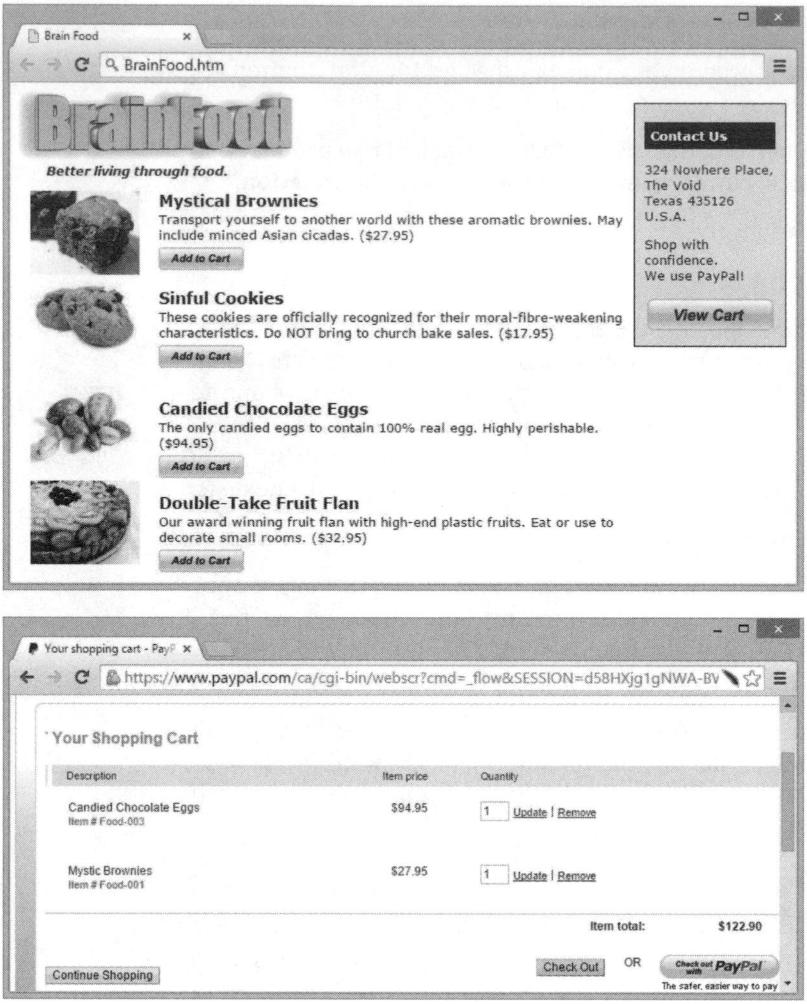

FIGURE 13-24

Top: Here's the revised BrainFood page, with shopping cart buttons.

Bottom: After clicking a few "Add to Cart" buttons, here's the shopping cart page your visitors will see (in a separate window). All they need to do is click Check Out to complete a purchase.

To get started with any of these approaches, log in, click the My Account tab, and then click the Withdraw link underneath and follow the instructions.

Interactivity and Multimedia

JavaScript: Adding Interactivity

JavaScript is a simplified programming language designed to beef up web pages with interactive features. It gives you just enough programming muscle to add some fancy effects, but not enough to cause serious damage to your site if your code goes wonky. JavaScript is perfect for creating pop-up windows, embedding animated effects, and modifying the content on your web page. On the other hand, it can't help you build a hot ecommerce storefront; for that, you need the PayPal tools described in Chapter 13 or a server-side programming platform (see page 458).

The goal of this chapter isn't to teach you the details of JavaScript programming—it's to give you enough background so you can find great free JavaScript code online, understand it well enough to make basic changes, and then paste it into your pages to get the results you want.

NOTE In fact, you've already used JavaScript (perhaps unwittingly) in some of the examples in this book. You used it to track visitors to your site with Google Analytics (page 332), to fetch a suitable block of ads for your AdSense-enabled web page (page 427), and to grab a list of your recent tweets to show on your site (page 362). In all these cases, you used a block of ready-made JavaScript code (or a reference to a ready-made JavaScript file). You got the benefits of JavaScript interactivity without needing to write a line of code yourself. Now you'll learn how JavaScript actually works.

■ Understanding JavaScript

The JavaScript language has a long history; it first hit the scene with the Netscape Navigator 2 browser in 1995. Internet Explorer jumped on the bandwagon with version 3. Today, all modern browsers run JavaScript, and it's become wildly popular as a result.

Here's what JavaScript can do:

- Dynamically insert new content into a web page or modify an existing HTML element. For example, you can display a personalized message to your visitors ("Hello, Joe!") or make titles grow and shrink perpetually (see the example on page 477).

- Gather information about the current date, your visitor's browser, or the text your visitor types into a form. You can display any of this information on a web page or use it to make decisions about what your page does next. For example, you could stop visitors from going any further in your site until they type in an email address.

- React to events that take place in a browser. For example, you can add JavaScript code that runs when a page finishes loading or when a visitor clicks a picture.

- Talk to a program running on a web server. JavaScript can poll the server for a recent stock quote, for example, or for a bunch of records from a company database. This is one task you won't see covered in this chapter, because it requires some serious programming mojo to write the non-JavaScript code that runs on the web server.

It's just as important to understand what JavaScript *can't* do. JavaScript code is *sandboxed*, which means that a browser locks JavaScript-containing pages into a carefully controlled place in your guests' computer memory, known as a sandbox. As a result, the code can't perform any potentially risky tasks on your visitor's computer, like sending orders to a printer, opening files, running other programs, reformatting a hard drive, and so on. This design ensures good security.

> **NOTE** JavaScript is thoroughly different from the Java language (although the code sometimes looks similar, because the two share some code-writing rules). Java is a full-fledged programming language, every bit as powerful—and complicated—as languages like C# and Visual Basic.

Server-Side and Client-Side Programming

To understand how JavaScript fits into the web universe, it's important to understand the two types of programming on the Web.

When you use a search engine like Google or go to an ecommerce site like Amazon, you connect to a high-powered piece of software known as a *server-side application*, which runs on a web server. When you visit one of these sites, you send the server-side program information, like the keywords you want to search for or the book you want to buy. The program, in turn, consults a massive database and spits out some HTML that creates the page you see in your browser.

Server-side applications rule the web world, because there's virtually nothing they can't do. However, they're difficult to program. Not only do developers need to worry about getting server-side programs to generate HTML for a browser, but they also need to make sure the programs can run all kinds of complex code and tap giant databases—all the while ensuring that the site runs just as well when millions of people view it as it does when only one person visits it. This is hard work, and it's best handled by the poor souls we call programmers.

Client-side applications, on the other hand, use a completely different model. They embed small, lightweight programs inside an ordinary HTML page. When a browser downloads the page, the browser itself runs the program (assuming your security settings or compatibility issues haven't disabled the program). Client-side programs are much less powerful than those on the server side—they can't reliably poll the huge databases stored on web servers, for example, and for security reasons they can't directly change most things on your computer. However, they're much simpler to create.

> **NOTE** The distinction between server-side and client-side programs is sometimes muddied by the fact that top-flight websites use both. For example, Amazon uses fine-tuned JavaScript for its pop-up menus and "Look Inside" feature, which lets you browse a book. However, all the serious stuff, like tracking orders, processing credit cards, and storing customer reviews, happens on the web server.

The Evolution of JavaScript

JavaScript started out life as a bit of a toy. It wasn't as powerful as a full-fledged programming language or browser plug-in like Flash. Professional coders sneered at it.

However, JavaScript had simplicity on its side. Hobbyists loved the fact that you could embed basic instructions (like "scroll that heading from left to right" or "pop up an ad for fudge-flavored toothpicks in a new window") right inside your web pages. And even web novices who didn't know all the ins and outs of the JavaScript language could copy a cool script from a free website, paste it into a page, and get instant gratification.

But these conveniences paled next to JavaScript's real winning feature: its universality. Today, JavaScript runs on any browser and on virtually every device, including tablets, smartphones, and Apple devices that don't support Flash. And you never need to install JavaScript or configure it—it just works. That makes it the safe choice for any type of site, from an ecommerce storefront to a FreeCell clone. These days, when big companies create web applications, they use one of a variety of server-side programming platforms (including ASP.NET, PHP, JSP, Perl, Ruby, Node.js, and more) but stick with ordinary JavaScript to power the client-side parts.

This trend is accelerating with HTML5. The latest version of the HTML language comes bundled with a pile of next-generation standards that extend JavaScript. In fact, that's a large part of the reason why HTML5 attracted so much attention and went from outsider status to an accepted standard in record time. When HTML5 is finalized and implemented in modern browsers, developers will be able to use JavaScript to locate a web surfer's geographic location, draw dynamic graphics, and even take control of webcams and microphones. So consider the time you spend learning JavaScript today an investment in the future of your web page-building skills.

▉ JavaScript 101

Now that you've learned a bit about JavaScript and why it exists, it's time to dive in and start creating your first real script.

The <script> Element

Every JavaScript program starts with a <script> block you slot somewhere into an HTML document. Really, you have only two options:

- **The <body> section.** Put scripts you want your browser to run right away in the <body> section of your HTML. The browser runs your script as soon as it reaches the <script> element. Usually, JavaScript fans put their scripts at the *end* of the <body> section. That way, you avoid errors that might occur if you use a script that relies on another part of the page, and the browser hasn't read that section yet.

- **The <head> section.** If you place an ordinary script in the <head> section of your HTML, it runs immediately, before the browser processes any part of the markup. However, it's more common to use the <head> section for scripts that contain *functions* (see page 467). Functions don't run immediately—instead, you summon them when your visitor takes some kind of action on a page, like moving a mouse.

> **NOTE** You can place as many <script> blocks in a web page as you want.

A typical script block holds a series of programming instructions, wedged in between the opening <script> tag and the closing </script> tag. To get a handle on how these instructions work, consider the following example, which displays a JavaScript alert box on your page:

```
<!DOCTYPE html>
<html>
<head>
  <title>JavaScript Test</title>
</head>
<body>
  <h1>You Will Be Wowed</h1>
  <p>This page uses JavaScript.</p>
  <script>
    alert("Welcome, JavaScript coder.")
  </script>
</body>
</html>
```

This script pops up a window that displays a message, as shown in Figure 14-1. When you click OK, the message disappears, and it's back to life as usual for your web page.

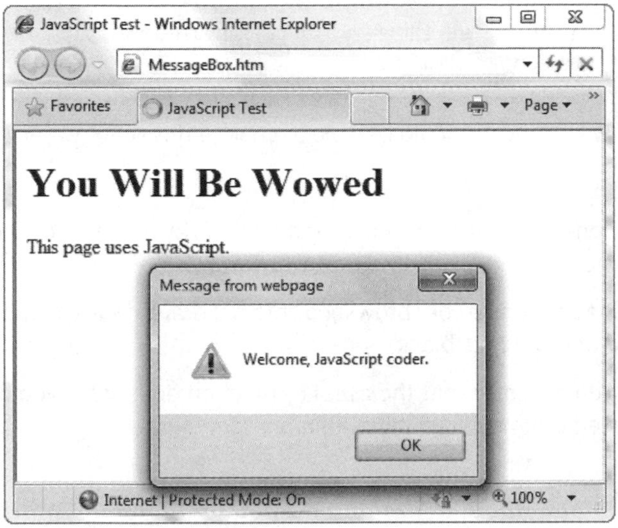

FIGURE 14-1

Because you positioned the <script> element for this page at the end of the HTML markup, the browser displays all the HTML first and then pops up the alert box. If you put the <script> element at the beginning of the <body> section (or in the <head> section), the alert box would appear earlier, while the page is still blank. The browser would then wait until you clicked OK in the box before reading the rest of the HTML page and displaying its contents.

You're probably wondering exactly how this script works its magic. When a browser processes it, the script runs all the code, going one line at a time. In this case, there's only one line:

```
alert("Welcome, JavaScript coder.")
```

This line uses a built-in JavaScript function called alert. A *function* is a piece of code that performs a certain well-defined task and that you can use over and over again. JavaScript has many built-in functions, but you can also build your own.

JavaScript's alert() function requires one piece of information, known as an *argument* in programmer-speak. In this case, that piece of information is the text you want the alert box to display. If you want to see an ordinary number, say 6, you could type it in as is—that is, you don't need to put it in quotes. But with text, there's no way for a browser to tell where text starts and stops. To compensate for this in JavaScript, you put text inside single quotation marks (') or double quotation marks ("), as in the previous example.

> **NOTE** Programmers call a distinct piece of text used in a program a *string*. "The friendly fox," "a," and "Rumpelstiltskin" all qualify as strings.

That's it. All this simple script does is call JavaScript's alert() function. (Spend enough time around programmers and JavaScript fans, and you'll soon learn that "call" is the preferred way to describe the action that triggers a function.) The alert() function does the rest, popping up a pre-sized window that displays an exclamation-point logo and whatever message you typed in. The box stays onscreen until your visitor clicks OK.

> **NOTE** To write this script, you need to know that there's an alert() function ready for you to use—a fact you can find out on one of the many JavaScript tutorial sites.

Based on what you now know, you should be able to change this script to:

- Display a different message (by changing the argument).

- Display more than one message box, one after the other (by adding more lines in your <script> block).

- Display the message box before your browser displays the web page (by changing the position of the <script> block).

It's not much to keep you occupied, but the alert() function does show you how easily you can get started using and changing a simple script.

GEM IN THE ROUGH

Dealing with Internet Explorer's Paranoia

If you run the alert example above in the Firefox browser, you'll find that everything works seamlessly. If you run it in Internet Explorer, you won't get the same satisfaction. Instead, you'll see a security warning in a yellow bar at the top of the page. Until you click that bar and then choose Allow Blocked Content, your JavaScript code won't run.

At first glance, IE's security warning seems like a surefire way to scare off the bravest web visitor. But you don't need to worry; the message is just part of the quirky way Internet Explorer deals with web pages that you store on your hard drive. When you open the same page over the Web, Internet Explorer won't raise the slightest objection.

That said, the security warning is still an annoyance while you're testing your web page, because it forces you to keep ex-

plicitly telling the browser to allow the page to run JavaScript. To avoid the security notice altogether, you can tell Internet Explorer to pretend you downloaded your page from a web server. You do this by adding a special comment called the *Mark of the Web*. You place this comment immediately after the <html> element that begins your page:

```
<html>
<!-- saved from url=(0014)about:internet
-->
```

When IE sees the Mark of the Web, it treats the page as though it came from a web server, skipping the security warning and running your JavaScript code without hesitation. To all other browsers, the Mark of the Web just looks like an ordinary HTML comment.

■ BROWSERS THAT DON'T SUPPORT JAVASCRIPT

It's rare, but some browsers will recognize the <script> element but refuse to run your code. This can happen if a browser doesn't support JavaScript (for example, a dusty text-only browser like Lynx) or if JavaScript has been switched off (which is possible in paranoid corporate environments, but still very rare).

To deal with the occasional situation like this, you can use the <noscript> element, which lets you supply alternate HTML content. You place the <noscript> element immediately after the closing </script> tag. Here's an example that displays a paragraph of text for browsers that lack JavaScript support:

```
<script>
  alert("Welcome, JavaScript coder.")
</script>
<noscript>
  <p>Welcome, non-JavaScript-enabled browser.</p>
</noscript>
```

Variables

Every programming language includes the concept of *variables*, which are temporary containers that store important information. Variables can store numbers, objects, or pieces of text. As you'll see throughout this chapter, variables play a key role in many scripts, and they're a powerful tool in any programmer's arsenal.

■ DECLARING VARIABLES

To create a variable in JavaScript, you use the var keyword, followed by the name of the variable. You can choose any name that makes sense to you, as long as you're consistent (and avoid spaces or special characters). This example creates a variable named myMessage:

```
var myMessage
```

You'll often want to create a variable and fill it with useful content all in the same step. To store information in a variable, you use the equal sign (=), which copies the data on the right side of the equal sign into the variable on the left. Here's an example that puts some text into myMessage:

```
myMessage = "Everybody loves variables"
```

Remember, you need to use quotation marks whenever you include a text string. In contrast, if you want to copy a *number* into a variable, you don't need quotation marks:

```
myNumber = 27.3
```

JavaScript variables are case-sensitive, which means a variable named myMessage differs from one named MyMessage. This detail seems innocent enough, but it's the source of plenty of headaches (see the box on page 464).

■ MODIFYING VARIABLES

One of the most useful things you can do with numeric variables is perform *operations* on them to change your data. For example, you can use arithmetic operators to perform mathematical calculations:

```
var myNumber = (10 + 5) * 2 / 5
```

Phantom Variables

To make matters a little confusing, JavaScript lets you refer to variables you haven't yet declared. Doing so is considered extremely bad form and is likely to cause all sorts of problems. However, it's worth knowing that these undeclared variables are permissible, because they're the source of many an unexpected error.

For example, a common mistake is to declare a variable (say, bodyWeight) but then refer to it with a slightly different name (like bodyWght) or slightly different capitalization (like BodyWeight). In this situation, you've unwittingly created *two* variables. The usual result is a page that behaves strangely—for example, a page that performs a calculation but gets the wrong answer.

There's no easy way to defend yourself against this sort of mistake. If you suspect you have a variable with multiple personalities, you can add *undefined variable* checks to your code. Essentially, this means you check whether a suspect variable has been defined before you attempt to use it. You can read more about this technique at *http://tinyurl.com/undef-js*.

These calculations follow the standard order of operations (parentheses first, then multiplication and division, then addition and subtraction). The result of this calculation is 6.

You can also use operations to join together multiple pieces of text into one long string. In this case, you use the plus sign (+):

```
var firstName = "Sarah"
var lastName = "Smithers"
var fullName = firstName + " " + lastName
```

Now the fullName variable holds the text "Sarah Smithers." (The " " in the code above tells JavaScript to leave a space between the two names).

■ AN EXAMPLE WITH VARIABLES

Although you'd need to read a thick volume to learn everything there is to know about variables, you can pick up a lot from a simple example. The following script inserts the current date into a web page. The relevant lines of code are numbered for easy reference.

```
<!DOCTYPE html>
<html>
<head>
  <title>JavaScript Test</title>
</head>
<body>
  <h1>What Day Is It?</h1>
  <p>This page uses JavaScript.</p>
```

```
      <p>
      <script>
1         var currentDate = new Date()
2         var message = "The current date is: "
3         message = message + currentDate.toDateString()
4         document.write(message)
      </script>
      </p>
   </body>
   </html>
```

Here's what's happening, line by line:

1. **This line creates a variable named currentDate.**

   It fills the variable with a new Date object (see number 3 below). You'll know JavaScript is creating an object when you see the keyword new. (You'll learn more about objects on page 474; for now, it's enough to know that they come with built-in functions that work more or less the same way as the functions you learned about earlier.)

2. **This line creates a new variable named message.**

   It fills the variable with the beginning of a sentence that announces the date.

3. **This line adds some new text to the end of the message you created in line 2.**

   The text comes from the currentDate object. The tricky part is understanding that the currentDate object comes with a built-in function, toDateString(), that converts the date information it gets from your computer into a piece of text suitable for display in a browser (see Figure 14-2). Once again, this is the kind of detail you can only pick up by studying a good JavaScript reference.

4. **This line uses JavaScript's document object, which has a function named write().**

   The write() function displays a piece of text on a web page at the current location. The final result is a page that shows your welcome message (see Figure 14-3).

Scripts can get much more complex than this. For example, they can use loops to repeat a single action several times or make decisions using conditional logic. You'll see examples of some of these techniques later in this chapter, but you won't get a blow-by-blow exploration of the JavaScript language—in fact, that would require a small book of its own. If you want to learn more, check out a book like *JavaScript: The Missing Manual* (O'Reilly).

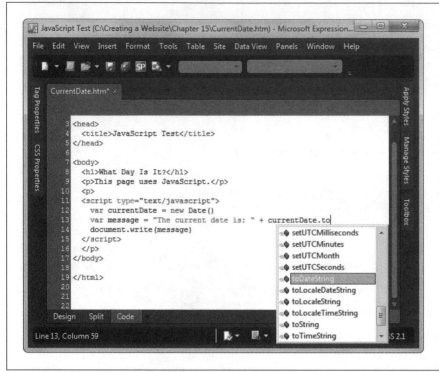

FIGURE 14-2

Some web page editors help out when you write JavaScript code. For example, Expression Web displays a drop-down menu that shows you all the functions an object provides. Although there probably isn't enough context for you to determine how to use the date object the first time out, it's a great way to refresh your memory later on.

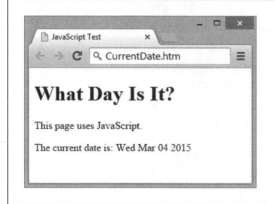

FIGURE 14-3

The document.write() *command inserts text directly into a page, wherever you position the script block. In this case, the command displays the current date.*

Spaces and Line Breaks in JavaScript

JavaScript code is quite tolerant of extra spaces. In this chapter, most of the examples use some sort of indenting to help you see the structure of the code. But, as with HTML, you don't absolutely have to add these spaces.

The only rule in JavaScript is that every code statement needs to be on a separate line. You can get around this limitation by using the line-termination character, which is a semicolon (;). For example, here's how you can compress three code statements onto one line:

```
alert("Hi"); alert("There"); alert("Dude");
```

Each semicolon designates the end of a code statement. This strange convention comes from the Bizarro world of the C and Java programming languages.

If you don't want to put more than one code statement on the same line, you don't need the semicolons. However, they can clarify your code, and they may help you catch certain types of mistakes. Web experts almost always use semicolons, and you'll find them in most any script that you download from the Web.

Functions

So far, you've seen scripts that use only a few lines of code. More realistic JavaScript scripts can run to dozens of lines, and if you're not careful, they can grow into a grotesque tangle that leaves the rest of your page difficult to edit. To control the chaos, smart JavaScripters almost always use *custom functions*.

A *function* is a series of code instructions you group together and give a name. In a way, functions are like miniature programs, because they can perform a series of operations. The neat thing about them is that once you create a function, you can use it over and over again.

■ DECLARING A FUNCTION

To create a JavaScript function, start by deciding what your function should do (like display an alert message), and then choose a suitable name for it (like ShowAlert-Box). As with most things in the programming world, function names can't have any spaces or special characters.

Now you're ready to put the ShowAlertBox <script> block in the <head> section of your page. But this <script> block looks a little different from the examples you've seen so far. Here's a complete function that shows an alert box with a predefined message:

```
<script>
  function ShowAlertBox() {
  alert("I'm a function.")
  }
</script>
```

To understand what's going on here, it helps to break down this example and consider it piece by piece.

Every time you declare a function, you start with the word *function*, which tells JavaScript what you're up to:

```
function
```

Then you add the name of your function, followed by two parentheses. You'll use the parentheses later to send extra information to your function, as you'll see shortly:

```
function ShowAlertBox()
```

At this point, you've finished *declaring* the function. All that remains is to add the code to the function that actually makes it work. To do this, you need the funny curly braces shown in the alert box function above. The { brace indicates the start of your function code, and the } brace indicates the end of it. You can put as many lines of code as you want in between.

One tricky part of function writing is the fact that JavaScript sets notoriously loose standards for line breaks. That means you can create an equivalent JavaScript function and put the curly braces on their own lines, like this:

```
<script>
  function ShowAlertBox()
  {
    alert("I'm a function.")
  }
</script>
```

But don't worry—both functions work exactly the same way.

TIP You can put as many functions as you want in a single `<script>` block. Just add them one after the other.

■ CALLING A FUNCTION

Creating a function is only half the battle. On their own, functions don't do anything. You have to *call* the function somewhere in your page to actually run the code. To call a function, you use the function name, followed by parentheses:

```
ShowAlertBox()
```

NOTE Don't leave out the parentheses after the function name. Otherwise, browsers will assume you're trying to use a variable rather than call a function.

You can call `ShowAlertBox()` anywhere you'd write ordinary JavaScript code. For example, here's a script that displays the alert message three times in a row to really hassle your visitors:

```
<script>
  ShowAlert()
  ShowAlert()
  ShowAlert()
</script>
```

This is the same technique you used to call the `alert()` function earlier. The difference is that `alert()` is built into JavaScript, while `ShowAlertBox()` is something you created. Also, the `alert()` function requires one argument, while `ShowAlertBox()` doesn't use any.

■ FUNCTIONS THAT RECEIVE INFORMATION

The `ShowAlertBox()` function is beautifully simple. You just call it, and it displays an alert box with the message you supplied. Most functions don't work this easily. In many cases, you need to send specific information to a function, or take the results of a function and use them in another operation.

For example, imagine you want to display a welcome message with some standard information in it, like the current date. But you also want the flexibility to change part of the message by substituting your own witty words each time you call the function. To do so, you need a way to call a function *and* to supply a text string with your message in it.

To solve this problem, you can create a `ShowAlertBox()` function that accepts a single *parameter*, or piece of information. In this case, that parameter is the customized text you want displayed in the alert box. To add the parameter, you must first give it a name, say `customMessage`, and put it in parentheses after the function name, like so:

```
function ShowAlertBox(customMessage) {
    ...
}
```

NOTE Technically, the pieces of information that a function receives (in this case, that's `customMessage`) are called *parameters*. When you call a function that has parameters, you pass the function one value for each parameter. The value you supply is called an *argument*.

In other words, the same piece of information is called a parameter from the function's point of view and an argument from the calling code's point of view. Sometimes, you'll hear the terms "parameter" and "argument" used interchangeably, but now you know the official difference.

There's no limit to how many pieces of information a function can accept. You just need to separate each parameter with a comma. Here's an example of the Show-AlertBox() function with three parameters, named `messageLine1`, `messageLine2`, and `messageLine3`:

```
function ShowAlertBox(messageLine1, messageLine2, messageLine3) {
    ...
}
```

Here's another example that shows a finished ShowAlertBox() function. It accepts a single parameter named customMessage, and it uses that parameter to create the text it displays in the alert box:

```
<script>
1    function ShowAlertBox(customMessage)
2    {
3        // Get the date.
4        var currentDate = new Date()
5
6        // Build the full message.
7        var fullMessage = "** IMPORTANT BULLETIN **\n\n"
8        fullMessage += customMessage + "\n\n"
9        fullMessage += "Generated at: " + currentDate.toTimeString() + "\n"
10       fullMessage += "This message courtesy of MagicMedia Inc."
11
12       // Show the message.
13       alert(fullMessage)
14   }
</script>
```

Here are some notes to help you wade through the code:

- Any line that starts with // is a comment (see lines 3 and 6). Good programmers include lots of comments to help others understand how a function works (and to help themselves remember what they did during a late-night coding binge). The browser ignores them.

- To put line breaks into an alert box, use the code \n (lines 7, 8, and 9). Each \n is equivalent to one line break. (This rule is for message boxes only. When you want a line break in HTML, use the familiar <br /> element.)

- To build the text for the fullMessage variable (lines 7 to 10), the code uses a shortcut in the form of the += operator. This operator automatically takes whatever's on the *right* side of the equal sign and pastes it onto the end of the variable on the *left* side. In other words, this:

```
8        fullMessage += customMessage + "\n\n"
```

is equivalent to this longer line:

```
8        fullMessage = fullMessage + customMessage + "\n\n"
```

Using this function is easy. Just remember that when you call it, you need to supply one argument for each parameter, separating them with a comma. In the case of the ShowAlertBox() function above, you only need to supply a single value for the customMessage variable. Here's an example:

```
<script>
  ShowAlertBox("This web page includes JavaScript functions.")
</script>
```

Figure 14-4 shows the result of this script.

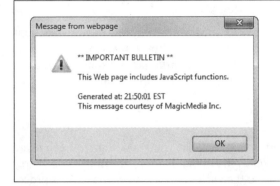

JAVASCRIPT 101

FIGURE 14-4

This message is built out of several pieces of text, one of which you supplied as an argument to the ShowAlertBox() function.

■ FUNCTIONS THAT RETURN INFORMATION

Parameters let you send information *to* a function. You can also create functions that send information *back* to the script that called the function in the first place. The key to doing this is the return command, which you put right at the end of your function. The return command ends the function immediately and spits out whatever information your function generates.

Of course, a sophisticated function can accept *and* return information. For example, here's a function that multiplies two numbers (the numberA and numberB parameters) and returns the result to anyone who's interested:

```
<script>
  function MultiplyNumbers(numberA, numberB)
  {
    return numberA * numberB
  }
</script>
```

Here's how you use this function elsewhere on your web page:

```
<p>The product of 3202 and 23405 is
<script>
  var product = MultiplyNumbers(3202, 23405)
  document.write(product)
</script>
</p>
```

This HTML includes a single line of text, followed by a block of script code. The script calls the `MultiplyNumbers()` function, gets the result (the number 74942810), and stuffs it in a variable named product for later use. The code then uses the `document.write()` command to display the contents of the product variable on the page. The final result is a paragraph with this text:

```
The product of 3202 and 23405 is 74942810
```

To use a typical script you get from the Web, you need to copy one or more functions into your page, and they're likely to look a lot more complex than what you've seen so far. However, now that you understand the basic structure of a function, you can wade through the code to get a fundamental understanding of what's taking place (or to at least pinpoint where the action goes down).

External Script Files

Reusing scripts inside a web page is neat, but did you know that you can share scripts *between* individual pages and even among different websites? You simply put your script into an external file and then link to it from a web page. This procedure is similar to the way you learned to link external style sheets back in Chapter 3.

For example, imagine you perfect the `ShowAlertBox()` routine so that it performs a complex task exactly the way you want it to, but it requires a couple of dozen lines of code. To simplify your life and your HTML document, create a new file to store that script.

Script files are always plain text files. Usually, they have the extension *.js* (for JavaScript). You put all your code inside a script file, but you don't include the `<script>` element. For example, you could create this JavaScript file named *ShowAlert.js*:

```
function ShowAlertBox()
{
  alert("This function is in an external file.")
}
```

Now save the file, and put it in the same folder as your web page. In your web page, define a script block but don't supply any code. Instead, add the `src` attribute and indicate the script file you want to link to:

```
<script src="ShowAlert.js">
</script>
```

When a browser comes across this script block, it requests the *ShowAlert.js* file and treats it as though the code were right inside the page. Here's a complete HTML test page that uses the *ShowAlert.js* file. The script in the body of the page calls the `ShowAlertBox()` function:

```
<!DOCTYPE html>
<html>
<head>
  <title>Show Alert</title>
```

```
<!-- Make all the functions in the ShowAlert.js file
  available in this page. Notice there's no actual content here. -->
<script src="ShowAlert.js">
</script>
</head>
<body>
  <!-- Test out one of the functions. -->
  <script>
    ShowAlertBox()
  </script>
</body>
</html>
```

There's no difference in the way an embedded or external script works. However, storing your scripts in separate files helps keep your website organized and makes it easy to reuse scripts across several pages. In fact, you can even link to JavaScript functions on another website—just remember that the src attribute in the <script> block needs to point to a full URL (like *http://SuperScriptSite.com/ShowAlert.js*) instead of just a filename. Of course, this technique is risky because the website owner might rename, move, or modify the JavaScript file. If you really want to use the code, it's far better to copy it to your own server to avoid this problem.

NOTE Using separate script files doesn't improve your security one iota. Because anyone can request your script file, a savvy web visitor can figure out what scripts your page uses and take a look at them. So never include any code or secret details in a script that you don't want the world to know about.

■ Dynamic HTML

JavaScript underwent a minor revolution in the late 1990s, adding support for a set of features called *dynamic HTML* (also shortened to DHTML). Dynamic HTML isn't a new technology—it's a fusion of three distinct ingredients:

- Scripting languages like JavaScript, which let you write code.

- The CSS (Cascading Style Sheet) standard, which lets you control the position and appearance of an HTML element.

- The HTML *document object model* (or DOM), which lets you treat an HTML page as a collection of *objects*.

The last point is the most important. Dynamic HTML sees a web page as a collection of *objects*. It treats each HTML element, including images, links, and even the lowly paragraph, as a separate programming ingredient that your JavaScript code can play with. Using these objects, you can change what each element looks like, or even where your browser places them on a page.

HTML Objects

Clearly, dynamic HTML requires a whole new way of thinking about web page design. Your scripts no longer look at your web page as a static block of HTML. Instead, they see a combination of *objects*.

Understanding Objects

In many programming languages, including JavaScript, everything revolves around objects. So what, exactly, is an object?

In the programming world, an object is nothing more than a convenient way to group some related features or information. For example, say you want to change the picture shown in an `<img>` element on a web page (which is useful if you want to write a script that flashes a series of images). In JavaScript, the easiest way to interact with an `<img>` element is to use the corresponding image object. In effect, the image object is a container holding all sorts of potentially useful information about what's happening inside an `<img>` element (including its dimensions, its position, the name of the image file associated with it, and so on). The image object also gives you a way to manipulate the `<img>` element—that is, to change some or all of these details.

For example, you can use an image object to get information about the image, like this:

```
document.write("The tooltip says" +
image.title)
```

You can even change one of these details. For example, you can modify the actual image that an `<img>` element shows by using this code:

```
image.src = "newpic.jpg"
```

You'll know an object's at work by the presence of a dot (.) in your code line. The dot separates the name of the variable (the first part) from one of the built-in functions it provides (called *methods*), or from one of the related variables (called *properties*). You always put methods and properties after a period.

In the previous examples, `src` and `title` are two of the image object's properties. In other words, the code statement `image.src = "newpic.jpg"` is equivalent to saying "Hey, Mr. Object named Image: I have a new picture for you. Change your `src` attribute to point to *newpic.jpg*."

Programmers embraced objects long ago because they're a great way to organize code conceptually (not to mention a great way to share and reuse it). You might not realize it at first, but working with the image object is actually easier than memorizing a few dozen different commands that manipulate the image itself.

Before you can manipulate an object on your web page, you need a way to uniquely identify it. Once you do, your code can find the object whenever it needs to. The best way to identify an object is with the `id` attribute. Add this attribute to the start tag for the element you want to manipulate and choose a unique name, as shown here:

```
<h1 id="PageTitle">Welcome to My Page</h1>
```

Once you give your element a unique ID, JavaScript can find it in your code and act on it.

JavaScript includes a handy way to locate an object: the `document.getElementById()` method. Basically, `document` is an object that represents your whole HTML document. It's always available, and you can use it anytime you want. This document object, like any object worthy of its name, lets you take advantage of some handy properties and methods. The `getElementById()` method is one of the coolest: It scans a page looking for a specific HTML element.

NOTE   In the example on page 465, you saw the document object at work on a different task—displaying information on a web page. To accomplish this feat, the script used the write() method of the document object.

When you call the document.getElementById() method, you supply the ID of the HTML element you're looking for. Here's an example that digs up the object for an HTML element that has the ID *PageTitle*:

```
var titleObject = document.getElementById("PageTitle")
```

This code gets the object for the <h1> element shown earlier and stores it in a variable named titleObject. By storing the object in a variable, you can perform a series of operations on it without having to look it up more than once.

So what, exactly, can you do with HTML objects? To a certain extent, the answer depends on the type of element you're working with. For example, if you have a hyperlink, you can change its URL. If you have an image, you can change its source. And you can apply some actions, like changing an element's style or modifying its text, to almost any HTML element. As you'll see, these actions are a good way to make your pages feel more dynamic—for example, you can change a page when a visitor takes an action, like clicking a link. Interactions like these make visitors feel as though they're using an intelligent, responsive program instead of a plain, inert web page.

Here's how you modify the text inside the just-mentioned <h1> element, for example:

```
titleObject.innerHTML = "This Page Is Dynamic"
```

If you use this code in a script, the headline text changes as soon as your browser runs the script.

This script works because it uses the *property* named innerHTML, which sets the content that's nested inside an element (in this case, the <title> element). Like all properties, innerHTML is just one aspect of an HTML object you can alter. To write JavaScript code like this, you need to know what properties the language lets you play with. Obviously, some properties apply to specific HTML elements only, like the src attribute of an image. But modern browsers boast a huge catalog of DOM properties you can use with just about any HTML element. Table 14-1 lists some of the most useful.

TIP   To figure out what properties you can use with a specific HTML element, check out the reference at *www.w3schools.com/jsref*.

Currently, the example above works in two steps (getting the object and then manipulating it). Although this two-step maneuver is probably the clearest approach, it's possible to combine these two steps into one line, which scripts often do. Here's an example:

```
document.getElementById("PageTitle").innerHTML = "This Page Is Dynamic"
```

This approach is more concise but also a bit more difficult to read.

TABLE 14-1 *Common HTML object properties.*

PROPERTY	DESCRIPTION
className	Lets you retrieve or set the class attribute (see page 85). In other words, this property determines what style (if any) this element uses. Of course, you need to define this style in an embedded or linked style sheet, or you'll end up with the plain-Jane default formatting.
innerHTML	Lets you read or change the HTML inside an element. This property is insanely useful, but it has two quirks. First, you can use it on all HTML content, including text and tags. So if you want to put bold text inside a paragraph, you can set innerHTML to `<b>Hi</b>`. Special characters aren't welcome—you need to replace them with the character entities described on page 63. Second, when you set innerHTML, you replace all the content inside this element, including any other HTML elements. So if you set the innerHTML of a `<div>` element that contains several paragraphs and images, all these items disappear, to be replaced by your new content. To modify just part of a paragraph, wrap that part in a `<span>` element.
parentElement	Provides the HTML object for the element that contains this element. For example, if the current element is a `<b>` element in a paragraph, this gets the object for the `<p>` element. Once you have this object, you can modify the paragraph. Using this technique (and other similar techniques in dynamic HTML), you can jump from one element to another.
style	Bundles together all the CSS attributes that determine the appearance of the HTML element. Technically, the style property returns a full-fledged style object, and you need to add another dot (.) and the name of the style attribute you want to change, as in myObject.style.fontSize. You can use the style object to dictate colors, borders, fonts, and even positioning.
tagName	Provides the name of the HTML element for this object, without the angle brackets. For example, if the current object represents an `<img>` element, this returns the text "img."

■ USING HTML OBJECTS IN A SCRIPT

The easiest way to come to grips with how HTML objects work is to look at an example. The web pages shown in Figure 14-5 include a paragraph that continuously grows and then shrinks, as your code periodically tweaks the font size.

The way this example works is interesting. First of all, you define two variables in the `<head>` section of your HTML. The size variable keeps track of the current size of the text (which starts out at 10 pixels). The growIncrement variable determines how much the text size changes each time your browser runs the code (initially, it grows by 2 pixels at a time):

```
<!DOCTYPE html>
<html>
<head>
  <title>Dynamic HTML</title>
  <script>
    // The current font size.
    var size = 10
    // The amount the font size is changing.
    var growIncrement = 2
```

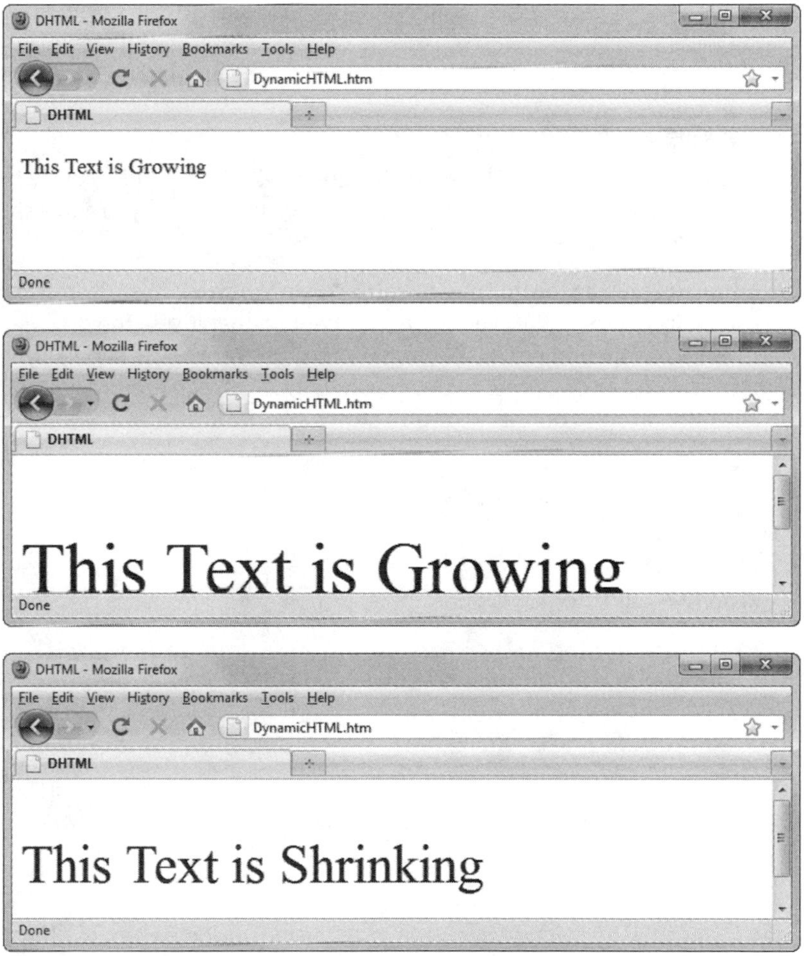

FIGURE 14-5

If you were looking at
this heading in a live web
browser, you'd see that the
text is always changing
size, making it difficult to
ignore.

Next, the script defines a function named ChangeFont(). This function retrieves the
HTML object, here the <p> element holding the text that will grow and shrink. Once
again, the getElementById() function does the job:

```
function ChangeFont() {
  // Find object that represents the paragraph
  // whose text size you want to change.
  var paragraph = document.getElementById("animatedParagraph")
```

Now, using the `size` and `growIncrement` variables, you define a variable that performs a calculation to determine the new size for the paragraph:

```
size = size + growIncrement
```

In this example, the + performs a numeric addition, because both the size and grow-Increment variables store a number.

It's just as easy to set the new size using the `paragraph.style.fontSize` property. Just tack the letters *px* on the end to indicate that your style setting is measured in pixels:

```
paragraph.style.fontSize = size + "px"
```

If this code runs perpetually, you'll eventually end up with text so ridiculously huge you can't see any of it on the page. To prevent this from happening, you add a safety valve to the code.

Say you decide that, when the text size hits 100 pixels, you want to stop enlarging it and start shrinking it. To do this, you write the script so that it sets the `growIncrement` variable to −2 when the text size reaches 100. The text starts shrinking from that point on, two pixels at a time. To detect when the message has grown too big, you use conditional logic courtesy of the `if` statement. Here's what it looks like:

```
// Decide whether to reverse direction from
// growing to shrinking (or vice versa).
if (size > 100) {
  paragraph.innerHTML = "This Text is Shrinking"
  growIncrement = -2
}
```

Of course, you don't want the shrinking to go on forever, either. So it makes sense to add a check that determines whether the text has shrunk to 10 pixels or less, in which case the script goes back to enlarging the text by setting growIncrement back to 2:

```
if (size < 10) {
  paragraph.innerHTML = "This Text is Growing"
  growIncrement = 2
}
```

Now, here comes the really crafty bit. JavaScript includes a `setTimeout()` function that lets you instruct a browser to "call this function, but wait a bit before you do." In this example, the `setTimeout()` function instructs the browser to call the Change-Font() method again in 100 milliseconds (one-tenth of a second):

```
    setTimeout("ChangeFont()", 100)
  }
  </script>
</head>
```

Because the `ChangeFont()` function always uses `setTimeout()` to call itself again, the shrinking and growing never stop. However, you can alter this behavior. You could, for example, add conditional logic so that JavaScript calls the `setTimeout()` method only a certain number of times.

The last detail is the <body> section, which contains the actual paragraph that you resize and a script that calls `ChangeFont()` for the first time, starting off the whole process:

```
<body>
  <p id="animatedParagraph">This Text is Growing</p>
  <script>
    ChangeFont()
  </script>
</body>
</html>
```

Although the resizing-paragraph example is absurdly impractical, the technique it uses is the basis for many much more impressive scripts. (To get the whole script and play around with it, download it from the companion site at *http://prosetech. com/web*.) For example, you can easily find scripts that animate text in various ways, like making it sparkle, fly in from the side of the page, or appear one letter at a time, typewriter-style.

Events

The most exciting JavaScript-powered pages are *dynamic*, which means they perform various actions as your visitor interacts with them (moving his mouse, typing in text, clicking things, and so on). A dynamic page is far more exciting than an ordinary HTML page, which appears in a browser and then sits there, immobile.

To create dynamic pages, you program them to react to JavaScript *events*. Events are notifications that an HTML element sends out when specific things happen.

For example, JavaScript gives every <a> hyperlink element an event named onmouseover (a compressed version of "on mouse-over"). As the name suggests, this event takes place (or *fires*, to use programmer-speak) when a visitor points to an HTML element like a paragraph, link, image, table cell, or text box. That action triggers the onmouseover event, and your code flies into action.

Here's an example that displays an alert message when a visitor points to a link:

```html
<!DOCTYPE html>
<html>
<head>
  <title>JavaScript Test</title>
</head>
<body>
  <h1>You Will Be Wowed (Again)</h1>
  <p>When you hover over <a href="SomePage.htm"
  onmouseover="alert('Colorless green ideas sleep furiously.')">this link</a>
  you'll see a secret message.
  </p>
</body>
</html>
```

When you write the code that makes a page react to an event, you don't absolutely need a script block (although it's a good idea to use one anyway, as shown in the next section). Instead, you can just put your code between quotation marks next to the event attribute:

```html
<a onmouseover="[Code goes here]">...</a>
```

Notice that, in this example, the text value ('Colorless green...') uses single quotation marks instead of double quotes. That's because the event attribute itself uses double quotes, and simultaneously using double quotes for two different purposes will horribly confuse your browser.

Figure 14-6 shows the result of running this script and pointing to the link.

FIGURE 14-6

In this example, the alert box doesn't pop up until you point to the link.

To use events effectively, you need to know what events each HTML element triggers. For example, almost any element can trigger an onClick event when it's clicked, but it takes a text box or a list box to notify you about changes with the onChange event. Table 14-2 provides a list of commonly used JavaScript events and the HTML elements they apply to (and you can find a more complete reference at *www.w3schools.com/jsref*).

In the following sections, you'll learn about two common scenarios that use some of these events.

TABLE 14-2 *Common HTML object events.*

EVENT NAME (WITH UPPERCASE LETTERS)	DESCRIPTION	APPLIES TO THESE HTML ELEMENTS
onClick	Triggered when you click an element.	Almost all
onMouseOver	Triggered when you point to an element.	Almost all
onMouseOut	Triggered when you move your mouse away from an element.	Almost all
onKeyDown	Triggered when you press a key.	<select>, <input>, <textarea>, <a>, <button>
onKeyUp	Triggered when you release a pressed key.	<select>, <input>, <textarea>, <a>, <button>
onFocus	Triggered when a control receives focus (in other words, when you position your cursor in the control so you can type something in). Controls include text boxes, checkboxes, and so on—see page 490 to learn more.	<select>, <input>, <textarea>, <a>, <button>
onBlur	Triggered when focus leaves a control.	<select>, <input>, <textarea>, <a>, <button>
onChange	Triggered when you change a value in an input control. In a text box, this event doesn't fire until you move to another control.	<select>, <input type="text">, <textarea>
onSelect	Triggered when you select a portion of text in an input control.	<input type="text">, <textarea>
onError	Triggered when your browser fails to download an image (usually due to an incorrect URL).	<img>
onLoad	Triggered when your browser finishes downloading a new page or finishes loading an object, like an image.	<img>, <body>
onUnload	Triggered when a browser closes ("unloads") a page. (This typically happens after you enter a new URL or when you click a link. It fires just *before* the browser downloads the new page.)	<body>

Image Rollovers

One of the most popular mouse events is the *image rollover*. To write one, you start by creating an <img> element that displays a picture. Then, when a visitor points to the image, her browser displays a new picture, thanks to the onmouseover event. Creating an image rollover is fairly easy. All you do is get the HTML object for the <img> element and then modify the src property.

But you can't do that with a single line of code. While you could pile your entire script into the event attribute (using semicolons to separate each line), the markup would look confusing. A better choice is to write the code as a function. You can then hook the element up to the function using the event attribute.

Here's the function that swaps an image, for example. In this script, the function is written in a very generic way using parameters, so you can use it over and over, as you'll see in a moment. Every time you call the function, you indicate which image you want to change (by supplying the corresponding ID) and what new image you want to use. Because the function uses parameters, you can use it anywhere on your page.

```
<script>
  function ChangeImage(imageName, newImageFile) {
    // Find the object that represents the img element.
    var image = document.getElementById(imageName)

    // Change the picture.
    image.src = newImageFile
  }
</script>
```

When you create an image rollover, you use two events. The onmouseover event switches to the rollover picture, and the onmouseout event (triggered when your visitor moves her mouse *off* the HTML element) switches back to the original picture. Figure 14-7 shows the result.

```
<img id="SwappableImage" src="ClickMe.gif" alt=""
onmouseover="ChangeImage('SwappableImage', 'LostInterestMessage.gif')"
onmouseout="ChangeImage('SwappableImage', 'ClickMe.gif')" />
```

To add more rollover images, just add a new <img> element with a different name. The following element uses the same initial image (*ClickMe.gif*) but shows a different rollover image (*PleasePleaseMessage.gif*) when a visitor points to the image:

```
<img id="SwappableImage2" src="ClickMe.gif" alt=""
onmouseover="ChangeImage('SwappableImage2', 'PleasePleaseMessage.gif')"
onmouseout="ChangeImage('SwappableImage2', 'ClickMe.gif')" />
```

If you want to get really fancy, you can even use the onclick event (which guests trigger when they click an element) to throw yet another picture into the mix.

FIGURE 14-7

A rollover image in action.

NOTE In Chapter 15, you'll see a different way to approach image rollovers—using CSS. Although the CSS technique doesn't work in every situation, it's a great tool for building basic rollover buttons.

Collapsible Text

Another nifty way to use events is to create *collapsible pages*. The basic idea behind a collapsible page is this: If you've got a lot of information to show your visitors but don't want to overload them with a lengthy page, you hide (or collapse) chunks of text behind headlines that guests can click to see the details (see Figure 14-8).

Dynamic HTML gives you many ways to trick browsers into hiding text, and the next example shows one of the best. The technique involves the CSS display property. When you set this property to block, an item appears in the HTML page in the normal way. But when you set it to none, the element disappears, along with everything inside it.

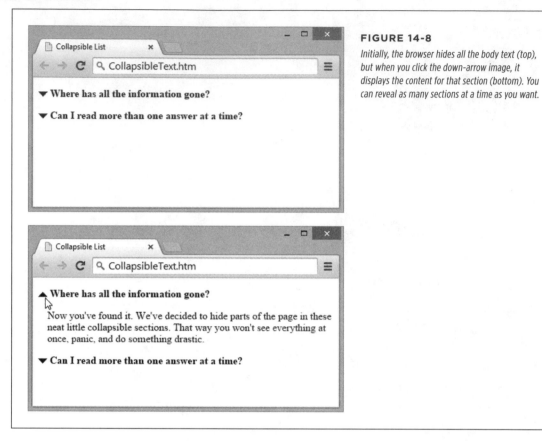

FIGURE 14-8
Initially, the browser hides all the body text (top), but when you click the down-arrow image, it displays the content for that section (bottom). You can reveal as many sections at a time as you want.

Your first task in building a collapsible page is creating the function that hides and then shows your content. The function requires two parameters: the name of the open/close arrow image and the name of the element you want to hide or show. The function actually does double-duty: It checks the current state of the section, and then it changes that state. In other words, it automatically shows a hidden section and automatically hides a displayed section, thanks to conditional logic. And while the function's doing that, it swaps the open/close image to display a different type of arrow.

NOTE The practice where you reverse the current state of an item is called *toggling* by jargon-happy programmers.

```
<script>
  function ToggleVisibility(image, element){
    // Find the image.
    var image = document.getElementById(image)

    // Find the element to hide/unhide.
    var element = document.getElementById(element)

    // Check the element's current state.
    if (element.style.display == "none"){
      // If hidden, unhide it.
      element.style.display = "block"
      image.src = "open.png"
    }
    else
    {
      // If not hidden, hide it.
      element.style.display = "none"
      image.src = "closed.png"
    }
  }
</script>
```

The code starts out by looking up the two objects you need (the arrow and the text block) and storing them in the variables image and element. Then it gets to work. It looks at the current state of the paragraph and makes a decision (using an if statement) about whether it needs to show or hide the text. Only one part of this conditional code runs. For example, if a browser is currently hiding the image (that is, if you set the display style to none), the function runs just these two lines of code, skips to the bottom of the function, and then ends:

```
element.style.display = "block"
image.src = "open.png"
```

On the other hand, if the browser is displaying the image, this code gets a chance to prove itself:

```
element.style.display = "none"
image.src = "closed.png"
```

To use this function, you need to add the <img> element that guests click to see or hide the text, along with the HTML element that contains the text. You can show or hide virtually any HTML element, but a good all-purpose choice is a <div> element because you can stuff whatever you want to hide inside it. Here's an example:

```
<p>
  <img id="Question1Image" src="closed.png" alt=""
  onclick="ToggleVisibility('Question1Image','HiddenAnswer1')" />
  <b>Where has all the information gone?</b>
</p>

<div id="HiddenAnswer1">
  <p>Now you've found it. We've decided to hide parts of the
  page in these neat little collapsible sections. That way you won't
  see everything at once, panic, and do something drastic.</p>
</div>
```

The first part of the markup, between the first set of <p> tags, defines the question heading, which visitors always see. It contains the arrow image and the question (in bold). The second part (in the <div> element) is the answer, which your code alternately shows or hides.

Best of all, because you put all the complicated stuff into a function, you can reuse the function to make additional collapsible sections. These sections have the same structure but different contents:

```
<p>
  <img id="Question2Image" src="closed.png" alt=""
  onclick="ToggleVisibility('Question2Image','HiddenAnswer2')" />
  <b>Can I read more than one answer at a time?</b>
</p>

<div id="HiddenAnswer2" style="display:none">
  <p>You can expand as many or as few sections as you want.
  Once you've expanded a section, just click again to collapse it back up
  out of sight. The only rule is that when you leave this page and come back
  later, everything will be hidden all over again. That's just the way
  JavaScript and Dynamic HTML work.</p>
</div>
```

Notice that you have to give each <img> and <div> element a unique ID or your function won't know which picture to change and which section to hide.

Optionally, you can change this page to give it a different feel but keep the same collapsing behavior. For example, you can make the page easier to use by letting your visitor expand and collapse sections by clicking the heading text (instead of just the image). The easiest way to do this is to pop the image and the bold heading into a <div> element and then add the onclick event attribute to it. Here's the change you'd make:

```
<div onclick="ToggleVisibility('Question1Image','HiddenAnswer1')">
  <p>
  <img id="Question1Image" src="closed.png">
  <b>Where has all the information gone?</b>
  </p>
</div>
```

You could even underline the heading text so that it looks like a link, which lets viewers know something will happen if they click it. Use the text-decoration style sheet property to do that (page 96).

Finally, if you want all your collapsible sections to start off as collapsed, you need to add another script that performs this service. Here's the <script> block you need, which you can position at the end of your page, just before the closing </body> tag:

```
<script>
  // Hide all sections, one by one.
  ToggleVisibility('Question1Image','HiddenAnswer1')
  ToggleVisibility('Question2Image','HiddenAnswer2')
  ...
</script>
```

You could hide your collapsible sections more easily by setting the display style property on each <div> element with an inline style rule (page 80). However, this approach can cause trouble in the unlikely event that a visitor has turned JavaScript off in his browser. In this situation, every section will remain permanently hidden. By using the code approach shown here, you ensure that JavaScript-challenged browsers will simply display all the content, including the collapsible sections. The page won't be as impressive, but at least nothing goes missing. This approach, called *progressive enhancement*, makes sure a page works for everyone but adds benefits where possible.

> **NOTE** You'll see more collapsible text effects when you tackle collapsible menus in Chapter 15.

Interactive Forms

HTML forms inhabit a corner of the HTML standard you haven't explored yet. You can use form elements to create the graphical widgets that make up forms, like text boxes, buttons, checkboxes, and lists. Visitors interact with these components, which are commonly called *controls*, to answer questions and provide information. Figure 14-9 shows an example of an HTML form in action.

HTML forms are an indispensable technology for many websites, but you probably won't get much mileage out of them. That's because they're a hallmark of server-side web applications (page 458). In a typical form, a visitor types in information and then clicks a Submit button. The browser then collects that information and sends it back to the web server for further processing. This processing might involve storing the information in a database or sending back another page with different HTML (for example, an error message if the application detects a problem).

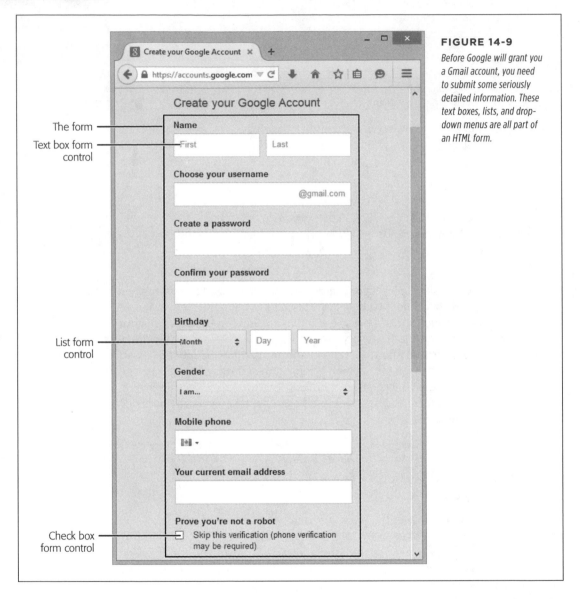

The form

Text box form control

List form control

Check box form control

FIGURE 14-9

Before Google will grant you a Gmail account, you need to submit some seriously detailed information. These text boxes, lists, and drop-down menus are all part of an HTML form.

However, a crafty JavaScript developer can still put a basic form to good use. The difference is that instead of sending information back to a web server, the form collects the data and sends it to a JavaScript routine. That JavaScript code then takes the next step, such as performing a calculation or updating the page.

■ FORM ELEMENTS

Every HTML form starts out with a `<form>` element. Because `<form>` is a container element, HTML interprets everything inside it as part of your form.

```
<form>
  ...
</form>
```

Form elements are also block elements (page 30). When you create a form, your browser adds a little bit of space and starts you off on a new line.

What goes inside your `<form>` element? You can put ordinary content (like paragraphs of text) inside or outside it—it really doesn't matter. But you should always put form controls (those graphical components, like buttons, text boxes, and lists) *inside* a `<form>` element. Otherwise, you won't have any way to capture the information a visitor types in.

To create controls, you use yet another set of HTML elements. Here's the weird part: most form controls use the *exact same* element. That element is named `<input>`, and it represents information you want to get *from* a visitor. You choose the type of input control using a type attribute. For example, to create a checkbox, you use the checkbox type:

```
<input type="checkbox" />
```

To create a text box (where a visitor types in whatever text he wants), you use the text attribute:

```
<input type="text" />
```

Every `<input>` element also supports a value attribute, which you usually use to set the initial state of a control. For example, to put instructions inside a text box when a page first appears, you could use this markup:

```
<input type="text" value="Enter the first name here" />
```

Checkboxes are a little different. You can start them off so that they're turned on by adding the checked attribute, as shown here:

```
<input type="checkbox" checked />
```

Not all controls use the `<input>` element. In fact, there are two notable exceptions. You use the `<textarea>` element to grab large amounts of text—copy that spans more than one line, like a comment a guest leaves. And you use the `<select>` element to create a list from which a visitor must select an item. Table 14-3 lists the most common controls. It doesn't include the new form ingredients that have been added in HTML5 (and that Internet Explorer 8 and earlier don't recognize).

TABLE 14-3 *Form controls.*

CONTROL	HTML ELEMENT	DESCRIPTION
Single-line text box	`<input type="text" />` `<input type="password" />`	Displays a box where visitors can type in text. If you use the password type of text box, the browser won't display the text. Instead, visitors see an asterisk (*) or a bullet (•) in place of each letter they type, hiding it from prying eyes.
Multiline text box	`<textarea>...</textarea>`	Shows a large text box that can fit multiple lines of text.
Checkbox	`<input type="checkbox" />`	Shows a checkbox you can turn on or off.
Radio button	`<input type="radio" />`	Shows a radio button (a circle) you can turn on or off. Usually, you have a group of radio buttons next to one another, in which case the visitor can select only one.

Button	`<input type="submit" />`
	`<input type="image" />`
	`<input type="reset" />`
	`<input type="button" />`
		Shows the standard clickable button. A *submit* button always gathers up the form data and sends it to its destination. An *image* button does the same thing but lets you display a clickable picture instead of the standard text-on-a-button. A *reset* button clears the visitor's selections and text from all the input controls. A *button* button doesn't do anything unless you add some JavaScript code.

List	`<select>...</select>`	Shows a list where your visitor can select one or more items. You add an `<option>` element for each item in the list.

■ A BASIC FORM

To create a complete form, you mix and match `<input>` elements with ordinary HTML. Consider the page shown in Figure 14-10. It provides several text boxes where a visitor types in numbers, and then it uses those numbers to determine the guest's body mass index (BMI) when he clicks the Calculate button.

Building this form is surprisingly easy. The trickiest part is creating the function that powers the underlying calculations.

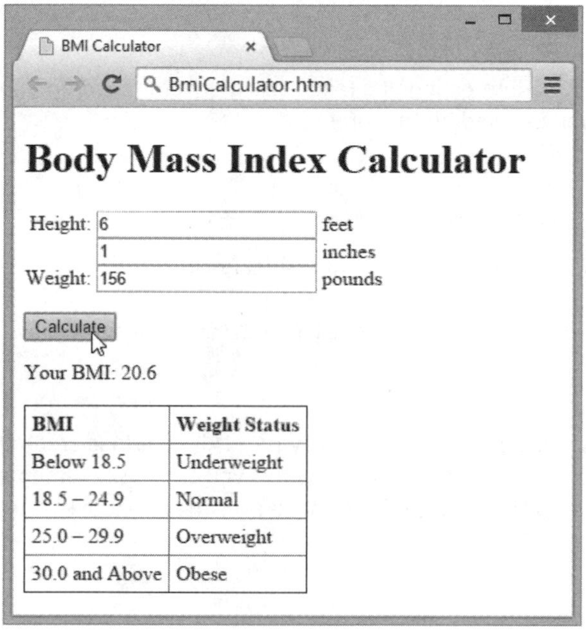

FIGURE 14-10

Most visitors are concerned about what this BMI calculator says about their health, but you can see single-line text boxes and a submit button (labeled "Calculate" here) at work.

This function needs several pieces of information, corresponding to the values in the three text boxes (feet, inches, and pounds). It also needs the name of the element where it should display the results. Here's how the function starts:

```
<script>
    function CalculateBMI(feet, inches, pounds, resultElementName) {
```

> **NOTE** You could create a CalculateBMI() function that doesn't use any parameters. Instead, the function could just search for all the controls on the page by name. However, using parameters is always a good idea, because it makes your code more flexible. For example, if you decide to change the names of the controls in your form, you don't need to change the code inside the CalculateBMI() function, just the line of code that calls CalculateBMI(). You're also able to move your function to a different page, or—in a more advanced scenario—to use it with data that you've retrieved from somewhere else other than a form.

The function code that follows isn't much different from what you've seen before. It begins by using a Number() function that's part of the JavaScript standard. This function converts the text a visitor types in to numbers that the function can use in calculations. If you don't take this step, you might still get the right answer (sometimes), because JavaScript can automatically convert text strings into numbers as needed. However, there's a catch—if you try to *add* two numbers and JavaScript thinks they're strings, it will just join the two strings into one piece of text, so 1+1 would get you 11. This mistake can really scramble your calculations, so it's best to always use the Number() function, like so:

```
inches = Number(inches)
pounds = Number(pounds)
feet = Number(feet)
```

The actual calculation isn't too interesting. It's taken straight from the definition of body mass index, which you can find on the Internet.

```
var totalInches = (feet * 12) + inches
```

Finally, the function displays the result:

```
var resultElement = document.getElementById(resultElementName)
resultElement.innerHTML =
  Math.round(pounds * 703 * 10 / totalInches / totalInches) / 10
}
</script>
```

Building the form that uses this function is the easy part. All you do is create the text boxes with <input> elements and give them names you can easily remember. In the example below, the form uses a table to make sure the text boxes line up neatly next to one another:

```
<form action="">
  <table>
    <tr>
    <td>Height: </td>
    <td><input type="text" name="feet" /> feet</td>
    </tr>
    <tr>
    <td> </td>
    <td><input type="text" name="inches" /> inches</td>
    </tr>
    <tr>
    <td>Weight: </td>
    <td><input type="text" name="pounds" /> pounds</td>
    </tr>
  </table>
```

Finally, at the bottom of the form, you create a button that calls the CalculateBMI() function using the form's values. To have the button make this call, you need to program your page to react to the onclick event. To look up a value in a form, you don't need the getElementById() function. Instead, you find it by name, using the this.form object, which represents the current form:

```
<p>
    <input type="button" name="calc" value="Calculate"
    onclick="CalculateBMI(this.form.feet.value, this.form.inches.value,
this.form.pounds.value, 'result')" />
    </p>
</form>
```

The final ingredient is the element that displays the result. In this case, because you want the result to appear inside another paragraph, the <span> element makes more sense than a <div> element.

```
<p>
    Your BMI: <span id="result"></span>
</p>
```

You can use all sorts of other form-related scripts. For example, you can check the information that people enter into forms for errors before letting them continue from one page to another. To learn more about these scripts, you need to take your search to the Web, as described in the next section.

■ Scripts on the Web

JavaScript is a truly powerful tool. If you're a die-hard alpha nerd who likes to program your TiVo to talk to your BlackBerry, you'll enjoy long nights of JavaScript coding. However, if you don't like to lie awake wondering what var howMany = (trueTop>1?"s" :""); really means, you'll probably be happier letting someone else do the heavy lifting.

If you fall into the nonprogrammer camp, this chapter has some good news. The Web is flooded with free JavaScript. Most of the time, these scripts include step-by-step instructions that explain where to put the functions, what elements to use in your page, and how to hook your elements up to functions using events.

However, there's a downside to free JavaScript. As you learned at the beginning of this chapter, JavaScript dates back to the early days of the Internet, and many JavaScript sites are nearly as old. As a result, they may feature garish formatting, out-of-date browser compatibility information (for example, they might warn you that a script doesn't work on the long-deceased Netscape browser), and old approaches that have been replaced with more modern techniques. Many JavaScript sites are also chock-full of ads.

If these issues haven't discouraged you, here are a few starting points for your JavaScript search:

www.dynamicdrive.com

>This site provides a set of respectable scripts that emphasize Dynamic HTML. Some scripts create exotic effects, like glowing green letters that tumble down the page, *Matrix*-style.

http://lokeshdhakar.com/projects/lightbox2

This site has just a single script, but it's one of the most popular effects on the Web. If you've ever clicked a picture thumbnail and had it expand to full size (while the rest of the page goes subtly dark), you've seen a variation of this effect.

http://tinyurl.com/webmonkey-js

The Web Monkey site offers a small set of old but still useful JavaScript tutorials, which can help you get oriented in the language—and pick up a few core techniques.

Using this list, you can dig up everything from little frills to complete, functioning Tetris clones. But keep in mind that a script is only as good as the coder who created it. Even on sites with good quality control, you could stumble across a script that doesn't work on all browsers or slows your page down to a crawl. As a rule of thumb, always try out each script thoroughly before you start using it on your site.

> **TIP** The hallmark of a good script site is that it's easy to navigate. You'll know you've found a bad script site if it's so swamped with ads and pop-ups that you can't find the scripts themselves.

Finding a Simple Script

Ready to hunt for scripts online? The next series of steps takes you through the process from beginning to end.

1. **Fire up your browser and choose your site from the list above.**

   For this example, use *www.dynamicdrive.com*.

2. **Choose the category you want from the site's home page.**

   In this case, go to the Documents Effects category. For a sample of what else you can find, see the box on page 495.

3. **Scroll through the list of scripts in your category (Figure 14-11), and then click one.**

   In this case, use the Top-Down Stripy Curtain script.

4. **The next page shows an example of the script (Figure 14-12).**

   Once the demo is over, you'll see a script description, the author's name, and a link to the script (if it isn't already displayed on the page). Underneath all this information are the step-by-step instructions for using the script.

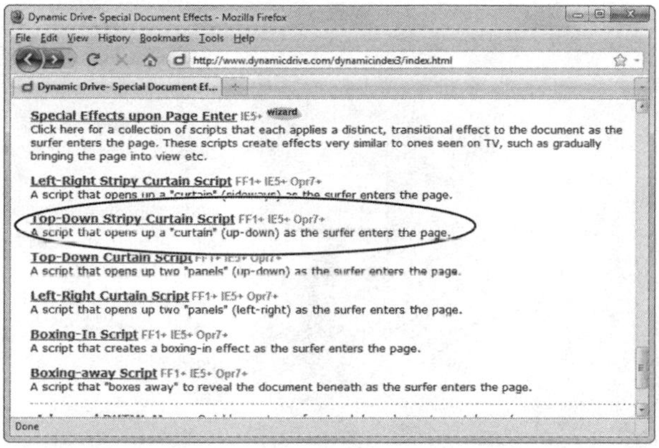

FIGURE 14-11

The Top-Down Stripy Curtain script is good to go, with support for all modern browsers.

Script Categories

To get a handle on the types of dynamic HTML scripts available, look through the categories at Dynamic Drive (*www.dynamic drive.com*). Here's a sampling of what you'll find:

- The Calendars category scripts produce nifty HTML that creates calendars—great for displaying important dates or letting visitors plan in advance.

- The Date & Time category offers virtual timekeepers and countdown clocks.

- The Document Effects category provides page transitions and background effects (like fireworks or floating stars).

- The Dynamic Content category has sliding menus, sticky notes, and scrollable panels.

- The Form Effects category includes scripts that let you manage forms (see page 487). You can use them to make sure visitors submit forms only once, to check for invalid entries, and more.

- The Games category offers full-blown miniature games, like tic-tac-toe and Tetris. These games stretch the capabilities of JavaScript and dynamic HTML as far as they can go.

- The Image Effects category has slideshow and image-gallery scripts, along with images that change when you point to them.

- The Links & Tooltips category includes fancy links that flash, button tricks, and pop-up text boxes that capture your visitors' attention.

- The Menus & Navigation category provides handy collapsible menus and navigation bars that let visitors move through your site, like the components you'll see in Chapter 15.

- The Mouse and Cursor category offers scripts that change the mouse pointer and add those annoying mouse trails (pictures that follow the mouse pointer wherever it goes).

- The Scrollers category has marquee-style scrolling text, like you might see in a news ticker.

- The Text Animations category scripts bring text to life, making it shake, fly, glow, or take on even more bizarre characteristics.

- The User/System Preference category scripts dig up information about the browser that's currently displaying your page.

- The Window and Frames category has scripts for a dozen types of pop-up windows.

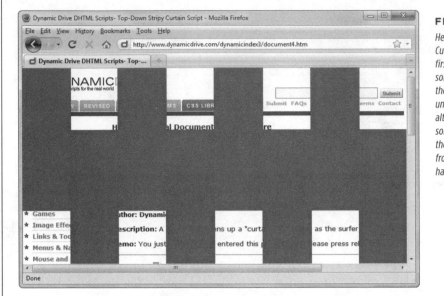

FIGURE 14-12

Here's the Top-Down Stripy Curtain script in action. It first fills the page with a solid green foreground and then exposes the content underneath by removing alternating strips of color, some of which fall from the top, while others rise from the bottom. It all happens in a flash.

5. **Follow the instructions to copy and paste the different parts of the script into your page (Figure 14-13).**

   You often get a set of functions you need to put in the <head> portion of your page and then some HTML elements you need to place in the <body> section. In some cases, you can customize the scripts—for example, you might modify numbers and other values to tweak the script code, or change the HTML elements to provide different content.

   NOTE Many scripts include a set of comments with author information. If they do, the standard practice is to keep these comments in your script file, so other developers who check out your site will know where the code came from. This practice is just part of giving credit where credit's due. Ordinary web visitors won't even think to look at the script code, so they won't have any idea whether or not you wrote the script from scratch.

JavaScript Libraries

In the years since JavaScript was first created, coders have shifted focus to JavaScript *libraries*. These libraries go beyond a hodgepodge of individual scripts—they offer a whole new set of JavaScript capabilities, extending the language so you don't need to write every piece of interactive code from scratch.

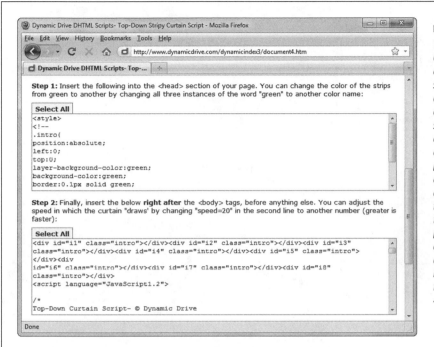

FIGURE 14-13

The Top-Down Stripy Curtain script has two components. The first is a style definition that produces the curtain's solid-color background. The second part creates the curtain itself (as a <div> element), which disappears to expose the page's content and includes the code that performs the transition. Copy both of these components to any page, and you're set. (For even better organization, consider placing the code in a separate JavaScript file, as described on page 472.)

Even better, the programs you find in JavaScript libraries have been tested to ensure that they work in all of today's browsers—sometimes using huge reams of behind-the-scenes code to do so. And super-smart programmers use JavaScript libraries to build even more useful scripts and self-contained web widgets, like slideshows, product carousels, dynamic charts, and image magnifiers. These slick scripts go far beyond the examples you'll find on an old-fashioned JavaScript site. For all these reasons, professional web developers almost always use JavaScript libraries.

When you first dip your toe into the world of JavaScript libraries, the best starting point is the wildly successful jQuery library (*http://jquery.com*). It's by far the most popular JavaScript library, playing a major or minor role in more than half of the world's most trafficked websites. More than a dozen other JavaScript libraries also flourish on the Web, including MooTools (*http://mootools.net*) and Dojo (*http://dojotoolkit.org*).

If you've never touched a line of programming until this chapter, JavaScript libraries might not be for you. That's because they're designed for other programmers—people who want to create their own JavaScript-fueled web pages, but don't want to reinvent the wheel. Mere mortals can use them, but there's a steep learning curve. If you're just getting started, you can check out *JavaScript: The Missing Manual* (O'Reilly), which describes JavaScript basics and the ins and outs of the jQuery library.

Dynamic Buttons and Menus

O ver the past 14 chapters, you've absorbed a fair amount of web wisdom. You learned to structure web pages using HTML, clothe them with style sheets, and breathe life into them with JavaScript. Now it's time to reap some of the rewards.

In this chapter, you'll consider two common (and practical) web page components. First, you'll learn how to create fancy buttons—for example, ones that light up when a guest points to them. Next, you'll learn to build a pop-up or pop-open navigation menu, so visitors can cruise around your site in style. These features give you the chance to take the skills you've developed in CSS and JavaScript one step further. In other words, it's time for your hard slogging to pay off with some snazzy website frills.

■ Fancy Buttons

The trends and styles of web design are always changing. In the early days of the Web, everyone used ordinary text links, like the ones you learned about in Chapter 6:

```
<a href="graceland.html">Visit Elvis</a>
```

Over time, these run-of-the-mill links started to look drab. Creative webmasters wanted more, and they decided to use small, clickable pictures, drawn to resemble buttons, instead.

Ordinary Picture Buttons

The most straightforward approach to creating a graphical button is to wrap the button image in an anchor, as described in Chapter 6. Here's what that looks like:

```
<a href="graceland.html"><img src="VisitElvis.jpeg" alt="Visit Elvis" /></a>
```

When you use this method, HTML adds an ugly blue border around the image to indicate that it's a link. To get rid of the border, you set CSS's border-style attribute to none.

The second, alternative approach is to use the <img> element in conjunction with JavaScript's onclick event attribute (page 481). Here's what that looks like:

```
<img onclick="GoToGraceland()" src="VisitElvis.jpeg" alt="Visit Elvis" />
```

This method doesn't generate an ugly blue border, so you don't need to set the border-style attribute, but you do need to create a JavaScript function named GoToGraceland() and write some code to do whatever you want the button to do. For example, a JavaScript element could change the content in other elements on your page or perform a calculation. You used this approach with the BMI calculator in Chapter 14 (page 491). In that example, visitors clicked a button to have JavaScript perform an arithmetic operation and display the result.

Dynamic Picture Buttons

Pretty soon, web designers weren't happy with text links *or* fancy button pictures. They wanted more, and they used JavaScript to get it. The basic idea was to create a new sort of button that uses the JavaScript image-swapping technique you learned about on page 482. These dynamic buttons (also known as *rollover buttons*) subtly but noticeably change when a visitor points to them. This effect tells her she's poised over a real, live button, and all she needs to do is click it to trigger an action, like going to a new page.

For a while, rollover buttons were wildly popular, and virtually everyone used them. And then leading website designers grew a bit tired of all the whirly, glowy button effects, and they decided to strip their pages down to a leaner, classier look. They reduced their use of rollover buttons and made the rollover effects themselves simpler. For example, web designers might change a button's background color on rollover but plop ordinary HTML text on top of it instead of embedding the text as part of the image. Not only does this create pages that are less busy and less distracting, but it also makes them easier to maintain, because you don't need to generate dozens of different button pictures. Figure 15-1 shows some examples.

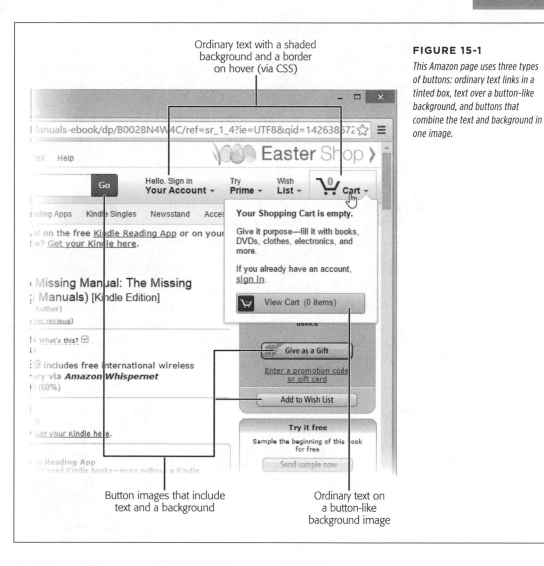

Ordinary text with a shaded
background and a border
on hover (via CSS)

Button images that include
text and a background

Ordinary text on
a button-like
background image

FIGURE 15-1

*This Amazon page uses three types
of buttons: ordinary text links in a
tinted box, text over a button-like
background, and buttons that
combine the text and background in
one image.*

■ Choosing Your Approach

Before you create any buttons, you need to pick your approach. You have three
distinct options for building rollover buttons:

- Create a background button picture and superimpose HTML text on top of it
  (Figure 15-2, top). If you use this approach, you need just two pictures, no matter
  how many buttons you have: a regular button background and a highlighted

button background. You reuse those pictures for every button you create. That means that you need to regenerate only two pictures if you want to change the style or size of a button. And if you need to alter the text on a button, you don't need to touch your pictures at all. Web developers who choose this approach sleep well at night.

- Create a picture for the entire button, text and all (Figure 15-2, bottom). This approach gives you the most control and allows the most impressive effects. However, it's also more awkward and requires more effort, because it forces you to create a separate pair of pictures for each button. For example, if you want to put eight graphical buttons on your web page, you need 16 button pictures, one for each button's normal state and one for its highlighted (mouseover) state.

- Create a background effect with CSS style settings, and superimpose some HTML text on top of it. This sounds even better, because you don't need to craft even a single image for your button. However, this choice is also more restrictive. It means that you'll only be able to create effects that are part of the CSS language. And even though CSS has plenty of slick formatting features (like rounded corners) that lend themselves to glowy buttons, older browsers, like IE 8 and IE 9, which still constitute roughly 10% of the web browsing world, don't work with these features. So unless you're willing to leave these visitors out, you need to stick with more boring border and shading choices.

NOTE You haven't learned about gradients and other cutting-edge CSS3 settings in this book because they're still too new to use without a carefully planned fallback strategy. If you want to learn more about the bleeding edge, check out *HTML5: The Missing Manual* (O'Reilly).

FIGURE 15-2

Top: This button uses ordinary text with a green background that darkens when a visitor points to it.

Bottom: This graphical button swaps pictures when a guest points to it.

So which strategy is right for your site? The first approach (all-picture buttons) makes sense if you want striking effects on part of your site. For example, you might use a few of them on your home page to direct new arrivals to different sections of your site. But for the majority of buttons, the second and third approaches are more convenient and easier to work with.

NOTE There's another reason to prefer ordinary text superimposed on a button background: search engines prefer it. As you learned on page 319, search engines give special weight to the text inside an anchor link. But if you use the image-only approach, you lose the chance to get that extra bit of attention.

UP TO SPEED

Making Button Pictures

If you decide to go with button pictures, you need a way to create them. Your options are:

- **Draw them yourself.** If you're graphically inclined, you can create button pictures by hand using just about any graphics program (Adobe Photoshop and Adobe Fireworks are two popular choices). However, getting buttons to look good isn't always easy. It's also hard to mass-produce them, because you need to make every button consistent: same text position, size, color palette, and background.

- **Use a button-creation website.** If your artistic abilities are feebler than those of Koko the painting gorilla, there's an easier option. You can use a specialized *button-creation* program. These programs have no purpose in life other than to help you create attractive buttons with the text, colors, and backgrounds you choose. The Web teems with

a range of these tools. They usually start by asking you to specify button details (like the text, color, background, and so on). Once you finish, you simply click a button and the program creates the button image (or images) and displays them in a new page. All you need to do is download the images and start using them on your site. Two examples of online button-making tools include *www.buttongenerator.com* and *www.grsites.com/button*.

- **Use Expression Web.** The popular web design tool has a feature that lets you create a whole whack of button pictures and the JavaScript code that manages them. The chief disadvantage is that this feature relies on a slightly cumbersome JavaScript-based approach, rather than the CSS technique that most web designers now prefer. To try it out, choose Insert→Interactive Button from the Expression Web menu.

Tutorial: Creating a Rollover Button

You already know how to build links, and you know the basics of the JavaScript image-swapping technique (described on page 482). But what you don't yet know is how to put it all together in a modern package—one that ensures that your buttons look understated but cool, that loads your pictures with no annoying lag, and that uses clever CSS tricks to keep your website free of messy JavaScript. The best way to get a handle on these details is to build a few buttons of your own.

In this tutorial, you'll start with a rollover button that uses a background picture and taps CSS to manage its states. Next, you'll see how to tweak a page to use the more complicated picture-with-text approach. Finally, you'll consider what you need to make an all-CSS, no-picture button for the ultimate in convenience.

TIP As with all the tutorials in this book, you can get the files from the companion site (*http://prosetech. com/web*). Look for the Tutorial-15-1 folder (which stands for "Chapter 15, first tutorial"). Inside is the Start folder, which has the set of pages you begin the exercise with, and the End folder, which shows the solution.

The Starter Page

Figure 15-3 shows the page you start with. It uses a standard two-column layout, like the ones you learned to make in Chapter 8. Right now, the column on the left holds a list of ordinary links that use the <a> element. Your challenge is to turn these links into rollover buttons.

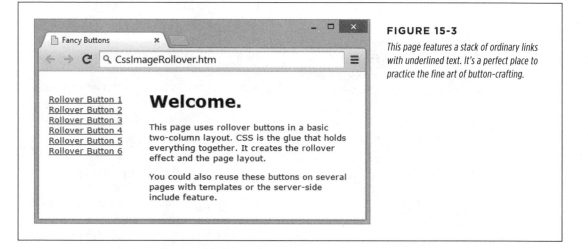

FIGURE 15-3

This page features a stack of ordinary links with underlined text. It's a perfect place to practice the fine art of button-crafting.

Structurally, this is a simple page. It uses two <div> elements, one for the list of links on the left, and one for the main content that occupies the rest of the space.

```
<div class="MenuBar">
  <a href="...">Rollover Button 1</a>
  <a href="...">Rollover Button 2</a>
  <a href="...">Rollover Button 3</a>
  <a href="...">Rollover Button 4</a>
  <a href="...">Rollover Button 5</a>
  <a href="...">Rollover Button 6</a>
</div>

<div class="MainContent">
  <h1>Welcome.</h1>
  <p>...</p>
  <p>...</p>
</div>
```

The magic that underpins this page is all in the style sheet. First, it applies a basic style rule to the <body> element, so that the page gets a consistent font:

```
body {
    font-family: Verdana,sans-serif;
    font-size: small;
}
```

Then, it positions the menu bar on the left side of the page, using the layout properties you picked up in Chapter 8:

```
.MenuBar {
    position: absolute;
    top: 20px;
    left: 0px;
    margin: 15px;
}
```

Another rule gives the main content extra margin space on the left, so it can't overlap the menu:

```
.MainContent {
    margin-left: 165px;
    margin-top: 30px;
    margin-right: 20px;
}
```

Finally, a contextual selector (page 217) picks out all the anchor elements in the menu bar:

```
.MenuBar a {
    display: block;
}
```

This rule uses the display property to transform each <a> element from an inline element into a block element (like a paragraph or a heading). That way, a browser puts each link on a separate line, so you don't need to add line breaks using the <br> element.

NOTE   Another approach is to make each <a> element a separate item in an unordered list (as represented by the <ul> element). You can then use style sheets to format the list so that it doesn't show the standard bullet next to each item. Many of the dynamic, pop-up, and collapsible menus you'll come across on the Web are actually unordered lists on the inside.

Preparing the Button Pictures

The next step is to ready your button images. In this example, you've got a relatively simple picture preparation job, because you're using a button background with superimposed text. That means you need to create an image that looks like the surface of a blank button, and a second image that looks like a highlighted version of the same button (perhaps using a different shade of the same color).

You'll find two ready-made button backgrounds in the tutorial's Start folder: *NormalButtonBackground.jpg* and *HighlightedButtonBackground.jpg*. Open them and take a look. On their own, they don't look like much. The *NormalButtonBackground.jpg* image is a gray, shaded button face, while *HighlightedButtonBackground.jpg* shows the same button in yellow.

> **NOTE** Just about anyone can develop two good-looking rectangles in a drawing program. And because you create just two buttons and no text, you won't face the headaches of trying to get text to line up correctly in each button (which, if done incorrectly, can create maddeningly inconsistent buttons). If you don't want to make your own graphics, you can take to the Web and use Google's image-search tool to find a ready-made button background you want to adopt.

Once you have the button images you need, you're ready to incorporate them into your page. Figure 15-4 shows the result you're after.

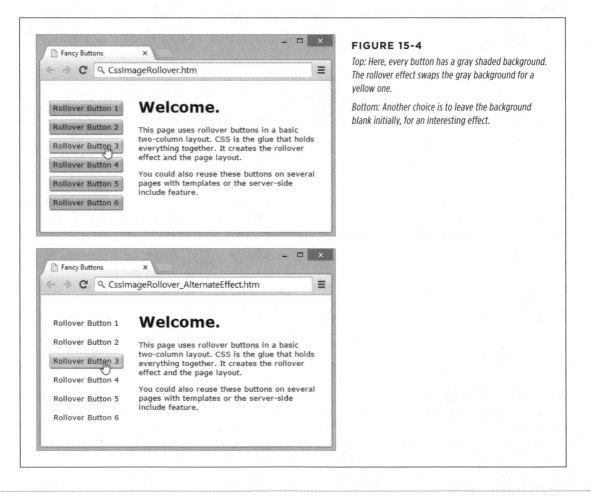

FIGURE 15-4

Top: Here, every button has a gray shaded background. The rollover effect swaps the gray background for a yellow one.

Bottom: Another choice is to leave the background blank initially, for an interesting effect.

Making the Rollover Effect

To create the rollover effect, you need to refine the styles for the <a> elements. Start by opening the *CssImageRollover.css* style sheet in a text editor.

Your first step is to refine the style that formats the links. Use the text-decoration and color properties to change the text from its standard look (underlined blue) to something that looks more appropriate on a button:

```
.MenuBar a {
    display: block;

    text-decoration: none;
    color: black;
```

The real magic starts when you specify the background property. It grabs the image *NormalButtonBackground.jpg* and puts it behind each anchor:

```
    background: url("NormalButtonBackground.jpg") no-repeat 0 0;
```

The no-repeat attribute makes sure the browser doesn't tile the image, and the 0 0 values position the picture's top-left corner at the top-left corner of the anchor.

Finally, the width and height properties size the anchor to match the size of the background button (125 x 23 pixels), while the margin and padding properties separate the buttons from one another and pad the text inside.

```
    width: 125px;
    height: 23px;

    margin-bottom: 5px;
    padding-top: 5px;
    padding-left: 7px;
}
```

Of course, none of this creates the rollover effect. To get that, you need the hover *pseudo-class* (first described on page 193). It springs into action when a guest points to an element. In this case, it changes the background picture:

```
.MenuBar a:hover {
    background: url("HighlightedButtonBackground.jpg") no-repeat 0 0;
}
```

> **TIP** If you use a less button-like, more box-like background, you might want to set the text-decoration property to underline in the hover pseudo-class. That way, the link becomes underlined when someone points to it, making its page-navigating purpose clear. Amazon uses this trick in its pop-up menus and in the category-browsing bar that sits across the top of some windows (for instance, the one in Figure 15-1).

This completes the example. However, you may remember that CSS defines a few more pseudo-classes, and you can use them with your button, too. Use visited to control what a link looks like once a guest visits the linked page, and use active to control what a link looks like in the brief moment when a visitor clicks it. For example, you could shift the button slightly to the side to make it look like it's being pushed in:

```
.MenuBar a:active {
  margin-left: 1px;
}
```

Alternatively, you could supply another background image.

Picture-with-Text Buttons

You can adapt the previous example to work with full button pictures—that is, images that include both the button background and the button text. Figure 15-5 shows an example.

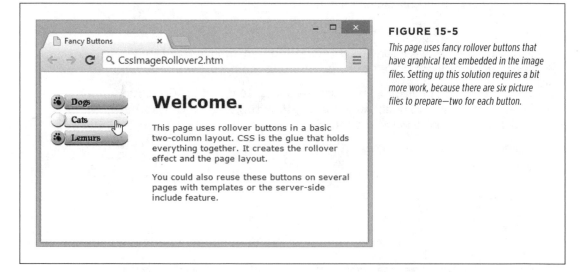

FIGURE 15-5

This page uses fancy rollover buttons that have graphical text embedded in the image files. Setting up this solution requires a bit more work, because there are six picture files to prepare—two for each button.

When you use a pile of fancy button pictures (instead of one pair of button background images), you need to use a technique called image *preloading*. This practice ensures that a browser downloads all the button "state" images when it processes the page for the first time, instead of waiting until a visitor points to a button. Although you won't notice the difference when you run the page from your computer's hard drive, preloading images makes the buttons more responsive when visitors interact with them over the Internet, particularly if they have a slow connection, and especially if the page holds a lot of buttons.

Web designers have tried a number of techniques for preloading images. Eventually, they settled on packing both button images (the normal and the selected states) into a single image file. Your style sheet dictates which part of the picture a browser shows, so that guests see only one version of the button at a time.

Consider the buttons in Figure 15-5, which were created using an online button-builder, in this case the one at *www.buttongenerator.com*. You save each pair of button pictures as a single file, as shown in Figure 15-6.

FIGURE 15-6

This graphic combines a normal (top) and a highlighted (bottom) button image. Your style sheet rules can grab just one part of the picture to use as a button. Note that it doesn't matter how much space you put between the paired pictures, so long as you keep the space consistent across all your picture pairs.

You can go to *www.buttongenerator.com* to make your own images, or you can use the images in the Start folder for this tutorial. They are *DogsButton.png* (the one in Figure 15-6), *CatsButton.png*, and *LemurButton.png.*

You can expand this double-button system into a triple-button system if you use the active pseudo class. And some performance-mad web designers pack a whole page worth of buttons and other graphical embellishments into a single background image. They then use carefully targeted style rules to slice and dice the graphic and spread it around all the elements that need it. This system ensures that a browser loads all the button graphics from the start, and that the rollover effects work without lag. It also simplifies your button management, because you have fewer files to keep track of and fewer files to reference in your markup.

NOTE Not all button-makers can create images for different button states (unclicked, pointed to, clicked, and visited). However, you can usually run the button generator multiple times and choose a slightly different color scheme to create the highlighted button image.

Once you prepare some buttons, you're ready to build an example page like the one shown in Figure 15-5. You simply take the example you completed in the previous step, change the links, and alter the link-formatting rules in the style sheet.

Your first task is to remove all the text ("Rollover Button 1" and so on) from your anchors, so that the only thing a browser will display is the button images themselves. Then you need to supply the URL of the button pictures. But here's where things start to get messy. In the previous example, you stored the background pictures using two style rules. But if you want each button to use a different set of pictures, you need a separate style rule for every button—and that's sure to make a mess of even the best-organized style sheet.

A better solution is to use a style rule that stores all the button information *except* the picture filenames. Here's the slightly shorter style rule for formatting anchor elements:

```
.MenuBar a {
  display: block;

  width: 115px;
  height: 18px;

  margin-bottom: 5px;
  padding-top: 5px;
  padding-left: 7px;

  background-repeat: no-repeat;
}
```

Now you can specify the filename for each button using an inline style. First, remove the old set of links from the MenuBar <div>. Then, add these three links in their place:

```
<a href="..." style="background-image: url('DogButton.png')"> </a>
<a href="..." style="background-image: url('CatButton.png')"> </a>
<a href="..." style="background-image: url('LemurButton.png')"> </a>
```

The style rule explicitly sets the width and height of the buttons so that a browser displays only the top part of the button file.

The final ingredient is the rule that displays the pointed-to buttons. It repositions the view of the button image file just a shade (by using a negative number of pixels for background-position), effectively pulling the picture up, so the top portion of the image, which holds the button's normal state, falls outside the top margin of the anchor button, and the bottom portion of the image, which holds the pointed-to button, is visible. In Figure 15-5, the highlighted button sits 23 pixels below the normal-state button, so the style sheet rule looks like this:

```
.MenuBar a:hover {
  background-position: 0 -23px;
}
```

Picture-less Buttons

Many minimalist web designers build buttons without any pictures at all. They use CSS properties to create a shaded box for the button and then superimpose a label on it using HTML.

If you go this route, you have a choice. You can accept boring buttons that change their borders, text color, background color, or underlining for a relatively modest effect. For example, Amazon uses the basic border-adding trick as a rollover effect in the page on Figure 15-1.

Your other choice is to use fancier CSS3 properties that some browsers will ignore. These include properties for gradients, shadows, and rounded borders. Taken together, these features can turn an ordinary background into a reasonable facsimile of a fancy button. The problem is that versions of Internet Explorer before IE 9 won't understand these properties and won't properly display your buttons. Depending on the properties you choose and the way you apply them, the change could be minor or nearly catastrophic.

To try the CSS-only approach with CSS3 properties, check out the button-maker on the CSS-Tricks site (*http://css-tricks.com/examples/ButtonMaker*). It lets you adjust colors and shading to create a picture-less button (Figure 15-7).

FIGURE 15-7

To create a button at CSS-Tricks, just play with the sliders and click "View the CSS" when you like what you see. But be warned: The curvy, shaded button shown here turns into a plain blue box for guests using any version of Internet Explorer before IE 9, which isn't that bad.

If you're even more ambitious, you can look at more complex JavaScript libraries that pile on even more CSS3 frills. For example, you can find animated buttons and medallions in the iHover library at *http://tiny.cc/ihover*. They include eye-popping effects like spins and fades that superimpose graphics and text. But once again, IE 9 fans need not apply.

■ Fancy Menus

When rollover buttons first came into vogue, they were wildly popular. There's something irresistible about a button that lights up when you point to it. You can, however, have too much of a good thing, and stuffing too many rollover buttons on a page is a surefire way to create an overdone turkey of a website.

In recent years, the Web has seen a small renaissance in simplicity and a trend away from excessive rollover buttons. Part of the reason is the increasing complexity of websites—quite simply, a handful of rollover buttons no longer offer enough navigational aid for today's typically complex sites. Instead, these sites use more detailed multilevel menus, replacing dozens of rollover buttons with a clearer, more streamlined set of hierarchical links.

A typical menu starts with a collection of anchor elements you group together on a page. The key is to organize these links into logical groups. For example, the website for a company might include a group of product pages, a group of pages with contact and location information, and another group of tech support pages. By arranging links into groups, visitors can find what they're looking for more easily.

So far, this menu design doesn't require anything special. Using the linking skills you picked up in Chapter 6 and the layout smarts you gained in Chapter 8, you can easily create a side panel with a grouped list of links. But really neat menus add another flourish—they're *collapsible*. That means you don't see the whole set of links at once. Initially, you see only the group headings, like Products, Contact Information, and Tech Support. When you click a group heading, a list of related links pops open just underneath.

You can create collapsible menus in several ways. Some are easy, while others are dizzyingly complex. In the following sections, you'll learn how to build a simple collapsible menu of your own, and then use a more complicated menu courtesy of a free JavaScript site.

Do-It-Yourself Collapsible Menus

You can create a respectable menu of your own using dynamic HTML and the collapsible text example from Chapter 14 (page 48). The basic idea is to use JavaScript to hide and show specific HTML elements by changing the CSS `display` property.

Imagine you want to create the cool tabbed menu shown in Figure 15-8. You split the links into three groups and display the topmost link for each group as an onscreen tab. When a guest clicks a tab, the page shows the sublinks for that tab.

In the rest of this section, you'll get a chance to look at the solution piece by piece. To see the complete page, check out the *SimpleTabs.htm* page, available from the companion site at *http://prosetech.com/web*.

■ THE MENU MARKUP

The design in Figure 15-8 might seem a little intimidating at first, but it consists of only two parts: the tabs at the top of the page and the link boxes (menus) that appear underneath them when a visitor points to a tab. To make these regions easy to deal with, so you can style and manipulate them with JavaScript, you need to wrap them in `<div>` and `<span>` elements, as you've seen throughout this book.

FIGURE 15-8

Top: When this page first loads, it presents visitors with three tabs.

Middle and bottom: As a visitor moves her mouse over a tab box, a set of related links appears underneath. These links "float" above the page content.

The three tabs are grouped together in a `<div>` with the name *TabGroup*. Inside, a separate `<span>` element represents each tab, like this:

```
<div class="TabGroup">
  <span class="Tab">About Me</span>
  <span class="Tab">My Store</span>
  <span class="Tab">Really Cool Stuff</span>
</div>
```

The <span> element is the best choice for the tabs, because they need to appear next to one another on the same line. If you used a <div>, you'd get a line break and some space between each element.

These <span> elements have the descriptive class name *Tab*. That associates them with the following style sheet rule, which gives the tabs the correct font and borders:

```
.Tab {
  font-weight: bold;
  padding: 5px;
  border-style: solid;
  border-width: 1px;
  cursor: hand;
}
```

This rule includes something you haven't seen yet—the cursor property. It styles the mouse cursor when a guest points to a link element. In this case, the cursor changes to a hand icon (Figure 15-8, middle).

You wrap all the tabs in a <div> that uses the *TabGroup* class so you can put the *TabGroup* <div> at a specific position on the page:

```
.TabGroup {
  position: absolute;
  top: 16px;
  left: 10px;
}
```

After you declare the tabs, it makes sense to add the floating submenus. Each submenu is simply a box with borders and a yellow background. A group of links sits inside the box. The <div> element makes sense here, because you want each submenu to exist independently of the others on the page (rather than stuffed together into a single line). You also need to give each <div> element a unique ID, so you can change its visibility based on the tab a visitor clicks.

Here are the <div> elements for the three link groups:

```
<div id="AboutMe" class="Links">
  <a href="...">My Traumatic Childhood</a>
  <a href="...">My Education</a>
  <a href="...">Painful Episodes</a>
</div>

<div id="MyStore" class="Links">
  <a href="...">Buy Something</a>
  <a href="...">Request a Refund</a>
  <a href="...">File a Complaint</a>
</div>
```

```
<div id="ReallyCoolStuff" class="Links">
  <a href-"...">Pie Eating</a>
  <a href="...">Harvesting Bananas</a>
  <a href="...">Blindfolded Heart Surgery</a>
</div>
```

The <div> elements float above the page, which means you need to absolutely position them. Here's the style rule for that:

```
.Links {
  position: absolute;
  top: 40px;
  left: 10px;
  border-width: 1px;
  border-style: solid;
  padding: 10px;
  background-color: lightyellow;
  font-size: small;
  display: none;
}
```

Along with the absolute positioning coordinates (40 pixels from the top of the browser window, 10 pixels from the left), this style also sets a few formatting details (the border, background, padding, and text size). More importantly, it uses the display property to explicitly hide all the submenus when the page first loads. So even though this example stacks the submenu <div> elements one on top of the other, you won't ever see them that way on a page, because you won't ever see them all at once.

Give the <a> elements inside the floating boxes a bit of margin space so they don't run into one another:

```
.Links a {
  margin-right: 5px;
}
```

TIP If you want a menu with the tabs stacked one above the other, you can tweak this style rule to use the display: block property, just as you did with the panel of rollover buttons on page 506.

And, finally, wrap the rest of the content for the page in a <div> element that has the class name *MainBody*. Give this <div> a generous top margin, so that it clears the tabs:

```
.MainBody {
  margin-top: 70px;
  margin-left: 15px;
}
```

These style sheet rules and <span> and <div> elements create the basic framework for the collapsible menus. The final step is to create a script that displays one of the hidden <div> elements, depending on which tab your visitor selects.

■ THE CODE THAT SHOWS THE SUBMENUS

The code that shows each tab is similar to the code you used for the ToggleVisibility() function in Chapter 14 (page 485). But in this case, you're not interested in hiding and showing individual sections. Instead, you want to show a single section, depending on the tab selected, and hide everything else. Two custom functions handle the job: MakeVisible(), which shows the submenu for a specific tab; and ResetAllMenus(), which hides all the submenus.

Here's a simplified version of the MakeVisible() function. As you can see, it takes an element name, finds the element, and changes its style settings so that it appears on the page.

```
function MakeVisible(element){
  // Find the element and unhide it.
  var element = document.getElementById(element)
  element.style.display = "block"
}
```

TIP If you need to change a bunch of style properties, or if you just want to keep all your style sheet settings in your style sheet (which is always a good idea), there's another way to write this example. Instead of modifying the style in the MakeVisible() function, you can *switch* the style. Start by creating two class-based styles in your style sheet, one for visible tabs (say, *SelectedTab*) and one for hidden tabs (*NonSelectedTabs*). Then, in the MakeVisible() function, change the element.className property to point to the style you need, like this:

```
element.className = "NonSelectedTabs"
```

Once you write the code for the MakeVisible() function, you're ready to hook it up to all the tab buttons. You have a choice here: MakeVisible() could react to either a click using the onclick event or to a mouse pointing to the tab using the onmouseover event. This example uses the latter approach.

```
<span class="Tab" onmouseover="MakeVisible('AboutMe')">About Me</span>
<span class="Tab" onmouseover="MakeVisible('MyStore')">My Store</span>
<span class="Tab" onmouseover="MakeVisible('ReallyCoolStuff')">Really Cool
  Stuff</span>
```

The page still isn't quite right. Although the MakeVisible() function shows the correct tabs, it doesn't hide anything. That means that if you point to all three tabs, you see all three groups of links at the same time, one above the other.

To hide the irrelevant tabs, you need to get a little craftier. The problem is that Make Visible() knows what tab it's supposed to show, but it doesn't know the status of the other two tabs. To find that out, your code needs to search through the rest of the page. In this example, the basic approach is to look for any `<div>` element that has the class name *Links* and hide it. The `ResetAllMenus()` function handles that:

```
function ResetAllMenus() {
  // Get an array with div elements.
  var links = document.getElementsByTagName("div")

  // Search the array for link boxes, and hide them.
  for (var j = 0; j < links.length; j++) {
    if (links[j].className == 'Links') links[j].style.display = "none"
  }
}
```

This code is a little tricky. First, the `getElementsByTagName()`function retrieves a programming object called an *array*. An array is special because it doesn't hold just one object; it holds a whole group of them at once. In this case, the array named *links* holds three objects, one for each `<div>` element on the page.

Then you use a programming construct called a for loop. It processes code a certain number of times using a built-in counter. In this case, the counter is a variable named j that starts at 0 and keeps increasing until it matches `links.length`—in other words, until it gets to the last `<div>` object in the `links` array. Assuming the `links` array has three items, your browser executes this statement three times:

```
if (links[j].className == 'Links') links[j].style.display = "none"
```

The first time, j is 0, and the code loads up the first object in the list. The second time, j is 1, and it digs up the second object. You can guess what happens the third time. As the code moves through this list, it checks the class name of each `<div>` element. If it indicates that you found a link box, the code makes it disappear from the page by changing its display style.

> **NOTE** If the stranger aspects of JavaScript still look like Danish, don't worry. If you're inclined, you can learn about JavaScript programming features like arrays, loops, and if statements from a website or a dedicated book (like *JavaScript & jQuery: The Missing Manual* [O'Reilly]). Or you can keep your sanity and rely on the examples in this book, or find great free scripts online.

Now you can fix the `MakeVisible()` function so that it first hides all the menus and then reveals just the one you want:

```
function MakeVisible(element){
  ResetAllMenus()

  // Find the element and unhide it.
  var element = document.getElementById(element)
  element.style.display = "block"
}
```

A good practice is to hide all the floating menu boxes if your guest moves his mouse pointer off the floating link box and over the rest of the page. This suggests that the visitor decided not to click a menu command and went back to reading the page:

```
<div class="MainBody" onmouseover="ResetAllMenus()">
```

The code in the downloadable example gets slightly fancier. It hides a selected tab's border and changes its background color. However, the basic approach is the same.

Third-Party Menus

If you've had enough fun writing your own JavaScript code, you'll be happy to hear that the Web is chock-full of free menu scripts. Many of them have more dazzle than the tabbed menu in the previous example. Some of the extra features you might find include the following:

- Multilevel menus that let visitors drill down to specific subcategories.

- Menus that let you collapse and expand subsections, so you can show all the links that interest you.

- Ridiculously showy effects, like shaded highlighting and transparent backgrounds.

To find a good menu, use a JavaScript sample site (page 493), or search for "JavaScript menus" or "CSS menus" on the Web. You'll find that there's quite a bit more diversity in menus than in rollover buttons. Every menu looks and behaves a little differently. Some pop up, others slide out, and others try to emulate the look and feel of popular programs like Microsoft Outlook.

TIP Stay away from menus that force you to bury your links in a block of JavaScript. Not only does this approach make it harder to edit the menus should you add or remove a link, but it also can cause problems for search engines, which might not be able to discover (and index) all the pages on your website. Today's webmasters put the links in real <a> elements, which you can then stack one after the other or place inside an unordered list.

To get a glimpse of what's out there, head over to Dynamic Drive (*www.dynamicdrive. com/dynamicindex1*), which has a nifty set of menus, and a particularly interesting one called Slashdot (*www.dynamicdrive.com/dynamicindex1/slashdot.htm*). Figure 15-9 shows Slashdot with the same structure as the tabbed menu you saw earlier in this chapter.

TIP Before you choose a navigation bar for your own site, test drive quite a few. This section walks you through the process, but you'll want to compare the results with other navigation bars before you commit to one.

In the following sections, you'll download the script for a Slashdot menu and put it to use.

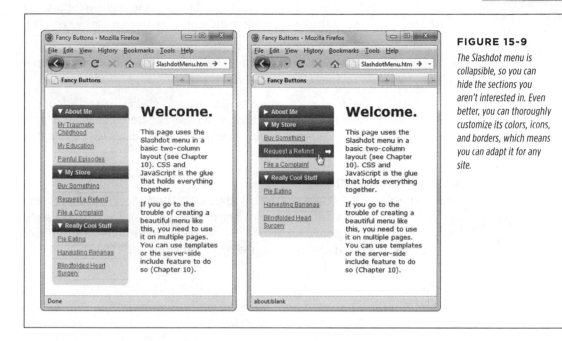

FIGURE 15-9

The Slashdot menu is collapsible, so you can hide the sections you aren't interested in. Even better, you can thoroughly customize its colors, icons, and borders, which means you can adapt it for any site.

■ GETTING THE SCRIPT

To download the Slashdot menu, follow these steps:

1. **Go to *www.dynamicdrive.com/dynamicindex1/slashdot.htm*.**

   This page displays a sample menu and provides instructions for using it. It also cites browser compatibility for the menu, and the news is good—it works in every mainstream browser.

2. **Look for the download link for the *sdmenu.zip* file. Click it, and then save the ZIP file somewhere on your computer.**

   The Slashdot menu consists of a JavaScript file, some images, and a style sheet, all of which you'll find in the ZIP file.

3. **Unzip the contents of *sdmenu.zip*. Put it in your site folder on your computer, along with the rest of your site pages.**

   Altogether, *sdmenu.zip* contains a sample page that includes the menu (*index. html*) and a subfolder (*sdmenu*) that contains all the support files. Drag both of these into your site folder.

   You don't need to touch the contents of the *sdmenu* folder (although you might if you want to refine the menu to match your website). By carefully replacing some of the graphics, you can modify the background of the title sections (*top-*

title.gif and *title.gif*), the arrows (*collapsed.gif*, *expanded.gif*, and *linkarrow.gif*), and the bottom border (*bottom.gif*). By cracking open the style sheet (*sdmenu. css*), you can change the background colors, borders, and spacing for the rest of the menu. Finally, the *sdmenu* folder includes a JavaScript file (*sdmenu.js*), which you probably won't edit at all.

4. **Create a new web page (or start editing one that already has a set of menu links you want to adapt into a Slashdot menu).**

    You could edit your *index.html* page (and that's a good way to get started with most examples). However, the Slashdot menu is straightforward and similar to the do-it-yourself collapsible menu you created earlier, so it's easy enough to incorporate into a new page.

■ CREATING THE MENU

The first step to using the Slashdot menu is to attach its style sheet to your page and add a reference to the JavaScript file that powers the menu. You also need a scrap of script that creates your menu when the page loads. All three of these ingredients go in the <head> section of your page, and here's what they look like:

```
<head>
  <title>Fancy Buttons</title>
  <link rel="stylesheet" type="text/css" href="sdmenu/sdmenu.css" />
  <script src="sdmenu/sdmenu.js"></script>
  <script>
    var myMenu;
    window.onload = function() {
      myMenu = new SDMenu("my_menu");
      myMenu.init();
    };
  </script>
  ...
</head>
```

The script code is generic. You can copy it word-for-word into every page that uses the Slashdot menu. The only point to note is that the menu name it uses (*my_menu* in this example) must match the ID of the <div> element that contains the Slashdot menu on your page.

You probably also want to add an embedded style sheet or link to another style sheet in your <head> section. The example in Figure 15-9 uses three basic style rules. One assigns a font to the page, another positions the sidebar that has the Slashdot menu, and the third positions the main content section:

```
body {
  font-family: Verdana,sans-serif;
  font-size: small;
}
```

```
.MenuBar {
  position: absolute;
  top: 20px;
  left: 0px;
  margin: 15px;
}

.MainContent
{
  margin-left: 180px;
  margin-top: 30px;
  margin-right: 20px;
}
```

These styles are nothing new. You saw them in earlier examples.

Now it's time to build the menu. Its structure is remarkably similar to the examples you've seen in this chapter. Essentially, each collapsible section of the menu consists of a <div> container full of anchor elements. The only added feature is the title text, which a <span> element at the top of the <div> provides:

```
<div>
  <span>About Me</span>
  <a href="...">My Traumatic Childhood</a>
  <a href="...">My Education</a>
  <a href="...">Painful Episodes</a>
</div>
```

A typical Slashdot menu contains several collapsible submenus. You wrap them all together in another <div> element and give it a name that matches the menu name in the script:

```
<div class="sdmenu" id="my_menu">
  ...
</div>
```

This is enough to create the Slashdot menu with all its formatting and functionality intact. However, you probably want to wrap the Slashdot <div> in another <div>, one that represents the menu sidebar. That way, you can place the sidebar exactly where you want it, without worrying about style sheet conflicts or modifying the *sdmenu.css* file.

```
<div class="MenuBar">
  <div class="sdmenu" id="my_menu">
    ...
  </div>
</div>
```

Here's the complete markup used to create the menu in Figure 15-9:

```
<div class="MenuBar">
  <div class="sdmenu" id="my_menu">
    <div>
      <span>About Me</span>
      <a href="...">My Traumatic Childhood</a>
      <a href="...">My Education</a>
      <a href="...">Painful Episodes</a>
    </div>
    <div>
      <span>My Store</span>
      <a href="...">Buy Something</a>
      <a href="...">Request a Refund</a>
      <a href="...">File a Complaint</a>
    </div>
    <div>
      <span>Really Cool Stuff</span>
      <a href="...">Pie Eating</a>
      <a href="...">Harvesting Bananas</a>
      <a href="...">Blindfolded Heart Surgery</a>
    </div>
  </div>
</div>
```

NOTE Once you perfect your website and you're ready to take it live, remember to upload the *sdmenu* subfolder and all its files.

POWER USERS' CLINIC

The Menus and Widgets That jQuery UI Offers

Although the Slashdot menu gives your site a quick, shake-and-bake menu, it's probably not the best tool to underpin a big, professional website. Instead, you might prefer to outfit your site with the features and frills of a JavaScript *library*. That way, you won't need to continuously trawl the Web for bits and pieces of code to improve your pages. Instead, you can use a library's comprehensive and unified set of tools.

For example, many web developers use jQuery, a small but wildly popular library that extends the features of ordinary JavaScript. jQuery offers graphical effects like fading and simple animations, and includes plenty of time-saving shortcuts, too. One of the most interesting things about jQuery is the way that other web developers can extend it and add their own plug-ins. One example is the powerful jQuery UI library, which adds a set of slick, interactive widgets for web creators to play with. These include autocomplete text boxes, accordion-style collapsible panels, tabs, and a customizable menu.

If you're one of the many web developers who use the jQuery library, it's worth seeing if the jQuery UI menu can help you out. And if you're using a different JavaScript library, like jQuery or Dojo (page 496), you might find that it includes a similar menu that you can use (or that someone else has created a menu based on your JavaScript library of choice).

Here's where life gets a bit sticky, simply because there are so many paths to your goal: a nice-looking menu for your web pages. To learn more about the jQuery solution, consider reading *JavaScript & jQuery: The Missing Manual* (O'Reilly), or visit the jQuery learning center at *http://learn.jquery.com*.

Audio and Video

I n the early days of the Internet, websites were about as jazzy as an IRS form. You'd see pages filled with an assortment of plain text, links, and more plain text. Over time, the Web matured, and web pages started to change as designers embraced the joys of color, pictures, and tacky clip art. But when that excitement started to wear off, it was time for a new trick—multimedia.

Multimedia is a catch-all term for a variety of technologies and file types, which have different computer requirements and pose different web design challenges. Multimedia includes everything from the irritating jingle that plays in the background of your best friend's home page to the wildly popular video clip of a cat playing the piano. (Depressing fact: That cat has over 40 million views, and you're unlikely to ever create a web page that's half as popular.)

In this chapter, you'll learn how to put audio players and video playback windows into your web pages. You'll also learn to overcome the limitations of old browsers by using a Flash fallback system, which ensures that pretty much any web-connected computer can listen to your music and watch your videos. And finally, once you've learned how to do all this on your own, you'll see how to simplify your life by hosting your video files on YouTube.

▓ Understanding Multimedia

There comes a point when all new web designers want more than mere text and pictures on their pages. Even spruced-up fonts and elegant page layouts don't satisfy the design envy many newcomers feel when they spot a site loaded with sound and motion. That's understandable: You, too, want to trick out your pages with audio and video. But before you can jazz up your site, you need to understand a few basics of multimedia.

Linking and Embedding

One of the key choices you make when you outfit your pages with multimedia is whether to link to or embed the files.

Linking to multimedia content is the simplest but least glamorous approach. The link *points to* an audio or video file stored along with all your other website files. There's really nothing to creating linked multimedia. You use the same lowly anchor element and href attribute you used in Chapter 6. Here's an example:

```
Would you like to hear <a href="IndustrialNoiseBand.mp3">Industrial Noise</a>?
```

Figure 16-1 shows what happens when you click one of these babies.

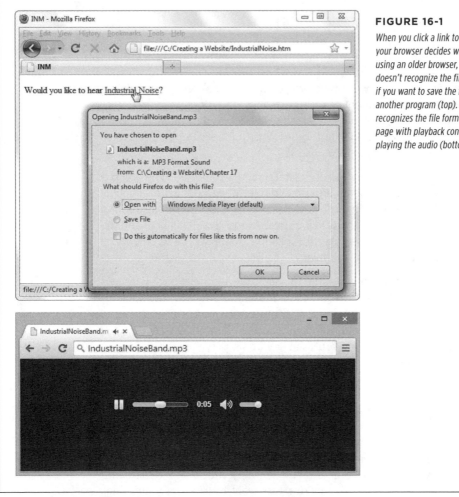

FIGURE 16-1

When you click a link to a multimedia file, your browser decides what to do. If you're using an older browser, or if your browser doesn't recognize the file format, it asks if you want to save the file or open it in another program (top). But if your browser recognizes the file format, it opens a blank page with playback controls and starts playing the audio (bottom).

NOTE It makes absolutely no difference what kind of software your web host's server runs. When someone clicks a link to an audio file, the browser downloads the file to the visitor's computer and plays it there, not from the server.

Embedding multimedia is a more advanced approach. It *integrates* music or video into your HTML page. As a result, you can create rich combinations of text, sound, and video.

NOTE The distinction between linking and embedding multimedia is the same as the distinction between linking to a picture (with the <a> element), and embedding it right in your page (with the <img> element).

You use the <audio> element to embed an audio player on your page and the <video> element to show a video on your page. These two newer elements didn't exist until HTML5. Before that, web developers had to fiddle around with the clunky <embed> element, which was notoriously finicky and never managed to work for every visitor.

Today, browsers understand both the <audio> and <video> elements. Even mobile browsers work with them. In fact, there's just one browser still kicking around that doesn't know what to do with <audio> and <video> elements, and that's Internet Explorer 8, which commands around 3 percent of the worldwide browser market at the time of this writing. If this worries you, don't panic—you can create audio- and video-enhanced pages that have a Flash-powered fallback player for ancient browsers. You'll learn how to add one on page 536.

Hosted Multimedia

One way to avoid all these browser headaches is to use *hosted multimedia*—audio and video files stored on someone else's server but displayed on your web page. The best-known example of hosted multimedia is YouTube, a ridiculously popular site that plays back hundreds of millions of video clips every day.

Hosted multimedia is an excellent choice if you want to include really large files, particularly movie clips, on your page. It won't tap out your website's bandwidth (page 289). Best of all, you don't need to worry about making sure your media files work with different browsers and operating systems, because the media hosting service does all that work. The only drawback is that you give up a fair bit of control. For example, if you host your videos on YouTube, you need to abide by its rules, which restrict you from posting videos with nudity, dangerous acts, violence, or copyrighted material. (And even if you think your video is using copyrighted material fairly—for example, in the context of a larger work of commentary, criticism, or satire—the copyright holder can probably persuade YouTube to yank it down unless you pay a small army of lawyers to argue otherwise.)

Despite these conditions, YouTube is still far and away the most practical way to share clips. You'll learn to use YouTube on page 541.

■ Playing Audio Files

The first ingredient you need to create a music-playing page is an audio file. Your best bet is one encoded using the popular MP3 standard. That way, you can rest assured that your page will work on the latest version of every browser in existence.

> **TIP** For best results, take an audio track in an uncompressed format (like WAV) and use it to generate an MP3 audio file. Most basic audio editors can perform this task. Audacity (*http://audacity.sourceforge.net*) is a free editor for Mac and Windows that fits the bill, although you'll need to install the LAME MP3 encoder to get MP3 support (*http://lame1.buanzo.com.ar*). Goldwave (*www.goldwave.com*) is a similarly capable audio editor that's free to try but sold for a nominal fee.

Here's an example of a page that uses the <audio> element in the simplest way possible:

```
<!DOCTYPE html>
<html>
<head>
  <title>A Taste of Scarlatti</title>
</head>
<body>
<h1>Relax, Music</h1>
<p>I've picked some music for you. Press the play button to listen to
Scarlatti's K. 184 sonata.</p>
<audio src="scarlatti.mp3" controls></audio>
</body>
</html>
```

The src attribute identifies the audio file you want to play. In this example, a browser looks for that file in the same folder as the page. Of course, you could also put your music file in a subfolder on your server and then use a relative path in the markup (page 177).

> **NOTE** It goes without saying that you shouldn't put an audio file on your website unless you created it, the content creator has given you permission, or you can verify that it's in the public domain. Plenty of websites provide royalty-free music you can use on your pages, so long as you give credit to the composer somewhere on your site. For some good examples of free music catalogs, visit *http://incompetech.com/music* or *www.bensound. com* or *http://musopen.org/music*.

The controls attribute tells a browser to display a basic set of playback controls. Each browser has a slightly different version of these controls, but they always serve the same purpose—to let your guest start and stop playback, jump to a new position in the file, and change the volume (Figure 16-2). To try out this example, find it on the companion site (*http://prosetech.com/web*), which has both the HTML page and the corresponding MP3 file.

NOTE The `<audio>` and `<video>` elements must have both a start and an end tag. You can't use empty element syntax, like `<audio />`.

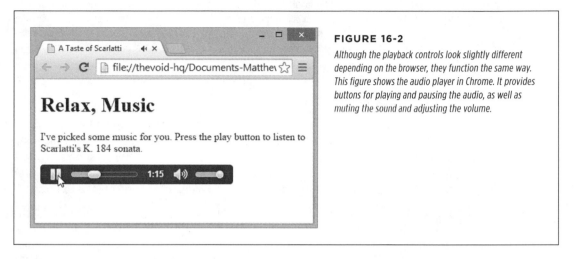

FIGURE 16-2

Although the playback controls look slightly different depending on the browser, they function the same way. This figure shows the audio player in Chrome. It provides buttons for playing and pausing the audio, as well as muting the sound and adjusting the volume.

Along with the basic `src` and `controls` attributes, the `<audio>` element offers several other options, which you'll read about below.

Automatic Playback

Most people like to browse the Web in peaceful silence. That means no trance-hypno-ambient background tracks, no strange disco beats, and no sudden cymbal crashes. This aversion to noise may be due to the fact that something like 98 percent of all web browsing takes place on company time.

But if you like to startle and annoy people, or if you're absolutely convinced that your audience really *does* want some funky beats, you can bring on the background music by adding the `autoplay` attribute, which tells a browser to start playback as soon as it finishes loading the page. It looks like this:

```
<p>The music now blaring from your speakers is
Scarlatti's K.184 sonata.</p>
<audio src="scarlatti.mp3" controls autoplay></audio>
<p>I hope you didn't tell your colleagues you were working!</p>
```

Without autoplay, it's up to the person viewing the page to click the Play button, which is obviously a politer way of handling things.

If you're really determined to annoy your visitors, you can use the `<audio>` element to play background music mercilessly by adding the `autoplay` attribute and removing the `controls` attribute. This creates an automatic music player that guests can't shut off. The only reason to take this step is if you create your own controls, using JavaScript. For example, you might create a JavaScript-powered button that switches off the audio, or you might use the <audio> element to play music and sound effects for a JavaScript game embedded in the page.

> **NOTE** Creating your own music players and controlling the <audio> and <video> elements with JavaScript are two tasks beyond the scope of this book. You can learn more from the book *HTML5: The Missing Manual* (O'Reilly), which demonstrates how to create custom players, or you can dive in headfirst with a custom-player-building tutorial from the Web. (There are many, but you can find one popular article at *http://tinyurl. com/custom-player*.)

Preloading Media Files

One useful HTML5 attribute for multimedia files is preload, which tells a browser when to download a file. Set preload to auto, and the browser starts downloading the whole media file once it opens the page, so the file's available as soon as a guest clicks Play. Of course, the download takes place in the background, so your visitor can scroll around and read the page without waiting for the download to finish.

The preload attribute works with two other values, too. Use metadata to tell the browser to grab the first small chunk of data from the file, which is enough to determine some basic details, like the total length of the audio. Or you can use none, which tells the browser to hold off on the download. You might use one of these options to save bandwidth, for example, if you have a page stuffed full of <audio> elements and you don't expect the visitor to play more than a few of them.

```
<audio src="scarlatti.mp3" controls preload="metadata"></audio>
```

When you use the metadata or none values, the browser downloads the audio file as soon as someone clicks Play. Happily, browsers can play one chunk of audio while downloading the next without a hiccup unless you're working over a slow network connection.

If you don't set the preload attribute, browsers can do what they want, and different browsers make different assumptions. Most browsers assume auto as the value, but Firefox uses metadata. Furthermore, it's important to note that the preload attribute isn't a rigid rule, but a recommendation you give the browser—one that it might ignore, depending on other factors. (And some slightly older versions of browsers don't pay attention to the preload attribute at all.)

> **NOTE** If you have a page stuffed with <audio> elements, the browser creates a separate strip of playback controls for each one. Your visitor can listen to one audio file at a time or play them all at once.

Looping Playback

Finally, the loop attribute tells a browser to start over at the beginning when playback ends. You can use this technique to keep your visitors happy with endlessly looping background music:

```
<audio src="scarlatti.mp3" controls loop></audio>
```

In most browsers, playback is fluid enough that you can use this technique to cre-ate a seamless, looping soundtrack. The trick is to choose a loopable piece of audio that ends where it begins.

Although many websites sell audio loops, you can download one for free at Flash Kit (*www.flashkit.com/loops*). Flash Kit offers a large and excellent catalog of nearly 10,000 loops ranging in style from ambient to urban. They were originally designed for Flash players, but you can also download them in MP3 format, which is what the <audio> element requires.

NOTE Loops are the audio equivalent of a wallpaper tile. They're short snippets of music specially designed so that the beginning picks up where the end leaves off. You can play an audio loop over and over again, and the result is a seamless background track. In a first-rate loop, the repetition isn't immediately obvious, and you can happily listen to it for several minutes.

■ Showing Video Clips

Now that you've conquered the challenges of audio and learned to put music into your web pages, you're ready to move on to the challenge of video content.

To show video content, you use the <video> element, which works for video files much like the <audio> element works for audio files. Here's an example that plays an MP4 video file:

```
<!DOCTYPE html>
<html>
<head>
  <title>Embarrassing Party Video</title>
</head>
<body>
<h1>It's Less Fun (When the Police Come)</h1>
<p>Party was going great until the fine fellows at 24th division
came by on a noise complaint.</p>
<video src="arrest.mp4" controls></video>
<p>Click the play button to see what happened to us.</p>
</body>
</html>
```

Once again, the controls attribute adds a handy set of playback controls to your page (Figure 16-3). In most browsers, these controls disappear when you click somewhere else on the page and return when you point to the movie link.

To build this simple page on your own, download the *arrest.mp4* file from the com-panion site (*http://prosetech.com/web*). Create a new web page in the same folder, and add the <video> element inside.

FIGURE 16-3

Every browser has a slightly different style for the video window, but the playback buttons are all virtually the same. Chrome's video player offers the same buttons as its audio player, plus one—a button in the bottom-right corner that expands the video to fill the entire screen.

NOTE If you right-click a video window that uses the `<video>` element, you'll get a simple menu that includes the option to save the video file on your computer. Depending on the browser, it may also include commands for changing the playback speed, looping the video, taking it full screen, and muting the sound.

Video formats aren't quite as simple as audio formats. That's because you need to consider two details: the *codec*, which is a sort of recipe that compresses your video, and the *container*, which is the package that holds the encoded video and audio. In the video world, there's a dizzying range of codec-and-container combinations. To ensure that your video plays back on the widest range of browsers, your video file should meet two criteria:

- You should encode it with the popular H.264 codec. These days, H.264 is the recording format of choice for most consumer devices, from smartphones to video cameras.

- You should store it in an MP4 (also known as MPEG-4) container. You can usually tell that you have the right type of container by looking at the file extension, which should be *.mp4*.

Follow these rules, and your video will play on the modern version of every browser.

NOTE Even if you have the right type of file (an MP4 file that holds H.264-encoded content), it's probably too big to be practical for your website. Page 532 explains a bit more about how to convert and slim down video files.

NOSTALGIA CORNER

The Format Wars

Browser makers spent several years battling it out over different multimedia formats. The war over video formats was particularly nasty, and it still hasn't completely subsided. At the moment, every browser supports H.264 (sometimes reluctantly). However, there's no way to know if format disagreements might erupt again. For example, Google, the creator of Chrome, has officially pledged to remove H.264 support in favor of the free WebM codec in a future browser release (although it now seems unlikely that that will actually happen).

If the format wars do erupt again, the <audio> and <video> elements are ready. That's because they both support a format fallback system. Here's how it works: Instead of supplying a single source file in a single format with the src attribute,

you offer up a list of files by adding a <source> element for each one. For example, if you have a web video in two different formats, you add two <source> elements inside the <video> element, one for each file. When a browser processes your page, it scans through this list until it finds a video in a format that it supports.

This multiple-file system is messy and awkward. It also wastes your time and your web space, because it's up to you to encode each media file in multiple formats. To learn more, check out the reference for the <source> element in Appendix B (page 572). Or read a detailed tutorial of the format fallback system at *http://tinyurl.com/vid-for-ev*.

Configuring the Video Window

The <video> element has the same src, controls, preload, autoplay, and loop attributes as the <audio> element. However, if you choose automatic playback, you can make it slightly less obnoxious by throwing in the muted attribute, which shuts off the sound on most browsers. Your guest can switch the audio back on by clicking the speaker icon, as usual.

The <video> element also adds three more attributes: height, width, and poster.

The width and height attributes set the size of the playback window (in pixels). Here's an example that creates a playback window that measures 400 x 300 pixels:

```
<video src="arrest.mp4" controls width="400" height="300"></video>
```

If you decide to supply the width and height attributes, make sure they match the true dimensions of the video. Technically, you don't need to add these details, because a browser can figure out what size to make the video box when it loads the video file. However, there's an advantage to making these details explicit. That's because it forces the browser to reserve the right amount of space for the playback window right off the bat, preserving your carefully crafted layout as the video loads (or even if the video fails to load altogether).

Finally, the `poster` attribute lets you supply an image that browsers display in place of the video in three situations: if the browser hasn't downloaded the first frame of the video yet, if it couldn't find the selected video file, or if you set the `preload` attribute to none.

```
<video src="arrest.mp4" controls poster="police_cuffs.jpg"></video>
```

Preparing Video for the Web

Audio and video files exhibit some hefty differences. Most importantly, video files are big. Even the smallest of them is many times the size of an audio recording of a full-length Mahler symphony.

Handling this much data without trying your visitors' patience is a true test. In the following sections, you'll learn how to prepare your video for the Web and let your visitors view it.

Hosting your own video files is a task meant for ambitious multimedia mavens. The key stumbling block is the sheer size of digital video. On a digital camcorder, every second of video can chew through 1 to 3 MB of storage (depending on the recording quality and format you use). Put together a 5-minute clip, and you're looking at a staggering 300 to 900 MB file. Not only is this awkward to manage, but it's also enough to take a bite out of any webmaster's server and bandwidth allocations.

What can you do to make a web video both look good and perform well? You can always use someone else's web-ready video (or pay a video-editing company lots of money to trim yours down to web proportions). Assuming that's not what you want, you have two choices:

- **Record at lower quality.** Many video cameras let you record using lower-quality settings for the sole purpose of putting video on the Web. This way, you can dodge conversion headaches and send video straight to your site.

- **Lower the quality afterward.** More commonly, you need to go through a long process of *re-encoding* your high-quality video to convert it to a size suitable for the Web. To do this, you need a video-editing or video-conversion program (see the box on page 533 for tips on choosing one). It may take a bit of time to get this approach working, because you need to pick a program, settle on the right settings, and check your results. But once you iron out the kinks, this is the best solution, because it gives you the flexibility to retain as much quality as you can in your web video. It's a particularly handy strategy if you plan to use a hosting service like YouTube. YouTube does best with high-quality video, because it does its own re-encoding when you upload your video files.

Encoding Your Media

Plenty of programs can edit and convert video files. Some are free, while others are professional tools with prices to match. However, there are good choices out there for even casual video creators. If you need to edit your video (for example, snip out pieces, add fades and transitions, or superimpose captions over the action), you should consider a video editing tool. Two basic choices are Windows Movie Maker, included with Windows, and iMovie for the Mac. If you use Windows Movie Maker, however, you'll need one of the free conversion programs described below to convert the final Windows Media Video file (.wmv) into a legitimate MP4 file (.mp4).

If you already have the video you want and simply need a way to convert it to MP4 format or compress it to a web-friendly size, two free, open-source conversion tools can help: HandBrake (available at *http://handbrake.fr*, and shown in Figure 16-4) and Miro Video Converter (*www.mirovideoconverter.com*). Both programs offer Windows and Mac versions and can convert a wide range of formats. Miro is slightly simpler to use, while HandBrake lets you tweak a few more advanced options for the encoding.

Here's how to get your video ready for the Web:

1. **Film your movie.**

   Take a couple of lessons from video aficionados and film your video in a way that makes it easier to compress and introduces less distortion: Keep camera movements smooth and gradual, and don't film complex patterns. Your compressed video will look better.

   If you're using a smartphone or a tablet, remember to *always* film in landscape orientation (so the long edge of the device is horizontal). In other words, you want the picture to be short and wide, like a computer monitor or a television screen. If you ignore this advice and film in portrait mode, you'll be disappointed when you play your video in a web page. That's because the video player will shrink down your tall, skinny video and pad the sides with oceans of black space.

2. **Connect your device to your computer using a USB cable.**

   Other modes of transport are possible, but usually less practical. For example, if you have a video on a smartphone, you can upload it to a web storage service or email the video file to yourself. But because video files are so big, these approaches are often slow and awkward.

3. **Copy your video file from your device to your computer.**

   You may have a program that automatically copies pictures and movie files to your computer. Examples include a photo and media management program like Adobe Lightroom, Picasa, or iPhoto (if you're moving videos from an iPhone to a Mac).

   If you plug in your device and no program offers to perform the import, you may need to transfer the files on your own. Fortunately, it's a relatively simple job. Just browse the folders on your device until you find a video file (look for big files with extensions like *.mp4* or *.mov*). Then drag one or more files to a folder on your computer so you can work with them.

4. **Use a video-editing program to snip out just the video segment you want.**

Some programs let you add music or special effects at this point, too. There's no shortage of options here, from simple, budget-friendly editors like iMovie and Windows Movie Maker to professional packages like Adobe Premiere Elements and Apple's Final Cut Pro.

5. **Re-encode that piece of video in a highly compressed format.**

If all the format information in your program sounds like gobbledy-gook, look for an option that clearly says "web video" when you save your clip. (If you're still looking for a program that can perform this sort of conversion, check out the box on page 533.)

Technically, you make three choices in this step:

- **Video format.** As discussed earlier, the best choice is to create an MP4 file encoded using the H.264 codec.

- **Video dimensions.** If your source video already has the dimensions you want, you don't need to change anything. But if you want to show a smaller video window in your web page, you might decide to scale down your video to match, because this reduces its file size. These days, videos are usually recorded in a widescreen aspect ratio, and they commonly fall into one of these pixel dimensions: 640 x 360 (usually the smallest you'll want to go), 854 x 480, 1280 x 720 (known as 720p, or High Definition), and 1920 x 1080 (known as 1080p, or Full High Definition).

- **Video quality.** As with JPEG pictures, the greater the compression, the more detail you lose. Some video conversion tools let you pick a quality setting (Figure 16-4). Others let you choose the bitrate (the number of bits set aside to store each second of video). The smaller the bitrate, the lower the quality and the smaller the final video file.

Re-encoding video is time-consuming—even a speedy computer can take several times as long as the length of the original clip. The good news is that at the end of the process, you'll have a more manageable web-ready file—say, a 20 MB file for a full 3-minute clip.

NOTE If you plan to create a website with a lot of digital audio and video, you need to reconsider your site's storage and bandwidth requirements (see page 291). Unlike ordinary HTML pages and web graphics, multimedia files can grow quite large, threatening to overwhelm your space and bandwidth allotment. You can avoid this problem by using a hosted multimedia service like YouTube, in which case the video views cost you neither web space nor bandwidth.

The Picture tab lets you
change the video dimensions

Click here to start
the conversion

The converted file will
have this name

FIGURE 16-4

*Although HandBrake is
full of settings, you need
to consider changing
only a few of them. Pull
the Quality slider to the
left to create a video file
that's smaller and of lower
quality.*

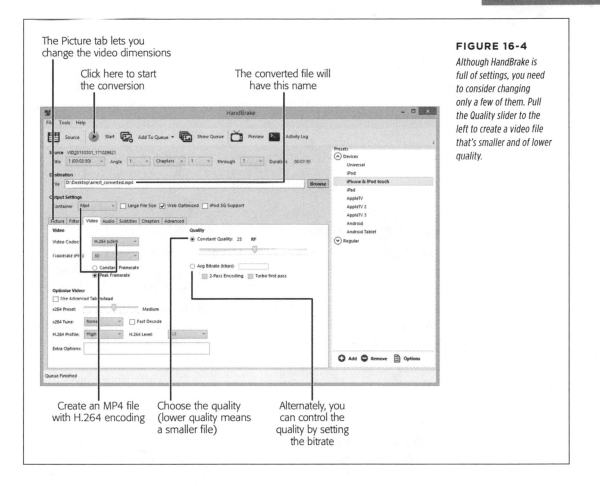

Create an MP4 file
with H.264 encoding

Choose the quality
(lower quality means
a smaller file)

Alternately, you
can control the
quality by setting
the bitrate

Fallbacks for Old Browsers

The <audio> and <video> elements are great tools when they work, which is most of the time. But if your page runs into an old browser that doesn't recognize HTML5 attributes, things aren't quite so smooth.

Usually, the only browser you need to worry about is Internet Explorer (specifically, IE 8 and older). Even though IE 8 is more than six years old, it's still kicking around on ancient Windows XP computers that can't run newer versions of the browser. IE 8 doesn't know anything about HTML5. If it sees the <audio> and <video> elements, it ignores them and displays the rest of your page with no playback controls or video window.

To deal with this situation, you need to include fallback content nestled inside the <audio> or <video> element. That way, if a browser doesn't understand the element, it displays alternate content. For example, instead of showing a video player window, your page can show a link to download the video:

```
<video src="arrest.mp4" controls>
    Click here to download the <a href="arrest.mpg">arrest.mpg</a> video.
</video>
```

Browsers that don't understand HTML5 (like IE 8) will act as though they saw this:

```
    Click here to download the <a href="arrest.mpg">arrest.mpg</a> video.
```

Of course, a link isn't nearly as good as a real video window. To compensate, you can use another type of playback window if the <video> element fails. There are two reliable ways to do that without HTML5:

- **Use a YouTube video window.** The drawback is that you'll need to upload your video to YouTube, as described on page 536.

- **Use a Flash video player.** The world has plenty of Flash players, and many of them are free for noncommercial use. And best of all, most support H.264, which means you don't need to go to the work of re-encoding your files.

Either way, you need to take a bunch of markup and paste it inside the <video> element, so that the Flash plug-in becomes the fallback for browsers that don't understand HTML5. You can see the HTML for a YouTube player on page 549. You'll find the markup for a Flash player in the next section.

UP TO SPEED

The Role of Flash

Flash is a versatile plug-in that's slowly being replaced by HTML5. Just a few years ago, Flash was a top tool for programmers who wanted to create rich, interactive websites and games. Today, a mixture of HTML5 and JavaScript is more likely to fill that role, but Flash lives on as a way to play video without relying on HTML.

Visitors can't use Flash unless they have a Flash plug-in installed. That said, good estimates suggest that an overwhelming 99 percent of web-connected desktop computers already have the plug-in. The real strength of Flash is that even very old computers are likely to have the Flash plug-in.

It might occur to you that you could add a Flash player to your page and leave out HTML5 altogether. After all, doesn't virtually every computer have Flash? The problem is that Flash doesn't play well with mobile devices. In particular, Flash doesn't work at all on iPhones and iPads for reasons that are partly technical and partly political. In other words, if you want people to see your videos on Apple's current crop of mobile devices, you need to start with HTML5 and use Flash as a last resort for browsers that don't do HTML5.

Adding a Flash Fallback

If you're interested in a Flash video player, your first step is to pick the one you want to use. Two popular choices are JW Player (*http://www.jwplayer.com*) and

Flowplayer Flash (*http://flash.flowplayer.org*). With either one, you need to sign up at the website and then pick a plan. You're interested in the free plan, which gets you the Flash player only. (You can pay money for them to host your videos and to get extra features in the Flash player.)

For example, the process of using JW Player goes like this:

1. **Visit *www.jwplayer.com*.**

2. **Click the Order Now button.**

   A detailed page appears with different pricing plans. Ignore the option of paying for hosting (which gets JW Player to host your video files on its site, instead of keeping it on your own site).

3. **Under the Free option, click Get It Now.**

4. **Provide your email address, and then click Get Started.**

   JW Player sends you a confirmation email, with a link you need to click.

5. **Confirm your account by clicking the link in your email.**

   Once you click the link, the JW Player site asks you to create a password.

6. **Choose a password to complete your account registration.**

   Now you go to JW Player's Publish Wizard page.

7. **Click "Publish a Video Now" to get the ball rolling.**

   JW Player needs three pieces of information to create your Flash player (Figure 16-5).

8. **Fill in the information for your video.**

   - **Media File** is the crucial detail. Identify the MP4 video file that you want to show in your video window. Just type in its name, as you do with the <video> element. The JW Player can then play your video as long as it's in the same folder as your page. If you want to get fancy, you can use a relative path, like *videos/arrest.mp4* to point to a video in a subfolder on your website.

   - **Poster Image** is an optional image that appears in the video window before playback starts. It plays the same role as the poster attribute in the <video> element.

   - **Media Title** is an optional descriptive name for your video. It appears in the middle of the video window, before playback starts. It's also used if you create a playlist with this video.

NOTE You don't need to upload the media file or poster image. You just need to tell JW Player what their filenames are. That way, the JW Player site can create the right markup to show the player on your page.

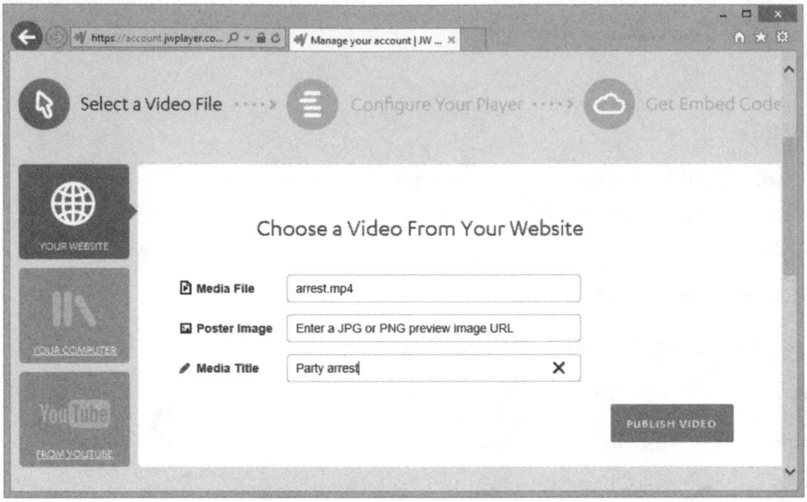

FIGURE 16-5

In this example, you're about to create the markup for a JW Player-powered video window. The player will show the arrest.mp4 video that's on your site.

9. **Click Publish Now.**

   The next step asks you to configure your player (Figure 16-6).

10. **Choose the size of your video window. Optionally, you can specify any of the other settings on this page.**

    Usually, you'll pick Responsive, which means the player sizes itself to match your video file. Your other choice is Fixed Dimensions, in which case you need to set the exact height and width of the window in pixels.

    You can also choose a *skin* for your player, which sets the color scheme and the styling for the video box border and its controls. But because you've opted to use the free version of JW Player, you're limited to the standard black-and-gray skin.

    In the Playback Options section, you can make a few more minor adjustments. For example, you can check the Autostart setting to start playback as soon as the browser loads the page, and Repeat to make the video loop continuously. Make sure you set the Primary State option to Flash, not HTML5. That's because you want to use JW Player as a fallback only, not an all-purpose player.

11. **Click Get Embed Code.**

    Now you're rewarded with the markup and JavaScript code you need to put your customized version of the JW Player on your site.

FIGURE 16-6

When you create the JW Player markup, you pick a few options to style the video box, and the website spits out the code you need.

12. **Copy the first `<script>` element and put it in the `<head>` section of your web page.**

    The first `<script>` element points to a block of JavaScript code stored on the JW Player website. Your page uses this code to create the player. Here's an example:

    `<script src="http://jwpsrv.com/library/VgIvAsOOEeSUiw4AfQhyIQ.js"></script>`

    Part of this URL looks like a string of gibberish letters. In truth, it's a unique code that identifies you to the JW Player site.

13. **Copy the rest of the markup, and then put it inside the `<video>` element in your web page.**

    Once you add the `<script>` element, you can put the playback window wherever you want in your page using a second block of HTML markup that the JW Player site provides. It consists of an empty <div> container and a <script> element with a bit more JavaScript code:

```
<div id='playernCvWpRtuIEqB'></div>
<script type='text/javascript'>
  jwplayer('playernCvWpRtuIEqB').setup({
      file: 'arrest.mp4',
      image: '//www.longtailvideo.com/content/images/jw-player/lWMJeVvV-876.jpg',
      title: 'Party arrest',
      width: '100%',
      aspectratio: '16:9',
      primary: 'flash'
  });
</script>
```

The code in the <script> element creates the playback window according to the options you specified and places it in the <div> container. But you don't see the messy JavaScript and Flash details that make everything happen, because the JW Player site stores them.

Remember, the JW Player is a fallback. You don't want to use it unless the <video> element fails. That means you need to put the JW Player inside your <video> element. Here's a complete page that puts the pieces together:

```
<!DOCTYPE html>
<html>
<head>
  <title>Embarrassing Party Video</title>
  <script src="http://jwpsrv.com/library/VgIvAsOOEeSUiw4AfQhyIQ.js"></script>
</head>
<body>
<h1>It's Less Fun (When the Police Come)</h1>
<p>Party was going great until the fine fellows at 24th division
came by on a noise complaint. </p>
<video src="arrest.mp4" controls>
  <div id='playernCvWpRtuIEqB'></div>
  <script type='text/javascript'>
    jwplayer('playernCvWpRtuIEqB').setup({
        file: 'arrest.mp4',
        image: '//www.longtailvideo.com/content/images/jw-player/
        lWMJeVvV-876.jpg',
        title: 'Party arrest',
        width: '100%',
        aspectratio: '16:9',
        primary: 'flash'
    });
  </script>
</video>
```

```
<p>Click the play button to see what happened to us.</p>
</body>
</html>
```

To see how the JW Player works, find an old browser that doesn't understand HTML5, or cheat by removing the <video> element from your page, so that it contains the JW Player script and nothing else. That way, you'll see the same content as ancient, HTML5-ignorant browsers.

> **NOTE** With Flash's standard security settings, you can't play a movie from your hard drive. That means that if you create a test page with JW Player and you try to run it from your computer, it won't work. You need to upload the page to a web server (along with your video file), and then try it out.

■ Uploading Videos to YouTube

Before YouTube hit the scene, video clips hadn't really taken off on the Web. They were all-around inconvenient: slow to download, with often jerky and sporadic playback. Today, the landscape has shifted. Web connections are faster and every browser supports video playback through HTML5 or Flash. Ordinary people own all sorts of digital video gadgets that can shoot short movies, from true video cameras to digital cameras, smartphones, and webcams. Popular clips rocket around the world, going from unknown to Internet sensation in a matter of hours. Family members, adventurers, and wannabe political commentators all regularly use video to keep in touch, show their skills, and dish the dirt.

YouTube (*www.youtube.com*) is at the forefront of this revolution. It currently ranks as the world's third most-popular site (behind Google and Facebook), and it's held that spot for years. And YouTube's range of content is staggering. With a quick search, you can turn up both amateur and professional content, including funny home videos, product reviews and announcements, homemade music videos, clips from movies and television shows, and ordinary people spouting off on just about any topic.

If you're still considering options for putting your video online, there are three great reasons to use YouTube:

- **It's easy.** When you use YouTube, you don't need to worry about converting your video to the right format, re-encoding it to make it smaller, or adding a Flash fallback. YouTube handles all these concerns gracefully, using HTML5 or Flash, depending on what your visitor's browser understands. It even encodes your video into several different resolutions, so that people on slow connections get a smaller video file that won't choke up halfway through, while people on fast connections can enjoy your video in high quality.

- **It extends the reach of your website.** YouTube is one of the most popular sites on the Web. If you're lucky, a YouTube video can increase your audience from a few people to millions of eager clip-watchers. By putting your movies on YouTube, you increase the odds that someone will discover it and possibly visit your site afterward. For example, many of the most popular clip-makers capitalize on their YouTube popularity by selling themed merchandise on their sites. Others use AdSense (page 415), which includes special ad boxes that sit unobtrusively at the bottom of the playback window.

- **The bandwidth is free.** If you put a video on your site, you need to worry about the space it takes up and whether you have enough bandwidth to satisfy every visitor. This is a particular problem if your video goes viral (becomes briefly and instantly popular). If you have a basic shared hosting account, this attention can crash your site.

In the following sections, you'll see how to upload your first YouTube video and how to embed it in one of your pages.

Preparing a Video for YouTube

Before you upload a video, it helps to understand how YouTube works and the sort of files it expects. Here are some essential bits of YouTube wisdom:

- YouTube accepts video in virtually any format, including MPEG2, MPEG4, MOV, DivX, WMV, WebM, AVI, and FLV. That means you probably won't need to convert your file before submitting it.

- YouTube automatically re-encodes the videos you upload so that web visitors can watch them without teeth-gnashing delays. For this reason, YouTube recommends that you upload the original version of your clip. In other words, don't re-encode your video. Doing so only wastes your time and lowers the movie's quality because YouTube re-encodes the clip anyway to prepare it for playback.

NOTE Depending on the length of your clip and the video format you used, your original file could be gargantuan (easily running into hundreds of megabytes). Even though YouTube allows uploads of files up to 128 GB, videos of this size aren't practical for everyone (they take forever to upload, for one thing). If you have a slow web connection, or if your Internet service provider limits how much data you can transfer in a month, you might need to ignore YouTube's recommendation and shrink your video files before you upload them. If so, use one of the tools described on page 533.

- YouTube plays back both standard and widescreen video. For best results, use the largest dimensions your recording device allows. When you upload your file, YouTube creates different copies of it at different sizes. That way, viewers get a video optimized for their playback window, whether that's a standard desktop-browser window, a full-screen window, or a tiny window on a mobile device.

- Read the YouTube Help section. From time to time, YouTube changes its recommendations or accepts new formats. To get the lowdown before you upload, visit *http://tinyurl.com/66onkub*.

Uploading a Video

Once your video's ready, it's time to put it online. The process is refreshingly straightforward:

1. **Go to** *www.youtube.com*. **Click the Sign In link in the top-right corner of the page. Then log in with your Google account.**

   Anyone can browse and view YouTube videos (you can choose from over a billion clips at the time of this writing). But to upload your own movies, you need a Google account. If you've somehow made it to this point in the book without creating one, you need one now. Supply the usual particulars, including your email address, password, location, and date of birth, and then sign yourself up.

2. **Click the Upload button at the top of the page.**

   You'll see an upload "drop box" (Figure 16-7).

FIGURE 16-7

To get started with YouTube, you need to drop a video file in the big white box (or click the big arrow in the middle).

3. **Drag and drop a file into the upload box, or click "Select file to upload" to browse for it on your hard drive.**

   Either way, you can upload more than one video at a time.

   As soon as you pick your clips, YouTube begins uploading them (Figure 16-8). With the time-consuming upload process under way, you can add information about your video at your leisure.

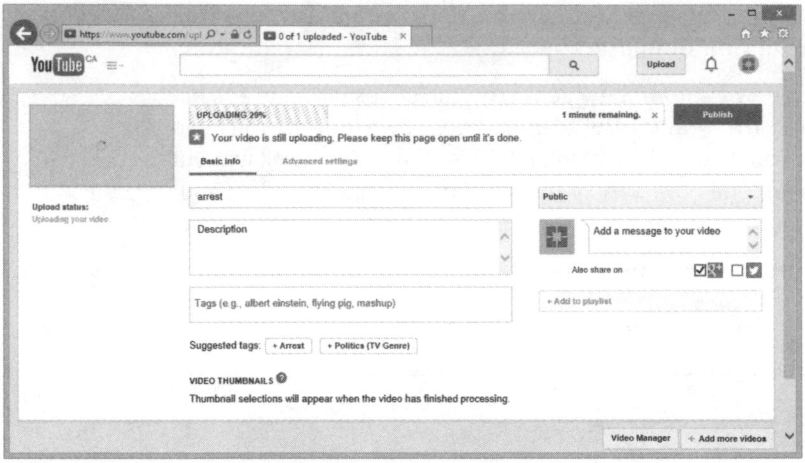

FIGURE 16-8

As YouTube uploads a file, it estimates how long the transfer will take. While you wait, you can fill out the descriptive information for your video.

4. **Fill in the details about your video.**

   You need to supply a title and description, which YouTube displays on your video page and in its search results. You also need to specify a category for your video and add one or more *tags*. When other people search YouTube using keywords that match your category or tags, there's a better chance that your video will turn up in the search results.

   NOTE Don't worry if the information you enter isn't perfect. You can change it anytime. Just find your video in the My Videos section, select it, and then click Edit.

5. **Choose a privacy setting (Public, Unlisted, or Private).**

   • **Public.** A public video turns up in YouTube search results, and anyone can watch it.

   • **Unlisted.** Anyone can also watch an unlisted video, but people will need the right URL to find it—the video won't turn up in an ordinary search.

   • **Private.** If you mark a clip as private, only YouTubers you explicitly identify can see it, and only after they log into YouTube.

6. **Optionally, click Advanced Settings to configure a few more settings.**

   Here are some options you might find useful:

   • Use the "Allow comments" and "Users can view ratings for this video" settings to let people respond to your video. For example, you can ban people from commenting (turn off "Allow comments"), or allow only comments you approve (turn "Allow comments" on and then choose "Approved" instead of "All"). Ordinarily, YouTube allows all comments, giving the site a raucous community atmosphere. In some cases, it makes sense to limit comments and ratings (for example, if you cover a sensitive topic and you're worried about attracting abusive comments). But the vast majority of videos on YouTube allow comments and are heavily commented. Videos that don't let people opine are likely to be ignored.

- Choose a category to classify your video and help make sure it turns up in the right searches. YouTube has categories like Comedy, Education, Gaming, and News.

- Use the "Recording date" and "Video location" settings to identify when and where you recorded your video.

- Use the "Allow embedding" setting to control whether other people can embed your video on their web pages. But take note: If you don't allow this, it not only stops *other* people from showcasing your video; it also prevents *you* from embedding your own video on your website.

7. **Wait.**

YouTube says it typically takes 1 to 5 minutes to upload each megabyte of video if you have a high-speed connection, so this is a good time to get a second cup of coffee.

While you're waiting, you can drag another video file onto the upload page and start uploading it as well. Or, if you've given up completely, click the tiny X icon next to the progress bar to stop the upload.

Once YouTube uploads and converts your video, it replaces the progress bar with a "Processing Done" message.

If you get really tired of waiting, consider skipping ahead to step 9. That's right, you can tell YouTube to publish your video even before it finishes uploading the file. YouTube then schedules your movie for publication, which means it will become live on the site as soon as YouTube finishes processing it.

8. **Pick a thumbnail for your video from the Video Thumbnails section.**

The video thumbnail is a single frame from your movie that appears in the YouTube video window before playback starts. It also shows up when YouTube lists your film in a search result.

As YouTube processes your video, it takes a frame grab every few seconds and adds it as a possible thumbnail.

9. **Click Publish.**

Now your video is completely configured and live before the entire web world (Figure 16-9).

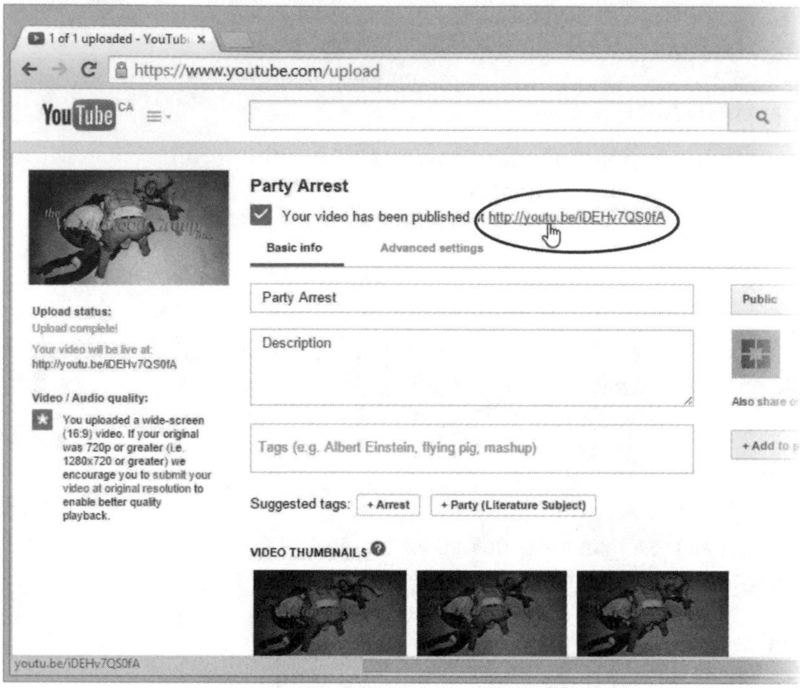

FIGURE 16-9

Once you publish your video, YouTube gives you a link to it.

TIP If you want to edit the information for an already-uploaded video, remove the video, or get some fascinating statistics about the people who've seen it, you need to use the YouTube video manager. Scroll down to the bottom of the upload page and click the Video Manager button in the bottom-right corner. (Or, if you're somewhere else on YouTube, click the Account button in the top-right corner, click Creator Studio, and then choose Video Manager from the menu of links on the left.)

Showing a YouTube Video in a Web Page

Once your video is ready, you can watch it in several ways:

- You can search for it on YouTube.

- You can put a link on your web page that leads to your YouTube video page. Just visit that page and copy the URL from the address bar.

- You can play it back in a YouTube window on one of your web pages. This is the most powerful approach. It lets you combine the look and feel of a self-hosted video with YouTube's high performance and solid browser support.

Embedding videos is as easy as copying a snippet of HTML into your page. Here's what you do:

1. **Go to the YouTube page for your video.**

   You can use the URL you got when you published your video (Figure 16-9). If you've already moved on, you can browse through the videos in your account. Click the Account button at the top right of any YouTube page, choose Creator Studio, and then click your recently uploaded video.

2. **Click the Share button underneath the video window.**

   It sits between your video's title and description. When you click it, YouTube shows a small panel of sharing information.

3. **Click Embed.**

   This gives you the HTML markup you need (Figure 16-10), instead of a mere link.

FIGURE 16-10

Here's the markup you need to display this video on your web page. The code's crammed into a single line.

4. **Right-click the box with the HTML markup and choose Copy.**

5. **Edit your HTML page and paste in the YouTube markup.**

   Put the markup where you want the video window to appear (Figure 16-11).

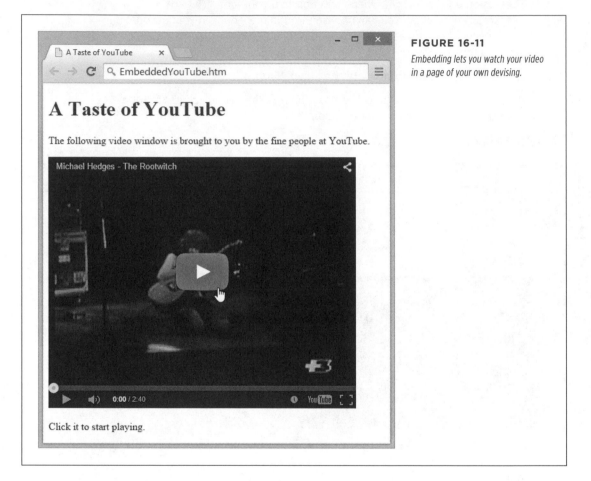

FIGURE 16-11

Embedding lets you watch your video in a page of your own devising.

Here's the complete markup that creates the page in Figure 16-11:

```
<!DOCTYPE html>
<html>
<head>
  <title>Embarrassing Party Video</title>
</head>
<body>
<h1>It's Less Fun (When the Police Come)</h1>
<p>The following video window is brought to you by the fine people
at YouTube.</p>
```

```
<iframe width="560" height="315" src=https://www.youtube.com/embed/
iDEHv7OSOfA?rel=0
frameborder="0" allowfullscreen></iframe>

<p>Click it to start playing.</p>
</body>
</html>
```

To embed your video, YouTube uses the `<iframe>` element (page 565) to stake out a small rectangular section of your page and insert some content there. To place the playback window in a specific spot, put the `<iframe>` element inside a `<div>` element, and then use style rules to position the `<div>`.

TIP To change the color of the border around your video window, start playback automatically, display the movie in full-screen mode, or tweak several other details, you need to adjust the markup (see the bolded line in the code above). For the complete scoop, check out *http://tinyurl.com/2kxnv3*.

Appendixes

Where to Go from Here

B y this point, you've taken a long voyage across the Web. You began by learning the fundamentals of site building, first by considering the HTML markup that structures every web page, and then by using the CSS styling language to transform the appearance of those pages. After that, you explored a range of web-based services for your site, from search engine optimization and visitor tracking to social media promotion and ad sales. Finally, you dipped your toe into the deep waters of web programming with a bit of JavaScript.

So now that you've explored so much, where should you go next?

The obvious answer is "To your computer!" To get the most out of your new skills, you need to practice them—starting with the tutorials in this book, and then by building websites on your own. That's because there's no substitute for experimentation. The hours you spend fiddling with your markup, changing the design of a page, and building a menu will give you a practical understanding of what works in the web world and where the traps lie.

Another reason to take to your keyboard is to check out the websites mentioned in this book. Using them, you can dig deeper into specialized topics and see more examples. Don't worry, you don't need to search through chapter after chapter to find these sites; they're listed and linked on this book's companion site at *http:// prosetech.com/web*.

If you're more ambitious, there's plenty more to learn. Here are a few other resources you might use to make the jump from competent personal website builder to expert web designer:

- **Master CSS.** The styling language of the Web offers plenty of advanced tricks for creating slick sites. You can find many of them in the latest version of the standard, CSS3, which is only now gaining widespread browser support. For a gentle review of all things CSS, including an introduction to many of the newer CSS3 features, check out *CSS3: The Missing Manual* (O'Reilly), or read one of the many other books on the subject.

- **Learn to program with JavaScript.** When the Web was new, JavaScript was little more than a quirky gimmick. Today, JavaScript is where all the action is. Fancy-pants designers adorn entire pages with sliding, swooping, expanding, and fading effects powered by JavaScript. Hardcore programmers build apps, like browser-based versions of solitaire, using nothing but JavaScript. And many of the newer features in CSS3 and HTML5 can't shine without at least a bit of JavaScript. Learning JavaScript is no small undertaking, but it unlocks worlds of possibilities. If you're curious, check out a book like *JavaScript & jQuery: The Missing Manual* (O'Reilly).

- **Brush up on HTML5.** Every page you've seen in this book is an authentic HTML5 document. Even so, you haven't covered all the features and frills of the latest version of the standard. In particular, you haven't learned anything about the many JavaScript-powered HTML extensions that let you tap capabilities like geolocation (finding where a visitor is in the world), web storage (saving personal information between site visits), and browser-based drawing (to paint shapes, text, and pictures onscreen). If you decide to learn more about JavaScript, you might also want to explore more about these features of HTML5, which are covered in *HTML5: The Missing Manual* (O'Reilly).

- **Optimize your site for mobile devices.** Thanks to tablets and indispensable smartphones, mobile browsing has exploded. But your desktop site will look like little more than a tiny version of itself if you don't dynamically refashion your pages for the small screen. Page 250 introduces this issue, but you can learn how to truly make your site mobile-friendly in *HTML5: The Missing Manual* (O'Reilly). Or, for a more thorough and technical discussion of web design in the mobile world, check out the Smashing Magazine book *The Mobile Web Handbook* (learn more about it at *http://tinyurl.com/mobile-web-h*).

- **Try out a content-management system.** Understanding the standards that underpin a page is only part of the challenge of site building. To create a beautiful, content-filled, frequently updated website, you need to juggle a lot of details. That's where content-management systems and blogging-and-more platforms like WordPress come in. With WordPress, you pick a layout and write the page content, but WordPress combines the two into a flawless site. Of course, it's up to you to decide if you want to give up that much control to get the sort of features that WordPress offers. If you do, you'll find that your understanding of HTML markup and CSS styling still comes in handy when you customize the templates and style sheet that govern a WordPress-powered site. To step off in this direction, check out *WordPress: The Missing Manual* (O'Reilly).

And no matter which path you take, happy travels!

HTML Quick Reference

H TML is the language of the Web. You can use it to create any web page, whether you're promoting a local bake sale or running a Fortune 500 company. Chapter 1 introduced you to HTML, and since then, you've steadily added to your arsenal of HTML elements.

This appendix provides a quick reference of all the HTML elements you've seen in this book (and a few more). Each entry features a brief description of the element, and many entries provide cross-references to more detailed examples in the book. The list includes the most usable new elements from the latest version of HTML, HTML5. You'll also get a quick refresher on HTML character entities, which let you display special characters on a web page.

HTML Elements

As you know, the HTML standard is based on *elements*—specialized codes in angle brackets that tell a browser how to format text, when to insert images, and how to link different documents together.

The elements listed below are arranged in alphabetical order. The beginning of each section details the type of element it is:

- **A block or inline element.** Block elements are separated from other elements with a bit of extra white space. For example, the <h1> block element adds a heading to your page on its own line and separates it from the preceding and following content with some padding and margin space. (Of course, you can alter or remove this space using the margin and padding style properties.)

NOTE In official HTML5 lingo, block elements are called *flow elements*, and inline elements are called *phrasing elements*.

- **A container or standalone element.** A container element holds text or other elements inside it. A standalone element can't contain anything, so you usually write it as only one tag using the empty element syntax (page 15). HTML limits where you can put some standalone elements, meaning you can associate them only with certain other elements. For example, you can associate the <area> element, which defines an image-map hotspot, only with the <map> element, which defines an image map.

The section below doesn't include any of the new elements from HTML5—you'll find those in a separate section, starting on page 577.

<a> (Anchor Element)

Inline Element, Container Element

The anchor element (<a>) has two roles. The most common is to create a link that, when clicked, takes a visitor from one page to another. The second role is to place a hidden marker, called a bookmark, in a web page. You'll learn about both uses below.

To create a link, you supply the destination URL using the href attribute. You put the clickable link text between the opening and closing tags:

```
<a href="LinkedPage.htm">Click Me</a>
```

When setting the href attribute, you can use a *relative* URL, which points to a page on your own website, or an *absolute* URL, which starts with *http://* and can point to any page on the Web. For a review of the differences between relative and absolute links and when to use each, see page 177.

You can also use the anchor element to create clickable image links. They're just as easy to write as clickable text links. The trick is to put the <img> element inside an <a> element, like this:

```
<a href="LinkedPage.htm"><img src="MyPic.gif" alt="My Pic" /></a>
```

Finally, you can use the anchor element to create a link that, instead of sending a visitor to a new page, opens an email message with the address information already filled in. You do this by creating a *mailto* link, as shown here:

```
<a href="mailto:me@myplace.com">Email Me</a>
```

For more information about the ins and outs of the mailto link, see page 188.

You can also apply the target attribute to an anchor, which instructs a browser to open the destination page in a new browser window or in a specific frame, like this:

```
<a href="LinkedPage.htm" target="_blank">Click Me</a>
```

The anchor element also works with *bookmarks*, letting you lead website guests to a specific spot on a web page. To create a bookmark, you simply add an identifying name to the target element using the id attribute, like this:

```
<h2 id="Canaries">Pet Canaries</h2>
```

Once you create a bookmark like this, you can use the anchor element to write a URL that points to it by adding the bookmark information to the end of the URL. To do this, add the number-sign symbol (#) followed by the bookmark name, as shown here:

```
Learn about recent developments in <a href="sales.htm#Canaries">canary
sales</a>.
```

You can learn more about bookmarks and ordinary links in Chapter 6.

<address> (Contact Information)
Block Element, Container Element

Webmasters use the <address> element only occasionally; by convention, they use it only as a way to contact the authors of the web page. The contact information could be an email address, a web link (the two most common options), or a postal address. Here's an example:

```
Our website is managed by:
<address>
<a href="mailto:jsolo@mysite.com">John Solo</a>,
<a href="mailto:lcheng@mysite.com ">Lisa Cheng<a>, and
<a href="mailto:rpavane@mysite.com ">Ryan Pavane</a>.
</address>
```

Most browsers format text in the <address> element in italics, just as though you had used the <i> element. The only value in using <address> is that it lets automated programs that scan web pages extract useful address information.

To put other address information on your page, like your store's physical address, don't use the <address> element to style it. Remember that, by convention, it's reserved for address details for the person or people who maintain the web page.

<area> (Image Map)
Standalone Element, Allowed in <map> Only

The <area> element defines a clickable region (known as a *hotspot*) inside an image map (which you create using the <map> element). When defining an area, you need to supply the target URL (using the href attribute), the type of shape the area is (using the shape attribute), and the coordinates of that shape (using the coords attribute). For shape, you can specify a circle, square, or polygon.

For a circle, specify the coordinates in this order: center point x-coordinate, center point y-coordinate, radius. For any other shape, supply the corners, in order, as a series of x-y coordinates, like this: x1, y1, x2, y2, and so on. Here's an example that creates a square hotspot:

```
<area href="page1.htm" shape="square" coords="5,5,95,195" alt="A clickable
square" />
```

This square is invisible to your site guests. But if they click anywhere inside it, they'll go to *page1.htm*. For more information, see the <map> element on page 567. For a full-fledged image map example, see page 189.

<audio> (Sound Player)
Block Element, Container Element

The <audio> element creates an audio player, a small set of playback controls that visitors can use to listen to an audio file.

You specify the filename using the src attribute. Browsers differ in which audio formats they'll play, but MP3 files are by far the most reliable choice. In addition, you should always include the controls attribute. Without it, guests have no idea that there's a player on the page (unless you create a set of controls for it using JavaScript).

Here's a fully configured <audio> element at its simplest:

```
<audio src="rubberduckies.mp3" controls></audio>
```

You can set a few options for the <audio> element. Use the obnoxious autoplay attribute to tell the audio player to start playing as soon as the page loads. Use the loop attribute to tell the audio player to replay the audio file when it ends, unless a visitor clicks the Pause button. Use the muted attribute to start the player with the sound muted (in which case a visitor can click the speaker icon to restore sound).

You can specify fallback content for the <audio> element, too. That way, if a browser doesn't understand HTML5 (for example, if a visitor checks out your page with a dusty old copy of IE 8), the browser displays the fallback content instead of the audio player:

```
<audio src="rubberduckies.mp3" controls>
  Your browser is old. Click here to download the
  <a href="rubberduckies.mp3">rubberduckies.mp3</a> audio file.
</audio>
```

Optionally, you can give the <audio> element a list of audio files in different formats. The player then plays the first audio file whose format it understands. To do this, you need to remove the src attribute and then, inside the <audio> element, add one or more <source> elements, like this:

```
<audio controls>
  <source src="rubberduckies.ogg" type="audio/ogg">
  <source src="rubberduckies.mp3" type="audio/mpeg">
  Your browser is old. Click here to download the
  <a href="rubberduckies.mp3">rubberduckies.mp3</a> audio file.
</audio>
```

Now the player will play *rubberduckies.ogg* if the browser supports it (Chrome, Firefox, and Opera do). Otherwise, it will play *rubberduckies.mp3*, if the browser supports that (Safari and Internet Explorer, please step forward). And if the browser doesn't understand the <audio> element at all, it will show the fallback content, which is the link to the audio file.

To see what the <audio> element looks like in a full web page, see page 526.

<b> (Bold Text)
Inline Element, Container Element

The <b> element displays text in boldface. The official rules suggest that you use <b> for "stylistically offset" text, that is, text that should be presented in bold but that doesn't have greater importance than the words around it. This could include keywords, product names, and anything else that might be bold in print:

```
Make sure you buy the <b>Super-Fraginator</b> today!
```

If you want to format text in bold *and* convey additional importance, <strong> is the recommended choice (although the visual result is the same). This subtle difference in meaning is the official position of the people who created the HTML5 standard, although few web developers actually pay attention to the difference.

<base> (Base URL)
Standalone Element, Allowed in <head> Only

The <base> element defines a document's *base URL*, which is a starting-point web address used to interpret all relative paths. You have to place the <base> element in the <head> section of a page, and you can use two attributes: href (which identifies the base URL) and target (which supplies a target frame for links).

For example, if you have a link that points to a file named *MySuperSunday.htm* and the base URL is *http://www.SundaysForever.com/Current/*, a browser interprets the link as *http://www.SundaysForever.com/Current/MySuperSunday.htm*.

Web-heads rarely use the base URL this way because it almost always makes more sense for the browser to use the current page as a starting point for all relative URLs. In other words, if you're looking at *http://www.SundaysForever.com/Current/Intro.htm*, the browser already knows that the base URL is *http://www.SundaysForever.com/Current/*. For more information about the difference between absolute and relative links, see page 177.

<blockquote> (Block Quotation)
Block Element, Container Element

The <blockquote> element identifies a long quotation as a block element. It stands on its own, separate from paragraph block elements:

```
<blockquote><p>It was the best of times, it was the worst of times.</p>
</blockquote>
```

Usually, browsers indent the <blockquote> element on the left and right sides. However, you shouldn't use <blockquote> as a formatting tool. Instead, use it where it makes sense—to highlight a passage quoted from a book. As with any element, you can use a style sheet rule to change the way a browser formats <blockquote> text.

To put a brief quotation inside a block element like a paragraph, use the <q> element instead of <blockquote>.

<body> (Document Body)
Container Element, Allowed in <html> Only

The <body> element is a basic part of the structure of any HTML document. You put it immediately after the <head> section ends, and it contains all the content of your web page, including its text, image URLs, tables, and links.

 (Line Break)
Inline Element, Standalone Element

The line break (<br>) is an inline element that forces the text following it onto a new line, with no extra spacing. For example, you can use the <br> element to split address information in a paragraph:

```
<p>Johnny The Fever<br />
200 Easy Street<br />
Akimbo, Madagascar</p>
```

<button> (Button)
Inline Element, Container Element

The <button> element lets you create a clickable button within a form, and you can put a phrase or an image between the <button> element's start and end tags. As with any other form control, you need to supply a unique name and a value that the form will submit when a visitor clicks the button. You put the button content between the opening and closing tags:

```
<button name="submit" value="order" type="button">Place Order</button>
```

You can create three types of buttons, depending on the value you choose for the type attribute. A value of button creates an ordinary button with no built-in smarts (add JavaScript code to make it do something). A reset button clears all the information a visitor has filled out in a form, and a submit button sends the information in a form (like a guest's name or email address) back to a web server, which is useful if you create an application that uses the information (say, to build a list of customers).

The <button> element is more powerful than the <input> element for creating buttons, because it puts whatever content you want on the face of the button, including images:

```
<button name="submit" value="order" type="button">
  <img src="Order.gif" alt="Place Order" />
</button>
```

<caption> (Table Caption)

Container Element, Allowed in <table> Only

The <caption> element defines the title text for a table. If you use it, you have to make it the first element in a <table> element:

```
<table>
  <caption>Least Popular Vacation Destinations</caption>
  ...
</table>
```

HTML applies no automatic formatting to the caption; it simply positions the caption at the top of a table as ordinary text (and wraps it, if necessary, to fit the width of the table). You can apply whatever formatting you want through style sheet rules.

<cite> (Citation)

Inline Element, Container Element

The <cite> element identifies a *citation*, which is a reference to a book, print article, or other published resource:

```
<p>Charles Dickens wrote <cite>A Tale of Two Cities</cite>.</p>
```

Usually, browsers render the <cite> element as italic text. But you shouldn't use the <cite> element for formatting alone. Instead, use it when it makes sense (for example, when you refer to a published work you quote) and add style sheet rules that apply the specific formatting you want.

<code> (Code Listing)

Inline Element, Container Element

Use the <code> element to wrap snippets of example code (for instance, in a web page that presents a programming tutorial). Browsers display this code in a mono-spaced font.

<dd> (Dictionary Description)

Container Element, Allowed in <dl> Only

The <dd> element defines a word in a dictionary list. For more information, see the example in the <dl> element description below, or refer to page 54.

<del> (Deleted Text)

Block Element or Inline Element, Container Element

Webmasters rarely use the <del> element; it identifies text that was present but has now been removed. Browsers that support it display crossed-out text to represent the deleted material. Another element web-heads sometimes use to indicate a revision trail is <ins>.

\<dfn\> (Defined Term)

Inline Element, Container Element

Site authors rarely use the \<dfn\> element; it indicates the defining instance of a term. For example, the first time you learn about a new term in this book, like *froopy*, it's italicized. That's because it's the defining instance, and a definition usually follows. Browsers render the \<dfn\> element in italics.

\<div\> (Generic Block Container)

Block Element, Container Element

The \<div\> element groups together one or more block elements. For example, you could group together several paragraphs, a paragraph and a heading, and so on. Here's an example:

```
<div>
  <p>...</p>
  <p>...</p>
</div>
```

On its own, the \<div\> element doesn't do anything, but it's a powerful way to apply style sheet formatting. In the example above, you can apply formatting to the \<div\> element, and the browser passes that formatting along to the two nested paragraphs (assuming the style properties you're using support inheritance, as described on page 82).

To learn more about using the \<div\> element to apply style rules, see page 213. You should also refer to the \<span\> element, which applies formatting *inside* a block element. And if you want to apply more meaning to your containers, consider replacing your \<div\> with one of the HTML5 semantic elements discussed on page 577.

\<dl\> (Dictionary List)

Block Element, Container Element

The \<dl\> element defines a definition list (also known as a dictionary list), which is a series of terms, each followed by a definition in an indented block of text. In theory, you could put any type of content in a dictionary list, but it's recommended that you follow its intended use and include a list of terms and explanations. Here's an example:

```
<dl>
  <dt>tasseomancy</dt>
  <dd>Divination by reading tea leaves.</dd>
  <dt>tyromancy</dt>
  <dd>Divination by studying how cheese curds form during cheese making.</dd>
</dl>
```

<dt> (Dictionary Term)
Container Element, Allowed in <dl> Only

The <dt> element identifies the dictionary term that you're about to define. For more information, see the simple example under the <dl> element description above, or refer to page 54.

<em> (Emphasis)
Inline Element, Container Element

The <em> element has the same effect as the <i> (italic text) element, but a slightly different meaning. It's for emphasized text that would have a different inflection if read out loud (say, by a screen reader), like this:

```
Make sure you <em>don't</em> use the wrong element for your italics.
```

By comparison, the <i> element is for italicized text that doesn't have this emphasis.

Using style sheet rules, you can change the formatting of the <em> element, and emphasize its content in a way that doesn't use italic formatting (like by coloring the text red).

<form> (Interactive Form)
Block Element, Container Element

You use the <form> element to create a page that collects information from your guests. In it, you put graphical widgets like text boxes, checkboxes, selectable lists, and so on (represented by the <input>, <textarea>, <button>, and <select> elements, respectively). By putting these widgets in a <form> element, your browser can collect the information and then send it to a web server for use in another program, like a database that records guests' email addresses. Web applications are outside the scope of this book, but you can see how to use a <form> element with JavaScript on page 490, and you can consider free form-submission services on page 357.

<h1>, <h2>, <h3>, <h4>, <h5>, <h6> (Headings)
Block Element, Container Element

Headings are section titles. They appear as boldface letters at various sizes. The size of the text depends on the heading level. The six heading levels start at <h1> (the biggest) and move down to <h6>. Both <h5> and <h6> are actually smaller than regularly sized text. Here's an <h1> element in action:

```
<h1>Important Information</h1>
```

When you use headings, nest them on the page following a logical structure. Start with <h1> for the most important heading, and then use lower heading levels for subtopics under the main heading. Don't start with <h3> just because the formatting looks nicer. Instead, use the heading levels to delineate the structure of your document, and use style sheets to change the formatting of each heading to suit you.

\<head\> (Document Head)

Container Element, Allowed in \<html\> Only

The \<head\> section of a page goes before the \<body\> section. While the \<body\> element contains the web page content, the \<head\> element includes other information, like the title of the web page (the \<title\> element), descriptive metadata (one or more \<meta\> elements), and styles (the \<style\> or \<link\> elements).

\<hr\> (Horizontal Rule)

Block Element, Standalone Element

The \<hr\> element produces a horizontal rule (a solid line) that you use to separate block elements:

```
<p>...</p>
<hr />
<p>...</p>
```

Although the \<hr\> element still works perfectly well, HTML whizzes prefer using border settings in a style sheet rule to get much more control over the line style and its color. Here's an example that defines a style sheet rule for a solid blue line:

```
.border { border-top: solid medium navy }
```

And here's how you could apply it:

```
<p>...</p>
<div class="border"></div>
<p>...</p>
```

For more information about the style sheet border settings, refer to page 108.

\<html\> (Document)

Container Element

The \<html\> element is the first one that should appear in any HTML document. It wraps the rest of the document. If you create an ordinary web page, the \<html\> element contains two other essential ingredients: the \<head\> element, which defines the title, metadata, and linked style sheets; and the \<body\> element, which contains the actual content.

\<i\> (Italic Text)

Inline Element, Container Element

The \<i\> element displays text in italics, without conveying any extra emphasis or inflection. Here's an example:

```
The mattress label says <i>do not remove under penalty of law</i>
```

If you want to provide italics that suggest an emphasis in the way they are spoken, the <em> element is a better choice. However, both elements provide the same formatting, and the difference is acknowledged only by serious HTML5 wonks.

<iframe> (Inline Frame)
Inline Element, Container Element

The <iframe> element creates an *inline frame*—a scrollable window that's embedded in a page and that displays another web page inside it. You supply the attributes src (the page you want your browser to display in the frame), name (the unique name of the frame), and width and height (the dimensions of the frame in pixels). You can turn off the automatic border by setting the frameborder="0" attribute, and turn off scrolling by adding the scrolling="no" attribute. Here's one use of the <iframe> element:

```
<iframe src="MyPage.html" width="100" height="250"></iframe>
```

You can include instructions with the <iframe> element that a browser will display if it doesn't support <iframe>:

```
<iframe src="MyPage.html" width="100" height="250">
  <p>To see more details, check out <a href="MyPage.html">this page</a>.</p>
</iframe>
```

<img> (Image)
Inline Element, Standalone Element

The <img> element points to a picture file you want to display in a page. The src attribute identifies the picture using a relative or absolute link (see page 177). The alt attribute supplies text that a browser displays if it can't display the picture.

```
<img src="OrderButton.gif" alt="Place Order" />
```

Internet Explorer displays alternate text in a pop-up box, while some more standards-aware browsers (namely Firefox) don't. No matter; you can display a pop-up text box in just about any browser using the title attribute. It's the best way to add cross-browser pop-up text to an image.

The <img> element also supports height and width attributes you can use to explicitly size a picture:

```
<img src="photo01.jpg" alt="A photo" width="100" height="150" />
```

In this example, the picture has a width of 100 pixels and a height of 150 pixels. If these dimensions don't match the actual size of the picture, your browser stretches and otherwise mangles the picture to match the dimensions.

Never use the width and height attributes to resize an image; make those kinds of edits in a proper image-editing program. You can use the width and height attributes to tell a browser how big your picture is so it can lay out the page before it downloads the whole image, and to preserve your layout even if the browser can't find your picture.

To learn more about the image types you can use and how to organize pictures on a page, refer to Chapter 4.

Finally, you can create clickable regions on an image by defining an image map, and then by linking that image map to your image with the usemap attribute of the <img> element. For more information, see the <map> section (page 567).

<input> (Input Control)

Standalone Element, Allowed in <form> Only

The <input> element is the most common ingredient in an HTML form (which itself uses the <form> element). The <input> element can represent different widgets (called *controls*) that collect information from a web visitor.

The type attribute specifies the kind of control you want to create. Table B-1 lists the most common types. Additionally, you should give every control a unique name using the name attribute.

TABLE B-1 *HTML form controls.*

CONTROL	HTML ELEMENT	DESCRIPTION
Single-line text box	<input type="text" />	Displays a box where a visitor can type in text.
Password text box	<input type="password" />	Shows a box where a visitor can type in text, but the browser doesn't display the text. Instead, it displays an asterisk (*) or bullet (•) in place of every letter, to hide the text from prying eyes.
Checkbox	<input type="checkbox" />	Displays a checkbox you can set as turned on or off.
Radio button	<input type="radio" />	Shows a radio button (a circle you can set as turned on or off). Usually, you have a group of radio buttons next to one another, in which case a visitor selects exactly one.
Submit button	<input type="submit" />	Shows a standard clickable button that submits a form and all its data.
Reset button	<input type="reset" />	Displays a standard clickable button that clears any text a visitor has typed in and any selections she's made.
Image button	<input type="image" />	Shows a Submit button with a difference—you supply its visuals as a picture. To specify the picture file you want, set the src attribute.
Ordinary button	<input type="button" />	Shows a standard clickable button that doesn't do anything unless you hook it up to some JavaScript code (Chapter 14).

Here's an `<input>` element that creates a text box. When a visitor submits the page, whatever he typed into the box will be sent, along with the descriptive identifier LastName:

```
<input type="text" name="LastName" />
```

Of course, forms are useful only if you have code that processes their data. On page 490, you saw how guests can interact with forms using JavaScript, but forms are more commonly used with server-side web programs. For example, a server-side script might receive some visitor information from a form and store it in a database.

`<ins>` (Inserted Text)
Block Element or Inline Element, Container Element

The `<ins>` element identifies newly inserted text (for example, text added to a web page during its most recent edit). By design, browsers underline the text inside the `<ins>` element. Because of its specialized purpose, you'll rarely come across pages that use the `<ins>` element.

You can use the `<ins>` element around block elements or inside a block element. The `<del>` element is a complementary revision element, and you might want to use it in conjunction with `<ins>`.

`<li>` (List Item)
Container Element, Allowed in `<ol>` and `<ul>` Only

The `<li>` element represents a single item in an ordered (numbered) or unordered (bulleted) list. For more information, see the `<ol>` element for ordered lists and the `<ul>` element for unordered lists.

`<link>` (Document Relationship)
Standalone Element, Allowed in `<head>` Only

The `<link>` element describes a relationship between the current document and another document. For example, you might use it to point to the previous version of the current document. More commonly, you use it to point to an *external style sheet* that provides formatting instructions for the current page. You always put the `<link>` element in the `<head>` section of a page. Here's one possible use:

```
<link rel="stylesheet" href="MyStyles.css" />
```

By using external style sheets, you can define the styles for your site in a single file and then link all your site's pages to it. Chapter 3 has much more on style sheets and how to use them.

`<map>` (Image Map)
Inline Element, Container Element

The `<map>` element defines an *image map*—a picture with one or more clickable regions. When you create an image map, you assign it a unique name using the name attribute. You then add one <area> element inside the <map> element for each clickable region, specifying the coordinates of the clickable area and the destination URL. (See the <area> element on page 557 for more on how the coords attribute works.) Here's an example of an image map with three clickable regions:

```
<map id="Three Squares" name="ThreeSquares">
  <area href="page1.htm" shape="square" coords="5,5,95,195"
  alt="Square #1" />
  <area href="page2.htm" shape="square" coords="105,5,195,195"
  alt="Square #2" />
  <area href="page3.htm" shape="square" coords="205,5,295,195"
  alt="Square #3" />
</map>
```

Finally, to use your image map, you need to apply it to an image using the usemap attribute. The usemap attribute matches the name of the map but starts with a number sign (#), which tells browsers that the image map is on the current page:

```
<img src="image.gif" usemap="#ThreeSquares" alt="Image with Hotspots" />
```

You can't see the clickable regions of an image map (unless you outline them in the image). However, when you point to a hotspot, your mouse cursor changes to a hand. Clicking a hotspot has the same effect as clicking an ordinary <a> link—you immediately go to the new URL. For a full-fledged image map example, see page 189.

<meta> (Metadata)
Standalone Element, Allowed in <head> Only

Meta elements let you embed descriptive information in your web pages. Your visitors never see this information, but automated programs like web search engines can find it as they scan your site. You add metadata by placing <meta> elements in the <head> section of your page.

Every <meta> element includes a name attribute (which identifies the type of information you're adding) and a content attribute (which supplies the information itself). Although you can have an unlimited number of potential <meta> elements, the two most common are description and keywords, because some search engines use them:

```
<meta name="description" content="Sugar Beat Music for Children offers age-
appropriate music classes for children 4 months to 5 years old" />
```

Page 317 describes meta elements in more detail and explains how search engines use them.

<noscript> (Alternate Script Content)
Block Element, Container Element

The <noscript> element defines the content a browser should display if it can't run a script, a mini-program embedded in your page. You place it immediately after the

<script> element. The most common reason a browser can't run a script is because a visitor has turned off his browser's script feature.

For more information about scripts, refer to Chapter 14.

<object> (Embedded Object)
Inline Element, Container Element

The <object> element embeds specialized, nonstandard objects in your page. For example, you might use an <object> element to place a Flash movie inside a web page, although this practice is becoming steadily less common.

<ol> (Ordered List)
Block Element, Container Element

An ordered list starts with the <ol> element and contains multiple list items, each of which you represent with an <li> element. In an ordered list, your browser arranges each item consecutively, using your choice of numbers, letters, or Roman numerals.

Here's a simple ordered list that numbers items from 1 to 3:

```
<ol>
  <li>Buy bread</li>
  <li>Soak stamps off letters</li>
  <li>Defraud government with offshore investment scheme</li>
</ol>
```

To start at a number other than 1, use the start attribute and supply the starting number. To change the list's number or letter format, use the type attribute with one of these values: 1 (numbers), a (lowercase letters), A (uppercase letters), i (lowercase Roman numerals), I (uppercase Roman numerals).

HTML5 adds a feature for backward-counting lists. To create one, you add the reversed attribute to the <ol> element. However, older browsers don't support this feature.

For more information on ordered lists, see page 51.

<option> (Menu Option)
Container Element, Allowed in <select> Only

The <option> element defines the items you want to appear in a list, and you put the element inside a <select> element. For example, to create a drop-down menu that lets visitors choose a color from a list of options including Blue, Red, and Green, you need one <select> element with three <option> elements inside it.

When you define the <option> element, you can use the selected attribute to tell a browser to pre-select an item when it displays the page for the first time. You can also use the value attribute to associate a unique identifying piece of information with an option, which is included with the form data when a visitor submits the form.

For a basic example, see the description of the <select> element.

<p> (Paragraph)
Block Element, Container Element

The <p> element contains a paragraph of text:

```
<p>It was the best of times, it was the worst of times ...</p>
```

Because paragraphs are block elements, a browser automatically adds a line break and a little extra space between two paragraphs, or between a paragraph and another block element, like a list or a heading.

Browsers ignore empty paragraphs. To create a blank paragraph, use a nonbreaking space like this:

```
<p> </p>
```

<param> (Object Parameter)
Standalone Element, Allowed in <object> Only

The <param> element defines extra information in an <object> element, which a browser sends to an applet or a plug-in.

<pre> (Preformatted Text)
Block Element, Container Element

Preformatted text breaks the normal rules of HTML formatting. When you put content inside a <pre> element, a browser duplicates every space and line break it sees, retaining the formatting you used originally. Additionally, the browser puts all the content in a monospaced font (typically Courier), which means the results aren't always pretty.

The <pre> element is an easy and quick way to get text to appear exactly the way you want it, which is useful if you want to represent visual poetry or display a snippet of programming code. However, you shouldn't use it to align large sections of ordinary text; use CSS positioning rules for that (see Chapter 8).

```
<pre>
Tumbling-hair
                    picker of buttercups
                                       violets
     dandelions
And the big bullying daisies
                         through the field wonderful
     with eyes a little sorry
Another comes
                 also picking flowers
</pre>
```

\<q\> (Short Quotation)

Inline Element, Container Element

The \<q\> element defines a short quotation inside another block element, like a paragraph.

```
<p>As Charles Dickens once wrote, <q>It was the best of times, it was the
worst of times</q>.</p>
```

Usually, browsers display the \<q\> element as italic text, and some browsers, like Firefox, add quotation marks around the text. However, don't use the \<q\> element as a formatting tool. Instead, use it to identify quotations in your text, and then add style sheet rules to apply the formatting you want.

If you want a longer quotation that stands on its own as a block element, use the \<blockquote\> element instead.

\<samp\> (Sample Output)

Inline Element, Container Element

Use the \<samp\> element to mimic the way computer code looks when it's printed out or displayed on a computer console. This rarely used element simply formats its contents with a monospaced font, like \<pre\> and \<code\>.

\<script\> (Client-Side Script)

Block Element, Container Element

The \<script\> element lets you include a client-side script inside your web page. A script is a set of instructions written in a simplified programming language like JavaScript. Web designers use scripts to create interactive web pages that add effects like buttons that change color when you point to them. To learn some of the basics of JavaScript and to see scripts in action, check out Chapter 14.

\<select\> (Selectable List)

Container Element, Allowed in \<form\> Only

The \<select\> element creates a list you can use in a form. Your visitor selects a single item from the list (or multiple items, if you add the multiple attribute). You use the name attribute to give the list a unique name, as in the following example:

```
<select name="PromoSource">
  <option value="Ad">Google Ad</option>
  <option value="Search">Google Search</option>
  <option value="Psychic">Uncanny Psychic Intuition</option>
  <option value="Luck">Bad Luck</option>
</select>
```

Ordinarily, you create selection lists as drop-down menus. However, you can create a scrollable list box using the size attribute. Just specify the number of rows you want to show at once:

```
<select name="PromoSource" size="3">
  ...
</select>
```

For an example of a form, refer to page 490.

<small> (Small Print)

Inline Element, Container Element

Use the <small> element to hold "small print," like the legalese at the bottom of a contract. Visually, small print steps the text size down one notch, although you can change this effect through a style sheet if it's not appropriate.

<source> (Audio or Video File)

Standalone Element, Allowed in <video> or <audio>

You can use the <source> element to identify the file you want an audio or video player to play. Usually, you do this to list a set of files that provide the same content in different file formats. That way, you can ensure that the largest possible range of browsers can play your file. (The obvious drawbacks are that you need to make multiple copies of the files, encode them in different formats, and then find space to store the files on your website.)

The <source> element takes two attributes: src (which identifies the file) and type (which identifies the file format and, optionally, its codec). Here's an example with the <audio> element:

```
<audio controls>
  <source src="rubberduckies.ogg" type="audio/ogg">
  <source src="rubberduckies.mp3" type="audio/mpeg">
</audio>
```

The most common and reliable formats for audio are MP3 (set the type to audio/mp3) and OGG (set the type to audio/ogg). The most common formats for video are MP4 (video/mp4), WebM (video/webm), and OGG (video/ogg). You can get detailed format information at *http://tinyurl.com/html5-formats*.

<span> (Generic Inline Container)

Inline Element, Container Element

Use the <span> element to mark text you want to format inside a block element. For instance, you could format a single word in a paragraph, a few words, a whole sentence, and so on. Here's an example:

```
<p>In this paragraph, some of the text is wrapped in a span element.
That <span>gives you the ability</span> to format it in some fancy
way later on.</p>
```

On its own, the `<span>` element doesn't do anything. However, it's a powerful way to apply style sheet formatting in a flexible, reusable way.

You should also refer to the `<div>` element, which can apply formatting to several block elements at once (see page 213).

`<strong>` (Strong Importance)
Inline Element, Container Element

The `<strong>` element has the same effect as the `<b>` (bold text) element, but the official rules of HTML suggest you use it for text that has greater importance than the surrounding words. Here's an example:

```
I'm <strong>very</strong> sorry for all the trouble.
```

To customize the way the `<strong>` element emphasizes important text (say, to make the text both bold and italicized), use a style sheet rule. On the other hand, if you want bold text that doesn't give one word more emphasis than the surrounding words, you're better off using the `<b>` element.

`<style>` (Internal Style Sheet)
Container Element, Allowed in `<head>` Only

The `<style>` element lets you define a style right inside a web page. This is known as an *internal style sheet*. Use it to supply style sheet rules for the current page. Always put the `<style>` element inside the `<head>` section of a web page.

Here's an example of an internal style sheet that gives `<h1>` headings fuchsia text:

```
<style>
  h1 { color: fuchsia }
</style>
```

More commonly, you'll use the `<link>` element in your pages to connect to a central style sheet. That way, you can apply the same styles to all the pages in your site without cluttering up your markup. Chapter 3 has much more about style sheets and how to use them.

`<sub>` (Subscript)
Inline Element, Container Element

The `<sub>` element makes text smaller and positions it lower than the surrounding text (the midpoints of subscript characters line up with the bottom of the surrounding text). It's best not to rely on this trick for formatting (use style sheets instead), but it's a handy way to deal with scientific terms like H_2O. Here's how you use it:

```
Water is H<sub>2</sub>O
```

<sup> (Superscript)
Inline Element, Container Element

The <sup> element makes text smaller and positions it higher than the surrounding text (the middle of superscript text lines up with the top of the current line). It's best not to rely on this trick for formatting (use style sheets instead), but it's a handy way to deal with exponents like 3^3. Here's the <sup> element in action:

```
3<sup>3</sup> is 27
```

<table> (Table)
Block Element, Container Element

The <table> element is the outermost element that defines a table. Inside it, you define rows with the <tr> element, and inside each row, you use the <td> element to define individual cells and specify the content they hold. Here's a basic table:

```
<table>
  <tr>
    <td>Row 1, Column 1</td>
    <td>Row 1, Column 2</td>
  </tr>
  <tr>
    <td>Row 2, Column 1</td>
    <td>Row 2, Column 2</td>
  </tr>
</table>
```

It looks like this:

Row 1, Column 1	Row 1, Column 2
Row 2, Column 1	Row 2, Column 2

See page 57 for more on creating tables and page 259 for information on sizing them.

<td> (Table Data Cell)
Container Element, Allowed in <tr> Only

The <td> element represents an individual cell inside a table row (a <tr> element). Each time you add a <td> element, you create a column. However, it's perfectly valid to have different numbers of columns in subsequent rows (although it might look a little wacky). For a basic table example, see the <table> element definition above, and for a detailed explanation of tables, check out Chapter 2.

<textarea> (Multiline Text Input)
Container Element, Allowed in <form> Only

The <textarea> element displays a large text box in a form (the <form> element) that can fit multiple lines of text. As with all input controls, you need to identify the control by giving it a unique name. Additionally, you can set the size of the text box using the rows and cols attributes.

To preload text in the `<textarea>` element, put it between the start and end tags, like so:

```
<textarea name="Comments">Enter your comments here.</textarea>
```

`<th>` (Table Header Cell)
Container Element, Allowed in `<tr>` Only

The `<th>` element represents an individual cell with table heading text. Use the `<th>` element in the same way you use the `<td>` element. The difference is that you usually reserve the `<th>` element for the first row of a table (because it represents column headings), and `<th>` text appears boldfaced and centered (which you can tailor using style sheets).

`<title>` (Document Title)
Container Element, Allowed in `<head>` Only

The `<title>` element specifies the title of a web page. A browser displays this text in its title bar and uses it as the bookmark text if a visitor bookmarks the page. You have to put the `<title>` element in the `<head>` section of a page.

```
<title>Truly Honest Car Mechanics</title>
```

`<tr>` (Table Row)
Container Element, Allowed in `<table>` Only

The `<tr>` element represents an individual row inside a table (a `<table>` element). To add cells of information, you need to add the `<td>` element inside the `<tr>` element. For a basic table example, see the `<table>` element definition above.

`<ul>` (Unordered List)
Block Element, Container Element

An unordered list starts with the `<ul>` element and includes multiple list items, each of which you represent with an `<li>` element. The browser indents each item in the list and draws a bullet next to it.

Here's a simple unordered list:

```
<ul>
  <li>Buy bread</li>
  <li>Soak stamps off letters</li>
  <li>Defraud government with offshore investment scheme</li>
</ul>
```

Webmasters often use the `<ul>` element to create a menu of commands. (You can also use multiple levels of nested lists to create a hierarchical menu.) When using

`<ul>` to create a navigation menu, use a style sheet rule to remove the bullets (set `list-style-type` to none) and tweak the `margin` and `padding` settings.

`<video>` (Video Player)

Block element, Container element

The `<video>` element creates a playback window with a small set of playback controls underneath it. A visitor uses these controls to watch a video.

You specify the video you want to appear in the window using the `src` attribute. Browsers differ in the video file formats they play back, but you can't go wrong with MP4 files that use H.264 encoding (see page 530). In addition, you should always include the `controls` attribute. Without it, you'll create a playback window that has no buttons (and that therefore won't play a video unless you create an alternative set of controls using JavaScript).

Here's a fully configured `<video>` element at its simplest:

```
<video src="butterfly.mp4" controls></video>
```

The `<video>` element lets you set a few options.

The `height` and `width` properties set the size of the video window. If you don't set these attributes, browsers create a video window that matches the dimensions of the video you want to play. The `poster` attribute specifies an image that appears in the video window initially, before a visitor clicks Play. The obnoxious `autoplay` attribute tells the player to start playback as soon as the page loads, and the `loop` attribute tells the player to restart the video file when it ends, unless a visitor clicks the Pause button. Finally, you can use the `muted` attribute to start the player with the sound muted (visitors can click the speaker icon to restore sound).

You can specify fallback content inside the `<video>` element. That way, very old browsers that don't understand HTML5, like IE 8, display the fallback content instead of the video player. (Without the fallback content, old browsers ignore the video player altogether.)

```
<video src="butterfly.mp4" controls>
  No video for you. But you can still download the
  <a href="butterfly.mp4">butterfly.mp4</a> video file.
</audio>
```

Optionally, you can give the `<video>` element a list of files in different formats. The player shows the first video file that has a format it understands. To do this, you need to remove the `src` attribute and then, inside the `<video>` element, add one or more `<source>` elements, like this:

```
<video controls>
  <source src="butterfly.webm" type="video/webm">
  <source src="butterfly.mp4" type="video/mp4">
  Your browser is old. Click here to download the
```

```
        <a href="butterfly.mp4">butterfly.mp4</a> video file.
    </audio>
```

If a browser understands the WebM video standard, the video player loads *butterfly. webm* (as you'll see in Chrome, Firefox, and Opera). Browsers that don't play WebM files but do play MP4 (like Internet Explorer and Safari) will load *butterfly.mp4*. And if the browser doesn't understand the <video> element at all, it displays the fallback content and a link to download the video file.

To see what the <video> element looks like in a full web page, see page 529.

■ HTML5 Semantic Elements

As you learned in Chapter 1, the latest version of the HTML language is known as HTML5. And although it's full of improvements, it also comes with a significant caveat. Because it's relatively new, many browsers don't recognize all its features. Internet Explorer is a particular laggard; you'll won't be able to tap into any HTML5 features unless you use IE 9 or later.

Because of these browser support issues, web designers need to approach HTML5 with caution. Workaround techniques let you use many HTML5 features without leaving older browsers in the dark. (For example, page 535 explains how you should use a Flash fallback with the HTML5 <video> element to make sure your videos work even on old browsers.) However, these solutions aren't always simple, and sometimes they're more trouble than they're worth.

You can use one group of elements right now, however, and without much extra effort. These are HTML5's *semantic elements*, which add meaning to the structure of your pages. Semantic elements let you identify the logical purpose of different portions of your page. For example, you can indicate in your markup where your header is, where you placed your navigation links, and so on. Your visitors never see this information, but you can employ it in a variety of other useful ways. For example, search engines can use it to learn more about your website, screen reading programs can present your content more effectively to people with disabilities, and other tools can extract your data and reuse it in dozens of ways. All of these scenarios are still evolving, but if you plan to stick with your website for a long time, it's worth getting used to some of these new conventions so you can take advantage of them when HTML5 works in all browsers.

If you decide to use HTML5's semantic elements, you still need to worry about one issue. Older browsers (like IE 8) won't recognize these elements, so they'll just ignore them. That's fine up to a point, because the semantic elements aren't about formatting; they're about structure. But many of the new semantic elements are block elements, which means a browser should display them on a separate line on the resulting web page, with a little bit of space between them and the preceding (and following) elements. Browsers that don't recognize HTML5 elements won't know to display some of the semantic elements as block elements, so it's up to you to add a style sheet rule that tells these browsers what to do. Here's a style super-rule that applies block formatting to the nine HTML5 semantic elements in one step:

```
article, aside, figure, figcaption, footer, header, hgroup, nav, section,
summary {
  display: block;
}
```

This rule won't have any effect on browsers that already recognize HTML5, because they already set the `display` property to `block`.

The super style sheet rule above solves part of the problem but not all of it. It works with old browsers that don't understand HTML5, except Internet Explorer (which, in practice, is probably the only non-HTML5 browser still traveling the Web in significant numbers). The problem is that IE won't apply style sheet formatting to elements it doesn't recognize. Fortunately, you have a workaround: You can trick Internet Explorer into recognizing a foreign element by registering it using a JavaScript command. Here's a script block that gives IE the ability to recognize and style the <header> element:

```
<script>
  document.createElement('header')
</script>
```

Rather than write this sort of code yourself, you can make use of a ready-made script that does it for you (described at *http://tinyurl.com/nlcjxm*). To use this script, you simply add a reference to it in the <head> section of your page, like this:

```
<head>
  <title>...</title>
  <script src="http://html5shim.googlecode.com/svn/trunk/html5.js"></script>
</head>
```

This grabs the script from the *html5shim.googlecode.com* web server and runs it before the browser starts processing the rest of the page. The script is short and to the point—it uses the JavaScript trick described above to simulate all the new HTML5 elements. That way, you can format the elements with style sheet rules. Add the super-rule shown above to your style sheet, and the new elements will display as proper block elements. The only remaining task is for you to use the elements and add your own style sheet rules to format them.

The following sections list all of HTML5's new semantic elements. Notably missing are the HTML5 elements that don't have handy workarounds for old browsers. This includes the new HTML5 widgets for creating forms (page 487), and the <canvas> element that lets you draw shapes with the help of JavaScript.

TIP To see the latest version of the HTML5 specification, complete with all the features that leave older browsers out in the cold, see *http://dev.w3.org/html5/markup*. To learn about all of HTML5's new features, including those that let you build better web programs with JavaScript, you can read *HTML5: The Missing Manual* (O'Reilly).

<article> (Article)

Block Element, Container Element

Represents whatever you think of as an article—a section of self-contained content like a newspaper article, a forum post, or a blog entry (not including frills like comments or an author bio).

As with almost all the HTML5 semantic elements, the <article> element doesn't apply any built-in formatting. Think of it as a more specific version of the generic <div> container.

<aside> (Sidebar)

Block Element, Container Element

Represents a complete chunk of content that's separate from the main content of the page. For example, it makes sense to use <aside> to create a sidebar with content related to a main article. You can also use it for a block of links or ads.

<figcaption> (Figure Caption)

Block Element, Container Element

The <figcaption> element wraps the caption text that goes with a <figure> (see below). The goal is to clearly indicate the association between an image and its caption. Of course, <figcaption> isn't limited to text alone. You can use any HTML elements that make sense; good choices include links and tiny icons.

<figure> (Figure)

Block Element, Container Element

The <figure> element wraps a picture and its associated caption. Here's an example:

```
<figure>
   <img src="planetree.jpg" alt="Plane Tree" />
   <figcaption>The bark of a plane tree</figcaption>
</figure>
```

In most cases, you want to use a style sheet class to position the <figure> element. For example, you might choose to float it on the left or right side of your page.

<footer> (Footer)

Block Element, Container Element

The <footer> element holds a chunk of content that sits at the bottom of a page (or at the bottom of a well-defined section of content, like an <article>) element. The footer may include small print, a copyright notice, and a small set of links (for example, links that take you to About Us or Get Support pages).

\<header\> (Header)

Block Element, Container Element

The \<header\> element represents a heading that includes a title and some content. For example, a heading at the beginning of an article might include a title and a byline, or a title and some links to subtopics in the article. Here's an example:

```
<header>
  <h1>An HTML5 Investigation</h1>
  <p>Prepared by Steven Smith</p>
</header>
```

The \<header\> can also wrap the heading section of a website (for example, a banner with a company logo). It's perfectly acceptable for a web page to have more than one \<header\> section, as long as each header belongs to a distinct section of content. (For example, a news site that shows several articles on one page could have a header section for each article.)

\<mark\> (Highlighted Text)

Inline Element, Container Element

The \<mark\> element represents a section of text you want to highlight for reference. For example, you could use it to flag changes, mistakes, or keywords in a page.

If you decide to use the \<mark\> element now, you'll need to supply the formatting for browsers that don't recognize HTML5. Here's the sort of style rule you need:

```
mark {
  background-color: yellow;
  color: black;
}
```

\<nav\> (Navigation Links)

Block Element, Container Element

The \<nav\> element represents a section of a page that contains links. These links may point to topics on the current page or to other pages on a website. In fact, it's not unusual to have a page with multiple \<nav\> sections—one for a site-wide navigation menu, another for topics in the current article, and so on.

It's worth noting that you don't have to wrap every block of links in a \<nav\> element. Web designers generally reserve it for the largest and most important navigational sections on a page. You can place \<nav\> inside another HTML5 element as well. For example, if you have a set of navigation links right in the header, you're free to place the \<nav\> element inside the \<header\> element. Or, if you decide the links aren't clearly part of the header, you may choose to add the \<header\> element followed by the \<nav\> element. The HTML5 specification is explicit in saying that decisions like these are a matter of taste.

\<section> (Section)

Block Element, Container Element

Of all of HTML5's semantic elements, the \<section> element is the most general. It represents a document that should start with a heading of any level.

If possible, you should use a more specific container for your content than \<section>. For example, both \<article> or \<aside> have more specific meanings, which makes them better choices than \<section>. If you can't really describe your content as an article or an aside, however (for example, say it's a patient record pulled out of a database), then a \<section> element is a perfectly reasonable way to identify it.

One confusing detail is that you can use a \<section> for *parts* of a page. For example, on your website's home page you could put blog postings, news, and a sidebar of ads into their own separate \<section> elements.

> **NOTE** As web designers become more accustomed to using elements like \<section>, people will begin to settle on a few widely accepted usage patterns. Until then, HTML5 leaves some ambiguity about the best ways to use its new elements.

\<time> (Date or Time)

Inline Element, Container Element

Date and time information appears frequently in web pages. For example, it turns up at the end of most blog postings. Unfortunately, there's no standardized way to tag dates, so there's no easy way for other programs (like search engine crawlers) to extract them without guessing. The \<time> element solves this problem in two ways. Not only does it let you flag an existing date for later use, but it also adds a datetime attribute that you can use to provide the date in a standardized form that any program can understand.

Here are a few examples of the \<time> element at work:

```
<time datetime="2011-11-30">30<sup>th</sup> of November</time>
<time datetime="20:00">8:00pm</time>
<time datetime="2011-11-30T20:30">8:30 PM on November 11, 2011</time>
```

Remember, the information in the datetime attribute won't appear on your web page. It's there for other programs to read.

Because the \<time> element is purely informational and doesn't have any associated formatting, you can use it with any browser.

■ HTML Character Entities

HTML character entities are codes that browsers translate into other characters when they display a page. All HTML character entities start with an ampersand (&) and end with a semicolon (;).

There are two principal reasons to use HTML character entities. First of all, you might want to use a character that has a special meaning in the HTML standard. For example, if you type < in an HTML document, a browser assumes you're starting to define an element, which makes it difficult to write a pithy bit of logic like "2 < 3." To get around this, you replace the < symbol with a character entity that *represents* the less-than symbol. The browser then inserts the actual < character you want when it displays the page.

The other reason to use HTML character entities is because you want to use a special character that's not easy to type, like an accented letter or a currency symbol. In fact, characters like these are quite possibly not on your keyboard at all.

Table B-2 has the most commonly used HTML entities. For the complete list, which includes many more international language characters, see *www.webmonkey.com/ reference/Special_Characters*. You can also type in certain special characters using a non-English keyboard or pick international language characters from a utility program. See page 66 for more information about these options.

TABLE B-2 *HTML character entities.*

CHARACTER	NAME OF CHARACTER	WHAT TO TYPE
<	Less-than	&lt;
>	Greater-than	&gt;
&	Ampersand	&amp;
"	Quotation mark	&quot;
©	Copyright mark	&copy;
®	Registered trademark symbol	&reg;
¢	Cent sign	&cent;
£	Pound sterling sign	&pound;
¥	Yen sign	&yen;
€	Euro sign	€ (but € is better supported)
°	Degree sign	&deg;
±	Plus or minus sign	&plusmn;
÷	Division sign	&divide;
×	Multiply sign	&times;

CHARACTER	NAME OF CHARACTER	WHAT TO TYPE
µ	Micron sign	µ
¼	One-quarter fraction	¼
½	One-half fraction	½
¾	Three-quarters fraction	¾
¶	Paragraph sign	¶
§	Section sign	§
«	Left angle quote, guillemotleft	«
»	Right angle quote, guillemotright	»
¡	Inverted exclamation mark	¡
¿	Inverted question mark	¿
æ	Small ae diphthong (ligature)	æ
ç	Small c, cedilla	ç
è	Small e, grave accent	è
é	Small e, acute accent	é
ê	Small e, circumflex accent	ê
ë	Small e, dieresis or umlaut mark	ë
ö	Small o, dieresis or umlaut mark	ö
É	Capital E, acute accent	É

HTML Color Names

The HTML standard officially recognizes only 16 color names. Table B-3 lists them.

TABLE B-3 *HTML color names.*

Aqua	Navy
Black	Olive
Blue	Purple
Fuchsia	Red
Gray	Silver
Green	Teal
Lime	White
Maroon	Yellow

Although many browsers recognize more names, the best way to specify color is with a *color code* (see page 89).

Index

T

Creating a Website

THE MISSING CD

There's no CD with this book; you just saved $5.00.

Instead, every single Web address, practice file, and piece of downloadable software mentioned in this book is available at *missingmanuals.com* (click the Missing CD icon). There you'll find a tidy list of links, organized by chapter.

Don't miss a thing!
Sign up for the free Missing Manual email announcement list at missingmanuals.com. We'll let you know when we release new titles, make free sample chapters available, and update the features and articles on the Missing Manual website.